Cultural Anthropology
in a Globalizing World

Cultural Anthropology
in a Globalizing World

Fourth Edition

Barbara Miller
George Washington University

PEARSON

Boston   Columbus   Indianapolis   New York   San Francisco   Amsterdam
Cape Town   Dubai   London   Madrid   Milan   Munich   Paris   Montréal   Toronto
Delhi   Mexico City   São Paulo   Sydney   Hong Kong   Seoul   Singapore   Taipei   Tokyo

VP, Product Development: Dickson Musslewhite
Publisher: Charlyce Jones-Owen
Editorial Assistant: Laura Hernandez
Program Team Lead: Maureen Richardson
Project Team Lead: Melissa Feimer
Program Manager: Rob DeGeorge
Project Manager: Cheryl Keenan
Art Director: Maria Lange
Cover Art: Travel Pictures/Alamy Stock Photo

Director, Digital Studio: Sacha Laustein
Digital Media Project Manager: Amanda A. Smith
Procurement Manager: Mary Fischer
Procurement Specialist: Mary Ann Gloriande
Full-Service Project Management and Composition:
    Lumina Datamatics, Inc./Andrea Stefanowicz
Printer/Binder: LSC Communications
Cover Printer: LSC Communications
Text Font: Palatino LT Pro 9.5/11

Acknowledgements of third party content appear on pages 285–290, which constitutes an extension of this copyright page.

Library of Congress Cataloging-in-Publication Data

Names: Miller, Barbara D.
   Title: Cultural anthropology in a globalizing world / Barbara Miller,
George Washington University.
   Description: Fourth edition. | Boston : Pearson, 2017. | Includes
bibliographical references and index.
   Identifiers: LCCN 2015051276| ISBN 9780134518299 |
   ISBN 0134518292
Subjects: LCSH: Ethnology. | Globalization--Social aspects.
Classification: LCC GN316 .M49 2017 | DDC 305.8—dc23
   LC record available at http://lccn.loc.gov/2015051276

KV 11.08.2018 0817

Student
ISBN-10:   0-13-451829-2
ISBN-13: 978-0-13-451829-9

Books á la Carte
ISBN-10:   0-13-445847-8
ISBN-13: 978-0-13-445847-2

PEARSON

Brief Contents

Contents

Features

Anthropology Works

Think Like an Anthropologist

Culturama

Eye on the Environment

Maps

Preface

"I had no idea all those cultures were out there," said one of my students after taking my introductory cultural anthropology course. Another commented, "I'm a business major, but I am going to keep the books from this course because they will help me in my career. I need to understand people."

Cultural anthropology opens up whole new worlds. Not just "out there," but here, there, and everywhere. The subject matter of cultural anthropology may seem distant, exotic, and "other"—jungle drumbeats and painted faces, for example. This book helps students to encounter those faraway cultures and also to realize that their culture has its own versions of jungle drumbeats and painted faces. "Making the strange familiar" is essential learning in a globalizing world where cultural diversity may equal cultural survival for all of us. "Making the familiar strange" is a priceless revelation because it reduces the divide between "us" and the "other." "We" become "other" through the insights of cultural anthropology.

To achieve this double goal, *Cultural Anthropology in a Globalizing World*, Fourth Edition, delivers rich and exciting information about the world's cultures and promotes critical thinking and reflective learning. Students will find many points at which they can interact with the material, view their own culture as a culture, and make connections between anthropology and their everyday life in, for example, hairstyles, food symbolism, sleep deprivation, doctor–patient dialogues, racism and sexism, and the meaning of gestures.

The study of the world's cultures involves learning new words and analytical categories, but the effort will pay off in terms of bringing the world's peoples and cultures closer to you. If this book achieves my aspirations, anyone who reads it will live a life that is more culturally aware, enriched, and tolerant.

How This Book Is Organized

The book's organization and pedagogical features are designed to help ensure student engagement and enhanced learning. The 13 chapters are organized in the following way—but professors will find it easy to assign chapters out of order.

The first chapter describes the discipline of anthropology as a whole and provides the foundation for the rest of the book. The second chapter moves to the subject of how cultural anthropologists define research topics, carry out research, and present their findings.

The next three chapters discuss how people make a living and their patterns of consumption and exchange, how they reproduce and raise children, and how different cultures deal with illness, suffering, and death. While these three chapters address basic questions of how people feed themselves, reproduce, and stay alive and well, the discussion in each case fans out to include a wide array of cultural interpretations and practices that go far beyond sheer basics.

The next three chapters look at people in groups. One chapter addresses kinship and its changing forms. Another looks at social ties that are not based on kinship. The third considers how people organize themselves politically, how they seek to maintain order, and how they deal with conflict.

Although symbolic behavior permeates the entire book, three chapters most directly focus on meaning and symbolism. The chapter on communication pulls much of the book together as it considers the origins and evolution of communication and language, with special attention to contemporary change. The chapter on religion provides cross-cultural categories of religious belief and practice as well as linking "world religions" to specific local transformations. Expressive culture is a wide-ranging subject, and the chapter on it embraces expected topics such as art and music and unexpected topics such as sports, leisure, and travel.

The last two chapters consider two of the most important topics shaping cultural change in our times: migration and international development. These chapters explicitly put culture into motion and show how people are affected by larger structures, such as globalization or violence, and exercise agency in attempting to create meaningful and secure lives.

Features

Several new and continued features make this textbook distinctive and effective.

Learning Objectives

Learning Objectives are listed at the beginning of each chapter and below the three major chapter headings. At the end of the chapter, Learning Objectives Revisited provides a helpful review of the key points related to the three Learning Objectives.

Anthro Connections

Each chapter begins with an attention-getting short piece on an aspect of culture that relates to recent events and connects to the chapter opening photo. This feature helps students see the relevance of anthropology to contemporary issues around the world.

Culturama

All chapters include a one-page profile of a cultural group with a mini-panorama of two photographs and a map with captions. These brief summaries provide an enticing glimpse into the culture presented.

Anthropology Works

Although students may appreciate the interesting material that cultural anthropology offers, they are still likely to ask, "Does this knowledge have any practical applications?" Every chapter contains a compelling example of how knowledge and methods in cultural anthropology can prevent or solve social problems. Anthropology Works examples include: Paul Farmer's role in providing health care in Haiti, Laura Tabac's applied research on men's risky sexual practices in New York City and Australian Aboriginal women's collaboration with an anthropologist to document and preserve their cultural heritage.

Think Like an Anthropologist

These examples connect anthropology to everyone's lives and prompt reflective learning. Others introduce a problem and show how it has been studied or analyzed from different anthropological perspectives, providing links to the major theoretical debates in cultural anthropology presented in Chapter 1, and prompt critical thinking.

Eye on the Environment

This feature highlights the important relationship between culture and environment. Along with many in-text references to how culture and the environment interact, students will recognize culture-environment connections through examples from many cultures.

Map Program

The maps are carefully chosen and designed to provide the right amount of information to complement the text. Detailed captions lead students on to connect the map with other topics such as livelihood, population, and language.

In-Text Glossary

Definitions of the Key Concepts are provided where the concept is first mentioned and defined. A paginated list of the Key Concepts appears at the end of each chapter. The glossary at the end of the book contains a complete list of Key Concepts and their definitions.

Thinking Outside the Box

This feature provides two or three thought-provoking questions in each chapter, displayed at the end of the chapter. These questions prompt readers to relate a topic to their cultural experiences or provide an avenue for further research. They can promote class discussion or serve as a basis for a class project.

What's New in This Edition?

Each chapter contains updated material including examples from the latest research, current population statistics, and new and revised Key Concepts. Chapters now begin with an Anthro Connections box that relates to contemporary issues around the world.

- Chapter 1: the relevance of cultural anthropology in addressing the Ebola epidemic
- Chapter 2: computational anthropology as a new Key Concept, discussion of "diffraction" in commodity studies; updates in the Culturama on the Trobriand Islands; and sexual discrimination within the discipline
- Chapter 3: discussion of hyperconsumerism; example of effects of global consumer demand driving phosphate mining in a small Pacific island and displacement of the indigenous population; new Key Concepts on division of labor, subjective well-being, and mobile money
- Chapter 4: update on China's One Child Policy as more flexible; update in the Culturama on the Amish; heteronormativity is a new Key Concept
- Chapter 5: discussion of zoonotic diseases as a subtype of infectious diseases; stigma is a new Key Concept
- Chapter 6: new example of touch as a way of communicating kinship in Central India
- Chapter 7: material on emerging social inequality within "racial" categories in South Africa based on life histories; update in the Culturama on the Roma
- Chapter 8: revised statistics about incarceration; update in the Culturama on the Kurdish people
- Chapter 10: new material about the Ngarrindjeri and their land claims in Australia; revised Key Concept definition of revitalization movements
- Chapter 11: material on the role of art in post-conflict situations
- Chapter 12: updated migration statistics throughout the chapter
- Chapter 13: updated statistics on indigenous peoples; material on careers in international development and how students can best pursue such careers

The Importance of Names

Since the beginning of modern humanity, people have been naming each other, naming their groups and other groups, and naming features of the places they inhabit. People of earlier times often referred to themselves in terms that translate roughly into "The People." As far as they were concerned, they were The People: the only people on earth.

Things are more complicated now. European colonialism, starting in the fifteenth century, launched centuries of rapid contact between Europeans and thousands of indigenous groups around the world. The Europeans named and described these groups in their European languages. The names were not those that the people used for themselves, or if they were, the transliteration into a European language altered local names into something very different from the original.

The Spanish explorers' naming of all the indigenous peoples of North America as Indians is a famous example of a misnomer. Beyond being wrong by thinking they had reached India, the Spanish conquerors who renamed thousands of people and claimed their territory simultaneously erased much of the indigenous people's heritage and identity.

The challenge of using the preferred names for people and places of the world faces us today as people worldwide wrestle with the issue of what they want to be called. Until recently, indigenous peoples of the present-day United States mainland preferred to be called Native Americans, rejecting the pejorative term "Indian." Now, they are claiming and recasting the term "Indian." In Alaska, the preferred term is "Alaska Native," and in Hawai'i it is "Native Hawai'ian." In Canada, preferred terms are "First Nations," "Native Peoples," and "Northern Peoples."

From small-scale groups to entire countries, people are attempting to revive precolonial group names and place names. Bombay is now Mumbai, and Calcutta is Kolkata. Group names and place names are frequently contested. Is someone Hispanic or Latino? Is it the Persian Gulf or the Arabian Gulf? Is it Greenland or Kalaallit Nunaat? Does it matter? The answer is yes, resoundingly, yes.

This book strives to provide the most currently accepted names for people, places, objects, activities, and ideas. By the time it is printed, however, some names and their English spellings will have changed. It is an ongoing challenge to keep track of such changes, but doing so is part of our job as citizens of a transforming world.

The Cover Image

Mongolia is one of the most sparsely populated countries in the world, with a population of around three million people. It contains very little farmable land, as much of its area is grassy steppe, with mountains to the north and west and the Gobi Desert to the south. Approximately 30 percent of the population depend on herding animals for their livelihoods. Freedom of movement, horse riding, and yert domestic architecture are central parts of the culture. The majority of its population are Buddhists. Women's economic and political roles in Mongolian history were often important. Genghis Khan appointed his daughters as combatant generals. Throughout history, many Mongolian women have been skilled horse riders and archers. Since 1999, two women have filled the post of Minister of Foreign Affairs. More than 70 percent of students in higher education are women. We have yet to see how changing gender roles will shape Mongolia's future.

In Thanks

The breadth, depth, and quality of this edition are the result of many people's ideas, comments, corrections, and care. For the first edition of *Cultural Anthropology*, four anthropologists carefully reviewed multiple drafts of the book. I will always be grateful to them for their monumental contribution that helped make this book what it is today: Elliot Fratkin, Smith College; Maxine Margolis, University of Florida; Russell Reid, University of Louisville; and Robert Trotter II, University of Arizona.

The author thanks the following reviewers who provided comments and advice in preparation for this edition: Lisa Beiswenger, The Ohio State University; Lesley Daspit, Purdue University; Alexa Dietrich, Wagner College; Henri Gooren, Oakland University; William Jankowiak, University of Nevada, Las Vegas; Patricia Jolly, University of Northern Colorado; Jing Lei, State University of New York at Oswego; Andrew Nelson, University of North Texas; Simone Poliandri, Framingham State University; and Frank Salamone, Iona College.

The cultural anthropologists who have reviewed previous editions of this textbook and offered their critiques and detailed suggestions have shaped this book from start to finish: Warren D. Anderson, Southeast Missouri State University; Jason Antrosio, Hartwick College; Diane Baxter, University of Oregon; Monica L. Bellas, Cerritos College; Joyce Bishop, California State University, Sacramento; Ronald Bolender, Mount Vernon Nazarene University; Barbara Bonnekessen, University of Missouri–Kansas City; Peter Brown, University of Wisconsin, Oshkosh; Howard Campbell, University of Texas, El Paso; (the late) Charles R. de Burlo, University of Vermont; Elizabeth de la Portilla, University of Texas at San Antonio; William W. Donner, Kutztown University; Lisa Pope Fischer, Santa Monica College; Pamela J. Ford, Mount San Jacinto College; Monica Frolander-Ulf, University of Pittsburgh, Johnstown; Mary Kay Gilliland, Pima Community College; Nancy Gonlin, Bellevue Community College; Jeanne Humble, Bluegrass Community & Technical College; Ann Kingsolver, University of South Carolina; Courtney Kurlanska, University of New Hampshire; Leslie Lischka, Linfield College; William M. Loker, California State University, Chico; Martin F. Manalansan IV, University of Illinois; Roberta Martine, Fort Hays State University; Corey Pressman, Mt. Hood Community College; Ed Robbins, University of Wisconsin; Jacquelyn Robinson, Albany State University;

Harry Sanabria, University of Pittsburgh; Kathleen M. Saunders, Western Washington University; G. Richard Scott, University of Nevada, Reno; Wesley Shumar, Drexel University; David Simmons, University of South Carolina; Kimberly Eison Simmons, University of South Carolina; Lori A. Stanley, Luther College; Margaret Weinberger, Bowling Green State University; Jim Wilce, Northern Arizona University; Peter Wogan, Willamette University; Katrina Worley, Sierra College; Sabrina Adleman, Lansing Community College, Mott Community College; Annalisa Alvrus, Mesa Community College; John Baker, Moorpark College; Suzanne Baldon, University of Texas At Arlington; Sally Billings, College of Southern Nevada; Adriana Bohm, Delaware County Community College; Vicki Bradley, University of Houston; Angela Bratton, Augusta State University; Liam Buckley, James Madison University; Howard Campbell, UTEP; Jenny Chio, University of California Berkeley; Heather Claussen, Cabrillo College; Pearce Creasman, Blinn College; Julie David, Orange Coast College; Phyllisa Eisentraut, Santa Barbara City College; Jack Eller, Metropolitan State College of Denver; Diana Fox, Bridgewater State College; Renee Garcia, Saddleback College; Erik Gooding; Jane Goodman, Indiana University; Kathryn Grant, University of North Florida; William Griffin, St. Charles Community College; Corinna Guenther, Southwestern College; Melissa Hargrove, Miami University of Ohio; Julie Hartley, Brigham Young University; Alanson Hertzberg, Cosumnes River College; Robin Hicks, Ball State University; J. Dwight Hines, Point Park University; Elizabeth Hirsh, Community College of Aurora; Brian Hoey, Marshall University; Barbara Hughes, Metropolitan State College of Denver; Francisca James Hernandez, Pima Community College; William Jankowiak, UNLV; Hannah Jopling, Fordham University; Ronald Kephart, University of North Florida; Andrew Kinkella, Moorpark College; Tracy Kopecky, College of Dupage; Hollie Kopp, Front Range Community College; Elizabeth Lamble, Mott Community College; Alison Lee, UC Riverside; William Leggett, Middle Tennessee State University; Jennifer Malicher, Bergen Community College; Roberta Martine, Fort Hays State University; Chad Morris, George Mason University; Laurie Occhipinti, Clarion University; Carlos Ochoa, University of Arkansas; Pamela Pacheco, Golden West College; James Preston, Sonoma State University; Kathleen Ragsdale, Mississippi State University; Karaleah Reichart, UNC-Chapel Hill And UNC-Greensboro; Margaret Sabom Bruchez, Blinn College; Suzanne Scheld, California State University, Northridge; Edward Snajdr, John Jay College of Criminal Justice, CUNY; R. Sophie Statzel, Baruch College; Susan Speigel, College of Dupage; Megan Springate, Monmouth University; Ayse Taskiran, Butte College; Mary Taylor, Hunter College; Shelly Tiley, California State University, Sacramento; Andria Timmer, Texas Christian University; Alan Trevithick, Fordham University; Salena Wakim, Orange Coast College; Margaret Weinberger, Bowling Green State University; and Katrina Worley, Sierra College.

Many anthropologists and others have provided encouragement, suggestions, feedback, references, and photographs: Lila Abu-Lughod, Abigail Adams, Vincanne Adams, Catherine Allen, Joseph Alter, Matthew Amster, Myrdene Anderson, Donald Attwood, Christopher Baker, Isabel Balseiro, Nancy Benco, Marc Bermann, Alexia Bloch, Elson Boles, Lynne Bolles, John Bowen, Don Brenneis, Alison Brooks, Judith K. Brown, D. Glynn Cochrane, Jeffery Cohen, Carole Counihan, Brian Craik, Liza Dalby, Loring Danforth, Patricia Delaney, Alexander Dent, Linus Digim'rina, Timothy Earle, Daniel Everett, Johannes Fabian, Ilana Feldman, Janina Fenigsen, Elliot Fratkin, Martin Fusi, Maris Boyd Gillette, Richard A. Gould, David Gow, Richard Grinker, Daniel Gross, (the late) Marvin Harris, Tobias Hecht, Cornelia Mayer Herzfeld, Michael Herzfeld, Barry Hewlett, Danny Hoffman, Michael Horowitz, (the late) Robert Humphrey, Lanita Jacobs-Huey, Vicki Jensen, Anstice Justin, Barry D. Kass, Patty Kelly, Laurel Kendall, David Kideckel, Diane E. King, Stuart Kirsch, Dorinne Kondo, Conrad Kottak, Jennifer Kramer, Donald B. Kraybill, Ruth Krulfeld, Joel Kuipers, Takie Lebra, David Lempert, Lamont Lindstrom, Susan Orpett Long, Luisa Maffi, Beatriz Manz, Debra Martin, Samuel Martínez, Catherine McCoid, Leroy McDermott, Kimber Haddox McKay, Jerry Milanich, Laura Miller, Madhushree Mukerjee, Kirin Narayan, Sarah Nelson, Gananath Obeyesekere, Ellen Oxfeld, Hanna Papanek, Michael G. Peletz, Deborah Pellow, (the late) Gregory Possehl, David Price, Joanne Rappaport, Jennifer Robertson, Nicole Sault, Joel Savishinsky, David Z. Scheffel, Nancy Scheper-Hughes, Pankaj Sekhsaria, Bob Shepherd, Richard Shweder, Jennie Smith-Pariola, Chunghee Soh, Kate Spilde Contreras, Anthony Stocks, Patricia Tovar, Sita Venkateswar, Martha Ward, James (Woody) Watson, Rubie Watson, Van Yasek, and Kevin Yelvington.

I am grateful to Charlyce Jones-Owen, my editor at Pearson, for her support. I have enjoyed working closely with Ohlinger Publishing Services in Columbus, Ohio, during the revision process, especially Brooke Wilson.

I thank the Millers—my parents, siblings, aunts and uncles, and nieces and nephews—for their interest and support. My father's two comments about the book were that it has a lot of long words and how do I know so much about sex? "From reading, Dad," was my truthful reply. I am grateful to the Heatons—my former in-laws, including my ex-husband, (late) ex-parents-in-law, brothers- and sisters-in-law, and nieces and nephews—for their enduring friendship.

I thank, especially, my son, Jack Heaton. He was a superb traveling companion on our trip around the world with the Semester at Sea Program in 1996, when I wrote much of the first edition of *Cultural Anthropology*. He continues to be excellent company during our time together in DC. This book is dedicated to him.

Barbara Miller
Washington, DC

Support for Instructors and Students

This book is accompanied by an extensive learning package to enhance the experience of both instructors and students. The author played a major role in developing and updating the material in the Instructor's Resource Manual with Tests, MyTest, and the PowerPoint™ slides.

Instructor's Resource Manual and Test Bank

(0-13-445839-7)

For each chapter, this supplement provides a lecture outline, learning objectives, key concepts, Thinking Outside the Box questions, video suggestions, suggested readings, and a list of REVEL interactives. Test questions in multiple choice, true-false, and essay formats are available for each chapter. This manual is available for download at www.pearsonhighered.com/irc.

MyTest (0-13-445840-0)

This computerized software allows instructors to create personalized exams, to edit any or all of the existing test questions, and to add new questions. Other features include the random generation of test questions, the creation of alternative versions of the same test, scrambling question sequences, and test previews before printing. This software is available for download at www.pearsonhighered.com/irc.

Powerpoint™ Presentation for Cultural Anthropology in a Globalizing World

(0-13-445841-9)

These PowerPoint slides combine text and graphics for each chapter to help instructors convey anthropological principles and examples in a clear and engaging way. They are available for download at www.pearsonhighered.com/irc.

REVEL™ Educational Technology Designed for the Way Today's Students Read, Think, and Learn

When students are engaged deeply, they learn more effectively and perform better in their courses. This simple fact inspired the creation of **REVEL**: an immersive learning experience designed for the way today's students read, think, and learn. Built in collaboration with educators and students nationwide, **REVEL** is the newest, fully digital way to deliver respected Pearson content. **REVEL** enlivens course content with media interactives and assessments—integrated directly within the authors' narrative—that provide opportunities for students to read about and practice course material in tandem. This immersive educational technology improves student engagement and understanding of concepts, improving performance throughout the course. Learn more about **REVEL** at http://www.pearsonhighered.com/revel/

Strategies in Teaching Anthropology, Sixth Edition

(0-205-71123-5)

This book focuses on the "how" of teaching anthropology across all of the discipline's four fields and provides a wide array of associated learning outcomes and student activities. It is a compendium of strategies and teaching tips from anthropologists, teaching in a variety of settings, who share their pedagogical techniques, knowledge, and observations.

About the Author

Barbara D. Miller

Barbara Miller is Professor of Anthropology and International Affairs in the Elliott School of International Affairs of the George Washington University in Washington, DC. She is Director of the Elliott School's Institute for Global and International Studies as well as Director of two of its affiliated research groups, the Culture in Global Affairs Program and the Global Gender Program. Before coming to GW in 1994, she taught at Syracuse University, the University of Rochester, SUNY Cortland, Ithaca College, Cornell University, and the University of Pittsburgh.

For over 30 years, Barbara's research has focused on gender-based inequalities in India, especially the nutritional and medical neglect of daughters in northern regions of the country, and sex-selective abortion. She has also conducted research on culture and rural development in Bangladesh, on low-income household dynamics in Jamaica, and on Hindu adolescents in Pittsburgh. Her current interests include continued research on gender inequalities in health in South Asia and the role of cultural anthropology in informing policy, especially as related to women, children, and other disadvantaged groups.

She teaches course on introductory cultural anthropology, medical anthropology, development anthropology, culture and population, health and development in South Asia, migration and mental health, and global gender policy.

Barbara has published many scholarly articles and book chapters and several books including *The Endangered Sex: Neglect of Female Children in Rural North India*, Second Edition (Oxford University Press 1997), an edited volume, *Sex and Gender Hierarchies* (Cambridge University Press 1993), and a co-edited volume with Alf Hiltebeitel, *Hair: Its Power and Meaning in Asian Cultures* (SUNY Press 1998). In addition to *Cultural Anthropology*, Eighth Edition, she is the author of *Cultural Anthropology in a Globalizing World*, Fourth Edition (Pearson 2017) and the lead author of a four-field textbook entitled *Anthropology*, Second Edition (Pearson 2008).

She launched a blog in 2009 called anthropologyworks where she and other contributors present informed opinion pieces about important social issues, a weekly feature covering anthropology in the mainstream media, and other features. Since its beginning, the blog has had 120,000 visits from people in nearly every country of the world. You can follow her, along with over 17,000 people worldwide, via Twitter @ anthroworks and Facebook. In 2010, she launched a second blog called globalgendercurrent, which highlights new research and debates about global women's issues as informed by grounded research and cutting-edge policy questions. She Tweets and Facebooks about global gender issues.

"Cultural Anthropology is exciting because it

connects with everything, from **food** to **art**. And it can

help prevent or **solve** world problems related to *social*

inequality and injustice."

Chapter 1
Anthropology and the Study of Culture

Learning Objectives

1.1 Define what is anthropology.

1.2 Recognize what is cultural anthropology.

1.3 Summarize the distinctive features of cultural anthropology.

Anthro Connections

A Zhuang (zhoo-ANG) girl works in the famously beautiful rice terraces of southern China near its border with Vietnam. The Zhuang number about 18 million, making them the largest ethnic minority in China. In addition to growing tourism in the Zhuang region, it is now a favored retirement destination for elderly Chinese. One major attraction is the quality of the drinking water that comes from natural springs (Lin and Huang 2012). Another is the area's reputation for having many people who live for a long time, including China's oldest person who is 127 years old. An elderly resident comments, "My high blood pressure was brought under control after I spent a month here. I would get epileptic attacks about once in two months, but it never strikes now."

Cannibalism, *Jurassic Park,* hidden treasure, *Indiana Jones and the Temple of Doom,* ancient prehuman fossils, and the Fountain of Youth in China? The popular impression of anthropology is based mainly on movies and television shows that depict anthropologists as adventurers and heroes. Many anthropologists do have adventures and discover treasures such as ancient pottery, medicinal plants, and jade carvings. But most of their research is not glamorous. Some anthropologists spend years in difficult physical conditions, searching for the earliest fossils of our ancestors. Others live among people in Silicon Valley, California, and study how they work and organize family life in a setting permeated by modern technology. Some anthropologists conduct laboratory analyses of tooth enamel to learn where an individual once lived. Others study designs on prehistoric pottery to understand trade relations between cities. And others observe nonhuman primates such as chimpanzees or orangutans in the wild to learn how they live.

Anthropologists study the entire diversity of humanity, past and present. Cultural anthropologists study living people including (LEFT) contemporary Silicon Valley culture in California and (RIGHT) the Dani people of West Papua, the Indonesian part of the island of New Guinea, who still value their stone tools in addition to steel tools.

■ *As you read this chapter, make a list of the kinds of data (information) that anthropologists in the four fields collect during their research.*

Anthropology is the study of humanity, including prehistoric origins and contemporary human diversity. Compared with other disciplines that study humanity such as history, psychology, economics, political science, and sociology, anthropology is broader in scope. Anthropology covers a much greater span of time than these disciplines, and it encompasses a broader range of topics.

Introducing Anthropology's Four Fields

1.1   Define what is anthropology.

In North America, anthropology is divided into four fields (Figure 1.1) that focus on separate, but connected, subject matter related to humanity:

- **Biological anthropology** or physical anthropology—the study of humans as biological organisms, including evolution and contemporary variation.
- **Archaeology**—the study of past human cultures through their material remains.
- **Linguistic anthropology**—the study of human communication, including its origins, history, and contemporary variation and change.
- **Cultural anthropology**—the study of living peoples and their cultures, including variation and change. **Culture** refers to people's learned and shared behaviors and beliefs.

Some anthropologists argue that a fifth field, applied anthropology, should be added. **Applied anthropology** is the use of anthropological knowledge to prevent or solve problems or to shape and achieve policy goals.

Biological or Physical Anthropology

Biological anthropology encompasses three subfields. The first, primatology, is the study of the nonhuman members of the order of mammals called primates, which includes a

---

anthropology the study of humanity, including its prehistoric origins and contemporary human diversity.

biological anthropology the study of humans as biological organisms, including evolution and contemporary variation.

archaeology the study of past human cultures through their material remains.

linguistic anthropology the study of human communication, including its origins, history, and contemporary variation and change.

cultural anthropology the study of living peoples and their cultures, including variation and change.

culture people's learned and shared behaviors and beliefs.

applied anthropology the use of anthropological knowledge to prevent or solve problems or to shape and achieve policy goals.

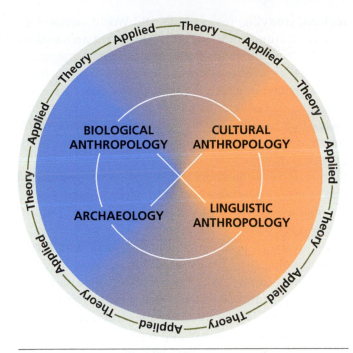

Figure 1.1 The Four Fields of Anthropology

wide range of animals from very small, nocturnal creatures to gorillas, the largest members. Primatologists study nonhuman primates in the wild and in captivity. They record and analyze how the animals spend their time, collect and share food, form social groups, rear offspring, develop leadership patterns, and experience and resolve conflicts. Primatologists are alarmed about the decline in numbers, and even the extinction, of nonhuman primate species. Many apply their knowledge to nonhuman primate conservation.

The second subfield is paleoanthropology, the study of human evolution on the basis of the fossil record. Paleoanthropologists search for fossils to increase the amount of evidence related to the way human evolution occurred.

The third subfield is the study of contemporary human biological variation. Anthropologists working in this area seek to explain differences in the biological makeup and behavior of contemporary humans. They study such biological factors as DNA within and across populations, body size and shape, human nutrition and disease, and human growth and development.

Archaeology

Archaeology means, literally, the "study of the old," but "the old" is limited to human culture. Therefore, the time depth of archaeology goes back only to the beginnings of *Homo sapiens*, between 300,000 and 160,000 years ago, when they first emerged in Africa. Archaeology encompasses two major areas: prehistoric archaeology, which concerns the human past before written records, and historical archaeology, which deals with the human past in societies that have written documents. Prehistoric archaeologists often identify themselves with broad geographic regions, studying, for example, Old World archaeology (Africa, Europe, and Asia) or New World archaeology (North, Central, and South America).

Another set of specialties within archaeology is based on the context in which the archaeology takes place. For example, underwater archaeology is the study of submerged archaeological sites. Underwater archaeological sites may be from either prehistoric or historic times. Some prehistoric sites include early human settlements in parts of Europe, such as household sites discovered in Switzerland that were once near lakes but are now submerged.

The archaeology of the recent past is an important research direction. An example of the archaeology of contemporary life is the "Garbage Project" conducted by archaeologists at the University of Arizona at Tucson (Rathje and Murphy 1992). They have excavated part of the Fresh Kills landfill on Staten Island, near New York City. It is one of the largest human-made structures in North America. The excavation of pop-top can tabs, disposable diapers, cosmetics containers, and newspapers reveals much about recent consumption patterns and how they affect the environment. One surprising finding is that the

Underwater archaeology is a focus of some archaeologists. Stephen Lubkemann, trained as both a cultural anthropologist and an underwater archaeologist, documents the remains of the hull of DRTO-036, a vessel that wrecked in the Dry Tortugas in the mid-nineteenth century. The vessel lies within Dry Tortugas National Park in the Florida Keys.

▌ *You can access UNESCO's Convention on the Protection of Underwater Heritage on the Internet.*

kinds of garbage people often blame for filling up landfills, such as fast-food packaging and disposable diapers, cause less serious problems than paper. Newspaper is a major culprit because of its sheer quantity. This information can improve recycling efforts worldwide.

Linguistic Anthropology

Linguistic anthropology is devoted to the study of communication, mainly (but not exclusively) among humans (Chapter 9 is devoted to this field). Linguistic anthropology has three subfields: historical linguistics, the study of language change over time and how languages are related; descriptive linguistics or structural linguistics, the study of how contemporary languages differ in terms of their formal structure; and sociolinguistics, the study of the relationships among social variation, social context, and linguistic variation, including nonverbal communication.

Linguistic anthropologists are studying important current issues, as discussed in Chapter 9. First, they study language in everyday use, or discourse, and how it relates to power structures at local, regional, and international levels (Duranti 1997a). Second, they look at the role of information technology in communication, including the Internet, social media such as Facebook, and cell phones. Third is attention to the increasingly rapid extinction of indigenous languages and what can be done about it.

Cultural Anthropology

Cultural anthropology is the study of contemporary people and their cultures. The term culture refers to people's learned and shared behaviors and beliefs. Cultural anthropology considers variations and similarities across cultures,

Maya people watch as a forensic anthropologist conducts an exhumation of more than 50 bodies in a highland Guatemalan village in 1997. Such work is ongoing in Guatemala and many other places in the world. It gives closure to the survivors.

▌ *Are courses in forensic anthropology offered at your school?*

Anthropology Works

Delivering Health Care in Rural Haiti

Journalist Tracy Kidder's book, *Mountains Beyond Mountains: The Quest of Paul Farmer, a Man Who Would Cure the World* (2003), is an inspiring story about an inspiring person: Paul Farmer. Farmer earned a Ph.D. in anthropology and a degree in medicine from Harvard University. His training in cultural anthropology and medicine is a powerful prescription for providing health care to the poor.

In his first book, *AIDS and Accusation: Haiti and the Geography of Blame* (1992), he wrote about the coming of HIV/AIDS to Haiti and a rural community's attempt to understand and cope with this devastating new disease. He also describes how the wider world mistakenly blamed Haiti for being the source of the disease. Farmer focuses attention on poverty and social justice as primary causes of health problems worldwide. This position has shaken the very foundations of Western medicine.

In addition to his scholarly publications, Farmer is an influential health practitioner and activist. As one of the cofounders of Partners in Health, he has helped heal thousands of people. In 2009, Farmer was named U.S. deputy special envoy to Haiti. Since the earthquake in January 2010, he has worked tirelessly to alleviate suffering in Haiti.

In my undergraduate cultural anthropology class, when I ask who has heard of Paul Farmer, many hands shoot up. Of these students, most have read *Mountains Beyond Mountains*. A few have heard him speak. This level of awareness of Farmer's contributions to health and anthropology prompted me to create a label that captures Farmer's inspirational role: the Paul Farmer Effect (PFE).

A woman cares for her sick child while he receives treatment for cholera at a clinic in Port-au-Prince, Haiti, in 2011. Cholera has affected more than 450,000 people in this country of 10 million, or nearly five percent of the population, and it has killed more than 6,000. Haiti continues to seek reparations from the United Nations because it was their staff who brought cholera to Haiti.

This label refers to the Pied Piper role he plays for students: They want to follow his lead; they want to be a Paul Farmer. Students are choosing courses and selecting majors and minors to help them achieve that goal.

I began to notice the PFE in 2010, and it is still growing. Because of the PFE, more students each year combine their academic interests in anthropology, global health, and international affairs. These students are beginning to graduate and are going on to pursue humanitarian careers. Thanks to Paul Farmer and the PFE, they are more powerfully informed to make the world a better place.

and how cultures change over time. Cultural anthropologists learn about culture by spending a long time, typically a year or more, living with the people they study (see Chapter 2).

Prominent areas of specialization in cultural anthropology include economic anthropology, psychological anthropology, medical anthropology, political anthropology, and international development anthropology.

Applied Anthropology: Separate Field or Cross-Cutting Focus?

In the United States, applied anthropology emerged during and after World War II. Its first concern was with improving the lives of contemporary peoples, so it was more closely associated with cultural anthropology than with the other three fields.

Many anthropologists feel that applied anthropology should be considered a fifth field of anthropology, standing on its own. Many others think that the application of

knowledge to solve problems, just like theory, should be part of each field (see Figure 1.1). The latter is the author's position, and therefore, many examples of applied anthropology appear throughout this book.

Applied anthropology can be found in all four fields of anthropology:

- Archaeologists are employed in cultural resource management (CRM), assessing the presence of possible archaeological remains before construction projects, such as roads and buildings, can proceed.

- Biological anthropologists are employed as forensic anthropologists, participating in criminal investigations through laboratory work identifying bodily remains. Others work in nonhuman primate conservation, helping to protect their habitats and survival.

- Linguistic anthropologists consult with educational institutions about how to improve standardized tests for bilingual populations and conduct policy research for governments.

- Cultural anthropologists apply their knowledge to poverty reduction, education, health care, international business, and conflict prevention and resolution (see Anthropology Works throughout this book for examples).

Introducing Cultural Anthropology

1.2 Recognize what is cultural anthropology.

Cultural anthropology is devoted to studying human cultures worldwide, both their similarities and differences. Cultural anthropology makes "the strange familiar and the familiar strange" (Spiro 1990). It teaches us to look at ourselves from the "outside" as a somewhat "strange" culture. A compelling example of making the familiar strange is the case of the Nacirema (nah-see-RAY-muh), a culture first described in 1956:

> The Nacirema are a North American group living in the territory between the Canadian Cree, the Yaqui and the Tarahumara of Mexico, and the Carib and the Arawak of the Antilles. Little is known of their origin, though tradition states that they came from the east. According to Nacirema mythology, their nation was originated by a culture hero, Notgnihsaw, who is otherwise known for two great feats of strength—the throwing of a piece of wampum across the river Pa-To-Mac and the chopping down of a cherry tree in which the Spirit of Truth resided (Miner 1965 [1956]:415).

The anthropologist goes on to describe the Nacirema's intense focus on the human body. He provides a detailed account of a daily ritual performed within the home in a specially constructed shrine area:

> The focal point of the shrine is a box or chest which is built into the wall. In this chest are kept the many charms and magical potions without which no native believes he could live. These preparations are secured from a variety of specialized practitioners. The most powerful of these are the medicine men, whose assistance must be rewarded with substantial gifts. . . . Beneath the charm-box is a small font. Each day every member of the family, in succession, enters the shrine room, bows his head before the charm-box, mingles different sorts of holy water in the font, and proceeds with a brief rite of ablution (415–416).

If you do not recognize this tribe, try spelling its name backwards. (*Note:* Please forgive Miner for his use of the masculine pronoun in describing Nacirema society; he wrote this piece several decades ago.)

Highlights in the History of Cultural Anthropology

The beginning of cultural anthropology goes back to writers such as Herodotus (fifth century BCE; note: BCE stands for Before the Common Era, a secular transformation of BC, or Before Christ), Marco Polo (thirteenth to fourteenth centuries

CE, or Current Era), and Ibn Khaldun (fourteenth century), who traveled extensively and wrote reports about cultures they encountered. More recent conceptual roots are found in writers of the French Enlightenment, such as the philosopher Montesquieu, who wrote in the first half of the eighteenth century. His book *The Spirit of the Laws*, published in 1748 [1949], discussed the temperament, appearance, and government of various peoples around the world. He thought that different climates caused cultural variations.

In the second half of the nineteenth century, the discovery of the principles of biological evolution by Charles Darwin and others offered for the first time a scientific explanation for human origins. Biological evolution says that early forms evolve into later forms through the process of natural selection, whereby the most biologically fit organisms survive to reproduce while those that are less fit die out. According to Darwin's model, continuous progress toward increasing fitness occurs through struggle among competing organisms.

The concept of evolution was important in the thinking of early cultural anthropologists. The most important founding figures of cultural anthropology in the late eighteenth and early nineteenth centuries were Sir Edward Tylor and Sir James Frazer in England and Lewis Henry Morgan in the United States (see Figure 1.2). They developed a model of cultural evolution whereby all cultures evolve from lower to higher forms over time. This view placed non-Western peoples at a "primitive" stage and Euro-American culture as "civilization." It assumed that non-Western cultures would either catch up to the level of Western civilization or die out.

Bronislaw Malinowski, a major figure in modern cultural anthropology of the first half of the twentieth century, established a theoretical approach called **functionalism**. It says that a culture is similar to a biological organism: The parts work together to support the operation of the whole. Religion and family organization, for example, contribute to the functioning of the whole culture. Franz Boas is considered the founder of North American cultural anthropology. Born in Germany and educated in physics and geography, he came to the United States in 1887 (Patterson 2001:46ff). He brought with him a skepticism toward Western science gained from a year's study with the Inuit, indigenous people of Baffin Island, Canada (see Map 2.3, page 36). He learned from the Inuit that people in different cultures may have different perceptions of even basic physical substances, such as "water." Boas came to recognize the individuality and validity of different cultures. He introduced the concept of **cultural relativism**, or

---

functionalism the theory that a culture is similar to a biological organism, in which parts work to support the operation and maintenance of the whole.

cultural relativism the perspective that each culture must be understood in terms of the values and ideas of that culture and not judged by the standards of another culture.

Figure 1.2 Key Contributors to Euro-American Cultural Anthropology

Late Nineteenth Century	
Sir Edward Tylor	First definition of culture, armchair anthropology
Sir James Frazer	Comparative study of religion, armchair anthropology
Lewis Henry Morgan	Insider's view, cultural evolution, comparative method
Early Twentieth Century	
Bronislaw Malinowski	Functionalism, holism, participant observation
Franz Boas	Cultural relativism, historical particularism, advocacy
Margaret Mead	Personality and culture, cultural constructionism, public anthropology
Ruth Benedict	Personality and culture, national character studies
Zora Neale Hurston	African American, women's roles, ethnographic novels
Mid- and Late Twentieth Century and Early Twenty-First Century	
Claude Lévi-Strauss	Symbolic analysis, French structuralism
Beatrice Medicine	Native American anthropology
Eleanor Leacock	Anthropology of colonialism and indigenous peoples
Marvin Harris	Cultural materialism, comparison, theory building
Mary Douglas	Symbolic anthropology
Michelle Rosaldo	Feminist anthropology
Clifford Geertz	Interpretive anthropology, thick description of local culture
Laura Nader	Legal anthropology, "studying up"
George Marcus	Critique of culture, critique of cultural anthropology
Gilbert Herdt	Gay anthropology
Nancy Scheper-Hughes	Critical medical anthropology
Leith Mullings	Anti-racist anthropology
Sally Engle Merry	Globalization and human rights
Lila Abu-Lughod	Gender politics, politics of memory

the view that each culture must be understood in terms of the values and ideas of that culture and not be judged by the standards of another. According to Boas, no culture is "better" than any other, a view that contrasted markedly with that of the nineteenth-century cultural evolutionists.

Margaret Mead, the most famous student of Boas, contributed to understanding how culture, specifically child-rearing, shapes personality and gender roles. Her writings had wide influence on U.S. child-care patterns in the 1950s. Mead was thus an early public anthropologist who took seriously the importance of bringing cultural anthropology knowledge to the general public to create positive social change.

Following World War II, cultural anthropology expanded substantially in terms of the number of trained anthropologists and departments of anthropology in colleges and universities. Along with this growth came increased theoretical diversity. Several anthropologists developed theories of culture based on environmental factors. They suggested that similar environments (for example, deserts or tropical rainforests or mountains) would predictably lead to the emergence of similar cultures.

At this time, French anthropologist Claude Lévi-Strauss was developing a different theoretical perspective, known as French structuralism. He maintained that the best way to understand a culture is to collect its myths and stories and analyze the underlying themes in them. French structuralism inspired the development of symbolic anthropology, or the study of culture as a system of meanings, which was especially prominent in the United States in the latter part of the twentieth century.

In the 1960s, Marxist theory emerged in anthropology, stating the importance of people's access to the means of livelihood. It inspired the emergence of a new theoretical school in the United States called **cultural materialism**. Cultural materialism is an approach to studying culture by emphasizing the material aspects of life, including people's environment, how people make a living, and differences in wealth and power. Also arising in the 1960s was the theoretical position referred to as **interpretive anthropology**, or interpretivism. This perspective developed from both

cultural materialism an approach to studying culture by emphasizing the material aspects of life, including people's environment, how people make a living, and differences in wealth and power.

interpretive anthropology or a symbolic approach, seeks to understand culture by studying what people think about, their ideas, and the meanings that are important to them.

U.S. symbolic anthropology and French structural anthropology. It says that understanding culture should focus on what people think about, their ideas, and the symbols and meanings that are important to them. These two positions are discussed in more detail later in this section.

Since the 1990s, two other theoretical directions have gained prominence. Both are influenced by postmodernism, an intellectual pursuit that asks whether modernity is truly progress and questions such aspects of modernism as the scientific method, urbanization, technological change, and mass communication. The first theory is termed **structurism** (the author coined this term), the view that powerful structures such as economics, politics, and media shape cultures, influencing how people behave and think, even when they do not realize it. The second theory emphasizes human **agency**, or free will, and the power of individuals to create and change culture by acting against structures.

Three Debates

Three debates in anthropology go to the heart of basic questions of why people differ and are similar across cultures, why they behave and think the way they do, and how anthropologists should proceed to understand these questions. The first debate engages biological anthropology with cultural anthropology. The second and third are debates specifically within cultural anthropology.

BIOLOGICAL DETERMINISM VERSUS CULTURAL CONSTRUCTIONISM Biological determinism seeks to explain people's behavior and thinking by considering biological factors such as people's genes and hormones. Thus, biological determinists search for the gene or hormone that contributes to behavior such as homicide, alcoholism, or adolescent stress. They also examine cultural practices in terms of how they contribute to the "reproductive success of the species," that is, they contribute to the gene pool of subsequent generations by boosting the number of surviving offspring produced. In this view, behaviors and ideas that have reproductive advantages are more likely than others to be passed on to future generations. Biological determinists, for example, explain why human males apparently have "better" spatial skills than females. They say that these differences are the result of evolutionary selection because males with "better" spatial skills would have an advantage in securing both food and mates. Males

with "better" spatial skills impregnate more females and have more offspring with "better" spatial skills.

Cultural constructionism, in contrast, maintains that human behavior and ideas are best explained as products of culturally shaped learning. In terms of the example of "better" male spatial skills, cultural constructionists would provide evidence that such skills are passed on culturally through learning, not genes. They would say that parents and teachers socialize boys and girls differently in spatial skills and are more likely to promote learning of certain kinds of spatial skills among boys. Though recognizing the role of biological factors such as genes and hormones, anthropologists who favor cultural construction and learning as an explanation for behaviors such as homicide and alcoholism point to childhood experiences and family roles as being perhaps even more important than genes or hormones. Most cultural anthropologists are cultural constructionists, but some connect biology and culture in their work.

INTERPRETIVE ANTHROPOLOGY VERSUS CULTURAL MATERIALISM Interpretive anthropology, or interpretivism, focuses on understanding culture by studying what people think about, their explanations of their lives, and the symbols that are important to them. For example, in understanding the dietary habits of Hindus, interpretivists ask why Hindus do not eat beef. Hindus point to their religious beliefs, where cows are sacred and it is a sin to kill and eat them. Interpretivists accept this explanation as sufficient.

Cultural materialism attempts to learn about culture by first examining the material aspects of life: the environment and how people make a living within particular environments. Cultural materialists believe that these basic facts of life shape culture, even though people may not realize it. They use a three-level model to explain culture. The bottom level is infrastructure, a term that refers to basic material factors such as natural resources, the economy, and population. According to this model, infrastructure tends to shape the other two domains of culture: structure (social organization, kinship, and political organization) and superstructure (ideas, values, and beliefs). This book's chapters are organized roughly in terms of these three categories, but with the recognition that the layers are not neat and tidy but have interconnections.

A cultural materialist explanation for the taboo on killing cows and eating beef involves the fact that cattle in India play a more important role alive than dead or carved into steaks (Harris 1974). The many cattle wandering the streets of Indian cities and villages look useless to Westerners. A closer analysis, however, shows that the seemingly useless population of bovines serves many

---

structurism a theoretical position concerning human behavior and ideas that says large forces such as the economy, social and political organization, and the media shape what people do and think.

agency the ability of humans to make choices and exercise free will even within dominating structures.

biological determinism a theory that explains human behavior and ideas as shaped mainly by biological features such as genes and hormones.

---

cultural constructionism a theory that explains human behavior and ideas as shaped mainly by learning.

An urban scene in India (LEFT) and in the United States (RIGHT) showing two patterns of traffic congestion.

With growing aspirations of people worldwide to own a car, what do you think urban planners need to consider in the immediate future and for ten years from now?

useful functions. Ambling along, they eat paper trash and other edible refuse. Their excrement is "brown gold," useful as fertilizer or, when mixed with straw and formed into dried patties, as cooking fuel. Most important, farmers use cattle to plow fields. Cultural materialists take into account Hindu beliefs about the sacred meaning of cattle, but they see its relationship to the material value of cattle, as symbolic protection keeping these extremely useful animals out of the meat factory.

Some cultural anthropologists are strong interpretivists, whereas some are strong cultural materialists. Many combine the best of both views.

INDIVIDUAL AGENCY VERSUS STRUCTURISM This debate concerns the question of how much individual will, or agency, affects the way people behave and think, compared with the power of forces, or structures, that are beyond individual control. Western philosophical thought gives much emphasis to the role of agency, the ability of individuals to make choices and exercise free will. In contrast, structurism emphasizes that free choice is an illusion

because choices are structured by larger forces such as the economy, social and political organization, and media.

A prime example is the study of poverty. Those who emphasize agency focus their research on how individuals attempt to act as agents, even in situations of dire poverty, in order to change their situation as best they can. Structurists, by contrast, would emphasize that the poor are trapped by large and powerful forces. They would describe how the political economy and other forces provide little room for agency for those at the bottom. An increasing number of cultural anthropologists seek to blend a structural perspective with attention to agency.

Changing Perspectives

Cultural anthropology continues to be rethought and refashioned. Several new theoretical perspectives have transformed and enriched the field. Feminist anthropology is a perspective that emphasizes the need to study female roles and gender-based inequality. Early feminist anthropologists, starting in the 1970s, realized that anthropology had

Colombian anthropologist Patricia Tovar (center) at an anthropology conference in Colombia. In Central and South America, applied anthropology is an integral part of cultural anthropology.

overlooked women. To address this gap, feminist anthropologists undertook research that explicitly focused on women and girls, half of the world's people. A related area is gay and lesbian anthropology, or queer anthropology, a perspective that emphasizes the need to study gay people's cultures and discrimination based on sexual identity and preferences. This book presents findings from these areas.

In North American anthropology, African American, Latino, and Native American anthropologists are increasing in number and visibility. Yet, anthropology in North America and Europe remains one of the "whitest" professions (Shanklin 2000). Some steps for moving the discipline toward being more inclusive include (Mullings 2005):

- Examine and recognize anthropology's history of racism.
- Work to increase the diversity of professors, researchers, staff, and students in the discipline.
- Teach about racism in anthropology classes and textbooks.

Worldwide, non-Western anthropologists are questioning the dominance of Euro-American anthropology, and they are offering new perspectives (Kuwayama 2004). Their work provides useful critiques of anthropology as a largely Western-defined discipline and promises to lead it in new directions in the future.

The Concept of Culture

Although cultural anthropologists are united in the study of culture, the question of how to define it has been debated for decades. This section discusses definitions of culture, characteristics of culture, and bases for cultural identity.

DEFINITIONS OF CULTURE Culture is the core concept in cultural anthropology, so it might seem likely that cultural anthropologists would agree about what it is. In the 1950s, an effort to collect definitions of culture produced 164 different ones (Kroeber and Kluckhohn 1952). Since then, no one has tried to count the number of definitions of culture used by anthropologists.

British anthropologist Sir Edward Tylor proposed the first definition in 1871. He stated, "Culture, or civilization. . . is that complex whole which includes knowledge, belief, art, law, morals, custom, and any other capabilities and habits acquired by man as a member of society" (Kroeber and Kluckhohn 1952:81). The phrase "that complex whole" has been the most durable feature of his definition.

In contemporary cultural anthropology, the cultural materialists and the interpretive anthropologists support two different definitions of culture. Cultural materialist Marvin Harris says, "A culture is the total socially acquired life-way or life-style of a group of people. It consists of the patterned repetitive ways of thinking, feeling, and acting that are characteristic of the members of a particular society or segment of society" (1975:144). In contrast, Clifford Geertz, speaking for the interpretivists, believes that culture consists of symbols, motivations, moods, and thoughts and does not include behavior as a part of culture. This book defines culture as learned and shared behavior and beliefs, a definition broader than Geertz's.

Culture exists among all human beings. Some anthropologists refer to this universal concept of culture as Culture with a capital "C." Culture also exists in a more specific way. The term **microculture**, or local culture, refers to

microculture a distinct pattern of learned and shared behavior and thinking found within a larger culture.

distinct patterns of learned and shared behavior and ideas found in local regions and among particular groups. Microcultures are based on ethnicity, gender, age, and more.

CHARACTERISTICS OF CULTURE   Understanding of the complex concept of culture can be gained by looking at its characteristics.

Culture Is Not the Same as Nature   The relationship between nature and culture is of great interest to cultural anthropologists in their quest to understand people's behavior and thinking. This book emphasizes the importance of culture.

A good way to see how culture diverges from, and shapes, nature is to consider basic natural demands of life within different cultural contexts. Universal human functions that everyone must perform to stay alive are eating, drinking, sleeping, and eliminating. Given the primary importance of these four functions in supporting a human being's life, it seems logical that people would fulfill them in similar ways everywhere. But that is not the case.

Eating   Culture shapes what people eat, how they eat, when they eat, and the meanings of food and eating. Culture also defines foods that are acceptable and unacceptable. In China, most people think that cheese is disgusting, but in France, most people love cheese. Throughout China, pork is a widely favored meat. The religions of Judaism and Islam, in contrast, forbid the consumption of pork. In many cultures where gathering wild plant foods, hunting, and fishing are important, people value the freshness of food. They would consider a package of frozen food on a grocery store shelf as way past its time.

Perceptions of taste vary dramatically. Western researchers have long defined four supposedly universal taste categories: sweet, sour, bitter, and salty. Cross-cultural research disproves these categories as universals. A prominent East Asian flavor, recently added to the Western list, is umami, or savoriness. Providing even more complexity, the Weyéwa (wuh-YAY-wuh) people of the highlands of Sumba, Indonesia (see Map 1.1), define seven categories of taste: sour, sweet, salty, bitter, tart, bland, and pungent (Kuipers 1991).

How to eat is also an important aspect of food behavior. The proper way to eat is one of the first things a person needs to learn when living in a foreign culture. Dining rules in India require using only the right hand. The left hand is considered polluted because it is used for personal cleansing after elimination. A person's clean right hand is the preferred eating utensil. Silverware that has been touched by others, even if it has been washed, is considered unclean. In some cultures, it is important to eat only from one's own plate, whereas in others, eating from a shared central platter is considered proper.

Map 1.1   Weyéwa Region in Indonesia

Sumba, one of Indonesia's many islands, is 75 miles long. The Weyéwa people number about 85,000 and live in small settlements on grassy plateaus in the western part of the island. They grow rice, maize, and millet, and they raise water buffaloes and pigs.

An Ethiopian family eating a meal together (LEFT). A typical Ethiopian meal consists of several meat and vegetable dishes, cooked with distinctive spices and laid out on injera bread, a soft, flat bread that is torn into small pieces and used to wrap bits of meat and vegetables (RIGHT). The entire meal can be eaten without utensils.

■ *How does this meal in terms of social arrangements and food resemble or differ from a recent meal that you have had?*

Another area of cultural variation involves who is responsible for cooking and serving food. In many cultures, domestic cooking is women's responsibility, but cooking for public feasts is more often something that men do. Power issues may arise about who cooks what for whom (see Think Like an Anthropologist).

Drinking   Cross-cultural variations related to drinking are also complex. Every culture defines the appropriate substances to drink, when to drink and with whom, and the meanings of the beverages and drinking occasions. French culture allows for the consumption of relatively large amounts of table wine with family meals, including lunch. In the United States, water is generally served and consumed during family meals. In India, water is served and consumed at the end of the meal. Around the world, different categories of people drink different beverages. In cultures where alcoholic beverages are consumed, men tend to consume more than women.

Culture often defines the meaning of particular drinks and the style of drinking and serving them. Social drinking—whether the beverage is coffee, beer, or vodka—creates and reinforces bonds. Beer-drinking rituals in U.S. college fraternities are a good example. In an ethnographic film entitled *Salamanders*, filmed at a large university in the northeastern United States, the fraternity brothers run to various "stations" in the fraternity house, downing a beer at each (Hornbein and Hornbein 1992). At one point, a brother chugs a beer, turns with a stagger toward the next station, falls flat on his face, and passes out. The movie documents another drinking ritual in which both young men and women at fraternity parties swallow live salamanders, sometimes two or three

at a time, with large gulps of beer. (This practice is now forbidden by law.)

Sleeping   Common sense might say that sleep is the one natural function that is not shaped by culture because people tend to do it at least once every 24 hours, everyone shuts their eyes to do it, everyone lies down to do it, and most people sleep at night. Going without sleep for an extended period can lead to insanity and even death.

Sleep, however, is at least as much culturally shaped as it is biologically determined. Cultural influences on sleep include the questions of who sleeps with whom, how much sleep a person should have, and why some people have insomnia or other sleep disorders. Across cultures, marked variation exists in rules about where infants and children should sleep: with the mother, with both parents, or by themselves in a separate room. Among indigenous peoples of the Amazon region of South America, mothers and babies share the same hammock for many months, and breastfeeding occurs whenever the baby is hungry.

Culture shapes the amount of time a person sleeps. In rural India, women sleep fewer hours than men because they have to get up early to start the fire for the morning meal. In fast-track, corporate North America, "type A" males sleep relatively few hours and are proud of that fact—to sleep too much is to be a wimp. A disorder in Japan called excessive daytime sleepiness (EDS) is common in Tokyo and other large cities (Doi and Minowa 2003). Excessive daytime sleepiness is correlated with more accidents on the job, more absenteeism, decreased productivity, deteriorated personal and professional relationships, and increased rates of illness and death. Women are almost twice as likely as men to experience EDS, and married women are especially vulnerable.

Think Like an Anthropologist

Power in the Kitchen

Within a family, cooking food for other members can be a sign of love and devotion. It may carry a message that love and devotion are expected in return. Among Tejano (tay-HAH-no) migrant farm workers in the United States, preparing tamales is a symbol of a woman's commitment to her family and thus of the "good wife" (Williams 1984). The Tejanos are people of Mexican descent who live in Texas. Some of them move to Illinois in the summer, where they are employed as migrant workers.

For Tejanos, tamales are a central cultural iden-tity marker. Tamales contain a rich inner mash of pig's head meat wrapped in corn husks. Making tamales is extremely time-consuming, and it is women's work. Typically, several women work together over a few days to do the necessary tasks: buying the pigs' heads, strip-ping the meat, preparing the stuffing, wrapping the stuff-ing with the corn husks, and baking or boiling the tamale.

Tamales symbolize and emphasize women's nurturance of their husbands. One elderly woman, at home in Texas for Christmas, made 200 tamales with her daughters-in-law, nieces, and goddaughter. They distributed the tamales to friends, relatives, and local taverns. The effort and expense involved were enormous. But for the women, it was worth it. Through their tamale making, they celebrate the holiday, build ties with people whom they may need to call on for support, and maintain communication with tavern owners so that they will watch over male kin who drink at their bars.

Tejano women also use tamale making as a state-ment of domestic protest. A woman who is dissatisfied with her husband's behavior will refuse to make tamales, a serious statement on her part. The link between being

Tamales consist of fried meat and peppers in a cornmeal dough that is encased in cornhusks.

a good wife and making tamales is strong, so a husband can take his wife's unwillingness to make tamales as grounds for divorce. One young Tejano sued his wife for divorce in Illinois on the grounds that she refused to cook tamales for him, in addition to dancing with other men at fiestas. The judge refused to grant a divorce.

Food for Thought

Provide an example from your microcultural experience about food being used as a way of expressing social solidarity or social protest.

Eliminating In spite of its basic importance to people everywhere, elimination receives little attention from anthropologists.

The first question is where to eliminate. Differences emerge in the degree to which elimination is a private act or can be done in more or less public areas. In many European cities, public options include street urinals for males but not for females. In most villages in India, houses do not have interior bathrooms. Instead, early in the morning, groups of women and girls leave the house and head for a certain field, where they squat and chat. Men go to a different area. Everyone carries, in their left hand, a small brass pot full of water with which they splash themselves clean. Think about the ecological advantages: This system adds fertilizer to the fields and leaves no paper litter. Westerners may consider the village practice unclean and unpleasant, but village-dwelling people in India would think that the Western system is unsanitary because using toilet paper does not

clean one as well as water does, and they would find the practice of sitting on a toilet less comfortable than squatting.

In many cultures, urine and feces are considered polluting and disgusting. Among some groups in Papua New Guinea (Map 1.2), people take great care to bury or otherwise hide their fecal matter for fear that someone will find it and use it for magic against them. A negative assessment of the products of elimination is not universal, however. Among some Native American cultures of the Pacific Northwest region of Canada and the United States, urine, especially women's urine, was believed to have medicinal and cleansing properties and was considered the "water of life" (Furst 1989). In some death rituals, it was sprinkled over the corpse in the hope that it might rejuvenate the deceased. People stored urine in special wooden boxes for ritual use, including for a baby's first bath. (The urine was diluted with water.)

What about hand-washing practices among people in rich countries? One study investigated fecal bacteria on the

The United Nations seeks to convey a message worldwide that handwashing with soap is an effective way of preventing disease. (LEFT) Women in a village in Bangladesh look out a window beside a poster showing how to wash one's hands properly. (RIGHT) Students participate in an event in the Philippines that teaches children the principles of handwashing with soap to promote hygiene and help prevent an outbreak of swine flu.

Be prepared to discuss how the UN's promotion of handwashing with soap might need to take into account contexts where people do not have access to soap and clean water.

hands of 404 commuters in five cities in the United Kingdom (Judah et al. 2010). It found that 28 percent of commuters' hands had fecal bacteria on them, and men were more likely to have fecal bacteria on their hands than women.

Culture Is Based on Symbols   Our entire lives—from eating breakfast to greeting our friends, working, creating art, practicing religion, and having fun—are based on and organized through symbols. A **symbol** is an object, word, or action with a culturally defined meaning that stands for something else with which it has no necessary or natural relationship. Symbols are arbitrary (bearing no necessary

---

symbol an object, word, or action with culturally defined meaning that stands for something else; most symbols are arbitrary.

relationship to that which is symbolized), unpredictable, and diverse. Because symbols are arbitrary, it is impossible to predict how a particular culture will symbolize something. Although one might assume that people who are hungry would have an expression for hunger involving the stomach, no one could predict that in Hindi, the language of northern India, a colloquial expression for being hungry is saying that "rats are jumping in my stomach." The linguistic history of Barbara—the name of the author of this book—reveals that originally, in the Greek, it referred to people who were outsiders, "barbarians," and, by extension, uncivilized and savage. On top of that, the Greek term referred to such people as "bearded." The symbolic content of the American name Barbara does not immediately convey a sense of beardedness in its current

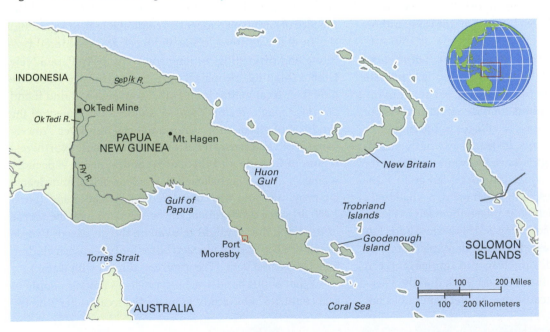

Map 1.2 Papua New Guinea

The Independent State of Papua New Guinea (PNG), the eastern half of the island of New Guinea, gained its autonomy from Australia in 1975. Mostly mountainous with coastal lowlands, PNG is richly endowed with gold, copper, silver, natural gas, timber, oil, and fisheries. Its population is over seven million. Port Moresby, the capital, has a high rate of HIV/AIDS infection among the working-age population.

In India, a white sari (women's garment) symbolizes widowhood.

▌*What might these women think about the Western custom of a bride wearing white?*

context because symbolic meaning can change. It is through symbols, arbitrary and amazingly rich in their attributions, that culture is shared, stored, and transmitted over time.

Culture Is Learned   Because culture is based on symbols that are arbitrary, culture must be learned anew in each context. Cultural learning begins from the moment of birth, if not before. (Some people think that an unborn baby takes in and stores information through sounds heard from the outside world.) A large but unknown amount of people's cultural learning is unconscious, occurring as a normal part of life through observation. Learning in schools, in contrast, is a formal way to acquire culture. Throughout prehistory and much of history, cultures have not passed on learning through formal schooling. Instead, children acquired culture patterns through observation and practice and advice from family members and elder members of the group. Such informal learning still goes on, of course.

Cultures Are Integrated   To state that cultures are internally integrated is to assert the principle of **holism**. Thus, studying only one or two aspects of culture provides an understanding so limited that it is more likely to be misleading or wrong than are more comprehensive approaches.

Consider what would happen if a researcher were to study intertribal warfare in highland Papua New Guinea (see Map 1.2) and focused only on the actual practice of warfare without examining other aspects of culture.

A key feature of highland culture is the exchange of pigs at political feasts. To become a political leader, a man must acquire many pigs. Pigs eat yams, which men grow, while women harvest yams and feed the yams to the pigs. This division of labor means that a man with more than one wife will be able to maintain more pigs and rise politically by giving more feasts. Such feasting enhances an aspiring leader's status and makes his guests indebted to him. With more followers attracted through feasting, a leader can gather forces and wage war on neighboring villages. Success in war brings gains in territory. So far, this example pays attention mainly to economics, politics, and marriage systems. But other aspects of culture are involved, too. Supernatural powers affect the success of warfare. Painting spears and shields with particular designs is believed to increase their power. At feasts and marriages, body decoration (including paint, shell ornaments, and elaborate feather headdresses) is an important expression of identity and status. Looking at warfare without attention to its wider cultural context yields an incomplete picture.

Cultural integration is relevant to applied anthropologists interested in proposing ways to promote positive change. Years of experience show that introducing programs for change in one aspect of culture without considering their effects in other domains is often detrimental to the welfare and survival of a culture. For example, Western missionaries and colonialists in parts of Southeast Asia banned the practice of head-hunting. This practice was connected to many other aspects of the people's culture, including politics, religion, and psychology. A man's sense of identity depended on the taking of a head. While preventing head-hunting might seem like a good thing, outlawing it had disastrous consequences for the cultures in which it was practiced because of its central importance to the entire culture.

Cultures Interact and Change   Cultures interact with each other and change each other through contact such as trade networks, international development projects, telecommunications, education, migration, and tourism. **Globalization**, the process of intense global interconnectedness and movement of goods, information, and people, is a major force of contemporary cultural change. It has gained momentum through technological change, especially in information and communication technology (ICT).

Globalization does not spread evenly, and its interactions with, and effects on, local cultures vary substantially from positive change to cultural destruction and extinction. Four models of cultural interaction capture some of the variation (Figure 1.3).

The clash of civilizations argument says that the spread of Euro-American capitalism and lifeways throughout the

---

holism the view that one must study all aspects of a culture to understand it.

globalization increased and intensified international ties related to the movement of goods, information, and people.

Clash of civilizations	Conflict model
Westernization	Western culture takeover and homogenization model
Hybridization	Blending model
Localization	Local cultural remaking and transformation of global culture

Figure 1.3 **Four Models of Cultural Interaction**

world has created disenchantment, alienation, and resentment among other cultural systems. This model divides the world into the "West and the rest."

The Westernization model says that, under the powerful influence of the United States and Europe, the world is becoming culturally homogeneous. A variant of Westernization is McDonaldization, a model defined by "fast-food culture," with its principles of mass production, speed, standardization, and impersonal service.

Hybridization, also called syncretism and creolization, occurs when aspects of two or more cultures combine to form something new—a blend. In Japan, for instance, a grandmother might bow in gratitude to an automated banking machine. In the Amazon region and in the Arctic, indigenous people use satellite imagery to map and protect the boundaries of their ancestral lands.

A fourth pattern is **localization**, the transformation of global culture by local microcultures into something new. Localization is happening all around us, all the time. Consider the example of McDonald's restaurants. In many Asian settings, people resist the pattern of eating quickly and insist on leisurely family gatherings (Watson 1997). The McDonald's managers accommodate this preference and alter the pace of service to allow for a slower turnover of tables. In Saudi Arabia, McDonald's provides separate areas for families, including women accompanied by a husband or father or brother, and for single men. Single women cannot enter a McDonald's, but they use delivery services. Examples of localization raise questions about whether Western "mono-culture" is taking over the world and erasing cultural diversity.

Multiple Cultural Worlds

Within large cultures, a variety of microcultures exist, as discussed in this section (Figure 1.4). A particular individual in such a complex situation is likely to be a member of

Class	Gender, sexuality
"Race"	Age
Ethnicity, indigeneity	Institution

Figure 1.4 **Some Bases of Microcultures**

A view into the yard of a house in a low-income neighborhood of Kingston, Jamaica. People in these neighborhoods prefer the term "low-income" to "poor."

several microcultures. Microcultures may overlap or may be related to each other hierarchically in terms of power, status, and rights.

In discussing microcultures, the contrast between difference and hierarchy is important. People and groups can be considered different from each other in terms of a particular characteristic, but they may or may not be unequal on the basis of it. For example, people with blue or brown eyes might be recognized as different, but this difference does not entail unequal treatment or status. In other instances, such differences may become the basis for inequality.

CLASS **Class** is a category based on people's economic position in society, usually measured in terms of income or wealth and exhibited in terms of lifestyle. Class societies may be divided into upper, middle, and lower classes. Separate classes are, for example, the working class (people who trade their labor for wages) and the landowning class (people who own land on which they or others labor). Classes are related in a hierarchical system, with upper classes dominating lower classes. Class struggle, in the classic Marxist view, is inevitable, as those at the top seek to maintain their position while those at the bottom seek

localization the transformation of global culture by local cultures into something new.

class a way of categorizing people on the basis of their economic position in society, usually measured in terms of income or wealth.

to improve theirs. People at the bottom may attempt to improve their class position by gaining access to resources and by adopting aspects of upper-class symbolic behavior, such as speech, dress, and leisure and recreation activities.

Class is a recent social development in human history, extending back in time for only about 10,000 years. It does not exist today in remote local cultures where everyone has equal wealth and sharing food and other resources among the group is expected.

"RACE," ETHNICITY, AND INDIGENOUS PEOPLES

"Race" refers to groups of people with supposedly homogeneous biological traits. The term "race" is extremely complicated, as it is used in diverse ways in different parts of the world and among different groups of people. Therefore, it makes sense to put the word in quotation marks to indicate that it has no single meaning. In South Africa, as in the United States, "race" is defined mainly on the basis of skin color. In pre–twentieth-century China, body hair was the key biological basis for racial classification (Dikötter 1998). The "barbarian" races had more body hair than the "civilized" Chinese people. Chinese writers referred to bearded, male missionaries from Europe as "hairy barbarians." Into the twentieth century, some Chinese anthropologists divided humans into evolutionary stages on the basis of amounts of body hair.

Ethnicity refers to a sense of identity among a group based on a sense of a common heritage, language, religion, or other aspect of culture. Examples include African Americans and Italian Americans in the United States, the Croats of Eastern Europe, the Han of China, and the Hutu and Tutsi of Rwanda. This sense of identity may be expressed through political movements to gain or protect group rights and recognition or more quietly stated in how one lives one's daily life. Compared with the term "race," "ethnicity" appears to be a more neutral, less stigmatizing term. But it, too, has been, and still is, a basis for discrimination, segregation, and oppression.

Indigenous peoples, according to guidelines laid down by the United Nations, are defined as groups that have a long-standing connection with their home territories, a connection predating colonial or other societies that prevail in that territory (Sanders 1999). They are typically a numerical minority and often have lost the rights to their original territory. The United Nations distinguishes between indigenous peoples and minority ethnic groups such as the Roma, the Tamils of Sri Lanka, and African Americans. The San peoples of Southern Africa, as well as their several subgroups, are an important example of indigenous peoples whose way of life was dramatically affected first by colonialism and now by globalization (see Culturama).

GENDER Gender refers to culturally constructed and learned behaviors and ideas attributed to males, females, or sometimes a blended, or "third," gender. Gender differs from sex, which is based on biological markers, such as genitals and hormones, to define categories of male and female. Cultural anthropology shows that a person's biological makeup does not necessarily correspond to gender. Biology directly determines only a few roles and tasks, such as giving birth and nursing infants.

Cross-culturally, gender differences vary from societies in which male and female roles and worlds are similar or overlapping to those in which gender roles are sharply differentiated. In much of rural Thailand, men and women are about the same size, their clothing is similar, and their agricultural tasks are complementary and often interchangeable (Potter 1977). In contrast, among many groups in highland New Guinea, extreme gender segregation exists in most aspects of life, including the kinds of food men and women eat (Meigs 1984). The men's house physically and symbolically separates the worlds of men and women. Men engage in rituals that purge them of female substances: nose or penis bleeding, vomiting, tongue scraping, sweating, and eye washing. Men possess sacred flutes, which they parade through the village from time to time. If women dare to look at the flutes, men have the right, by tradition, to kill them.

AGE The human life cycle, from birth to old age, takes people through cultural stages for which appropriate behavior and thinking must be learned anew. In many African herding societies, elaborate age categories for males define their roles and status as they move from being boys with few responsibilities and little status, to young men who are warriors and live apart from the rest of the group, to adult men who are allowed to marry, have children, and become respected elders. "The Hill," or the collective members of the U.S. Senate and the House of Representatives, is a highly age-graded microculture (Weatherford 1981). The Hill is a gerontocracy (a group ruled by senior members) in which the older politicians dominate younger politicians in terms of

"race" a way of categorizing people into groups on the basis of supposedly homogeneous and largely superficial biological traits such as skin color or hair characteristics.

ethnicity a way of categorizing people on the basis of the shared sense of identity based on history, heritage, language, or culture.

indigenous people people who have a long-standing connection with their home territories that predates colonial or outside societies.

gender a way of categorizing people based on their culturally constructed and learned behaviors and ideas as attributed to males, females, or blended genders.

Culturama

San Peoples of Southern Africa

San is a cluster name for many groups of people in southern Africa who speak related languages that have glottal click sounds. Around 2,000 years ago, the San were the only people living in southern Africa, but today they are restricted to scattered locations throughout the region.

European colonialists referred to San people as "Bushmen," a derogatory term at the time but one that San people now prefer over what some locals call them. Some San also refer to themselves with the English term "First People."

For many centuries, the San supported themselves through collecting food such as roots and birds' eggs and by hunting eland, giraffe, and other animals. Now, pressure from African governments, farmers, ranchers, game reserves, diamond companies, and international tourism has greatly reduced the San's access to their ancestral land and their ability to survive. Some have been arrested for hunting on what they consider their land.

The Ju/wasi (True People) are a subgroup of San numbering between 10,000 and 15,000 people who live in a region crossing the borders of Namibia and Botswana. As described by Richard Lee in the early 1960s, they were highly mobile food collectors and quite healthy (1979).

Today, most San have been forced from their homeland and live as poor, urban squatters or in government-built resettlement camps. Many work as farm laborers or in the international tourist industry, serving as guides and producing and selling crafts. Others are unemployed. The living conditions of the San people depend on government policy toward indigenous people in the country where they live.

Transnational advocacy organizations, including the Working Group of Indigenous Minorities in Southern Africa (WIMSA) and First People of the Kalahari (FPK), are making progress in protecting the rights of San peoples.

Recently, WIMSA waged an international legal case with a large pharmaceutical company and succeeded in ensuring that the San receive a portion of the profits from the commercial development of hoodia (*Hoodia gordonii*). Hoodia is extracted from a cactus indigenous to the Kalahari region. An effective appetite suppressant, it is widely available as diet pills, though controversy exists about its efficacy and safety.

Thanks to Alison Brooks, George Washington University, for reviewing this material.

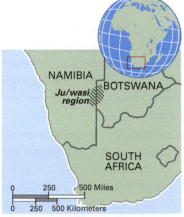

Map 1.3 Ju/wasi Region in Namibia and Botswana

(LEFT) Richard Lee (wearing a shirt) asks Ju/wasi men about food plants of the Kalahari Desert. This photograph was taken in 1968. Lee and many other researchers affiliated with the Harvard Kalahari research project learned to speak the Ju/wasi language.

(CENTER) San people eat part of the hoodia cactus when on long treks in the desert because it suppresses hunger and thirst. Now they cultivate it for commercial production in a diet pill sold in high-income countries.

Before country boundaries were drawn, the Ju/wasi ranged freely across their traditional territory (shaded area), depending on the seasonal availability of food and water. Now they must show a passport when crossing from one country to another.

amount of time they speak and how much attention their words receive. It may take a junior member between 10 and 20 years to become as effective and powerful as a senior member.

INSTITUTIONS Institutions, or enduring group settings formed for a particular purpose, have their own characteristic microcultures. Institutions include hospitals, schools and universities, and prisons. Anyone who has entered such an institution has experienced a feeling of strangeness. Until you gain familiarity with the unwritten cultural rules, you may do things that offend or puzzle people, that fail to get you what you want, and that make you feel marginalized and insecure.

Anthropologists who study educational institutions have shown that schools often replicate and reinforce stereotypes, power relations, and inequalities of the wider society. A study of middle schools in the southwestern Rocky Mountain region of the United States found a situation in which teachers marginalized Mexican immigrant girls (Meador 2005). In this school, Mexican immigrant students are labeled as ESL (English as a Second Language) students because they are not fluent in English and take special courses designed to improve their English. In addition, the teachers' mental model of a "good student" is a student who is

- motivated to do well in school and gets good grades.
- an athlete.
- popular and has good students as friends.
- comes from a stable family.

It is difficult for many Mexican immigrant children to conform to this image. Mexican immigrant girls, or Mexicanas, are especially disadvantaged because most are not interested in, or good at, sports. The few Mexicanas who are motivated to try to get good grades are consistently overlooked by the teachers, who instead call on students who are confident, bright, and popular, and who sit in front of the classroom and raise their hands eagerly.

Applied anthropologists sometimes study institutions to make recommendations about how to improve their effectiveness. In 2014, the American Anthropological Association led an effort to bring together cultural anthropologists with expertise on West Africa to generate suggestions about how to improve health-care institutions in addressing Ebola (http://www.aaanet.org/about/Governance/upload/AAA-Ebola-Report.pdf). Their findings indicate that health-care workers have to learn about local cultures and people's beliefs and values to be more effective in delivering health care to sick people and preventing future outbreaks.

Health-care workers inside a clinic with their Ebola virus protective gear in Monrovia, Liberia, in 2015. The three most affected countries during the 2014 outbreak were in West Africa: Guinea, Sierra Leone, and Liberia.

Distinctive Features of Cultural Anthropology

1.3 **Summarize the distinctive features of cultural anthropology.**

Over the course of its history, cultural anthropology has developed distinctive guiding principles and concepts that emerge from its objectives of understanding and describing different cultures worldwide and how they change. Some of these distinctive aspects have been adopted by other disciplines, and this is something of which cultural anthropology can be proud.

Ethnocentrism and Cultural Relativism

Cultural anthropology has contributed two concepts that are now accepted, and sometimes debated, beyond anthropology. The first is **ethnocentrism**: judging other cultures by the standards of one's own culture rather than by the standards of other cultures. Most people grow up thinking that their culture is the best way of life and that other ways of life are strange and inferior. Ethnocentrism has fueled centuries of efforts to change "other" people in the world, sometimes through religious missionary work, sometimes in the form of colonial domination.

The opposite of ethnocentrism is cultural relativism, the idea that each culture must be understood in terms of its own values and beliefs and not by the standards of another culture. Cultural relativism assumes that no culture is better than any other. This concept has great merit but also has some problems.

---

ethnocentrism judging another culture by the standards of one's own culture rather than by the standards of that particular culture.

| Absolute cultural relativism | Whatever goes on within a particular culture cannot be questioned or changed by outsiders as that would be ethnocentric. |
| Critical cultural relativism | Anyone can pose questions about what goes on in various cultures, including their own culture, in terms of how particular practices or beliefs may harm certain members; follows Lévi-Strauss's comment that no society is perfect and that, therefore, all societies may be able to learn from others and improve. |

Figure 1.5 Cultural Relativism: Two Views

One way that some anthropologists have interpreted cultural relativism is absolute cultural relativism, which says that whatever goes on in a particular culture must not be questioned or changed because it would be ethnocentric to question any behavior or idea anywhere (Figure 1.5). The position of absolute cultural relativism, however, can lead in dangerous directions. Consider the example of the Holocaust during World War II, in which millions of Jews, Roma, homosexuals, disabled people, and other minorities in much of Eastern and Western Europe were killed as part of the German Nazis' Aryan supremacy campaign. The absolute cultural relativist position becomes boxed in, logically, to saying that because the Holocaust was undertaken according to the values of the culture, outsiders have no business questioning it. Can anyone feel comfortable with such a position?

Critical cultural relativism offers an alternative view that poses questions about cultural practices and ideas in terms of who accepts them and why, and whom they might be harming or helping. In terms of the Nazi Holocaust, a critical cultural relativist would ask, "Whose culture supported the values that killed millions of people on the grounds of racial purity?" Not the cultures of the Jews, Roma, and other victims. It was the culture of Aryan supremacists, who were just one group among many. In other words, the situation was far more complex than a simple absolute cultural relativist statement suggests. Rather, it was a case of cultural imperialism, in which one dominant group claimed supremacy over minority cultures and took actions in its own interests and at the expense of the subjugated cultures. Critical cultural relativism avoids the trap of adopting a homogenized view. It recognizes internal cultural differences: winners and losers, and oppressors and victims. It pays attention to the interests of various power groups. It can illuminate the causes and consequences of recent and contemporary conflicts.

Many cultural anthropologists seek to critique (which means "to probe underlying power interests," not "to offer negative comments," as in the general usage of the term "criticism") the behavior and values of groups from the standpoint of a set of generally agreed-on human rights and values. Two issues emerge in this endeavor. First, it is difficult, if not impossible, to generate a universal list of what all cultures would agree to as good and right. Second, as Claude Lévi-Strauss said, "No society is perfect" (1968:385).

Valuing and Sustaining Diversity

Cultural anthropology's findings come largely from firsthand experience in the field, as described in Chapter 3. The perspectives and on-the-ground knowledge of cultural anthropologists lead directly to their commitment to the importance of valuing and sustaining cultural diversity. Different cultural blueprints for life, around the world, show how people in diverse contexts can adapt to changing situations.

Anthropologists therefore value and are committed to maintaining cultural diversity throughout the world, as part of humanity's rich heritage. Many cultural anthropologists share their expertise and knowledge to support the survival of indigenous peoples and other small-scale groups worldwide.

In the United States, an organization called Cultural Survival helps indigenous peoples and ethnic minorities deal as equals in their interactions with outsiders. Cultural Survival's guiding principle is outlined in the preface of this book. Cultural Survival sponsors programs to help indigenous peoples and ethnic minorities protect and manage their natural environment, claim land rights, and protect their cultural heritage.

Cultural Anthropology Is Relevant to Careers

Some of you reading this book may take only one anthropology course to satisfy a requirement. Others may become interested in the subject matter and take a few more. Some will decide to major or minor in anthropology. Just one course in anthropology may change your way of thinking about the world and your place in it. More than that, anthropology coursework may enhance your ability to get a job.

MAJORING IN ANTHROPOLOGY An anthropology B.A. is a liberal arts degree. It is not, however, a professional degree, such as a business degree or a degree in physical therapy. It provides a solid education relevant to many career directions that are likely to require further study, such as law, criminal justice, medicine and health services, social services, education, humanitarian assistance, international development programs, and business. Students interested in pursuing a B.A. major in anthropology should know that anthropology is at least as useful as other liberal arts majors for either graduate study or a professional career.

Anthropology has several clear advantages over other liberal arts majors, and employers and graduate schools are increasingly recognizing these features. Cultural anthropology provides knowledge about the world's people and diversity. It offers insights into a variety of specialized research methods. Cross-cultural awareness and communication skills are valuable assets sought by business, government, health-care providers, and nongovernmental organizations.

The recurrent question is this: Will it be possible to get a good job related to anthropology with a B.A. in anthropology? The answer is yes, but it takes planning and hard work. Do the following: Gain expertise in at least one foreign language, study abroad, do service learning during your undergraduate years, and conduct an independent research project and write up the results as a professional report or conference paper. Package these skills on your résumé so that they appear relevant to employers. Do not give up. Good jobs are out there, and coursework and skills in anthropology are increasingly valued.

Anthropology is also an excellent minor. It complements almost any other area of study by adding a cross-cultural perspective. For example, if you are majoring in music, courses about world music will enrich your primary interest. The same applies to subjects such as interior design, psychology, criminal justice, international affairs, economics, political science, and more.

GRADUATE STUDY IN ANTHROPOLOGY Some of you may go on to pursue a master's degree (M.A.) or doctoral degree (Ph.D.) in anthropology. If you do, here is some advice: Be passionate about your interest, but also be aware that a full-time job as a professor or as a professional anthropologist is not easy to get.

To expand your possibilities of getting a good job, it is wise to consider combining a professional skill or degree with your degree program in anthropology, such as a law degree, an M.A. degree in project management, a master of public health (M.P.H.), a certificate in disaster relief, or participation in a training program in conflict prevention and resolution.

LIVING AN ANTHROPOLOGICAL LIFE Studying cultural anthropology makes for smart people and people with breadth and flexibility. In North America, college graduates are likely to change careers (not just jobs, but careers) several times in their lives. Because you never know where you are going to end up working, or in what endeavor, it pays to be broadly informed about the world.

Cultural anthropology prompts you to ask original and important questions about the world's people and their relationships with one another, and it helps provide some useful answers.

Beyond career value, cultural anthropology will enrich your daily life by increasing your exposure to the world's cultures. When you read a newspaper, you will find several articles that connect with what you have learned in your anthropology classes. You will be able to view your own everyday life as culturally constructed in interesting and meaningful ways. You will be a different person, and you will live a richer life.

---

1 Learning Objectives Revisited

1.1   Define what is anthropology.

Anthropology is an academic discipline, like history or economics. It comprises four interrelated fields in its attempt to explore all facets of humanity from its origins through the present. Biological or physical anthropology is the study of humans as biological organisms, including their evolution and contemporary variation. Archaeology is the study of past human cultures through their material remains. Linguistic anthropology is the study of human communication, including its origins, history, and contemporary variation and change. Cultural anthropology is the study of living peoples and their cultures, including variation and change. Culture is people's learned and shared behaviors and beliefs.

Each field makes both theoretical and applied contributions. The perspective of this book is that applied anthropology, just like theoretical anthropology, should be an integrated and important part of all four fields rather than a separate fifth field. Examples of applied anthropology in the four fields include forensic anthropology, nonhuman primate conservation, global health programs, literacy programs for refugees, and social marketing.

1.2   Recognize what is cultural anthropology.

Cultural anthropology is the field within general anthropology that focuses on the study of contemporary humans and their cultures. It has several distinctive features that set it apart from the other fields of general anthropology and from other academic disciplines. The concept of cultural relativism, attributed to Franz Boas, is a guiding principle that other disciplines have widely adopted.

Cultural anthropology values and works to sustain cultural diversity.

Cultural anthropology has a rich history of theoretical approaches and changing topical focuses. Three important theoretical debates are biological determinism versus cultural constructionism, interpretive anthropology versus cultural materialism, and individual agency versus structurism. Each, in its own way, attempts to understand and explain why people behave and think the way they do and to account for differences and similarities across cultures.

Culture is the key concept of cultural anthropology, and many definitions for it have been proposed throughout the history of anthropology. Many anthropologists define culture as learned and shared behavior and ideas, whereas others equate culture with ideas alone and exclude behavior as a part of culture. It is easier to understand culture by considering its characteristics: Culture is related to nature but is not the same as nature; it is based on symbols and it is learned; cultures are integrated within themselves; and cultures interact with other cultures and change. Four models of cultural interaction involve varying degrees of conflict, blending, and resistance. People participate in cultures of different levels, including local microcultures shaped by such factors as class, "race"/ethnicity/indigeneity, gender, age, and institutions.

1.3 **Summarize the distinctive features of cultural anthropology.**

Cultural anthropology has contributed two powerful concepts that have been widely adopted by other disciplines: cultural relativism and ethnocentrism. These principles continue to shape thinking in cultural anthropology.

Knowledge about culture forms "on the ground." Cultural anthropology's findings come largely from firsthand experience in the field. The perspectives and on-the-ground knowledge of cultural anthropologists lead directly to their commitment to the importance of valuing and sustaining cultural diversity. Different cultural blueprints for life, around the world, show how people in diverse climates can adapt to changing situations.

Cultural anthropology can be an important foundation or complement to your career. Coursework in cultural anthropology expands one's awareness of the diversity of the world's cultures and the importance of cross-cultural understanding. Employers in many fields—such as public health, humanitarian aid, law enforcement, business, and education—increasingly value a degree in cultural anthropology. In today's diverse and connected world, being culturally informed and culturally sensitive is essential.

Graduate degrees in cultural anthropology, either at the M.A. or Ph.D. level, may lead to professional positions that directly use your anthropological education and skills; such jobs are highly competitive. Combining graduate coursework in anthropology with a professional degree, such as a master's degree in public health or public administration, or a law degree, is a successful route to a meaningful career outside academia. Cultural anthropology, beyond its career relevance, will enrich your life everyday with its insights.

Key Concepts

agency, p. 8
anthropology, p. 3
applied anthropology, p. 3
archaeology, p. 3
biological anthropology, p. 3
biological determinism, p. 8
class, p. 16
cultural anthropology, p. 3
cultural constructionism, p. 8

cultural materialism, p. 7
cultural relativism, p. 6
culture, p. 3
ethnicity, p. 17
ethnocentrism, p. 19
functionalism, p. 6
gender, p. 17
globalization, p. 15
holism, p. 15

indigenous people, p. 17
interpretive anthropology, p. 7
linguistic anthropology, p. 3
localization, p. 16
microculture, p. 10
"race," p. 17
structurism, p. 8
symbol, p. 14

Thinking Outside the Box

1. What are your impressions of anthropology? How did you acquire them? Make notes of these impressions and review them at the end of the course.
2. Think about your everyday drinking patterns and your drinking patterns on special occasions. What beverages do you consume, and with whom, and what are the meanings and wider social implications involved?
3. Over one week, keep track of how often you wash your hands each day and whether or not you use soap each time. Compare the data from your mini–self-study to those of your classmates. What patterns emerge?

Chapter 2
Researching Culture

Learning Objectives

2.1 Discuss how cultural anthropologists do research.

2.2 Recognize what fieldwork in cultural anthropology involves.

2.3 List some urgent issues in cultural anthropology research.

Anthro Connections

Cultural anthropologist Robert Bailey and biological anthropologist Nadine Peacock, members of a Harvard University team, conversing with some Ituri people in the rainforests of the eastern part of the Democratic Republic of Congo in the 1980s. Local conflicts starting in 1999 in a small corner of Ituri grew into a brutal and prolonged conflict because of the influence and manipulation of local, national, and regional powers. The UN Organization Mission in the Democratic Republic of Congo (MONUNC) has tried to bring peace to Ituri through military and diplomatic actions (Fahey 2011), but the likelihood of conflict in the region continues because it is rich in oil and precious minerals including gold. The interests of powerful international corporations in the region continue to fuel ongoing local conflict.

This chapter describes how cultural anthropologists do research to learn about people's shared and learned behavior and beliefs. The first section discusses how methods in cultural anthropology have changed since the late nineteenth century. The second section covers the steps involved in a research project. The chapter concludes by addressing two urgent topics in cultural anthropology research.

Changing Research Methods

2.1 **Discuss how cultural anthropologists do research.**

Methods in cultural anthropology today are different in several ways from those used during the nineteenth century. Most cultural anthropologists now gather data by doing **fieldwork**, going to the field, which is wherever people and cultures are, to learn about culture through direct observation. They also use a variety of specialized research techniques depending on their particular goals.

From the Armchair to the Field

The term armchair anthropology refers to how early cultural anthropologists conducted research by sitting at home in their library and reading reports about other cultures written by travelers, missionaries, and explorers. These early thinkers never visited the places they wrote about and had no direct experience with the people whose customs they discussed.

In the late nineteenth and early twentieth centuries, anthropologists hired by European colonial governments moved a step closer to learning directly about people of other cultures. They traveled to their home country's colonies in Africa and Asia, where they lived near, but not with, the people they were studying. This approach is called verandah anthropology because, typically, the anthropologist would send out for "natives" to come to his verandah, or porch for interviewing. Verandah anthropologists, like armchair anthropologists, were men.

In the United States during the mid-nineteenth century, Lewis Henry Morgan took steps toward learning

Ethnographic research in the early twentieth century often involved photography. This Andaman girl wears the skull of her deceased sister. Indigenous people of the Andaman Islands, located off the coast of Myanmar but under control of India, revered the bones of their dead relatives and would not want them to be taken away, studied, or displayed in a museum.

---

fieldwork research in the field, which is any place where people and culture are found.

Lanita Jacobs-Huey's field sites include hairstyling competitions throughout the United States and in London, England. Here, a judge evaluates the work of a student stylist at the Afro Hair & Beauty Show in London.

about people and their culture through direct observation and interactions with more than just a few individuals out of context. A lawyer, Morgan lived in Rochester, New York, near the Iroquois territory. He became well acquainted with many of the Iroquois and gained insights into their everyday lives (Tooker 1992). Morgan showed that Iroquois behavior and beliefs make sense if an outsider spends time learning about them, in context and through direct interactions and experience. His writings changed the prevailing Euro-American perception of the Iroquois, and other American Indian tribes, as "dangerous savages."

Participant Observation

Another major turning point occurred in the early twentieth century, during World War I, laying the foundation for the cornerstone method in cultural anthropology: fieldwork combined with participant observation. **Participant observation** is a research method for learning about culture that involves living in a culture for an extended period while gathering data.

- Living with the people for an extended period of time
- Participating in and observing people's everyday life
- Learning the local language

Figure 2.1 Three Elements of Field Methods in Cultural Anthropology

The "father" of participant observation is Bronislaw Malinowski. He is credited with inventing a new approach to learning about culture while he was in the Trobriand Islands in the South Pacific during World War I (see Culturama, page 28). For two years, he resided in a tent alongside the local people, participating in their activities and living, as much as possible, as one of them. He also learned their language.

With these innovative approaches that are now standard features of field research in cultural anthropology (Figure 2.1), Malinowski was able to learn about Trobriand culture first hand, rather than through secondhand reports or by verandah interviews. By being able to speak the local language, he could bypass the use of interpreters and thus gain a much more accurate understanding of the culture.

Through the mid-twentieth century, a primary goal of cultural anthropologists was to record as much as possible of a people's language, songs, rituals, and social life because many cultures were disappearing. At this time, most cultural anthropologists did fieldwork in small, relatively isolated cultures, and they thought they could study everything about such cultures, following the principle of holism (defined in Chapter 1), the view that one must study all aspects of a culture to understand it. Holism is related to the theoretical perspective of functionalism that recognizes the complex interactions of all aspects of culture.

Today, few, if any, such seemingly isolated cultures remain due to globalization and mass communication including the Internet. Cultural anthropologists have devised new research methods so that they can study larger-scale cultures, global–local connections, and cultural change. One methodological innovation of the late twentieth century helps to address these new issues: **multisited research**, which is fieldwork conducted on a topic in more than one location (Marcus 1995). Although especially helpful in studying migrant populations in both their place of origin and their new location, multisited research is useful for studying many topics.

Lanita Jacobs-Huey conducted multisited fieldwork to learn about the language and culture of hair styles among African American women (2002). She chose a range of sites

---

participant observation basic fieldwork method in cultural anthropology that involves living in a culture for a long time while gathering data.

multisited research fieldwork conducted in more than one location to understand the culture of dispersed members of the culture or relationships among different levels of culture.

throughout the United States and in London, England, to explore the many facets of the far-from-simple topic of hair: beauty salons, regional and international hair expos and training seminars, Bible study meetings of a nonprofit group of Christian cosmetologists, stand-up comedy clubs, a computer-mediated discussion about the politics of Black hair, and a cosmetology school in Charleston, South Carolina.

Doing Fieldwork in Cultural Anthropology

2.2 **Recognize what fieldwork in cultural anthropology involves.**

Fieldwork in cultural anthropology can be exciting, frustrating, boring, and sometimes dangerous. One thing is true: It transforms the lives of everyone involved. This section explores the stages of a fieldwork research project, starting with the initial planning and ending with the analysis and presentation of the findings.

Beginning the Fieldwork Process

Before going to the field, the prospective researcher must select a research topic and prepare for the fieldwork itself. These steps are critical to the success of the project.

PROJECT SELECTION Finding a topic for a research project is a basic first step. The topic should be important and feasible. Cultural anthropologists often find a topic to research by carrying out a literature review, which is the formal term for reading studies on the subject and then assessing their strengths and gaps. Such a review is called a desk study or gap analysis. For example, cultural anthropologists realized during the 1970s that anthropological research to date had ignored women and girls, and this awareness led to feminist anthropology (Miller 1993).

Bronislaw Malinowski during his fieldwork in the Trobriand Islands, 1915–1918.

Important events and trends often inspire a research project. The HIV/AIDS epidemic and its rapid spread continue to prompt much research as do other new health threats. The plight of many international migrants and refugees provides a pressing topic for study. Conflicts in Afghanistan, Iraq, Syria, and other places spur cultural anthropologists to ask what causes such conflicts and how postconflict reconciliation and reconstruction can be accomplished (Lubkemann 2005). Climate change and environmental problems have gained a prominent place in public attention since the 1990s, and cultural anthropologists are busy documenting how local groups are affected by drought, declining animal and fish populations, and rising temperatures.

Some cultural anthropologists examine a particular item or commodity within its cultural context, such as sugar (Mintz 1985), money (Foster 2002), shea butter (Chalfin 2004), wedding dresses (Foster and Johnson 2003), coca (Allen 2002), cars (Lutz and Lutz Fernandez 2010), or guns (Springwood 2014). The particular item provides a window into understanding the social relations surrounding its production, consumption, use, and trade, and what it means in terms of people's identities. Anthropologists who do this kind of research use the metaphor of diffraction, given that a focused examination of one commodity can produce insights from many angles around it.

Another advance in methods is related to the need for applied research to produce knowledge with usable results for governments, nongovernmental organizations (NGOs) and businesses (see Anthropology Works). Rather than spending a year or more in the field, they rely on expert knowledge of the culture, a teamwork approach, and shortcut methods, or rapid-research methods, to provide information within a few weeks. Admittedly such research lacks the depth and nuance of traditional extended fieldwork, but it has the advantage of providing "good enough" insights into practical applications.

Another idea for a research project is a restudy, or fieldwork, conducted in a previously researched community. Many previous studies offer a foundation on which later studies can build, providing insights into changes that have occurred or offering a new angle. One of Bronislaw Malinowski's major contributions to anthropology is his classic study, *Argonauts of the Western Pacific* (1961 [1922]) and its detailed examination of the Trobriand Island **kula**, a trading network linking many islands through which men maintain long-standing partnerships involving the exchange of everyday goods, such as food, as well as highly valued necklaces and armlets (see Culturama, page 28). More than half a century later, Annette Weiner traveled to

kula a trading network, linking many of the Trobriand Islands, in which men have long-standing partnerships for the exchange of everyday goods, such as food, as well as highly valued necklaces and armlets.

Anthropology Works

What's for Breakfast in California?

Cultural anthropologist Susan Squires is one of the brains behind the General Mills breakfast food Go-Gurt®. During its first year of production in 1991, Go-Gurt® generated sales of $37 million.

Squires, who earned a Ph.D. in cultural anthropology from Boston University, is a pioneer in consumer anthropology, or the use of anthropological research methods to identify what people do and say in their everyday lives to inform product development and design. In contrast to traditional anthropological methods that involve long-term participant observation, consumer research relies on short-term, drop-in visits, often of a small sample of people who are representative of a larger population. Typically, an

anthropologist and a designer work as a team in the field.

Research into the development of Go-Gurt® took Squires and an industrial designer into the homes of middle-class families in suburban California to observe their breakfast behavior and food choices. On their first day of research, they arrived at a residence at 6:30 a.m. laden with video cameras and other equipment, prepared to have breakfast with a family they had never met. They repeated this process with more families at breakfast time and were able to build up a picture of habits and preferences.

Squires found that a major factor shaping breakfast food choice was the need to leave home early for work or school. Breakfast time is often a rushed affair, cut short by the need to get in the car or meet the bus. At the same time, she learned that parents

want their children to eat healthy food for breakfast, while children are frequently uninterested in eating anything so early in the morning.

Squires realized that the ideal breakfast food for such busy families should be portable, healthy, fun, and come in a disposable container. The answer: yogurt packaged so that it can be eaten by squeezing it out of the package, bypassing the need for a spoon. One mother said that her daughter thinks she is eating a popsicle when she has Go-Gurt® for breakfast.

The work of Susan Squires demonstrates how cultural anthropology can benefit business and the everyday lives of consumers. Two assets of consumer anthropology are its attention to people's behavior and preferences in everyday life and its ability to describe cultural variation and similarities that can translate to effective product design.

A middle-class family breakfast in California. Recent studies claim that multitasking involving telephone conversations and being on the Internet detracts from the quality of social relationships and the ability to concentrate. Whether or not such claims are true, a media-saturated lifestyle does affect eating in terms of the kind of food consumed and social interaction at mealtime.

---

the Trobriand Islands to study wood carving. She settled in a village near the place Malinowski had done his research and immediately began making startling observations: "On my first day in the village, I saw women performing a mortuary [death] ceremony in which they distributed thousands of bundles of strips of dried banana leaves and hundreds of beautifully decorated fibrous skirts" (1976:xvii). Weiner was intrigued and decided to change her research project to investigate women's exchange

patterns. Power and prestige derive from both men's and women's exchange networks. Reading Malinowski alone informs us about the former, but in isolation from half of the islands' population: women. Weiner's book *Women of Value, Men of Renown* (1976) provides an account of women's trading and prestige activities as well as how they are linked to those of men. Building on the work of her predecessor, Weiner shows how a full understanding of one gender requires knowledge of the other.

Culturama

The Trobriand Islanders of Papua New Guinea

The Trobriand Islands are named after eighteenth-century French explorer Denis de Trobriand. They include 22 flat coral atolls east of the island of New Guinea. The indigenous Trobriand population lives on four main islands. Kiriwina is by far the most populated, with about 28,000 people (digim'Rina, personal communication 2006). The Papua New Guinea (PNG) district office and an airstrip are located on Kiriwina at Losuia.

The islands were first colonized by Great Britain and then ceded to Australia in 1904 (Weiner 1988). The British attempted to stop local warfare and to change many other aspects of Trobriand culture. Christian missionaries introduced the game of cricket as a substitute for warfare (Chapter 13). In 1943, Allied troops landed as part of their Pacific operations. In 1975, the islands became part of the state of PNG.

Island-to-island cultural differences exist. Even within one island, people may speak different dialects, although everyone speaks a version of the language called Kilivila (Weiner 1988).

The Trobrianders grow much of their own food, including root crops such as yams, sweet potatoes, and taro; beans and squash; and bananas, breadfruit, coconuts, and betel nuts. Pigs are the main animal raised for food and as prestige items.

Two major economic changes have occurred since the late twentieth century. Trobrianders have become increasingly dependent on money sent to them by relatives working elsewhere in PNG. Development projects encourage people to plant more fruit trees, such as mango (digim'Rina 2005).

Kinship emphasizes the female line, and mothers and daughters form the core of household groups along with males related by blood. A woman's husband, and her child's father, lives with his female relatives by blood, and not with his wife and children. Fathers, even though just visitors, spend as much time caring for their children as mothers do (Weiner 1988). Fathers of political status give their children, both boys and girls, highly valued shell earrings and necklaces to wear. Mothers give daughters prized red skirts.

Trobriand children attend Western-style schools on the islands, and many go to mainland PNG and beyond for further studies. Elders worry that young people do nothing but dream about money and fail to care for the heritage of their ancestors. The elders say, "We don't live on money here. We have our gardens" (MacCarthy 2014:10).

At the same time, the people of the Trobriands increasingly face the threat of HIV/AIDS that is affecting the so-called "islands of love" (Lepani 2012).

Thanks to Linus S. digim'Rina, University of Papua New Guinea, and Robert Foster, University of Rochester, for reviewing this material.

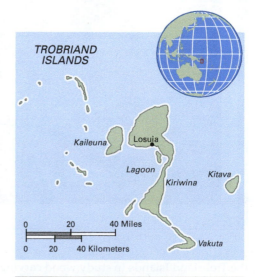

(LEFT) Trobriand men's coveted trade goods include this shell necklace and armlet.

(CENTER) A Trobriand girl wears a valued skirt at a dance in honor of the ancestors on Kiriwina Island. She and other female participants coat their skin with coconut oil and herbs and wear decorative flowers.

Map 2.1 Trobriand Islands of Papua New Guinea

Also known as the Kiriwina Islands, the Trobriands are an archipelago of coral atolls lying off the eastern coast of the island of New Guinea.

PREPARING FOR THE FIELD After defining the research topic, it is important to secure funding to carry out the research. Academic anthropologists can apply for grants from a variety of sources, governmental and nongovernmental. Several sources of funding are also available for advanced graduate students. Undergraduate students have a more difficult time finding grants to support fieldwork, but some succeed.

Related to the funding question is whether it is appropriate for an anthropologist to conduct research while employed in the research setting. Employment provides financial support for the research, but it raises some problems. A basic dilemma, discussed later in the chapter, is the ethical principle that anthropologists cannot do "undercover" research. If you are working in a factory, for example, while studying what goes on in the factory, you must get people's permission for your study, something that is not always easy. More positively, a work role can help gain people's trust and respect. A British graduate student worked as a bartender in a tourist town in Ireland (Kaul 2004). This position placed him at the center of the village, and people respected him as a hard-working person, thus greatly adding to his ability to learn about the local culture, at least as revealed from a bartender's perspective.

If the project involves international travel, the host government may require a visa and an application for permission to conduct research. These formalities may take a long time and may even be impossible to obtain. The government of India, for example, restricts research by foreigners, especially research related to "sensitive" topics such as tribal people, border areas, and family planning. China's restrictions against foreign anthropologists doing fieldwork have been eased since the 1980s, but it is still not easy to get permission to do fieldwork and participant observation.

Many countries require that researchers follow official guidelines for the protection of human subjects. In the United States, universities and other institutions that support or conduct research with living people must establish institutional review boards (IRBs) to monitor research to make sure that it conforms to ethical principles. IRB guidelines follow a medical model related to the need to protect people who participate as "subjects" in medical research. Normally, IRBs require informed consent, in writing, from the research participants. **Informed consent** is an aspect of research ethics requiring that the researcher inform the research participants of the intent, scope, and possible effects of the study and seek their agreement to be in the study. Obtaining written consent from research participants is reasonable and feasible in many anthropological research projects. Written consent, however, is often not reasonable or feasible, especially in oral-based cultures where most people are not literate. Fortunately, IRBs are gaining more experience with the contexts in which

cultural anthropologists do research. Some universities' IRBs will waive the requirement for written informed consent, allowing oral informed consent instead. IRB guidelines do change, so check your institution's website for the latest policy.

Depending on the project's location, preparation for the field may involve buying specialized equipment, such as a tent, warm clothing, waterproof clothing, and sturdy boots. Health preparations may require immunization against contagious diseases such as yellow fever. For research in a remote area, a medical kit and basic first-aid training are essential. Research equipment and supplies are another important aspect of preparation. Cameras, video recorders, tape recorders, and laptop computers are now basic field equipment.

If a researcher is unfamiliar with the local language, intensive language training before going to the field is critical. Even with language training in advance, cultural anthropologists often find that they cannot communicate in the local version of the language they studied in a classroom. Therefore, many fieldworkers rely on help from a local interpreter throughout their study or at least in its early stages.

Working in the Field

Another key step in establishing a fieldwork project is to decide on the particular location or locations for the research. The second is to find a place to live.

SITE SELECTION A research site is the place where the research takes place. The researcher often has a basic idea of the area where the fieldwork will occur—for example, a favela (shantytown) in Brazil, a village in Scotland, or a factory in Malaysia. But it is often impossible to know in advance exactly where the project will be located. Selecting a research site depends on many factors. It may be necessary to find a large village if the project involves class differences in work patterns, or a clinic if the study concerns health-care behavior. It may be difficult to find a village, neighborhood, or institution in which the people welcome the researcher and the project. Often, housing shortages mean that even the most welcoming community cannot provide space for an anthropologist.

GAINING RAPPORT Rapport is a trusting relationship between the researcher and the study population. In the early stages of research, the primary goal is to establish rapport with key leaders or decision makers in the

---

informed consent an aspect of fieldwork ethics requiring that the researcher inform the research participants of the intent, scope, and possible effects of the proposed study and seek their consent to be in the study.

rapport a trusting relationship between the researcher and the study population.

community who may serve as gatekeepers (people who formally or informally control access to the group or community). Gaining rapport involves trust on the part of the study population, and that trust depends on how the researcher presents herself or himself. In many cultures, people have difficulty understanding why a person would come to study them because they do not know about universities and research and cultural anthropology. They may provide their own explanations based on previous experience with outsiders whose goals differed from those of cultural anthropologists, such as tax collectors, family planning promoters, and law-enforcement officials.

Stories about false role assignments can be humorous. During his 1970s fieldwork in Northwest Pakistan, Richard Kurin reports that, in the first stage of his research, the villagers thought he was an international spy from America, Russia, India, or China (1980). Over time, he convinced them that he was not a spy. So what was he? The villagers came up with several roles for Kurin. First, they speculated that he was a teacher of English because he was tutoring one of the village boys. Second, they guessed that he must be a doctor because he gave people aspirin. Third, they thought he might be a lawyer who could help them in local disputes because he could read court orders. Last, they decided that he was a descendant of a local clan because of the similarity of his last name and that of an ancestral king. For Richard Kurin, the last of these—being a true "Karan"—was best of all.

Being labeled a spy continues to be a problem for anthropologists. Christa Salamandra, a Western-trained graduate student in anthropology, went to Damascus, Syria (Map 2.2), to do research for her doctoral dissertation in anthropology (2004). Although Damascus has an ancient history, it is increasingly cosmopolitan. Damascenes, however, have little exposure to anthropology. Syria has no university with a department of anthropology, and there are no Syrian anthropologists. Salamandra's research interests in popular culture (movies, cafés, and fashion) perplexed the local people, who decided she must be a foreign spy. One person said to her, "Your question is CIA, not academic" (2004:5). Nevertheless, she managed to carry out her study and write a book about popular culture in Damascus.

GIFT-GIVING AND EXCHANGE Giving gifts to people involved in the research can help the project proceed, but gifts should be culturally and ethically appropriate. Learning the local rules of exchange is important (Figure 2.2).

Matthews Hamabata, a Japanese American who did fieldwork in Japan, learned about the complexities of gift-giving among Japanese business families (1990). He developed a close relationship with one family, the Itoos, and helped their daughter apply for admission to universities in the United States. When the applications were completed, Mrs. Itoo invited him to an expensive restaurant to celebrate. After the dinner, she handed him a small, carefully wrapped

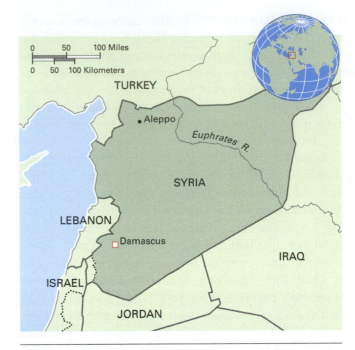

Map 2.2 Syria

The Syrian Arabic Republic historically included the present-day territories of Lebanon, Israel, the Palestinian Territories, and parts of Jordan. The population of Syria is 18 million people. The capital city, Damascus, with a population of 2.5 million people, is one of the oldest continually inhabited cities in the world. Since the onset of the civil war in 2011, over nine million Syrians have been displaced internally, and over four million are refugees living outside Syria in dire conditions.

package, expressing her embarrassment at the inadequacy of her gift in relation to all that he had done for her daughter. When he returned home, he opened the gift. It was a box of chocolates. Upon opening the box, he discovered 50,000 yen (about US$250). Hamabata felt insulted: "Who do the Itoos think they are? They can't buy me or my services!" (1990:21–22). He asked some Japanese friends what he should do. They told him that the gift signaled the Itoos' wish to have a long-standing relationship and that returning the money to the Itoos would be an insult. They advised him to give a return gift later on, to maintain the relationship. His gift should leave him in debt by about 25,000 yen, given his status as an anthropologist in relation to the Itoos' status as a rich business family. This strategy worked, and the relationship between Hamabata and the Itoos remained intact.

- What is an appropriate gift
- How to deliver a gift
- How to behave as a gift-giver
- How to behave when receiving a gift
- Whether and how to give a follow-up gift

Figure 2.2 Culture and Gift-Giving in the Field

MICROCULTURES AND FIELDWORK Class, "race"/ ethnicity, gender, and age all affect how the local people will perceive and welcome an anthropologist. Some examples illustrate how microcultures influence rapport and affect the research in other ways.

Class In most fieldwork situations, the anthropologist is more wealthy and powerful than the people studied. This difference is obvious to the people. They know that the anthropologist must have spent hundreds or thousands of dollars to travel to the research site. They see the anthropologist's expensive equipment (camera, tape recorder, video recorder, even a vehicle) and valuable material goods (stainless steel knives, cigarettes, flashlights, canned food, and medicines).

Many years ago, Laura Nader urged that anthropologists should also "study up" by doing research among powerful people such as members of the business elite, political leaders, and government officials (1972). As one example of this approach, research on the high-fashion industry of Japan placed the anthropologist in touch with members of the Japanese elite—influential people capable of taking her to court if they felt she wrote something defamatory about them (Kondo 1997). Studying up has prompted greater attention to accountability to the people being studied, whether or not they are able to read what the anthropologist has written about them or are wealthy enough to hire a lawyer if they do not like how they and their culture have been presented.

"Race"/Ethnicity For most of its history, cultural anthropology has been dominated by Euro-American White researchers who study "other" cultures that are mainly non-White and non-Euro-American. The effects of "Whiteness" on role assignments range from the anthropologist being considered a god or ancestral spirit to being reviled as a representative of a colonialist past or neocolonialist present. While doing research in a village in Jamaica, Tony Whitehead learned how "race" and status interact (1986). Whitehead is an African American from a low-income family. Being of a similar "race" and class as the rural Jamaicans with whom he was doing research, he assumed that he would quickly build rapport because of a shared heritage. The people of Haversham, however, have a complex status system that relegated Whitehead to a position that he did not predict, as he explains:

> I was shocked when the people . . . began talking to me and referring to me as a "big," "brown," "pretty-talking" man. "Big" was not a reference to my weight but to my higher social status as they perceived it, and "brown" referred not only to my skin color but also to my higher social status. . . . More embarrassing than bothersome were the references to how "pretty" I talked, a comment on my Standard English speech pattern. . . . Frequently mothers told me that their children were going to school so that they could learn to talk as pretty as I did. (1986:214–215)

This experience prompted Whitehead to ponder the complexities of "race" and status cross-culturally.

Gender If a female researcher is young and unmarried, she is likely to face more difficulties than a young unmarried man or an older woman, married or single, because people in most cultures consider a young unmarried female on her own as extremely unusual. Rules of gender segregation may dictate that a young unmarried woman should not move about freely without a male escort, attend certain events, or be in certain places. A woman researcher who studied a community of gay men in the United States says:

> I was able to do fieldwork in those parts of the setting dedicated to sociability and leisure—bars, parties, family gatherings. I was not, however, able to observe in those parts of the setting dedicated to sexuality—even quasi-public settings such as homosexual bath houses. . . . Thus my portrait of the gay community is only a partial one, bounded by the social roles assigned to females within the male homosexual world. (Warren 1988:18)

Gender segregation may also prevent male researchers from gaining access to a full range of activities. Liza Dalby, a White American, lived with the geishas of Kyoto, Japan,

American anthropologist Liza Dalby in formal geisha dress during her fieldwork on geisha culture in Kyoto, Japan.

▌ *Besides learning to dress correctly, what other cultural skills did*
▌ *Liza Dalby probably have to learn?*

Tobias Hecht plays a game with some of the street children in his study in Rio de Janeiro, Brazil.

and trained to be a geisha (1998). This research would have been impossible for a man to do.

Age Anthropologists are adults, and this fact tends to make it easier for them to gain rapport with people their age than with children or the aged. Although some children and adolescents welcome the participation of a friendly adult in their daily lives and respond to questions openly, others are more reserved.

CULTURE SHOCK Culture shock is the feeling of uneasiness, loneliness, and anxiety that occurs when a person shifts from one culture to a different one. The more different the two cultures are, the more severe the shock is likely to be. Culture shock happens to many cultural anthropologists, no matter how much they have tried to prepare themselves for fieldwork. It also happens to students who study abroad, Peace Corps volunteers, and others who spend a long time living in another culture.

Culture shock can range from problems with food to language barriers and loneliness. Food differences were a major problem in adjustment for a Chinese anthropologist who came to the United States (Huang 1993). American food never gave him a "full" feeling. An American anthropologist who went to Pohnpei (pona-pay), an island in the Federated States of Micronesia (see Map 5.6, page 106), found that

---

culture shock persistent feelings of uneasiness, loneliness, and anxiety that often occur when a person has shifted from one culture to a different one.

deductive approach (to research) a research method that involves posing a research question or hypothesis, gathering data related to the question, and then assessing the findings in relation to the original hypothesis.

etic an analytical framework used by outside analysts in studying culture.

inductive approach (to research) a research approach that avoids hypothesis formation in advance of the research and instead takes its lead from the culture being studied.

---

her lack of skills in the local language caused her the most serious adjustment problems (Ward 1989). She says, "Even dogs understood more than I did. . . . [I will never] forget the agony of stepping on a woman's toes. Instead of asking for forgiveness, I blurted out, 'His canoe is blue' " (1989:14).

A frequent psychological aspect of culture shock is the feeling of reduced competence as a cultural actor. At home, the anthropologist is highly competent, carrying out everyday tasks, such as shopping, talking with people, and mailing a package, without thinking. In a new culture, the simplest tasks are difficult and one's sense of self-efficacy is undermined.

Reverse culture shock may occur after coming home. An American anthropologist describes his feelings on returning to San Francisco after a year of fieldwork in a village in India:

> We could not understand why people were so distant and hard to reach, or why they talked and moved so quickly. We were a little frightened at the sight of so many white faces and we could not understand why no one stared at us, brushed against us, or admired our baby. (Beals 1980:119)

Fieldwork Techniques

The goal of fieldwork is to collect information, or data, about the research topic. In cultural anthropology, variations exist about what kinds of data to emphasize and the best ways to collect data.

DEDUCTIVE AND INDUCTIVE RESEARCH A **deductive approach** is a form of research that starts from a research question or hypothesis, and then involves collecting relevant data through observation, interviews, and other methods. This approach produces **etic** (pronounced like the last two syllables of "phonetic," or eh-tik) data, or data collected according to the researcher's questions and categories, with the goal of being able to test a hypothesis (Figure 2.3). An **inductive approach** is a form of research

Research Approach	Type of Data	Data
Inductive (emic)	Qualitative	Participation observation, interviews, video, archival data, life history
Deductive (etic)	Quantitative	Participant observation, interviews, survey, time allocation, census data, other statistical data
Mixed	Qualitative and Quantitative	A combination of the above as relevant to the study objectives

Figure 2.3 Methods in Cultural Anthropology

that proceeds without a hypothesis and involves gathering data through unstructured, informal observation, conversation, and study of stories, myths, and performance. It generates **emic** (pronounced like the last two syllables of "phonemic," or ee-mik) data that reflect what insiders say and understand about their culture, and insiders' categories of thinking.

Deductive methods are more likely to collect **quantitative data**, or numeric information, such as the amount of land in relation to the population or the numbers of people with particular health problems. The inductive approach in cultural anthropology emphasizes **qualitative data**, or nonnumeric information, such as recordings of myths and conversations and filming of events. Most anthropologists, to varying degrees, combine deductive and inductive approaches as well as quantitative and qualitative data.

Again, most cultural anthropologists collect both types of data. This approach is called **mixed methods**: the combined use of qualitative and quantitative data on people's individual experiences as well as data about the community and regional and global levels to provide a more comprehensive view.

The latest trend is to use what is called big data, massive sets of quantitative information generated by computerized sources such as Google. Such data can provide information about behavior patterns at the local level. Thus, a new area in anthropology is developing called **computational anthropology**, a research approach that uses massive datasets available through Google (see Chapter 9 for further discussion of big data), telephone use, and other computer-based sources, to provide information about social patterns. For example, a study used data from a location-based social network in China. Their research question is: Do locals visit different places than nonlocals? Using check-ins for over 1.3 million people in relation to their home towns, the study shows that locals and non-locals do indeed have different spatial mobility patterns. Notably, the next destination of nonlocals is likely to be a major tourist site. While this finding may sound like common sense, it provides an idea of what such large datasets may provide in the future, as research questions become more well defined (MIT Technology Review 2014).

PARTICIPANT OBSERVATION The term participant observation includes two processes: participating, or being part of the people's lives, and, at the same time, carefully observing. These two activities may sound simple, but they are actually quite complex.

Being a participant means that the researcher adopts the lifestyle of the people being studied, living in the same kind of housing, eating similar food, wearing similar clothing, learning the language, and participating in the daily round of activities and in special events. The rationale is that participation over a long period improves the quality of the data. The more time the researcher spends living among the people, the more likely it is that the people will live their "normal" lives. In this way, the researcher is able to overcome the Hawthorne effect, a research bias that occurs when participants change their behavior to conform to the perceived expectations of the researcher. The Hawthorne effect was discovered in the 1930s in a study of a factory in the United States. During the study, research participants altered their behavior in ways they thought would please the researcher.

TALKING WITH PEOPLE While participant observation is the cornerstone of anthropological fieldwork, the label omits the critical aspect of talking to people. Anthropologists in the field are constantly asking questions such as "What is going on here?" "What does that mean?" and "Why are you doing that?" The process of talking to people and asking them questions is such an important component of participant observation that the basic fieldwork method of participant observation should actually be called participant observation and conversation. Cultural anthropologists use a variety of data-collection techniques that rely on talking with people, from informal, casual, and unplanned conversations to more formal methods.

An **interview** is a technique for gathering verbal data through questions or guided conversation. It is more purposeful than a casual conversation. An interview may involve only two people, the interviewer and the interviewee, or several people in what are called group interviews or focus groups. Cultural anthropologists use different interview styles and formats, depending on the kinds of information they seek, the amount of time they have, and their language skills. The least structured type of interview is an open-ended interview, in which the respondent (interviewee) takes the lead in setting the direction of the conversation, determining the topics to be covered, and choosing how much time to devote to a particular topic. The interviewer does not interrupt or provide prompting questions. In this way, the researcher discovers what themes are important to the person.

---

emic insiders' perceptions and categories, and their explanations for why they do what they do.

quantitative data numeric information.

qualitative data nonnumeric information.

mixed methods data collection and analysis that integrates quantitative and qualitative approaches for a more comprehensive understanding of culture.

computational anthropology a research approach that uses large quantitative datasets available through Google, telephone use, and other computer-based sources to provide large-scale information about human preferences, values, and behavior.

interview a research technique that involves gathering verbal data through questions or guided conversation between at least two people.

A **questionnaire** is a formal research instrument containing a preset series of questions that the anthropologist asks in a face-to-face setting, by mail, e-mail, or telephone. Cultural anthropologists who use questionnaires favor a face-to-face setting. Like interviews, questionnaires vary in the degree to which the questions are structured (close ended) or unstructured (open ended). Structured questions limit the range of possible responses—for example, by asking research participants to rate their positions on a particular issue as "very positive," "positive," "negative," "very negative," or "no opinion." Unstructured interviews generate more emic responses.

When designing a questionnaire, the researcher should have enough familiarity with the study population to be able to develop questions that make cultural sense. Researchers who take a ready-made questionnaire to the field with them should ask another researcher who knows the culture to review the questionnaire in advance to see whether it makes sense. Further revisions may be required in the field to make the questionnaire fit local conditions. A pilot study using the questionnaire among a small number of people in the research area can expose areas that need further revision.

COMBINING OBSERVATION AND TALKING A combination of observation of what people actually do with verbal data about what people say they do and think is essential for a well-rounded view of a culture (Sanjek 2000). People may say that they do something or believe something, but their behavior may differ from what they say. For example, people may say that sons and daughters inherit equal shares of family property when the parents die. Research into what really happens may reveal that daughters do not, in fact, inherit equal shares. Similarly, an anthropologist might learn from people and their laws that discrimination on the basis of skin color is illegal. Research on people's behavior might reveal clear examples of discrimination. It is important for an anthropologist to learn about both what people say and what happens. Both are "true" aspects of culture.

SPECIALIZED METHODS Cultural anthropologists also use several kinds of specific research methods. The choice depends on the anthropologist's research goals.

Life History A life history is a qualitative, in-depth description of an individual's life as narrated to the researcher. Anthropologists differ in their views about the value of the life history as a method in cultural anthropology. Early in the twentieth century, Franz Boas rejected this method as unscientific because research participants might lie or exaggerate (Peacock and Holland 1993). Others

disagree, saying that a life history reveals rich information on individuals and how they think, no matter how "distorted" their reports are. For example, some anthropologists have questioned the accuracy of parts of *Nisa: The Life and Times of a !Kung Woman* (Shostak 1981), which is probably the most widely read life history in anthropology. It is a book-length story of Nisa, a Ju/wasi (!Kung) woman of the Kalahari Desert of southern Africa (review Culturama, Chapter 1, page 18). Presented in Nisa's voice, the book offers details about her childhood and several marriages. The value of the narrative is not so much whether it is "true" or not; rather, the value is that we learn from Nisa about what she wants to tell, her view of her experiences. That counts as "data" in cultural anthropology, for it is "truly" what she reported to Marjorie Shostak.

In the early days of life history research, anthropologists tried to choose an individual who was somehow typical, average, or representative. It is not possible, however, to find one person who is representative of an entire culture in the scientific sense. Instead, anthropologists seek individuals who occupy particularly revealing social niches. For example, Gananath Obeyesekere (oh-bay-yuh-sek-eruh) analyzed the life histories of four Sri Lankan people, three women and one man (1981). Each became a Hindu religious devotee and ascetic, distinguished by their hair, which is permanently matted into long, twisted coils that look like snakes. If they try to comb out the tangles, they cannot succeed because, according to the devotees, a deity is present in their matted hair. Obeyesekere suggests that all four people had suffered deep psychological afflictions during their lives, including sexual anxieties. Their matted hair symbolizes their suffering and provides them with a special status as holy, thus placing them beyond the rules of married life including marital sexual relations.

Time Allocation Study A time allocation study is a quantitative method that collects data on how people spend their time each day on particular activities. This method relies on standard time units and then labeling or coding the activities that occur within certain time segments (Gross 1984). Activity codes must be adapted to fit local contexts. For example, activity codes for various kinds of work would not be useful in a time allocation study in a retirement home. Data can be collected through observation that may be continuous, at fixed intervals (for instance, every 48 hours), or on a random basis. Continuous observation is extremely time-consuming and means that the number of people observed is limited. Spot observations help increase the number of observations but may inadvertently miss important activities. Another option for data collection is to ask people to keep daily time logs or diaries.

Texts Many cultural anthropologists collect and analyze textual material, a category that includes written or oral stories, myths, plays, sayings, speeches, jokes,

---

questionnaire a formal research instrument containing a preset series of questions that the anthropologist asks in a face-to-face setting, by mail, e-mail, or telephone.

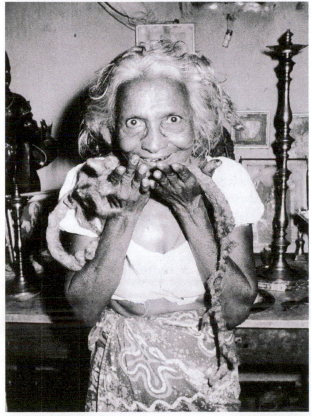

Life histories are a long-standing method of data collection in cultural anthropology. (TOP) Marjorie Shostak interviewing Nisa during fieldwork among the Ju/wasi in 1975. (BOTTOM) This Sri Lankan woman, whose life story Gananath Obeyesekere analyzed, is a priestess to a deity. She stands in the shrine room of her house, holding her matted, snaky hair.

What would you tell an anthropologist about your life and what might you decide to not discuss?

transcriptions of people's everyday conversations, and material on the Internet and social media outlets.

In the early twentieth century, Franz Boas recorded thousands of pages of texts from American Indians of the Northwest Coast of Canada, including myths, songs, speeches, and accounts of how to perform rituals. These collections provide valuable records of cultures that have changed since the time of his fieldwork. Surviving tribal members have consulted them to recover forgotten aspects of their culture.

Boas would be interested to know about new studies in cultural anthropology that analyze Internet websites for their social meaning. The Internet has been labeled a modern-day Pandora's box because it makes available to the viewing public any and all knowledge and opinions, right or wrong, evidence-based or not. Anna Kata, a graduate student in anthropology at McMaster University in Canada, examined several Internet sites for the social discourse, or shared themes, about the dangers of vaccination (2010). As background, she consulted published data showing that around 74 percent of Americans and 72 percent of Canadians are online. Of them, between 75 and 80 percent of users search for health information, and of them, 70 percent say that the information they access influences their medical treatment decisions, so the Internet plays a large role in people's medical decision making. Using Google as her search engine, Kata applied several criteria to label a particular website as "anti-vaccination." In all, she examined eight American and Canadian sites for content analysis. The prominent themes that emerged are safety (vaccines are poisons), effectiveness (vaccines are not effective), alternative medicine favored over vaccines ("back to nature"), civil liberties (parental rights), conspiracy theories (accusations of cover-up), religion (go with God-given immune system), misinformation about vaccine studies, and emotional appeals (personal testimonies). Combating anti-vaccination views with education is necessary but not sufficient, Kata concludes. Analysis of the social discourse on the Internet can help pinpoint areas that need further study.

Multiple Research Methods and Team Projects Most cultural anthropologists use a mix of several methods for their research because just one would not provide all the varieties of data necessary to understand a given topic. For example, consider what interviews with people in 100 households would provide in breadth of coverage, and then add what you could learn from life histories collected from a subset of five men and five women to provide depth, as well as what long-term participant observation with these people would contribute.

Anthropologists, with their in-depth insights about real people and real people's lives, are increasingly taking part in multidisciplinary research projects, especially projects with an applied focus. Such teamwork strengthens the research by adding more perspectives and methods. For example, a team project uses mixed methods such as data from group interviews, one-on-one interviews, participant observation, and mapping to provide detailed information on Inuit place names and environmental knowledge (see Eye on the Environment).

Eye on the Environment

Inuit Place Names and Landscape Knowledge

The South Baffin Island Place Name Project is dedicated to collecting and recording Inuit place names and landscape knowledge as a means to preserving climatically important information (Henshaw 2006).

Inuit is a cluster name for many indigenous peoples who live in the Arctic region of Canada, Alaska, and Greenland. Before contact with Europeans, Inuit life was one of constant mobility. Now, most Inuit are settled in villages and towns. As a result, their detailed knowledge of migration routes, locations along these routes, and how to adapt to changing conditions when on the move is being lost.

A recent study looks at toponymy (to-PAH-nuh-mee), or the naming of places. Inuit toponymy is one aspect of a rich set of **indigenous knowledge**, or local understanding of the environment, climate, and other matters related to livelihood and well-being.

The South Baffin Island Place Names Project used several methods for collecting data. The first step was community-wide workshops, with 10 to 15 people gathered together in a community hall. The researchers laid out large maps, and the Inuit added place names to the map and explained their importance.

The second step was conducting one-on-one interviews with Inuit elders. These elders have lived in particular

---

indigenous knowledge   local understanding of the environment, climate, and other matters related to livelihood and well-being.

areas and can provide specialized knowledge about their use (for shelter, fishing and hunting, and storage), routes to and from the site, and likely weather conditions.

In the third step, anthropologists and Inuit collaborators went to many of the sites. They gained firsthand experience about travel conditions to and from the sites and conditions at the sites. They made video recordings and took photographs.

The fourth step was analytical and archival. The researchers created a computer database, linking the ethnographic data to maps.

This research project has many uses. It will provide a data baseline, starting with elders' memories and narratives of important sites and migration routes. It will show, over time, environmental changes that have occurred and how people are adapting to them. It will create an archive of indigenous knowledge that can be used by future generations of Inuit in protecting their cultural heritage.

Food for Thought

Choose an ordinary day in your week, create a map of where you go, and take notes about how key locations are named (such as your dorm room, dining hall, classrooms, and other locations). What names do you use for key sites, and what do the place names mean to you? How would you change your daily route depending on differences in the weather or season?

Map 2.3 Baffin Island in Northeast Canada

Baffin Island, the largest island in the Canadian Arctic, has a population of 11,000. The Inuit name for the island is Qikiqtaaluk. It is part of the territory of Nunavut, and Iqaluit, a town of about 3,000 people, is the capital.

Map 2.4 **Spain**

The Kingdom of Spain is the largest of the three countries occupying the Iberian Peninsula (France, Spain, Portugal). The geography is dominated by high plateaus and mountain ranges. Spain's population exceeds 47 million of which more than five million are foreign residents. Within the European Union, Spain has the highest immigration rate after Cyprus. Spain's administrative structure is complex, including autonomous communities, such as Andalucia and Catalonia, and provinces. The central government is granting more autonomy to some localities, including the Basque area.

Asturias is located in the far north of Spain. It has extensive coastal beaches but the inland is mainly mountainous. The traditional economy was based in fishing and agriculture. Coal mining and steel production were important in the mid-twentieth century but have declined.

Recording Culture

How does an anthropologist keep track of all the information collected in the field and record it for future analysis? As with everything else about fieldwork, things have changed since the early times when a notebook and pencil were the major recording tools. Taking detailed notes, nonetheless, is still a cultural anthropologist's trademark method of recording data.

FIELD NOTES Field notes consist of daily logs, personal journals, descriptions of events, and notes about those notes. Ideally, researchers should write up their field notes each day. Trying to capture, in the fullest way possible, the events of even a single day is a monumental task and can result in dozens of pages of handwritten or typed field notes. Laptop computers now enable anthropologists to enter their daily observations directly into the computer.

AUDIO RECORDINGS, PHOTOGRAPHS, AND VIDEOS Audio or video recorders are a major aid to fieldwork. Their use may raise problems, however, such as research participants' suspicions about a machine that can capture their voices and faces, and the ethical issue of protecting the identities of people. María Cátedra reports on her use of audio recording during her research in the Asturias region of rural Spain (Map 2.4):

At first the existence of the "apparatus," as they called it, was part wonder and part suspect. Many had never seen one before and were fascinated to hear their own voice, but all were worried about what I would do with the tapes. . . . I tried to solve the problem by explaining what I would do with the tapes: I would use them to record correctly what people told me, since my memory was not good enough and I could not take notes quickly enough. . . . One event helped people to accept my integrity in regard to the "apparatus." In the second *braña* [small settlement] I visited, people asked me to play back what the people of the first *braña* had told me, especially some songs sung by a group of men. At first I was going to do it, but then I instinctively refused because I did not have the first people's permission. . . . My stand was quickly known in the first *braña* and commented on with approval. (1992:21–22)

To be useful for analysis, audio recordings have to be transcribed (typed up), either partially or completely. Each hour of recorded talk takes between five and eight hours to transcribe.

Like tape recordings, photographs or videos capture more detail than written notes. Any researcher who has watched people performing a ritual, taken written notes, and then tried to reconstruct the details of the ritual later on will know how much of the sequencing and related activity is lost to memory within just a few hours. Reviewing photographs or a video recording of the ritual provides a surprising amount of forgotten or missed material. The trade-off, however, is that if you are using a camera or video recorder, you cannot take notes at the same time.

Data Analysis

During the research process, an anthropologist collects a vast amount of data in many forms. How does he or she put the data into a meaningful form? In data analysis, as with data collection, two basic varieties of data exist: qualitative (prose-based description) and quantitative (numeric presentation).

ANALYZING QUALITATIVE DATA Qualitative data include descriptive field notes, narratives, myths and stories, songs and sagas, and more. Few guidelines exist for undertaking a qualitative analysis of qualitative data. One procedure is to search for themes or patterns. This approach involves exploring the data, or "playing" with the data, either "by hand" or with the use of a computer.

Many qualitative anthropologists use computers to help sort the data for tropes (key themes). Computer scanning offers the ability to search vast quantities of data more quickly and perhaps more accurately than with the human eye. The range of software available for such data management is expanding. The quality of the results, though, still depends on careful and complete inputting of the data, as well as an intelligent coding scheme that will tell the computer what it should be scanning for in the data.

The presentation of qualitative data relies on people's own words—their stories, explanations, and conversations. Lila Abu-Lughod followed this approach in conveying Egyptian Bedu (bed-oo) women's narratives in her book *Writing Women's Worlds* (1993). Abu-Lughod offers a light authorial framework that organizes the women's stories into thematic clusters such as marriage, production, and honor. Although she provides an introduction to the narratives, she offers no conclusion, thereby prompting readers to think for themselves about the meanings of the stories and what they say about Egyptian Bedu women's lives.

Some anthropologists question the value of such artistic, interpretive approaches because they lack scientific verifiability. Too much depends, they say, on the individual selection process of the anthropologist, and interpretation often depends on a small number of cases. Interpretive anthropologists respond that verifiability, in the scientific sense, is not their goal and, in fact, is not a worthwhile goal for cultural anthropology. Instead, they seek to provide a plausible interpretation or a fresh understanding of people's lives that offers detail and richness.

ANALYZING QUANTITATIVE DATA Analysis of quantitative, or numeric, data can proceed in several directions.

In the Xingu (zeen-goo) region of the Brazilian Amazon, a Kayapo Indian uses a video camera to document public events. Since the 1980s, and largely as the result of cultural anthropologist Terry Turner's work with the Kayapo, they have used video to record ceremonies and other traditional events as well as their political encounters with Brazilians who have been pushing, for decades, to build a large dam that will affect thousands of acres of Indian lands.

Some of the more sophisticated methods require knowledge of statistics, and many require the use of a computer and a software package that can perform statistical computations. The author's research on low-income household budgets in Jamaica involved the use of computer analysis, first to divide the sample households into three income groups (lower, medium, and higher) and second to calculate percentages of expenditures in three categories of goods and groups of goods: food, housing, and transportation (Figure 2.4). Because the number of households was quite small (120), the analysis could have been done "by hand," but using the computer made the analysis proceed more quickly and more accurately.

REPRESENTING CULTURE Ethnography, or a detailed description of a living culture based on participant observation, is the main way that cultural anthropologists

---

ethnography a firsthand, detailed description of a living culture, based on personal observation.

Item	Urban				Rural			
	Group 1	Group 2	Group 3	Total	Group 1	Group 2	Group 3	Total
Number of Households	26	25	16	67	32	30	16	78
Food	60.5	51.6	50.1	54.7	74.1	62.3	55.7	65.8
Alcohol	0.2	0.4	1.5	0.6	0.5	1.1	1.0	0.8
Tobacco	0.8	0.9	0.9	0.9	1.1	1.7	1.2	1.4
Dry Goods	9.7	8.1	8.3	8.7	8.8	10.2	14.3	10.5
Housing	7.3	11.7	10.3	9.7	3.4	5.7	3.9	4.4
Fuel	5.4	6.0	5.0	5.6	3.7	3.9	4.1	3.9
Transportation	7.4	8.2	12.4	8.9	3.0	5.3	7.6	4.9
Health	0.3	0.6	0.7	0.5	1.5	1.4	1.7	1.5
Education	3.5	2.8	3.1	3.2	1.2	2.1	3.0	1.9
Entertainment	0.1	0.9	1.1	0.6	0.0	0.1	0.3	0.2
Other	5.2	8.3	6.9	6.8	2.1	6.0	6.9	4.6
Total*	100.4	99.5	100.3	100.2	99.4	99.8	99.7	99.9

*Totals may not add up to 100 due to rounding.
Sources: From "Social Patterns of Food Expenditure Among Low-Income Jamaicans" by Barbara D. Miller in *Papers and Recommendations of the Workshop on Food and Nutrition Security in Jamaica in the 1980s and Beyond*, ed. by Kenneth A. Leslie and Lloyd B. Rankine, 1987.

Figure 2.4 **Mean Weekly Expenditure Shares (Percentage) in 11 Categories by Urban and Rural Expenditure Groups, Jamaica, 1983–1984**

present their findings. These early ethnographers tended to treat a particular local group or village as a unit unto itself with clear boundaries, and they attempted to provide a holistic view of the supposed unit. Since the 1980s, ethnographies have changed in several ways:

- Ethnographers treat local cultures as connected with larger regional and global structures and forces.
- Ethnographers focus on one topic of interest and avoid a more holistic approach.
- Ethnographers study Western, industrialized cultures as well as other cultures.

Urgent Issues in Cultural Anthropology Research

2.3 **List some urgent issues in cultural anthropology research.**

This section considers two urgent issues in cultural anthropology research: fieldwork ethics and safety during fieldwork.

Ethics and Collaborative Research

Anthropology was one of the first disciplines to create and adopt a code of ethics. Two events in the 1950s and 1960s prompted cultural anthropologists to reconsider their role in research in relation to the sponsors of their research and to the people with whom they were studying. The first was *Project Camelot* of the 1950s; it was a plan of the U.S. government to influence political leadership in South America in order to strengthen U.S. interests (Horowitz 1967). The U.S. government employed several anthropologists to collect information on political leaders and events, without revealing their purpose to the people from whom they collected information.

The second major event was the Vietnam War (or the American War, as people in Vietnam refer to it). It brought to the forefront of anthropology questions about government interests in ethnographic information, the role of anthropologists during wartime, and the protection of the people with whom anthropologists conduct research. Two bitterly opposed positions emerged within anthropology. On one side was the view that all Americans, as citizens, should support the U.S. military effort in Vietnam. People on this side said that any anthropologist who had information that could help subvert communism should provide it to the U.S. government. The other position stated that an anthropologist's responsibility is, first and always, to protect the people being studied, a responsibility that takes priority over politics. Anthropologists supporting this position opposed the war and saw the people of South Vietnam as victims of Western imperialism. They uncovered cases in which some anthropologists submitted information about people's political affiliations to the U.S. government, with the result being military actions and death of the people exposed by the research.

This period was the most divisive in the history of U.S. anthropology. It led, in 1971, to the adoption by the American Anthropological Association (AAA) of a code of ethics. The AAA code of ethics states that an anthropologist's primary responsibility is to ensure the safety of the people participating in the research. A related principle is that cultural anthropology does not condone covert, or "undercover," research.

Both of these principles created controversy among anthropologists about whether or not cultural anthropologists should participate in the U.S. Human Terrain System (HTS) that was part of the U.S. war effort in Afghanistan and Iraq. The HTS was designed to reduce wartime casualties of the U.S. military and civilians by employing cultural anthropologists and others who were knowledgeable about the local culture in on-the-ground operations. The rationale is reasonable: Culturally informed and sensitive militaries will avoid offending local people, will be able to learn about them, and will be more effective in bringing closure to war or counterinsurgency operations (González 2009). While that sounds good, a major problem arises because joining the HTS is likely to place the anthropologist in a position of providing politically sensitive information about local people to the military whose war interests may, in fact, end up harming people. The principle of "do no harm" is impossible, some argue, to reconcile with military action.

COLLABORATIVE RESEARCH A new direction in methods explicitly seeks to involve members of the study population in collaborative research, from data collection to analysis and presentation. **Collaborative research** is an approach to learning about culture that involves the anthropologist working with members of the study population as partners and teammates rather than as "subjects." This strategy, from the start, forces a reconsideration of how anthropologists refer to the people being studied, especially the long-standing term "informant." The term sounds related to espionage or war and implies a passive role on

---

collaborative research an approach to learning about culture that involves anthropologists working with members of the study population as partners and participants rather than as "subjects."

handing over information to someone else. As noted earlier in this chapter, IRBs use the term "human subject," which cultural anthropologists reject for similar reasons. Cultural anthropologists favor the term research participant.

Luke Eric Lassiter is a pioneer in collaborative methods. In a recent project, Lassiter involved his undergraduate anthropology students in a partnership with members of the African American community of Muncie, Indiana. This project resulted in a book with shared authorship among Lassiter, the students, and the community members (2004). The project collected information about African American life that is now housed in a library archive.

Safety in the Field

Fieldwork can involve physical and psychological risks to the researcher and to members of his or her family and research team. Dangers from the physical environment are often serious and can be fatal. In the 1980s, the slippery paths of the highland Philippines claimed the life of Michelle Zimbalist Rosaldo, a major figure in late twentieth-century cultural anthropology (review Figure 1.2, page 7). Disease is a frequent problem. Many anthropologists have contracted infectious diseases that have chronic effects or that may be fatal.

Anthropological research may involve danger from political violence or even war. War zone anthropology, or research conducted within zones of violent conflict, can provide important insights into topics such as the militarization of civilian lives, civilian protection, the cultural dynamics of military personnel, and postconflict reconstruction (Hoffman and Lubkemann 2005). This kind of research requires skills and judgment that anthropology classes or books on research methods do not typically address (Nordstrom 1997, Kovats-Bernat 2002). Previous experience in conflict zones as a worker in international aid organizations or the military can provide life-saving skills.

What about fieldwork danger in supposedly normal situations? After more than 20 years of fieldwork in the Kalahari Desert in southern Africa, Nancy Howell confronted the issue of danger in the field when one of her teenage sons was killed and another injured in a truck accident in Botswana, while with their father, Richard Lee, who was doing fieldwork there (1990). In the months following the accident, she heard from many anthropologist friends who shared stories about fieldwork accidents.

Howell contacted the AAA to see what advice it provides to prospective fieldworkers about safety. The answer was "not much." The AAA responded with financial support for her to undertake a detailed inquiry into fieldwork hazards in anthropology. Howell drew a sample of 311 anthropologists listed as employed in the AAA's *Guide to Departments*. She sent them a questionnaire asking for information on gender, age, work status, health status, and work habits in the field; she also asked about health problems and other hazards they had experienced. She received 236 completed questionnaires, a high response rate indicating strong interest in the study.

Her analysis revealed regional variation in risk and danger. The highest rates were in Africa, followed by India, the Asia/Pacific region, and Latin America. Howell offers recommendations about how anthropologists can prepare themselves more effectively for preventing and dealing with fieldwork risks. They include increasing risk awareness, training in basic medical care, and learning about fieldwork safety in anthropology classes.

Howell's landmark study did not include any questions about safety and security related to threats from colleagues during fieldwork. In 2013–2014, biological anthropologist Kate Clancy and some colleagues carried out research on sexual harassment and abuse in the field by colleagues and mentors (Clancy et al. 2014). Their findings are dramatic, showing that a large proportion of younger, and mainly female, researchers experience sexual harassment and abuse during fieldwork.

Research methods in cultural anthropology have come a long way from the time of the armchair anthropologists. Topics have changed, as have techniques of data gathering and data analysis. New concerns such as ethics, collaboration, and safety continue to arise.

---

2   Learning Objectives Revisited

2.1   Discuss how cultural anthropologists do research.

Cultural anthropologists conduct research by doing fieldwork and using participant observation. In the nineteenth century, early cultural anthropologists did armchair anthropology, meaning that they learned about other cultures by reading reports written by explorers and other untrained observers. The next stage was verandah anthropology, in which an anthropologist went to the field but did not live with the people. Instead, the anthropologist would interview a few members of the study population, typically on the verandah. Early anthropologists were all men and usually employed by colonial countries to study lifeways in the colonies.

Fieldwork and participant observation became the cornerstones of cultural anthropology research only after Malinowski's innovations in the Trobriand Islands during World War I. His approach emphasized the value of living for an extended period in the field, participating in the daily activities of the people, and learning the local language. These features are the hallmarks of fieldwork in cultural anthropology today.

New techniques have developed in recent decades. They include multisited research, in which the anthropologist studies a topic at more than one location, and consumer research that relies on rapid research techniques to deliver information for product design and development that responds to users' needs and preferences.

2.2   Recognize what fieldwork in cultural anthropology involves.

Fieldwork in cultural anthropology involves several stages. The first is to choose a research topic. A good topic is timely, important, and feasible. Ideas for topics can come from a literature review, restudies, current events and pressing issues, and sheer luck. Once in the field, the first steps include site selection, gaining rapport, and dealing with culture shock.

Microcultures affect how anthropologists gain rapport and shape their access to particular cultural domains. Participating appropriately in the culture involves learning local forms of gift-giving and other types of exchange to express gratitude for people's hospitality, time, and trust.

Research techniques vary between being more deductive or more inductive and accordingly will emphasize gathering quantitative or qualitative data. Political economy-oriented anthropologists are more likely to gather quantitative data, whereas interpretivists gather qualitative data, but considerable overlap exists with many cultural anthropologists increasingly open to collecting both. When in the field, anthropologists take daily notes, often by hand but now also using computers. Other methods of recording culture include photography, audio recording, and video recording.

Anthropologists' theoretical orientation, research goals, and the types of data collected affect their approach to data analysis and presentation. Quantitative data may involve statistical analysis and presentation in graphs or tables. The presentation of qualitative data is more likely to be descriptive.

2.3   List some urgent issues in cultural anthropology research.

Since the mid-twentieth century, cultural anthropologists have discussed research ethics. In 1971, U.S. anthropologists adopted a set of ethical guidelines for research to define the role, if any, anthropologists should play in research that might harm the people being studied. The AAA code of ethics states that an anthropologist's primary responsibility is to avoid doing harm to the people involved. Further, cultural anthropologists should never engage in covert research and should always explain their purpose to the people in the study and preserve the anonymity of the location and of individuals.

Collaborative research is a recent development that responds to ethical concerns by pursuing research that involves the participants as partners rather than as subjects.

Safety of the researcher during fieldwork is an important issue. Danger to anthropologists can come from physical sources such as infectious diseases, violence in the research context, and from their research colleagues in terms of sexual harassment and abuse. A survey of anthropologists in the 1980s produced recommendations about increasing safety during fieldwork provides a baseline but needs updating in terms of sexual harassment and abuse.

Key Concepts

collaborative research, p. 40
computational anthropology, p. 33
culture shock, p. 32
deductive approach (to research), p. 32
emic, p. 33
ethnography, p. 38
etic, p. 32

fieldwork, p. 24
indigenous knowledge, p. 36
inductive approach (to research), p. 32
informed consent, p. 29
interview, p. 33
kula, p. 26

mixed methods, p. 33
multisited research, p. 25
participant observation, p. 25
qualitative data, p. 33
quantitative data, p. 33
questionnaire, p. 34
rapport, p. 29

Thinking Outside the Box

1. Think of a situation in which you experienced culture shock, even as the result of just a brief cross-cultural encounter. How did you feel? How did you cope? What did you learn from the experience?
2. Given the emphasis on observation in fieldwork, is it possible for a blind person to become a cultural anthropologist?
3. Have you ever had the experience of taking photographs of a place, event, or people and then being terribly disappointed because the results did not capture the essence of your experience? What was missing from the photographs?

Chapter 3
Economic Systems

Learning Objectives

3.1 Know what are the characteristics of the five modes of livelihood.

3.2 Recognize how modes of livelihood are related to consumption and exchange.

3.3 Illustrate how livelihood, consumption, and exchange are changing in contemporary times.

Anthro Connections

Dharavi is a low-income neighborhood of Mumbai, formerly called Bombay, India, and perhaps the largest slum in Asia. Most residents are poor and, if employed, work in low-paying and insecure jobs. Dharavi has been depicted in many Indian films, including the award winning movie, *Slumdog Millionaire*. Recently, a two-room dwelling, eight feet by eight feet, with no plumbing or electricity, was on sale for the equivalent of US$43,000 (Nolen 2012), and prices are rising because of its location in Mumbai which has some of the highest real estate prices in the world. Developers have long

been eyeing Dharavi, hoping that the city would relocate its residents and open up the area for "redevelopment." The Mumbai government has pledged to upgrade the slum, maintaining most of it as a low-income neighborhood but with services such as piped water. Slum tourism brings many well-off tourists to Dharavi to see how poor people live. Efforts are ongoing to try to bring some of the benefits of this tourism to Dharavi and its residents.

http://www.theglobeandmail.com/news/world/two-room-shack-mumbai-slum-asking-price-43000/article2388735/

During the many thousands of years of human prehistory, people made their living by collecting food and other necessities from nature. All group members had equal access to life-sustaining resources. Now, most people live in economies much different from this description.

Economic anthropology is the subfield of cultural anthropology that focuses on economic systems cross-culturally. The term economic system includes three areas: livelihood, or making goods or money; consumption, or using up goods or money; and exchange, or the transfer of goods or money between people or institutions.

This chapter first discusses the subject of production and introduces the concept of **mode of livelihood**: the dominant way of making a living in a culture. Ethnographic examples illustrate each of the five major modes of livelihood.

The section provides cross-cultural examples of the other two components of economic systems: the **mode of consumption**: the dominant pattern, in a culture, of using up goods and services, and the **mode of exchange**: the dominant pattern, in a culture, of transferring goods, services, and other items between and among people and groups. The chapter's last section presents examples of contemporary change in consumption and exchange.

mode of livelihood the dominant way of making a living in a culture.

mode of consumption the dominant pattern, in a culture, of using things up or spending resources to satisfy demands.

mode of exchange the dominant pattern, in a culture, of transferring goods, services, and other items between and among people and groups.

Making a Living: Five Modes of Livelihood

3.1 Know what are the characteristics of the five modes of livelihood.

Anthropologists define five major modes of livelihood. The modes of livelihood are discussed in order of their appearance in the human record (Figure 3.1). This continuum does not mean that a particular mode of livelihood evolves into the one following it. For example, foragers do not necessarily transform into horticulturalists, and so on. Nor does this model imply a judgment about the sophistication or superiority of more recent modes of livelihood. The oldest system involves complex and detailed knowledge about the environment that a contemporary city dweller would find difficult to learn quickly enough to ensure survival.

Terminology is important in looking at the various ways people make a living. Some anthropologists use the term subsistence to refer to making a living at a minimum level with no surpluses and no luxuries. It conveys a negative view that people who do not have surpluses and luxuries are backward and inferior, and implies that they should change to be more like people in contemporary capitalist cultures. The author of this book rejects the term subsistence but uses the term poverty to convey material deprivation. **Poverty** is the lack of access to tangible or

poverty lack of access to tangible or intangible resources that contribute to life and the well-being of a person, group, country, or region.

Foraging	Horticulture	Pastoralism	Agriculture	Industrial/Digital
Reason for Production Production for use				**Reason for Production** Production for profit
Division of Labor Family-based Overlapping gender roles				**Division of Labor** Class-based High degree of occupational specialization
Property Relations Egalitarian and collective				**Property Relations** Stratified and private
Resource Use Extensive and temporary				**Resource Use** Intensive and expanding
Sustainability High degree				**Sustainability** Low degree

Figure 3.1 Modes of Livelihood

intangible resources that contribute to life and the well-being of a person, group, country, or region. Although development organizations seek to measure poverty across the world using standard criteria, anthropologists show that local definitions of what it means to be poor vary widely (Cochrane 2009, Tucker et al. 2011), along with the causes of poverty. Furthermore, many people reject being termed "poor" because it seems degrading to them. Given its importance and complexity, poverty will be discussed again in this book. A more productive way of looking at how well people are doing in a particular society is to consider **subjective well-being** (Kant et al. 2014). Instead of assessing what people do not have in material terms, well-being considers people's values and perceptions of what is a good life that can include things like family ties, a sense of home and personal security. Subjective well-being cannot be measured by externally defined, global indicators, such as annual monetary income.

While reading this section, please bear in mind that most anthropologists are uneasy about typologies because they often do not reflect the complexity of life in any particular context. The purpose of the categories is to help you organize the ethnographic information presented in this book.

Foraging

Foraging is a mode of livelihood based on resources that are available in nature through gathering, fishing, or hunting. The oldest way of making a living, foraging is a strategy that humans share with our nonhuman primate relatives. Although foraging supported humanity since

our beginnings, it is in danger of extinction. Only around 250,000 people worldwide provide for their livelihood predominantly from foraging now. Most contemporary foragers live in what are considered marginal areas, such as deserts, tropical rainforests, and the circumpolar region. These areas, however, often contain material resources that are in high demand in core areas, such as oil, diamonds, gold, and expensive tourist destinations. Thus, the basis of their survival is threatened by what is called the resource curse: People in high-income countries desire the natural resources in their areas, which leads to conversion of foraging land to mines, plantations, or tourist destinations, in turn leading to the displacement of foragers from their homeland.

Depending on the environment, foragers' food sources include nuts, berries, and other fruits, as well as surface-growing vegetables such as melons, roots, honey, insects, and eggs. Foragers trap and hunt a wide variety of birds, fish, and animals. Successful foraging requires sophisticated knowledge of the natural environment and seasonal changes in it. Most critical is knowledge about the location of water sources and of various foods, how to follow animal tracks, how to judge the weather, and how to avoid predators. This unwritten knowledge is passed down over the generations (review Eye on the Environment, Chapter 2, page 36).

Foragers rely on many kinds of tools for gathering, transporting, and processing wild foods. Tools include digging sticks for removing roots from the ground and for penetrating the holes dug by animals to get the animals out, bows and arrows, spears, nets, and knives. Baskets are important for carrying food. For processing raw materials into edible food, foragers use stones to mash, grind, and pound. Meat can be dried in the sun or over fire, and fire is used for cooking either by boiling or by roasting. These activities involve few nonrenewable fuel sources beyond wood or other combustible substances

---

subjective well-being how people experience the quality of their lives based on their perception of what is a good life.

foraging obtaining food available in nature through gathering, hunting, or scavenging.

	Temperate-Region Foragers	Circumpolar-Region Foragers
Diet	Wide variety of nuts, tubers, fruits, small animals, and occasional large game	Large marine and terrestrial animals, small seasonal plants
Gender division of labor in food procurement	Men and women forage; men hunt large game	Men hunt and fish
Shelter	Casual construction, nonpermanent, little maintenance	Time-intensive construction and maintenance, some permanent

Figure 3.2 **Temperate and Circumpolar Foraging Systems Compared**

for cooking. Foraging is an **extensive strategy**, a mode of livelihood requiring access to large areas of land and unrestricted population movement. Cultural anthropologists distinguish two major varieties of foraging that are related to different environmental contexts: temperate-climate foraging and circumpolar foraging (Figure 3.2).

The Ju/wasi people of southern Africa, as studied in the early 1960s, moved several times during a year, depending on the seasonal availability of water sources (review Culturama, Chapter 1, page 18). Each cluster of families regularly returned to "their" territory, reconstructing or completely rebuilding their shelters with sticks for frames and leaf or thatch coverings. Shelters are sometimes attached to two or three small trees or bushes for support. The amount of time involved in gathering and processing food and constructing shelters is modest.

In contrast to foragers of temperate climates, those living in the circumpolar regions of North America, Europe, and Asia devote more time and energy to obtaining food and providing shelter. The specialized technology of circumpolar peoples includes spears, nets, and knives, as well as sleds and the use of domesticated animals to pull them. Dogs or other animals used to pull sleds are an important aspect of circumpolar peoples' technology and social identity (see Think Like an Anthropologist). Much work and skill are needed to construct and maintain igloos and log houses. Another time-intensive activity is making and maintaining clothing, including coats, gloves, and boots.

DIVISION OF LABOR Among foraging peoples, the **division of labor**, assigning particular tasks to particular individuals or groups, is shaped by factors of gender and age. Among temperate foraging cultures, a minimal gender-based division

of labor exists. Temperate foragers obtain most of their everyday food by gathering roots, berries, larvae, small birds and animals, and fish, and both men and women collect these basic foods. Hunting large animals, however, tends to involve only men, who go off together in small groups on long-range expeditions. Large game provides a small and irregular part of the diets of temperate-climate foragers. In circumpolar groups, a significant part of people's diet comes from large animals such as seals, whales, bears, and fish. Men do most of the hunting and fishing. Among circumpolar foragers, therefore, the division of labor is strongly gender-divided.

Age is an important factor affecting what tasks people do in all modes of livelihood. Boys and girls in foraging cultures often help by collecting and carrying food, fuel, and other daily requirements as well as younger siblings. Elderly people tend to stay at the camp area where they help care for young children.

PROPERTY RELATIONS The concept of private property, in the sense of owning something that can be sold to someone else, does not exist in foraging societies. Instead, the term **use rights** is more appropriate. It means that a person or group has socially recognized priority in access to particular resources such as gathering areas, hunting and fishing areas, and water holes. This access is willingly shared with others by permission. Among the Ju/wasi, family groups control

extensive strategy a form of livelihood involving temporary use of large areas of land and a high degree of spatial mobility.

division of labor how a society distributes various tasks depending on factors such as gender, age, and physical ability.

use rights a system of property relations in which a person or group has socially recognized priority in access to particular resources such as gathering, hunting, and fishing areas and water holes.

A Ju/wasi traditional shelter in southern Africa in the 1960s.

Think Like an Anthropologist

The Importance of Dogs

Dogs were the first domesticated animal, with archaeological evidence of their domestication from sites in Eastern Europe and Russia dating to around 18,000 years ago. In spite of dogs' long-standing importance to humans around the world, few cultural anthropologists have focused attention on humans and their dogs. One of the rare ethnographies to do so provides insights into the economic, social, and psychological importance of dogs among a group of circumpolar foragers.

At the time of Joel Savishinsky's fieldwork, fewer than 100 Hare Indians lived in the community of Colville Lake in Canada's Northwest Territories (1974). Their livelihood was based on hunting, trapping, and fishing in one of the coldest environments in the world. Savishinsky went to Colville Lake to study how people cope with environmental stress. Environmental stress factors include extremely cold temperatures, long and severe winters, extended periods of isolation, hazardous travel conditions along with the constant need for mobility during the harshest periods of the year, and sometimes food scarcity. Social and psychological stress factors also exist, including contact with outsiders. In addition to learning about stress, Savishinsky discovered the importance of dogs to the Hare people:

> ... when I obtained my own dogteam, I enjoyed much greater freedom of movement, and was able to camp with many people whom I had previously not been able to keep up with. Altogether I travelled close to 600 miles by dogsled between mid-October and early June. This constant contact with dogs, and the necessity of learning how to drive, train and handle them, led to my recognition of the social and psychological, as well as the ecological, significance of these animals in the lives of the people. (1974:xx)

The 14 households owned 224 dogs for an average of nearly 14 dogs per household. People estimate that six dogs are required for travel.

More than being economically useful, dogs play a significant role in people's emotional lives. They are a frequent topic of conversation: "Members of the community constantly compare and comment on the care, condition, and growth of one another's animals, noting special qualities of size, strength, color, speed, and alertness." (p. 169)

Emotional displays, uncommon among the Hare, are frequent and visible between people and their dogs. According to Savishinsky, "Pups and infants are . . . the only recipients of unreserved positive affect in the band's social life. . . . (pp. 169–170).

Food for Thought

Think of a culture (perhaps yours) in which dogs or some other domesticated animals are a focus of intense, positive human interest. How do people and the animals in question interact? Are there age and gender differences in human relationships with domesticated animals?

Map 3.1 Hare Region Is Near Colville Lake in Northwest Canada

Early European colonialists named the local people Hare because of their reliance on snowshoe hares for food and clothing. The Hare people became involved in the wage-labor economy and were afflicted by alcoholism, tuberculosis, and other diseases. Efforts to reestablish claims to ancestral lands began in the 1960s. Over 600 First Nations in Canada continue to fight for rights from the Canadian government.

Hare Indian children use their family's sled to haul drinking water to their village.

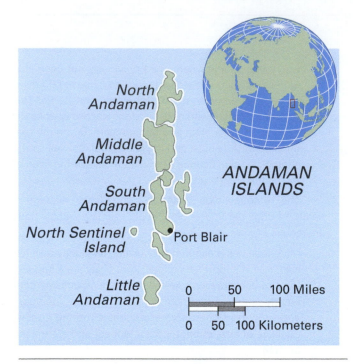

Map 3.2 Andaman Islands of India

The 576 islands are geologically part of Myanmar and Southeast Asia. The British Empire controlled them until India's independence in 1947.

access to particular water holes and the territory surrounding them (Lee 1979:58–60). Visiting groups are welcome and will be given food and water. In turn, the host group, at another time, will visit other camps and be offered hospitality there.

FORAGING AS A SUSTAINABLE SYSTEM When untouched by outside influences and with abundant land available, foraging systems are sustainable, which means that crucial resources are regenerated over time in balance with the demand that the population makes on them. North Sentinel Island, one island in the Andaman Islands, provides a clear case of foraging as sustainable, because its inhabitants have long lived in a "closed" system (see Map 3.2). So far, the few hundred indigenous people live in almost complete isolation from the rest of the world, other than the occasional helicopter flying overhead and the occasional attempt by outsiders to land on their territory.

One reason for the sustainability of foraging is that foragers' needs are modest. Anthropologists have typified the foraging lifestyle as the original affluent society because needs are satisfied with minimal labor efforts. This term is used metaphorically to remind people living in contemporary consumer cultures that foraging is not a miserable, inadequate way to make a living, contrary to most ethnocentric thinking.

Because foragers' needs for goods are limited, minimal labor efforts are required to satisfy them. Foragers typically work fewer hours a week than the average employed North American. In traditional (undisturbed) foraging societies, the people spend as few as five hours a week collecting food and making and repairing tools. They have

much time for storytelling, playing games, and resting. Foragers also traditionally enjoyed good health. During the early 1960s, the age structure and health status of the Ju/wasi compared well with people in the United States of around 1900 (Lee 1979:47–48). They had few infectious diseases or health problems related to aging such as arthritis.

Horticulture

Horticulture is a mode of livelihood based on cultivating domesticated plants in gardens using hand tools. Garden crops are often supplemented by foraging and by trading with pastoralists for animal products. Horticulture is still practiced by many thousands of people throughout the world. Prominent horticultural regions are found in sub-Saharan Africa, South Asia, Southeast Asia and the Pacific, Central America, South America, and the Caribbean islands. Major horticultural crops include yams, corn, beans, grains such as millet and sorghum, and several types of roots, all of which are rich in protein, minerals, and vitamins.

Horticulture involves the use of handheld tools, such as digging sticks, hoes, and carrying baskets. Rain is the sole source of moisture. Horticulture requires rotation of garden plots for them to regenerate. Thus, another term for horticulture is shifting cultivation. Average plot sizes are less than 1 acre, and 2.5 acres can feed a family of five to eight members for a year. Yields can support semi-permanent villages of 200 to 250 people. Overall population density per square mile is low because horticulture, like foraging, is an extensive strategy. Horticulture is more labor intensive than foraging because of the energy required for plot preparation and food processing. Anthropologists distinguish five phases in the horticultural cycle (Figure 3.3).

Clearing: A section of the forest is cleared, partially or completely, by cutting down trees and brush and then setting the area on fire to burn off other growth. The fire creates a layer of ash that is rich fertilizer. The term slash-and-burn cultivation refers to this stage of clearing.

Planting: People use digging sticks to loosen the soil. They plant seeds by scattering them (called broadcasting) or they insert cuttings of plants in the loose soil.

Weeding: Horticulture involves little weeding because the ash cover and shady growing conditions keep weed growth down.

Harvesting: This phase requires substantial labor to cut or dig crops and carry them to the residential area.

Fallowing: Depending on the soil and the crop grown, the land must be left unused for a specified number of years so that it regains its fertility.

Figure 3.3 Five Stages in Horticulture

horticulture a mode of livelihood based on growing domesticated crops in gardens, using simple hand tools.

DIVISION OF LABOR Gender and age are the key factors structuring the division of labor, with men's and women's work roles often being clearly differentiated. Typically, men clear the garden area while both men and women plant and tend the staple food crops. This pattern exists in Papua New Guinea, much of Southeast Asia, and parts of West and East Africa. Food processing involves women often working in small groups, whereas men more typically form small groups for hunting and fishing for supplementary food.

Two unusual horticultural cases involve extremes in terms of gender roles and status. The first is the pre-contact Iroquois of central New York State, that is, before the arrival of Europeans (Brown 1975) (Map 3.3). Iroquois women cultivated maize, the most important food crop, and they controlled its distribution. This control meant that they were able to decide whether the men would go to war, because a war effort depended on the supply of maize to support it. A contrasting example, in terms of the gender division of labor and women's status in relation to men, is that of the Yanomami of the Venezuelan Amazon (Chagnon 1992) (Map 3.4). Among the Yanomami, men are the dominant decision makers and have more social power than Yanomami women do. Yanomami men clear the fields and tend and harvest the crops. They also do much of the cooking for ritual feasts. Yanomami women,

Map 3.4 Yanomami Region in Brazil and Venezuela

The Yanomami region is supposedly protected from outsiders. But miners, ranchers, loggers, and other commercial developers have encroached on the reserve, extracting natural resources and sexually exploiting women and children.

though, are not idle. They play an important role in providing the staple food, **manioc** or **cassava**, a starchy root crop that grows in the tropics. Manioc requires lengthy processing to make it edible, including soaking it in water to remove toxins and then scraping it into a mealy consistency. We will learn about Yanomami life later in this book.

No one can explain the origins of the different divisions of labor in horticulture, but we do know that the differences are related to men's and women's status (Sanday 1973). Most importantly, analysis of many horticultural societies shows that women's contribution to food production is a necessary but not sufficient basis for women's high status. In other words, if women do not contribute to producing food, their status will be low. If they do contribute, their status may, or may not, be high. The critical factor appears to be control over the distribution of what is produced, especially public distribution beyond the family. Slavery is a clear example of how a major role in production does not bring high status because slaves have no control over the product and its distribution.

Children do more productive work in horticultural societies than in any other mode of livelihood (Whiting and Whiting 1975). The *Six Cultures Study* is a research project that examined children's behavior in horticultural, farming, and industrial settings. It found that children among a horticultural group, the Gusii (goo-see-eye) of western Kenya, performed the most tasks at the youngest ages. Gusii boys and girls care for siblings, collect fuel, and carry water. Children do so many tasks in horticultural societies because adults, especially women, are busy working in the fields and markets.

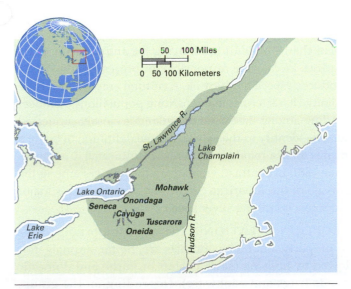

Map 3.3 Precolonial Iroquois Region

At the time of the arrival of the European colonialists, the six nations of the Iroquois extended over a wide area. The Mohawk stood guard over the eastern door of the confederacy's symbolic longhouse, and the Seneca guarded the western door. The six nations worked out a peace treaty and established a democracy. A great orator named Hiawatha promoted the treaty throughout the tribes, and a Mohawk woman was the first to approve it.

manioc, or cassava a starchy root crop that grows in the tropics and requires lengthy processing to make it edible, including soaking it in water to remove toxins and then scraping it into a mealy consistency.

Shopping for cassava in a small town in Colombia. Cassava is widely grown throughout the tropics and goes by many different names. A staple part of the diet of 500 million people in low-income countries; it is a rich source of carbohydrates but not protein.

■ *Do research to find recipes that include cassava or manioc.*

PROPERTY RELATIONS Private property, as something that an individual can own and sell, is not characteristic of horticultural societies. Use rights are typically important and more clearly defined and formalized than among foragers. By clearing and planting an area of land, a family puts a claim on it and its crops. The production of surplus goods allows the possibility of social inequality in access to goods and resources. Rules about sharing within the larger group decline in importance as some people gain higher status.

HORTICULTURE AS A SUSTAINABLE SYSTEM Fallowing is crucial in maintaining the viability of horticulture. Fallowing allows the plot to recover lost nutrients and improves soil quality by allowing the growth of weeds whose root systems keep the soil loose. The benefits of a well-managed system of shifting cultivation are clear as are the two major constraints involved: the time required for fallowing and the related need for extensive access to land so that some land is in use while other land is fallowed. Using a given plot for too many seasons or reducing fallowing time quickly results in depletion of soil nutrients, decreased crop production, and soil erosion.

Pastoralism

Pastoralism is a mode of livelihood based on domesticated animal herds and the use of their products, such as meat and milk, for at least half of the diet. Pastoralism has long existed in the Middle East, Africa, Europe, and Central Asia, especially where rainfall is limited and unpredictable. In the Western Hemisphere, the only indigenous pastoralist system in existence before the arrival of the Spanish in the fifteenth century was in the Andean region of the

New World; it was based on domesticated llamas (Barfield 2001). Sheep, goats, horses, and cattle became prominent after the Spanish conquest. Some American Indian tribal groups in the southwestern United States still rely on herding animals.

Worldwide, the six major species of herd animals are sheep, goats, cattle, horses, donkeys, and camels. Three others have more restricted distribution: yaks at high altitudes in Asia, reindeer in northern sub-Arctic regions, and llamas in highland South America. Many pastoralists keep dogs for protection and for help with herding.

In terms of food, pastoralism provides primarily milk and milk products, with occasional slaughtering of animals for meat. Thus, pastoralists typically form trade links with foragers, horticulturalists, or farmers to obtain food and other goods that they cannot produce themselves. Prominent trade items are food grains and manufactured items, such as cooking pots, for which they offer milk, animals, hides, and other animal products.

Like foraging and horticulture, pastoralism is an extensive strategy. A common problem for all pastoralists is the continued need for fresh pasture and water for their animals. Herds must move or else the grazing area will become depleted.

DIVISION OF LABOR Families and clusters of related families are the basic production unit. Gender and age are, again, key factors in the allocation of work. In many pastoralist cultures, gender roles are clearly divided. Men are in charge of herding—moving the animals from place to place. Women are responsible for processing the herd's products, especially the milk. A cultural emphasis on masculinity characterizes many herding populations. Reindeer herding among the Saami of Finland is closely connected to male identity to the extent that the definition of being a man is to be a reindeer herder (see Culturama, Chapter 9, page 188). In contrast, women are the herders among the Navajo of the American Southwest. Navajo men's major work role is crafting silver jewelry.

PROPERTY RELATIONS The most important forms of property among pastoralists are, by far, animals, followed by housing (such as tents or yurts) and domestic goods (rugs and cookware). Depending on the group, ownership of animals is inherited through males, most commonly, or, less frequently, through females, as among the Navajo. A concept of private property exists for animals, which the family head may trade for other goods. A family's housing materials are also their own. Use rights, however, regulate pasture land and migratory routes, and these rights tend to be informally regulated through an oral tradition.

PASTORALISM AS A SUSTAINABLE SYSTEM Pastoralists have developed sustainable cultures in extremely varied environments, from the relative lushness of Iran to

pastoralism a mode of livelihood based on keeping domesticated animals and using their products, such as meat and milk, for most of the diet.

Men and Plowing Hypothesis

This hypothesis is based on the importance of plowing fields in preparation for planting and on the fact that plowing is almost exclusively a male task (Goody 1976). Some anthropologists say that men plow because they are stronger than women and have the advantage of greater aerobic capacity. In southern India, for example, weather patterns require that plowing be accomplished in a very narrow time period (Maclachlan 1983). Assigning the task to the physically stronger gender ensures that the work is done more quickly and is thus an adaptive cultural strategy because it increases the chances for a good crop.

Women and Child-Care Hypothesis

This hypothesis says that women are not involved in plowing and other agricultural field labor as much as men because such tasks are incompatible with child care (J. K. Brown 1970).

Women and Food Processing Hypothesis

This hypothesis notes that agriculture increases the demand for labor within and near the house (Ember 1983). Winnowing, husking, grinding, and cooking agricultural products are extremely labor-intensive processes. Linked to women's primary roles in child care and increased fertility in farm families, these labor demands restrict women to the household domain.

Figure 3.4 **Three Hypotheses to Explain Male Dominance in the Gender Division of Labor in Family Farming**

the more depleted situation of Mongolia. Pastoralism is a highly successful and sustainable economic system that functions in coexistence with other economic systems. As with foraging and horticulture, however, when outside forces reduce the space available for migration, overexploitation of the environment soon results.

Agriculture

Agriculture is a mode of livelihood that involves growing crops on permanent plots with the use of plowing, irrigation, and fertilizer; it is also called farming. In contrast to foraging, horticulture, and pastoralism, agriculture is an **intensive strategy**. Intensification involves the use of techniques that allow the same plot of land to be used repeatedly without losing its fertility. Crucial inputs include substantial amounts of labor for weeding, use of natural and chemical fertilizers, and control of water supply. The earliest agricultural systems are documented from the time of the Neolithic period, beginning around 12,000 years ago in the Middle East. Agricultural systems now exist worldwide, on all continents except Antarctica.

Agriculture relies on the use of domesticated animals for plowing, transportation, and organic fertilizer either in the form of manure or composted materials. It is highly dependent on artificial water sources such as irrigation channels or terracing the land. Like the modes of livelihood already discussed, agriculture involves complex knowledge about the environment, plants, and animals, including soil types, precipitation patterns, plant varieties, and pest management. Long-standing agricultural traditions are now being increasingly displaced by methods introduced from the outside, and so the world's stock of indigenous knowledge about agriculture is declining rapidly. In many cases, it has become completely lost, along with the cultures and languages associated with it.

Two types of agriculture are discussed next: family farming and industrial agriculture.

FAMILY FARMING **Family farming** (formerly termed peasant farming) is a form of agriculture in which production is geared to support the family and to produce goods for sale. Today, more than one billion people, or about one-sixth of the world's population, make their living from family farming. Found throughout the world, family farming is more common in countries such as Mexico, India, Poland, and Italy than in more industrialized countries. Family farmers exhibit much cross-cultural variety. They may be full-time or part-time farmers; they may be more or less closely linked to urban markets; and they may be poor and indebted or wealthy and powerful. Activities in family farming include plowing, planting seeds and cuttings, weeding, caring for irrigation systems and terracing, harvesting crops, and processing and storing crops.

Division of Labor The family is the basic labor unit of production, and gender and age are important in organizing work. Most family farming societies have a marked gender-based division of labor. Cross-cultural analysis of gender roles reveals that men perform most of the labor in over three-fourths of the societies (Michaelson and Goldschmidt 1971). Anthropologists have proposed various theories to explain why productive work on so many family farms is male dominated (Figure 3.4).

In family farms in the United States and Canada, men typically have the main responsibility for daily farm operations; women's participation ranges from equal to minimal (Barlett 1989). Women do run farms in the United States and Canada but generally only when they are divorced or widowed. Women are usually responsible for managing

agriculture a mode of livelihood that involves growing crops with the use of plowing, irrigation, and fertilizer.

intensive strategy a form of livelihood that involves continuous use of the same land and resources.

family farming a form of agriculture in which farmers produce mainly to support themselves but also produce goods for sale in the market system.

the domestic domain. On average, women's daily work hours are 25 percent more than those of men.

Balanced work roles between men and women in family farming frequently involve a pattern in which men do the agricultural work and women do marketing. This gender division of labor is common among highland indigenous groups of Central and South America. For example, among the Zapotec Indians of Mexico's southern state of Oaxaca (wuh-HAH-kuh), men grow maize, the staple crop, and cash crops such as bananas, mangoes, coconuts, and sesame (Chiñas 1992) (see Map 4.3, page 75). Women sell produce in the town markets, and they make tortillas, which they sell from their houses. The family thus derives its income from the labor of both men and women working interdependently. Male status and female status are roughly equal in such contexts.

Female farming systems, in which women and girls play the major role in livelihood, are found mainly in southern India and Southeast Asia where wet rice agriculture is practiced. This is a highly labor-intensive way of growing rice that involves starting the seedlings in nurseries and transplanting them to flooded fields. Men are responsible for plowing the fields using teams of water buffaloes. Women own land and make decisions about planting and harvesting. Women's labor is the backbone of this type of farming. Standing calf-deep in muddy water, they transplant rice seedlings, weed, and harvest the rice. Why women predominate in wet rice agriculture is an intriguing question but impossible to answer. Its consequences for women's status, however, are clear. In female farming systems, women have high status: They own land, play a central role in household decision making, and have substantial personal autonomy (Stivens et al. 1994).

Children's roles in agricultural societies range from prominent to minor, depending on the context (Whiting and Whiting 1975). The *Six Cultures Study*, mentioned earlier, found low rates of child labor in agricultural villages in North India and Mexico compared to high rates among the horticultural Gusii in Kenya. In many agricultural contexts, however, children's labor participation is high. In villages in Java, Indonesia, (see Map 1.2, page 14) and Nepal (see Map 5.5, page 105), children spend more time caring for farm animals than adults do (Nag, White, and Peet 1978).

Property Relations   Family farmers make substantial investments in land, such as clearing, terracing, and fencing, and these investments are linked to the development of firmly defined and protected property rights. Rights to land can be acquired and sold. Formalized, often written, guidelines exist about inheritance of land and transfer of rights to land through marriage. Social institutions such as law and police exist to protect private property rights.

Family farmers typically know their land, inch by inch, and their animals. Commercial farming separates owners from the vast amount of land and the many animals involved. (TOP) Family farming in highland Ecuador. A man plows while women in the family follow, planting seed potatoes. (BOTTOM) Commercial dairy farming is not exactly hands-on.

In family farming systems where male labor and decision making predominate, women and girls are excluded from land rights. Conversely, in female farming systems, inheritance rules regulate the transmission of property rights more often through females.

INDUSTRIAL CAPITAL AGRICULTURE Industrial capital agriculture produces crops through capital-intensive means, using machinery and inputs such as processed fertilizers instead of human and animal labor (Barlett 1989).

---

industrial capital agriculture a form of agriculture that is capital-intensive, substituting machinery and purchased inputs for human and animal labor.

- Increased use of complex technology including machinery, chemicals, and genetic research on new plant and animal varieties.
  Social effects: This feature results in displacement of small landholders and field laborers. For example, replacing mules and horses with tractors for plowing in the U.S. South during the 1930s led to the eviction of small-scale sharecroppers from the land because the landowners could cultivate larger units.
- Increased use of capital (wealth used in the production of more wealth) in the form of money or property.
  Social effects: The high ratio of capital to labor enables farmers to increase production but reduces flexibility. If a farmer invests in an expensive machine to harvest soybeans and then the price of soybeans drops, the farmer cannot simply switch from soybeans to a more profitable crop. Capitalization is most risky for smaller farms, which cannot absorb losses easily.
- Increased use of energy (primarily gasoline to run the machinery and nitrates for fertilizer) to grow crops. This input of energy often exceeds the calories of food energy yielded in the harvest. Calculations of how many calories of energy are used to produce a calorie of food in industrial agricultural systems reveal that some 2.5 calories of fossil fuel are invested to harvest 1 calorie of food—and more than 6 calories are invested when processing, packaging, and transport are taken into account.
  Social effects: This energy-heavy mode of production creates farmers' dependence on the global market of energy supplies.

Source: Adapted from "Industrial Agriculture" by Peggy F. Barlett in *Economic Anthropology*, ed. by Stuart Plattner. Copyright © 1989. Published by Stanford University Press.

Figure 3.5 **Three Features of Industrial Agriculture and Their Social Effects**

It is commonly practiced in the United States, Canada, Germany, Russia, and Japan and is increasingly being adopted in developing countries such as India, Brazil, Mexico, and China.

Industrial agriculture has brought with it the corporate farm, a huge agricultural enterprise that produces goods solely for sale and are owned and operated by companies entirely reliant on hired labor. Industrial agriculture has major social effects (Figure 3.5). Much of the labor demand in industrial agriculture is seasonal, creating an ebb and flow of workers, depending on the task and time of year.

THE SUSTAINABILITY OF AGRICULTURE Agriculture requires labor inputs, technology, and nonrenewable natural resources than the economic systems discussed earlier. The ever-increasing spread of corporate agriculture worldwide is now displacing other long-standing practices and resulting in the destruction of important habitats and cultural heritage sites in its search for land, water, and energy sources. Intensive agriculture is not a sustainable system. For many years, anthropologists have pointed to the high costs of agriculture to the environment and to humanity.

Industrialism and the Digital Age

Industrialism/digital economy is the mode of livelihood in which goods and services are produced through mass employment in business and commercial operations and through the creation, manipulation, management, and transfer of information through electronic media and the Internet. Most people work to produce goods not to meet basic needs but to satisfy consumer demands for essential and, increasingly, nonessential goods. Employment in agriculture decreases while jobs in manufacturing, the service sector, and electronic-based jobs increase. Unemployment is an increasingly serious problem in industrial/digital societies.

Modes of Consumption and Exchange

3.2 **Recognize how modes of livelihood are related to consumption and exchange.**

Imagine that it is the late eighteenth century and you are a member of the Kwakwaka'wakw (KWA-kwuh-kayuh'-wah-kwah) of British Columbia in Canada's Pacific Northwest region (see Culturama at the end of this chapter, page 63). You and your tribal group are invited to a **potlatch**, a feast in which the host lavishes the guests with abundant quantities of the best food and many gifts (Suttles 1991). The most honorable foods are fish oil, high-bush cranberries, and seal meat, and they will be served in ceremonial wooden bowls. Gifts include embroidered blankets, household articles such as carved wooden boxes and woven mats, canoes, and items of food. The more the chief gives, the higher his status rises and the more his guests are indebted to him. Later, when it is the guests' turn to hold a potlatch, they will give away as much as, or more than, their host did.

The Pacific Northwest region is rich in fish, game, berries, and nuts, among other foods. Nonetheless, given regional climatic variation, food supplies were often uneven, with some groups each year having surpluses while others faced scarcity. The potlatch system helped to smooth out these variations: Groups with a surplus

industrialism/digital economy a mode of livelihood in which goods are produced through mass employment in business and commercial operations and through the creation and movement of information through electronic media.

potlatch a grand feast in which guests are invited to eat and to receive gifts from the hosts.

Foraging	Horticulture	Pastoralism	Agriculture	Industrial/Digital
Mode of Consumption Minimalism Finite needs				**Mode of Consumption** Consumerism Infinite needs
Social Organization of Consumption Equality/sharing Personalized products are consumed				**Social Organization of Consumption** Class-based inequality Depersonalized products are consumed
Primary Budgetary Fund Basic needs				**Primary Budgetary Fund** Rent/taxes, luxuries
Mode of Exchange Balanced exchange				**Mode of Exchange** Market exchange
Social Organization of Exchange Small groups, face-to-face				**Social Organization of Exchange** Anonymous market transactions
Primary Category of Exchange The gift				**Primary Category of Exchange** The sale

Figure 3.6 Modes of Livelihood, Consumption, and Exchange

would sponsor a potlatch and those experiencing a leaner year were guests. In this way, potlatching established a social safety net across a wide area of the Northwest. This brief sketch of potlatching shows the linkages among the three economic processes of livelihood, consumption, and exchange (review Figure 3.1, page 45). Potlatches are related to food supply; they are opportunities for consumption, and involve exchange, the topics of this section.

Modes of Consumption

Consumption has two meanings: First, it is a person's "intake" in terms of eating or other ways of using things; second, it is "output" in terms of spending or using resources to obtain those things. Thus, for example, "intake" is eating a sandwich; "output" is spending money at the store to buy a sandwich. Both activities fit within the term consumption.

People consume many things. Food, beverages, clothing, and shelter are the most basic consumption needs in most cultures. People also may acquire tools, weapons, means of transportation, computers, books and other items of communication, art and other luxury goods, and energy for heating and cooling their residence. In noncash economies, such as that of foragers, people "spend" time or labor in order to provide for their needs. In money-based economies, such as industrialized contexts today, most consumption depends on having cash or some virtual form of money.

In categorizing varieties of consumption, it makes sense to consider two contrasting modes, with mixed modes in the middle (Figure 3.6). They are based on the relationship between demand (what people need or want) and supply (the resources available to satisfy demand):

- **Minimalism:** a mode of consumption characterized by few and finite consumer demands and an adequate and sustainable means to achieve them. It is most characteristic of free-ranging foragers but is also found to some degree among horticulturalists and pastoralists.

- **Consumerism:** a mode of consumption in which people's demands are many and infinite, and the means of satisfying them are never sufficient, thus driving colonialism, globalization, and other forms of expansionism. Consumerism is the distinguishing feature of industrial/digital economy cultures. Globalization is spreading consumerism throughout the world and, in some cases, leading to hyperconsumerism, as among the very wealthy people around the world. Hyperconsumerism is consumption for its own sake, often driven by the perceived need to purchase certain brands and related to constructing and maintaining identity in a socially competitive context.

How and what people consume, with whom, where, and how, and the meaning of consumption to individuals and groups vary cross-culturally. Consumption patterns

---

minimalism a mode of consumption that emphasizes simplicity, is characterized by few and finite consumer demands, and involves an adequate and sustainable means to achieve them.

consumerism a mode of consumption in which people's demands are many and infinite and the means of satisfying them are insufficient and become depleted in the effort to satisfy these demands.

are related to livelihoods. As noted previously, foragers are generally egalitarian, whereas social inequality characterizes most agricultural and industrial/digital societies. In foraging peoples, sharing within the group is the norm, and everyone has equal access to all resources. Among the Ju/wasi (review Culturama in Chapter 1, page 18): "Even though only a fraction of the able-bodied foragers go out each day, the day's return of meat and gathered foods are [sic] divided in such a way that every member of the camp receives an equitable share" (Lee 1979:118).

The distribution among the group of personal goods such as clothing, beads, musical instruments, or smoking pipes is also equal. **Leveling mechanisms** are unwritten, culturally embedded rules that prevent an individual from becoming wealthier or more powerful than anyone else. They are maintained through social pressure and gossip. An important leveling mechanism among the Ju/wasi requires that any large game animal killed be shared with the group, and its killer must be modest, insisting that the meat is meager (Lee 1969). Ju/wasi hunters gain no social status or power through their provision of meat. The same applies to other foragers. Leveling mechanisms are important in horticultural and pastoralist societies, too. For example, when someone's herd grows "too large," that person will be subject to social pressure to sponsor a large feast in which many of the herd animals are eaten.

The mode of consumption that contrasts with minimalism is consumerism, with the United States being the major consumerist country of the world. Since the 1970s, consumption levels in the United States have been the highest of any society in human history, and they show no sign of decline. Since China adopted features of capitalism, it has quickly become a consumerist giant. In the world's poorest countries, too, rising numbers of middle- and upper-class people pursue consumerism.

As consumerism spreads throughout the world, changes in the social relations involved in consumption also occur. In small-scale societies—such as those of foragers, horticulturalists, and pastoralists—consumption items are typically produced by the consumers themselves for their own use. If not, they are likely to be produced by people with whom the consumer has a personal, face-to-face relationship—in other words, personalized consumption. Everyone knows where products came from and who produced them. This pattern contrasts markedly with consumption in our contemporary globalized world, which is termed depersonalized consumption. Depersonalized consumption, by distancing consumers from workers who actually produce goods, makes it more possible for workers to be exploited.

Apple juice on sale at a farmers market stall in Tewkesbury, a small city in England. Farmers markets are a modern version of historic periodic markets with an emphasis on locally grown produce and locally made crafts and other goods.

Even in the most industrialized/digital economy contexts, though, depersonalized consumption has not completely replaced personalized consumption. The popularity of farmers' markets in urban centers in North America is an example of personalized consumption in which the consumer buys produce from the person who grew it and with whom the consumer may have a friendly conversation, perhaps while sampling an apple.

CONSUMPTION MICROCULTURES This section provides examples of three consumption microcultures: class, gender, and "race." Microcultures have distinct entitlement patterns, related levels of health and welfare, and identity associated with consumption. Depending on the cultural context, social inequality may play an important role and have major effects on human welfare.

Women's Deadly Diet in Papua New Guinea Consumption patterns are often marked by gender and related to discrimination and inequality. Specific foods may be considered "men's food" or "women's food." An example of lethal gender inequalities in food consumption comes from highland Papua New Guinea (Map 3.5).

The story begins with the eruption of a mysterious disease, with the local name of *kuru* (koo-roo), among the Fore (for-ay), a horticultural people of the highlands (Lindenbaum 1979). Between 1957 and 1977, about 2,500 people died of kuru. The first signs of kuru are shivering tremors, followed by a progressive loss of motor ability along with pain in the head and limbs. Kuru victims could walk unsteadily at first but would later be unable to get up. Death occurred about a year after the first symptoms appeared. Most victims were women.

American medical researchers revealed that kuru was a neurological disease. Australian cultural anthropologist Shirley Lindenbaum pinpointed the cultural cause of kuru:

---

leveling mechanism an unwritten, culturally embedded rule that prevents an individual from becoming wealthier or more powerful than anyone else.

Map 3.5 **Location of the Kuru Epidemic in Papua New Guinea**

cannibalism. Kuru victims had eaten the flesh of deceased people who had died of kuru.

Why were most of the kuru victims women? Lindenbaum learned that among the Fore, it was considered acceptable to cook and eat the meat of a deceased person, although it was not a preferred food. The preferred source of animal protein is meat from pigs, and men receive preferential access to the best food. Fore women had begun to eat human flesh more often because of increased scarcity of pigs. Population density in the region had risen, more land was being cultivated, and forest areas had decreased. Pigs live in forest areas, so as their habitat became more restricted, their numbers declined. The Fore could not move to more pig-abundant areas because they were bounded on the east, west, and north sides by other groups. The south was a harsh and forbidding region. These factors, combined with the Fore's male-biased system of protein consumption, forced women to turn to the less-preferred protein source of human flesh. By eating the flesh, including brains, of kuru victims, they contracted the disease.

"Race" and Children's Shopping in New Haven Throughout the world, in countries with "race"-based social categories, inequalities in consumption and quality of life exist, often in spite of anti-discrimination legislation. In the United States, racism affects many areas of life from access to housing, neighborhood security and services, schooling, health, and whether a person is likely to be ignored or picked up by a taxi or be stopped by a police officer for speeding. Racial inequality between Black and White Americans has

risen steadily since the 1970s in terms of income, wealth, and property ownership, especially house ownership (Shapiro 2004). Those at the top of the income distribution have increased their share of the wealth most. The share of total income that goes to the top one percent of families is nearly the same size as the total income share of the bottom 40 percent.

How could this happen in a country dedicated to equality of opportunity? A large part of the answer lies in the simple fact that, in a capitalist system, inequality leads to more inequality through the transfer of wealth and property across generations. Those who have wealth and property are able to establish their children's wealth through college tuition payments, house down payments, and other financial gifts. The children of poor parents have to provide for their education and housing costs from their wages alone, a fact that makes it far less likely that they will be able to pursue higher education or buy a home.

As a graduate student in anthropology at Yale University, Elizabeth Chin decided to do her dissertation research on consumption patterns among schoolchildren in a poor, African American neighborhood in New Haven, Connecticut (2001). In terms of per capita income, Connecticut is the wealthiest state in the United States. It also harbors some of the most severe poverty and racial inequality in its major cities. New Haven exemplifies this racialized inequality in its clearly defined neighborhoods in the fear and suspicion with which Whites and Blacks view each other. During her research in a Black neighborhood, Chin found that 50 percent of the children age five and under were living in poverty.

Chin formed a relationship with one fifth-grade class of 22 students. She spent time in the classroom, visited the children and their families in their homes, and accompanied the children on shopping trips to the mall. While the children are bombarded with media messages about consumption, they have little money to spend. Some receive an allowance for doing household chores; some receive small amounts of pocket money on an ad hoc basis; and some earn money from small-scale ventures such as a cucumber stand. They learn about the basics of household finances and the costs of daily life early on. Seeing their families strain every day to put meals on the table teaches them about the negative effects of overindulgence: "From divvying up the milk to figuring out where to sleep there is an emphasis on sharing and mutual obligation" (2001:5).

These practical lessons shape how the children spend their money when they go to the mall. Practicality and generosity guide their shopping choices. To learn about the children's decisions, Chin would give a child $20 and go with him or her to the mall. Most of the girls spent over half their money on gifts for family members, especially their mothers and grandmothers (2001:139). The girls knew their mothers' shoe sizes and clothing sizes. One boy, just before school was to start in the fall, spent $10 on a T-shirt to wear on the first day of school, $6 on a pair of shorts, and the rest on school supplies: pencils, pens, notebook paper, and a binder (2001:135). In her two years of research, Chin never heard a child nag a caretaker about buying him or her something.

Modes of Exchange

Exchange is the transfer of something that may be material or immaterial between at least two persons, groups, or institutions. Cultural anthropologists have done much research on gifts and other forms of exchange, such as Malinowski's early work on the kula in the South Pacific (review Culturama, Chapter 2, page 28). In all economic systems, individuals and groups exchange goods and services with others. But variation exists in what is exchanged, how goods are exchanged, when exchange takes place, and the meaning of exchange.

In contemporary industrial/digital societies, money is the major item of exchange, and such economies are referred to as monetized. In nonindustrialized economies, money plays a less important role, and time, labor, and goods are prominent exchange items. As nonindustrialized economies are connected, through globalization, they are confronted with the (to them) peculiar and mysterious meaning of Western money. Often, they give local meaning to money by treating particular bills as more special than others. Money is rapidly replacing other valued items of exchange throughout the world. Beyond coins and paper money, **mobile money** is on the rise throughout the world, including in low-income countries with many countries in Africa leading the way (see Map 3.6). Mobile money refers to financial transactions that take place through a cell phone, also called a mobile phone.

Parallel to the two contrasting modes of consumption described earlier (minimalism and consumerism), two distinct modes of exchange can be delineated (Figure 3.7):

- **Balanced exchange:** a system of transfers in which the goal is either immediate or eventual balance in value.

- **Unbalanced exchange:** a system of transfers in which one party attempts to make a profit.

BALANCED EXCHANGE The category of balanced exchange contains two subcategories based on the social relationship of the two parties involved in the exchange and the degree to which a "return" is expected. **Generalized reciprocity** is a transaction that involves the least

mobile money financial transactions that take place through a cell phone, also called a mobile phone.

balanced exchange a system of transfers in which the goal is either immediate or eventual equality in value.

unbalanced exchange a system of transfers in which one party seeks to make a profit.

generalized reciprocity exchange involving the least conscious sense of interest in material gain or thought of what might be received in return.

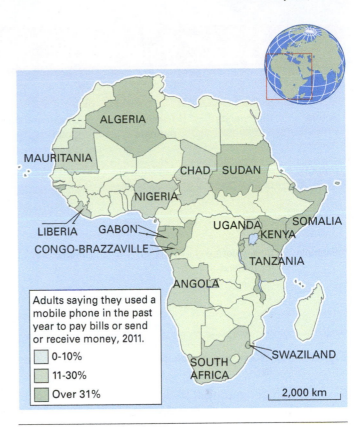

Map 3.6 Use of Mobile Money in Africa

As a percentage of its total population, Africa is the world's leading region in the management of money, including banking and transfers, via mobile technology. Within Africa, Kenya is way ahead with nearly 70 percent of the population involved in mobile money transactions, with Sudan next at 50 percent.

conscious sense of interest in material gain or thought of what might be received in return, and when. Such exchanges often involve goods and services of an everyday nature, such as a cup of coffee. Generalized reciprocity is the main form of exchange between people who know each other well and trust each other. Therefore, it is the main form of exchange in foraging societies. It is also found among close kin and friends cross-culturally.

A **pure gift** is something given with no expectation or thought of a return. The pure gift is an extreme form of generalized reciprocity. Examples of a pure gift might include donating money for a food drive, or a blood drive, donating one's organs after death, or giving money to disaster relief and religious organizations. Some people argue that a truly pure gift does not exist because one always gains something in giving, no matter how difficult to measure—even if it is just the good feeling of generosity. How selfish is that! Parental care of children is said to be a pure gift by some, but others do not agree. Those who say that parental care is a pure gift argue that most parents do not consciously calculate how much they have spent on their children with

pure gift something given with no expectation or thought of a return.

	Balanced Exchange			Unbalanced exchange		
	Generalized Reciprocity	Expected Reciprocity	Redistribution	Debt	Market Exchange	Theft, Exploitation
Actors	Kin, friends	Trading partners	Leader and pooling group	Nonpersonal lender/borrower	Buyers/Sellers	Nonkin, nonfriends, unknown
Return	Not calculated or expected	Expected at some time	Feast and give-away	Long-term, Interest on loan to lender accrues over time	Immediate payment	No return
Example	Buying coffee for a friend	Kula	Moka	Countries who owe money to the World Bank; student college loans	Internet shopping	Shoplifting

Figure 3.7 Keeping Track of Exchange

the intention of "getting it back" later on. Those who do not consider parental care a pure gift say that even if the "costs" are not consciously calculated, parents have unconscious expectations about what their children will "return" to them, whether the return is material (care in old age) or immaterial (making the parent feel proud).

Expected reciprocity is the exchange of approximately equally valued goods or services, usually between people of roughly equal social status. The exchange may occur simultaneously between both parties, or it may involve an understanding about the time period within which the exchange will be completed. This aspect of timing contrasts with generalized reciprocity, in which there is no fixed time limit for the return. In expected reciprocity, if the second party fails to complete the exchange, the relationship will break down. Balanced reciprocity is less personal than generalized reciprocity and, according to Western definitions, more "economic" in that it may involve consideration of costs and benefits.

The kula system as found in the Trobriand Islands (review Culturama, Chapter 2, page 28) is an example of an expected reciprocity. Men throughout a vast region of Melanesia exchange necklaces and armlets, giving them to their exchange partners after keeping them for a while. Partners include neighbors as well as people on faraway islands who are visited via long canoe voyages on high seas. Trobriand men are distinguished by the particular armlets and necklaces that they exchange, and certain armlets and necklaces are more prestigious than others. One cannot keep one's trade items for long because the kula code dictates that "to

possess is great, but to possess is to give." Generosity is the essence of goodness, and stinginess is the most despised vice. Kula exchanges should involve items of equivalent value. If a man trades a very valuable necklace with his partner, he expects to receive in return a very valuable armlet as an equivalent gift. The equality of exchange ensures a strong bond between the trading partners and is a statement of trust. When a man arrives in an area where it may be dangerous because of previous raids or warfare, he can count on having a friend to give him hospitality.

Redistribution is a form of exchange in which one person collects goods or money from many members of a group and provides a social return at a later time. At a public event, even several years later, the organizer "returns" the pooled goods to everyone who contributed by sponsoring a generous feast. Compared to the two-way pattern of exchange involved in reciprocity, redistribution involves some "centricity." It contains the possibility of inequality because what is returned may not always equal, in a material sense, what each individual contributed. The pooling group may continue to exist, however, because it benefits from the leadership skills of the person who mobilizes contributions. If a neighboring group threatens a raid, people turn to their redistributive leader for political leadership (discussed further in Chapter 8). Over time, redistribution should balance out, with givers of goods and sponsors of festivities both feeling they benefited from the arrangement. But, as we will discuss later in this book, the leader tends to gain more in prestige than the followers.

expected reciprocity an exchange of approximately equally valued goods or services, usually between people roughly equal in social status.

redistribution a form of exchange that involves one person collecting goods or money from many members of a group, who then, at a later time and at a public event, "returns" the pooled goods to everyone who contributed.

Scenes at two permanent markets. (LEFT) In China, many marketers are women. These two women display their wares in a permanent food market in a city about an hour's drive from Shanghai. (RIGHT) Workers at Tsukiji, the world's largest fish market in Tokyo, transport frozen tuna on hand carts for the upcoming auction.

■ *For a research project, learn more about Ted Bestor's research on Tsukiji.*

UNBALANCED EXCHANGE Debt, in industrial/digital societies, differs from balanced exchange in terms of the lack of a personal connection between the parties involved and the possibility that a debt may become so large that it may never be repaid (Graeber 2011). In this sense, according to David Graeber, author of a monumental study entitled *Debt*, modern debt did not emerge until a period when settled states began to engage in warfare in the Middle East around 5,000 years ago. Graeber argues that contemporary patterns of massive national debt are inextricably linked to warfare and a pervasive value of military solutions to national security of major world powers.

Market exchange, a prominent form of unbalanced exchange, is the buying and selling of commodities under competitive conditions in which the forces of supply and demand determine value and the seller seeks to make a profit. In market transactions, the seller and buyer may or may not have a personal relationship. They may or may not be social equals. Their exchange is not likely to generate social bonding. Many market transactions take place in a marketplace, a physical location in which buying and selling occur. The market system evolved from other, less formal contexts of **trade**, formalized exchange of one thing for another according to set standards of value, in which the party with the sought-after good seeks to make a profit from the party seeking the good.

The market system is associated with regional specialization in producing particular goods and trade between regions. Certain products are often identified with a town or region. In Morocco, the city of Fez (see Map 4.2, page 73) is famous for its blue-glazed pottery, whereas the Berber people of the Atlas Mountains are known for their fine wool blankets and rugs. In Oaxaca, Mexico (see Map 4.3, page 75), some villages are known for their blankets, pottery, stone grinders, rope, and chili peppers (Plattner 1989). Increasingly, producers of regionally distinct products, such as champagne, are legally copyrighting the regional name to protect it from use by producers of similar products from outside the region.

Marketplaces range from informal, small stands that appear in the morning and disappear at night, to huge multistoried shopping centers. One variety found in many parts of the world is a periodic market, a site for buying and selling that takes place on a regular basis (for example, monthly) in a particular location but without a permanent physical structure. Sellers appear with their goods and set up a table with perhaps an awning. In contrast, permanent markets are built structures situated in fixed locations. Marketplaces, however, are more than just places for buying and selling. They involve social interactions and even performances. Sellers solicit customers, shoppers meet and chat, government officials drop by, religious organizations may hold services, and traditional healers may treat toothaches.

Ted Bestor conducted research over many years in Tsukiji (tsee-kee-jee), the world's largest fish market, located in Tokyo (2004). Tsukiji connects large-scale

---

market exchange the buying and selling of commodities under competitive conditions, in which the forces of supply and demand determine value.

trade the formalized exchange of one thing for another according to set standards of value.

corporations that supply most of the seafood with small-scale family-run firms that continue to dominate Tokyo's retail food trade. Bestor describes the layout of the huge market, with inner and outer sections, as a basic division. The outer market attracts younger, hipper shoppers looking for unusual, trendy gourmet items and a more authentic-seeming shopping experience. It contains sushi bars, noodle stalls, knife shops, and chopstick dealers, as well as temples and graveyards. The inner market contains 11 fresh produce market subdivisions. The seafood section by far overshadows the "veggie" markets in size and transaction level. It is subdivided into several main buildings where auctions occur, activities such as deliveries and dispatches take place, and rows of retail stalls serve 14,000 customers each morning. Bestor gained insight into the verbally coded conversations between experienced buyers and sellers in the stalls that are more likely to yield a better price than what an inexperienced first-time buyer will get. Stalls do not typically post prices, so buyers and sellers have to negotiate them. The verbal codes involve phrases such as "morning mist on a white beach" which, depending on the number of syllables in the phrase, conveys a price offer.

OTHER FORMS OF UNBALANCED EXCHANGE Several other forms of unbalanced exchange exist outside the market. In extreme instances, no social relationship is involved; in others, sustained unequal relationships are maintained over time between people. These forms include taking something with no expectation of giving any return. They can occur in any mode of livelihood but are most likely to be found in large-scale societies where more options (other than face-to-face) for balanced exchange exist.

Gambling Gambling, or gaming, is the attempt to make a profit by playing a game of chance in which a certain item of value is staked in hopes of acquiring the much larger return that one receives if one wins the game. If one loses, that which was staked is lost. Gambling is an ancient practice and is common cross-culturally. Ancient forms of gambling include dice throwing and card playing. Investing in the stock market can be considered a form of gambling, as can gambling of many sorts through the Internet. Although gambling may seem an odd category within unbalanced exchange, its goals of making a profit seem to justify its placement here. The fact that gambling within "high" capitalism is on the rise justifies anthropological attention to it.

Indian tribal gambling establishments in the United States have mushroomed in recent years. Throughout the United States, Indian casinos are so financially successful that they are perceived as an economic threat to many

state lotteries. The Pequot Indians of Connecticut, a small tribe of around 200 people, now operate the most lucrative gaming establishment in the world, Foxwoods Resort and Casino, established in 1992. Through gaming, many other Indian tribal groups have become successful capitalists. An important question is what impact casinos will have on Indian tribal people, and anthropologists are involved in trying to answer this question (see Anthropology Works).

Theft Theft is taking something with no expectation or thought of returning anything to the original owner for it. It is the logical opposite of a pure gift. Anthropologists have neglected the study of theft, no doubt a reasonable response because theft is an illegal activity that is difficult to study and might involve danger.

A rare study of theft focused on food stealing by children in West Africa (Bledsoe 1983). During fieldwork among the Mende people of Sierra Leone (see Map 4.5, page 83), Caroline Bledsoe learned that children in town stole fruits such as mangoes, guavas, and oranges from neighborhood trees. Bledsoe at first dismissed cases of food stealing as exceptions, but then she realized that she "rarely walked through town without hearing shouts of anger from an adult and cries of pain from a child being whipped for stealing food" (1983:2). Deciding to look into children's food stealing more closely, she asked several children to keep diaries. Their writings were dominated by themes of *tiefing*, the local term for stealing. Fostered children, who are temporarily placed in the care of friends or relatives, do more food tiefing than children living with their birth families do. Such food stealing can be seen as children's attempts to compensate for their less-than-adequate food shares in their foster homes.

While much theft worldwide is motivated by skewed entitlements and need, much is also driven by greed. Cultural anthropologists, for obvious reasons, have not done research on high-level theft involving expensive commodities such as drugs, gems, and art, nor have they examined corporate financial malpractice as a form of theft. Given the ethical requirement of informed consent, it is highly unlikely that any anthropologist would be given permission to study such criminal activity.

Exploitation Exploitation, or getting something of greater value for less in return, is a form of extreme and persistent unbalanced exchange. Slavery is a form of exploitation in which people's labor power is appropriated without their consent and with no recompense for its value. According to many scholars, it still exists in the form of human trafficking, in which ruthless people exploit the labor, sexual or otherwise, of other people through international as well as within-country networks of human smuggling.

Anthropology Works

Evaluating the Social Effects of Indian Gaming

In 2006, the Center for California Native Nations (CCNN) at the University of California at Riverside released an evaluation of the effects of Indian gaming in California (Spilde Contreras 2006). *Note:* According to current preferences of the people involved, the terms Indian and Indian tribe are used instead of Native American.

Kate Spilde Contreras, applied cultural anthropologist, directed the multidisciplinary team of anthropologists, political scientists, economists, and historians. The research objective was to evaluate the social and economic effects of Indian gaming operations on tribal and local governments in California. The study relies mainly on public data, especially the 1990 and 2000 U.S. Censuses, to supply a "before" and "after" picture during the initial growth phase of Indian gaming in the state. To learn about more recent changes, the research team conducted surveys of tribal and local government officials and in-depth case studies of individual tribal governments.

Findings indicate two important factors that shape the effects of Indian gaming in California: Gaming establishments are owned by tribal governments, and gaming establishments are located on existing tribal trust lands. Therefore, gaming revenues support community and government activities of the tribal communities, and employment generation is localized within the tribal communities.

Indian reservations in California are more economically heterogeneous than elsewhere in the United States. Since the development of gaming, California also has greater economic inequality between gaming and nongaming reservations than is found in other states. By 2000, the fastest average income growth on California reservations occurred on gaming reservations. A policy response to this situation is a tribal-state gaming contract, the Revenue Sharing Trust Fund (RSTF) that provides for sharing of gaming revenue with nongaming communities.

Spilde Contreras's team considered the effects on gaming beyond the reservation. They found that areas within 10 miles of gaming reservations experienced significant employment increases, greater income growth, and more educational expansion than those farther away. Given the fact that reservations in California are located in the poorest regions, this location effect is progressive; that is, it helps poorer communities in favor of helping better-off communities.

Although the income and other effects of gaming in California are clearly substantial for Indians and their neighbors, Spilde Contreras points to the large gaps that still exist between conditions on Indian reservations and those for most Americans.

Food for Thought

How does the development of Indian casinos connect with the theoretical perspectives of structure versus agency? (Review Chapter 1.)

Casino Sandia, located in the Sandia Pueblo in northern New Mexico, is one of many casinos in the state established in the hope of raising funds to improve the lives of Indian people.

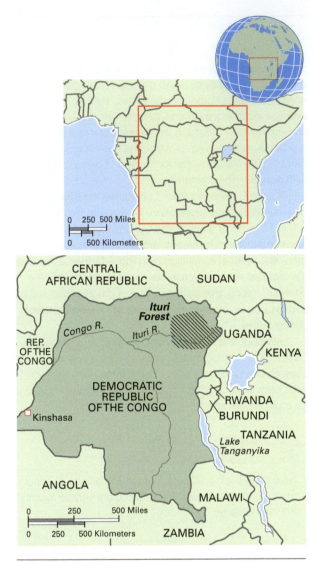

Map 3.7 Lese and Efe Region in the Democratic Republic of Congo

The Lese and Efe live in the Ituri Forest, a dense tropical rainforest in the northern part of the Congo River Basin. Cultural survival supports the Ituri Forest Peoples Fund, which promotes the health and education of Efe foragers and Lese farmers. Go to the Internet to learn about the projects of the Ituri Forest Peoples Fund.

Slavery is rare among foraging, horticultural, and pastoralist societies. Social relationships that involve sustained unequal exchange may exist between members of different social groups that, unlike pure slavery, involve no overt coercion and entail a certain degree of return by the dominant member to the subdominant member. Some degree of covert (hidden, indirect) compulsion or dependence is likely to be present, however, in order for relationships of unequal exchange to endure.

Relationships between the Efe (eff-ay), who are "pygmy" foragers, and the Lese (less-ay), who are farmers, in the Ituri region of the Democratic Republic of Congo are an example of such sustained unequal exchange (Grinker 1994) (Map 3.7). The Lese live in small villages. The Efe are seminomadic and live in temporary camps near Lese villages. Men of each group maintain long-term, hereditary exchange partnerships with each other. The Lese give cultivated foods and iron to the Efe, and the Efe give meat, honey, and other forest goods to the Lese.

Each Efe partner is considered a member of the "house" of his Lese partner, although he lives separately. Their main link is the exchange of food items, a system conceptualized by the Lese not as trade but as sharing of coproduced goods by partners living in a single unit. Evidence of inequality exists, however, in these relationships, with the Lese having the advantage. The Efe provide much-wanted meat to the Lese, but this role gives them no status. Rather, it is the giving of cultivated foods by the Lese to the Efe that conveys status to the Lese. Another area of inequality is marital and sexual relationships. Lese men may marry Efe women, and their children are considered Lese. Efe men, however, cannot marry Lese women.

Globalization and Changing Economies

3.3 Illustrate how livelihood, consumption, and exchange are changing in contemporary times.

Powerful market forces controlled by powerful, high-income countries are the main factors affecting change in consumption and exchange. High-income countries create markets, extract material resources, and exploit cheaper labor in low-income countries. Local cultures, though, variously adopt and adapt globalizing products, practices, and their meanings. Sometimes they resist them outright. And some global movements are afoot to create consumption and exchange practices and meanings that are more geared toward the local, toward sustainability, and toward social relationships.

Sugar, Salt, and Steel Tools in the Amazon

Katherine Milton, a biological anthropologist, has studied the nutritional effects of Western contact on the consumption patterns and health of indigenous foragers in the Brazilian Amazon. She reports on the strong attraction of indigenous peoples to Western goods, starting in the early twentieth century, when the Brazilian government sought to "pacify" Amazonian groups by placing cooking pots, machetes, axes, and steel knives along trails.

Culturama

The Kwakwaka'wakw of Canada

Several Northern First Nations recently adopted the name Kwakwaka'wakw to refer to a cluster of 20 linguistically related groups of Canada's Pacific Northwest region (Macnair 1995). Kwakwaka'wakw means "the people who speak Kwak'wala." It replaces the earlier term Kwakiutl, which refers to only one of the several groups and is therefore insulting to members of the other groups.

Their territory includes many islands as well as the waterways and deep inlets penetrating the Coast Mountains, a region of dense forests and sandy beaches. In earlier times, travel was mainly by canoe. Families moved seasonally with all their belongings packed in the canoe (Macnair 1995).

The Kwakwaka'wakw are famous for aspects of their material culture, including tall, carved wooden totem poles, canoes, masks, and serving bowls, as well as richly decorated capes, skirts, and blankets.

Cedar is vital to the Kwakwaka'wakw. They use its wood for the objects just mentioned and the inner bark for garments. Women pounded the bark strips with a whalebone beater until the fibers separated and became soft.

They wove the strips on a loom or handwove them into mats used for sleeping on.

The first contact with Whites occurred in 1792, when explorer Captain George Vancouver arrived (Macnair 1995). At that time, the Kwakwaka'wakw numbered around 8,000 people. Franz Boas arrived in 1886 and carried out research with the help of George Hunt, born of an English father and a high-ranking Tlingit (Northwest Coast) mother.

In the late nineteenth century, colonial authorities and missionaries disapproved of matters such as marriage arrangements and the potlatch, and enacted legislation to promote change, including a ban on potlatching from 1884 to 1951. The people continued, however, to potlatch in secret.

The Royal British Columbia Museum (RBCM) in Victoria, British Columbia, Canada, worked closely with Kwakwaka'wakw communities to document their potlatches and promote cultural revitalization (Kramer, personal communication 2005). The first legal potlatch of recent times, hosted by Mungo Martin in 1953, was held outside the RBCM.

Thanks to Jennifer Kramer, University of British Columbia, for reviewing this material.

(LEFT) Canoes and their crews from other Kwakwaka'wakw villages gather at Alert Bay in 1999 to help celebrate the opening of the newly built Big House.

(CENTER) Kwakwaka'wakw students practice the hamat'sa dance at a school in Alert Bay, under the tutelage of K'odi Nelson.

Map 3.8 The Kwakwaka'wakw Region in Canada

The Kwakwaka'wakw are Pacific Northwest Coast indigenous people. Their current population is approximately 5,500. Most live in British Columbia on northern Vancouver Island and the adjoining mainland. Some live outside their homelands in urban areas such as Victoria and Vancouver. Their language, now spoken by about 250 people, consists of four dialects. They are organized into 13 band governments.

Adoption of Western processed foods, such as salt and sugar, has negatively affected the nutrition and health of indigenous Amazonian peoples. Previously, they consumed small quantities of salt made by burning certain leaves and collecting the ash, and sugar came from wild fruits, in the form of fructose. Sucrose, in contrast, tastes exceptionally sweet, and the Indians get hooked on it. Tooth decay, obesity, and diabetes are new and growing health risks. Milton comments, "The moment manufactured foods begin to intrude on the indigenous diet, health takes a downward turn" (1992:41).

Global Demand for Phosphate Eats an Island

Phosphate is found in rock deposits in several parts of the world. It is in high demand in agriculture, for fertilizer. Huge corporate businesses deal in phosphates, and their interest is in mining phosphate as cheaply as possible. In the Pacific region, an important source of phosphate is Banaba Island, or Ocean Island, which is part of the Republic of Kiribati (see Map 12.1, page 244). Ethnographic research documents the effects of the global demand for phosphate on Banaba (2015). Phosphate was discovered on Banaba Island in 1900. From that time through 1979 when the phosphate mines were closed, a British company stripped 90 percent of the island's surface. Most of the residents were forcibly displaced, many to Fiji. Some have returned.

The Kiribati government would like to reopen the mines, but it is facing resistance from Banaba Island residents as well as members of the Banaban diaspora.

Alternative Food Movements in Europe and North America

Starting in Europe in the 1980s, several alternative food movements have grown in Europe and North America (Pratt 2007). Alternative food movements seek to reestablish direct links between food producers, consumers, and marketers by promoting consumption of locally grown food and food that is not mass produced. Such movements exist in direct opposition to the agro-industrial food system, which:

- leads to economic ruin of small-scale producers who promote biodiversity.

- shifts diet to fast foods, convenience food, take-away food, and microwave preparation.
- transforms meals into eating on the run.
- promotes a depersonalized, global market and supply chain, with Walmart as the prime example.
- has little regard for the environmental consequences of mass production and global marketing.

Many alternative food movements exist. One of the first, Italy's Slow Food Movement, started in the late 1980s and has spread around the world. Naming itself in opposition to Western "fast food," the Slow Food Movement celebrates local agricultural traditions, seeks to protect consumers in terms of food quality, and advocates for social cooking, dining, and conviviality.

The Enduring Potlatch

Potlatching among native peoples of the northwest coast of the United States and Canada was subjected to decades of opposition from Europeans and Euro-Americans (Cole 1991). The missionaries opposed potlatching as an un-Christian practice. The government thought it was wasteful and excessive, out of line with their goals for the "economic progress" of the Indians. In 1885, the Canadian government outlawed the potlatch. Of all the Northwest Coast tribes, the Kwakwaka'wakw (see Culturama) resisted this prohibition most strongly and for the longest time. In Canada, potlatches are no longer illegal. But it took a long battle to remove restrictions.

Reasons for giving a potlatch today are similar to those in the past: naming children, mourning the dead, transferring rights and privileges, celebrating marriages, and raising totem poles (Webster 1991). The length of time devoted to planning a potlatch, however, has changed. In the past, several years were involved compared to about a year now. Still, it takes much organization and work to accumulate enough goods to ensure that no guest goes away empty-handed, and the guest list may include between 500 and 1,000 people. Another change is in the kinds of goods exchanged. Typical potlatch goods now include crocheted items (such as cushion covers, blankets, and potholders), glassware, plastic goods, manufactured blankets, pillows, towels, articles of clothing, and sacks of flour and sugar. The potlatch endures but changes.

3 Learning Objectives Revisited

3.1 Know what are the characteristics of the five modes of livelihood.

The five modes of livelihood among contemporary people are foraging, horticulture, pastoralism, agriculture, and industrialism.

In foraging societies, the division of labor is based on gender and age, and temperate foragers exhibit more gender overlap in tasks than circumpolar foragers. Property is shared, and all people have equal rights to resources such as land and water holes. Foraging has long-term sustainability when not affected by outside pressure.

Horticulture and pastoralism are extensive strategies that depend on domesticated plants (horticulture) and animals (pastoralism). Horticulture requires fallowing, and pastoralism requires the constant movement of animals to fresh pastures. The division of labor varies, including situations in which men do more productive work, those where women do more work, and those in which workloads are shared between men and women. Use rights are the prominent form of property relations. Both have long-term sustainability when not affected by encroachments.

Family farming systems produce crops for their own use and for sale in the market. Most family farming systems involve more male labor in the fields and more female labor in the domestic domain. Agriculture's sustainability is limited by the need to replenish the land.

In industrial/digital societies, the division of labor is highly differentiated by class, gender, and age. Widespread unemployment is found in many industrial economies. In capitalist societies, private property is the dominant pattern. Industrial/digital societies lack sustainability, given the high demand for nonrenewable energy.

3.2 Recognize how modes of livelihood are related to consumption and exchange.

Anthropologists contrast modes of consumption in nonmarket and market-based systems of production. In the former, minimalism is the dominant mode of consumption, with finite needs. In the latter, consumerism is the dominant mode of consumption, with infinite needs. Foraging societies typify the minimalist mode of consumption. Industrial capitalist/informatics societies typify the consumerist mode. The modes of livelihood between foraging and industrialism/digital exhibit varying degrees of minimalism and consumerism.

In nonmarket economies, most consumers produce the goods they use themselves or they know who produced them. In market economies, consumption is depersonalized through globalized mass production.

Modes of exchange also correspond to the modes of livelihood and consumption. In foraging societies, the mode of exchange is balanced exchange, with the goal of keeping the value of the items exchanged roughly equal over time. Balanced exchange involves people who have a social relationship with each other, and the relationship is reinforced through continued exchange.

Market exchange is a transaction in which the seller's goal is to make a profit. Compared to balanced exchange, the people involved in market exchanges are less likely to know each other or to have an enduring social relationship.

3.3 Illustrate how livelihood, consumption, and exchange are changing in contemporary times.

Economic globalization is changing livelihood, consumption, and exchange around the world. Western goods, such as steel axes, are in high demand by people in non-Western, nonindustrialized contexts. Such goods must be purchased, a fact that impels people to work for cash so that they can buy things.

In spite of the powerful effects of globalization on local economic patterns, many groups seek to restore traditional patterns of livelihood, consumption, and exchange. The rise of new food movements that promote small farm and local food production is an example of an attempt to localize and personalize food production and exchange. The revival of potlatching in the Pacific Northwest is an example of the revitalization of traditional consumption and exchange practices.

Key Concepts

agriculture, p. 51

balanced exchange, p. 57

consumerism, p. 54

division of labor, p. 46

expected reciprocity, p. 58

extensive strategy, p. 46

family farming, p. 51

foraging, p. 45

generalized reciprocity, p. 57

horticulture, p. 48

industrial capital agriculture, p. 52

industrialism/digital economy, p. 53

intensive strategy, p. 51

leveling mechanism, p. 55

manioc or cassava, p. 49

market exchange, p. 59

minimalism, p. 54

mobile money, p. 57

mode of consumption, p. 44

mode of exchange, p. 44

mode of livelihood, p. 44

pastoralism, p. 50

potlatch, p. 53

poverty, p. 44

pure gift, p. 57

redistribution, p. 58

subjective well-being, p. 45

trade, p. 59

unbalanced exchange, p. 57

use rights, p. 46

Thinking Outside the Box

1. Propose some examples of what might qualify as a "pure gift."
2. Some people think that child sex workers should be unionized to protect them. Others argue that unionization signals acceptance of this role for children. Where do you stand on this issue and why?
3. You have invited Jesus, the Buddha, Muhammad, and Moses to dinner. What are you serving?

Chapter 4
Reproduction and Human Development

Learning Objectives

4.1 Illustrate how modes of reproduction are related to modes of livelihood.

4.2 Discuss how culture shapes fertility in different cultural contexts.

4.3 Identify how culture shapes personality over the life cycle.

Anthro Connections

In Havana, Cuba, a girl celebrates her fifteenth birthday known as a *fiesta de quince*. In Hispanic culture globally, a girl's fifteenth birthday is a coming-of-age ceremony marked by lavish expenditures on an elegant gown and a party including a fancy cake. Whereas sons are preferred in many Asian populations, in much of Latin America, daughters are equally or even more desired than sons. In Havana, Cuba, most women prefer to have a daughter (Härkönen 2010). Mothers who have a daughter spend a lot of money on frilly baby outfits and hair ornaments, while mothers who have a son console themselves by saying that it is cheaper to have a son because they do not have to buy the pretty clothes and accessories. Cuba has the lowest rate of fertility in the Western hemisphere, at 1.5 births per woman, which is lower than the United States and Canada. Given the odds of fairly equal chances of having a boy or a girl, many Cuban mothers are likely disappointed when they have a son.

This chapter covers cross-cultural patterns of sexuality and having children and the formation of personality and identity over the life cycle. The first section provides an overview of reproduction in relation to modes of livelihood. The second section traces the connections between culture and reproduction, especially birth rates. The third section provides insights into how culture shapes personality and identity throughout the life cycle.

Modes of Reproduction

4.1 **Illustrate how modes of reproduction are related to modes of livelihood.**

A **mode of reproduction** is the dominant pattern, in a culture, of population change through the combined effect of **fertility**, or number of births in a given population or per woman, and **mortality**, or the number of deaths in a given population. Cultural anthropologists have enough cross-cultural data to provide the general characteristics of only three modes of reproduction (Figure 4.1) that correspond to three of the five modes of livelihood discussed in Chapter 3.

The Foraging Mode of Reproduction

Evidence about the foraging mode of reproduction comes from a classic study based on fieldwork conducted with the Ju/wasi in the 1970s (Howell 1979) (review Culturama in Chapter 1, page 18). The study shows that birth intervals (the time between a birth and the next birth) among the Ju/wasi are often several years in duration. What accounts for these long birth intervals? Two factors are most important: breast-feeding and women's low level of body fat. Frequent and long periods of breastfeeding inhibit progesterone production and suppress ovulation. Also, a certain level of body fat is required for ovulation. Ju/wasi women's diets contain little fat, and their regular physical exercise as foragers keeps their body fat level low, further suppressing ovulation. Thus, diet and work are key factors underlying Ju/wasi population dynamics.

Ju/wasi women, during the time of the study, typically had between two and three live births, of which two children survived into adulthood. This mode of reproduction is adaptive to the Ju/wasi environment and sustainable over time. Among the Ju/wasi who have become farmers or laborers, the number of births per woman is higher. This change is related to the facts that their diet contains more grains and dairy products and women are less physically active.

The Agricultural Mode of Reproduction

The agricultural mode of reproduction is associated with the highest birth rates of the three modes discussed here. **Pronatalism**, an attitude or policy that encourages

---

mode of reproduction the predominant pattern, in a culture, of population change through the combined effect of fertility (births) and mortality (deaths).

fertility the rate of births in a population or the rate of population increase in general.

mortality the rate of deaths in a population.

pronatalism an attitude or policy that encourages childbearing.

Foraging	Agriculture	Industrial/Digital
Population Growth Moderate birth rates Moderate death rates	**Population Growth** High birth rates Declining death rates	**Population Growth** Industrialized countries—negative population growth Developing countries—high
Value of Children Moderate	**Value of Children** High	**Value of Children** Mixed

Fertility Control
Indirect means
  Low-fat diet of women
  Women's work and exercise
  Prolonged breastfeeding
  Spontaneous abortion
Direct means
  Induced abortion
  Infanticide
	Fertility Control
	Increased reliance on direct means
	  Induced abortion
	  Infanticide
	Pronatalist techniques
	  Herbs
		Fertility Control
		Direct methods grounded in science and medicine
		Chemical forms of contraception
		In vitro fertilization
		Abortion

Social Aspects
Homogeneous fertility
Few specialists
	Social Aspects
	Emerging class differences
	Increasing specialization
	  Midwifery
	  Herbalists
		Social Aspects
		Stratified fertility
		  Globally, nationally, and locally
		Highly developed specialization

Figure 4.1 Modes of Livelihood and Reproduction

childbearing, is prevalent among farm families cross-culturally. It is prompted by the need for a large labor force to work the land, care for animals, process food, and do marketing. In this context, having many children is a rational reproductive strategy related to the mode of livelihood. Thus, farming people who live in family farming systems have their own "family planning," but one that promotes rather than prevents the birth of many children.

High birth rates of seven or more children per woman exist in several low-income agricultural countries of Africa, such as Niger (7.4 births per woman), Somalia, (6.7 births per woman), Uganda (6.7 births per woman), and Angola (6.5 births per woman) (Population Reference Bureau 2009). Lower rates, of two or three children per woman, however, are found in many agricultural countries in South America, such as Venezuela, Chile, and Argentina.

Within countries, groups with the highest birth rates in the world are the Mennonites and Hutterites. They are Christians of European descent living mainly in the United States and Canada. Women in these groups typically have between 8 and 10 children who survive into adulthood. High birth rates also characterize the Amish, a closely related group (see Culturama).

In another pronatalist context, rural North India, having many children—especially sons—is important in farming families. Young boys learn to do farm work with their father. As adults, they are responsible for plowing the farm and for protecting the family land from takeovers by neighboring farmers. When Western family planning experts visited villages in North India in the late 1950s to promote the idea of small families, the farmers expressed dismay (Mamdani 1972). To them, a large family, especially one with many sons, is a sign of wealth and success, not poverty and failure.

The Industrial/Digital Mode of Reproduction

In industrial countries, reproduction is at the point of either replacement-level fertility, in which the number of births equals the number of deaths, leading to maintenance of the current population size, or below-replacement-level fertility, in which the number of births is less than the number of deaths, leading to population decline. Children in these contexts are less useful in production because of the reduced labor demands of industrialism. Furthermore, children must attend school and therefore cannot work for their families much during the school year. People respond to these factors, unconsciously, by having fewer children and by investing more resources in the children they have.

Population changes that take place during the transition to the industrial/digital mode of reproduction

Culturama

The Old Order Amish of the United States and Canada

The Amish are Christians who live in rural areas of the United States and Canada. Their total population in the United States and Canada is estimated at 250,000. Their ancestry traces to German-speaking Swiss Anabaptists (a sect opposed to baptism) in the sixteenth century. To escape religious persecution, they migrated to North America, starting in the early eighteenth century and continuing into the mid-nineteenth century. There are no Amish in Europe today.

The term Old Order Amish refers to the main body of the Amish people. A small minority, known as New Order Amish, broke off from the Old Order in the late 1960s. Both groups use horse-drawn transportation, but the New Order Amish accept more technology.

The Amish speak a German-derived dialect. They wear modest clothing and dress similarly to each other. They avoid using electricity from power grids, but solar-generated electricity and 12-volt batteries are allowed. Education beyond the eighth grade is seen as unnecessary. A basic theme in Amish life is the need to guard against "worldly" (non-Amish, mainstream United States) values, dependencies, and hurriedness, and to maintain the family as a unit that lives and works together. Working with one's own hands is valued, as are humility and modesty. Farming is the traditional means of livelihood among the Amish. Beyond these generalizations, many variations exist across communities in terms of how strictly people interpret teaching in the Bible (Kraybill 2014).

The Amish have many children, typically six or seven per woman. Even though some children leave and join "the English" (non-Amish), their population is doubling every 20 years. In Lancaster County, Pennsylvania, the heartland of the Old Order Amish, a steep rise in population growth starting in the 1970s has exceeded the availability of farmland (Kraybill and Nolt 2004).

Now, several hundred Amish businesses exist. Many are small scale and operate from the home, but many others are large scale and earn millions of dollars per year. Amish who enter business try to retain Amish values of family solidarity by working at home and selling products from their homes, but many increasingly work in businesses outside their homes, alongside the English.

Amish youth have the opportunity of deciding whether to be baptized into the faith when they are 16 years old. At this time, called *rumspringa* in Pennsylvania Dutch, or "running around," the young people are allowed to explore the customs of the English world, including television. Most stay at home during rumspringa, spending time with Amish friends on the weekends. In rare cases, some experiment with alcohol, drugs, and sex (Shachtman 2006). Around 90 percent of Amish teenagers decide to accept Amish ways and be baptized, choosing a lifestyle that emphasizes humility and community solidarity rather than the "worldly" lifestyle of individualism and competition.

Thanks to Donald B. Kraybill, Elizabethtown College, for reviewing this material.

(LEFT) Members of an Amish household sit around their kitchen table.

(CENTER) In Pennsylvania, a farmer mows alfalfa with a team of mules and a gasoline engine to power the mower. This mechanism enhances his farm work but does not break the Old Order Amish rule against using tractors in the field.

Map 4.1 Old Order Amish Population of North America

Ohio, Pennsylvania, and Indiana have the largest number of Old Order Amish in the United States.

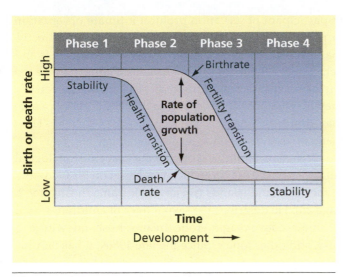

Figure 4.2 Model of the Demographic Transition

Source: Nebel, Bernard J.; Wright, Richard T.; *Environmental Science: The Way The World Works*, 7th edition. Copyright © 2000. Electronically reproduced by permission of Pearson Education, Inc. Upper Saddle River, New Jersey.

correspond to what is called the **demographic transition**, a process during which the agricultural pattern of high fertility and high mortality becomes the industrial pattern of low fertility and low mortality. There are two phases in the demographic transition model (Figure 4.2). In the first phase, mortality declines because of improved nutrition and health, so population growth rates increase. The second phase occurs when fertility also declines. At this point, low rates of population growth occur to the extent that many industrial/digital countries have below-replacement fertility including Japan, Canada, the United States, and countries in Europe. While such low rates of population growth are welcomed by many thinkers as reducing the burden on the environment, leaders of some

countries worry about labor shortages and a declining tax base.

The industrial/digital mode of reproduction has three distinguishing features:

- **stratified reproduction:** middle-class and upper-class people tend to have few children with high survival rates while among the poor, both fertility and mortality rates are high. Brazil, a newly industrializing state, has the world's most extreme income inequality and extremely stratified reproduction.

- **population aging:** when the proportion of older people increases relative to younger people. In Japan, the national fertility rate declined to replacement level in the 1950s and later reached the below-replacement level. Japan is currently experiencing a decline in population growth of about 15 percent per generation and, simultaneously, rapid aging of the population. As many people enter the senior category, they create a population bulge that is not balanced by the number of younger people (Figure 4.3). A population projection for the year 2050 suggests that the bulge will increase.

- **high level of involvement of scientific (especially medical) technology in all aspects of pregnancy:** becoming pregnant, through artificial insemination, preventing pregnancy, and terminating pregnancy (Browner and Press 1996). This trend is accompanied by increasing levels of specialization in providing new services (discussed below).

---

demographic transition the change from the agricultural pattern of high fertility and high mortality to the industrial pattern of low fertility and low mortality.

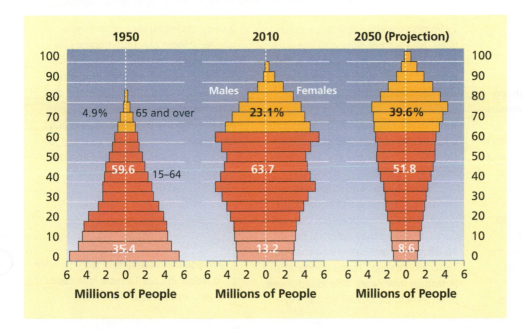

Figure 4.3 Changes in the Population Pyramid of Japan

Source: Statistics Bureau, MIC, Ministry of Health, Labor and Welfare. Reproduced with permission.

Culture and Fertility

4.2 **Discuss how culture shapes fertility in different cultural contexts.**

Culture shapes human fertility from its very start, if conception is considered to be the fertilization of an ovum (egg). The following discussion begins with sexual intercourse and continues through pregnancy and birth.

Sexual Intercourse

Sexual intercourse usually involves private, sometimes secret, beliefs and behaviors. Anthropological research on sexual practices is thus particularly challenging. The ethics of participant observation prohibit intimate observation or participation, so data can be obtained only indirectly. Biases in people's verbal reports about sexual beliefs and behavior are likely for several reasons. People may be too shy or otherwise unwilling to discuss sex or, conversely, they may be boastful and inflate the truth. Many people may simply be unable to answer questions such as "How many times did you have sexual intercourse last year?"

Bronislaw Malinowski wrote the first anthropological study of sexuality (1929) which was based on his fieldwork in the Trobriand Islands (review Culturama in Chapter 2, page 28). He describes the sexual lives of children, sexual techniques, love magic, erotic dreams, husband–wife jealousy, and other topics. Since the late 1980s, it has become

Anthropology Works

Studying Sexual Behavior among MSM in New York City

Lara Tabac, medical anthropologist, worked at the New York City Department of Health and Mental Hygiene (DOHMH), along with another cultural anthropologist and 6,000 other employees (2003). Her unit was the DOHMH's Epidemiology Services. Epidemiology is the study of the factors that cause health and disease in different populations, and it provides information to public health-care providers so that they can improve their programs.

Tabac was hired to collect qualitative information from New Yorkers about their behavior and how it related to their health, specifically MSM (men who have sex with men).

Tabac describes her job as a challenging mix of words and numbers (2003). The department is highly quantitative, using statistics to shape health-action agendas. Tabac explains that while the numbers tell us how many people do X or Y and suffer from X or Y disease, they say nothing about why people behave the way they do and therefore put themselves at risk for certain health problems. Tabac's expertise as a cultural anthropologist allowed her to provide insights into the "why" question and help make the work of the DOHMH more effective.

Anthropological training reinforced and shaped Tabac's personal

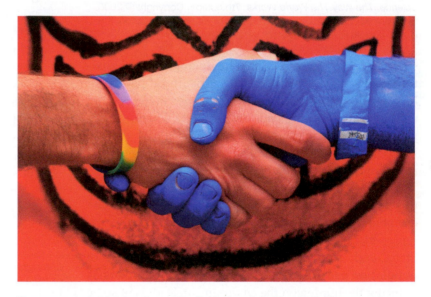

Two gay men shaking hands at a Gay Pride Parade in New York City.

inclination to observe and ask questions. She put her skills and interests to work, listening to people on a wide range of topics. With her MetroCard, she reached people in far-flung neighborhoods who were willing to share with her their health dilemmas and life struggles as well as their suggestions for improving services and programs that they needed.

Tabac's goal was to learn about condom use among the MSM population: who uses or does not use condoms, and why they do or do not do so. To gather qualitative information, Tabac spent many hours conducting individual interviews. She found these interviews to be crucial for gaining a deep understanding of sensitive issues. People are more honest in a one-on-one interview with someone they trust compared to talking about their sexual lives in a focus group that includes several people. Tabac found her job with the DOHMH challenging and socially relevant. She took the job because she wanted to help improve people's lives. She has not been disappointed.

Food for Thought

Are you inspired by this story to want to follow in Lara Tabac's footsteps? If yes, why? If not, why not?

A bride wearing traditional wedding clothing in the city of Meknès, Morocco.

Map 4.2   Morocco

The Kingdom of Morocco is the westernmost country of the Arab world. A border dispute continues with the Western Sahara, which Morocco has administered since 1975. Morocco's population is 33 million. The terrain ranges from coastal lowlands to rugged interior mountains. Morocco's economy is based on mining phosphates, remittances, and tourism. It is one of the world's largest producers and exporters of cannabis and the world's largest per capita consumer of sugar. Most Moroccans are Sunni Muslims. The official language is classical Arabic, but Moroccan Arabic is widely spoken. More than 40 percent of the people speak a variety of Berber.

increasingly important to study how culture affects sexuality because of the spread of sexually transmitted diseases (STDs), including HIV/AIDS. Without understanding variations in sexual values and practices, it is impossible to design effective programs for preventing and controlling STDs (see Anthropology Works).

WHEN TO BEGIN HAVING INTERCOURSE? Biologically speaking, sexual intercourse between a fertile female and a fertile male is normally required for human reproduction, although artificial insemination is becoming a widely used option in some contexts. Biology, interacting with environment and culture, defines the time span within which a female is fertile: from **menarche** (pronounced MEN-ar-kee), the onset of menstruation, to **menopause**, the end of menstruation. Globally, the beginning of menarche varies from 12 to 14 years of age (Thomas et al. 2001). Generally, girls in high-income countries reach menarche a few years earlier than girls in low-income countries. For example, the estimated age at menarche in Japan is 12.5 years, but in Haiti it is 15.5 years.

Cultures socialize children regarding the appropriate age to begin sexual intercourse, and cultural rules are more variable than the biological marker of menarche. Cultural guidelines vary by gender, class, race, and ethnicity. In many cultures, sexual activity should begin only with marriage. This rule often applies more strictly to females than to males. In Zawiya (zuh-WEE-yuh), a Muslim town of northern Morocco (Map 4.2), a bride's virginity is highly valued, whereas that of the groom is ignored (Davis and Davis 1987). Most brides conform to the ideal. Some unmarried young women do engage in premarital sex, however. If they choose to have a traditional wedding, they must somehow meet the requirement of producing blood-stained wedding sheets after the first night. If the bride and the groom have been having premarital sexual relations, the groom may assist in the deception by nicking a finger with a knife and bloodying the sheets himself. Another option is to buy fake blood sold in drugstores.

INTERCOURSE FREQUENCY AND FERTILITY Cross-culturally, the frequency of sexual intercourse varies widely. The relationship between frequency of sexual intercourse and fertility, though, is not simple. A common assumption is that people in cultures with high fertility rates have sexual intercourse frequently. Without modern

---

menarche the onset of menstruation.

menopause the cessation of menstruation.

birth control, such as condoms, birth control pills, and intrauterine devices (IUDs), frequent intercourse would seem, logically, to produce high rates of fertility.

A classic study of reported intercourse frequency among Euro-Americans in the United States and Hindus in India, however, throws this assumption into question (Nag 1972). The Indians had intercourse less frequently (less than twice a week) than the Euro-Americans did (two to three times a week) in all age groups. Several features of Indian culture limit the frequency of sexual intercourse. First, the Hindu religion teaches the value of sexual abstinence, thus providing ideological support for limiting sexual intercourse. Hinduism also suggests that one should abstain from intercourse on many sacred days: the first night of the new moon, the first night of the full moon, the eighth day of each half of the month (the light half and the dark half), and sometimes on Fridays. As many as 100 days each year could be observed as days of abstinence. Another factor is Hindu men's belief in what anthropologists term the lost semen complex, which links men's health and strength to the retention of semen. An anthropologist learned about this complex during his fieldwork in North India:

> Everyone knew that semen was not easily formed; it takes forty days and forty drops of blood to make one drop of semen. . . . Semen of good quality is rich and viscous, like the cream of unadulterated milk. . . . Celibacy was the first requirement of true fitness, because every sexual orgasm meant the loss of a quantity of semen, laboriously formed. (Carstairs 1967:83–86, quoted in Nag 1972:235)

The fact remains, however, that fertility is higher in India than in many other parts of the world where such religious restrictions on sexual intercourse do not exist. Obviously, sheer frequency of intercourse is not the explanation because it takes only one act of sexual intercourse at the right time of the month to create a pregnancy. The point of this discussion is to show that reverse reasoning (assuming that high fertility means people have nothing better to do than have sex) is wrong. The cultural dynamics of sexuality in India function to restrain sexual activities and thus keep fertility lower than it otherwise would be.

Fertility Decision Making

Within the context of the family unit, decision makers weigh factors influencing why and when to have a child. At the state level, governments plan their overall population target on the basis of fertility goals that are sometimes pronatalist and sometimes antinatalist (opposed to many births). At the global level, powerful economic and political interests influence the reproductive policies of countries and, in turn, of families and individuals.

AT THE FAMILY LEVEL Within the family, parents and other family members consider, consciously and unconsciously,

the value and costs of children (Nag 1983). Cross-cultural research indicates that four factors are most important underlying factors in affecting the desire for children:

- Children's labor value
- Children's value as old-age support for parents
- Infant and child mortality rates
- Economic costs of children

The first three factors increase fertility: When children's value is high in terms of labor or old-age support, fertility is likely to be high and when infant and child mortality rates are high, fertility rates tend to be high to "replace" offspring who do die. In the case of the last factor, child costs—including direct costs (for food, education, and clothing, for example) and indirect costs (employment opportunities that the mother gives up)—the relationship is negative. Higher costs reduce the desire for children. In industrial/digital economy contexts, child costs are high and child labor value declines dramatically. Mandatory school attendance also pulls children out of the workforce and may involve direct costs for fees, uniforms, and supplies. In countries that provide old-age security and pension plans, the need for children is reduced.

Husbands and wives may not always have the same preferences about the number of children they desire. In a highland village in the Oaxaca region of Mexico (Map 4.3), men want more children than women do (Browner 1986). Of women with only one child, 80 percent were content with a family of that size. Most men (60 percent) who were satisfied with their present family size had four or more children. One woman said, "My husband sleeps peacefully through the night, but I have to get up when the children need something. I'm the one the baby urinates on; sometimes I have to get out of bed in the cold and change both our clothes" (1986:714).

A family planning clinic in Baghdad, Iraq. Throughout much of the world, Western-style family planning advice is controversial because it may conflict with local beliefs and values.

❚ *In your cultural experience, what is the prevailing attitude about family planning?*

Map 4.3 Mexico

The United Mexican States is the most populous Spanish-speaking country in the world. It was subjected to Spanish rule for three centuries before gaining independence. Its population is 125 million, and the capital, Mexico City, has a population of 21 million people. Mexico has a mixed economy of industry, agriculture, and trade. It is the tenth-largest oil producer in the world and the world's leading producer of silver. Ethnically, the population consists of Mestizos (60 percent), Indians (30 percent), and Whites (nine percent). Southern states have the highest proportion of Indians. Among the Organisation for Economic Co-operation and Development (OECD) countries, Mexico has the second highest degree of economic disparity between the extremely poor and extremely rich, after Chile.

Depending on the gender division of labor and on other social features, families may prefer sons, daughters, or a balance of each. Preference for sons is widespread, especially in South Asia (including India and Pakistan) and East Asia (China and Korea), but it is not universal. Throughout much of Southeast Asia, for example, people prefer a balanced number of sons and daughters. A preference for daughters exists in some parts of Africa south of the Sahara and in some Caribbean populations.

AT THE STATE LEVEL State governments formulate policies that affect rates of population growth within their boundaries. These policies vary from being antinatalist to pronatalist, and they vary in terms of the methods of fertility management promoted. Factors that affect government policies include economic factors, such as projected jobs and employment levels, public services, and maintaining the tax base, as well as other factors, such as filling the ranks of the military, maintaining ethnic and regional proportions, and dealing with population aging.

AT THE GLOBAL LEVEL The most far-reaching layer that affects fertility decision making occurs at the international level, where global power structures such as pharmaceutical companies and religious leaders influence country-level and individual-level decision making. In the 1950s, there was a wave of enthusiasm among Western nations for promoting family planning programs of many types in developing countries. In the 1990s, the United States adopted a more restrictive policy toward family planning, withdrew

support for such options as abortion, and began to promote abstinence as the foundation of population control.

Fertility Control

People in all cultures since prehistory have had ways of influencing fertility, including ways to increase it, reduce it, and regulate birth spacing. Some ways are direct, such as using herbs or medicines that induce abortion. Others are indirect, such as long periods of breastfeeding, which reduce the chances of conception.

INDIGENOUS METHODS Hundreds of direct indigenous fertility control methods are available cross-culturally (Newman 1972, 1985).

Research in Afghanistan during the 1980s found over 500 fertility-regulating techniques in just one region (Hunte 1985). In Afghanistan, as in most nonindustrial cultures, it is women who possess this information. Specialists, such as midwives or herbalists, provide further expertise. Of the total number of methods in the Afghanistan study, 72 percent were for increasing fertility, 22 percent were contraceptives, and six percent were used to induce abortion. Most methods involve plant and animal substances. Herbs are made into tea and taken orally. Some substances are formed into pills, some are steamed and inhaled as vapors, some are vaginally inserted, and others are rubbed on the woman's stomach.

INDUCED ABORTION A review of 400 societies found that induced abortion was practiced in virtually all of them (Devereaux 1976). Cross-culturally, attitudes toward induced abortion range from absolute acceptability to conditional approval (abortion is acceptable but only under specified conditions), tolerance (abortion is regarded with neither approval nor disapproval), and opposition and punishment for offenders. Methods of inducing abortion include hitting the abdomen, starving oneself, taking drugs, jumping from high places, jumping up and down, lifting heavy objects, and doing hard work. Some methods clearly are dangerous to the pregnant woman. In Afghanistan, a midwife inserts an object such as a wooden spoon or stick treated with copper sulfate into the pregnant woman to cause vaginal bleeding and eventual abortion of the fetus (Hunte 1985).

The reasons women seek to induce abortion are usually related to economic and social factors. Pastoralist women, for example, frequently carry heavy loads, sometimes for long distances. This lifestyle does not allow women to care for many small children at one time. Poverty is another frequent motivation. A woman who is faced with a pregnancy in the context of limited resources may find abortion preferable to bearing a child who cannot be fed. Culturally defined "legitimacy" of a pregnancy and social penalties for bearing an illegitimate child provide long-standing motivations for abortion, especially in Western societies.

Some governments regulate access to abortion, either promoting it or forbidding it. Since the late 1980s, China has pursued a rigorous campaign to limit population growth (Greenhalgh 2008). Its One-Child-per-Couple Policy, announced in 1978, restricted most families to having only one child. The policy involved strict surveillance of pregnancies, strong group disapproval directed toward women pregnant for the second time or more, and forced abortions and sterilizations. In 2014, the Chinese government loosened its policy and said that a couple could apply to have a second child if the mother or father was an only child (Levin 2014). Religion and abortion are often related, but there is no simple relationship between what a particular religion teaches about abortion and what people actually do. Catholicism forbids abortion, but thousands of Catholic women have sought abortions throughout the world. Predominantly Catholic countries have laws making induced abortion illegal. This is the case in Brazil where, in spite of Catholic beliefs and the law, many women, especially poor women, resort to abortion. In one impoverished shantytown in the city of Recife in the northeast, one-third of the women said that they had aborted at least once (Gregg 2003). Illegal abortions are more likely to have detrimental effects on women's health than safe, legal abortion services. Several local studies conducted in the northeastern part of Brazil, the country's poorest region, report high percentages, up to one-fourth, of maternal deaths due to complications from illegal abortion (McCallum 2005).

Islamic teachings forbid abortion. Abortion of female fetuses is nonetheless practiced covertly in Pakistan and by Muslims in India. Hinduism teaches *ahimsa*, or nonviolence

In Japan, people regularly visit and decorate *mizuko*, small statues in memory of their "returned" fetuses.

toward other living beings, including a fetus whose movements have been felt by the mother. Thousands of Hindus, however, seek abortions every year. In contrast, Buddhism provides no overt rulings against abortion. Japanese Buddhism teaches that all life is fluid and that an aborted fetus is simply "returned" to a watery world of unshaped life and may later come back (LaFleur 1992). This belief is compatible with people's frequent use of induced abortion as a form of birth control in Japan.

THE NEW REPRODUCTIVE TECHNOLOGIES Since the early 1980s, new forms of reproductive technology, or methods that seek to bypass biology to offer options for childbearing to infertile couples, have emerged and are now available in many places around the world.

In vitro fertilization (IVF), in which egg cells are fertilized outside the womb, is highly sought after by many couples in Western countries, especially middle- and upper-class couples, among whom infertility is high. It is also available in many cities worldwide (Inhorn 2003). As IVF spreads globally, people interpret it within their own cultural frameworks. A study of male infertility in two Middle Eastern cities—Cairo in Egypt and Beirut in Lebanon—reveals the close connection between masculine identity and fertility (Inhorn 2004). While married couples want to have children, if the husband is infertile, IVF is not a clear option. In these cities, infertile men face social stigma and feelings of deep inadequacy. In addition, third-party donation of sperm is not acceptable according to Islam. These couples are trying to balance their desire for children with Muslim values.

Infanticide

Infanticide, or the killing of an infant or child, is widely practiced cross-culturally, although it is rarely a frequent or common practice. Infanticide takes two major forms: direct infanticide and indirect infanticide (Harris 1977).

---

infanticide the killing of an infant or child.

A study by Nancy Scheper-Hughes, carried out among the urban poor of northeastern Brazil, found that indirect infanticide in the late twentieth century was related to extreme poverty (Scheper-Hughes 1992). From the 1960s through the 1990s, Brazil experienced what Scheper-Hughes calls the modernization of mortality. In Brazil, the modernization of mortality means that infant and child mortality is class-based, mirroring a deep division in entitlements between the rich and the poor. Economic growth in Brazil in the latter part of the twentieth century brought rising standards of living for many, and the infant mortality rate (deaths of children under the age of one year per 1,000 births) declined dramatically. This decline, however, was unevenly distributed with high infant death rates concentrated among the poorest social classes of society. When Scheper-Hughes did fieldwork in the later twentieth century, poverty forced mothers to selectively, and unconsciously, neglect babies who seem sickly or weak, sending them to heaven as "angel babies" rather than struggling to keep them alive. People's religious beliefs, a form of Catholicism, provided psychological support for indirect infanticide by allowing mothers to believe that their dead babies went safely to heaven. In an update to her earlier research, Scheper-Hughes reports that young women in her fieldwork area now, in the early twenty-first century, give birth to only three babies, and most of them survive. A major factor creating this change is government-provided health services. Unfortunately, while the infants now have a better chance of surviving, as adolescents they face new challenges of drug-related gang violence (2012).

Personality and the Life Cycle

4.3   **Identify how culture shapes personality over the life cycle.**

Personality is an individual's patterned and characteristic way of behaving, thinking, and feeling. Cultural anthropologists think that personality is formed largely through enculturation (also called socialization), or the learning of culture through both informal and formal processes. They study how various cultures enculturate their members into having different personalities and identities. Cultural anthropologists also investigate how personalities vary according to cultural context, and some ask why such variations exist. Others study how changing cultural contexts affect personality, identity, and well-being over the life cycle.

Birth, Infancy, and Childhood

This section first considers the cultural context of birth itself. It then discusses cultural variations in infant care and

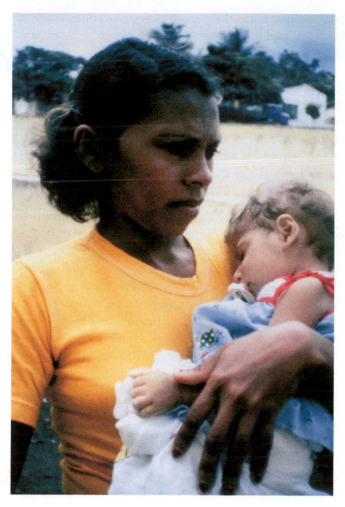

A mother and her malnourished son in Bom Jesus, a shantytown in northeastern Brazil. Nancy Scheper-Hughes first lived as a Peace Corps volunteer in Bom Jesus in the 1960s and then returned to do fieldwork in the 1980s. At that time, extreme poverty meant that mothers could not provide good food for their children, and they had to deal psychologically with frequent child death. Now, children in northeast Brazil are more likely to survive, but adolescent boys especially experience high mortality because of drugs and violence.

Have you studied bonding theory in a psychology class? What did you learn?

Direct infanticide is the death of an infant or child resulting from actions such as beating, smothering, poisoning, and drowning. Indirect infanticide, a more subtle process, may involve prolonged practices such as food deprivation, failure to take a sick infant to a clinic, and failure to provide warm clothing in winter.

The most frequent motive for direct infanticide reported cross-culturally is that the infant was "deformed" or very ill (Scrimshaw 1984). Other motives for infanticide include the infant's sex, an adulterous conception, an unwed mother, the birth of twins, and too many children in the family. A study of 148 cases of infanticide in contemporary Canada found that the mothers convicted of killing their offspring were relatively young and lacked financial and family resources to help them (Daly and Wilson 1984).

---

personality an individual's patterned and characteristic way of behaving, thinking, and feeling.

how they may shape personality and identity. Last, it deals with the topic of gender identity formation in infancy.

THE BIRTH CONTEXT The cultural context of birth affects an infant's psychological development. Brigitte Jordan (1983), a pioneer in the cross-cultural study of birth, conducted comparative research on birth practices in Mexico, Sweden, the Netherlands, and the United States. She studied the birth setting, including its location and who is present, the types of attendants and their roles, the birth event, and the postpartum period. Among Maya women in Mexico, the midwife is called in during the early stages of labor. One of her tasks is to give a massage to the mother-to-be. She also provides psychological support by telling stories, often about other women's birthing experiences. The husband is expected to be present during the labor so that he can see "how a woman suffers." The woman's mother should be present, too, along with other female kin, such as her mother-in-law, godmother, sisters, and friends. Thus, a Maya mother is surrounded by a large group of supportive people.

In the United States, hospital births are typical. Some critics argue that the hospital-based system of highly regulated birth is extremely technocratic and too managed, alienating the mother—as well as other members of the family and the wider community—from the birthing process and the infant (Davis-Floyd 1992). This critique has prompted a consideration of how to improve the way birth is conducted in the United States.

BONDING Many contemporary Western psychological theorists say that parent–infant contact and bonding at the time of birth is crucial for setting in motion parental attachment to the infant. Western specialists say that if bonding is not established at the time of the infant's birth, the infant will not develop later. Explanations for juvenile delinquency or other unfavorable child-development problems often include references to a lack of proper infant bonding at birth.

Nancy Scheper-Hughes (1992) questions Western bonding theory on the basis of her research in northeastern Brazil from the 1960s through the 1990s. She argues that bonding does not necessarily have to occur at birth to be successful. Her observations reveal that many low-income mothers at the time did not exhibit bonding with their infants at birth. Instead, bonding occurred later, if the child survived infancy, and when the child was several years old and clearly likely to survive. Scheper-Hughes proposes that this pattern of later bonding is related to the high rate of infant mortality among poor people of northeast Brazil at the time. She suggested that, if women were to develop strong bonds with their newborn infants, the mothers would suffer untold amounts of grief. Thus, Western bonding is adaptive in low-mortality, low-fertility societies in which strong maternal attachment is reasonable because infants are likely to survive. Close bonding would be disastrous for mothers in contexts where infant and child mortality rates are high.

The Western medical model of birth contrasts sharply with non-Western practices. Sometimes they come into direct conflict. In such situations, anthropological expertise can mediate the conflict by providing what medical specialists now refer to as **cultural competence**, or awareness of and respect for, among Western-trained professionals, beliefs and practices that differ from those of Western medical practice (Gálvez 2011).

GENDER IN INFANCY Anthropologists distinguish between sex and gender (see Chapter 1). Sex is something that everyone is born with. In the view of Western science, it has three biological markers: genitals, hormones, and chromosomes. A male has a penis, more androgens than estrogens, and the XY chromosome. A female has a vagina, more estrogens than androgens, and the XX chromosome. Increasingly, scientists are finding that these two categories are not airtight. In all populations, up to 10 percent of people are born with indeterminate genitals, similar proportions of androgens and estrogens, and chromosomes with more complex distributions than simply XX and XY.

Gender, in contrast, is a cultural construction and is highly variable across cultures (Miller 1993). In the view of most cultural anthropologists, a high degree of human "plasticity" (or personality flexibility) allows for substantial variation in personality and behavior. More biologically inclined anthropologists, however, continue to insist that many sex-linked personality characteristics are inborn.

Proving the existence of innate (inborn) gender characteristics is made difficult by two factors. First, it is impossible to collect data on infants before they are subject to cultural treatment. Culture may begin to shape infants even in the womb, through exposure to sound and motion, but current scientific data on the cultural effects on the prenatal stage are slim. Once birth takes place, culture shapes infants in many ways, including how people handle and interact with them. There is thus no such thing as a "natural" infant.

Second, it is difficult, if not impossible, to study and interpret the behavior of infants to try to ascertain what is "natural" and what is "cultural" without introducing biases from the observers. Studies of infants have focused on assessing the potential innateness of three major Euro-American personality stereotypes (Frieze et al. 1978:73–78):

- That infant males are more aggressive than infant females

---

cultural competence among Western-trained health professionals, awareness of and respect for beliefs and practices that differ from those of Western medicine.

- That infant females are more social than infant males
- That infant males are more independent than infant females

What is the evidence? Studies conducted in the United States indicate that boy babies cry more than girl babies, and that some people accept this difference as evidence of higher levels of inborn aggression in males. An alternative interpretation is that baby boys, on average, tend to weigh more than girls at birth. They therefore are more likely to have a difficult delivery from which it takes time to recover. So they cry more, but not because of aggressiveness. In terms of sociability, baby girls smile more often than boys, and some researchers claim that this difference confirms innate personality characteristics. But culture, not nature, may be the explanation because American caretakers smile more at baby girls than they smile at baby boys. Thus, the more frequent smiling of girls is likely to be a learned behavior. In terms of independence or dependence, studies thus far reveal no clear differences in how upset baby boys and girls are when separated from their caretakers. Taken as a whole, studies seeking to document innate differences between girls and boys are not convincing.

Cultural anthropologists who take a constructionist view make two further points. They note that, if gender differences are innate, it is odd that cultures go to so much trouble to enculturate offspring into a particular gender. Also, if gender differences are innate, then they should be the same throughout history and across all cultures, which they clearly are not. The following material explores cross-cultural cases of how culture constructs gender, beginning with childhood.

Socialization during Childhood

The *Six Cultures Study*, mentioned in Chapter 3, was designed to provide cross-cultural data on how children's activities and tasks shape their personalities (Whiting and Whiting 1975). Researchers used similar methods at six sites (Figure 4.4), observing children between the ages of 3 and 11 years. They recorded the children's behavior, such as caring for and being supportive of other children; hitting other children; and performing tasks such as child care, cooking, and errands. The data collected were analyzed in terms of two major personality types: nurturant-responsible and dependent-dominant. A nurturant-responsible personality is characterized by caring and sharing acts toward other children. The dependent-dominant personality involves fewer acts of caregiving, more acts that assert dominance over other children, and more need for care by adults.

Of the six cultures, the Gusii children of southwestern Kenya had the highest frequency of a nurturant-responsible personality type. They were responsible for the widest range of tasks and at earlier ages than children in any other culture in the study, often performing tasks that an Orchard Town, United States, mother does. Although some children in all six cultures took care of other children, Gusii children (both boys and girls) spent the most time

(LEFT) A Yanomami boy acquiring skills necessary for hunting and warfare through play. (RIGHT) An American boy playing a video game.

■ *Consider examples of children's games that may provide learning and skills related to adult roles in your culture.*

Horticultural Groups
Gusii people, Kenya
Maya people, Oaxaca, Mexico
Tarong people, Philippines
Intensive Agriculture or Industrial/Digital Groups
Taira village, Okinawa, Japan
Rajputs, village in North India
Middle-class Euro-Americans, Orchard Town, New England, United States
Source: Whiting and Whiting (1975).

Figure 4.4 Groups in the Six Cultures Study

doing so. They began taking on this responsibility at a very young age, between five and eight years old.

In contrast, Orchard Town children had the highest frequency of the dependent-dominant personality type. The differences correlate with the mode of livelihood. In the research sites in Kenya, Mexico, and the Philippines, all reliant on horticulture, children were more nurturant-responsible. Livelihood in the sites in Japan, India, and the United States was based on either intensive agriculture or industry.

How do these different modes of livelihood influence child personality? The key underlying factor is women's work roles. In the horticultural societies, women are an important part of the labor force and spend much time working outside the home. Their children take on many family-supportive tasks and thereby develop personalities that are nurturant-responsible. When women are mainly occupied in the home, as in the second group of cultures, children have fewer tasks and less responsibility. They develop personalities that are more dependent-dominant.

This study has many implications for Western child-development experts. For one thing, what happens when the dependent-dominant personality develops to an extreme level—into a narcissistic personality? A narcissist is someone who constantly seeks self-attention and self-affirmation, with no concern for other people's needs. Consumerism supports the development of narcissism via its emphasis on identity formation through ownership of self-defining goods (clothing, electronics, cars) and access to self-defining services (vacations, therapists, fitness salons). The *Six Cultures Study* suggests that involving children more in household responsibilities might result in less self-focused personality formation and more nurturant-responsible people.

Adolescence and Identity

The transition from "childhood" to "adulthood" involves certain biological events, as well as cultural events, that shape the transition to adulthood. Cultural anthropologists provide rich data demonstrating how this transition is at least as much a cultural transformation as a biological one.

IS ADOLESCENCE A UNIVERSAL LIFE-CYCLE STAGE? Puberty is a time in the human life cycle that occurs universally and involves a set of biological markers. In males, the voice deepens and facial and body hair appear; in females, menarche and breast development occur; in both males and females, pubic and underarm hair appear and sexual maturation is achieved. **Adolescence**, in contrast, is a culturally defined period of maturation from around the time of puberty until the attainment of adulthood, usually marked by becoming a parent, getting married, or becoming economically self-sufficient.

Some scholars say that all cultures define a period of adolescence. A comparative study using data on 186 societies argues for the universal existence of a culturally defined phase of adolescence (Schlegel 1995). The researchers point to supportive evidence in the fact that people in cultures as diverse as the Navajo and the Trobriand Islanders have special terms comparable to the American term "adolescent" to refer to a person between puberty and marriage. Following a biological determinist, Darwinian model, they interpret the supposedly universal phases of adolescence as being adaptive in an evolutionary sense. The logic is that adolescence provides training for parenthood and thus contributes to enhanced reproductive success and survival of parents' genes.

Other anthropologists view adolescence as culturally constructed, highly variable, and thus impossible to explain on only biological grounds. These researchers point out that people in many cultures recognize no period of adolescence. In some others, identification of an adolescent phase is recent. Moroccan anthropologist Fatima Mernissi (1987), for example, states that adolescence became a recognized life-cycle phase for females in Morocco only in the late twentieth century:

> The idea of an adolescent unmarried woman is a completely new idea in the Muslim world, where previously you had only a female child and a menstruating woman who had to be married off immediately so as to prevent dishonorable engagement in premarital sex. (1987:xxiv)

Another line of evidence supporting a cultural constructionist view is that, in different cultures, the length and elaboration of adolescence varies for males and females. In many horticultural and pastoralist societies in which men are valued as warriors, a long period between

puberty a time in the human life cycle that occurs universally and involves a set of biological markers and sexual maturation.

adolescence a culturally defined period of maturation from the time of puberty until adulthood that is recognized in some, but not all, cultures.

Before their initiation and circumcision, Maasai male youth braid each other's hair. As a later part of the initiation, the initiate's mother will shave his head.

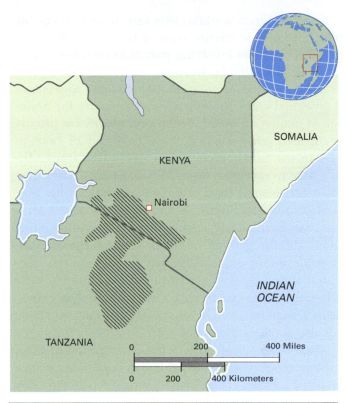

Map 4.4 Maasai Region of Kenya and Tanzania

An estimated 350,000 Maasai live in Kenya and 150,000 in Tanzania. The climate is semiarid.

boyhood and adulthood is devoted to training in warfare and developing solidarity among males of similar ages. This pattern occurs, for example, among the Maasai (sometimes spelled Masai). The Maasai are pastoralists, numbering over 500,000, who live in a large area crossing Kenya and Tanzania (Map 4.4). The extended adolescent period for males has nothing to do with training for parenthood. Maasai females, by contrast, move directly from being girls to being wives with no adolescent period in between. They learn adult roles when they are children.

In some cultures, especially in sub-Saharan Africa and the Amazon region of South America, girls go through lengthy adolescent phases during which they live separated from the wider group and gain special knowledge and skills (Brown 1978). After this period of seclusion, they reemerge as women, get married, and have children.

A cultural explanation exists for whether a young male or young female goes through a marked adolescent phase. Cultural materialism (Chapter 1) says that a long and marked period of adolescence is preparation for culturally valued adult roles such as worker, warrior, or parent. Confirmation of this hypothesis comes from the finding that an extended adolescence for females in nonindustrial societies occurs in cultures where adult females are important as food producers (Brown 1978). Whether or not this theory holds up in industrialized societies has yet to be examined. Some scholars might argue that an extended adolescent period among middle class youth in wealthy countries is a way of deferring their entry into a saturated labor market where jobs for them are scarce.

COMING OF AGE AND GENDER IDENTITY Margaret Mead made famous the phrase "coming of age" in her book *Coming of Age in Samoa* (1961 [1928]). The phrase can refer generally to the period of adolescence or specifically to a ceremony or set of ceremonies that marks the boundaries of adolescence. What are the psychological aspects of such special events for the children who go through them? Some ceremonies have a sacrificial element, with symbolic death and rebirth. Most coming-of-age ceremonies are gender specific, highlighting the importance of adult roles of men and women. These ceremonies often involve marking the body of the initiate in some way. Such marking may include scarification, tattooing, and genital surgery.

In many societies, adolescent males undergo genital surgery that involves the removal of part of the skin around the tip of the penis (circumcision); without this operation, the boy would not become a full-fledged male. Among many African pastoralist groups, such as the Maasai, adolescent males go through a circumcision ceremony that marks the end of adolescence and the beginning of manhood and full membership in the group. A young Maasai male, in a first-person account of his initiation into manhood, describes the "intolerable pain" he experienced following the circumcision, as well as his feeling of accomplishment two weeks later when his head was shaved and he became a warrior: "As long as I live, I will never forget the day my head was shaved and I emerged a man, a Maasai warrior. I felt a sense of control over my destiny so great that no words can accurately describe it" (Saitoti 1986:71).

Less common worldwide is **female genital cutting (FGC)**, or female circumcision, a term that refers to a range of practices involving partial or total removal of the clitoris and labia. In some contexts, FGC is practiced along with infibulation, the stitching together of the vaginal entry, leaving a small aperture for drainage of menstrual blood. These procedures are usually performed when a girl is between 7 and 15 years of age. In the Sahelian countries, extending from Africa's west to east coast (Map 12.5, page 254), many people practice some form of female genital cutting. FGC is also found in Egypt, in some groups of the Middle East, particularly among Bedu tribes, and among some Muslim groups in South and Southeast Asia. In terms of religion, FGC is often, but not always, associated with people who are Muslim. In Ethiopia, some Christian groups practice it. Genital cutting occurs in many groups in which female labor participation is high, but also in others where it is not.

Scholars cannot explain the distribution of FGC. Anthropologists who study this practice ask the people involved for their views. Many young girls say they look forward to the ceremony so that they will be free from childhood tasks and can take on the more respected role of an adult woman. In other cases, anthropologists have reported hearing statements of resistance (Fratkin 1998:60). Few issues force the questioning of cultural relativism more clearly than female genital cutting (see Think Like an Anthropologist).

Initiation rites often involve themes of death and rebirth as the initiate loses his or her former identity and emerges with a new one. During the early 1990s, Abigail Adams conducted research on initiation rituals at what was then a men's military school, the Virginia Military Institute (VMI) (2002). Freshmen students, called "Rats," are each assigned to an upperclassman, called a "Dyke." The freshman year involves continuous humiliation and other forms of abuse for the Rats. Dykes treat their Rats like infants, telling them how to eat, bathe, and talk and yelling at them in baby talk. The culminating initiation ritual for the Rats takes place during March. The town's fire truck sprays the outskirts of the campus to create a large area of mud. The Rats have to crawl through the mud while sophomores and juniors attack them, shout at them, push them down, sit on them, and fill their eyes, ears, faces, and clothes with mud. The Rats can barely see as they grope their way along, and many lose their pants. The ordeal continues over two banks of earth and a ditch, with continuous harassment from the sophomores and juniors. When the Rats finally reach the top of the second

bank, the Dykes rush to greet them, tenderly wash the mud off them, and wrap them in blankets. The moment when the mud is washed away is the transition of the Rat into a cadet.

Adams interprets this ritual as a birthing event, with the newborn emerging blinded by and covered with fluids, then cleaned and blanketed. One senior said that being a Dyke "is like having my own child" (2002:39). Many aspects of this ritual, however, are ambiguous, not least of which is the term "Dyke" for male "mothers" (or "fathers"?). The Breaking Out initiation ritual is no longer practiced at VMI. In the mid-1990s, VMI, as the recipient of public funds, was under pressure to admit women to be compliant with the law. After a drawn-out legal battle that ended up in the Supreme Court, VMI admitted its first women students in 1997. Breaking Out has been replaced with a long weekend series of events involving physical and field challenges.

SEXUAL IDENTITY AND GENDER PLURALISM Scholars have long debated whether gender identity and sexual preferences are biologically determined (ruled by genetic or hormonal factors) or culturally constructed and learned. Biological anthropologist Melvin Konner (1989) takes a middle position, saying that both factors play a part, but simultaneously warning that no one has a simple answer to the question of why an individual is gay.

The cultural constructionist position emphasizes socialization and childhood experiences as more powerful than biology in shaping sexual orientation. These anthropologists find support for their position in the cross-cultural record and its cases in which people change their sexual orientation once, or sometimes more than once, during their lifetimes. In the Gulf state of Oman, the *xanith* (hah-neeth) is one example (Wikan 1977). A xanith is a man who, for a time, becomes more like a woman, wears female

Breaking Out, a rite of passage at a military academy in Virginia when it was an all-men's school.

❙ *What rite of passage have you been through, and how would you analyze it anthropologically?*

---

female genital cutting (FGC) a range of practices involving partial or total removal of the clitoris and labia.

Think Like an Anthropologist

Cultural Relativism and Female Genital Cutting

Female genital cutting (FGC) is a necessary step toward full womanhood in cultures that practice it. People believe that an uncircumcised daughter is unmarriageable and that removing the labia makes a woman beautiful by removing "male" parts. The prevailing Western view, increasingly being shared by many people who have long practiced FGC, is that FGC is both an indication of women's low status and an unnecessary cause of women's suffering.

FGC is linked with several health risks, including those related to the surgery itself (shock, infection) and subsequent genitourinary complications (Gruenbaum 2001). Infibulation scars the vaginal canal and may lead to problems during childbirth, sometimes causing the death of the infant and mother. Having an infibulated bride's husband "open" her, using a stick or knife to loosen the aperture, is both painful and an opportunity for infection. After giving birth, a woman is usually reinfibulated, and the process begins again. Health experts say that repeated trauma to the woman's vaginal area increases the risk of contracting HIV/AIDS.

Besides the pain and health risks, outsiders argue that clitoridectomy severely reduces a woman's sexuality since it makes clitoral orgasm impossible. Others point out that FGC and infibulation may cause infertility, which lowers a woman's marital value. Thus, a practice done to ensure a woman's marriageability may reduce her value and happiness as a mother. So far, however, studies have not found a clear relationship between FGC or infibulation and infertility (Larsen and Yan 2000).

What are the views of insiders? Is there any evidence for female agency in these practices? Or is it all structure and should anthropologists support FGC liberation movements? Insights that transcend insider–outsider divisions come from cultural anthropologist Fuambai Ahmadu, who was born and raised in Washington, DC, and is descended from a prominent Kono lineage in Sierra Leone (2000). In 1991, Ahmadu traveled to Sierra Leone with her mother and other family members for what she refers to as her "circumcision." Upon her return, she wrote about her initiation experience and what it meant to her. Although the physical pain was excruciating (in spite of the use of anesthetics), "the positive aspects have been much more profound" (2000:306). Through the initiation, she became part of a powerful female world. Her analysis addresses the effects of genital cutting on health and sexuality. Ahmadu argues that Westerners exaggerate these issues by focusing on infibulation rather than on the less extreme forms. She adds, however, that if global pressures against the practice continue, she will go along with that movement and support "ritual without cutting" (2000:308).

Map 4.5 Sierra Leone

The Republic of Sierra Leone was an important center of the transatlantic slave trade. Its capital, Freetown, was established in 1792 as a home for African slaves who fought with the British during the American Revolution. Sierra Leone's coast is covered with mangrove swamps, while the interior is plateau, forests, and mountains. The population is six million. Sierra Leone suffered a terrible civil war from 1991 to 2002, causing thousands of deaths and the displacement of two million people. It has the lowest per capita income in the world. English is the official language, but most people speak local, tribal languages.

Food for Thought

- Why do you think FGC is a prominent issue in human rights debates in the West, whereas male circumcision and other forms of sometimes dangerous forms of adolescent initiation (such as fraternity and sorority hazing) are not?
- Where do you stand on FGC and why?
- What kinds of cultural remodeling of the female body are practiced in your culture?

clothing, and has sex with other men. Later, the xanith returns to a standard male role, marries a woman, and has children. Thus, given the same biological material, some people assume different sexual identities over their lives.

Some cultures allow for a third gender, which is neither purely "male" nor purely "female," according to a particular culture's definition of those terms. As with the xanith of Oman, these gender categories offer ways for "males" to cross gender lines and assume more "female" behaviors, personality characteristics, and dress. Among some American Indians, a "two-spirit person" is someone whose work roles and sexual orientation may or may not conform to their genital endowment, usually a male who adopts stereotypically female behaviors (Williams 1992). Someone may become a two-spirit person in a variety of ways. Sometimes parents, especially if they have several sons, choose one to become a two-spirit person, or it may be that a boy shows interest in typically female activities or who likes to wear female clothing. Such a child is a focus of pride for the family, never a source of disappointment or stigma. During decades of contact with Euro-American colonizers, including Christian missionaries, the outsiders viewed the two-spirit role with disapproval and ridicule (Roscoe 1991) and American Indian cultures began to suppress their two-spirit tradition. Starting in the 1980s, as American Indians' cultural pride began to grow, the open presence of the two-spirit has revived. Many contemporary American Indian cultures, compared with mainstream White culture, are more accepting of gender role fluidity.

In India, the counterpart of the two-spirit person is a **hijra** (hij-ruh). Hijras dress and act like women but are neither truly male nor truly female (Nanda 1990). Many hijras were born with male genitals or with genitals that were not clearly male or female. Hijras have the traditional right to visit the home of a newborn, inspect the newborn's genitals, and claim him or her for their group if the genitals are neither clearly male nor clearly female. Hijras born with male genitals may opt to go through an initiation ceremony that involves cutting off their penis and testicles. Hijras roam large cities of India, earning a living by begging from store to store and threatening to lift their skirts if not given money. Because women do not sing or dance in public, hijras play an important role as performers in public events, especially as dancers or musicians. Mainstream Indians do not admire or respect hijras, and no family would be delighted to hear that their son has decided to become a hijra.

In mainland and island Southeast Asia, the situation is even more flexible, with a wide range of gender options, or **gender pluralism**. Gender pluralism is the existence in a culture of multiple categories of femininity, masculinity, and blurred genders that are tolerated and legitimate (Peletz 2006:310). In Thailand, three gender categories have long existed: *phuuchai* (male), *phuuyung* (female), and *kathoey* (transvestite/transsexual/hermaphrodite) (Morris 1994). A kathoey is "originally" a male who crosses into the

The South Korean transgender musical group "Lady" includes four transsexuals.

body, personality, and dress defined as female. The sexual orientation of kathoeys is flexible, including either male or female partners. In contemporary Thailand, explicit discussion and recognition of homosexuality exists, usually couched in English terms, conveying a sense of its foreignness. The words for lesbian are *thom* (from the word "tomboy") and *thut* (an ironic usage from the U.S. movie *Tootsie*, about a heterosexual man playing the part of a woman).

Yet another variation in defining one's sexuality results from the combination of Islamic values, urban modernity, and the rejection of Western binary labels of heterosexual and homosexual among youth in Tehran, the capital of Iran (see Map 8.3, page 169) (Mahdavi 2012). Many young women in Tehran have their first sexual experience with another woman, given the gender segregation that exists and the likelihood that young women will become close with one another. Yet they do not self-define as gay and would even make occasional homophobic comments. Politically, however, many male and female youths in Tehran are subscribing to international human rights standards in protesting the execution of gay men in Iran.

Beyond sexuality and its many complications, another category exists that challenges all the existing terms:

---

hijra in India, a blurred gender role in which a person, usually biologically male, takes on female dress and behavior.

gender pluralism the existence within a culture of multiple categories of femininity, masculinity, and blurred genders that are tolerated and legitimate.

asexuality. An asexual person is someone who does not experience sexual attraction. Asexuals exist around the world and are beginning to come out and identify themselves through websites and in public arenas, such as gay rights parades, even though asexuals are not gay (Scherrer 2008).

All the above examples speak against **heteronormativity,** the belief that all people fit into two distinct genders, male and female, with corresponding distinct social roles and adhering to heterosexual relations.

No matter what one's theoretical or personal perspective is on sexuality, homosexuality, and asexuality, it is clear that homophobia (hatred of people whose sexual preferences are toward the same sex) is widespread worldwide, and homosexuals are discriminated against wherever heterosexuality is the standard. In the United States, homosexuals are disproportionately victims of hate crimes, housing discrimination, and problems in the workplace, including wage and benefits discrimination. They often suffer from being stigmatized by their parents, peers, and the wider society. The psychological damage to their self-esteem by social stigma and discrimination is related to the fact that homosexual youth in the United States have substantially higher suicide rates than heterosexual youth (Suicide Prevention Resource Center 2008). A public health study shows that lesbian Hispanic women in the United States have higher rates of several health problems compared to heterosexual Hispanic women, including asthma (Kim and Fredriksen-Goldsen 2012).

Adulthood

For most people, adulthood means entering into some form of marriage or long-term domestic relationship and having children. The following discussion considers the psychological aspects of parenthood and the "senior years."

BECOMING A PARENT In Euro-American culture, a woman becomes a mother when she gives birth. Matrescence is the cultural process of becoming a mother (Raphael 1975). Like adolescence, matrescence varies cross-culturally in terms of duration and meaning. In some cultures, a woman is transformed into a mother as soon as she thinks she is pregnant. In others, she becomes a mother and is granted full maternal status only when she delivers an infant of the "right" sex, as in much of northern India, where son preference is strong.

In many nonindustrial cultures, matrescence occurs in the context of supportive family members. Some cultures promote prenatal practices, abiding by particular food taboos, which can be regarded as part of matrescence. Such rules make the pregnant woman feel that she has a role in ensuring that the pregnancy turns out well. In the West, medical experts increasingly define the prenatal period as an important phase of matrescence, and they have issued many scientific and medical rules for potential parents, especially mothers (Browner and Press 1996). Pregnant women are urged to seek prenatal examinations, be under the regular supervision of a doctor who monitors the growth and development of the fetus, follow particular dietary and exercise guidelines, and undergo a range of tests such as ultrasound scanning. Some anthropologists think that such medical control of pregnancy leads to the greater likelihood of postpartum depression, as a result of the mother's lack of agency in the process of matrescence.

Patrescence, or the cultural process of becoming a father, is less marked cross-culturally than matrescence. One exception to this generalization is **couvade** (coo-VAHD), beliefs and customs applying to a father during his wife's pregnancy and delivery (Broude 1988). In some cases, the father takes to his bed before, during, or after the delivery, and he may experience pain and exhaustion. Couvade often involves rules for the expectant father: He may not hunt a certain animal, eat certain foods, or cut objects. Early theories of why couvade exists relied on Freudian interpretations that men were identifying with the female role in contexts where the father role was weak. Cross-cultural data indicate the opposite, because couvade occurs in societies where fathers have prominent roles in child care. In these contexts, couvade is a phase of patrescence: The father's proper behavior helps ensure a safe delivery and a healthy baby. Once the baby is born, who takes care of him or her? Most cultural anthropologists agree that child care is predominantly the responsibility of females worldwide—but not universally. They seek to provide a cultural construction explanation rather than a genetic or hormonal one. As evidence, they point to the cross-cultural variation in child-care roles. For example, throughout the South Pacific, child care is shared across families, and women breastfeed other women's babies. Paternal involvement varies cross-culturally as well. Among Aka foragers of the Central African Republic (Map 4.6), paternal child care is prominent (Hewlett 1991). Aka fathers are intimate, affectionate, and helpful, spending half their time each day holding or within close reach of their infants. Fathers are more likely to hug and kiss their infants than mothers are. The definition of good fatherhood among the Aka means being affectionate toward

---

asexuality lack of sexual attraction or interest in sexual activity.

heteronormativity the belief that all people fall into two distinct genders, male and female, with corresponding distinct social roles and adhering to heterosexual relations.

---

couvade customs applying to the behavior of fathers during and shortly after the birth of their children.

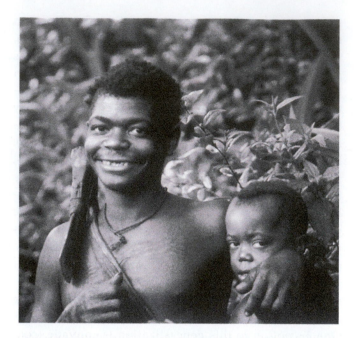

An Aka father and his son. Aka fathers are affectionate caretakers of infants and small children. Compared with mothers, they are more likely to kiss and hug children.

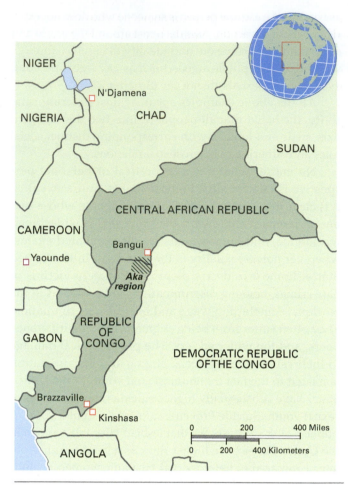

Map 4.6 Aka Region of the Central African Republic and the Democratic Republic of Congo

The 30,000 Aka are tropical forest foragers who know hundreds of plants and animals. They eat roots, leaves, nuts, fruits, mushrooms, honey, grubs, caterpillars, and meat from monkeys, rats, mongooses, and porcupines. They trade meat to farmers for manioc and other cultivated foods. They are socially egalitarian, and their religious beliefs are indigenous. Diaka, their main language, is tonal. The Aka territory is critically endangered by commercial loggers.

children and assisting the mother when her workload is heavy. Among the Aka, gender equality prevails and violence against women is unknown. This high level of paternal involvement is related to all these patterns and supports a constructionist view of parenting and gender roles rather than a biological determinist view.

MIDDLE AGE In many industrial/digital societies, a major turning point for men is the 40th birthday. According to a study of men turning 40 in the United States, the 40 syndrome involves feelings of restlessness, rebelliousness, and unhappiness that often lead to family break-ups (Brandes 1985). A possible reason behind the emphasis on the age 40 as a turning point for males is that it is the current midpoint of a typical life span for a middle-class American man. In cultures with shorter life spans, a so-called midlife crisis would necessarily occur at some point other than the age of 40 years.

Menopause, or the cessation of menstruation, is a significant aspect of middle age for women in many, but not all, cultures. A study examined differences in the perception and experience of menopause among Maya women of Mexico and rural Greek women (Beyene 1989). Among Maya women, menopause is not a time of stress or crisis. They consider menstruation an illness and look forward to its end. They do not experience negative physical or emotional symptoms. In contrast, the rural Greek women recognized menopause as a phase of hot flashes, especially at night, that may last about one year, and something that all women experience. The women did not think it was serious and did not regard it as worthy of medical attention. Postmenopausal women emphasized the relief and

freedom they felt. Postmenopausal women can go into cafes by themselves, something they would never do otherwise, and they can participate more fully in church ceremonies. In Japan, likewise, menopause is minimally stressful and women rarely consider it something that warrants medical attention (Lock 1993).

THE SENIOR YEARS The senior life-cycle stage may be a development of contemporary human society, because, like most other mammals, our early ancestors rarely lived beyond their reproductive years. In many cultures, elders are highly revered as having great wisdom based on their life experiences. In others, aged people become burdens to their families and to society.

Cross-cultural comparisons reveal that the status of elderly people is higher and their welfare more secure in contexts where they continue to live with their families (Lee and Kezis 1979). This pattern is, however, more likely to be found in nonindustrial societies than in industrialized ones, where the elderly live with younger kin less frequently. Instead, they are increasingly experiencing a shift to living in age-segregated residences such as "retirement homes," where they have to create new social roles and ties and find new ways of gaining self-esteem and personal satisfaction. Research conducted in a retirement home in a small town in central New York State shows that having a pet promotes a person's sense of well-being (Savishinsky 1991).

THE FINAL PASSAGE: DEATH AND DYING It may be that no one in any culture welcomes death, unless he or she is in very poor health and suffering greatly. The contemporary United States, with its dependence on medical technology, appears to play a leading role in resistance to death, often at high financial and psychological costs. In many other cultures, a greater degree of acceptance prevails.

A study of attitudes toward death and dying among Alaskan Inuits revealed a pervasive feeling that people are active participants in their death rather than passive victims (Trelease 1975). The person near death calls friends and neighbors together, is given a Christian sacrament, and then, within a few hours, dies. The author comments, "I do not suggest that everyone waited for the priest to come and then died right away. But the majority who did not die suddenly did some degree of planning, had some kind of formal service or celebration of prayers and hymns and farewells" (1975:35).

Terminally ill people, especially in industrial/digital economy societies with a high level of medical technology, are likely to be faced with choices about how and where they should die, at home or in a hospital, and whether they should prolong their lives with "unusual means" or opt for "physician-assisted suicide." Depending on the cultural context, the options are affected not only by the degree of medical technology and health-care services available but also by matters of kinship and gender role ideals (Long 2005). In urban Japan, terminally ill people have clear ideas of what is a "good death" and two major "scripts" for a "good death." A modern script of dying in a hospital is widely accepted because it reduces burdens on family members. But a value on dying surrounded by one's family members still prevails; this practice reassures the dying person that he or she will be remembered.

In many cultures, the inability to perform a proper burial and funeral for a deceased person is a cause of serious social suffering. Among refugees from Mozambique living in neighboring Malawi, the greatest cause of stress was being forced to leave behind deceased family members without providing a proper burial for them (Englund 1998). Such improperly treated deaths mean that the unhappy spirit of the deceased will haunt the living. This belief is related to the high rate of mental health problems among the refugees. A culturally informed recommendation for reducing their anxiety is to provide them with money to travel home and to perform a proper funeral for their deceased relatives. In that way, the living may carry on in greater peace.

Anthropologists know little about people's grief at the death of a loved one or a close community member. It might seem that sadness and grief, as well as a period of mourning, are only natural. But the outward expression of grief varies from extended, dramatic, public grieving that is overtly emotional to no visible sign of grief at all. The latter pattern is the norm in Bali, Indonesia (see Map 1.1, page 11), where people's faces remain impassive at funerals and no vocal lamenting occurs (Rosenblatt, Patricia, and Douglas 1976). Do impassive faces and silence mean that the Balinese feel no sadness? Different expressions of loss may be related to the healing process for the survivors by providing socially accepted rules of behavior—in other words, a script for loss. Either highly expressive public mourning or repressed grief may be equally effective, depending on the context.

4 Learning Objectives Revisited

4.1 Illustrate how modes of reproduction are related to modes of livelihood.

Cultural anthropologists define three modes of reproduction that are related to foraging, agriculture, and industrial/digital societies. They differ in terms of desired and actual fertility.

For thousands of years, foragers maintained a balanced level of population through direct and indirect means of fertility regulation. A classic study of the Ju/wasi shows how foragers' lifestyles, including a low-fat diet and women's physical activity, suppress fertility.

As sedentary lifestyles increased and food surpluses became more available and storable with agriculture, population growth increased. The highest rates of population growth in human prehistory and history are found among settled agriculturalists. Contemporary examples of high-fertility agriculturalists are the Amish and Mennonite people of North America.

4.2 Discuss how culture shapes fertility in different cultural contexts.

Cross-culturally, many techniques exist for increasing fertility, reducing it, and regulating its timing. From culture to culture, values differ about the right age for people to start having sexual relations and how often they do so. In terms of cultural practices that directly affect fertility, hundreds of different traditional methods exist, including the use of herbs and other natural substances for either preventing or promoting fertilization and for inducing abortion if an undesired pregnancy occurs.

In nonindustrialized societies, knowledge about fertility regulation, as well as its practice, is largely unspecialized and available to all women. In the industrial/digital mode of reproduction, scientific and medical specialization increases, and most knowledge and expertise are in the hands of professionals rather than of women. Class-stratified access to fertility-regulating methods now exists both globally and within nations.

Population growth is also shaped through the practice of infanticide, which, though of ancient origin, still exists today. It is sometimes performed in response to limited family resources, perceptions of inadequate "fitness" of the child, or preferences regarding the gender of offspring.

4.3 Identify how culture shapes personality over the life cycle.

Cultural anthropologists emphasize the effects of infant care practices on personality formation, including gender identity. Other cross-cultural studies show that variations in the gender division of labor and children's work roles in the family correspond to varying personality patterns. Adolescence, a culturally defined time beginning around puberty and running until adulthood, varies cross-culturally from being nonexistent to involving detailed training and elaborate ceremonies.

In contrast to the sharp distinction between "male" and "female" in Euro-American culture, many cultures have traditions of third or blurred gender identities. Gender pluralism is found in many cultures, especially in some American Indian and Asian cultures. Asexuality, when a person has no sexual attraction, is a newly recognized category of personal identity.

Cross-culturally, adult roles usually involve parenthood. In nonindustrial societies, learning about motherhood is embedded in other aspects of life and knowledge about birthing, and child care is shared among women. In industrial/digital societies, science and medicine play a large part in defining the maternal role.

The senior years are generally shorter in nonindustrialized societies than in industrial/digital societies, in which life spans tend to be longer. Elderly men and women in nonindustrial cultures are treated with respect, are assumed to know the most, and retain a strong sense of their place in the culture. Increasingly in industrial/digital societies, elderly people live apart from their families and spend many years in age-segregated institutions, such as retirement homes, or alone.

Key Concepts

adolescence, p. 80
asexuality, p. 85
cultural competence, p. 78
couvade, p. 85
demographic transition, p. 71
female genital cutting (FGC), p. 82

fertility, p. 68
gender pluralism, p. 84
heteronormativity, p. 85
hijra, p. 84
infanticide, p. 76
menarche, p. 73

menopause, p. 73
mode of reproduction, p. 68
mortality, p. 68
personality, p. 77
pronatalism, p. 68
puberty, p. 80

Thinking Outside the Box

1. In your microculture, is there a preference about the desired number of sons and daughters? Is there a preference for their birth order?
2. Try to recall your daily activities when you were 5 years old, 10 years old, and 15 years old. What tasks did you do? In terms of the *Six Cultures Study* categories, which type of personality do you have?

Chapter 5
Disease, Illness, and Healing

Learning Objectives

5.1 Describe the scope of ethnomedicine and how it has changed in recent times.

5.2 Explain the three major theoretical approaches in medical anthropology.

5.3 Recognize how globalization is affecting health, illness, and healing.

Anthro Connections

Traditional medicine in India includes such elements as herbs, pills, oil massages, dietary regimens, meditation, and exercise. Two major branches include Ayurvedic (eye-yur-vay-dik) healing, related to Hinduism, and Unani (oo-nah-nee) healing, related to Islam. They share many elements, and each requires a trained expert to diagnose problems and prescribe a treatment plan. In the past decade, Ayurvedic healing has gained global attention. Many five-star spas in India, especially in the southern state of Kerala, provide Ayurvedic treatments. Health tourism there is on the rise, drawing people from within India as well as from Europe and the Middle East. Aspects of Ayurvedic healing enjoy a large following around the world among Hindus and non-Hindus alike, and Ayurvedic techniques appear to be effective in addressing a variety of health problems. For example, a recent study in Norway indicates that women with fibromyalgia, which is considered a treatment-resistant condition, experienced significant, long-term reduction in symptoms, including pain and depression (Rasmussen et al. 2012).

Medical anthropology is one of the most rapidly growing areas in anthropology, probably because of its relevance to a major global challenge: people's health. This chapter first describes how people in different cultures think and behave regarding health, illness, and healing. The second section considers three theoretical approaches in medical anthropology. The chapter concludes by discussing how globalization is affecting health.

Ethnomedicine

5.1 Describe the scope of ethnomedicine and how it has changed in recent times.

Since the early days of anthropology, the topic of **ethnomedicine**, or the study of cross-cultural health systems, has been a focus of research. A health system encompasses many areas: perceptions and classifications of health problems, prevention measures, diagnosis, healing (magical, religious, scientific, healing substances), and healers.

In the 1960s, when the term ethnomedicine first came into use, it referred only to non-Western health systems and was synonymous with the now abandoned term primitive medicine. The early use of the term was ethnocentric. Contemporary **Western biomedicine (WBM)**, a

---

ethnomedicine the study of cross-cultural health systems.

Western biomedicine (WBM) a healing approach based on modern Western science that emphasizes technology for diagnosing and treating health problems related to the human body.

Melissa Gurgel is a Brazilian model and beauty pageant titleholder who was crowned Miss Brasil 2014 and represented her country at Miss Universe 2014. Her looks exemplify the global norm of female beauty and health. Many models and beauty queens, however, suffer from a range of health and behavioral problems.

healing approach based on modern Western science that emphasizes technology in diagnosing and treating health problems related to the human body, is an ethnomedical system, too. Medical anthropologists now study WBM as a cultural system intimately bound to Western values. Thus, the current meaning of the term ethnomedicine encompasses health systems everywhere.

Defining and Classifying Health Problems

Emic diversity in labeling health problems presents a challenge for medical anthropologists and health-care specialists. Western labels, which biomedically trained experts accept as true, accurate, and universal, often do not correspond to the labels in other cultures. One set of concepts that medical anthropologists use to sort out the many cross-cultural labels and perceptions is the disease–illness dichotomy. In this model, **disease** refers to a biological health problem that is objective and universal, such as a bacterial or viral infection or a broken arm. **Illness** refers to culturally specific perceptions and experiences of a health problem. Medical anthropologists study both disease and illness, and they show how each must be understood within their cultural contexts.

A first step in ethnomedical research is to learn how people label, categorize, and classify health problems. Depending on the culture, the following may be bases for labeling and classifying health problems: cause, vector (the means of transmission, such as mosquitoes), affected body part, symptoms, or combinations of these.

Often, knowledgeable elders are the keepers of ethnomedical knowledge, and they pass it down through oral traditions. Among groups of American Indians of the Washington–Oregon region, many popular stories refer to health (Thompson and Sloat 2004). The stories convey messages about how to prevent health problems, avoid bodily harm, relieve afflictions, and deal with old age. For example, here is the story of Boil, a story for young children:

> Boil was getting bigger.
>
> Her husband told her to bathe.
>
> She got into the water.
>
> She disappeared. (2004:5)

Other longer stories about Boil add complexities about the location of the boil and how to deal with particular boils, revealing indigenous patterns of classification.

A classic study among the Subanun (soo-BAH-nun) people focused on their categories of health problems (Frake 1961). In the 1950s, the Subanun were horticulturalists living in the highlands of Mindanao, in the Philippines (Map 5.1). Being egalitarian people, all Subanun, even young children, had substantial knowledge about health problems and how to deal with them. Of their 186 labels for health

problems, some are a single term, such as "itch," which can be expanded on by using two words, such as "splotchy itch." Skin diseases are common afflictions among the Subanun and have several degrees of specificity (Figure 5.1).

In WBM, panels of medical experts have to agree about how to label and classify health problems according to scientific criteria. Classifications and descriptions of thousands of afflictions are published in thick manuals, and online, that physicians consult before they give a diagnosis. In countries where medical care is privatized, the code selected may determine whether the patient's costs are covered by insurance or not.

Further, Western medical guidelines are biased toward diseases that WBM recognizes, and they ignore health problems that other cultures recognize. Anthropologists have discovered health problems around the world referred to as culture-specific syndromes or folk illnesses. A **culture-specific syndrome** is a health problem with a set of symptoms associated with a particular culture (Figure 5.2). Social factors such as stress, fear, or shock often are the underlying causes of culture-specific syndromes. Biophysical symptoms may be involved, and culture-specific syndromes can be fatal. **Somatization**, or embodiment, refers to the process through which the body absorbs social stress and manifests symptoms of suffering.

For example, **susto**, or "fright/shock disease," is found in Spain and Portugal and among Latino people wherever they live. People afflicted with susto attribute it to events such as losing a loved one or having a terrible accident (Rubel, O'Nell, and Collado-Ardon 1984). For example, in Oaxaca, southern Mexico (see Map 4.3, page 75), a woman said her susto was brought on by an accident in which pottery she had made was broken on its way to market, whereas a man said that his susto came on after he saw a dangerous snake. Susto symptoms include loss of appetite, lack of motivation, breathing problems, generalized pain, and nightmares. The researchers analyzed many cases of susto in three villages. They found that the people most likely to be afflicted were those who were socially marginal or experiencing a sense of role failure. For example, the woman with the broken pots had also suffered two spontaneous abortions and was worried that she would never have children. In Oaxaca, people with susto have higher mortality rates than

---

disease in the disease–illness dichotomy, a biological health problem that is objective and universal.

illness in the disease–illness dichotomy, culturally shaped perceptions and experiences of a health problem.

culture-specific syndrome a collection of signs and symptoms that is restricted to a particular culture or a limited number of cultures.

somatization the process through which the body absorbs social stress and manifests symptoms of suffering.

susto fright/shock disease, a culture-specific illness found in Spain and Portugal and among Latino people wherever they live; symptoms include back pain, fatigue, weakness, and lack of appetite.

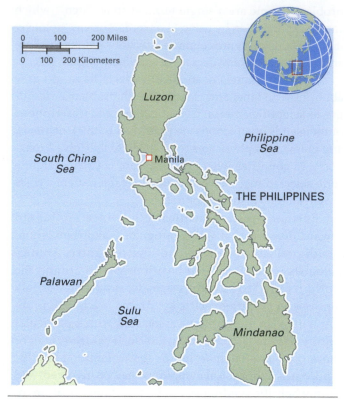

Map 5.1 The Philippines

The Republic of the Philippines comprises an archipelago of over 7,000 islands, of which around 700 are populated. The population is 104 million, with two-thirds living on Luzon. The economy is based on agriculture, light industry, and a growing business-processing outsourcing (BPO) industry. Over eight million Filipinos work overseas and remit more than $12 billion per year, a large part of the country's economy. Although Filipino and English are the official languages, more than 170 languages are spoken. Literacy rates are high for both males and females. Many different ethnic groups live in the country, with Tagalog people constituting the largest proportion of 30 percent. The Philippines has the world's third largest Christian population, among which Roman Catholicism is predominant.

- Rash
- Eruption
- Inflammation
    — Eruption
    — Inflamed/Quasi-Bite
    — Ulcerated
- Sore
    — Distal Ulcer
        Shallow
        Deep
    — Proximal Ulcer
        Shallow
        Deep
    — Simple Sore
    — Spreading Sore
- Ringworm
    — Exposed
    — Hidden
    — Spreading Itch
- Wound

Source: Adapted from Frake 1961:118, Figure 1.

Figure 5.1 Subanun Categories of Skin-Related Health Problems

other people. Thus, social marginality, or a deep sense of social failure, can place a person at a higher risk of dying. It is important to look at the deeper causes of susto.

Medical anthropologists first studied culture-specific syndromes in non-Western cultures. This focus created a bias in thinking that they exist only in "other" cultures. Now, anthropologists recognize that Western cultures also have culture-specific syndromes. Anorexia nervosa and a related condition, bulimia, are culture-specific syndromes found mainly among White middle-class adolescent girls of the United States, although some cases have been documented among African American girls in the United States and among young males (Fabrega and Miller 1995). Since the 1990s, and perhaps as a result of Western globalization, cases have been documented in Hong Kong and in cities in Japan and India. Anorexia nervosa's cluster of symptoms includes self-perception of fatness, aversion to food, hyperactivity, and, as the condition progresses, continued wasting of the body and often death.

No one has found a clear biological cause for anorexia nervosa, although some researchers claim that it has a genetic basis. Cultural anthropologists say that much evidence suggests a strong role for cultural construction. One logical result of the role of culture is that medical and psychiatric treatments are notably unsuccessful in curing anorexia nervosa (Gremillion 1992). Extreme food deprivation can become addictive and entrapping, and the affliction becomes intertwined with the body's biological functions. Extended fasting makes the body unable to deal with ingested food. Thus, medical treatment may involve intravenous feeding to override the biological block.

Pinpointing the cultural causes of anorexia nervosa, however, is also difficult. Some experts cite societal pressures on girls that lead to excessive concern with looks, especially body weight. Others feel that anorexia is related to girls' unconscious resistance to controlling parents. For such girls, food intake may be one thing over which they have power.

Ethno-Etiologies

People in all cultures, everywhere, attempt to make sense of health problems and try to understand their cause or etiology. The term **ethno-etiology** refers to a cross-culturally specific causal explanation for health problems and suffering.

Among the urban poor of northeastern Brazil, people consider several reasons when they are sick (Ngokwey 1988). In Feira de Santana, the second largest city in

ethno-etiology a culturally specific causal explanation for health problems and suffering.

Name of Syndrome	Distribution	Attributed Causes	Description and Symptoms
Anorexia nervosa	Middle- and upper-class Euro-American girls; globalizing	Unknown	Body wasting due to food avoidance; feeling of being too fat; in extreme cases, death
Hikikomori	Japan, males from adolescence through adulthood	Social pressure to succeed in school and pursue a position as a salaryman	Acute social withdrawal; refusal to attend school, or leave their room for months, sometimes years
Koro	China and Southeast Asia, men	Unknown	Belief that the penis has retracted into the body
Peito aberto (open chest)	Northeastern Brazil, especially women, perhaps elsewhere among Latino populations	Excessive worry about others	Enlarges the heart and "bursts" through it causing "openings in the heart"
Retired Husband Syndrome (RHS)	Japan, older women whose husbands are retired	Stress	Ulcers, slurred speech, rashes around the eyes, throat polyps
Sufriendo del agua (suffering from water)	Valley of Mexico, low-income people, especially women	Lack of access to secure and clean water	Anxiety
Susto	Spain, Portugal, Central and South America, Latino immigrants in the U.S. and Canada	Shock or fright	Lethargy, poor appetite, problems sleeping, anxiety

Sources: Chowdhury 1996; Ennis-McMillan 2001; Faiola 2005; Gremillion 1992; Kawanishi 2004; Rehbun 1994; Rubel, O'Nell, and Collado-Ardón 1984.

Figure 5.2 **Selected Culture-Specific Syndromes**

the state of Bahia in the northeast (see Map 3.3, page 49), ethno-etiologies include natural, socioeconomic, psychological, or supernatural factors. Natural causes include exposure to the environment. For example, people say that humidity and rain cause rheumatism, excessive heat causes dehydration, and some types of winds cause migraines. Other natural explanations for illness take into account the effects of aging, heredity, personality, and gender. Contagion is another natural explanation, as are the effects of certain foods and eating habits. In the psychosocial domain, emotions such as anger and hostility cause certain health problems. In the supernatural domain, spirits and magic can cause health problems. The African–Brazilian religions of the Bahia region encompass many spirits who can inflict illness. They include spirits of the unhappy dead and devil-like spirits. Some spirits cause specific illnesses; others bring general misfortune. In addition, envious people with the evil eye cast spells on people and cause much illness. People also recognize the lack of economic resources, proper sanitation, and health services as structural causes of health problems. In the words of one person, "There are many illnesses because there are many poor" (1988:796).

The people of Feira de Santana also recognize several levels of causality. In the case of stomachache, they might blame a quarrel (underlying cause), which prompted the aggrieved party to seek the intervention of a sorcerer (intermediate cause), who cast a spell (immediate cause), which led to the resulting illness. The multilayered causal understanding opens the way for many possible avenues of treatment.

The multiple understandings of etiology in Bahia contrast with the scientific understandings of causality in WBM. The most striking difference is the tendency for biomedical etiologies to exclude structural issues and social inequality as causing illness. Medical anthropologists use the term **structural suffering**, or social suffering, to refer to health problems caused by powerful forces such as poverty, war, famine, and forced migration. Such structural factors affect health in many ways, with effects ranging from anxiety and depression to death.

An example of a culture-specific syndrome that clearly implicates structural factors as causal is *sufriendo del agua*, or "suffering from water" (Ennis-McMillan 2001). Research in a low-income community in the Valley of Mexico, located in the central part of the country (see Map 4.3, page 75), reveals that sufriendo del agua is a common health problem, especially among women. The immediate cause is the lack of water for drinking, cooking, and washing.

structural suffering human health problems caused by such economic and political factors as war, famine, terrorism, forced migration, and poverty.

Women, who are responsible for cooking and doing the washing, cannot count on water coming from their taps on a regular basis. This insecurity makes the women feel constantly anxious and in a state of nervous tension. The lack of access to water also means that the people are at higher risk for cholera, skin and eye infections, and other biophysical problems. A deeper structural cause of sufriendo del agua is unequal development. The construction of piped water systems in the Valley of Mexico bypassed low-income communities in favor of servicing wealthier urban neighborhoods and supplying water for irrigation projects and the industrial sector. In Mexico, as a whole, nearly one-third of the population has inadequate access to clean drinking water and to a dependable supply of water for bathing, laundry, and cooking.

Healing Ways

The following material describes two healing modalities or approaches to healing that are likely unfamiliar to most readers. It then discusses cross-cultural examples of healers and healing substances.

COMMUNITY HEALING A general distinction can be drawn between private healing and **community healing**. The former addresses bodily ailments in social isolation, whereas the latter encompasses the social context as crucial to healing. Compared with WBM, many non-Western systems use community healing. An example of community healing comes from the Ju/wasi foragers of the Kalahari Desert in southern Africa (review Culturama, Chapter 1, page 18). Ju/wasi healing emphasizes the mobilization of community "energy" as a key element in the cure:

> The central event in this tradition is the all-night healing dance. Four times a month on the average, night signals the start of a healing dance. The women sit around the fire, singing and rhythmically clapping. The men, sometimes joined by the women, dance around the singers. As the dance intensifies, *num* or spiritual energy is activated by the healers, both men and women, but mostly among the dancing men. As num is activated in them, they begin to *kia* or experience an enhancement of their consciousness. While experiencing kia, they heal all those at the dance. (Katz 1982:34)

The dance is a community event in which the entire camp participates. The people's belief in the healing power of num brings meaning and efficacy to the dance through kia.

Does community healing "work"? In both ethnic and Western terms, the answer is yes. It "works" on several levels. People's solidarity and group sessions may support

---

community healing healing that emphasizes the social context as a key component and that is carried out within the public domain.

humoral healing healing that emphasizes balance among natural elements within the body.

A Ju/wasi healer in a trance, in the Kalahari desert, southern Africa. Most Ju/wasi healers are men, but some are women.

In your microculture, what are the patterns of gender, ethnicity, and class among various kinds of healers?

mental and physical health, acting as a health protection system. When people fall ill, the drama and energy of the all-night dances may act to strengthen the afflicted in ways that Western science would have difficulty measuring. In a small, close-knit group, the dances support members who may be ill or grieving.

An important aspect of the Ju/wasi healing system is its openness. Everyone has access to it. The role of healer is also open. There is no special class of healers with special privileges. More than half of all adult men and about 10 percent of adult women are healers.

HUMORAL HEALING **Humoral healing** is based on a philosophy of balance among certain elements within the body and within the person's environment (McElroy and Townsend 2008). In this system, food and drugs have different effects on the body and are classified as either "heating" or "cooling"—the quotation marks indicate that these properties are not the same as thermal measurements. Diseases are the result of bodily imbalances—too much heat or coolness—that must be counteracted through dietary and behavioral changes or medicines that will restore balance.

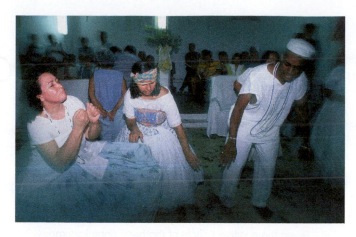

Umbanda is a popular religion in Brazil and, increasingly, worldwide. Its ceremonies are devoted to healing through spiritual means. In this session, tourists at the back of the room watch as Umbanda followers perform a dance related to a particular deity.

▌ *What is your opinion on the role of spirituality in health and healing, and on what do you base your view?*

Humoral healing systems have been practiced for thousands of years in the Middle East, the Mediterranean, and much of Asia. In the New World, indigenous humoral systems exist and sometimes blend with those that Spanish colonialists brought with them. Humoralism has shown substantial resilience in the face of WBM as a source of healing for many people. Local people also reframe WBM in classifying biomedical treatments as either heating or cooling.

In Malaysia (see Map 1.1, page 11), several humoral traditions coexist, reflecting the region's history of contact with outside cultures. Malaysia has been influenced by trade and contact between its indigenous culture and that of India, China, and the Arab-Islamic world for around 2,000 years. Indian, Chinese, and Arabic health systems all define health as the balance of opposing elements within the body, although each has its own variations (Laderman 1988). Indigenous belief systems may have been compatible with these imported models because they also were based on concepts of heat and coolness.

Insights into these indigenous systems before outsiders arrived come from accounts about the Orang Asli, indigenous peoples of the interior of the Malaysian peninsula who are relatively unaffected by contact. A conceptual system of hot–cold opposition dominates Orang Asli cosmological, medical, and social theories. The properties and meanings of heat and coolness differ from their counterparts in Islamic, Indian, and Chinese humoralism in several ways. In the Islamic, Indian, and Chinese systems, for example, death is the result of too much coolness. Among the Orang Asli, excessive heat is the primary cause of mortality. In their view, heat emanates from the sun and is associated with excrement, blood, misfortune, disease, and death. Humanity's hot blood makes people mortal, and their consumption of meat speeds the process. Heat

causes menstruation, violent emotions, aggression, and drunkenness.

Coolness, in contrast, is vital for health among the Orang Asli. Staying in the forest protects against the harmful effects of the sun. Following this logic, the treatment of illness aims to reduce or remove heat. If someone were to fall ill in a clearing, the entire group would relocate to the coolness of the forest. The forest is also a source of cooling leaves and herbs. Healers are cool and retain their coolness by bathing in cold water and sleeping far from the fire. Extreme cold, however, can be harmful. Dangerous levels of coolness are associated with the time right after birth, because the mother is believed to have lost substantial heat. The new mother should not drink cold water or bathe in cold water. She increases her body heat by tying sashes around her waist that contain warmed leaves or ashes, and she lies near a fire.

HEALERS In an informal sense, everyone is a "healer," because self-diagnosis and treatment are likely the first steps when anyone feels ill. Yet, in all cultures, some people become recognized as having special abilities to diagnose and treat health problems. Cross-cultural evidence indicates some common features of healers (Figure 5.3).

Selection: Certain individuals may show more ability for entry into healing roles. In Western medical schools, selection for entry rests on apparently objective standards, such as pre-entry exams and college grades. Among the indigenous Ainu of northern Japan, healers were men who had a special ability to go into a sort of seizure called *imu* (Ohnuki-Tierney 1980).

Training: The period of training may involve years of observation and practice and may be arduous and even dangerous. In some non-Western traditions, a shaman must make dangerous journeys, through trance or use of drugs, to the spirit world. In Western biomedicine, medical school involves immense amounts of memorization, separation from family and normal social life, and sleep deprivation.

Certification: Healers earn some form of ritual or legal certification, such as a shaman going through a formal initiation ritual that attests to his or her competence.

Professional image: The healer role is demarcated from that of ordinary people through behavior, dress, and other markers, such as the white coat in the West and the Siberian shaman's tambourine for calling the spirits.

Expectation of payment: Compensation in some form, whether in kind or in cash, is expected for formal healers. Payment level may vary, depending on the status of the healer and other factors. In rural northern India, strong preference for sons is reflected in payments to the midwife that are twice as high for the birth of a son as for a daughter. In the United States, medical professionals in different specializations receive markedly different salaries.

Figure 5.3 Criteria for Becoming a Healer

Eye on the Environment

Local Botanical Knowledge and Child Health in the Bolivian Amazon

The Tsimané (see-MAH-nay) are a foraging–horticultural society of Bolivia's northeastern Amazon region (Map 5.2), numbering about 8,000 (McDade et al. 2007). Although most Tsimané make a living from horticulture, complemented by some gathering and hunting, new opportunities for wage work are becoming increasingly available in logging camps or on cattle ranches, or by selling products from the rainforest. At the time of the study described here, in 2002–2003, the Tsimané were not much affected by outside forces and still relied heavily on local resources for their livelihood.

The study focused on mothers' botanical knowledge and the health of their children. The word botany refers to knowledge about plants. Household visits and interviews with mothers provided data on mothers' knowledge of plants. Children's health was assessed with three measures: concentrations of C-reactive protein (or CRP, a measure of both immunity and "infectious burden"), skinfold thickness (which measures body fat), and stature, or height (which indicates overall progress in growth and development).

The study showed a strong relationship between mothers' knowledge of plants and the health of their children. Botanical knowledge promotes healthier children through nutritional inputs; that is, more knowledgeable mothers tend to provide healthier plant foods to their children. It also improves children's health by providing herbal ways of treating their illnesses. The overall conclusion is that a mother's knowledge of local plant resources contributes directly to the benefit of her children. In contrast, levels of formal schooling of mothers and household wealth have little, if anything, to do with child health.

Given the positive effects of mothers' botanical knowledge and use of local plants to promote their children's health, it is critical that access to plant resources by indigenous people be protected and sustained and that local botanical knowledge be respected and preserved.

Food for Thought

When you eat food that contains herbs or spices such as oregano, parsley, or cinnamon, or when you consume plant-based drinks such as tea or coffee, do you think about their positive or negative health effects on you?

Map 5.2 The Republic of Bolivia

Situated in the Andes Mountains, Bolivia is the lowest-income country in South America, although it is rich in natural resources, including the second largest oil field in South America after Venezuela. The population of 10 million includes a majority of indigenous people of nearly 40 different groups. The largest are the Aymara-speaking (two million) and Quechua-speaking groups (1.5 million). Thirty percent of the population is mestizo, of mixed descent, and 15 percent is of European descent. Two-thirds of the people are low-income farmers. The official religion is Roman Catholicism, but Protestantism is growing. Religious syncretism is prominent. Most people speak Spanish as their first language, although Aymara and Quechua are also common. Bolivia's popular fiesta known as *El carnival de Oruro* is on UNESCO's list of Intangible Cultural Heritage. In 2014, the government started building a mass-transit aerial cable system linking the capital city, La Paz, with its neighbor city, El Alto, the highest city in the world and the city in Latin America with the largest Indian population.

In various cultures, specialists include midwives, bonesetters (those who reset broken bones), **shamans** or **shamankas** (male or female healers, respectively, who mediate between humans and the spirit world), herbalists, general practitioners, psychiatrists, nurses acupuncturists, chiropractors, dentists, and hospice care providers. Some healing roles may have higher status and more power and may receive higher pay than others.

shaman or shamanka a male and female healer, respectively, whose healing methods rely on communication with the spirit world.

Midwifery is an example of a healing role that is endangered in many parts of the world because birth has become increasingly medicalized and brought into the institutional realm of the hospital rather than the home. The term midwife refers to a person, usually female, who has formal or informal training in assisting a woman to give birth. In Costa Rica, a government campaign to promote hospital births with a biomedical doctor in attendance achieved a rate of 98 percent of all births taking place in hospitals by the end of the twentieth century (Jenkins 2003). This achievement means that midwives, especially in rural areas, can no longer support themselves, and they are abandoning their profession. The promotion of hospital births has destroyed the positive elements of community-based midwifery and its provision of social support and techniques such as massage for the mother-to-be.

HEALING SUBSTANCES Around the world, thousands of natural or manufactured substances are used as medicines for preventing or curing health problems. Anthropologists have spent more time studying the use of medicines in non-Western cultures than in the West, although a more fully cross-cultural approach is emerging that also examines the use and meaning of Western pharmaceuticals (Petryna, Lakoff, and Kleinman 2007).

Phytotherapy is healing through the use of plants. Cross-culturally, people use many different plants for a wide range of health problems, including gastrointestinal disorders, skin problems, wounds and sores, pain relief, infertility, fatigue, altitude sickness, and more (see Eye on the Environment). Increasing awareness of the range of potentially useful plants worldwide provides a strong incentive for protecting the world's cultural diversity, because it is people, especially indigenous people, who know about botanical resources (Posey 1990).

Leaves of the coca plant have for centuries been a key part of the health system of the Andean region of South America (Allen 2002). Coca is important in rituals, in masking hunger pains, and in combating the cold. In terms of health, Andean people use coca to treat gastrointestinal problems, sprains, swellings, and colds. The leaf may be chewed or combined with herbs or roots and water to make a *maté* (MAH-tay), a medicinal beverage. Trained herbalists have specialized knowledge about preparing matés. One maté, for example, is for treating asthma. The patient drinks the beverage, made of a ground root and coca leaves, three to four times a day until cured.

Minerals are also widely used for prevention and healing. For example, many people worldwide believe that bathing in water that contains high levels of sulfur or other minerals promotes health and cures ailments such as arthritis and rheumatism. Thousands of people every year go to the Dead Sea, which lies beneath sea level between Israel and Jordan, for treating skin diseases. Bathing in the sulfur springs near the Dead Sea and plastering oneself with mud from the shore provide relief from skin ailments such as psoriasis. Throughout East Asia, including Japan, bathing in mineral waters is popular as a health-promotion practice.

In a more unusual practice, thousands of people worldwide visit "radon spas" every year, seeking the therapeutic effects of low doses of radon gas to alleviate the symptoms of arthritis and other afflictions. In the United States, many radon spas are located in mines in the mountains of Montana (Erickson 2007). At one such spa, the Free Enterprise Mine, the recommended treatment is to go into the mine for one-hour sessions, two or three times daily, for up to a total of about 30 sessions. The mine contains benches and chairs, and clients read, play cards, chat, or take a nap. Some "regulars" come back every year and make plans to meet up with friends from previous visits.

Pharmaceutical medicines are increasingly popular worldwide. Although these medicines have many benefits, negative effects include overprescription and frequent use without a prescription. The sale of patent medicines is often unregulated, and self-treating individuals can buy them in a local pharmacy. The popularity and overuse of capsules and injections has led to a growing health crisis related to the emergence of drug-resistant disease strains.

These boys are selling hyssop, a medicinal herb, in Syria. In Unani (Islamic) traditional medicine, hyssop is used to alleviate health problems such as asthma.

▌ *Do research to learn more about hyssop and its medicinal uses.*

phytotherapy healing through the use of plants.

Guests are undergoing radon treatment at the Kyongsong Sand Spa in Haonpho-ri, North Korea. The spa, and its hot spring, has a 500-year history as a healing center. The treatment shown here is a "sand bath" used for chronic diseases such as arthritis, postoperative problems, and some female problems.

Three Theoretical Approaches

5.2 Explain the three major theoretical approaches in medical anthropology.

The first major theoretical approach to understanding health systems emphasizes the importance of the environment in shaping health problems and how they spread. The second highlights symbols and the meaning in people's expression of suffering and healing practices. The third points to the need to look at structural factors as the underlying causes of health problems and examines WBM as a cultural institution.

The Ecological/Epidemiological Approach

The **ecological/epidemiological approach** examines how aspects of the natural environment interact with culture to cause health problems and to influence their spread throughout the population. According to this approach, research should focus on gathering information about the environmental context and social patterns that affect health, such as food distribution within the family, sexual practices, hygiene, and degree of contact with outsiders. Research methods and data tend to be quantitative and etic, although a growing tendency is to include qualitative and emic data in order to provide a context for understanding the quantitative data (review Chapter 2).

The ecological/epidemiological approach seeks to yield findings relevant to public health programs. It can provide information about groups that are at risk for

specific problems. For example, although hookworm is common throughout rural China, epidemiological researchers learned that rice cultivators have the highest rates. The reason is that hookworm spreads through night soil (human excrement used as a fertilizer) that is applied to the rice fields in which the cultivators work.

Urbanization is another significant environmental factor that has important effects, both positive and negative, on health. On the positive side, urban areas offer access to modern health-care services. On the negative side, as archaeologists have documented, settled populations living in dense clusters are more likely than mobile populations to experience a range of health problems, including infectious diseases and malnutrition (Cohen 1989). Such problems are also apparent among many recently settled pastoralist groups in East and West Africa. One study compared the health status of two groups of Turkana men in northwest Kenya (see Map 4.4, page 81): those who were mobile pastoralists and those who lived in a town (Barkey, Campbell, and Leslie 2001). The two groups differ strikingly in diet, physical activities, and health. Pastoralist Turkana consume mainly animal foods (milk, meat, and blood), spend much time in rigorous physical activity, and live in large family groups. Settled Turkana men eat mainly maize and beans. Their sedentary (settled) life means less physical activity and exercise. In terms of health, the settled men had more eye infections, chest infections, backache, and cough/colds. Pastoralist Turkana men were not, however, free of health problems. One-fourth of the pastoralist men had eye infections, but among the settled men, half had eye infections. In terms of nutrition, the settled Turkana were shorter and had greater body mass than the taller and slimmer pastoralists.

Anthropologists have applied the ecological/epidemiological approach to the study of the negative effects of colonialism on the health and survival of indigenous peoples. The effects of colonial contact are overall negative,

Agricultural work done in standing water increases the risk of hookworm infection. Hookworm is endemic throughout China.

▌ *Is hookworm a threat where you live? What is the major infectious disease in your home region?*

---

ecological/epidemiological approach an approach within medical anthropology that considers how aspects of the natural environment and social environment interact to cause illness.

ranging from the quick and outright extermination of indigenous peoples, to resilient adjustment among other groups. In the Western Hemisphere, European colonialism brought a dramatic decline in the indigenous populations, although disagreement exists about the numbers involved (Joralemon 1982). Research indicates that the precontact New World was largely free of the major European infectious diseases, such as smallpox, measles, and typhus, and perhaps also of syphilis, leprosy, and malaria. Therefore, the exposure of indigenous peoples to these infectious diseases likely had a massive impact, given those people's complete lack of resistance. One analyst compared colonial contact to a "biological war":

> Smallpox was the captain of the men of death in that war, typhus fever the first lieutenant, and measles the second lieutenant. More terrible than the conquistadores on horseback, more deadly than sword and gunpowder, they made the conquest by the whites a walkover as compared to what it would have been without their aid. (Ashburn 1947:98, quoted in Joralemon 1982:112)

This quotation emphasizes the importance of the three major diseases in New World colonial history: smallpox, typhus fever, and measles. A later arrival, cholera, had devastating effects through contaminated water and food.

Besides being ravaged by infectious diseases, indigenous populations were decimated by outright killing, enslavement, and harsh labor practices. The psychological damage produced by losing one's land and livelihood, social ties, and access to ancestral burial ground produces ongoing generational trauma (Map 5.3 and Map 5.4).

Enduring effects of European colonialism among indigenous peoples worldwide include high rates of depression and suicide; low self-esteem; high rates of child and adolescent drug use; and high rates of alcoholism, obesity, and hypertension. **Historical trauma** refers to the intergenerational transfer of the emotional and psychological effects of colonialism from parents to children (Brave Heart 2004). It is closely associated with substance abuse as a way of attempting to cover the continued pain it induces. Troubled parents create a difficult family situation for children, who tend to replicate their parents' negative coping mechanisms. The concept of historical trauma helps to expand the scope of traditional epidemiological studies by drawing on factors from the past to explain the social and spatial distribution of contemporary health problems. Such an approach may prove more effective than

historical trauma the intergenerational transfer of the detrimental effects of colonialism from parents to children.

Map 5.3 **Precolonial Distribution of Indian Tribes in the 48 United States**

Before the arrival of European colonialists, Indians were the sole occupants of the area. The first English settlers were impressed by their height and robust physical health.

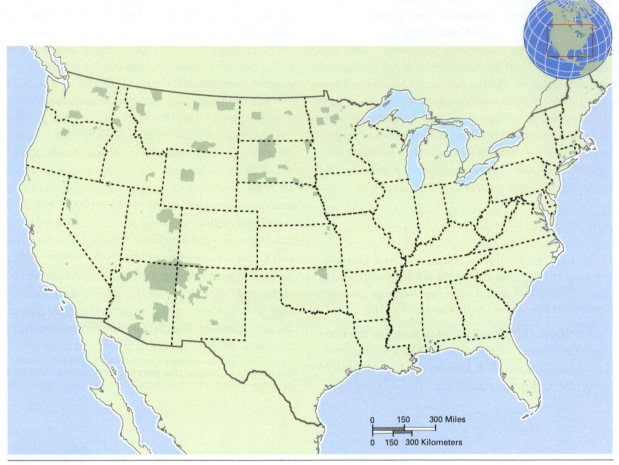

Map 5.4 Designated Reservations in the 48 United States

Federal Indian reservations today make up a small percentage of the U.S. landmass. Reservations are allocated to "recognized tribes." This map, however, does not show reservations designated by particular states. While such reservations are rare in the eastern states, they are extensive in several western states. Furthermore, this map underrepresents the presence of American Indians since many nonrecognized tribes exist, and many Indians live off the reservations.

a biomedical one in devising culturally appropriate ways to alleviate health problems.

The Symbolic/Interpretivist Approach

Some medical anthropologists examine health systems as systems of meaning. They study how people in different cultures label, describe, and experience illness and how healing systems offer meaningful responses to individual and communal distress. Symbolic/interpretivist anthropologists have examined aspects of healing, such as ritual trance, as symbolic performances. The French anthropologist Claude Lévi-Strauss established this approach in a classic essay called "The Effectiveness of Symbols" (1967). He examined how a song sung by a shaman among the Guna Indians of Panama helps women through a difficult delivery. The main point is that healing systems provide meaning to people who are experiencing seemingly meaningless forms of suffering. The provision of meaning offers psychological support to the afflicted and may enhance healing through what Western science calls the **placebo effect**, or meaning effect, a positive result from a healing method due to a symbolic or otherwise nonmaterial factor (Moerman 2002). In the United States, depending on the health problem, between 10 and 90 percent of the efficacy of medical prescriptions lies in the placebo effect. Several explanatory factors may be involved in the meaning effect: the confidence of the specialist prescribing a treatment; the act of prescription itself; and concrete details about the prescription, such as the color and shape of a pill.

Critical Medical Anthropology

Critical medical anthropology focuses on analyzing how structural factors—such as the global political economy,

placebo effect a positive result from a healing method due to a symbolic or otherwise nonmaterial factor.

critical medical anthropology an approach within medical anthropology involving the analysis of how economic and political structures shape people's health status, their access to health care, and the prevailing medical systems that exist in relation to them.

global media, and social inequality—affect the prevailing health system, including types of afflictions, people's health status, and their access to health care. Critical medical anthropologists show how WBM itself often serves to bolster the institution of medicine to the detriment of helping the poor and powerless. They point to the process of **medicalization**, or labeling a particular issue or problem as medical and requiring medical treatment when, in fact, its cause is structural. In this way, people are prescribed pills and injections for poverty, forced displacement from one's home, and being unable to provide for one's family.

SOCIAL INEQUALITY AND POVERTY
Substantial evidence indicates that poverty is the primary cause of morbidity (sickness) and mortality (death) in both high-income countries and low-income countries (Farmer 2005). It may be manifested in different ways— for example, in child malnutrition in Chad or Nepal, or through street violence among the urban poor in high-income countries.

Pharmaceutical companies invest significant resources in the design and color of new pills and advertising to promote sales. The tablets of Pfizer's erectile dysfunction drug Viagra are shaped to suggest energy and perkiness, and their arrangement in the photo also conveys activity and motion.

■ *What about the choice of the color blue?*

At the broadest level, comparing high-income countries with low-income countries, distinctions exist between the most common health problems of high-income countries and those of low-income countries. In the former, major causes of death are circulatory diseases, malignant cancers, HIV/AIDS, excess alcohol consumption, and the smoking of tobacco. In low-income countries, TB, malaria, and HIV/AIDS are the three leading causes of death.

Within the developing world, rates of childhood malnutrition are inversely related to income. In other words, as income increases, so does calorie intake as a percentage of recommended daily allowances (Zaidi 1988). Thus, increasing the income of the poor is the most direct way to improve child nutrition and health. Yet, in contrast to this seemingly logical approach, most health and nutrition programs around the world focus on treating the health results of poverty rather than its causes.

Critical medical anthropologists describe the widespread practice of medicalization, in developing countries. An example is Nancy Scheper-Hughes's research during the 1980s in Bom Jesus, a favela, or slum, northeastern Brazil (review Chapter 4, page 67 and see Map 3.3, page 49).

The people of Bom Jesus, poor and often unemployed, frequently experienced symptoms of weakness, insomnia, and anxiety (1992). Doctors at the local clinic gave them pills. The people were, however, hungry and malnourished. They needed food, not pills. In this case, as in many others, the medicalization of poverty serves the interests of pharmaceutical companies, not the poor and makes it possible for doctors to feel like they are doing something, since doctors are not trained to address structural violence and poverty.

CRITIQUE OF WESTERN BIOMEDICAL TRAINING
Since the 1980s, critical medical anthropologists have studied WBM as a cultural system. Despite recognizing many of its benefits, they point to ways in which WBM could be improved—for example, by reducing reliance on technology; broadening an understanding of health problems as they relate to structural conditions and not just biological conditions, and diversifying healing through alternative methods such as massage, acupuncture, and chiropractic.

Some critical medical anthropologists have conducted research on Western medical school training. One study of obstetric training in the United States involved interviews with 12 obstetricians, 10 males and 2 females (Davis-Floyd 1987). As students, they absorbed the technological model of birth as a core value of Western obstetrics. This model treats the body as a machine. The physician uses the assembly-line approach to birth in order to promote efficient production and quality control. One of the residents in the study explained, "We shave 'em, we prep 'em, we hook 'em up to the IV and administer sedation. We deliver the baby, it goes to the nursery and the mother goes to her room. There's no room for niceties around here. We just move 'em right on through. It's not hard to see it like an assembly line" (1987:292). The goal is the "production" of a healthy baby. The doctor is a technical expert in charge of achieving this goal, and the mother takes second place. One obstetrician said, "It is what we all were trained to always go after—the perfect baby. That's what we were trained to produce. The quality of the mother's experience—we rarely thought

---

medicalization the labeling of a particular issue or problem as medical and requiring medical treatment when, in fact, that issue or problem is economic or political.

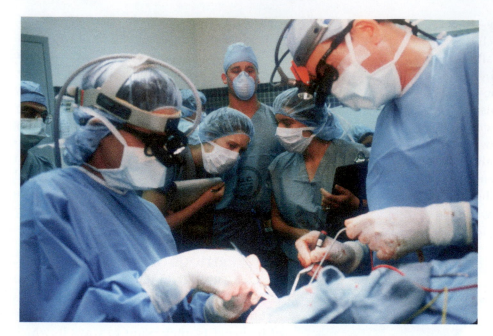

Medical students in training in a Western biomedical setting. These students are observing brain surgery.

▌ *What does this scene convey about values and beliefs of Western medicine?*

about that. Everything we did was to get that perfect baby" (1987:292).

This goal involves the use of sophisticated monitoring machines. One obstetrician said, "I'm totally dependent on fetal monitors, 'cause they're great! They free you to do a lot of other things. . . . I couldn't sit over there with a woman in labor with my hand on her belly, and be in here seeing 20 to 30 patients a day" (1987:291). The use of technology also conveys status to the physician. One commented, "Anybody in obstetrics who shows a human interest in patients is not respected. What is respected is interest in machines" (1987:291).

How do medical students learn to accept the technological model? Davis-Floyd's research points to three key processes. One way is through physical hazing, a harsh rite of passage involving, in this case, stress caused by sleep deprivation. Hazing extends throughout medical school and the residency period.

Second, medical school training in the United States involves a process of cognitive retrogression, in which students relinquish critical thinking and thoughtful ways of learning. During the first two years of medical school, most courses are basic sciences and students must memorize vast quantities of material. The sheer bulk of memorization forces students to adopt an uncritical approach. This mental overload socializes students into a uniform pattern, giving them tunnel vision in which the knowledge of medicine assumes supreme importance.

Third, in a process termed dehumanization, medical school training works to erase humanitarian ideals through an emphasis on technology and objectification of the patient. One obstetric student explained, "Most of us went into medical school with pretty humanitarian ideals. I know I did. But the whole process of medical education

makes you inhuman . . . by the time you get to residency, you end up not caring about anything beyond the latest techniques you can master and how sophisticated the tests are that you can perform" (1987:299).

Globalization and Change

5.3 **Recognize how globalization is affecting health, illness, and healing.**

With globalization, health problems move around the world and into remote locations and cultures more rapidly than ever before. At the same time, Western culture, including biomedicine, is on the move. Perhaps no other aspect of Western culture, except for the capitalist market system and the English language, has so permeated the rest of the world as WBM. But the cultural flow is not one-way: Many people in North America and Europe are turning to forms of non-Western and nonbiomedical healing, such as acupuncture and massage therapy. This section considers new and emerging health challenges, changes in healing, and examples of the relevance of applied medical anthropology.

Infectious Diseases

In the mid-twentieth century, scientific advances such as antibiotic drugs, vaccines against childhood diseases, and improved technology for sanitation dramatically reduced the threat from infectious disease. The 1980s, however, brought an era of shaken confidence, with the onset and rapid spread of the HIV/AIDS epidemic.

New contexts for exposure and contagion are created through increased international travel and migration,

Fighting AIDS in South Africa. (LEFT) Activist Noxolo Bunu demonstrates how to use a female condom. It is not clear if they will gain popularity and help reduce sexually transmitted diseases. (RIGHT) Social stigma often adds to the suffering of HIV/AIDS victims. The billboards, near Soweto in South Africa, promote condom use and seek to reduce social rejection and stigma.

deforestation, and development projects, among others. Increased travel and migration have contributed to the spread of HIV/AIDS, SARS, Ebola, and other new infectious diseases. A subcategory of infectious diseases is zoonotic diseases. A zoonotic disease is a disease that is spread from animals to people. Two examples are malaria and Lyme disease.

Deforestation is related to higher rates of malaria, which is spread by mosquitoes; mosquitoes thrive in pools of water in open, sunlit areas, as opposed to forests. Development projects such as constructing dams and clearing forests create unintended health problems for local people.

Diseases of Development

A **disease of development** is a health problem caused or increased by economic development projects. For example, the construction of dams and irrigation systems throughout the tropical world has brought dramatically increased rates of schistosomiasis (shish-to-suh-MY-a-sis), a disease caused by the presence of a parasitic worm in the blood system. Over 200 million people suffer from this debilitating disease, with prevalence rates the highest in sub-Saharan countries in Africa (Michaud, Gordon, and Reich 2005). The larvae hatch from eggs and mature in slow-moving water such as lakes and rivers. When mature, they can penetrate the human (or other animal) skin with which they come into contact. Once inside the human body, the adult schistosomes breed in the veins around the human bladder and bowel. They send fertilized eggs into the environment through urine and feces. These eggs then contaminate water, in which they hatch into larvae.

Anthropological research has documented steep increases in the rates of schistosomiasis at large dam sites in tropical countries (Scudder 1973). The risk is caused by the dams slowing the rate of water flow. Stagnant water

systems offer an ideal environment for development of the larvae. Opponents of the construction of large dams have used this information in support of their position.

Increased obesity in many countries can also be viewed as a disease of development, somewhat ironically. In high-income countries around the world, rising rates of childhood obesity have generated concern about the children's health and the toll they will take on public health systems as they age. The so-called child obesity epidemic surely has health implications, but its causes are not first and foremost medical and the most effective steps to its prevention are also outside the medical domain (Moffat 2010). In general, prevention has to do with changing the child's diet and activity patterns.

Medical Pluralism

Contact between cultures often leads to a situation in which aspects of both cultures coexist: two (or more) different languages, religions, systems of law, or health systems, for example. The term **medical pluralism** refers to the presence of several, separate health systems within a society. The coexistence of many forms of healing provides clients a range of choices and enhances the quality of health. While medical pluralism offers the advantage of choice, it also presents people with conflicting models of illness and healing, which can result in misunderstandings between healers and clients and in unhappy outcomes.

---

disease of development a health problem caused or increased by economic development activities that have detrimental effects on the environment and people's relationship with it.

medical pluralism the existence of more than one health system in a culture; also, a government policy to promote the integration of local healing systems into biomedical practice.

Award-winning English chef Jamie Oliver is also a food activist. He has worked to improve school lunches in England, and in 2010, he came to Huntington, West Virginia, to do the same. Huntington has been called the least healthy city in the least healthy state of the United States. His efforts to convince the cook at Central City Elementary School to improve the quality of school meals met with strong resistance from the cook, the students, and city administrators. The students even rejected his healthy chicken nuggets.

▌ *Is Jamie Oliver just an elitist food snob trying to change West Virginia food culture?*

SELECTIVE PLURALISM: THE CASE OF THE SHERPA The Sherpa of Nepal (see Culturama) are an unusual example of a culture in which the preference for traditional healing systems remains strong and is combined with the selective use of WBM (Adams 1988). Healing therapists available in the Upper Khumbu (khoom-boo) region in northeastern Nepal fit into three categories:

- Orthodox Buddhist practitioners, including *lamas*, whom Khumbu people consult for prevention and cure through their blessings, and *amchis*, who practice Tibetan medicine, a humoral healing system.
- Unorthodox religious or shamanic practitioners, who perform divination ceremonies for diagnosis.
- Biomedical practitioners who work in a clinic that was first established to serve tourists. The clinic was

established as a permanent medical facility in 1967, and many Sherpa selectively use it.

Thus, three varieties of health care exist in the region. Traditional healers are thriving, unthreatened by changes brought by the tourist trade, the influx of new wealth, and notions of modernity. The question of why WBM has not completely taken over other healing practices requires a complicated answer. One part of the answer is that high-mountain tourism does not deeply affect local production and social relations. Although it brings in new wealth, it does not require large-scale capital investment from outside as, for example, mega-hotel tourist developments have elsewhere. So far, the Sherpa maintain control of their productive resources, including trekking knowledge and skills.

CONFLICTING EXPLANATORY MODELS In many other contexts, however, anthropologists have documented conflicts and misunderstandings between WBM and local health systems. Miscommunication often occurs between biomedical doctors and patients in matters seemingly as simple as a prescription that should be taken with every meal. The Western biomedical doctor assumes that this means three times a day. But some people do not eat three meals a day and thus unwittingly fail to follow the doctor's instructions.

One anthropological study of a case in which death resulted from cross-cultural differences shows how complex the issue of communication across medical cultures is (review the discussion in Chapter 4 of cultural competence). The "F family" were immigrants from American Samoa (Map 5.6) living in Honolulu, Hawai'i (Krantzler 1987). Neither parent spoke English. Their children were "moderately literate" in English but spoke a mixture of English and Samoan at home. Mr. F was trained as a traditional Samoan healer. Mary, a daughter, was first stricken with diabetes at age 16. She was taken to the hospital by ambulance after collapsing, half-conscious, on the sidewalk near her home in a Honolulu housing project. After several months of irregular contact with medical staff, she was again brought to the hospital in an ambulance, unconscious, and she died there. Her father was charged with causing Mary's death through medical neglect.

In the biomedical view, her parents failed to give Mary adequate care, even though the hospital staff took pains to instruct her family about how to give insulin injections, and Mary was shown how to test her urine for glucose and acetone and counseled about her diet. She was to be followed up with visits to the outpatient clinic, and, according to the clinic's unofficial policy of linking patients with physicians from their own ethnic group, she was assigned to see the sole Samoan pediatric resident. Over the next few months, Mary was seen once in the clinic by a different resident, missed her next

Culturama

The Sherpa of Nepal

The word Sherpa means "person." About 150,000 Sherpa live in Nepal, mainly in the northeastern region. Several thousand live in Bhutan and Sikkim, and in cities of Europe and North America.

In Nepal, the Sherpa are most closely associated with the Khumbu region. Khumbu is a valley set high in the Himalayas, completely encircled by mountains and with a clear view of Mount Everest (Karan and Mather 1985). The Sherpa have a mixed economy involving animal herding, trade between Tibet and India, small businesses, and farming, with the main crop being potatoes.

Since the 1920s and the coming of Western mountaineers, Sherpa men have become increasingly employed as guides and porters for trekkers and climbers. Many Sherpa men and women now run guest houses or work in guest houses as cooks, food servers, and cleaners.

The Sherpa are organized into 18 separate lineages, or *ru* ("bones"), with marriage taking place outside one's birth lineage. Recently, they have begun marrying into other ethnic groups, thus expanding the definition and meaning of what it is to be Sherpa. Because of increased intermarriage, the number of people who can be considered Sherpa to some degree is 130,000.

Status distinctions include "big people," "middle people," and "small people," with the middle group being the largest by far (Ortner 1999:65). The main privilege of those in the top level is not to carry loads. Those in the "small people" category are landless and work for others.

The Sherpa practice a localized version of Tibetan Buddhism, which contains non-Buddhist elements having to do with nature spiritualism that connects all beings. The place name Khumbu refers to the guardian deity of the region.

External forces have long affected the Sherpa given their trade links beyond the region. Tourism has been, and still is, a major change factor for the Sherpa. In Khumbu, the number of international tourists per year exceeds the Sherpa population. International tourism is a major factor in monetizing the economy and affecting local cultural change through cross-cultural exposure.

Tourism dependence, specifically guiding mountain climbers, came into question in 2014 when five Sherpa guides were killed in an avalanche during a climb of Mount Everest. The Sherpa Organization demanded benefits for the families.

Thanks to Vincanne Adams, University of California at San Francisco, for reviewing this material.

(LEFT) A Sherpa porter carries a load up a steep mountain path in the Himalayas. Porters earn good wages compared to farmers, for example, because they work for international tourists.

(CENTER) Nepali children learn writing in a school supported by the Himalayan Trust, an organization founded by Sir Edmund Hillary in 1961 after he climbed Mount Everest and asked the local people he met how he could help them.

Map 5.5 **Nepal**

The Kingdom of Nepal has a population of almost 30 million, a number double from that of 30 years ago. Most of its territory is in the Himalayas. Nepal has eight of the world's 10 highest mountains.

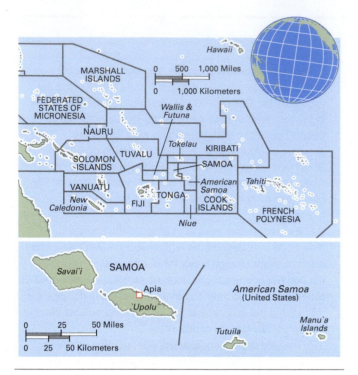

Map 5.6 **Samoa and American Samoa**

Samoa, or the Independent State of Samoa, was known as German Samoa (1900–1919) and Western Samoa (1914–1997) until recognized by the United Nations as a sovereign country. Its population is around 190,000. American Samoa, or Amerika Samoa in Samoan English, is a territory of the United States with a population of about 55,000. During World War II, U.S. Marines in American Samoa outnumbered the local population and had a strong cultural influence. Unemployment rates are high, and the U.S. military is the largest employer.

three appointments, came in once without an appointment, and was readmitted to the hospital on the basis of test results from that visit. At that time, she, her parents, and her older sister were once again advised about the importance of compliance with the medical advice they were receiving. Four months later, she returned to the clinic with blindness in one eye and diminished vision in the other. She was diagnosed with cataracts, and the Samoan physician again advised Mary about the seriousness of her illness and the need for compliance. The medical experts increasingly judged that "cultural differences" were the basic problem and that, in spite of all their attempts to communicate with the F family, they were basically incapable of caring for Mary.

The family's perspective, in contrast, was grounded in *fa'a Samoa*, the Samoan way. Their experiences in the hospital were not positive from the start. When Mr. F arrived at the hospital with Mary the first time, he spoke with several hospital staff, through a daughter as translator. It was a teaching hospital, so various residents and attending physicians had examined Mary. Mr. F was concerned that there was no single physician caring for Mary, and he was concerned that her care was inconsistent. The family observed

a child die while Mary was in the intensive care unit, reinforcing the perception of inadequate care and instilling fear over Mary's chance of surviving in this hospital.

Language differences between Mary's family and the hospital staff added to the problem. Some hospital staff told Mary's family that her problem was "sugar," using a folk term in English for diabetes (1987:330). Mary's mother thought that meant she needed more sugar in her diet. Miscommunications led to lack of trust in Mary's family of the hospital staff, and they began to resort more to their traditional resources including relying on Mary's father, a traditional Samoan healer.

From the Samoan perspective, the F family behaved logically and appropriately. The father, as household head and healer in his own right, felt he had authority. Dr. A, though Samoan, had been resocialized by the Western medical system and alienated from his Samoan background. He did not offer the personal touch that the F family expected. Samoans believe that children above the age of 12 are no longer children and can be expected to behave responsibly, so the family's assigning of Mary's 12-year-old sister to assist with her insulin injections and in recording results made sense to them. Also, the hospital in American Samoa does not require appointments. Cultural misunderstanding was the ultimate cause of Mary's death.

Applied Medical Anthropology

Applied medical anthropology is the application of anthropological knowledge to further the goals of health-care providers. It may involve improving doctor–patient communication in multicultural settings, making recommendations about culturally appropriate health intervention programs, or providing insights into factors related to disease that medical practitioners do not usually take into account. Applied medical anthropologists draw on ethnomedical knowledge and on any of the three theoretical approaches or a combination of them (see Anthropology Works).

REDUCING LEAD POISONING AMONG MEXICAN AMERICAN CHILDREN An example of the positive impact of applied medical anthropology is in the work of Robert Trotter on lead poisoning among Mexican American children (1987). The three most common sources of lead poisoning of children in the United States are the following:

- Eating lead-based paint chips
- Living near a smelter where the dust has high lead content
- Eating or drinking from pottery made with an improperly treated lead glaze

---

applied medical anthropology the application of anthropological knowledge to furthering the goals of health-care providers.

Anthropology Works

Promoting Vaccination Programs in Developing Countries

Vaccination programs in developing countries, especially as promoted by UNICEF, are introduced with much fanfare. But they are sometimes met with little enthusiasm by the target population. In India, many people are suspicious that vaccination programs are clandestine family planning programs (Nichter 1996). In other instances, fear of foreign vaccines prompts people to reject inoculations. In Pakistan and Afghanistan, some public health workers providing polio vaccines to children in remote areas have been killed on the assumption that they are spies for the West.

Overall, acceptance rates of vaccination are lower than Western public health planners expected. To understand why people reject vaccinations,

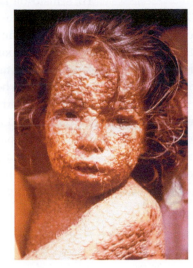

A girl in Bangladesh, photographed in 1975, has the raised bumps of smallpox. In 1977, the World Health Organization announced that smallpox had been eradicated in Bangladesh.

▌ *Has smallpox been eradicated worldwide?*

medical anthropologists conducted surveys in several countries. The results revealed that many parents have a partial or inaccurate understanding of what the vaccines protect against. Some people did not understand the importance of multiple vaccinations. Public health promoters incorporated findings from the survey in two ways:

- Educational campaigns for the public that addressed its concerns

- Education for the public health specialists about the importance of understanding and paying attention to local cultural practices and beliefs

Food for Thought

If your job was to promote wider acceptance of vaccinations in your home country, what would you want to know before you began an education campaign?

The discovery of an unusual case of lead poisoning by health professionals in Los Angeles in the 1980s prompted investigations that produced understanding of a fourth cause: the use by many Mexican Americans of a traditional healing remedy, *azarcon*, which contains lead, to treat a culture-specific syndrome called *empacho*. Empacho is a combination of indigestion and constipation believed to be caused by food sticking to the abdominal wall.

The U.S. Public Health Service asked Trotter to investigate the availability and use of azarcon. He went to Mexico and surveyed the contents of herbal shops. He talked with *curanderos* (traditional healers). His findings convinced the U.S. government to place restrictions on azarcon and a related remedy called *greta*. Trotter also made recommendations about the need to provide a substitute remedy for the treatment of empacho that would not have harmful side effects. He offered ideas about how to advertise the substitute in a culturally effective way. Throughout his involvement, Trotter played several roles—researcher, consultant, and program developer—all of which brought anthropological knowledge to the solution of a public health problem.

PUBLIC HEALTH COMMUNICATION Much work in applied medical anthropology involves health communication (Nichter 1996). Anthropologists can help health

educators in the development of more meaningful messages through these methods:

- Addressing local health beliefs and health concerns
- Taking seriously all local illness terms and conventions
- Adopting local styles of communication
- Identifying subgroups within the population that may be responsive to different types of messages and incentives
- Monitoring the response of communities to health messages over time and facilitating corrections in communication when needed
- Exposing and removing possible "blaming the victim" in health messages

These principles helped health-care officials understand local responses to public vaccination programs in several countries of Asia and Africa. In this, and so many other ways, an anthropologist can serve as a **cultural broker**, someone

---

cultural broker someone who is familiar with two cultures and can promote communication and understanding across them.

intercultural health an approach in health that seeks to reduce the gaps between local and Western health systems in promoting more effective prevention and treatment of health problems.

who is familiar with two cultures and can promote communication and understanding across them.

WORKING TOGETHER: WESTERN BIOMEDICINE AND NONBIOMEDICAL SYSTEMS The World Health Organization has endorsed the incorporation of traditional healing practices into national health systems since the late 1970s. This policy emerged in response to several factors. First is the increasing appreciation of the value of many non-Western healing traditions. Another is the shortage of trained biomedical personnel. Third is the growing awareness of the deficiencies of WBM in addressing a person's psychosocial context.

Debates continue about the efficacy of many traditional medical practices compared with biomedicine. For instance, opponents of the promotion of traditional medicine claim that it has no effect on such infectious diseases as cholera, malaria, TB, schistosomiasis, and leprosy. They insist that it makes no sense to allow for or encourage ritual practices against cholera, for example, when a child has not been inoculated against it. Supporters of traditional medicine as one component of **intercultural health** believe that intercultural health is an approach in health that seeks to reduce the gaps between local and Western health systems in promoting more effective prevention and treatment of health problems (Torri 2012). This combination of health systems would help fill the gap in much of biomedicine that neglects a person's mind, soul, and social setting and bring to traditional medicine some of the technical advantages of biomedicine in one place.

5   Learning Objectives Revisited

5.1   Describe the scope of ethnomedicine and how it has changed in recent times.

Ethnomedicine is the study of the health systems of specific cultures. Health systems include categories and perceptions of illness and approaches to prevention and healing. Research in ethnomedicine shows how perceptions of the body differ cross-culturally and reveals both differences and similarities across health systems in perceptions of illness and symptoms. Culture-specific syndromes are found in all cultures, not just in non-Western societies, and many are now becoming global.

Ethnomedical studies of healing, healing substances, and healers reveal a wide range of approaches. Community healing is more characteristic of small-scale nonindustrial societies. Community healing emphasizes group interaction and treating the individual within the social context. Humoral healing seeks to maintain balance in bodily fluids and substances through diet, activity, and behavior. In industrial/digital societies, biomedicine emphasizes the body as a discrete unit, and treatment addresses the individual body or mind and frames out the wider social context. Biomedicine is increasingly reliant on technology and is increasingly specialized.

5.2   Explain the three major theoretical approaches in medical anthropology.

Ecological/epidemiological medical anthropology emphasizes links between the environment and health. It reveals how certain categories of people are at risk of contracting particular diseases within various contexts in historical times and the present.

The symbolic/interpretivist approach focuses on studying illness and healing as a set of symbols and meanings. Cross-culturally, definitions of health problems and healing systems for these problems are embedded in meaning.

Critical medical anthropologists focus on health problems and healing within a structurist framework. They ask what power relations are involved and who benefits from particular forms of healing. They analyze the role of inequality and poverty in health problems.

5.3   Recognize how globalization is affecting health, illness, and healing.

Health systems everywhere are facing accelerated change in the face of globalization, which includes the spread of Western capitalism as well as new diseases and new medical technologies. The "new infectious diseases" are a challenge to health-care systems in terms of prevention and treatment. Diseases of development are health problems caused by development projects that change physical and social environments, such as dams and mines, and by the changing diets and activity patterns of people who live in developed settings, which can lead to chronic conditions such as diabetes and obesity.

The spread of Western biomedicine to many non-Western contexts is a major direction of change. As a consequence, medical pluralism exists in all countries. While the existence of plural, separate systems offers people some choice of what kind of healer to consult, such a situation can often be confusing and provide conflicting views with negative results. A new proposition, intercultural health, may help with its combination of different forms of knowledge and solutions. Applied medical anthropologists play several roles in improving health systems. They may inform medical care providers of more appropriate forms of treatment, guide local people about their increasingly complex medical choices, help prevent health problems by changing detrimental practices, or improve public health communication by making it more culturally informed and effective.

Key Concepts

applied medical anthropology, p. 106
community healing, p. 94
critical medical anthropology, p. 100
cultural broker, p. 107
culture-specific syndrome, p. 91
disease, p. 91
disease of development, p. 103
ecological/epidemiological
    approach, p. 98

ethno-etiology, p. 92
ethnomedicine, p. 90
historical trauma, p. 99
humoral healing, p. 94
illness, p. 91
intercultural health, p. 108
medicalization, p. 101
medical pluralism, p. 103
phytotherapy, p. 97

placebo effect, p. 100
shaman or shamanka, p. 96
somatization, p. 91
structural suffering, p. 93
susto, p. 91
Western biomedicine
    (WBM), p. 90

Thinking Outside the Box

1. In your microculture, what are some prevailing perceptions about the body and how are they related to medical treatment?

2. Discuss some examples of culture-specific syndromes in your microculture or on your campus.

3. What steps do you take to treat yourself when you have a cold or headache? If you take medicine, do you know what materials are in the medicine?

Chapter 6
Kinship and Domestic Life

Learning Objectives

6.1 Define the three ways cultures create kinship.

6.2 Recognize how anthropologists define and study households and domestic life.

6.3 Illustrate how kinship and households are changing.

Anthro Connections

Minangkabau (mee-NAN-ka-bow) women own the land and the houses, and they make the decisions about farming (see Culturama on page 117). Yet, the Minangkabau are devout Muslims. How do they combine female-centered kinship with Islam? The answer, for now at least, is a pluralistic approach to kinship and gender with non-Islamic tradition guiding "high" inheritance of land and home from mother to daughter and "low" inheritance from a father to his children out of his earnings (Shapiro 2011). "Low" inheritance follows Islamic law, which says that sons get twice as much as daughters. New Islamic practices are emerging, however, including girls and women wearing headscarves (Parker 2008). The Minangkabau are an important example of whether women can maintain high status in a Muslim society.

Learning how another culture's kinship system works is as difficult as learning another language. Robin Fox became aware of this challenge during his research among the Tory Islanders of Ireland (Map 6.1) (Fox 1995 [1978]). Some Tory Island kinship terms are similar to American English terms; for example, the word *muintir* means "people" in its widest sense, as in English. It can also refer to people of a particular social category, as in "my people," and to close relatives. Another similarity is in *gaolta*, the word for "relatives" or "those of my blood." Its adjectival form refers to kindness, like the English word kin, which is related to "kindness." Tory Islanders have a phrase meaning "children and grandchildren," also like the English term descendants. One major difference is that the Tory Island word for "friend" is the same as the word for "kin." This usage reflects the cultural context of Tory Island with its small population, all related through kinship. So, logically, a friend is also kin.

All cultures have ways of defining kinship, or a sense of being related to another person or persons. Cultures also provide guidelines about who are kin and the expected behavior of kin. Starting in infancy, people learn about their particular culture's **kinship system**, the predominant form of kin relationships in a culture and the kinds of behavior involved. Like language, one's kinship system is so ingrained that it is taken for granted as something natural rather than cultural.

This chapter first considers cultural variations in three features of kinship systems. It then focuses on a key unit of domestic life: the household. The last section provides examples of contemporary change in kinship, particularly marriage patterns and household organization.

How Cultures Create Kinship

6.1 Define the three ways cultures create kinship.

In all cultures, kinship is linked with modes of livelihood and reproduction (Figure 6.1). Nineteenth-century anthropologists found that kinship was the most important organizing principle in nonindustrial, non-state cultures. The kinship group performs the functions of ensuring the continuity of the group by arranging marriages; maintaining social order by setting moral rules and punishing offenders; and providing for the basic needs of members by regulating production, consumption, and distribution. In large-scale industrial/digital societies, kinship ties exist, but many other kinds of social ties draw people together as well.

Nineteenth-century anthropologists also discovered that definitions of who counts as kin in the cultures they studied differed widely from those of Europe and the United States. Western cultures emphasize primary "blood" relations, or relations through birth from a biological mother and biological father (Sault 1994). "Blood" is not a universal basis for kinship, however. Even in some cultures with a "blood"-based understanding of kinship, variations exist in defining who is a "blood" relative and who is not. For example, in some cultures, male offspring are considered of one "blood," whereas female offspring are not.

Among the Inuit of northern Alaska, behavior is a nonblood basis for determining kinship (Bodenhorn 2000). In this context, people who act like kin are kin. If a person stops acting like kin, then he or she is no longer a kinsperson. So, among the Inuit, someone might say that a certain person "used to be" his or her cousin.

---

kinship system the predominant form of kin relationships in a culture and the kinds of behavior involved.

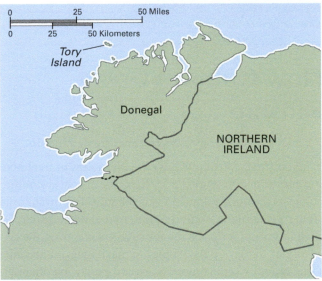

Map 6.1 Ireland

The Republic of Ireland's population is 4.6 million. The geography is low central plains surrounded by a ring of mountains. Membership in the European Union (EU) and the rising standard of living earned Ireland the nickname of the Celtic Tiger. Its economic opportunities attracted immigrants from places as diverse as Romania, China, and Nigeria. The financial crisis that began in 2008 has had major negative effects on the economy. Most people are Roman Catholics, followed by the Anglican Church of Ireland.

Studying Kinship: From Formal Analysis to Kinship in Action

Anthropologists in the first half of the twentieth century focused on finding out who, in a particular culture, is related to whom and in what way. Typically, the anthropologist would conduct an interview with a few people, asking questions such as "What do you call your brother's daughter?" "Can you (as a man) marry your father's brother's daughter?" and "What is the term you use to refer to your mother's sister?" The anthropologist would ask an individual to name all of his or her relatives, explain how they are related to the interviewee, and provide the terms by which he or she refers to them.

From this information, the anthropologist would construct a kinship diagram, a schematic way of presenting the kinship relationships of an individual, called ego, using a set of symbols to depict all the kin relations of ego (Figure 6.2). A kinship diagram depicts ego's relatives, as remembered by ego. In cultures in which kinship plays a major role in social relations, ego may be able to provide information on dozens of relatives. When I took a research methods course as an undergraduate, one assignment was to interview someone who was not an American and construct a kinship chart based on the information collected. I interviewed a student from an urban, middle-class business family in India. He recalled over 60 relatives on both his father's and mother's sides. My kinship diagram of his relatives required several sheets of paper taped together.

In contrast to a kinship diagram, a genealogy is a schematic way of presenting a family tree, constructed by beginning with the earliest ancestors that can be traced, then working down to the present. A genealogy, thus, does not begin with ego. When Robin Fox attempted to construct kinship diagrams beginning with ego, the Tory Islanders were uncomfortable with the approach. They preferred to proceed genealogically, so he followed their preference. Tracing a family's complete genealogy may involve archival research in the attempt to construct as complete a history as possible. In Europe and the United States, Christians have long followed a practice of recording their

Foraging	Horticulture	Pastoralism	Agriculture		Industrial/Digital
Descent and Inheritance Bilineal		Unilineal (matrilineal or patrilineal)			**Descent and Inheritance** Bilineal
Marital Residence Neolocal or bilocal		Matrilocal or patrilocal			**Marital Residence** Neolocal
Household Type Nuclear		Extended			**Household Type** Nuclear or single-parent or single-person

Figure 6.1 **Modes of Livelihood, Kinship, and Household Structure**

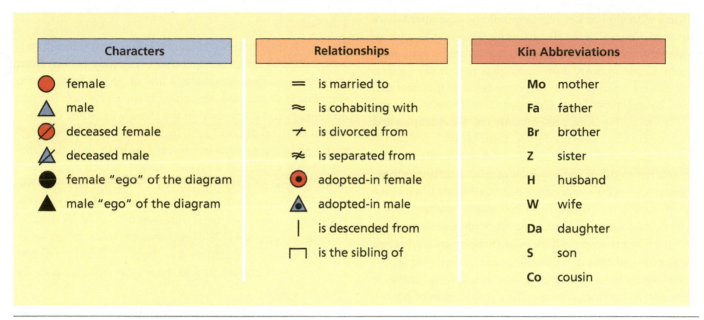

Figure 6.2 **Symbols Used in Kinship Diagrams**

genealogy in the front of the family Bible. Many African Americans and other people are consulting DNA analysts to learn about their ancestry and cultural heritage.

Decades of anthropological research have produced a mass of information on kinship terminology, or the words people use to refer to kin. For example, in Euro-American kinship, a child of one's father's sister or brother or one's mother's sister or brother is referred to by the kinship term "cousin." Likewise, one's father's sister and one's mother's sister are both referred to as "aunt," and one's father's brother and one's mother's brother are both referred to as "uncle." "Grandmother" and "grandfather" refer to the ascending generation on either one's father's or one's

mother's side. This merging pattern is not universal. In some cultures, different terms apply to kin on one's mother's and father's sides, so a mother's sister has a kinship term different from that referring to a father's sister. Another type of kinship system emphasizes solidarity along lines of siblings of the same gender. Among the Navajo of the American southwest, one's mother and one's mother's sisters have the same term, which translates into English as "mother."

Early anthropologists classified the cross-cultural variety in kinship terminology into six basic types, named after groups first discovered to have those systems. Two of the six types, for purposes of illustration, are the Iroquois type and the Eskimo type (Figure 6.3). Anthropologists place various

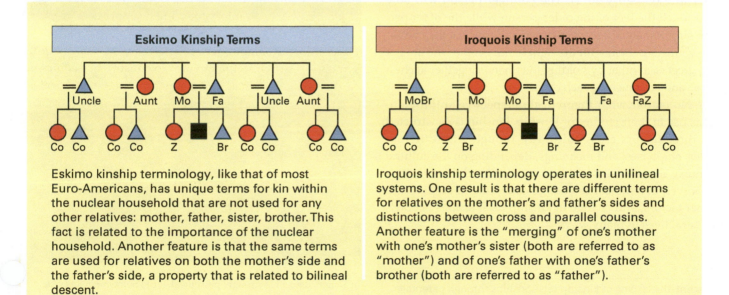

Eskimo kinship terminology, like that of most Euro-Americans, has unique terms for kin within the nuclear household that are not used for any other relatives: mother, father, sister, brother. This fact is related to the importance of the nuclear household. Another feature is that the same terms are used for relatives on both the mother's side and the father's side, a property that is related to bilineal descent.

Iroquois kinship terminology operates in unilineal systems. One result is that there are different terms for relatives on the mother's and father's sides and distinctions between cross and parallel cousins. Another feature is the "merging" of one's mother with one's mother's sister (both are referred to as "mother") and of one's father with one's father's brother (both are referred to as "father").

Figure 6.3 **Two Kinship Naming Systems**

cultures with similar kinship terminology, no matter where they lived, into one of the six categories. Thus, the Yanomami people of the Amazon are said to have an Iroquois naming system. Contemporary anthropologists who study kinship have moved beyond these categories because they feel that the six kinship types fail to illuminate actual kinship dynamics. This book, therefore, presents only the two examples and avoids going into detail on the six classic types.

Current interest in the study of kinship shows how it is related to other topics, such as globalization, ethnic identity, and even terrorism. Anthropologists have come a long way, from classifying kinship to showing how it matters, as documented in a recent book reviewing over a century of kinship studies in anthropology by French anthropologist Maurice Godelier (2012). Godelier, influenced by a materialist perspective, looks at how kinship is connected to economic issues, the organization of power, and the emerging forms of technology. His insights into how kinship is changing around the world today are particularly informed by aspects of modernity, including the role of new reproductive technologies (NRTs) including in vitro fertilization (IVF) and surrogate motherhood (review Chapter 4), two practices that address infertility, or the inability to conceive and complete a pregnancy. Both IVF and surrogate motherhood challenge traditional definitions of kinship in ways that play out differently depending on the cultural context and religious rulings. Islam, for example, forbids third-party donation of sperm (Inhorn 2004). Nonetheless, many Muslim couples who are unable to conceive are seeking this service.

Other anthropologists look at how people communicate kinship in everyday life. A study in rural central India found the importance of affirming kinship, and respect from younger kin to older kin, through a greeting that involves touching (Gregory 2011). The younger person will bow and touch the feet of the older person while the older person simultaneously reaches down and touches the chin of the younger person with the right hand. People who are not kin greet each other by holding their hands together at chest level, and not touching each other.

No matter what theoretical perspective anthropologists use in their studies of kinship, kinship is constructed on three factors cross-culturally, though with different rules, emphases, and meanings, depending on the cultural context: descent, sharing, and marriage. All three factors, however, are subject to change over time in response to other factors, and change in kinship itself shapes people's cultural lives in many ways.

Descent

Descent is the tracing of kinship relationships through parentage. It is based on the fact that everybody is born from someone else. Descent creates a line of people from whom someone is descended, stretching through history. But not all cultures reckon descent in the same way. Some cultures have a **bilineal descent** system, in which a child is recognized as being related by descent to both parents. Others have a **unilineal descent** system, which recognizes descent through only one parent, either the father or the mother. The distribution of bilineal and unilineal systems is roughly correlated with different modes of livelihood (see Figure 6.1, page 112). This correspondence makes sense because economic systems—livelihood, consumption, and exchange—are closely tied to the way people are socially organized.

UNILINEAL DESCENT Unilineal descent is the basis of kinship in about 60 percent of the world's cultures, making it the most common form of descent. This system tends to be found in societies with a fixed resource base. Thus,

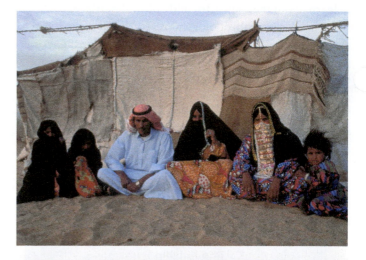

In Yemen, descent is strongly patrilineal. (TOP) Some members of a Bedu household in Yemen. The Bedu are a small proportion of the Yemeni population. (BOTTOM) Boys playing in Hababa, Yemen. In this patrilineal culture, public space is segregated by gender.

---

descent the tracing of kinship relationships through parentage.

bilineal descent the tracing of descent through both parents.

unilineal descent the tracing of descent through only one parent.

Think Like an Anthropologist

What's in a Name?

Naming children is a culturally significant act. Parents may follow cultural rules that a first-born son receives the name of his father's father or a first-born daughter receives the name of her mother's mother. Some parents believe that a new-born should not be formally named for a year or two, and the child is instead referred to by a nickname. Others think that a name must convey some special hoped-for attribute for the child or that a name should be unique.

The village of Ha Tsuen is located in the northwest corner of a rural area of Hong Kong (Watson 1986). About 2,500 people live in the village. All the males belong to the same patrilineage and all have the same surname of Teng. They are descended from a common male ancestor who settled in the region in the twelfth century. Daughters marry into families outside the village, and marital residence is patrilocal.

Women do not own property, and they have no control over the household economy. Few married women are employed in wage labor. They depend on their husbands for financial support. Local politics is male dominated, as is all public decision making. A woman's status as a new bride is low, and the transition from daughter to bride can be difficult psychologically. Women's primary role is in reproduction, especially of sons. As a woman bears children, especially sons, her status in the household rises.

The local naming system reflects the power, importance, and autonomy of males. All children are first given a name, referred to as their *ming*, when they are a few days old. If the baby is a boy, the 30-day ceremony is as elaborate as the family can afford. It may include a banquet for many neighbors and the village elders and the presentation of red eggs to everyone in the community. For a girl, the 30-day ceremony may involve only a special meal for close family members. Paralleling this expenditure bias toward sons is the thinking that goes into selecting the ming. A boy's ming is distinctive and flattering. It may have a classical literary connection. A girl's ming often has negative connotations, such as "Last Child," "Too Many," or "Little Mistake." One common ming for a daughter is "Joined to a Brother," which implies the hope that she will be a lucky charm, bringing the birth of a son to her mother next. Sometimes, though, people give an uncomplimentary name to a boy, such as "Little Slave Girl." The reason behind this naming practice is protection—to trick the spirits into thinking the baby is only a worthless girl so that the spirits will do no harm.

Marriage is the next formal naming occasion. When a male marries, he is given or chooses for himself a *tzu*, or marriage name. Gaining a tzu is a key marker of male adulthood. The tzu is not used in everyday address but appears mainly on formal documents. A man also has a *wai hao*, "outside name," which is his public nickname. As he enters middle age, he may take a *hao*, or courtesy name, which he chooses and which reflects his aspirations and self-perceptions.

In the case of a woman, her ming ceases to exist when she marries. She no longer has a name. Instead, her

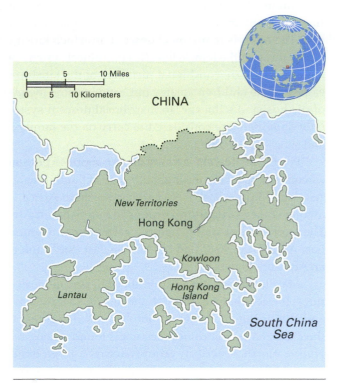

Map 6.2   Hong Kong

The formal name of Hong Kong is the Hong Kong Special Administrative Region of the People's Republic of China. A world center of finance and trade, it lacks natural resources and agricultural land, so it imports most of its food and raw materials. With seven million residents, Hong Kong's population density is extremely high while its fertility rate, at 1.1, is among the world's lowest. Most of the population is ethnic Chinese, and many practice ancestor worship. Ten percent of the population is Christian. Religious freedom is protected through Hong Kong's constitution.

husband refers to her as nei jen, "inner person," because now her life is restricted to the domestic world of the household, her husband's family, and the neighborhood. People may also refer to her by teknonyms, or names for someone based on their relationship to someone else, such as "Wife of So and So" or "Mother of So and So." In old age, she becomes ah po, "Old Woman."

Throughout their lives, men accumulate more and better names than women. They choose many of the names themselves. Over the course of their lives, women have fewer names than men have. Women's names are standardized, not personalized, and women never get to choose any of their names.

Food for Thought

Do Internet research on baby naming practices. Do you like your first name? If you would prefer a different first name, what would it be and why?

unilineal descent is most common among pastoralists, horticulturalists, and farmers. Inheritance rules that regulate the transmission of property through only one line help maintain cohesiveness of the resource base.

Unilineal descent has two major forms. One is **patrilineal descent**, in which kinship is traced through the male line. The other is **matrilineal descent**, in which kinship is traced through the female line. In a patrilineal system, only male children are considered members of the kinship lineage. Female children "marry out" and become members of the husband's lineage. In matrilineal descent systems, only daughters are considered to carry on the family line and sons "marry out."

Patrilineal descent is found among about 45 percent of all cultures. It occurs throughout much of South Asia, East Asia, the Middle East, New Guinea, northern Africa, and among some horticultural groups of sub-Saharan Africa. The world's most strongly patrilineal systems are found in East Asia, South Asia, and the Middle East (see Think Like an Anthropologist).

Matrilineal descent exists in about 15 percent of all cultures. It traces kinship through the female line exclusively, and the lineage consists of mothers and daughters and their daughters. Matrilineal descent is found among many Native North American groups; across a large band of central Africa; among many groups of Southeast Asia and the Pacific, and Australia; in parts of eastern and southern India; in a small pocket of northern Bangladesh; and in parts of the Mediterranean coast of Spain and Portugal. Matrilineal societies are found among foragers and in agricultural societies. Most matrilineal cultures, however, are horticulturalist economies in which women dominate the production and distribution of food and other goods. Often, but not always, matrilineal kinship is associated with recognized public leadership positions for women, as among the Iroquois and Hopi. The Minangkabau of Indonesia are the largest matrilineal group in the world (see Culturama).

BILINEAL DESCENT Bilineal descent traces kinship from both parents equally to the child. Bilineal descent is found in about one-third of the world's cultures (Murdock 1965 [1949]:57). The highest frequency of bilineal descent is found at opposite ends of the diagram of the modes of livelihood (see Figure 6.1, page 112). For example, Ju/wasi foragers have bilineal descent, as do most urban professionals in North America. Both foraging and industrial/digital cultures rely on a flexible gender division of labor in which both males and females contribute, more or less equally, to making a living. Bilineal descent makes sense for both foraging and industrial/digital groups because it promotes small kinship units and allows for spatial mobility of the small units.

Marital residence tends to follow the prevailing direction of descent rules (see Figure 6.1, page 112). Patrilocality, or marital residence with or near the husband's family, occurs in patrilineal societies, whereas matrilocality, or marital residence with or near the wife's family, occurs in matrilineal societies. Neolocality, or marital residence in a place different from either the bride's or groom's family, is common in Western industrialized society. Residence patterns have political, economic, and social implications. Patrilineal descent and patrilocal residence, for example, facilitate the formation of strongly bonded groups of men who can be mobilized for warfare.

Sharing

Many cultures emphasize kinship ties based on acts of sharing and support. These relationships may be either informal or ritually formalized. Godparenthood and blood brotherhood are examples of sharing-based kinship ties that are ritually formalized.

KINSHIP THROUGH FOOD SHARING Sharing-based kinship is common in mainland Southeast Asia, Australia, and Pacific island cultures (Carsten 1995). Among inhabitants of one of Malaysia's many small islands, sharing-based kinship starts in the womb when the mother's blood feeds the fetus. After birth, the mother's breast milk nourishes the infant, and it establishes a crucial tie between milk-giver and child. Breastfeeding is also the basis of the incest rule. People who have been fed from the same breast are kin and may not marry. After the baby is weaned, its most important food is cooked rice. Sharing cooked rice is another way that kinship ties are created and maintained, especially between women and children. Men are often away on fishing trips, in coffee shops, or at the mosque, and so they are less likely to establish rice-sharing kinship bonds with children.

ADOPTION AND FOSTERING Another form of sharing-based kinship is the transfer of a child or children from the birth parent(s) to the care of someone else. Adoption is a formal and permanent form of child transfer. Common motivations for adoption include infertility and the desire to obtain a particular kind of child (often a son). Motivations for

---

patrilineal descent a descent system that highlights the importance of men in tracing descent, determining marital residence with or near the groom's family, and providing for inheritance of property through the male line.

matrilineal descent a descent system that highlights the importance of women by tracing descent through the female line, favoring marital residence with or near the bride's family, and providing for property to be inherited through the female line.

Culturama

The Minangkabau of Indonesia

The Minangkabau are the world's largest matrilineal culture, numbering between four and five million (Sanday 2002). Most live in West Sumatra, Indonesia, and about 500,000 live in Malaysia. The Minangkabau are primarily farmers, producing substantial amounts of surplus rice. Many Minangkabau, both women and men, take up employment in Indonesian cities for a time and then return home.

In this strongly matrilineal kinship system, Minangkabau women hold power through their control of land passed down through the lineage, the products of that land, and agricultural employment on their land (Sanday 2002). Many have prominent positions in business, especially having to do with rice. Men are more likely to become scholars, merchants, and politicians.

Inheritance of property, including farmland and the family house, passes from mothers to daughters. Members of each sub-matrilineage, constituting several generations, live together in one house or several nearby houses.

Often, men and older boys live in a separate structure, such as the village mosque. In the household, the senior woman controls the power, and she makes decisions in all economic and ceremonial matters. The senior male of the sub-lineage has the role of representing its interests to other groups, but he is only a representative, not a powerful person in his own right.

Water buffaloes are important in both the Minangkabau rice economy and symbolically. The roofline of a traditional house has upward curves that echo the shape of water buffalo horns. Minangkabau women's festive headdresses have the same shape.

The Minangkabau are mostly Muslims, but they mix their Muslim faith with elements of earlier traditions and Hinduism. They have long-standing traditions of music, martial arts, weaving, wood carving, and making fine filigree jewelry of silver and gold.

Many of the traditional wooden houses and palaces in Western Sumatra are falling into a state of disrepair (Vellinga 2004). The matrilineal pattern of only women living in the house is changing, and today men and women are more likely to live together in small, nuclear households.

Thanks to Michael G. Peletz, Emory University, for reviewing this material.

(LEFT) A traditional wooden Minangkabau longhouse with its distinctive upward-pointing roof. The house interiors are divided into separate "bays" for sub-matrilineal groups. Many are no longer places of residence but are used as meeting halls or are falling into ruin.

(CENTER) The symbolic importance of water buffaloes, apparent in the shape of traditional rooftops, is reiterated in the shape of girls' and women's ceremonial headdress. The headdress represents women's responsibilities for the growth and strength of Minangkabau culture.

Map 6.3 Minangkabau Region in Indonesia

The shaded area shows the traditional heartland of Minangkabau culture in western Sumatra. Many Minangkabau people live elsewhere in Sumatra and in neighboring Malaysia.

the birth parent to transfer a child to someone else include a premarital pregnancy in a disapproving context, having "too many" children, and having "too many" of a particular gender. Among the Maasai pastoralists of East Africa, a woman with several children might give one to a friend, neighbor, or aged person who has no child to care for her or him.

Judith Modell, cultural anthropologist and adoptive parent, studied people's experiences of adoptees, birth parents, and adoptive parents in the United States (Modell 1994). She found that the legal process of adoption constructs the adoptive relationship to be as much like a biological one as possible. In closed adoption, the adopted child receives a new birth certificate, and the birth parent ceases to have any relationship to the child. A recent trend is toward open adoption, in which adoptees and birth parents have information about each other's identity and are free to interact with one another. Of the 28 adoptees Modell interviewed, most were interested in searching for their birth parents. The search for birth parents involves an attempt to discover "who I really am." For others, such a search is backward looking instead of being a path toward identity formation. Thus, in the United States, adoption legalizes sharing-based kinship but does not always replace a sense of descent-based kinship for everyone involved.

Fostering a child is similar to a formal adoption in terms of permanence and a sense of kinship. Or it may be temporary placement of a child with someone else for a specific purpose, with little or no sense of kinship. Child fostering is common throughout sub-Saharan Africa. Parents foster out children to enhance the child's chances for formal education or so that the child will learn a skill, such as marketing. Most foster children go from rural to urban areas and from poorer to better-off households. Fieldwork conducted in a neighborhood in Accra, Ghana (Map 6.4), sheds light on the lives of foster children (Sanjek 1990). Child fostering in the neighborhood is common: About one-fourth of the children were foster children. Of the foster children, there were twice as many girls as boys. School attendance is biased toward boys. All of the boys were attending school, but only 4 of the 31 girls were. An important factor affecting the treatment of the child is whether the fostered child is related to his or her sponsor. Although 80 percent of the foster children as a whole were kin of their sponsors, only 50 percent of the girls were kin. People who sponsor nonkin girls make a cash payment to the girl's parents. These girls cook, do housecleaning, and assist in market work by carrying goods or watching the trading area. Fostered boys do not perform such tasks because they attend school.

RITUALLY ESTABLISHED KINSHIP Ritually defined ties between adults and children born to other people are common among Christians, especially Catholics, worldwide. Relationships between godparents and godchildren often involve strong emotional ties and financial flows from the former to the latter.

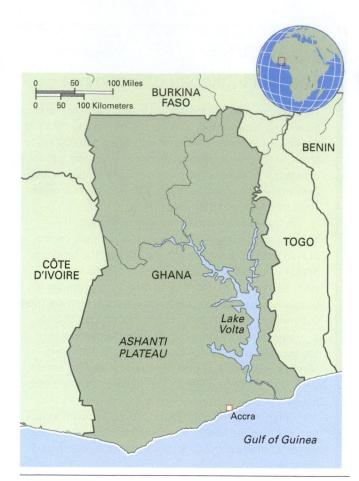

Map 6.4 Ghana.

The Republic of Ghana has over 25 million people. Ghana has rich natural resources and exports gold, timber, and cocoa. Agriculture is the basis of the domestic economy. Several ethnic groups exist, with the Akan people constituting over 40 percent of the population. English is the official language, but another 80 or so languages are also spoken. Over 60 percent of the people are Christian, 20 percent follow traditional religions, and 16 percent are Muslim.

Among the Maya of Oaxaca, Mexico (see Map 4.3, page 75), godparenthood is both a sign of the sponsor's status and the means to increased status for the sponsor (Sault 1985). A parent's request that a particular person sponsor his or her child is a public acknowledgment of the sponsor's standing. The godparent gains influence over the godchild and can call on the godchild for labor. Being a godparent of many children means that the godparent can amass a large labor force when needed and gain further status. Most godparents in Oaxaca are husband–wife couples, but many are women alone, a pattern that reflects the high status of Maya women.

Marriage

The third major basis for forming close interpersonal relationships is through marriage or other forms of "marriage-like" relationships, such as long-term cohabitation. The following material focuses on marriage.

TOWARD A DEFINITION Anthropologists recognize that some concept of marriage exists in all cultures, though it may take different forms and serve different functions. What constitutes a cross-culturally valid definition of marriage is, however, open to debate. A standard definition from 1951 is now discredited: "Marriage is a union between a man and a woman such that children born to the woman are the recognized legitimate offspring of both parents" (Barnard and Good 1984:89). This definition says that the partners must be of different genders, and it implies that a child born outside a marriage is not socially recognized as legitimate. Exceptions exist to both these features cross-culturally. Regarding the gender of partners, same-gender (or same-sex, or gay marriages) are increasingly recognized as legal around the world, from those first to do so (Denmark, Norway, and Holland) to many other countries that now do. The concept of marriage, and its legality, is a lively area of debate in and beyond anthropology (Feinberg 2012).

Regarding the "legitimacy of offspring," many cultures do not define the legitimacy of children on the basis of whether they were born within a marriage. Women in the Caribbean region, for example, typically do not marry until later in life. Before that, a woman has sequential male partners with whom she bears children. None of her children is considered more or less "legitimate" than any other.

Other definitions of marriage focus on rights over the spouse's sexuality. But not all forms of marriage involve sexual relations; for example, the practice of woman–woman marriage exists among the Nuer of South Sudan (see Map 13.6, page 275) and some other African groups (Evans-Pritchard 1951:108–109). In this type of marriage, a woman with economic means gives gifts to obtain a "wife," goes through the marriage rituals with her, and brings her into the residential compound just as a man would who married a woman. This wife contributes her productive labor to the household. The two women do not have a sexual relationship.

A lesbian couple's wedding ceremony in Vancouver, Canada. The rights of LGBT (lesbian, gay, bisexual, and transgender) people are contested around the world. Canada was the first country in the western hemisphere to legalize same-sex marriage.

Instead, the woman who marries into the household will have sexual relations with a man. Her children, though, will belong to the compound into which she married.

The many practices that come under the heading of marriage make it impossible to find a definition that will fit all cases. One might accept the following as a working definition of **marriage**: a more or less stable union, usually between two people, who may be, but are not necessarily, coresidential, sexually involved with each other, and procreative with each other.

SELECTING A SPOUSE All cultures have preferences about whom one should and should not marry or with whom one should and should not have sexual intercourse. Sometimes these preferences are informal and implicit, and other times they are formal and explicit. They include both rules of exclusion (specifying whom one should not marry) and rules of inclusion (specifying who is a preferred marriage partner).

An **incest taboo**, or rule prohibiting marriage or sexual intercourse between certain kinship relations, is one of the most basic and universal rules of exclusion. In his writings of the 1940s, Claude Lévi-Strauss proposes a reason for the universality of incest taboos by saying that, in non-state societies, incest avoidance motivated men to exchange women between families. In his view, this exchange is the foundation for all social networks and social solidarity beyond the immediate group. Such networks promote trade between areas with different resources and peace through ties established by bride exchange. So, for him, the incest taboo has important social and economic functions: It impels people to create social organization beyond the family.

Contemporary genetic research suggests an alternate theory for universal incest taboos. It says that larger breeding pools reduce the frequency of genetically transmitted conditions. Like the theory of Lévi-Strauss, the genetic theory is functional. Each theory attributes the universal existence of incest taboos to their adaptive contribution to human survival and success, though in two different ways. Anthropological data support both theories, but ethnographic data provide some puzzles to consider.

The most basic and universal form of incest taboo is against marriage or sexual intercourse between fathers and their children and between mothers and their children. Although most cultures forbid brother–sister marriage, a few exceptions exist. The most well-known example of brother–sister marriage as an accepted practice comes from Egypt at the time of the Roman Empire (Barnard

---

marriage a union, usually between two people who are likely to be, but are not necessarily, coresident, sexually involved with each other, and procreative.

incest taboo a strongly held prohibition against marrying or having sex with particular kin.

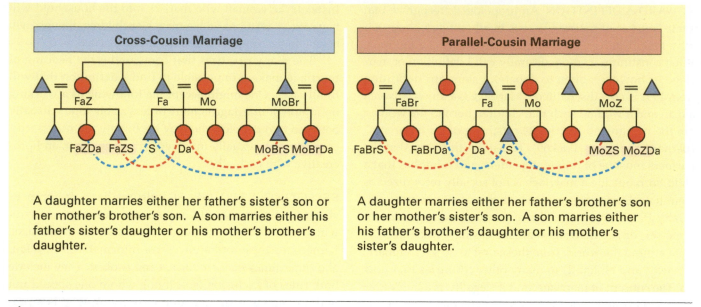

Figure 6.4 Two Types of Cousin Marriage

and Good 1984:92). Brother–sister marriage was the norm among royalty, and it was common among the general population, with between 15 and 20 percent of marriages between full brothers and sisters.

Further variations in close-relation marriage arise with regard to cousins. Incest taboos do not universally rule out marriage with cousins. In fact, some kinship systems promote cousin marriage, as discussed next.

Many preference rules exist cross-culturally concerning whom one should marry. Rules of **endogamy**, or marriage within a particular group, stipulate that the spouse must be from a defined social category. In kin endogamy, certain relatives are preferred, often cousins. Two major forms of cousin marriage exist. One is marriage between **parallel cousins**, either between children of one's father and one's father's brother or between children of one's mother and one's mother's sister—the term parallel indicates that the linking siblings are of the same gender (Figure 6.4). Parallel-cousin marriage is favored by many Muslim groups in the Middle East and northern Africa. The second form of cousin marriage is between **cross-cousins**, either between children of one's father and one's father's sister or between children of one's mother and one's mother's brother—the term cross indicates the different genders of the linking siblings. Hindus of southern India favor cross-cousin marriage. Although cousin marriage is preferred, it nonetheless is a minority of all marriages in the region. A survey of several thousand couples in the city of Chennai (formerly called Madras) in southern India showed that three-fourths of all marriages involved unrelated people, whereas one-fourth were between first cross-cousins or between uncle and niece, which is considered to be the same relationship as that of cross-cousins (Ramesh et al. 1989).

Readers who are unfamiliar with cousin marriage may find it objectionable on the basis of the potential genetic disabilities from close inbreeding. A study of thousands of such marriages in southern India, however, revealed only a small difference in rates of congenital problems compared to cultures in which cousin marriage is not practiced (Sundar Rao 1983). Marriage networks are diffuse, extending over a wide area and offering many options for "cousins." This situation contrasts to the much more closed situation of a single village or town. In cases where cousin marriage exists among a small and circumscribed population, the possibility of negative genetic effects is high.

Endogamy may also be based on location. Village endogamy is preferred in the eastern Mediterranean among both Christians and Muslims. It is also the preferred pattern among Muslims throughout India and among Hindus of southern India. Hindus of northern India, in contrast, forbid village endogamy and consider it a form of incest. Instead, they practice village **exogamy**, or marriage outside a defined social group. For them, a spouse should live in a far-off village or town. In India, marriage distance is greater in the north than in the south, and northern brides are thus far less likely to be able to maintain regular contact with their birth family. Many songs and stories of northern Indian women convey sadness about being separated from their birth families.

---

endogamy marriage within a particular group or locality.

parallel cousin offspring of either one's father's brother or one's mother's sister.

cross-cousin offspring of either one's father's sister or one's mother's brother.

exogamy marriage outside a particular group or locality.

Status considerations often shape spouse selection (Figure 6.5). (The following discussion pertains to hetero-sexual marriage.) Hypergyny, or "marrying up," refers to a marriage in which the bride's status is lower than the groom's. Hypergyny is widely practiced in northern India, especially among upper-status groups. It is also promi-nent among many middle- and upper-class people in the United States. Because of hypergyny, women in top pro-fessions such as medicine and law—especially women medical students in North America—have a difficult time finding appropriate partners, since there are few, if any, options for them to "marry up." The opposite pattern is hypogyny, or "marrying down," a marriage in which the bride has higher status than the groom. Hypogyny is rare cross-culturally. Isogamy, marriage between partners who are status equals, occurs in cultures where male and female roles and status are equal.

Subtypes of status-based hypergyny and hypogyny occur on the basis of factors such as age and even height. Age hypergyny refers to a marriage in which the bride is younger than the groom, a common practice world-wide. In contrast, age hypogyny is a marriage in which the bride is older than the groom. Age hypogyny is rare cross-culturally but has been increasing in the United States due to the marriage squeeze on women who would otherwise prefer a husband of equal age or some-what older.

Physical features, such as ability, looks, and appear-ance, are factors that may be explicitly or implicitly involved in spouse selection. Facial beauty, skin color, hair texture and length, height, and weight are vari-ously defined as important. Height hypergyny (in which the groom is taller than the bride) is more common in male-dominated contexts. Height-isogamous marriages are common in cultures where gender roles are relatively equal and where sexual dimorphism (differences in shape and size of the female body compared with the male body) is not marked, as in much of Southeast Asia.

The role of romantic love in spouse selection is debated by biological determinists and cultural constructionists. Biological determinists argue that feelings of romantic love are universal among humans because they play an adap-tive role in uniting males and females in offspring care. Cultural constructionists, in contrast, argue that cross-culturally romantic love is an unusual factor influencing spouse selection (Barnard and Good 1984:94). The cultural

constructionists point to variations in male and female economic roles to explain cross-cultural differences in the emphasis on romantic love. Romantic love is more likely to be an important factor in relationships in cultures where men contribute more to livelihood and where women are therefore economically dependent on men. Whatever the cause of romantic love, biological or cultural or both, it is an increasingly common basis for marriage in many cultures (Levine et al. 1995).

Within the United States, microcultural variations exist in the degree to which women value romantic love as a basis for marriage (Holland and Eisenhart 1990). One study interviewed young American women enter-ing college from 1979 to 1981 and again in 1987 after they had graduated and begun their adult lives. The research sites were two southern colleges in the United States, one attended mainly by White Euro-Americans and the other by African Americans. A contrast between the groups of women emerged. The White women were much more influenced by notions of romantic love than the Black women were. The White women were also less likely to have strong career goals and more likely to expect to be economically dependent on their spouse. The Black women expressed independence and strong career goals. The theme of romantic love supplies young White women with a model of the heroic male provider as the ideal, with her role being one of attracting him and pro-viding the domestic context for their married life. The Black women were brought up to be more economically independent. This pattern is related both to African tra-ditions in which women earn and manage their own earnings and to the racially discriminatory job market in the United States that places African American men at a severe disadvantage.

Arranged marriages are formed on the basis of par-ents' considerations of what constitutes a "good match" between the families of the bride and groom. Arranged marriages are common in many Middle Eastern, Afri-can, and Asian countries. Some theorists claim that arranged marriages are "traditional" and love mar-riages are "modern." They believe that arranged mar-riages will disappear with modernity. Japan presents a case of an industrial/digital economy with a highly educated population in which arranged marriages, as of the mid-1990s, constituted about 25 to 30 percent of all marriages (Applbaum 1995). Following the tsunami and

Hypergyny	The bride marries a groom of higher status.	The groom may be wealthier, more educated, older, taller.
Hypogyny	The bride marries a groom of lower status.	The bride may be wealthier, more educated, older, taller.
Isogamy	The bride and groom are status equals.	The bride and groom have similar wealth, education, age, height.

Figure 6.5 **Status Considerations in Partner Selection (Heterosexual Pairing)**

	Type	Where Practiced
Dowry	Goods and money given by the bride's family to the married couple	Europe and Asia; agriculturalists and industrialists
Groomprice	A form of dowry: goods and money given by the bride's family to the married couple and to the parents of the groom	South Asia, especially northern India
Brideprice (or bride-wealth)	Goods and money given by the groom's family to the parents of the bride	Asia, Africa, and Central and South America; horticulturalists and pastoralists
Brideservice	Labor given by the groom to the parents of the bride	Southeast Asia, the Pacific, and Amazonia; horticulturalists

Figure 6.6 Types of Marriage Exchanges

nuclear disaster of 2010, it appears that arranged marriages have risen in popularity to 40 percent of all marriages, perhaps due to increased challenges in traveling and a heightened sense of loneliness and personal insecurity (Millward 2012). The most important criteria for a spouse in Japan are the family's reputation and social standing; the absence of undesirable traits, such as a case of divorce or mental illness in the family; education; occupation; and income.

MARRIAGE GIFTS Most marriages are accompanied by exchanges of goods or services between the families of the bride and groom (Figure 6.6). The two major forms of marital exchanges cross-culturally are dowry and brideprice. **Dowry** is the transfer of goods, and sometimes money, from the bride's side to the new married couple for their use. The dowry includes household goods such as furniture, cooking utensils, and, sometimes, rights to a house. Dowry is the main form of marriage transfer in farming societies throughout Eurasia, from Western Europe through the northern Mediterranean and into China and India. In much of India, dowry is more accurately termed groomprice, because much of the goods and money pass not to the new couple but rather to the groom's family (Billig 1992). In China during the Mao era, the government considered dowry a sign of women's oppression and made it illegal. The practice of giving dowry in China has returned with increased personal wealth and consumerism, especially among the newly rich urban populations (Whyte 1993).

Brideprice, or bridewealth, is the transfer of goods or money from the groom's side to the bride's parents. It is common in horticultural and pastoralist cultures. **Brideservice**, a subtype of brideprice, is the transfer of labor from the groom to his parents-in-law for a designated period. It is practiced in some horticultural societies, especially in the Amazon.

Many marriages involve balanced gifts from both the bride's and the groom's side. A long-standing pattern in the United States places the major burden of the costs of

The Hausa are an important ethnic group of Ghana. This photograph shows a display of Hausa dowry goods in Accra, the capital city. The most valuable part of a Hausa bride's dowry is the *kayan dak'i* ("things of the room"), consisting of bowls, pots, ornamental glass, and cookware, which are conspicuously displayed in the bride's marital house so that the local women can get a sense of her worth. The bride's parents pay for these status items and for utilitarian items such as everyday cooking utensils.

dowry the transfer of cash and goods from the bride's family to the newly married couple.

brideprice the transfer of cash and goods from the groom's family to the bride's family and to the bride.

brideservice a form of marriage exchange in which the groom works for his father-in-law for a certain length of time before returning home with the bride.

the wedding and honeymoon on the bride's side, with the groom's side responsible for paying for the rehearsal dinner the night before the wedding. A trend toward shared costs by the bride and groom may indicate more equal relations in the marriage as well.

FORMS OF MARRIAGE Cultural anthropologists distinguish two forms of marriage on the basis of the number of partners involved. **Monogamy** is marriage between two people—a male or female if the pair is heterosexual, or two people of the same gender in the case of a homosexual pair. Heterosexual monogamy is the most common form of marriage cross-culturally, and in many countries it is the only legal form of marriage.

Polygamy is marriage involving multiple spouses, a pattern allowed in many cultures. Two forms of polygamous marriage exist. The more common of the two is **polygyny**, marriage of one man with more than one woman. **Polyandry**, or marriage between one woman and more than one man, is rare. The only place where polyandry is commonly found is in the Himalayan region that includes parts of Tibet, India, and Nepal. Nonpolyandrous people in the area look down on the people who practice polyandrous marriage as backward (Haddix McCay 2001).

Households and Domestic Life

6.2 **Recognize how anthropologists define and study households and domestic life.**

In casual conversation, North Americans might use the words family and household interchangeably to refer to people who live together. Social scientists, however, propose a distinction between the two terms. A **family** is a group of people who consider themselves related through kinship. In North American English, the term may include both "close" and "distant" relatives. All members of a family do not necessarily live together or have strong bonds with one another. But they are still "family."

A related term is the **household**, either a person living alone or one or more persons who occupy a shared living space and who may or may not be related by kinship. Most households consist of members who are related through kinship, but an increasing number do not. An example of a nonkin household is a group of friends who live in the same apartment. This section of the chapter looks at household forms and organization cross-culturally and at relationships between and among household members.

A polyandrous household in Nepal.

The Household: Variations on a Theme

Anthropologists define three forms of households, and they study the concept of household headship.

Household organization is divided into types according to how many married adults are involved. The **nuclear household** (which many people call the nuclear family) is a domestic group that contains one adult couple (married or "partners"), with or without children. An **extended household** is a domestic group that contains more than one adult married couple. The couples may be related through the father–son line (making a patrilineal extended household), through the mother–daughter line (a matrilineal extended household), or through sisters or brothers (a collateral extended household). Polygynous (multiple wives) and polyandrous (multiple husbands) households are complex households, domestic units in which one spouse lives with or near multiple partners and their children.

The precise cross-cultural distribution of these various types of households is not known, but some broad generalizations can be offered. First, nuclear households are found in all cultures but are the preferred household type in only about one-fourth of the world's cultures (Murdock 1965

---

monogamy marriage between two people.

polygamy marriage involving multiple spouses.

polygyny marriage of one husband with more than one wife.

polyandry marriage of one wife with more than one husband.

family a group of people who consider themselves related through a form of kinship, such as descent, marriage, or sharing.

household either one person living alone or a group of people who may or may not be related by kinship and who share living space.

nuclear household a domestic unit containing one adult couple (married or partners) with or without children.

extended household a coresidential group that comprises more than one parent–child unit.

[1949]:2). Extended households are the most important form in about half of all cultures. The distribution of these two household forms corresponds roughly with the modes of livelihood (see Figure 6.1, page 112). The nuclear form is most characteristic of economies at the two extremes of the continuum: foraging groups and industrial/digital societies. This pattern reflects the need for spatial mobility and flexibility in both modes of livelihood. Extended households constitute a substantial proportion of households in horticultural, pastoralist, and agricultural economies.

Intrahousehold Dynamics

How do household members interact with each other? What are their emotional attachments, rights, and responsibilities? What are the power relationships between and among members of various categories, such as spouses, siblings, and those of different generations? Kinship systems define what the content of these relationships should be. In everyday life, people may conform more or less to the ideal.

SPOUSE–PARTNER RELATIONSHIPS This section discusses two areas of spousal relationships: marital satisfaction and sexual activity over the life course.

A landmark study of marriages in Tokyo in 1959 compared marital satisfaction of husbands and wives in love marriages and in arranged marriages (Blood 1967). In all marriages, marital satisfaction declined over time, but differences between the two types emerged. The decline was greatest for wives in arranged marriages and least for husbands in arranged marriages. In love-match marriages, both partners' satisfaction dropped dramatically (a bit earlier for wives and a bit later for husbands), but both husbands and wives reported nearly equal levels of satisfaction after they had been married nine years or more.

Sexual activity of couples can be both an indication and a cause of marital satisfaction. Analysis of reports of marital

The stem household is still common in rural areas of China and Taiwan, but the nuclear household is on the rise. Sons still try to be responsible for their parents by hosting them for visits, providing meals, and making sure they are cared for in their old age.

sex from a 1988 survey in the United States shows that frequency per month declines steadily with the duration of marriage, from an average of 12 times per month for people ages 19 to 24 years to less than once a month for people 75 years of age and older (Call, Sprecher, and Schwartz 1995). Older married people have sex less frequently. Less happy people have sex less frequently. Within each age category, sex is more frequent among three categories of people:

- Those who are cohabiting but not married
- Those who cohabited before marriage
- Those who are in their second or later marriage

SIBLING RELATIONSHIPS Sibling relationships are an understudied aspect of intrahousehold dynamics. One example comes from research in a working-class neighborhood of Beirut, Lebanon (Joseph 1994). The anthropologist became friendly with several families and was especially close to Hanna, the oldest son in one of them. Hanna was an attractive young man, considered a good marriage choice, with friends across religious and ethnic groups. Therefore, the author reports her shock when she once heard Hanna shouting at his 12-year-old sister Flaur and slapping her across the face. Further observation of the relationship between the two suggested that Hanna was playing a fatherly role to Flaur. He was especially irritated with her if she lingered on the street near their apartment building, gossiping with other girls: "He would forcibly escort her upstairs to their apartment, slap her, and demand that she behave with dignity" (1994:51). Adults in the household thought nothing was wrong. They said that Flaur enjoyed her brother's aggressive attention. Flaur herself commented, "It doesn't even hurt when Hanna hits me." She said that she hoped to have a husband like Hanna.

An interpretation of this kind of brother–sister relationship, common in Arab culture, is that it is part of a socialization process that maintains and perpetuates male domination in the household: "Hanna was teaching Flaur to accept male power in the name of love . . . loving his sister meant taking charge of her and that he could discipline her if his action was understood to be in her interest. Flaur was reinforced in learning that the love of a man could include that male's violent control and that to receive his love involved submission to control" (1994:52).

DOMESTIC VIOLENCE BETWEEN PARTNERS Violence between domestic partners, with males dominating as perpetrators and women as victims, is found in nearly all cultures, although in varying forms and frequencies (Brown 1999). Wife beating is more common and more severe in contexts where men control the wealth. It is less common and less severe where women's work groups and social networks exist. The presence of women's work groups is related to a greater importance of women in livelihoods

Anthropology Works

Preventing Wife Abuse in Rural Kentucky

Domestic violence in the United States is reportedly highest in the state of Kentucky. Ethnographic study of domestic violence in Kentucky reveals several cultural factors related to the high rate of wife abuse (Websdale 1995). The study included interviews with 50 abused wives in eastern Kentucky, police officers, shelter employees, and social workers.

Three categories of isolation exist in rural Kentucky that make domestic violence particularly difficult to prevent:

1. Physical isolation: The women reported a feeling of physical isolation in their lives. Abusers' tactics were more effective because of geographical isolation. Tactics include disabling motor vehicles so the wife cannot leave the residence, destroying motor vehicles, monitoring odometer readings on motor vehicles, driving recklessly to intimidate the wife, and discharging firearms at, for example, a pet.

It is difficult or impossible for an abused woman to leave a home located many miles from the nearest paved road, especially if the woman has children. In rural Kentucky, no public transportation serves even the paved road. Nearly one-third of households at the time of the study had no phones. Getting to a phone to report abuse results in delay, gives police the impression that the call is less serious, and increases a woman's sense of hopelessness. Sheriffs have a reputation for not attending to domestic calls.

2. Social isolation: Gender roles promote a system of "passive policing." Men are seen as providers, and women are tied to domestic work and child rearing. When women do work outside the home, their wages are about 50 percent of men's wages. Marital residence is often in the vicinity of the husband's family. Thus, a woman is separated from the potential support of her natal family and is limited in seeking help in the immediate vicinity because the husband's family is likely to not be supportive of her. Local police officers view the family as a private unit, so they are not inclined to intervene in family problems. Because the home is the man's world and men are supposed to be dominant in the family, police are unwilling to arrest husbands accused of abuse. In some instances, the police take the batterer's side because they share the belief in a husband's right to control his wife.

3. Institutional isolation: Social services for battered women in Kentucky are scarce, especially in rural areas. The fact that abused women often know the people who run the services ironically inhibits the women from approaching them, given the value of family privacy. Other institutional constraints include low levels of schooling; lack of childcare centers to allow mothers the option to work outside the home; inadequate health services; and religious teaching of fundamentalist Christianity, which supports values such as the idea that it is a woman's duty to stay in a marriage and "weather the storm."

These findings suggest some recommendations. First, rural women need more and better employment opportunities to reduce their economic dependency on abusive partners. To address this need, rural outreach programs should be strengthened. Expanded telephone subscriptions would decrease rural women's institutional isolation. Because of the complexity of the social situation in Kentucky, however, no single solution will be sufficient.

Food for Thought

Since the study was conducted, cell phone use has expanded worldwide. Will cell phones be likely to reduce women's isolation in rural Kentucky?

Map 6.5 **Kentucky, United States**

Located in the southeastern United States, in the Appalachian region, Kentucky's population is over four million. It has more farmers per square mile than any other state. Per capita income is 47th in the 50 states. Before being occupied by British settlers in the late eighteenth century, Kentucky was the hunting grounds of the Shawnees and Cherokees. The current population is about 91 percent White, 7 percent Black, 0.6 percent American Indian, and 0.9 percent Asian. Kentucky is known for thoroughbred horse breeding and racing, bourbon and whiskey distilling, barbeque, and bluegrass music.

A widow and her son at a shelter in Nepal where widows are often rejected by their husband's family, cannot return to their family of birth, and are socially marginalized.

and a kinship system that keeps women together. These factors provide women with the means to leave an abusive relationship. For example, among the Garifuna (guh-REE-fuh-nuh), the African–Indian people of Belize, Central America, incidents of spouse abuse occur, but they are infrequent and not extended (Kerns 1999).

Increased domestic violence worldwide throws into question the notion of the house as a refuge or place. In the United States, evidence indicates high and increasing rates of intrahousehold abuse of children (including sexual abuse), violence between spouses or partners, and abuse of aged family members. Anthropological research helps policy makers and social workers better understand the factors affecting the safety of individuals within households so that they are able to design more effective programs to promote personal safety (see Anthropology Works).

HOUSEHOLDS WITHOUT A HOME The definition of a household includes "sharing a living space." In most cultures, that means a "home" of some sort—a structure in which people prepare and share meals, sleep, and spend time with each other in a secure environment. The ideal of a household living in a home is increasingly out of reach of millions of people around the world. The major reasons for homelessness, of families and individuals, are: poverty, warfare and conflict, natural disasters, mental illness and other disabilities, substance abuse, and domestic violence.

Addressing these causes, to prevent homelessness, is of critical importance. At the same time, providing services for those who are homeless is essential and must be based on knowledge about particular people's situation, potentials, and needs. Cultural anthropologist Philippe Bourgois and photographer Jeff Schonberg collaborated, in an effort they call photoethnography, to produce a book about homeless people in San Francisco who are addicted to

heroin (2009). They followed 12 people to learn about how they became homeless, how they cope with social marginality and addiction, and the social bonds they create with other homeless people. It is impossible to reduce the many lessons of their book into a few sentences here, but one takeaway is that, in the immediate term, social policies are needed to promote harm reduction through providing safe injection places and clean needle programs for addicts. Providing such care for homeless addicts is something that many countries are doing. Perhaps making it more possible for more people to live in homes would help, too.

A Syrian refugee family in Lebanon. Since the Syrian conflict began, more than two million Syrians have fled to neighboring countries. The number of Syrians displaced within the country is estimated at 6.5 million. In all, nearly half the population of Syria have had to leave their homes.

Changing Kinship and Household Dynamics

6.3 Illustrate how kinship and households are changing.

This section provides examples of how kinship and household patterns are changing. Many of these changes have roots in colonialism, whereas others are the result of recent changes caused by globalization.

Change in Descent

Matrilineal descent is declining worldwide as a result of both European colonialism and contemporary Western globalization. European colonial rule in Africa and Asia contributed to the decline in matrilineal kinship by registering land and other property in the names of assumed male heads of household, even where females were the heads (Boserup 1970). This process eroded women's previous rights and powers. Western missionaries contributed further to transforming matrilineal cultures into patrilineal systems (Etienne and Leacock 1980). For example, European colonial influences led to the decline of matrilineal kinship among Native North Americans. Before European colonialism, North America had one of the largest distributions of matrilineal descent worldwide. A comparative study of kinship among three reservation-based Navajo groups in Arizona shows that matrilineality is stronger where conditions most resemble the pre-reservation era (Levy et al. 1989).

Among the Minangkabau of Indonesia (review Culturama, this chapter), three factors explain the decline of matrilineal kinship (Blackwood 1995):

- Dutch colonialism promoted the image of male-headed nuclear families as an ideal.
- Islamic teachings idealize women as wives and men as household heads.
- The modernizing Indonesian state has a policy of naming males as household heads.

Change in Marriage

Although the institution of marriage in general remains prominent, many of its details, including courtship, the marriage ceremony, and marital relationships, are changing. New forms of communication are profoundly affecting courtship. In a village in western Nepal (see Map 5.5, page 105) people's stories of their marriages reveal that arranged marriages have decreased and elopement has increased since the 1990s.

Nearly everywhere, the age at first marriage is rising. The later age at marriage is related to increased emphasis on completing a certain number of years of education before marriage and to higher material aspirations, such as being able to own a house. Marriages between people of different countries and ethnicities are increasing, partly because of growing rates of international migration. Migrants take with them many of their marriage and family practices. They also adapt to rules and practices in their area of destination. Pluralistic practices evolve, such as conducting two marriage ceremonies—one conforming to the "original" culture and the other to the culture in the place of destination.

A marriage crisis is a cultural situation in which many people who want to marry cannot do so for one reason or another. Marriage crises are more frequent now than in the past, at least as perceived and reported by young people in the so-called marriage market. Throughout much of sub-Saharan Africa, many young men are unable to raise enough money for the brideprice and other marriage expenses. The reason these days often has to do with high rates of unemployment. A case study in a town of about 38,000 people in Niger, West Africa, illustrates these points (Masquelier 2005). Among the Mawri, who are Muslim, marriage is the crucial ritual that changes a boy into a man. The economy has been declining for some time, and typical farm or other wages are worth less than they were in earlier

A beluga whale watches while a Japanese couple holds a wedding ceremony at an aquarium in Yokohama, Japan. The ceremony, called "Dolphin Wedding," costs nearly $3,000 for 15 minutes and a maximum of 60 attendees.

What is your fantasy for a special wedding setting? How much would you be willing to pay for it? Consider how your culture may be shaping your answers to these questions.

times. Marriage costs for the groom, however, have risen. While wealthy young men can afford to give a car to the bride's parents, most young Mawri men cannot afford even a standard brideprice. They remain sitting at home in their parents' house, something that, ordinarily, only females do. The many young, marriage-age women who remain single gain a reputation of being immoral, occupying a new and suspect social space between girl and wife. In China, a different kind of marriage crisis exists and is growing. Population experts project that, by 2020, about two million men in China will not be able to find a woman to marry. This situation is due to the one-child policy, the preference for sons, and the resulting unbalanced sex ratio (*Global Times* 2010).

Weddings are important, culture-revealing events. Style changes in weddings worldwide abound, and they all mean something in terms of the choices people make to mark the event. Factors to consider in examining changes in wedding styles are the ceremony, costs, appropriate clothing, and the possibility of a honeymoon. The Western-style white wedding, so-named because the bride wears a white dress, is spreading around the world, though with fascinating local adaptations in terms of its features, including what the bride and groom wear, the design of the wedding cake, floral displays, and more. Throughout Asia, advertisements and upscale stores display the Western-style white wedding gown, but not in India, where white clothing for women signifies widowhood and is inauspicious. A resurgence of local, folksy styles is occurring in some contexts. In Morocco, for example, an urban bride may wear a Western-style white gown for one part of the wedding ceremony and an "exotic" Berber costume (long robes and ornate silver jewelry characteristic of the mountain pastoralists) at another stage of the ceremony. The blending of Western and non-Western elements signals a family's complex identity in a globalizing world.

Changing Households

Globalization is creating rapid change in household structure and intrahousehold dynamics. One assumption is that the frequency of extended households will decline with industrialization and urbanization and the frequency of nuclear households will rise. Given what this chapter mentioned earlier about the relationship between nuclear households and industrial/digital societies, it is highly possible that the spread of this mode of livelihood will cause an increase in the number of nuclear households, too.

This projection finds strong confirmation in the changes that have occurred in household structure among the Kelabit (kell-uh-bit) people of highland Borneo since the early 1990s

(LEFT) A modern-style Kelabit longhouse built in the 1990s. It is the home of six families who formerly lived in a 20-family longhouse, seen in the background, that is being dismantled. (RIGHT) Since the 1990s, houses built for a nuclear unit have proliferated in the highlands. These houses stand on the site of a former multiunit longhouse.

(Amster 2000). One Kelabit settlement was founded in 1963 near the Indonesian border. At the time, everyone lived in one longhouse with over 20 family units. It was a "modern" longhouse, thanks to roofing provided by the British army and the innovation of private sleeping areas. Like more traditional longhouses, though, it was an essentially egalitarian living space within which individuals could freely move. Today, that longhouse is no more. Most of the young people have migrated to coastal towns and work in jobs related to the offshore oil industry. Most houses are now single-unit homes with an emphasis on privacy. The elders complain of a "bad silence" in the village. No one looks after visitors with the old style of hospitality. There is no longer one common longhouse for communal feasts and rituals.

International migration is another major cause of change in household formation and internal relationships (discussed further in Chapter 12). A dramatic decline in fertility can occur in one generation when members of a farming household in, for example, Taiwan or Egypt migrate to England, France, Canada, or the United States. Having many children makes economic sense in their homeland, but not in the new destination. Many such migrants decide to have only one or two children. They tend to live in small, isolated nuclear households. International migration creates new challenges for relationships between parents and children. The children often become strongly identified with the new culture and have little connection with their ancestral culture. This rupture creates anxiety for the parents and conflict between children and parents over issues such as dating, dress, and career goals.

The shape of households is also changing. In the United States, at the beginning of the twenty-first century, three kinds of households are most common: households composed of couples living in their first marriage, single-parent households, and households formed through remarriage. A rising fourth category is the multigenerational household, a form of extended household, in which an adult child lives with his or her parent or parents. In the United States, the economic downturn appears to be related to the fact that the number of Americans living in multigenerational households rose by 5 percent from 2007 to 2008 (Pew Center 2010). The increase in multigenerational households began in the 1980s with the influx of immigrants, but it clearly accelerated during the economic crisis. Now 16 percent of the population lives in homes with multiple generations. Marriage age for young adults has risen as well, and these unmarried young people are most likely to live with their parent or parents. A fifth category is also emerging, related to the ever-rising age at which many women have children. Called late-forming families, this reproductive pattern corresponds with many women's career aspirations (Konvalinka 2013). One downside, in terms of child care, is that children in late-forming families cannot benefit from care and socialization from grandparents since they are often quite old by the time the grandchildren are growing up. Kinship, households, and domestic life are certainly not dull or static topics. Just trying to keep up with changing patterns in North America is a daunting task, to say nothing of tracking changes, and their causes, worldwide.

6   Learning Objectives Revisited

6.1   Define the three ways cultures create kinship.

Key differences exist between unilineal and bilineal descent systems. Within unilineal systems, further important variations exist between patrilineal and matrilineal systems in terms of property inheritance, residence rules for married couples, and the relative status of males and females. Worldwide, unilineal systems are more common than bilineal systems. Within unilineal kinship systems, patrilineal kinship is more common than matrilineal kinship.

A second important basis for kinship is sharing. Sharing one's child with someone else through either informal or formal processes is probably a cultural universal. Sharing-based kinship is created through food transfers, including breastfeeding (in some cultures, children breastfed by the same woman are considered kin and cannot marry). Ritualized sharing creates kinship, as in the case of godparenthood.

The third basis for kinship is marriage, another universal factor, even though definitions of marriage may differ substantially. All cultures have rules of exclusion and preference rules for spouses. These rules affect factors such as kinship relationships of potential spouses, region, class, wealth, education, perceptions of "looks," and more.

6.2   Recognize how anthropologists define and study households and domestic life.

A household may consist of a single person living alone or may be a group comprising more than one person, each of whom may or may not be related by kinship; these individuals share a living space and, often, financial responsibilities for the household.

Nuclear households consist of a mother and father and their children, but they also can be just a husband and wife without children. Nuclear households are found in all cultures but are most common in foraging and industrial/digital societies. Extended households include more than one nuclear household. They are most commonly found in cultures with a unilineal kinship system.

Household headship can be shared between two partners or can be borne by a single person, as in a woman-headed household. Studies of intrahousehold dynamics between parents and children and among siblings reveal complex power relationships as well as sharing and, sometimes, violence.

6.3 Illustrate how kinship and households are changing.

Recent forces of change, starting with European colonialism and now globalization, have had, and continue to have, marked effects on kinship formation and household patterns and dynamics. Matrilineal systems have been declining in distribution since European colonialist expansion began in the 1500s.

Many aspects of marriage are changing, including a trend toward later age at marriage in many low-income countries. Although marriage continues to be an important basis for the formation of nuclear and extended households, other options (such as cohabitation) are increasing in importance in many contexts, including urban areas in high-income countries. Wedding ceremonies provide a window into cultures and how they are changing. The globalizing white wedding is simultaneously being localized to fit with existing cultural values and practices.

Contemporary changes in kinship and in household formation raise several serious questions for the future, perhaps most importantly about the care of dependent members such as children, the aged, and disabled people. As fertility rates decline and average household size shrinks, kinship-based entitlements to basic needs and emotional support disappear.

Key Concepts

bilineal descent, p. 114
brideprice, p. 122
brideservice, p. 122
cross-cousin, p. 120
descent, p. 114
dowry, p. 122
endogamy, p. 120
exogamy, p. 120

extended household, p. 123
family, p. 123
household, p. 123
incest taboo, p. 119
kinship system, p. 111
marriage, p. 119
matrilineal descent, p. 116
monogamy, p. 123

nuclear household, p. 123
parallel cousin, p. 120
patrilineal descent, p. 116
polyandry, p. 123
polygamy, p. 123
polygyny, p. 123
unilineal descent, p. 114

Thinking Outside the Box

1. Do some research on Match.com or Chemistry.com to learn what cultural preferences people mention in their profiles.

2. What is your opinion about the relative merits of love marriages versus arranged marriages, and on what do you base your opinion?

3. In your microculture, what are the prevailing ideas about wedding expenses and who should pay for them?

Chapter 7
Social Groups and Social Stratification

 Outline

Social Groups

Think Like an Anthropologist: Making Friends

Social Stratification

Culturama: The Roma of Eastern Europe

Civil Society

Anthropology Works: Forensic Anthropology for the Maya of Guatemala

Learning Objectives

7.1 Explain what social groups are.

7.2 Define what is included in the term social stratification.

7.3 Discuss the concept of civil society.

Anthro Connections

The concept of the Uyghur (wee-ger) as a distinct people and a sense of their national identity emerged among Uyghur intellectuals during the early twentieth century, prompted by anti-colonialist sentiments against both the Chinese and Russians (Roberts 2010).

Tension continues to exist across the Uyghur region in Northwest China. At the same time, Uyghur cities such as Urumqi are emerging as important sites of Uyghur entrepreneurship (Harlan and Webber 2012).

In the early 1800s, when French political philosopher Alexis de Tocqueville visited the United States and characterized it as a "nation of joiners," he implied that people in some cultures are more likely to join groups than are people in other cultures. The questions of what motivates people to join groups, what holds people together in groups, and how groups deal with leadership and participation have intrigued scholars in many fields for centuries.

This chapter covers nonkin groups and nonkin microculture formation. Chapter 1 defines several factors related to microcultures: class, "race," ethnicity, indigeneity, gender, age, and institutions such as prisons and retirement homes. This chapter looks at how microcultures shape group identity and organization and the relationships among different groups in terms of hierarchy and power. It first examines a variety of social groups ranging from small scale to large scale and then considers inequalities among social groups. The last section presents the concept of civil society and examples of it.

Social Groups

7.1 Explain what social groups are.

A **social group** is a cluster of people beyond the household unit who are usually related on a basis other than kinship, although kinship relationships may exist between people in the group. Two basic categories exist: the **primary group**, consisting of people who interact with each other and know each other personally, and the **secondary group**, consisting of people who identify with one another on some common ground but who may never meet with one another or interact with each other personally.

Members of all social groups have a sense of rights and responsibilities in relation to the group. Membership

in a primary group, because of the face-to-face interaction, involves more direct accountability about rights and responsibilities than does membership in a secondary group.

Modes of livelihood affect the formation of social groups, with the greatest variety of groups found in agricultural and industrial/digital societies (Figure 7.1). One theory explaining this pattern is that mobile populations, such as foragers and pastoralists, are less likely to develop enduring social groups beyond kin relationships simply because they have lower population density and less continuous social interaction than more settled populations have. Although foragers and pastoralists have fewer types of social groups, they do not completely lack social groupings. A prominent form of social group among foragers and pastoralists is an **age set**, a group of people close in age who go through certain rituals, such as circumcision, at the same time.

Many informal and formal groups have been prominent throughout sub-Sahara Africa, Latin America, and Southeast Asia, in accordance with the generalization that settled populations have the social density to support such groups. In contrast, such groups were less prominent in South Asia, a region that includes Pakistan, India,

---

social group a cluster of people beyond the domestic unit who are usually related on grounds other than kinship.

primary group a social group in which members meet on a face-to-face basis.

secondary group a group of people who identify with one another on some basis but may never meet with one another personally.

age set a group of people close in age who go through certain rituals, such as circumcision, at the same time.

Foraging	Horticulture	Pastoralism	Agriculture	Industrial/Digital
Characteristics Informal and primary Egalitarian structure Ties based on balanced exchange		Ritual ties	**Characteristics** Formal and secondary Recognized leadership Dues and fees	**Characteristics**
Functions Companionship			Special purposes Work, war, lobbying government	**Functions**
Types Friendship	Friendship Age-based work groups Gender-based work groups		Status Groups: Class, "race," ethnicity, caste, age, gender Institutional Groups: Prisons, retirement homes Quasi-Political Groups: Human rights, environmental groups	**Types** Friendship Urban youth gangs Clubs, associations

Figure 7.1 **Modes of Livelihood and Social Groups**

Nepal, Bhutan, Bangladesh, and Sri Lanka, until the later part of the twentieth century. In Bangladesh (Map 7.1), for example, a densely populated and agrarian country of South Asia, indigenous social groups were rare. The most prominent ties beyond the immediate household were kinship based (Miller and Khan 1986). In spite of the lack of indigenous social groups, Bangladesh has gained world renown since the later twentieth century for its success in forming local groups through an organization called the Grameen Bank, which offers microcredit (small loans) to poor people to help them start small businesses. Likewise, throughout the rest of South Asia, since the later twentieth century, the rise of numerous active social groups is remarkable, including those dedicated to preserving traditional environmental knowledge, promoting women and children's health and survival, advocating for lesbian and gay rights, and poverty alleviation. The explanation for the rise of many of these groups lies in the global trend of nongovernmental groups to agitate for change in government policies and programs and to address problems that governments have overlooked.

This section describes a variety of social groups, starting with the most face-to-face, primary groups comprising two or three people based on friendship. It then moves to larger and more formal groups, such as countercultural groups and activist groups.

Friendship

Friendship refers to close social ties between at least two people in which the ties are informal, voluntary,

and involve personal, face-to-face interaction. Generally, friendship involves people who are nonkin, but in some cases kin are also friends. (Recall the Tory Islanders

Map 7.1 **Bangladesh**

The People's Republic of Bangladesh is located on a deltaic floodplain with rich soil and risk of flooding. One of the world's most densely populated countries, Bangladesh has around 160 million people living in an area about the size of the state of Wisconsin. Bangladesh is the world's third largest Muslim-majority country and the eighth largest country in the world in terms of population.

Think Like an Anthropologist
Making Friends

People's daily activities are often the basis of friendship ties. In Andalucia, southern Spain (see Map 2.4 on page 37), men and women pursue separate kinds of work and, relatedly, have different friendship patterns (Uhl 1991). Men's work takes place outside the house and neighborhood, either in the fields or in manufacturing jobs. Women devote most of their time to unpaid household work within the domestic domain. This dichotomy is somewhat fluid, however, as women's domestic roles sometimes take them to the market or the town hall.

For men, an important category of friend is an *amigo*, a friend with whom one casually interacts. This kind of friendship is acted out and maintained in bars where men drink together nightly. Bars are a man's world. Amigos share common experiences of school, sports and hobbies, and working together. In contrast, women refer to their friends using kin terms or as *vecina*, "neighbor," reflecting women's primary orientation to family and neighborhood.

Differences also emerge in the category of *amigos (as) de verdad*, or "true friends." True friends are those with whom one shares secrets without fear of betrayal. Men have more true friends than women do, a pattern that reflects their wider social networks.

A shepherd in Andalucia, southern Spain. In rural areas of Andalucia, as in much of the Mediterranean region, the gender division of labor is distinct, with men working outside the home and women working inside or near the home. Friendship formation follows this pattern. Men form ties with men in cafes and bars after work, while most women's ties are with other women in the neighborhood.

Food for Thought

What categories of friends do you have? Are friends in some categories "closer" or "truer" than others? What is the basis of close friendship?

---

discussed in Chapter 6.) Friendship fits into the category of a primary social group.

One question that cultural anthropologists ask is whether friendship is a cultural universal. Two factors make it difficult to answer this question. First, friendship is an understudied topic in cultural anthropology, so insufficient cross-cultural research exists to answer the question definitively. Second, defining friendship cross-culturally is problematic. It is likely, however, that something like "friendship" is a cultural universal but shaped in different degrees from culture to culture (see Think Like an Anthropologist).

SOCIAL CHARACTERISTICS OF FRIENDSHIP People choose their friends, and friends remain so on a voluntary basis. Even so, the criteria for who qualifies as a friend may be culturally structured. For instance, gender segregation may limit cross-gender friendships and promote same-gender friendships, and racial segregation limits cross-"race" friendships. Another characteristic of friendship is that friends are supportive of each other, psychologically

and sometimes materially. Support is mutual, shared back and forth in an expectable way as in balanced exchange (see Chapter 3). Friendship generally occurs between social equals, although there are exceptions, such as friendships between older and younger people, between a supervisor and a staff worker, or between a teacher and a student.

Sharing stories is often a basis of friendship groups. According to a study that focused on interactions among men's friendship groups in rumshops in Guyana (guy-AH-nuh) (Map 7.2 on page 135), Indo-Guyanese men who have known each other since childhood spend time every day at the rumshop, eating, drinking, and regaling each other with stories (Sidnell 2000). Through shared storytelling about village history and other aspects of local knowledge, men display their equality with each other. The pattern of storytelling, referred to as "turn-at-talk," in which efforts are made to include everyone as a storyteller in turn, also serves to maintain equality and solidarity. These friendship groups are tightly knit, and the members can call on one another for economic, political, and other kinds of support.

Map 7.2 **Caribbean Countries of South America**

The ethnically and linguistically diverse countries of the Caribbean region of South America include Guyana, Suriname, and French Guiana. Guyana, or the Co-operative Republic of Guyana, is the only South American country whose official language is English. Other languages are Hindi, Wai Wai, and Arawak. Its population is over 700,000. The Republiek Suriname, or Suriname, was formerly a colony of the Netherlands and is the smallest independent state in South America. Its population is 570,000. Dutch is the official language, but most Surinamese also speak Sranan Tongo, or Surinaams, a mixture of Dutch, English, Portuguese, French, and local languages. French Guiana is an overseas department of France and is thus part of the European Union. The smallest political unit in South America, its population is 260,000. Its official language is French, but several other languages are spoken, including indigenous Arawak and Carib.

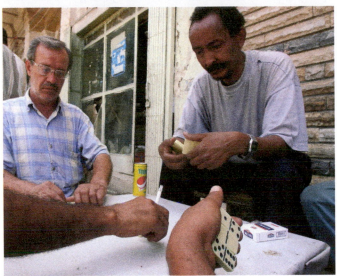

The game of dominoes is popular among men around the world. Men often play dominoes in public spaces, cheered on by male friends as in a low-income neighborhood in Rio de Janeiro (TOP), Brazil, in Baghdad, Iraq (CENTER), and in Beijing, China (BOTTOM).

▌ *Twenty years from now, do you think men in these same contexts will be playing dominoes? If not, what might they be playing?*

Participant observation and interviews with a sample of rural and urban, low-income Jamaicans reveal that cell phone use is frequent (Horst and Miller 2005). Jamaicans are keenly aware of their call lists and how often they

have kept in touch with the many individuals on their lists. Cell phones allow for "linking up," or creating extensive networks that include close friends, possible future sexual partners, and members of one's church. Phone numbers of kin are also prominent on people's cell phone number lists. By linking up periodically with people on their lists, low-income Jamaicans maintain friendship and other ties with people on whom they can call when they need support. Cell phones allow a more extensive network of friends and other contacts than was previously possible.

FRIENDSHIP AMONG THE URBAN POOR IN THE UNITED STATES Carol Stack (1974) wrote a landmark book in the early 1970s showing how friendship networks promote economic survival among low-income, urban African Americans. She conducted fieldwork in "The Flats," the poorest section of a Black community in a large midwestern city. She found extensive networks of friends "supporting, reinforcing each other—devising schemes for self-help, strategies for survival in a community of severe economic deprivation" (1974:28).

People in the Flats, especially women, maintain a set of friends through exchange: "swapping" goods (food, clothing) needed by someone at a particular time, sharing "child keeping," and giving or lending food stamps and money. Such exchanges are part of a clearly understood pattern—gifts and favors go back and forth over time. Friends thus bound together are obligated to each another and can call on each other in time of need. In opposition to theories that suggest the breakdown of social relationships among the very poor, this research documents how poor people strategize and cope through social ties.

In the intervening decades since the time of Stack's research, many other studies have documented the positive aspects of friendship among people of all social classes. Friendship, however, has its downside, since no one can be friends with everyone. So some people can feel left out. Bullying, or behavior that belittles and often viciously excludes individuals, can be considered the harsh opposite of befriending someone. While many sociologists and psychologists have studied bullying, cultural anthropologists have done so far less.

Clubs and Fraternities/Sororities

Clubs and fraternities/sororities are social groups that define membership in terms of a sense of shared identity and objectives. They may comprise people of the same ethnic heritage, occupation or business, religion, or gender. Although many clubs appear to exist primarily to serve functions of sociability and psychological support, deeper analysis often shows that these groups have economic and political roles as well.

College fraternities and sororities are highly selective groups that serve a variety of explicit functions, such as entertainment and social service. They also form bonds

A Cambodian boy dances to hip hop music in Phnom Penh, the capital city. Established by a former U.S. gang member who was deported after being convicted of armed robbery, the Tiny Toones center teaches disc-jockey skills and rapping to nearly 400 children. Tiny Toones and its founder, Tuy Sobil, better known as Kay Kay, have won praise for helping drug addicts and poor street kids transform their lives.

between members that may help in securing jobs after graduation. Few anthropologists have studied the "Greek system" on U.S. campuses. An exception is Peggy Sanday, who was inspired to study college fraternities after the gang rape of a woman student by several fraternity brothers at the campus where she teaches. Her book *Fraternity Gang Rape: Sex, Brotherhood, and Privilege on Campus* (1990) explores initiation rituals and how they are related to male bonding solidified by victimization and ridicule of women. Gang rape, or a "train," is a prevalent practice in some, not all, fraternities. Fraternity party invitations may hint at the possibility of a "train." Typically, the brothers seek out a "party girl"—a somewhat vulnerable young woman who may be especially needy of acceptance or especially high on alcohol or other substances (her drinks may have been "spiked"). They take her to one of the brothers' rooms, where she may or may not agree to have sex with one of the brothers, and she often passes out. Then a "train" of men have sex with her. Rarely prosecuted, the male participants reinforce their sense of privilege, power, and unity with one another through a group ritual involving abuse of a female outsider.

In many indigenous Amazonian groups, the men's house is fiercely guarded from being entered by women. If a woman trespasses on a male territory, men punish her by gang rape. One interpretation of this cultural practice is that men have a high degree of anxiety about their identity as fierce warriors and as sexually potent males (Gregor 1982). Maintaining their identity as fierce and forbidding toward outsiders involves taking an aggressive position in relation to women of their own group.

Cross-culturally, women do not tend to form androphobic ("man-hating" or otherwise anti-male) clubs, the logical parallel of gynophobic ("woman-hating" or otherwise anti-female) men's clubs. College sororities, for example, are not mirror images of college fraternities. Although some sororities' initiation rituals are psychologically brutal to the pledges, bonding among the members does not involve abusive behavior toward men.

Countercultural Groups

Several kinds of groups comprise people who, for one reason or another, are outside the "mainstream" of society and resist conforming to the dominant cultural pattern. The so-called hippies of the 1960s were one such group. One similarity among these groups, as with clubs and fraternities, is the importance of bonding through shared initiation and other rituals.

YOUTH GANGS The term **youth gang** refers to a group of young people, found mainly in urban areas, who are often

youth gang a group of young people, found mainly in urban areas, who are often considered a social problem by adults and law enforcement officials.

considered a social problem by adults and law enforcement officials (Sanders 1994).

Youth gangs vary in terms of how formally they are organized. Like clubs and fraternities, gangs often have a recognized leader, formalized rituals of initiation for new members, and symbolic markers of identity, such as tattoos or special clothing. An example of an informal youth gang with no formal leadership hierarchy or initiation rituals is that of the "Masta Liu" in Honiara, the capital city of the Solomon Islands in the South Pacific (Jourdan 1995) (Map 7.3). Unemployment is the primary unifying feature of the male youths who become Masta Liu. Most have migrated to the city from the countryside to escape what they consider an undesirable lifestyle there: working in the fields under control of their elders. Some Liu live with extended kin in

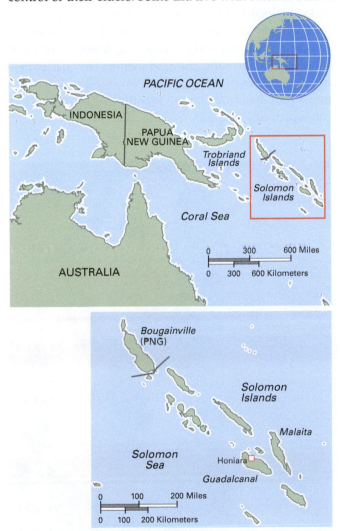

Map 7.3   The Solomon Islands

This country consists of nearly 1,000 islands. Its capital, Honiara, is located on the island of Guadalcanal. The population is nearly 600,000. Most of the people earn a living through small-scale farming and fishing. Commercial exploitation of local timber has led to severe deforestation. Over 70 languages are spoken, and an additional four have recently gone extinct. Most people are Christian, mainly Anglican. The Solomons were the site of some of the bitterest fighting during World War II.

the city; others organize Liu-only households. They spend their time wandering around town, referred to locally as going *wakabaot*, in groups of up to 10:

> They stop at every shop on their way, eager to look at the merchandise but afraid to be kicked out by the security guards; they check out all the cinemas only to dream in front of the preview posters ... not even having the $2 bill that will allow them to get in; they gaze for hours on end, and without moving, at the electronic equipment displayed in the Chinese shops, without saying a word: One can read in their gaze the silent dreams they create. (1995:210)

Street gangs are a more formal variety of youth gang. They generally have leaders and a hierarchy of membership roles and responsibilities. They are named, and their members mark their identity with tattoos or "colors." Much popular thinking associates street gangs with violence, but not all are involved in violence. An anthropologist who did research among nearly 40 street gangs in New York, Los Angeles, and Boston learned much about why individuals join gangs, providing insights that also contradict popular thinking (Jankowski 1991). One common perception is that young boys join gangs because they are from homes with no male authority figure with whom they identify. In the gangs studied, about half of the gang members were from intact nuclear households. Another common perception is that the gang replaces a missing feeling of family. This study showed that the same number of gang members reported having close family ties as those who did not.

Why, then, did young men join an urban gang? The research revealed that many gang members had a particular personality type called a defiant individualist. The defiant individualist type has five characteristics:

- Intense competitiveness
- Mistrust of others
- Self-reliance
- Social isolation
- A strong survival instinct

A structurist view suggests that poverty, especially urban poverty, leads to the development of this kind of personality as a response to the prevailing economic obstacles and uncertainty. To explain the global spread of urban youth gangs, structurists point to widespread economic changes in urban employment opportunities. In many countries, a declining urban industrial base has created persistent poverty in inner-city communities. At the same time, schooling and the popular media promote aspirations for a better life. Urban gang members, in this view, are the victims of large structural forces beyond their control that both inspire them to want aspects of a successful lifestyle and prevent them from achieving the legal means to obtain their aspirations. Many of these youths want to be economically successful, but social conditions channel their interests and skills into illegal pursuits rather than into legal pathways to achievement.

BODY MODIFICATION GROUPS One of the many countercultural movements in the United States includes people who have a sense of community strengthened through forms of body alteration. James Myers (1992) did research in California among people who feel that they are a special group because of their interest in permanent body modification, especially genital piercing, branding, and cutting. Fieldwork involved participant observation and interviews: Myers was involved in workshops organized for the San Francisco sadomasochist (SM) community; he attended the Fifth Annual Living in Leather Convention held in Portland, Oregon, in 1990; he spent time in tattoo and piercing studios; and he talked with students and others in his hometown who were involved in these forms of body modification. The study population included males and females, heterosexuals, gays, lesbians, bisexuals, and SMers. The single largest group was SM homosexuals and bisexuals. The study population was mainly White, and most had either attended or graduated from college.

Myers witnessed many modification sessions at workshops: Those seeking modification go up on stage and have their chosen procedure done by a well-known expert. Whatever the procedure, the volunteers exhibit little pain—usually just a sharp intake of breath at the moment the needle passes through or the brand touches skin. After that critical moment, the audience breathes an audible sigh of relief. The volunteer stands up and adjusts his or her clothing, and members of the audience applaud. This public event is a kind of initiation ritual that binds the expert, the volunteer, and the group together. Pain is an important part of many rites of passage. In this case, the audience witnesses and validates the experience and becomes joined to the initiate through witnessing.

The study revealed that a prominent motivation for seeking permanent body modification was a desire to identify with a specific group of people. One participant commented that piercing makes him feel like a part of a special group and that he can identify with someone else who is pierced (1992:292).

(LEFT) A Tahitian chief wears tattoos that indicate his high status. (RIGHT) A woman with tattooed arms in the United States.

■ *In your microcultural experience, what do tattoos mean to you when you see someone with them?*

Guna Indian woman sewing a mola, San Blas Islands, Panama.

■ *Learn more about molas from the Web.*

Map 7.4 Guna Region in Panama

The Guna are an indigenous people who live mainly in the eastern coastal region of Panama, including its offshore islands. Some live in cities, and a few live in villages in neighboring Colombia. The Guna population is around 150,000. Farming, fishing, and tourism are important parts of the economy. Each community has its own political organization, and the Guna as a whole are organized into the Kuna General Congress. Most speak Guna, or Dulegaya ("People's Language"), and Spanish. They follow traditional religious practices, often with a mixture of Christian elements.

Cooperatives

Cooperatives are a form of economic group in which surpluses are shared among the members and decision making follows the democratic principle of each individual member having one vote (Estrin 1996). Agricultural and credit cooperatives are the most common forms of cooperatives worldwide, followed by consumer cooperatives.

In Panama's eastern coastal region, indigenous Guna (goo-nuh) women long have sewn beautiful molas, or cloth with appliquéd designs (Map 7.4). Guna make this cloth for their own use as clothing, but since the 1960s, molas have been important items for sale both on the world market and to tourists who come to Panama (Tice 1995). Revenue from selling molas to tourists, as well as internationally, is now an important part of the household income of the Guna. Some women continue to operate independently, buying their own cloth and thread and selling their molas either to an intermediary who exports them or in the local tourist market. But many women have joined cooperatives that offer them greater economic security. The cooperative buys cloth and thread in bulk and distributes them to the women. The women are paid almost the entire sale price for each mola, with only a small amount of the eventual sale prices being taken out for cooperative dues and administrative costs. Their earnings are steadier than what the fluctuating tourist season offers. Other benefits from being a member of the cooperative include its use as a consumer's cooperative (buying rice and sugar in bulk for members), a source of mutual strength and support, and a place for women to develop greater leadership skills and to take advantage of opportunities for political participation in the wider society.

Social Stratifications

7.2 Define what is included in the term social stratification.

Social stratification consists of hierarchical relationships among different groups, as though they were arranged in layers, or strata. Stratified groups may be unequal on a variety of measures, including material resources, power, human welfare, education, and symbolic attributes. People

---

social stratification a set of hierarchical relationships among different groups as though they were arranged in layers, or "strata."

in groups in higher positions have privileges not experienced by those in lower echelon groups, and they are likely to be interested in maintaining their privileged positions. Social stratification appeared late in human history, most clearly with the emergence of agriculture. Now some form of social stratification is nearly universal.

Analysis of the categories—such as class, "race," gender, age, and indigeneity—within stratification systems reveals a crucial difference among them in the degree to which membership in a given category is an **ascribed position**, based on qualities of a person gained through birth, or an **achieved position**, based on qualities of a person gained through action. Ascribed positions may be based on one's "race," ethnicity, gender, age, or physical ability. These factors are generally out of the control of the individual, although some flexibility exists for gender (through surgery and hormonal treatments) and for certain kinds of physical conditions. Also, one can sometimes "pass" as a member of another "race" or ethnic group. Age is an unusual ascribed category because an individual goes through several status levels as they move through the life cycle. Achievement as a basis for group membership means that a person's membership in the group is based on some valued attainment. Ascribed systems are thus more "closed," and achievement-based systems are more "open," in terms of mobility, either upward or downward, within the system. Some scholars of social status believe that modernization during the twentieth century and increased social complexity led to a rise in achievement-based positions and a decline in ascription-based positions. The material that follows explores how social categories define group membership and relations of inequality among groups.

Societies place people into categories—student, husband, child, retired person, political leader, or member of Phi Beta Kappa—referred to as a person's **status**, or position or standing in society (Wolf 1996). Each status has an accompanying role, which is expected behavior for someone of a particular status, and a "script" for how to behave, look, and talk. Some statuses have more prestige attached to them than others. Within societies that have marked status positions, different status groups are marked by a particular lifestyle, including the goods they own, their leisure activities, and their linguistic styles. The maintenance of group position by the higher status categories is sometimes accomplished by exclusionary practices in relation to lower-status groups through a tendency toward group in-marriage and socializing only within the group. Groups, like individuals, have status, or standing, in society.

Achieved Status: Class

Social class (defined in Chapter 1) refers to a person's or group's position in society and is defined primarily in economic terms. In many cultures, class is a key factor in determining a person's status, whereas in others, it is less important than, for example, birth into a certain family. Class and status, however, do not always match. A rich person may have become wealthy in disreputable ways and never gain high status. Both status and class groups are secondary groups, because a person is unlikely to know every other member of the group, especially in large-scale societies.

In capitalist societies, the prevailing ideology is that the system allows for upward mobility and that every individual has the option of moving up. Some anthropologists refer to this ideology as meritocratic individualism, the belief that rewards go to those who earn them (Durrenberger 2001). In contrast, a structurist perspective points to the power of economic class position in shaping a person's lifestyle and his or her ability to choose a different one. Obviously, a person who was born rich can, through individual action, become poor, and a poor person can become rich. In spite of exceptions to the rule, a person born rich is more likely to lead a lifestyle typical of that class, just as a person born poor is more likely to lead a lifestyle typical of that class.

The concept of class is central to the theories of Karl Marx. Situated within the context of Europe's Industrial Revolution and the growth of capitalism, Marx wrote that class differences, exploitation of the working class by the owners of capital, class consciousness among workers, and class conflict were forces of change that would eventually spell the downfall of capitalism.

Ascribed Status: "Race," Ethnicity, Gender, and Caste

Four major ascribed systems of social stratification are based on divisions of people into unequally ranked groups on the basis of, respectively, "race," ethnicity, gender (defined in Chapter 1), and caste, the last a ranked group determined by birth and often linked to a particular occupation and to South Asian cultures. Like status and class groups, these four categories are secondary social groups, because no one can have a personal relationship with all other members of the entire group. Each system takes on local specificities, depending on the context. For example, "race" and ethnicity are interrelated and overlap with conceptions of culture in much of Latin America, although what they mean in terms of identity and status differs in different countries in the region (de la Cadena 2001). For some, the concept of **mestizaje** (mes-tee-SAH-hay),

---

ascribed position a person's standing in society based on qualities that the person has gained through birth.

achieved position a person's standing in society based on qualities that the person has gained through action.

status a person's position, or standing, in society.

mestizaje literally, a racial mixture; in Central and South America, indigenous people who are cut off from their Indian roots, or literate and successful indigenous people who retain some traditional cultural practices.

from the word mestizo, literally means "racial" mixture. In Central and South America, it refers either to people who are cut off from their Indian roots or to literate and successful people who retain some indigenous cultural practices. One has to know the local system of categories and meanings attached to them to understand the dynamics of inequality that go with them.

Systems based on differences defined in terms of "race," ethnicity, gender, and caste share some important features with each other and with class-based systems. First, they relegate large numbers of people to particular levels of entitlement to livelihood, power, security, esteem, and freedom (Berreman 1979 [1975]:213). This simple fact should not be overlooked. Second, those with greater entitlements dominate those with lesser entitlements. Third, members of the dominant groups tend to seek to maintain their position, consciously or unconsciously. They do this through institutions that control ideology among the dominated and through institutions that physically suppress potential rebellion or subversion by the dominated (Harris 1971, quoted in Mencher 1974:469). Fourth, in spite of efforts to maintain systems of dominance, instances of subversion and rebellion do occur, indicating the potential for agency among the oppressed.

"RACE" Racial stratification is a relatively recent form of social inequality. It results from the unequal meeting of two formerly separate groups through colonization, slavery, and other large-group movements (Sanjek 1994). Europe's "age of discovery," beginning in the 1500s, ushered in a new era of global contact. In contrast, in relatively homogeneous cultures, ethnicity is a more important distinction than "race." In contemporary Nigeria, for example, the population is largely homogeneous and ethnicity is the more salient term (Jinadu 1994). A similar situation prevails in other African states as well as in the Middle East, Central Europe and Eurasia, and China.

A key feature of racial thinking is its insistence that behavioral differences among peoples are "natural," inborn, or biologically caused. Throughout the history of racial categorizations in the West, such features as head size, head shape, and brain size have been accepted as reasons for behavioral differences. Writing early in the twentieth century, Franz Boas contributed to de-linking supposed inborn, racial attributes from behavior (review Chapter 1). He showed that people with the same head size but from different cultures behaved differently and that people with various head sizes within the same cultures behaved similarly. For Boas and his followers, culture, not biology, is the key explanation for behavior. Thus, "race" is not a biological reality; there is no way to divide the human population into "races" based on certain biological features. Yet social race and racism exist. In other words, in many contexts the concept of "race" has a social reality in terms of people's

entitlements, status, and treatment. In spite of some progress in reducing racism in the United States in the twentieth century, racial discrimination persists.

Racial classifications in the Caribbean and in Latin America involve complicated systems of status classification. The complexity results from the variety of contact over the centuries between peoples from Europe, Africa, Asia, and indigenous populations. Skin tone is one basis of racial classification, but it is mixed with other physical features and economic status as well. In Haiti, for example, racial categories take into account physical factors such as skin texture, depth of skin tone, hair color and appearance, and facial features (Trouillot 1994). Racial categories also include a person's income, social origin, level of formal education, personality or behavior, and kinship ties. Depending on how these variables are combined, a person occupies one category or another—and may even move between categories. Thus, a person with certain physical features who is poor will be considered to be a different "color" than a person with the same physical features who is well-off.

An extreme example of racial stratification was the South African policy of apartheid, the legally sanctioned segregation of dominant Whites from non-Whites. White dominance in South Africa (Map 7.5) began in the early 1800s with White migration and settlement. In the 1830s, slavery was abolished. At the same time, increasingly racist thinking developed among Whites (Johnson 1994:25). Racist images, including images of Africans as lazy and

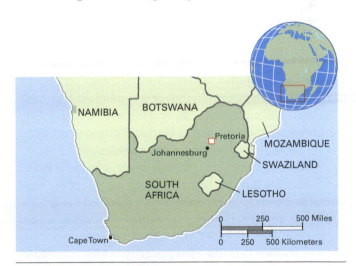

Map 7.5 South Africa

The Republic of South Africa experienced the highest level of colonial immigration of any African country. Its rich mineral wealth attracted interest from global powers throughout the Cold War era. Of its population of 52 million, 80 percent are Black South Africans. The rest are of mixed ethnic backgrounds and referred to as "Coloureds," Indian (from India), or White, who are mainly descendants of colonial immigrants. South Africa has 11 official languages, and it recognizes eight nonofficial languages. Afrikaans and English are the major languages of the administration. Nonofficial languages include those of the San and other indigenous peoples.

politically disorganized, served as part of the rationale for colonialist domination. In spite of years of African resistance to White domination, the Whites succeeded in maintaining and increasing their control for nearly two centuries. In South Africa, Blacks constitute 90 percent of the population, a numerical majority that was long dominated, through strict apartheid, by the White minority until 1994. During apartheid, every measure of the quality of life—infant mortality, longevity, education—showed great disparity between the Whites and the Africans. In addition to suffering from physical deprivation, Black South Africans experienced psychological suffering through constant personal insecurity caused by the threat and actuality of police raids and other forms of violence directed against them.

It is now more nearly 30 years after apartheid was officially abolished in 1991 and the first democratic elections were held in 1994. Although the country has come far, most Black South Africans continue to live in poverty and experience excess death and suffering from HIV/AIDS. A study based on the life histories of seven young South Africans reveals that frustration is growing as inequalities that once divided the races now are increasing within them (Newman and De Lannoy 2014). The stories of the seven youths, from varying backgrounds, offer an intimate look at the rising post-apartheid generation and how young people are navigating their way in this still-new democracy. One conclusion is that, while major Black–White differences continue to exist in opportunities and entitlements, new patterns of inequality are emerging within those groups. Some Blacks are gaining social and economic status while such standing is no longer guaranteed to Whites.

ETHNICITY Ethnicity is group membership based on a shared sense of identity that may be based on history, territory, language, or religion, or a combination of these (Comaroff 1987). Ethnicity can be a basis for claiming entitlements to resources (such as land, buildings, or artifacts) and for defending or regaining those resources.

States are interested in managing ethnicity to the extent that it does not threaten security. China has one of the most formalized systems for monitoring its many ethnic groups, and it has an official policy on ethnic minorities, meaning the non-Han groups (Wu 1990). The government lists 55 groups other than the Han majority, which constitutes about 92 percent of the total population. The other 8 percent of the population is made up of these 55 minority groups, about 67 million people. The non-Han minorities occupy about 60 percent of China's landmass and are mainly located in border or "frontier" areas in the west, south, and north such as Tibet, Yunnan, Xinjiang, and Inner Mongolia. Basic criteria for defining an ethnic group include language, territory, economy, and "psychological disposition." The Chinese government establishes strict definitions of group membership and group

In 2003, the Treatment Action Campaign (TAC) began a program of civil disobedience to prompt the government of South Africa to sign and implement a National Prevention and Treatment Plan for HIV/AIDS. The TAC uses images of Hector Peterson, the first youth killed in the Soweto uprising against apartheid, and slogans such as "The Struggle Continues: Support HIV/AIDS Treatment Now."

Take a position, and be prepared to defend it, on whether or not a country's government should have responsibility for preventing and treating HIV/AIDS.

characteristics; it even sets standards for ethnic costumes and dances. The Chinese treatment of the Tibetan people is especially severe and can be considered ethnocide, or annihilation of the culture of an ethnic group by a dominant group. In 1951, China forcibly incorporated Tibet, and the Chinese government undertook measures to bring about the social and economic transformation of what was formerly a decentralized, Buddhist feudal regime. This transformation has caused increasing ethnic conflict between Tibetans and Han Chinese, including demonstrations by Tibetans and crackdowns from the Chinese.

People of one ethnic group who move from one niche to another are at risk of exclusionary treatment by the local residents. Roma (often called Gypsies by outsiders, a term that Roma consider to be derogatory) are a **diaspora population**, a dispersed group living outside their original homeland. Roma are scattered throughout Europe and the United States (see Culturama). Their status within mainstream society is always marginal in terms of economic, political, and social measures.

GENDER AND SEXISM Like other forms of social inequality, gender inequalities, based on perceived differences between people born male or female or somewhere in between, vary from one culture to another. This book has already presented many examples of gender inequality, and more will appear in later chapters. The discussion

---

diaspora population a dispersed group of people living outside their original homeland.

Culturama

The Roma of Eastern Europe

The Roma (or Romani) are Europe's largest minority population. They live in nearly all the countries of Europe and Central Asia. In Europe, their total is between seven and nine million people (World Bank 2003). They are concentrated in Eastern Europe, where they constitute around 10 percent of the population.

The Roma have a long history of mobility and marginality ever since several waves of migrants left their original homeland in northern India between the ninth and fourteenth centuries CE (Crowe 1996). The lifestyle of many Roma in Europe continues to involve movement, with temporary camps of their wagons appearing overnight on the outskirts of a town. Most settled Roma live in marginalized areas that lack decent housing, clean water, and good schools. Members of mainstream society look down on, and even despise, the Roma.

In Budapest, Hungary, the Roma minority is the most disadvantaged ethnic group (Ladányi 1993). Not all Roma in Budapest, however, are poor. About 1 percent have gained wealth. The other 99 percent live in substandard housing in the slums of inner Pest.

Since the fall of state socialism in Hungary, social discrimination against the Roma has increased. Some Roma communities are mobilizing to improve their living conditions. The government instituted a policy allowing the Roma a degree of self-government (Schaft and Brown 2000).

In Slovakia, one-third of the Roma live in ghetto-like enclaves called *osada* (Scheffel 2004). These settlements lack clean water, sewage treatment, reliable electricity, access to decent housing, good schools, and passable roads. Osada exist in close proximity to affluent neighborhoods of ethnic Slovaks, or "Whites." In one village, Svinia (SVEEH-nee-yuh), roughly 700 Roma are crowded together on one hectare of swampy land while their 670 ethnic Slovak neighbors own over 1,400 hectares of land (2004:8).

As more Eastern European countries seek to enter the European Union, they are initiating programs to improve Roma living conditions and enacting laws to prevent discrimination. After Hungary joined the European Union in 2004, it elected two Roma to the EU Parliament. In Bulgaria, the Roma won a court case in 2005 declaring that segregated schools were unconstitutional. Fieldwork in Slovakia, however, indicates that the government is doing little to improve the lives of the Roma.

The global economic crisis that began in 2008 led to increased ethnic violence against Roma throughout Eastern Europe. The economic downturn hit European countries with large Roma populations particularly hard, including Hungary, Romania, Slovakia, and Serbia. Some politicians and extremist groups in these countries blame the Roma for taking away jobs from non-Roma people. Since 2010, France has been evicting Roma people from settlements there.

Thanks to David Z. Scheffel, Thompson Rivers University, for reviewing this material

(LEFT) The Roma settlement of Svinia in 1993. The standard of living has not improved since the 1990s, but the population has increased by nearly 50 percent, resulting in overcrowding and high levels of stress.

(CENTER) Roma children's access to school facilities is severely restricted. A few Romani schoolchildren participate in the school lunch program, but in a separate room next to the cafeteria.

Map 7.6 Roma Population in Eastern Europe

Romania has the highest number of Roma of any country in the world, between one and two million. Macedonia has the highest percentage of Roma in its population.

that follows highlights some features of male dominance cross-culturally.

Patriarchy, or male dominance in economic, political, social, and ideological domains, is common but not universal. It also varies in severity and results. In its most severe forms, women and girls are completely under the power of men and can be killed by men, with no societal response. So-called honor killings, for example, of girls and women who defy rules of virginity or arranged marriage and are murdered by male kin, are examples of extreme patriarchy (Kurkiala 2003). Less violent, but also serious, is the effect of patriarchy on girls' education. In many countries, girls are not sent to school at all, or if they are, they attend for fewer years or attend schools of lower quality than their brothers.

The logical opposite of patriarchy is **matriarchy**, or female dominance in economic, political, social, and ideological domains. Matriarchy is so rare in contemporary cultures that anthropologists are not certain that it even exists or has ever existed. Among the Iroquois at the time the European colonialists arrived, women controlled public finances, in the form of maize, and they determined whether or not war would be waged. They also chose the leaders, although the leaders were male. It is not clear whether the Iroquois were in fact matriarchal or might more accurately be considered gender egalitarian with a mixed and balanced gender system. A stronger case for a truly matriarchal society is found in the Minangkabau people of Malaysia and Indonesia (see Culturama in Chapter 6).

CASTE AND CASTEISM The **caste system** is a social stratification system linked with Hinduism and based on a person's birth into a particular group. It exists in its clearest form in India, among its Hindu population, and in other regions with large Hindu populations such as Nepal, Sri Lanka, and Fiji. The caste system is particularly associated with Hindu peoples because ancient Hindu scriptures are taken as the foundational sources for defining the major social categories called *varnas*, a Sanskrit word meaning "color" (Figure 7.2). The four varnas are the *brahmans*, priests; the *kshatriyas*, warriors; the *vaishyas*, merchants; and the *shudras*, laborers. Adolescent males of the first three varnas go through a ritual ceremony of initiation and "rebirth," after which they may wear a sacred thread across their chest, indicating their purity and high status as "twice born." Beneath the four varna groups are people ranked so low that they are outside the caste system itself, hence the English term "outcast." Another English term for them is "untouchables," because people of the upper varnas avoided any kind of contact with them to maintain their own purity. Mahatma Gandhi, himself a member of an upper caste, renamed them *harijans* ("children of god") in his attempt to raise their status into that of the shudras. Currently, members of this category have adopted the term **dalit** (dah-lit), which means "oppressed" or "ground down."

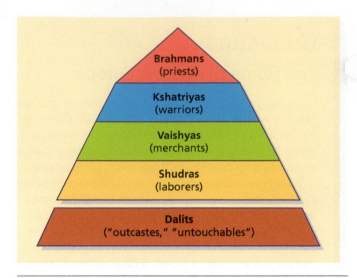

Figure 7.2 Model of India's Varna Categories

The four traditional varnas and the dalit category contain many hundreds of locally named groups called castes, or, more appropriately, *jatis* (jah-tees, or birth groups). The term caste comes from the Portuguese word *casta*, meaning "breed" or "type." Portuguese colonialists first used it in the fifteenth century to refer to the closed social groups they encountered. Jati, an emic term, conveys the meaning that a Hindu is born into his or her group. Jatis are ascribed status groups. Just as the four varnas are ranked relative to each other, so are all the jatis within them. For example, the jati of Brahmans is divided into priestly and nonpriestly subgroups; the priestly Brahmans are separated into household priests, temple priests, and funeral priests; the household priests are broken down into two or more categories; and each of those are divided into subgroups based on lineage ties (Parry 1996:77). Within all these categories exist well-defined status hierarchies.

The caste system involves several mechanisms that maintain it: marriage rules, spatial segregation, and ritual. Marriage rules strictly enforce jati endogamy (in-group marriage). Marriage outside one's jati, especially in rural areas and particularly between a higher caste female and lower caste male, is cause for punishment, often lethal, by

patriarchy the dominance of men in economic, political, social, and ideological domains.

matriarchy the dominance of women in economic, political, social, and ideological domains.

caste system a form of social stratification linked with Hinduism and based on a person's birth into a particular group.

dalit the preferred name for the socially defined lowest groups in the Indian caste system; the name means "oppressed" or "ground down."

Three views of caste in India. (TOP LEFT) Only a special category of Brahman priests can officiate at the Chidambaram temple in Tamil Nadu, southern India. Here, members of a mixed-age group sit for a moment's relaxation. (BOTTOM LEFT) A village carpenter in front of his house in a north Indian village. The status of carpenters is mid-level, between the elites and those who deal with polluting materials such as animal hides or refuse. (TOP RIGHT) In New Delhi, India, Dalit Christians and Dalit Muslims mobilize to assert their rights within the larger Dalit Movement that is dominated by Hindus.

caste elders and other local power holders. Nonetheless, a trend toward inter-jati marriages is emerging among educated people in urban areas.

Spatial segregation functions to maintain the privileged preserve of the upper castes and to remind the lower castes continually of their marginal status. In many rural villages, dalits live in a completely separate neighborhood into which no upper-caste person will venture.

Social mobility within the caste system has traditionally been limited, but instances have been documented of group "up-casting." Several strategies exist, including gaining wealth, affiliation or merger with a somewhat higher jati, education, migration, and political activism (Kolenda 1978). A group that attempts to gain higher jati status takes on the behavior and dress of twice-born jatis. These include men wearing the sacred thread, vegetarianism, nonremarriage of widows, seclusion of women from the public domain, and the giving of larger dowries for the marriage of a daughter.

The Indian constitution of 1949 declared that discrimination on the basis of caste is illegal. Constitutional decree, however, did not bring an end to these deeply structured inequalities. In the late twentieth century, the government of India instituted policies to promote the social and economic advancement of dalits, such as reserving for them places in medical schools, seats in the government, and public-sector jobs. This "affirmative action" plan infuriates many of the upper castes, especially Brahmans, who feel most threatened. Is the caste system on the decline? Surely, aspects of it are changing. Especially in large cities, people of different jatis can "pass" and participate on a more nearly equal basis in public life—if they have the economic means to do so.

Civil Society

7.3 **Discuss the concept of civil society.**

Civil society consists of the social domain of diverse interest groups that function outside the government to organize economic, political, and other aspects of life. According to the German philosopher G. W. F. Hegel, civil society encompasses social groups and institutions that exist between the individual and the state. The Italian social theorist Antonio Gramsci defined two types of civic institutions: those that support the state, such as the church and schools, and those that oppose state power, such as trade unions, social protest groups, and citizens' rights groups. This section discusses an example of a state-supporting group as well as an activist group that opposes state oppression.

Civil Society for the State: The Chinese Women's Movement

In some instances, governments seek to build civil society to further their own goals. The women's movement in China is an example of such a state-created organization. Canadian anthropologist Ellen Judd (2002) conducted a study of the women's movement in China, within the constraints that the government imposes on anthropological fieldwork by foreigners. Under the Mao leadership, foreign anthropologists were not allowed to do research of any sort in China. The situation began to change in the 1980s when some field research, within strict limitations, became possible.

Judd developed a long-term relationship with China over several decades, having lived there as a student from 1974 to 1977, undertaking long-term fieldwork there in 1986, and returning almost every year since for research or some other activity, such as being involved in a development project for women or attending the Beijing Fourth World Conference on Women. According to Judd, "These various ways of being in China all allowed me some interaction with Chinese women and some knowledge of their lives" (2002:14). In her latest project to study the Chinese women's movement, she wanted to conduct research as a cultural anthropologist would normally do, through intensive participant observation over a long time.

At the time of her research, Judd was not allowed to join the local women's organization or to speak privately with any of the women. Officials accompanied her on all household visits and interviews. She was allowed to attend meetings, however, and she had access to all the public information about the goals of the women's movement, which is called the Women's Federations.

A policy goal of the Chinese government is to improve the quality of women's lives, and the Women's Federations were formed to address that goal. The government oversees the operation at all levels, from the national level to the township and village. The primary objective is to mobilize women, especially rural women, to participate in literacy training and market activities.

Judd's fieldwork, constrained as it was by government regulations, nevertheless yielded insights. She learned, through interviews with women members, about some women who have benefited from the programs, and she discovered how important education for women is in terms of their ability to enter into market activities. The book she wrote is largely descriptive, focusing on the "public face" of the Women's Federations in one locale. Such a descriptive account is the most that can emerge from research in China at this time. Given that the women's organizations are formed by and for the government, this example stretches the concept of civil society.

Activist Groups: CO-MADRES

Activist groups are groups formed with the goal of changing certain conditions, such as political repression, violence, and human rights violations. In studying activist groups, cultural anthropologists are interested in learning what motivates the formation of such groups, what their goals and strategies are, and what leadership patterns they exhibit. Many anthropologists work for or with activist groups to support social justice (see Anthropology Works on page 147).

CO-MADRES of El Salvador (see Map 12.4, page 251) is a women-led social movement in Latin America (Stephen 1995). CO-MADRES is a Spanish abbreviation for an organization called, in English, the Committee of Mothers and Relatives of Political Prisoners, Disappeared and Assassinated of El Salvador. It was founded in 1977 by a group of mothers protesting the atrocities committed by the U.S.-backed Salvadoran government and military against a coalition of progressive groups including many indigenous people. During the civil war that lasted from 1979 until 1992, a total of 80,000 people died and 7,000 more disappeared, or one in every 100 Salvadorans.

---

civil society the collection of interest groups that function outside the government to organize economic and other aspects of life.

Anthropology Works

Forensic Anthropology for the Maya of Guatemala

Fredy Peccerelli, a forensic anthropologist, risks his personal safety working for victims of political violence in Guatemala, his homeland. Peccerelli is founder and executive director of the Guatemalan Forensic Anthropology Foundation (FAFG). FAFG is dedicated to the recovery and identification of the remains of thousands of indigenous Maya whom Guatemalan military forces "disappeared" or outright killed during the brutal civil war that raged from the mid-1960s to the mid-1990s.

Peccerelli was born in Guatemala. His family immigrated to the United States when his father, a lawyer, was threatened by death squads. He grew up in New York City and attended Brooklyn College in the 1990s. But he felt a need to reconnect with his heritage and began to study anthropology as a vehicle that would allow him to serve his country.

The FAFG scientists excavate clandestine mass graves, exhume the bodies, and identify them through several means, such as matching dental and/or medical records. In studying skeletons, they try to determine the person's age, gender, ancestry, and lifestyle. DNA studies are few because of the expense. The scientists also collect information from relatives of the victims and from eyewitnesses of the massacres. Since 1992, the FAFG team has discovered and exhumed approximately 200 mass gravesites.

Peccerelli sees the foundation's purpose as applying scientific principles to basic human concerns. Bodies of identified victims are returned to their families to allow them some sense of closure about what happened to their loved ones. Families can honor their dead with appropriate burial ceremonies.

The scientists also give the Guatemalan government clear evidence on the basis of which to prosecute the perpetrators of these atrocities. Members of the long-standing military rulers still hold powerful positions within the government.

Peccerelli, his family, and his colleagues have been harassed and threatened. Bullets have been fired into Peccerelli's home, and it has been burglarized. Eleven FAFG scientists have received written death threats. Nevertheless, the United Nations and other human rights organizations have made it clear to the government that they support FAFG's investigations, and exhumations continue with heightened security measures.

The American Association for the Advancement of Science honored Peccerelli and his colleagues in 2004 for their work in promoting human rights at great personal risk. In 1999, *Time* magazine and CNN chose Peccerelli as one of 50 "Latin American Leaders for the New Millennium." During the same year, the Guatemalan Youth Commission named him an "icon" for the youth of the country.

In Guatemala City, a woman, with her daughter, observes the pictures of people who lost their lives during the civil war. Some experts argue that the undeclared war against the indigenous Maya is not over.

A mural greets visitors on the exterior of Oakland's Ella Baker Center for Human Rights, a nonprofit social-justice organization that lobbies for green jobs programs for inner-city youth. The concept of green jobs programs was invented by Van Jones, the White House's Special Advisor for Green Jobs during 2009. Oakland is one of the most violent cities in the United States, with high levels of pollution, poverty, and unemployment. The green jobs program's goal is to prepare inner-city inhabitants to compete for the green jobs that will be created in the next 10 years.

The initial CO-MADRES group comprised nine mothers. One year later, it had grown to nearly 30 members, including some men. During the 1980s, the growing organization gained support from other Latin American countries, as well as from Australia, the United States, Canada, and European countries. Unfortunately, the group's increased visibility also attracted repression from the Salvadoran government. Its office was bombed several times during the 1980s, 48 members of CO-MADRES have been detained, and five have been assassinated. Harassment and disappearances continued even after the signing of the Peace Accords in January 1992: "In February 1993, the son and the nephew of one of the founders of CO-MADRES were assassinated in Usulutan. This woman had already lived through the experience of her own detention, the detention and gang rape of her daughter, and the disappearance and assassination of other family members" (1995:814).

In the 1990s, CO-MADRES focused on holding the state accountable for human rights violations during the civil war, providing protection for political prisoners, seeking assurances of human rights protection in the future, working against domestic violence, educating women about political participation, and initiating economic projects for women. The work of CO-MADRES, throughout its history, has incorporated elements of both the "personal" and the "political," concerns of mothers and other family members for lost kin and for exposing and halting human rights abuses of the state and the military. One lesson from the CO-MADRES is that activist groups formed by women based on kinship and domestic concerns, but their impact can have important high-level effects.

Social Capital, Social Movements, and Social Media

This chapter began with a discussion of factors that bring people together, such as friendship and forms of identity, and then moved on to discussing divisive factors. It concludes with the introduction of an important concept, social capital. The term **social capital** refers to the intangible resources that exist through social ties, trust, and cooperation. Many local organizations around the world use social capital to provide basic social needs, and they are often successful even in the poorest countries.

It is difficult to define, much less measure, social capital and its effects, both short-term and long-term. But few would disagree that being in a social group tends to have a multiplier effect. More and more, those who work with marginalized and oppressed people and groups show that by bringing people together, building social solidarity and a sense of group security, creates that indefinable multiplier effect of social capital—a non-monetized form of value that one can "bank" and "cash in hand" as needed. Examples in Chapters 14 and 15 illustrate how social capital works for migrants and the poor.

Social scientists use the term new social movements to refer to the many social activist groups that emerged in the late twentieth century around the world. These groups are often formed by oppressed minorities such as indigenous peoples, ethnic groups, women, and the poor. They are improving their lives through the strategic use of social capital as well as social media.

social capital the intangible resources existing in social ties, trust, and cooperation.

New social movements are taking advantage of ever-changing forms of communication through the Internet to broaden their membership, exchange ideas, and raise funds (Escobar 2002). Internet-enhanced social movements now often play important political roles. In a positive way, the Internet allows new social movements to build a following and potentially transform society.

Formal political leaders, as discussed in the next chapter, are paying increased attention to enhancing their personal websites and those of their parties and communicating through Facebook, Twitter, and many more channels. The author of this book gets frequent e-mails from (apparently) Barack Obama, Michelle Obama, Joe Biden, and Bill Clinton.

7 | Learning Objectives Revisited

7.1 Explain what social groups are.

Social groups can be classified in terms of whether all members have face-to-face interaction with one another, whether membership is based on ascription or achievement, and how formal the group's organization and leadership structure are. They extend from the most informal, face-to-face groups, such as those based on friendship, to groups that have formal membership requirements and whose members are widely dispersed and never meet each other. All groups have criteria for membership, often based on a perceived notion of similarity in terms of gender or class identity, work roles, opposition to mainstream culture, economic goals, or self-improvement.

Many groups require a formal ritual of initiation of new members. In some cases, initiation into the group involves dangerous or frightening activities that serve to bond members to one another through a shared experience of helplessness.

7.2 Define what is included in the term social stratification.

Social stratification consists of hierarchical relationships between and among different groups, usually on the basis of some culturally defined concept of status. The degree of social inequality among groups of different status is highly marked in agricultural and industrial/digital societies. Marked status inequalities are not characteristic of most foraging societies. Status inequalities are variable in pastoralist and horticultural societies, with leveling mechanisms typically at play to prevent the formation of severe inequalities.

Depending on the context, categories such as class, "race," ethnicity, gender, and rank may determine group and individual status. India's caste-based system is an important example of a rigid structure of severe social inequality based on a person's birth group. According to ancient Hindu scriptures, the population is divided into mutually exclusive groups with different rights and privileges. Discrimination on the basis of caste is banned by the Indian constitution, yet it still exists, as does racism in many other contexts, even though discrimination on the basis of "race" is illegal. Patterns of social inequality can and do change for the better (less inequality) or the worse (more inequality). Change can come from policy change at the top, such as the end of apartheid, or from grassroots social movements that contest unequal conditions.

7.3 Discuss the concept of civil society.

Civil society consists of the diverse interest groups that function outside the government to organize economic, political, and other aspects of life. It encompasses voluntary social groups and institutions.

Civil society groups can be divided into those that support government policies and initiatives, and thus further the interests of government, and those that oppose government policies and actions. The Chinese Women's Movement is an example of the former, and CO-MADRES in El Salvador is an example of the latter.

Starting at the end of the twentieth century, many new social movements have emerged around the world. Their activity is enhanced through cyberpower: the availability of new forms of information and communication technology. E-mail, the Internet, and cell phones help civil society groups gain visibility and stay in touch with their supporters.

Social capital arises from the benefits of people having social bonds and social solidarity. It creates a multiplier effect that can improve people's welfare.

Key Concepts

achieved position, p. 140
age set, p. 132
ascribed position, p. 140
caste system, p. 144
civil society, p. 146
dalit, p. 144

diaspora population, p. 142
matriarchy, p. 144
mestizaje, p. 140
patriarchy, p. 144
primary group, p. 132
secondary group, p. 132

social capital, p. 148
social group, p. 132
social stratification, p. 139
status, p. 140
youth gang, p. 136

Thinking Outside the Box

1. Think of some examples in which socially excluded groups have contributed to changing styles of music, dress, and other forms of expressive culture of so-called mainstream groups.

2. With which ethnic or other kind of social group do you identify? What are the bases of this identification? Is your social group relatively high or low in terms of social status?

3. Do Internet research to learn about CO-MADRES now: Does it still exist? If so, what are its objectives, activities, and achievements?

Chapter 8
Power, Politics, and Social Order

Learning Objectives

8.1 Recognize how anthropologists define and study public power.

8.2 Identify ways that cultures maintain social order and address conflict.

8.3 Illustrate changes in public power and social control.

Anthro Connections

A political leader of the Ashanti people of Ghana, West Africa. British colonialists referred to such leaders with the English term "chief." Perhaps the English word "king" might have been more appropriate. Nonetheless, the term chief has endured. In 2012, Ashanti people in the United States installed their New York chief who is laden with gold necklaces, bracelets, and a crown as well as wearing **kente cloth** (Semple 2012). At the ceremony elders poured libations, and drummers inspired hundreds of guests, draped in kente, to dance. The New York chief, as of 2011, is Acheampong-Tieku (try pronouncing it as you read it), who goes by

Michael in his civilian life and works in the Bronx as an accountant. He was nominated by a 10-member council of regional Ashanti elders and voted on by community members. His ceremonial and practical duties include mediating family and business disputes before they reach the courts and helping Ghanaian immigrants find work, housing, health care, and legal aid. His most pressing challenge, however, is the survival of his organization. Many of the New York Ghanaian association's original members have moved back to Ghana or died. Ghanaian-American youth are not interested in the association and its support of Ghanaian traditions.

This chapter covers topics in political and legal anthropology, two subfields of cultural anthropology. Political anthropology, discussed in the chapter's first section, addresses the area of human behavior and thought related to public power—who has it and who does not, degrees of power, bases of power, abuses of power, relationships between political and religious power, political organization and government, social conflict and social control, and morality and law. Legal anthropology, the subject of the second section, is the study of socially accepted ways of maintaining social order and resolving conflict.

Public Power: Political Organization and Leadership

8.1 Recognize how anthropologists define and study public power.

Compared with political scientists, cultural anthropologists take a broader view of politics that includes many kinds of behavior and thought beyond formal party politics and government as most readers of this book have experienced. Cultural anthropologists offer examples of

political systems and behavior that do not look "political" to people who have grown up in modern states.

This chapter uses the term politics to refer to the organized use of public power, not the private micropolitics of family and domestic groups. **Power** is the ability to bring about results with the potential or use of force. Closely related to power are authority and influence. **Authority** is the ability to bring about results based on a person's status, respect, and reputation in the community. Authority differs from power in two ways: Power is backed up by the potential use of force, and power can be wielded by an individual who lacks authority. **Influence** is the ability to bring about results by exerting social or moral pressure. Unlike authority, influence may be exerted from a low-status, marginal position.

All three terms are relational. A person's power, authority, or influence exists in relation to other people.

---

kente cloth a royal and sacred fabric associated with Ghana's Akan people and characterized by geometric shapes, bright colors, and designs associated with proverbs, leaders, events, and plants.

power the ability to take action in the face of resistance, through force if necessary.

authority the ability to take action based on a person's achieved or ascribed status or moral reputation.

influence the ability to achieve a desired end by exerting social or moral pressure on someone or some group.

Power, authority, and influence are variations on how a person can achieve desired outcomes. (TOP LEFT) Police in China practice how to protect schoolchildren from a possible attack. Police have power. (BOTTOM LEFT) Matilda House, an elder of the Ngambri-Ngunnawal people of Australia joins hands with Kevin Rudd, former prime minister and Brendan Nelson, leader of the Liberal Party, during a ceremony in 2008, marking the first time that Australia's parliament received a traditional indigenous welcome. She has authority. (TOP RIGHT) Irish singer Bono at a press conference in 2008 where he hammered G8 countries for falling far behind in aid pledges to Africa. He has influence.

Power implies the greatest likelihood of a coercive and hierarchical relationship, and authority and influence offer the most scope for consensual, cooperative decision making. Power, authority, and influence are all related to politics, power being the strongest basis for action and decision making—and potentially the least moral.

Anthropologists define **political organization** as the groups within a culture that are responsible for public decision making and leadership, maintaining social cohesion and order, protecting group rights, and ensuring safety from external threats.

The many forms of political organization that occur cross-culturally can be clustered into four types that are related to the modes of livelihood (Figure 8.1).

Bands

A **band**, the form of political organization associated with foraging groups, involves flexible membership and no formal leaders. Just as foraging has been the predominant mode of livelihood for almost all of human existence, the band is humanity's oldest form of political organization. And just as foraging is in danger of extinction as a way of life, so is band political organization.

A band typically comprises between 20 and a few hundred people at most, all related through kinship. These units come together at certain times of the year, depending on their foraging patterns and ritual schedule.

Band membership is flexible: If a person has a serious disagreement with another person or a spouse, one option is to leave that band and join another. Leadership is informal, with no one person named as a permanent leader. Depending on events, such as organizing the group to relocate or to send people out to hunt, a particular person may be a leader for that event, someone whose advice and knowledge are especially respected.

All members of the group are social equals, and a band leader has no special status. He has a certain degree of authority or influence, perhaps as a respected hunter or storyteller, but he does not have power and cannot force others to accept his views. Social leveling mechanisms prevent anyone from accumulating much authority or influence. Political activity in bands involves mainly decision making about migration, food distribution, and the resolution of interpersonal conflicts. External conflict between groups is rare because

political organization groups within a culture that are responsible for public decision-making and leadership, maintaining social cohesion and order, protecting group rights, and ensuring safety from external threats.

band the form of political organization of foraging groups, with flexible membership and minimal leadership.

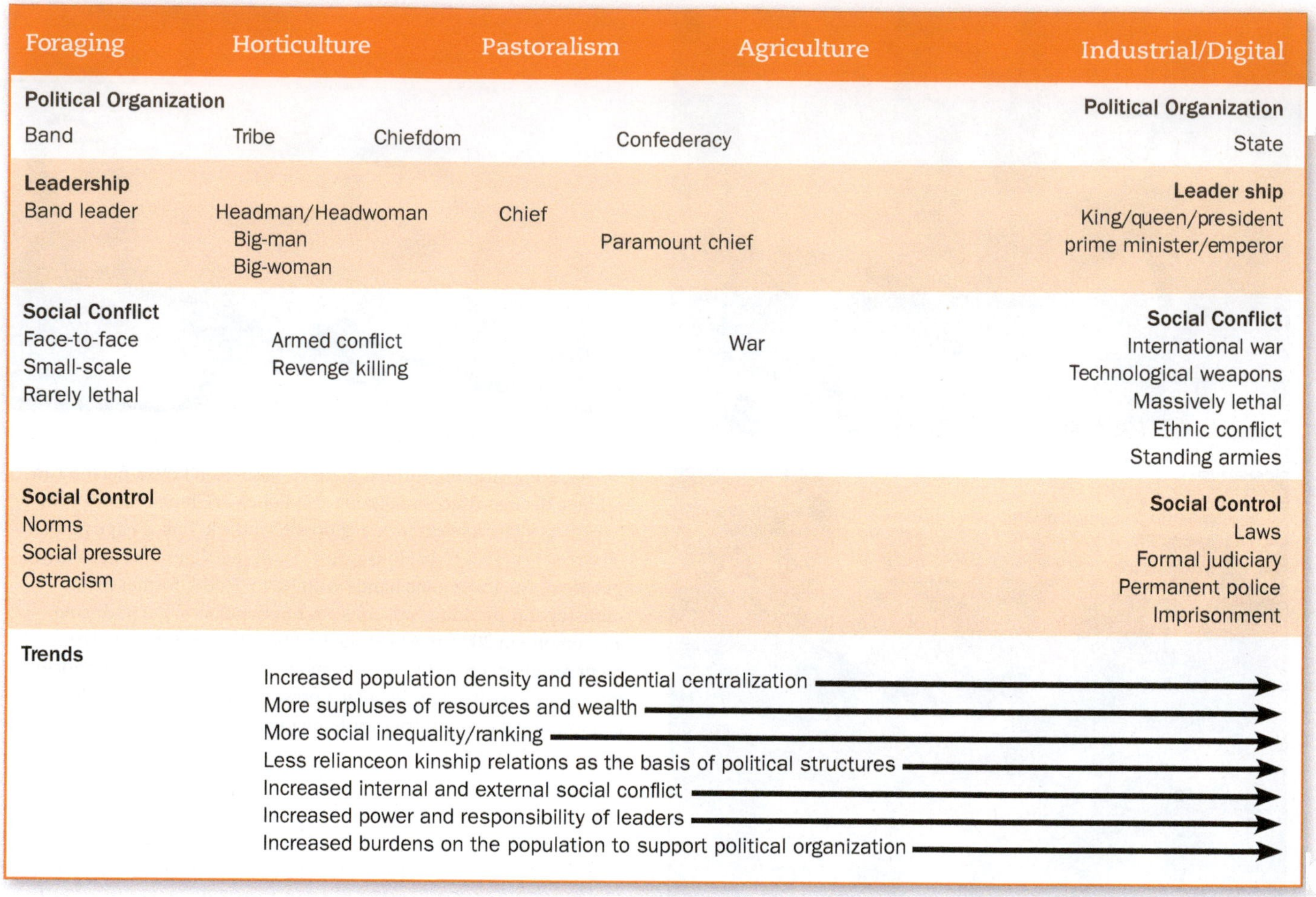

Foraging	Horticulture	Pastoralism	Agriculture	Industrial/Digital
Political Organization				**Political Organization**
Band	Tribe	Chiefdom	Confederacy	State
Leadership				**Leader ship**
Band leader	Headman/Headwoman	Chief		King/queen/president
	Big-man		Paramount chief	prime minister/emperor
	Big-woman			
Social Conflict				**Social Conflict**
Face-to-face	Armed conflict		War	International war
Small-scale	Revenge killing			Technological weapons
Rarely lethal				Massively lethal
				Ethnic conflict
				Standing armies
Social Control				**Social Control**
Norms				Laws
Social pressure				Formal judiciary
Ostracism				Permanent police
				Imprisonment
Trends				

Increased population density and residential centralization ⟶
More surpluses of resources and wealth ⟶
More social inequality/ranking ⟶
Less relianceon kinship relations as the basis of political structures ⟶
Increased internal and external social conflict ⟶
Increased power and responsibility of leaders ⟶
Increased burdens on the population to support political organization ⟶

Figure 8.1 Modes of Political Organization, Conflict, and Social Control

territories of different bands are widely separated and the population density is low.

The band level of organization barely qualifies as a form of political organization, because groups are flexible, leadership is ephemeral, and there are no signs or emblems of political affiliation. Some anthropologists argue, therefore, that true politics did not exist in undisturbed band societies. Bands still exist, but their members have had to learn to interact with other forms of political organization.

Tribes

A **tribe** is a more formal type of political organization than the band. Typically associated with horticulture and pastoralism, tribal organization arose between 10,000 and 12,000 years ago with the emergence of these modes of livelihood. A tribe is a political group that comprises several bands or lineage groups, each with a similar language and lifestyle and each occupying a distinct territory. Tribal groups may be connected through a clan structure, in which most people claim descent from a common ancestor although they may be unable to trace the exact relationship. Kinship is

the primary basis of membership. Tribal groupings contain from a hundred to several thousand people. Tribes are found in the Middle East, South Asia, Southeast Asia, the Pacific, Africa, and the Western Hemisphere.

A tribal headman (most tribal leaders are male) is a more formal leader than a band leader. A headman must be hardworking and generous and must possess good personal skills. A headman is a political leader on a part-time basis only. This role is more demanding than that of a band leader. Depending on the mode of livelihood, a headman will be in charge of determining the times for moving herds, planting and harvesting, and for setting the time for seasonal feasts and celebrations. Internal and external conflict resolution is also his responsibility. A headman relies mainly on authority and influence, rather than on power. These strategies are effective because tribal members are all kin and are loyal to each other.

tribe a form of political organization that comprises several bands or lineage groups, each with a similar language and lifestyle and occupying a distinct territory.

Chief Paul Payakan, leader of the Kayapo Payakan, was instrumental in mobilizing widespread resistance among the Kayapo and several other Amazonian tribes to the construction of a large hydroelectric dam at Altamira on the Xingu River.

▌*Find updated information on the Kayapo and the ongoing Altamira dam project on the Web.*

BIG-MAN AND BIG-WOMAN LEADERSHIP In between tribal and chiefdom organizations is the **big-man system or big-woman system**, a form of political organization in which individuals build a political base and gain prestige, influence, and authority through a system of redistribution based on personal ties and grand feasts (review Chapter 3). Anthropological research in Melanesia (Map 8.1), a large region in the South Pacific extending from New Guinea to Fiji, established the existence of big-man politics (Sahlins 1963). Similar favor-based political systems are found elsewhere, including in contemporary states.

Political ties of a successful big-man or big-woman include people in several villages. A big-man tends to have marginally greater wealth than his followers, although people continue to expect him to be generous. The core supporters of a big-man tend to be kin, with extended networks that include nonkin. A big-man has heavy responsibilities. He is responsible for regulating internal affairs, such as the timing of crop planting, and external affairs, such as intergroup feasts, trade, and war. In some instances, a big-man is assisted in carrying out

his responsibilities by a group of other respected men. These councils include people from the big-man's different constituencies.

In several tribes in the Mount Hagen (HAH-gen) area of the Papua New Guinea highlands (see Map 1.3, page 18), an aspiring big-man develops a leadership position through a process called **moka** (mawka) (Strathern 1971). Moka is a strategy for developing political leadership in Melanesia that involves exchanging favors and gifts, such as pigs, and sponsoring large feasts where further gift-giving occurs. A crucial factor in big-manship in the Mount Hagen area is having at least one wife. An aspiring big-man urges his wife or wives to work harder than ordinary women to grow more food to feed more pigs. The number of pigs a man has is an important measure of his status and worth.

An aspiring big-man builds moka relationships first with kin and then beyond. By giving goods to people, he gains prestige over them. The recipient is under pressure to make a return gift of equal or greater value. The exchanges go back and forth, over the years. The more the aspiring big-man gives, and the more people he can maintain in his exchange network, the greater prestige he develops.

A study on the island of Vanatinai reveals the existence of both big-women and big-men (Lepowsky 1990). In this gender-egalitarian culture, both men and women can gain power and prestige by sponsoring feasts at which valuables are distributed, especially mortuary feasts (feasts for the dead). Although more Vanatinai men than women are involved in political exchange and leadership, some women are extremely active as political leaders. These women lead sailing expeditions to neighboring islands to visit their exchange partners, who are both male and female, and they sponsor lavish feasts attended by many people.

Chiefdoms

A **chiefdom** is a form of political organization that includes permanently allied tribes and villages under one chief, a leader who possesses power. Compared with most tribes, chiefdoms have large populations, often numbering in the

---

big-man system or big-woman system a form of political organization midway between tribe and chiefdom and involving reliance on the leadership of key individuals who develop a political following through personal ties and redistributive feasts.

moka a strategy for developing political leadership in highland New Guinea that involves exchanging gifts and favors with individuals and sponsoring large feasts where further gift-giving occurs.

chiefdom a form of political organization in which permanently allied tribes and villages have one recognized leader who holds an "office."

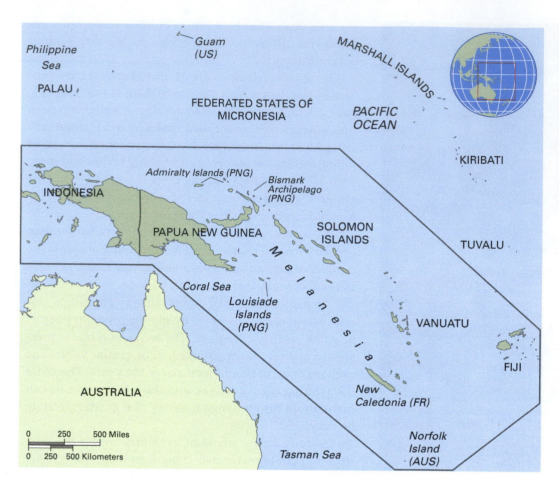

Map 8.1 Melanesia

Melanesia is a region in the South Pacific that includes the independent states of Papua New Guinea, the Republic of Vanuatu, the Solomon Islands, and Fiji as well as many islands that are controlled by other countries. It also encompasses the western part of the island of New Guinea, which is controlled by Indonesia, and islands to the west of it, though the people there do not identify themselves as Melanesians.

thousands. They are more centralized and socially complex. Hereditary systems of social ranking and economic stratification are a central feature of chiefdoms. Chiefs and their descendants have higher status than commoners, and intermarriage between members of the two strata is forbidden.

The chiefship must be filled at all times. When a chief dies or retires, he or she must be replaced. In contrast, the death of a band leader or of a big-man or big-woman does not require that someone else be chosen as a replacement. A chief has more responsibilities than a band or tribal leader. He or she regulates production and redistribution, solves internal conflicts, and plans and leads raids and warring expeditions. Criteria for becoming a chief include both ascribed and achieved qualities. Ascribed criteria include birth in a chiefly lineage and being the first son or daughter of the chief. Achievement is measured in terms of personal leadership skills, charisma, and accumulated wealth. Chiefdoms have existed throughout the world.

The Iroquois, located mainly in what today is New York State (see Map 3.2, page 48), provide a case of women's indirect political importance (Brown 1975). Men were chiefs, but women and men councilors were the appointing body. Most men were gone for extended periods, waging war as far away as Delaware and Virginia. Women controlled production and distribution of the staple crop, maize. If the women did not want warriors to leave for a particular campaign, they would refuse to provide them with maize, thereby vetoing the plan.

An expanded version of the chiefdom occurs when several chiefdoms are joined in a confederacy. Such a group is headed by a chief of chiefs—a "big chief" or paramount chief. Many prominent confederacies have existed, including the Iroquois league of five nations, the Cherokee of Tennessee, the Algonquins of the Chesapeake region in present-day Virginia and Maryland, and confederacies in Hawai'i in the late 1700s. In the Algonquin confederacy, each village had a chief and the regional council was composed of local chiefs and headed by the paramount chief. Powhatan, father of Pocahontas, was paramount chief of the Algonquins when the British arrived in the early 1600s.

Throughout much of the South Pacific, big-man and big-woman politics has long involved the demonstration of political leaders' generosity. (TOP) Leaders are expected to be able to mobilize resources for impressive feasts such as this one on Tanna Island, one of the many islands of the Republic of Vanuatu in the region of Melanesia. (BOTTOM) A sea turtle off the coast of Fiji, where local people consider them sacred and important as a feasting item.

▌ *How does public feasting play a role in politics in a context with which you are familiar?*

States

A **state** is a centralized political unit encompassing many communities, a bureaucratic structure, and leaders who possess coercive power. The state is now the form of political organization in which all people live. Band organizations, tribes, and chiefdoms exist, but they are incorporated to varying degrees within state structures. Before 1000 BCE, stateless societies were the norm. Now, the state rules as a form of political organization. Struggles exist around the world to define the boundaries of states and which group is or is not part of a particular state. Many groups would like to opt out of the state they are in and form their own state. The United Nations, when it was founded in 1945, recognized 51 states. It now recognizes 193 states.

STATE POWERS AND ROLES States have a wide range of powers and responsibilities:

- States engage in international relations to deal with other states about mutual concerns. The state may use force defensively to maintain its borders and offensively to extend its territory.

- States monopolize the use of force and the maintenance of law and order internally through laws, courts, and the police.

- States maintain standing armies and police (as opposed to part-time forces).

- States define citizenship and its rights and responsibilities. In complex societies, since early times, not all residents have been granted equal rights as citizens.

- States keep track of the number, age, gender, location, and wealth of their citizens through census systems that are regularly updated.

- States have the power to extract resources from citizens through taxation.

- States manipulate information. Information to protect the state and its leaders can be controlled both directly (through censorship, restricting access to certain information by the public, and promotion of favorable images via propaganda) and indirectly (through pressure on journalists, television networks, and other media to selectively present information or to present information in certain ways).

---

state a form of political organization in which a centralized political unit encompasses many communities, a bureaucratic structure, and leaders who possess coercive power.

(LEFT) Afghanistan President Hamid Karzai, 2004–2014, wears a carefully assembled collection of regional political symbols. The striped cape is associated with northern tribes. The Persian-lamb hat is an Uzbek style popular in the capital city, Kabul. He also wears a tunic and loose trousers, which are associated with villagers, and he sometimes adds a Western-style jacket. His clothing implies a statement of unity and diversity about his country. (CENTER) President Barack Obama typically wears a dark suit, white shirt, and necktie for formal occasions. During a Hawai'i-themed celebration at the White House, he sports a lei, which signals his close links to the state where he was born and spent much of his youth. (RIGHT) President Ellen Johnson-Sirleaf of Liberia and (then) U.S. Secretary of State Hillary Clinton make contrasting statements through their formal attire with Johnson-Sirleaf clearly signaling a connection to Africa and Clinton conveying a more neutral message in her trademark pantsuit.

SYMBOLS OF STATE POWER Religious beliefs and symbols are often closely tied to the power of state leadership: The ruler may be considered to be a deity or part deity, or may be a high priest of the state religion, or perhaps be closely linked with the high priest, who serves as advisor. Architecture and urban planning remind the populace of the greatness of the state.

In democratic states, where leaders are elected by popular vote, and in socialist states, where political rhetoric emphasizes social equality, expense and elegance are muted by the adoption of more egalitarian ways of dress (even though in private, these leaders may live relatively opulent lives in terms of housing, food, and entertainment). The earlier practice of all Chinese leaders wearing a "Mao jacket," regardless of their rank, was a symbolic statement of their antihierarchical philosophy. A quick glance at a crowd of people, including the prime minister of Canada or Britain or the president of the United States, would not reveal who was the leader, because dress differences are avoided. Even members of British royalty wear "street clothes" on public occasions where regalia are not required.

Beyond clothing, other commodities associated with top leadership positions include the quality of housing, food, and modes of transportation. State leaders live in grand mansions and often have more than one residence.

The King of Morocco, for example, has several official palaces around the country, and he travels regularly from one to another. President George W. Bush was considered "one of the people" because he liked to eat hamburgers. State leaders do not travel the way ordinary citizens do. For security reasons, their ground vehicles may have bulletproof windows, and a cavalcade of security vehicles protects the leader's vehicle. In many African countries, the most important new symbol of political power is an expensive imported car (Chalfin 2008).

GENDER AND LEADERSHIP IN STATES Most contemporary states are hierarchical and patriarchal, excluding members of lower classes and women from equal participation. Some states are less male dominated than others, but none is female dominated. One view of gender inequality in states suggests that increasing male dominance with the evolution of the state is based on men's control of the technology of production and warfare (Harris 1993). Women in most cultures have limited access to these areas of power. In more peaceful states, such as Finland, Norway, Sweden, and Denmark, women's political roles are more prominent.

Although women account for half of the world's population, they form only, on average, 19 percent of the world's parliamentary members (or the equivalent of parliament) (Franceschet, Krook, and Piscopo 2012). The highest percentage currently is in Rwanda, at over 50 percent, a result of the death of many men in the political violence that occurred between the Hutu and Tutsi people. Countries with over 25 percent of women parliamentarians are either African states, such as Rwanda and South Africa, that have recently experienced violence, or Scandinavian states, which are politically progressive.

Many countries with relatively high percentages of women in parliament (or the equivalent) have mandated gender quotas, or required percentages of seats that must be filled by women. Debate is ongoing as to whether such quotas will make a difference in international or domestic policy-making. That is, does having more women in leadership positions promote policies in support of "women's issues" such as peace, reproductive rights, and support for human capital investments (schools, children's programs)?

This discussion raises the question of gender essentialism: Does the fact of being a man or woman necessarily predict that the person will support policies that favor men or women, respectively? Some states have, or recently have had, women as prime ministers or presidents, including Indira Gandhi in India, Golda Meir in Israel, Margaret Thatcher in the United Kingdom, Benazir Bhutto in Pakistan, Michelle Bachelet in Chile, Angela Merkel in Germany, Ellen Johnson-Sirleaf in Liberia, and Tarja Halonen in Finland. Many female heads of state are related by kinship, as wife or daughter, to male heads of state. Indira Gandhi, for example, was the daughter of Jawaharlal Nehru, the popular first prime minister of independent India. It is unclear whether these women inherited the role or achieved it indirectly through socialization as a member of a political family, or both. Men who are heads of state, or members of parliament or its equivalent, may have also gained their position through kinship.

Social Order and Social Conflict

8.2 **Identify ways that cultures maintain social order and address conflict.**

Many Maasai people of Tanzania and Kenya work in cities and interact with international tourists, and some attend universities. But most rural Maasai, traditionally pastoralists who value their freedom to roam over vast areas, have limited knowledge of global events. Some rural villages lack electricity, so not everyone has access to a television. In 2002, when Kimeli Naiyomeh returned to his village in a remote area of Kenya following his medical studies at Stanford University in California, he told stories that stunned the villagers (Lacey 2002). They had not heard about the attacks on the United States on September 11, 2001. He described how massive fires destroyed buildings so high that they stretched into the clouds. The villagers could not believe that a building could be so tall that people jumping from it would die.

The stories about 9/11 saddened the villagers. They decided they should do something to help the victims. Cows are the most precious objects among the Maasai. As Kimeli Naiyomeh comments, "The cow is almost the center of life for us. . . . It's sacred. It's more than property. You give it a name. You talk to it. You perform rituals with it" (2002:A7). In June 2002, in a solemn ceremony, the villagers gave 14 cows to the United States. After the cows were blessed, they were transferred to the deputy chief of the U.S. Embassy in Kenya. He expressed his country's gratitude and explained that transporting the cows to the United States would be difficult. The cows were sold and the money went to support Maasai schools.

Violence, as well as the chances for peace, has global implications more than ever before. As Eben Kirksey, who has worked in West Papua for over a decade, says, we live in "entangled worlds" (2012). In West Papua, which may seem remote to most readers of this book, people have cell phones and pay attention to the world news on a daily basis. When Kirksey arrived to start his fieldwork, people there informed him that an anthropologist had been there before, and they asked him what he could do for them, pointing out their situation and needs. This initial meeting took Kirksey into a long exploration of how the people of West Papua have experienced terrifying forms of colonialism and, more recently, **militarism**. Militarism is the dominance of the armed forces in administration of the state and society. So far, the people of West Papua have responded with little direct resistance to outside forces but have displayed behavior that could be called collaboration for survival.

This section discusses social order and peace, including informal arrangements and formal laws and systems of crime prevention and punishment. It begins with the cross-cultural study of social order and then moves to a discussion of conflict and violence.

In anthropology, **social control** is the process by which people maintain orderly life in groups. Social control systems include informal social controls that exist through socialization for proper behavior, education, and peer pressure. They may also include formal systems of codified rules about proper behavior and punishments for deviation. In the United States and Canada, the Amish (review Culturama in Chapter 4, page 70) and Mennonites

---

militarism the dominance of the armed forces in administration of the state and society.

social control processes that, through both informal and formal mechanisms, maintain orderly social life.

Social norms and laws vary cross-culturally. Visitors queue at the site of the World Expo 2010 in Shanghai, China, the site of an expected 70 million visitors over the next six months with an average of 380,000 people expected daily. Queuing makes sense in densely populated situations.

rely on informal social controls far more than do most microcultural groups. The Amish and Mennonites have no police force or legal system; the way social order is maintained is through religious teaching and group pressure. If a member veers from correct behavior, punishment such as ostracism ("shunning") may be applied.

Norms and Laws

Cultural anthropologists distinguish two major instruments of social control: norms and laws. A **social norm** is an accepted standard for how people should behave that is usually unwritten and learned unconsciously through socialization. All societies have norms. Norms include, for example, the expectation that children should follow their parents' advice, that people standing in line should be orderly, and that an individual should accept an offer of a handshake (in cultures where handshakes are the usual greeting) when meeting someone for the first time. Enforcement of social norms is informal. For example, a violation may simply be considered rude and the violator would be avoided in the future. Sometimes, however, direct action may be taken, such as asking someone who disrupts a meeting to leave. A more recent concept in political science is that of a global norm: a value that many people believe should be universally held and enforced. An example of a global norm that is not universally accepted is women's equality in the public domain.

A **law** is a binding rule created through custom or official enactment that defines correct behavior and the punishment for misbehavior. Systems of law are more common and more elaborate in state-level societies, but many nonstate societies have formalized laws. Religion often provides legitimacy for law. Australian Aborigines believe that law came to humans during the Dreamtime (also called the Dreaming), a period in the mythological past when the ancestors created the world. The terms law and religion are synonymous in contemporary Islamic states. Secular Western states consider their laws to be religiously neutral, although, in fact, much Western law is based on Judeo-Christian beliefs.

Systems of Social Control

The material that follows considers forms of social control in small-scale societies as contrasted with large-scale societies. The former are characterized more by the use of norms. The latter, notably states, rely more on legal sanctions, although local-level groups, such as neighbors, practice social sanctions among themselves. A final topic considers the relationship between the law and social inequality.

SOCIAL CONTROL IN SMALL-SCALE SOCIETIES Anthropologists distinguish between small-scale societies and large-scale societies in terms of conflict resolution, social order, and punishment of offenses.

Bands are small, close-knit groups, so disputes tend to be handled at the interpersonal level through discussion or one-on-one fights. Group members may act together to punish an offender through shaming and ridicule. Emphasis is on maintaining social order and restoring social equilibrium, not hurtfully punishing an offender. Ostracizing an offending member (forcing the person to leave the group) is a common means of punishment. Capital punishment (execution) is rare.

social norm a generally agreed-upon standard for how people should behave, usually unwritten and learned unconsciously.

law a binding rule created through enactment or custom that defines right and reasonable behavior and is enforceable by the threat of punishment.

In some Australian Aboriginal societies, group laws restrict access to religious rituals and paraphernalia to men who have gone through a ritual initiation. If an initiated man shared secrets with an uninitiated person, the elders would delegate certain members of the group to kill the offender. In such instances, the elders act like a court.

In small-scale, nonstate societies, punishment is often legitimized through belief in supernatural forces and their ability to affect people. Among the highland horticulturalists of the Indonesian island of Sumba (see Map 1.2, page 14), one of the greatest offenses is to fail to keep a promise (Kuipers 1990). Breaking a promise will bring on "supernatural assault" by the ancestors of those who have been offended by the person's misbehavior. The punishment may come in the form of damage to crops, illness or death of a relative, destruction of the offender's house, or having one's clothing catch on fire. When such a disaster occurs, the only recourse is to sponsor a ritual that will appease the ancestors.

The overall goal in dealing with conflict in small-scale societies is to return the group to harmony. Village fission (breaking up) and ostracism are mechanisms for dealing with more serious conflict.

SOCIAL CONTROL IN STATES In densely populated societies with more social stratification and more wealth, increased social stress occurs in relation to the distribution of surplus, inheritance, and rights to land. In addition, increased social scale means that not everyone knows everyone else. Face-to-face accountability exists only in localized groups. Three important factors in state systems of social control are as follows:

- Specialization of roles involved in social control
- Formal trials and courts
- Power-enforced forms of punishment, such as prisons and the death penalty

Informal mechanisms of social control, however, exist alongside these formal systems at the local level.

Specialization The specialization of tasks related to law and order, such as those performed by police, judges, and lawyers, increases with the emergence of state organization. Full-time professionals such as judges and lawyers emerged with the state. These professionals are often members of powerful social groups, a fact that perpetuates elite biases in the justice process itself.

Policing is a form of social control that includes processes of surveillance and the threat of punishment related to maintaining social order (Reiner 1996). Police are the specific organization and personnel who discover, report, and investigate crimes. As a specialized group, police are associated with states.

Japan's low crime rate has attracted the attention of Western law-and-order specialists, who think that it may

be the result of the police system there. They ask whether solutions to U.S. crime problems can be found in such Japanese policing practices as neighborhood police boxes, or small, local police offices, staffed by foot patrolmen and volunteer crime-prevention groups organized on a neighborhood basis. Fieldwork among police detectives in the city of Sapporo reveals aspects of Japanese culture and policing that promote low crime rates (Miyazawa 1992). In Japan, the police operate under high expectations that no false arrests will be made and that all arrests should lead to confession. And, in fact, the rate of confession is high. The high rate of confession may be due to the fact that the police do an excellent job of targeting the guilty party, or it may result from the nearly complete control of interrogation by the police. The police are allowed to keep suspects isolated for long periods, a practice that wears down resistance. The suspect's statements are not recorded verbatim or taped; instead, the detectives write them down and the suspect is asked to sign them. Overall, policing culture in Japan gives more power to the police and less to the defendant than in the United States and has the potential to distort the process of justice.

Trials and Courts In societies where spirits and ancestors define wrongdoing and punishment, a person's guilt is proved simply by the fact that misfortune has befallen him or her. If lightning damaged a person's crops, for instance, then that person must have done something wrong. In other cases, guilt may be determined through **trial by ordeal**, a way of judging guilt or innocence in which the accused person is put through a test that is often painful. An accused person may be required to place his or her hand in boiling oil, for example, or to have a part of his or her body touched by a red-hot knife. Being burned is a sign of guilt, whereas not being burned means that the suspect is innocent.

The court system, with lawyers, judge, and jury, is used in many contemporary societies, although variation exists in how cases are presented and juries constituted. The goal of contemporary court trials is to ensure both justice and fairness. Analysis of courtroom dynamics and patterns of decision making in the United States and elsewhere, however, reveals ongoing problems in achieving these goals.

Prisons and the Death Penalty Administering punishment involves doing something unpleasant to someone who has committed an offense. As noted earlier, the most extreme form of punishment in small-scale societies is ostracism and only rarely death. A common form of punishment in the case of theft or murder in pastoralist societies,

---

policing the exercise of social control through processes of surveillance and the threat of punishment related to maintaining social order.

trial by ordeal a way of determining innocence or guilt in which the accused person is put to a test that may be painful, stressful, or fatal.

especially Islamic cultures of the Middle East, is that the guilty party must pay compensation to members of the family who have been harmed.

The number of imprisoned people varies widely around the world. The United States imprisons more people than any other country in the world (The Pew Charitable Trusts 2015). It is important to look at the rate of imprisonment as well as sheer numbers. The national incarceration rate is calculated as the number of people in prison per 100,000 people in a country. Countries vary widely in their incarceration rate. The United States has the highest incarceration rate, 743 per 100,000 people, followed by Rwanda 595, Russia, 568, and Georgia 547 (Walmsley 2010).

It is important to look inside national rates. In England and France, a disproportionate number of prisoners are Muslims (Moore 2008). Ethnic and gender differences in incarceration are marked in the United States (Pew Center 2015). One in 15 black men is in prison, and 1 in 9 black men 20 to 34 years of age is in prison. One in 355 white women ages 35 to 39 years is in prison, whereas 1 in 100 black women is behind bars. Among Hispanics, 1 in 36 adult Hispanic men is in prison. Within the United States, the state with the highest incarceration rate is Louisiana, and southern states in general have higher rates than northern states.

SOCIAL INEQUALITY AND THE LAW Critical legal anthropology is an approach within the cross-cultural study of legal systems that examines the role of law and judicial processes in maintaining the dominance of powerful groups through discriminatory practices rather than protecting members of less powerful groups. Systematic discrimination against ethnic minorities, indigenous peoples, and women, among other categories, has been documented in judicial systems around the world, including those of long-standing democracies. This section presents an example from Australia.

At the invitation of Aboriginal leaders in Australia, Fay Gale and her colleagues conducted research comparing the treatment of Aboriginal youth and White youth in the judicial system (1990). The question posed by the Aboriginal leaders was "Why are our kids always in trouble?" Two directions can be pursued to find the answer. First, structural factors—such as Aboriginal displacement from their homeland, poverty, poor living conditions, and bleak future prospects—can be investigated. Second, the criminal justice system can be examined to see whether it treats Aboriginal and White youth equally. The researchers decided to direct their attention to the judicial system because little work had been done in that area by social scientists.

Findings show that Aboriginal youth are overrepresented at every level of the juvenile justice system, from apprehension (being caught by the police) through pretrial processes, to the ultimate stage of adjudication (the judge's decision) and disposition (the punishment): "A far greater proportion of Aboriginal than other young people follow the harshest route. . . . At each point in the system where discretion operates, young Aborigines are significantly more likely than other young persons to receive the most severe outcomes of those available to the decision-makers" (1990:3). At the time of apprehension (being caught by the police), the suspect can be either formally arrested or informally reported. A formal arrest is made to ensure that the offender will appear in court. Officers ask suspects for a home address and whether they have a job. Aboriginal youth are more likely than White youth to live in an extended family in a poor neighborhood, and they are more likely to be unemployed. Thus, they tend to be placed in the category "undependable," and they are formally arrested more than White youth for the same crime (Figure 8.2). The next step determines whether the suspect will be tried in Children's Court or referred to Children's Aid Panels. The Children's Aid Panels in South Australia have gained acclaim worldwide for the opportunities they give to individuals to avoid becoming repeat offenders and take their proper place in society. But most Aboriginal youth offenders are denied access to them and instead have to appear in court, where the vast majority of youthful offenders end up pleading guilty. The clear and disturbing finding from this study is that the mode of arrest tends to determine each subsequent stage. To counter such unjust systems, many cultural anthropologists and others support

This man, in a military prison in Chechnya, is accused by the Russian government of participating with Chechen rebel forces. Human rights activists have been concerned about the mistreatment of prisoners in Chechnya for several years.

■ *What human rights do prisoners have in your country?*

critical legal anthropology an approach within the cross-cultural study of legal systems that examines the role of law and judicial processes in maintaining the dominance of powerful groups through discriminatory practices rather than protecting less powerful people.

	Aboriginal Youth (percent)	White Youth (percent)
Brought into system via arrest rather than police report	43.4	19.7
Referred to Children's Court rather than diverted to Children's Aid Panels	71.3	37.4
Proportion of court appearances resulting in detention	10.2	4.2

Note: Most of these youths are male; data are from 1979 to 1984.

Source: *Aboriginal Youth and the Criminal Justice System: The Injustice of Justice*, by Fay Gale, Rebecca Bailey-Harris, Joy Wundersitz, Copyright © Cambridge University Press 1990. Reprinted by permission of Cambridge UniversityPress.

Figure 8.2 **Comparison of Outcomes for Aboriginal and White Youth in the Australian Judicial System**

and work to promote **social justice**, a concept of fairness based on social equality that seeks to ensure entitlements and opportunities for disadvantaged members of society.

Social Conflict and Violence

All systems of social control have to deal with the fact that public conflict and violence may occur. This section considers several varieties of public conflict and violence.

ETHNIC CONFLICT Ethnic conflict and grievances may result from an ethnic group's attempt to gain more autonomy or more equitable treatment. It may also be caused by a dominant group's actions to subordinate, oppress, or eliminate an ethnic group by genocide (killing large numbers of a distinct ethnic, racial, or religious group) or ethnocide (destroying the culture of a distinct group).

In the past few decades, political violence has increasingly been enacted within states rather than between states. It is true that ethnic identity often provides people with an ideological commitment to a cause, but one should look beneath the labels to see whether deeper, structural issues exist. Consider Central Asia (Map 8.2), a vast region populated by many ethnic groups, none of which has a clear claim to the land on the grounds of indigeneity. Yet, in

social justice a concept of fairness based on social equality that seeks to ensure access to basic human needs and opportunities for disadvantaged members of society.

Map 8.2 **Central Asian States**

The five states of Central Asia are Kazakhstan, Turkmenistan, Uzbekistan, Kyrgyzstan, and Tajikistan. Central Asia is a large, landlocked region that is historically linked with pastoralism and the famous Silk Road, a trade route connecting the Middle East with China. The region's terrain encompasses desert, plateaus, and mountains. Given its strategic location near several major world powers, it has often been a battleground of other states' interests. The predominant religion is Islam, and most Central Asians are Sunnis. Languages are of the Turkic language group. Central Asia has an indigenous form of rap-style music in which lyrical improvisers engage in battles, usually accompanied by a stringed instrument. These musical artists, or *akyns*, use their art to campaign for political candidates.

Central Asia, every dispute appears on the surface to have an ethnic basis: "Russians and Ukrainians versus Kazakhs over land rights and jobs in Kazakhstan, Uzbeks versus Tajiks over the status of Samarkhand and Bukhara, conflict between Kirghiz and Uzbeks in Kyrgyzstan, and riots between Caucasian Turks and Uzbeks in the Fergana Valley of Uzbekistan" (Clay 1990:48). Attributing the causes of all such problems to ethnic differences overlooks competition for resources that is based on regional, not ethnic, differences. Uzbekistan has most of the cities and irrigated farmland, whereas Kyrgyzstan and Tajikistan control most of the water, and Turkmenistan has vast oil and gas riches.

SECTARIAN CONFLICT   **Sectarian conflict** is conflict based on perceived differences between divisions or sects within a religion, and often related to rights and resources. For hundreds of years, sectarian conflict has occurred within the British Isles, between Catholics and Protestants, both groups being Christian. Sectarian conflict between Muslims often follows a split between Shias and Sunnis (discussed in Chapter 12). This division is expressed in outright violence such as attacks on each other's sacred sites. It also takes the form of indirect, structural violence, as shown by a study conducted in northern Pakistan during a period of Shia–Sunni conflict (Varley 2010). During the conflict, exclusionary medical service provision occurred in which Sunni women experienced second-class treatment at obstetric clinics to the extent that they retreated to using alternative medicine.

WAR   One definition of war says that it is an open and declared conflict between two political units. This definition, however, rules out many warlike conflicts, including the American–Vietnam War because it was undeclared. Or, war may be defined simply as organized aggression. But this definition is too broad, because not all organized violence can be considered warfare. Perhaps the best definition is that **war** is organized conflict involving group action directed against another group and involving lethal force (Ferguson 1994, quoted in Reyna 1994:30).

Cultural variation exists in the frequency of war, the objectives of war, how war is waged, and how postwar social relations are rebuilt. Intergroup conflicts among free-ranging foragers that would fit the definition of war do not exist in the ethnographic record. The informal, nonhierarchical political organization among bands is not conducive to waging armed conflict. Bands do not have specialized military forces or leaders.

Although no evidence of warlike behavior among bands exists, it does among some tribal groups though one needs to take care in defining "war" because it can mean a situation in which contesting groups of men line up against each other with bows and arrows and shields, and the "war" stops when one man has been wounded. At one extreme, with reported high levels of warfare frequency, are the Yanomami of the Brazilian Amazon (see Map 3.3, page 49, and Think Like an Anthropologist).

In states, armies and complex military hierarchies are supported by increased material resources through taxation and other forms of revenue generation. Greater state power allows for more powerful and effective military structures, which in turn increase the state's power. Thus, a mutually reinforcing relationship emerges between the military and the state. Although most states are highly militarized, not all are, nor are all states equally militarized. Costa Rica (see Map 11.1, page 231) does not maintain an army.

Examining the causes of war between states has occupied scholars in many fields for centuries. Some experts have pointed to common, underlying causes, such as attempts to extend boundaries, secure more resources, ensure markets, support political and economic allies, and resist aggression from other states. Others point to humanitarian concerns that prompt participation in "just wars," to defend values such as freedom or to protect human rights that are defined as such by one country and are being violated in another.

Causes of war in Afghanistan, to take one case, have changed over time (Barfield 1994). Since the seventeenth century, warfare increasingly became a way in which kings justified their power in terms of the necessity to maintain independence from outside forces such as the British and Czarist Russia. The last Afghan king was murdered in a coup in 1978. When the Soviet Union invaded in 1979, no centralized ruling group existed to meet it. The Soviet Union deposed the ruling faction, set up one of its own, and then killed over one million people, caused three million to flee the country, and left millions of others to be displaced internally. Still, in spite of the lack of a central command, ethnic and sectarian differences, and being outmatched in equipment by Soviet forces, the Afghanis waged a war of resistance that eventually wore down the Soviets, who withdrew in 1989.

The long-standing, undeclared war in Afghanistan suggests that war was a more effective tool of domination in earlier times when war settled matters more definitively (Barfield 1994). Before "modern" war, fewer troops were needed to maintain dominance after a conquest, because continued internal revolts were less common and the main issue was defense against rivals from outside. Now, since the U.S. "shock and awe" attack of Iraq, leaders must know that attacking and taking over a country are only the first stages

---

sectarian conflict conflict based on perceived differences between divisions or sects within a religion.

war organized and purposeful group action directed against another group and involving lethal force.

Think Like an Anthropologist

Yanomami, The "Fierce People"?

The Yanomami are a horticultural people who live in dispersed villages of between 40 and 250 people in the Amazonian rainforest (Ross 1993). Since the 1960s, biological anthropologist Napoleon Chagnon has studied several Yanomami villages. He has written a widely read and frequently republished ethnography about the Yanomami, with early editions carrying the subtitle The Fierce People (1992 [1968]). He also helped produce classic ethnographic films about the Yanomami, including The Feast and The Ax Fight.

Chagnon's writings and films have promoted a view of the Yanomami as exceptionally violent and prone to lethal warfare. According to Chagnon, about one-third of adult Yanomami males die violently, about two-thirds of all adults lose at least one close relative through violence, and over 50 percent lose two or more close relatives (1992:205). He has reported that one village was raided 25 times during his first 15 months of fieldwork. Although village alliances are sometimes formed, they are fragile and allies may turn against each other unpredictably.

The Yanomami world, as depicted by Chagnon, is one of danger, threats, and counterthreats. Enemies, human and supernatural, are everywhere. Support from one's allies is uncertain. All of this uncertainty leads to what Chagnon describes as the waiteri (a Yanomami word) complex, a set of behaviors and attitudes that includes a fierce political and personal stance for men and forms of individual and group communication that stress aggression and independence. Fierceness is a dominant theme in socialization, as boys learn how to fight with clubs, participate in chest-pounding duels with other boys, and use a spear. Adult males are aggressive and hostile toward adult females, and boys learn to be aggressive toward girls from an early age.

Chagnon provides a biological, Darwinian explanation for the fierceness shown by the Yanomami. He reports that the Yanomami explain that village raids and warfare are carried out so that men may obtain wives. Although the Yanomami prefer to marry within their village, a shortage of potential brides exists because of the Yanomami practice of female infanticide. Although the Yanomami prefer to marry endogamously, taking a wife from another group is preferable to remaining a bachelor. Men in other groups, however, are unwilling to give up their women—hence the necessity for raids. Other reasons for raids are suspicion of sorcery or theft of food.

Chagnon argues that within this system warfare contributes to reproductive success because successful warriors are able to gain a wife or more than one wife (polygyny is allowed). Thus, successful warriors will have higher reproductive rates than unsuccessful warriors. Successful warriors, Chagnon suggests, have a genetic advantage for fierceness, which they pass on to their sons, leading to a higher growth rate of groups with violent males through genetic selection for fierceness. Male fierceness, in this view, is biologically adaptive.

Marvin Harris, taking the cultural materialist perspective, says that protein scarcity and population dynamics in the area are the underlying causes of warfare (1984). The Yanomami lack plentiful sources of meat, which is highly valued. Harris suggests that when game in an area becomes depleted, pressure rises to expand into the territory of neighboring groups, thus precipitating conflict. Such conflicts in turn result in high rates of adult male mortality. Combined with the effects of female infanticide, this meat-warfare complex keeps population growth rates down to a level that the environment can support.

A third view relies on historical data. Brian Ferguson (1990) argues that the high levels of violence among the Yanomami were caused by the intensified Western presence during the preceding 100 years. Furthermore, diseases introduced from outside, especially measles and malaria, severely depopulated the Yanomami and greatly increased their fears of sorcery (their explanation for disease). The attraction to Western goods such as steel axes and guns would also increase intergroup rivalry. Thus, Ferguson suggests that the "fierce people" are a creation of historical forces, especially contact with and pressure from outsiders.

Following Ferguson's position, but with a new angle, journalist Patrick Tierney points the finger of blame at Chagnon himself (2000). Tierney maintains that it was the presence of Chagnon, with his team of coresearchers and many boxes of trade goods, that triggered a series of lethal raids due to increased competition for those very

Napoleon Chagnon in the field with two Yanomami men, 1995. Chagnon distributed goods such as steel axes and tobacco to the Yanomami to gain their cooperation in his research.

goods. In addition, Tierney argues that Chagnon intentionally prompted the Yanomami to act fiercely in his films and to stage raids that created aggravated intergroup hostility beyond what had originally existed.

In 2001, the American Anthropological Association established a task force to examine five topics related to Tierney's allegations that Chagnon's and others' interactions with and representations of the Yanomami may have had a detrimental impact on them, contributing to "disorganization" among the Yanomami. The report of the El Dorado Task Force appears on the website http://www.aaanet.org of the American Anthropological Association. The task force rejected all charges against Chagnon and instead emphasized the harmfulness of false accusations that might jeopardize future scientific research.

Critical Thinking Questions

- Which perspective presented here on Yanomami men's behavior is most persuasive to you and why?
- What relevance does this case have to the theory that violence is a universal human trait?
- Do you think anthropological research could lead to increased violence among the study population?

in a more complicated process than the term regime change implies. Afghanistan is still attempting to recover and rebuild after over five decades of war (Shahrani 2002). Cultural factors influencing the country's recovery include codes of honor that value political autonomy and require vengeance for harm received, the moral system of Islam, the drug economy, and the effects of intervention from outside powers involving several foreign governments most notably the United States, and major resource extracting corporations. The challenge of constructing a strong state with loyal citizens in the face of competing internal and external factors is great.

GLOBAL–LOCAL CONFLICT The categories of conflict described previously involve units that are roughly parallel: ethnic groups, sectarian groups, or states. Another form of conflict has been taking place around the world since at least the fifteenth century when powerful European countries began to colonize tropical countries. This process, far from being over, is ongoing, though the major actors have shifted over time. The United States, known as the most powerful country in the world, has recently been involved in two simultaneous wars, in Iraq and Afghanistan. Although justified as "wars against terrorism," a more critical view would interpret them as neocolonial wars, that is, wars that seek to control strategic world areas for the material and political gain of the dominating country. Such wars are not formally declared, and they often do not conform to accepted international rules of engagement, including the treatment of prisoners.

Another type of conflict involves a private-sector (non-government) entity such as a multinational corporation versus a local group or groups that typically makes claims against, and often fights physically against, the corporation. Some cultural anthropologists work with multinational corporations to assist them in establishing and maintaining harmonious relations with people affected by their projects such as dams, mines, and oil drilling. The concept of **corporate social responsibility (CSR)** is increasingly adopted by large multinationals, though implemented to varying degrees. The definition of CSR is contested, but most would agree that it boils down to business ethics that seek to generate profits for the corporation while avoiding harm to people and the environment: The goal is to pursue profits in line with protecting people and the planet.

Other anthropologists work as advocates on behalf of the so-called "affected people" to document harm inflicted by businesses and to gain compensation, meager as it typically is, and late-coming due to extended legal processes (see Anthropology Works). Another role for anthropology is at the beginning of the process of a resource extraction process, documenting the legal steps involved in the Environmental Impact Assessment phase and how, typically, the process is tilted in favor of the companies due to their power networks. In one case, in Peru, the mining company was able to bring in scientific experts to attest on its behalf; the *campesinos* (small farmers), who resisted the mine, lacked the ability to bring in their own counter-experts (Li 2009).

Changing Public Power and Social Control

8.3 Illustrate changes in public power and social control.

Political and legal anthropologists do important research on global–local political and legal connections and change. This section provides three examples of change.

Nations and Transnational Nations

Many different definitions exist for a nation, and some of them overlap with definitions given for a state. One definition says that a **nation** is a group of people who share a language, culture, territorial base, political organization, and history (Clay 1990). In this sense, a nation is culturally homogeneous, and the United States would be considered not a nation, but rather a political unit composed of many nations. According to this definition, groups that lack a territorial base cannot be termed nations. A related term is the nation–state, which some say refers to a state that comprises only one nation, whereas others think that it refers to a state that comprises many nations. An example of the first view is the Iroquois nation (see Map 3.2, page 48).

Depending on their resources and power, nations and other groups may constitute a political threat to state stability and control. Examples include the Kurds in the Middle East (see Culturama), the Maya of Mexico and Central America, Tamils in Sri Lanka, Tibetans in China, and Palestinians in the Middle East. In response to such nonstate local political movements, states seek to create and maintain a sense of unified identity. Political scientist Benedict Anderson, in his classic study *Imagined Communities* (1991 [1983]), writes about the symbolic efforts that state builders employ to create a sense of belonging—an "imagined community"—among diverse peoples. Strategies include the imposition of one language as the national language; the construction of monuments and museums that emphasize unity; and the use of songs, dress, poetry, and other media messages to promote an image of a unified country. Some states, such as China, control religious expression in the interest of promoting loyalty to and identity with the state.

---

corporate social responsibility (CSR) business ethics that seek to generate profits for the corporation while avoiding harm to people and the environment.

nation a group of people who share a language, culture, territorial base, political organization, and history.

Anthropology Works

Advocacy Anthropology and Community Activism in Papua New Guinea

A controversial issue in applied anthropology is whether or not an anthropologist should take on the role of community activist on behalf of the people among whom they have conducted research (Kirsch 2002). Some say that anthropologists should maintain a neutral position in a conflict situation and simply offer information that may be used by either side. Others say that it is appropriate and right for anthropologists to take sides and help support less powerful groups against more powerful groups. Those who endorse anthropologists taking an activist role argue that neutrality is never truly neutral: By seemingly taking no position, one indirectly supports the status quo. Information provided to both sides will serve the interests of the more powerful side.

Stuart Kirsch took an activist role after conducting field research for over 15 years in a region of Papua New Guinea that has been negatively affected by a large copper and gold mine called the Ok Tedi (aka teddy) mine (see Map 1.2, page 14). The mine released 80,000 tons of mining wastes into the local river system daily, causing extensive environmental damage that in turn damaged local people's food and water sources. Kirsch joined the community in its extended legal and political campaign to limit further pollution and to gain compensation for damages suffered.

He explains his involvement with the community as a form of reciprocal exchange. The community members have provided him with information about their culture for many years. He believes that his knowledge is part of the people's cultural property and that they have a rightful claim to its use. Kirsch's support of the community's goals has taken three forms:

- Providing documentation of the problems of the people living downstream from the mine in terms of their ability to make a living and their health.

Yonggom people gather at a village meeting on the Ok Tedi River, Papua New Guinea, to discuss legal proceedings in 1996.

- Working with local leaders to help them to convey their views to the public and in the court.
- Serving as a cultural broker, a person familiar with two cultures who can mediate and prevent conflicts, in discussions among community members, politicians, mining executives, lawyers, and representatives of nongovernmental organizations (NGOs) to promote solutions for the problems faced by the Ok Tedi people living downstream from the mine.

In spite of official reports recommending that the mine be closed in 2001, its future remains uncertain. No assessment of past damages to the community has been prepared. As the case goes on, Kirsch continues to support the community's efforts. Indigenous people worldwide are increasingly invoking their rights to anthropological knowledge about themselves.

According to Kirsch, the Ok Tedi case, along with many others, requires cultural anthropologists to rethink

their roles and relationships with the people they study. Gone is old-fashioned fieldwork in which community members provide information that the anthropologist records and then keeps for his or her intellectual development alone. The overall goal must be one of collaboration and cooperation and, often, the anthropologist serving as an advocate for the people.

Food for Thought

Consider the pros and cons of anthropological advocacy in terms of the Ok Tedi case or another issue: Should an anthropologist side with the local people with whom he or she has done research against a powerful outside force? If the anthropologist does not side with the local people, is that equivalent to siding with the outsiders?

Thanks to Stuart Kirsch, University of Michigan, for providing updates.

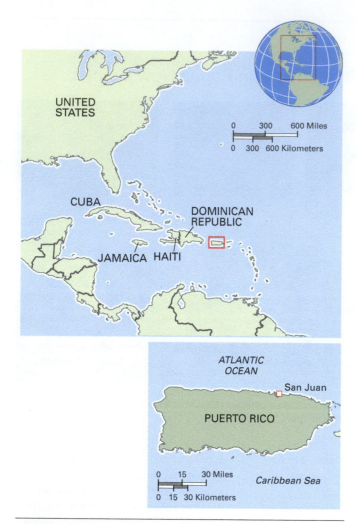

Map 8.4 Puerto Rico

The Commonwealth of Puerto Rico is a U.S. territory with commonwealth status. The indigenous population of the island, the Tainos, is extinct. Analysis of DNA of current inhabitants of Puerto Rico reveals a mixed ancestry, including the Taino, Spanish colonialists, and Africans who came to the island as slaves. The economy is based on agriculture, and sugarcane is the main crop. Tourism is also important, as are remittances. Official languages are Spanish and English. Roman Catholicism is the dominant religion, although Protestantism is increasing.

Globalization and increased international migration also prompt anthropologists to rethink the concept of the state (Trouillot 2001). The case of Puerto Rico (Map 8.4) is particularly illuminating because of its continuing status as a quasi-colony of the United States (Duany 2000). Puerto Rico is neither fully a state of the United States nor an autonomous political unit with its own national identity. Furthermore, Puerto Rican people do not coexist in a bounded spatial territory. By the late 1990s, nearly as many Puerto Ricans lived in the U.S. mainland as on the island of Puerto Rico. Migration to Puerto Rico also occurs, creating cultural diversity there. Migrants include returning Puerto Ricans and others from the United States, such as Dominicans and Cubans.

These migration streams—outgoing and incoming—pose a dual complication to the sense of Puerto Rico as constituting a nation. First, half of the "nation" lives outside the home territory. Second, within the home territory, ethnic homogeneity does not exist because of the diversity of people who migrate there. The Puerto Ricans who are return migrants are different from the islanders because many have adopted English as their primary language. All these processes foster the emergence of a transnational identity, which differs from a national identity centered in either the United States or Puerto Rico. (Chapter 12 provides additional material on transnationalism.)

Democratization

Democratization is the process of transformation from an authoritarian regime to a democratic regime. This process includes several features: the end of torture, the liberation of political prisoners, the lifting of censorship, and the toleration of some opposition (Pasquino 1996). In some cases, what is achieved is more a relaxation of authoritarianism than a true transition to democracy, which would occur when the authoritarian regime is no longer in control. Political parties emerge, some presenting traditional interests and others oppositional.

The transition to democracy appears to be most difficult when the change is from highly authoritarian socialist regimes. This pattern is partly explained by the fact that democratization implies a transition from a planned economy to one based on market capitalism (Lempert 1996). The spotty record of democratization efforts also has to do with the fact that many principles of democracy do not fit in with local political traditions that are based solely on kinship and patronage.

The United Nations and International Peacekeeping

What role might cultural anthropology play in international peacekeeping? Robert Carneiro (1994) has a pessimistic response. Carneiro says that during the long history of human political evolution from bands to states, warfare has been the major means by which political units enlarged their power and domain. Foreseeing no logical end to this process, he predicts that war will follow war until superstates become ever larger and one mega-state is the final result. He considers the United Nations powerless in dealing with the principal obstacle to world peace: state sovereignty interests. Carneiro indicts the United Nations for its lack of coercive power and its record of having resolved disputes through military intervention in only a few cases.

If war is inevitable, little hope exists that anthropological knowledge can be applied to peacemaking efforts. Nonetheless, and despite Carneiro's views, cultural

Culturama

The Kurds of the Middle East

The Kurds are an ethnic group of between 20 and 30 million people, most of whom speak some dialect of the Kurdish language, which is related to Farsi, the language spoken in Iran, among other countries (Major 1996). The majority are Sunni Muslims. Kurdish kinship is strongly patrilineal, and Kurdish family and social relations are male dominated.

Their home region, called Kurdistan ("Place of the Kurds"), extends from Turkey into Iran, Iraq, and Syria. This area is grasslands, interspersed with mountains, with no coastline. Before World War I, many Kurds were full-time pastoralists, herding sheep and goats. Following the war and the creation of Iraq, Syria, and Kuwait, many Kurdish herders were unable to follow their traditional grazing routes because they crossed the new country borders. Herders no longer live in tents year-round, though some do for part of the year. Others are farmers. In towns and cities, Kurds own shops, are professionals, and are employed in many different occupations.

Reliable population data for the Kurds in the Middle East do not exist, and estimates vary widely. About half of all Kurds—between 10 and 15 million—live in Turkey, where they constitute 20 percent, or perhaps more, of the total population. Approximately 6 million live in Iran, four to five million in Iraq, and 1.5 million in Syria. Others live in Armenia, Germany, France, and the United States.

For decades, the Kurds have attempted to establish, Kurdistan, an independent state (King 2014). So far, they have had no success. In Turkey, the state used to refer to them as "Mountain Turks" and still refuses to recognize them as a legitimate minority group. Use of the Kurdish language is restricted in Turkey.

The Kurds have faced similar repression in Iraq, especially following their support of Iran in the 1980–1988 Iran–Iraq war. Saddam Hussein razed villages and used chemical weapons against the Kurds. After the Persian Gulf War, two million Kurds fled to Iran. Many others have emigrated to Europe and the United States. Iraqi Kurds gained political autonomy from Baghdad in 1991 following a successful uprising aided by Western forces.

Many Kurds feel united by the shared goal of statehood, but several strong internal political factions and a guerrilla movement in Turkey also exist among the Kurds. Kurds in Turkey seek the right to have Kurdish-language schooling and television and radio broadcasts, and they would like to have their folklore recognized as well. The Kurds are fond of music and dancing, and Kurdish villages are known for their distinct performance styles.

Thanks to Diane E. King, University of Kentucky, for reviewing this material.

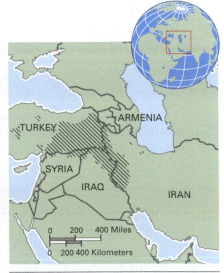

(LEFT) Herding goats and sheep is a major part of the economy throughout Kurdistan.

(CENTER) In Dohuk, Iraq, the Mazi Supermarket and Dream City are a combination shopping center and amusement park. The goods in the market come mainly from Dubai and Turkey.

Map 8.3   Kurdish Region in the Middle East

Kurdistan includes parts of Iran, Iraq, Syria, Turkey, and Armenia. About half of all Kurds live in Turkey.

anthropologists have shown that war is not a cultural universal and that some cultures solve disputes without resorting to war. The cultural anthropological perspective of critical cultural relativism (review this concept in Chapter 1) can provide useful background on issues of conflict and prompt a deeper dialogue between parties.

Two positive points emerge. The United Nations at least affords an arena for airing disputes. International peace organizations may thus play a role in world peace and order by providing a forum for analysis of the interrelationships among world problems and by exposing the causes and consequences of violence. Another positive direction is the role of NGOs and grassroots organizations in promoting local and global peacemaking through initiatives that bridge group interests.

8   Learning Objectives Revisited

8.1   Recognize how anthropologists define and study public power.

Political anthropology is the study of power relationships in the public domain and how they vary and change cross-culturally. Political anthropologists study the concept of power itself and related concepts such as authority and influence. They have discovered differences and similarities between politics and political organization in small-scale and large-scale societies in leadership roles and responsibilities and in the distribution of power.

Foragers have a minimal form of political organization in the band. Band membership is flexible. If a band member has a serious disagreement with another person or spouse, one option is to leave that band and join another. Leadership in bands is informal. The tribe is a more formal type of political organization than the band. A tribe comprises several bands or lineage groups with a headman or headwoman as leader. Big-man and big-woman political systems are an expanded form of the tribe, and leaders have influence over people in different villages. Chiefdoms may include several thousand people. Rank is inherited, and social divisions exist between members of the chiefly lineage and commoners.

The state is a centralized political unit encompassing many communities and possessing coercive power. States evolved in several locations with the emergence of intensive agriculture. Most states are hierarchical and patriarchal.

8.2   Identify ways that cultures maintain social order and address conflict.

Legal anthropology is the study of cultural variation in social order and social conflict. The more recent approach of critical legal anthropology points out how legal institutions often support and maintain social inequalities and injustice. Legal anthropologists also study the difference between norms and laws. Systems of social order and social control vary cross-culturally and over time.

Social control in small-scale societies seeks to restore order more than to punish offenders. The presence of a wide variety of legal specialists is more associated with the state than with small-scale societies, in which social shaming and shunning are common methods of punishment. In states, imprisonment and capital punishment may exist, reflecting the greater power of the state. Social conflict ranges from face-to-face conflicts, such as those among neighbors or domestic partners, to larger group conflicts between ethnic groups and states.

Cultural anthropologists are turning their attention to studying global conflict and peace-keeping solutions. Key issues involve the role of cultural knowledge in dispute resolution and how international or local organizations can help achieve or maintain peace.

8.3   Illustrate changes in public power and social control.

The anthropological study of change in public power and social control systems reveals several trends, many of which are related to the influences of European colonialism and contemporary globalization. Postcolonial states struggle with internal ethnic divisions and pressures to democratize.

Ethnic politics has emerged within and across states as groups seek to compete for increased rights within the state or for separation from it. The Kurds are an example of an ethnic group fighting for political autonomy.

Cultural anthropologists are increasingly doing research on international topics, including the internal dynamics of international organizations such as the United Nations. Their work demonstrates the relevance of cultural anthropology in global peacekeeping and conflict resolution.

Key Concepts

authority, p. 152
band, p. 153
big-man or big-woman system, p. 155
chiefdom, p. 155
corporate social responsibility (CSR),
    p. 166
critical legal anthropology, p. 162
influence, p. 152

kente cloth, p. 152
law, p. 160
militarism, p. 159
moka, p. 155
nation, p. 166
policing, p. 161
political organization, p. 153
power, p. 152

sectarian conflict, p. 164
social control, p. 159
social norm, p. 160
social justice, p. 163
state, p. 157
trial by ordeal, p. 161
tribe, p. 154
war, p. 164

Thinking Outside the Box

1. Consider the concepts of power, authority, and influence as defined in the chapter in the context of campus politics or in some other context with which you are familiar.

2. What are some prominent symbols of state power in your home country?

3. What is your position on states? Are they the best option for a peaceful world and for providing internal security and services for citizens? What are some examples of successful states?

Chapter 9
Communication

Learning Objectives

9.1 Summarize the ways that humans communicate.

9.2 Discuss how communication relates to cultural diversity and social inequality.

9.3 List examples of language change.

Anthro Connections

The Tuareg (TWAH-reg) are traditionally a pastoralist population that is widely distributed across the western part of Africa's Sahel region (see Map 12.5 on page 254). Among the Tuareg, men—not women—wear head and face coverings (Rasmussen 2010). Tuareg social practices include a mix of pre-Islamic matrilineal inheritance with Islamic laws and practices that favor patrilineal inheritance. Male veiling among the Tuareg shows social respect and, at the same time, social distance from settled peoples, constituting a form of visual signification. Many Tuareg male youths are now abandoning the veil, something seen by elders as a loss of dignity. Furthermore, states require a full-face photograph on identity cards, which requires removing the face veil, an act that Tuareg men regard as shameful.

This chapter is about human communication and language, drawing on work in both linguistic anthropology and cultural anthropology. It looks at communication with a wide-angle lens to include topics from word choice to language extinction. The chapter first discusses how humans communicate and what distinguishes human communication from that of other animals. The second section offers examples of language, microcultures, and inequality. The third section discusses language change from its origins in the distant past to contemporary concerns about language loss.

The Varieties of Human Communication

9.1 Summarize the ways that humans communicate.

Humans can communicate with words, either spoken or signed, with gestures and other forms of body language such as clothing and hairstyle, and using technology such as cellphones.

Language and Verbal Communication

Most people are in almost constant communication—with other people, with supernaturals, or with pets. We communicate in face-to-face situations or indirectly through old-fashioned mail or through the new media. **Communication** is the process of sending and receiving meaningful messages. Among humans, it involves some form of **language**, a systematic set of symbols and signs with learned and shared meanings. Language may be spoken, hand-signed, written, or conveyed through body movements, body markings and modifications, hairstyle, dress, and accessories.

Primatologist Sue Savage-Rumbaugh working with Kanzi, a male bonobo. Kanzi is involved in a long-term research project about ape language. He has learned to use several symbols. Some chimpanzees, bonobos, orangutans, and gorillas are able to communicate in American Sign Language and identify symbols on computer keyboards.

TWO FEATURES OF HUMAN LANGUAGE Over several centuries, scholars of language have proposed characteristics of human language that distinguish it from communication among other living beings. The following material describes the two most robust such characteristics.

communication the process of sending and receiving meaningful messages.

language a form of communication that is based on a systematic set of learned symbols and signs shared among a group and passed on from generation to generation.

A Pirahã shelter. According to Daniel Everett, who has spent many years learning about their culture and language, the Pirahã do not lead a culturally deprived life. The Pirahã are content with their lifestyle, which includes leisure activities such as playing tag and other games. In spite of their wish to remain living as they are, their reservation is not secure from outside encroachment.

Map 9.1   Pirahã Reservation in Brazil

Linguistic anthropologist Daniel Everett helped to define the boundaries of the Pirahã reservation in the 1980s. With support from Cultural Survival and other groups, the demarcation was legally declared in 1994.

First, human language has **productivity**, or the ability to create an infinite range of understandable expressions from a finite set of rules. This characteristic is a result of the rich variety of symbols and signs that humans use in their communication. In contrast, nonhuman primates have a more limited set of communicative resources. They rely on a **call system**, or a form of oral communication with a set repertoire of meaningful sounds generated in response to environmental factors. Nonhuman primates do not have the physiological capacity for speech that humans do. In captivity, however, some bonobos and chimpanzees have learned to communicate effectively with humans through sign language and by pointing to symbols on a chart. The world's most famous bonobo is Kanzi, who lives at the Great Ape Trust in Des Moines, Iowa. He can understand much of what humans say to him, and he can respond by combining symbols on a printed board. He can also play simple video games, such as Ms. Pac-Man (http://www.greatapetrust.org).

Second, human language emphasizes the feature of **displacement**, the ability to refer to events and issues beyond the immediate present. The past and the future, in this view, are considered to be displaced domains. They include reference to people and events that may never exist at all, as in fantasy and fiction.

Regarding productivity and displacement in human language, language among the Pirahã (pee-duh-hah) of Brazil raises many questions about supposed universal features of language (Everett 2008) (Map 9.1). Their language does not emphasize either productivity or displacement, though both exist to some degree. The Pirahã are a group of about 350 foragers living on a reservation in the Amazonian rainforest. Their language contains only three pronouns, few words associated with time, no past-tense verbs, no color terms, and no numbers other than a word that translates into English roughly as "about one." The grammar is simple, with no subordinate clauses. Kinship terms are simple and few. The Pirahã have no myths or stories and no art other than necklaces and a few rudimentary stick figures. In spite of over 200 years of regular contact with Brazilians and neighboring Indians who speak a different language, the Pirahã remain monolingual.

Since 1977, linguist Daniel Everett has frequently lived with the Pirahã and learned their language, so it is unlikely that he has overlooked major aspects of their language. He insists that their language is in no way "primitive" or inadequate. It has extremely complex verbs and rich and varied uses of stress and intonation, referred to in linguistics as prosody. The Pirahã enjoy verbal joking and teasing, both among themselves and with researchers.

Linguistic anthropologists have, for decades, learned about communication and language mainly through fieldwork and participant observation, and most of this chapter discusses findings from such studies. Recently, however, some scholars have pursued quantitative approaches using what is being called **big data**, collections of information

productivity a feature of human language whereby people are able to communicate a potentially infinite number of messages efficiently.

call system a form of oral communication among nonhuman primates with a set repertoire of meaningful sounds generated in response to environmental factors.

displacement a feature of human language whereby people are able to talk about events in the past and future.

big data sets of information including thousands or even millions of data points that are often generated from Internet and communication sources, such as cell phone use, Facebooking, and Tweeting.

including thousands, millions, or even billons of data points often generated from Internet and communication sources, such as cell phone use, Facebooking, and Tweeting (Palchykov et al. 2012). For example, one study analyzed cell phone calls in a European country over seven months, totaling 1.95 billion calls and nearly 500 million text messages. They analyzed the data by age and gender of the caller and the recipient, and they tracked frequency of calls. A striking finding is that, as women age, they trend away from calling men and more frequently call their parents and children. Younger women tend to call male contacts. This level of macroanalysis reveals fascinating patterns at the country level. Most cultural anthropologists would want to learn about more fine-grained patterns as well and the context that shapes the gender differences in cell phone contacts.

FORMAL PROPERTIES OF VERBAL LANGUAGE Human language can be analyzed in terms of its formal properties: sounds, vocabulary, and syntax (sometimes called grammar), which are the formal building blocks of all languages. But languages differ widely in which sounds are important, what words are important in the vocabulary, and how people put words together to form meaningful sentences. Learning a new language often involves learning different sets of sounds. The sounds that make a difference for meaning in a spoken language are called **phonemes**. The study of phonemes is called phonetics.

A native English-speaker learning to speak Hindi, the major language of North India, must learn to produce and recognize several new sounds. Four different "d" sounds exist. None is the same as an English "d," which is usually pronounced with the tongue placed on the ridge behind the upper front teeth (try it). One "d" in Hindi, which linguists refer to as a "dental" sound, is pronounced with the tongue pressed firmly behind the upper front teeth (try it) (Figure 9.1). Next is a dental "d" that is also aspirated (pronounced "with air"); making this sound involves the tongue being in the same position as it is in making the dental "d," but now a puff of air is expelled (try it, and try the regular dental "d" again with no puff of air at all). Next is what is referred to as a "retroflex" sound, made by flipping the tongue back to the central dome of the roof of the mouth (try it, with no puff of air). Finally, there is the aspirated retroflex "d" with the tongue in the center of the roof of the mouth and a puff of air. Once you can do this, try the whole series again with a "t," because Hindi follows the same pattern with this letter as with the "d." Several other sounds in Hindi require careful use of aspiration and placement of the tongue for communicating the right word. A puff of air at the wrong time can produce a serious

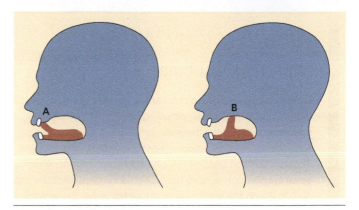

Figure 9.1   Dental and Retroflex Tongue Positions.
When making a dental sound, the speaker places the tongue against the upper front teeth (position A in the diagram). When making a retroflex sound, the speaker places the tongue up against the roof of the mouth (position B in the diagram)

error, such as saying the word for breast when you want to say the word for letter.

Every language has a vocabulary, or lexicon, which consists of all of the language's meaningful words. Speakers combine words into phrases and sentences to create meaning. Semantics refers to the study of the meaning of words, phrases, and sentences. Anthropologists add the concept of **ethnosemantics**, the study of the meaning of words, phrases, and sentences in particular cultural contexts. They find that languages classify the world in unpredictable ways, categorizing even such seemingly natural things as color and disease differently. (Recall the discussion of Subanun disease categories in Chapter 5.) Ethnosemantic research reveals much about how people define the world and their place in it, how they organize their social lives, and what is of value to them. Focal vocabularies are clusters of words that refer to important features of a particular culture. For example, many circumpolar languages have rich focal vocabularies related to snow (Figure 9.2), whereas in mountainous areas of Afghanistan, people use many terms for varieties of rocks.

- Firm, even snow that falls in mild weather
- Thickly packed snow caused by intermittent freezing/thawing and high winds
- Hard-packed snow formed by strong wind
- Dry, large-grained, water-holding snow at the deepest layers, closest to the ground, found in late winter and spring
- Snow that forms a hard layer after rain
- Ice sheet on pastures formed by rain on open ground that freezes
- A layer of frozen snow between other snow layers that acts as an ice sheet

Source: Jernsletten 1997.

Figure 9.2   Kinds of "Snow" the Saami Recognize Related to Reindeer Herding

---

phoneme a sound that makes a difference for meaning in a spoken language.

ethnosemantics the study of the meaning of words, phrases, and sentences in particular cultural contexts.

Anthropology Works

Narrating Troubles

Refugee survivors of violence are especially at risk of various mental health problems, including what psychiatrists call post-traumatic stress disorder, or PTSD. It includes symptoms such as depression, anxiety, sleep disorders, and changes in personality. In treating refugee survivors in North America, several approaches have been used, including narrative therapy, in which the sufferer tells about his or her experiences as a way of unloading the pent-up memories. It involves asking the individual to tell in detail, in a safe and caring interpersonal setting, the story of what happened to him or her.

A study of Bosnian refugees who now live in the United States sheds light on the positive effects of having survivors narrate their experiences of terror and suffering (Weine et al. 1995). Ten of the refugees in the study were male, and ten were female, ranging in age from 13 to 62 years. All but one were Muslims, and all adults were married and had worked either inside or outside the home. Analysis of their narratives showed that all had experienced many traumatic events, the frequency increasing with a person's age.

Almost all the refugees experienced the destruction of their homes, forced evacuation, food and water deprivation, disappearance of family members, exposure to acts of violence or death, detainment in a refugee camp, and forced emigration: "Nearly all the refugees emphasized the shock that came with the sudden occurrence of human betrayal by neighbors, associates, friends, and relatives" (1995:538).

The testimonies document the genocidal nature of the traumas directed at the entire Muslim Bosnian population. The traumas experienced were "extreme, multiple, repeated, prolonged, and communal" (1995:539). Some of the survivors carry with them constant images of death and atrocity. One man describes them as "films" that play in his head. In contrast, others have lost their memories of the events, and one woman was later unable to remember the trauma story she told three weeks earlier: "All kinds of things come together. Being expelled. Things we lost. Twenty years of work—then suddenly being without anything. . . . All the memories come at the same moment and it's too much" (1995:541).

The massiveness of their suffering, the psychiatrists report, extends beyond the bounds of the psychiatric diagnostic category of PTSD. Yet, in spite of their deep and extensive suffering, many Bosnian refugees in the United States are recovering and rebuilding their lives, perhaps in part because of the success of narrative therapy.

Studies of this therapeutic approach among refugees of other cultures, however, reveal that some people are extremely reluctant to discuss their experiences, even in a supportive setting. Thus, narrative therapy may not be effective in all cultures.

Map 9.2 Bosnia and Herzegovina

Formerly part of the Socialist Federal Republic of Yugoslavia, Bosnia and Herzegovina have a population of around four million. Bosnia occupies the northern areas of the country, about four-fifths of the total area, whereas Herzegovina occupies the southern part. The country still faces the challenges of reconstruction following the war of 1992–1995. On a brighter note, it has one of the best income equality rankings in the world.

A forensic expert clears the soil from a skull found in a mass grave in Bosnia. The grave is believed to contain bodies of perhaps 500 Muslim civilians killed by the Bosnian Serb forces during the 1992–1995 war.

Syntax, or grammar, consists of the patterns and rules by which words are organized to make sense in a sentence, or string. All languages have rules of syntax, although they vary in form. Even within the languages of contemporary Europe, syntactical variation exists. In German, for example, the verb often appears at the end of the sentence.

All the formal aspects of verbal communication allow people to convey, through speech, simple and complex messages about themselves and their experiences. Not all cultures shape their members to be equally "talky" as will be discussed below in the section on the importance of silence. In "talky" cultures, being able to share narratives (stories) about one's experiences, especially troubling or traumatic experiences, can be a path to healing (see Anthropology Works).

Nonverbal Language

Many forms of language and communication do not rely on verbal speech. Like verbal language, though, they are based on symbols and signs and have rules for their proper combination and meaning.

SIGN LANGUAGE Sign language is a form of communication that uses mainly hand movements to convey messages. A sign language provides a fully competent communication system for its users, just as spoken language does (Baker 1999). Around the world, many varieties of sign language exist, including American Sign Language, British Sign Language, Japanese Sign Language, Russian Sign Language, and many varieties of indigenous Australian sign languages. Most sign languages are used by people who are hearing impaired as their main form of communication. But in many indigenous Australian communities, people who are able to communicate verbally often opt to sign (Kendon 1988). They switch to sign language in situations in which verbal speech is forbidden or undesirable, for example, in some sacred contexts, for men during hunting, and for widows during mourning. Gestures are movements, usually of the hands, that convey meanings. Some gestures may be universally meaningful, but most are culturally specific and often completely arbitrary. Some cultures have more highly developed gesture systems than others. Black urban youths in the cities of Pretoria and Johannesburg in South Africa use a rich repertoire of gestures (Brookes 2004) (see Map 7.5, page 141). Some of the gestures are widely used and recognized, but many vary by age, gender, and situation (Figure 9.3). Men use more gestures than women do; the reason for this difference is not clear.

sign language a form of communication that uses mainly hand movements to convey messages.

---

child Fingers of one hand are brought together at the tips pointing upward. 	**girl/girlfriend** Thumb touches each breast starting with the breast opposite to the hand being used and then touches the first breast again. 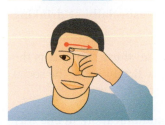
father/male elder/boyfriend Side of knuckle of forefinger, with thumb under chin, strokes chin downward once or twice. 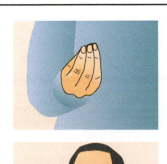	**secret lover** One hand placed under opposite armpit. 
friendship Sides of first fingers of each hand are tapped together several times. 	**drunk (she/he is drunk)** Side of curved first finger is drawn across the forehead. 

Figure 9.3 Some South African Gestures Used by a Man

Source: From *A Repertoire of South African Quotable Gestures*, from *The Journal of Linguistic Anthropology*, Copyright © 2004 Blackwell Publishers Ltd. Reproduced with permission of Blackwell Publishers.

Greetings, an important part of communication in every known culture, often involve gestures (Duranti 1997b). They are typically among the first communicative routines that children learn, as do tourists and anyone trying to learn a foreign language. Greetings establish a social encounter. They usually involve both verbal and nonverbal language. Depending on the context and the social relationship, many variations exist for both the verbal and the nonverbal component. Contextual factors include the degree of formality or informality. Social factors include gender, ethnicity, class, and age.

SILENCE Silence is another form of nonverbal communication. Its use is often related to social status, but in unpredictable ways. In rural Siberia, an in-marrying daughter-in-law has the lowest status in the household, and she rarely speaks (Humphrey 1978). In other contexts, silence is associated with power. For example, in U.S. courts, lawyers speak more than anyone else and the judge speaks rarely but has more power than a lawyer, while the silent jury holds the most power (Lakoff 1990).

Silence is an important component of communication among many American Indian cultures. White outsiders, including social workers, have sometimes misinterpreted this silence as a reflection of dignity or a lack of emotion or intelligence. How ethnocentric such judgments are is revealed by a study of silence among the Western Apache of Arizona (Basso 1972 [1970]) (Map 9.3). The Western Apache use silence in four contexts:

- When meeting a stranger, especially at fairs, rodeos, or other public events. Speaking with a stranger immediately indicates interest in something such as money, work, or transportation, all possibly serving as reasons for exhibiting bad manners.

- In the early stages of courting. Sitting in silence and holding hands for several hours is appropriate. Speaking "too soon" would indicate sexual willingness or interest.

- When a parent and child meet after the child has been away at boarding school. They should be silent for about 15 minutes. It may be two or three days before sustained conversations are initiated.

- When "getting cussed out," especially at drinking parties.

An underlying similarity of all these contexts is the uncertainty, ambiguity, and unpredictability of the social relationships involved.

BODY LANGUAGE Human communication, in one way or another, often involves the body in sending and receiving messages. Beyond the mechanics of speaking, hearing, gesturing, and seeing, the body itself can function as a "text" that conveys messages. The full range of body

Map 9.3 Western Apache Reservation in Arizona
Before European colonialism, the Apache lived in a wide area extending from Arizona to northwestern Texas. Originally foragers, they started planting some food crops in the 1600s. After the arrival of the Spanish, the Apache gained horses from them and became skilled equestrian warriors. In the second half of the nineteenth century, the U.S. government exterminated many Apache groups and forced those who survived to live on reservations to make way for White settlements.

language includes eye movements, posture, walking style, the way one stands and sits, cultural inscriptions on the body such as tattoos and hairstyles, and accessories such as dress, shoes, and jewelry. Body language follows patterns and rules just as verbal language does. As with verbal language, the rules and meanings are learned, often unconsciously. Without learning the rules and meanings, one will commit communication errors, which are sometimes funny and sometimes serious.

Different cultures emphasize different body language channels more than others. Some are more touch oriented than others, and some use facial expressions more. Eye contact is valued during Euro-American conversations, but in many Asian contexts direct eye contact is considered rude or perhaps a sexual invitation.

Clothing, hairstyles, and modification of or marks on the body convey messages about age, gender, sexual interest or availability, profession, wealth, and emotions. The color of one's clothing can send messages about a person's identity, class, gender, and more. In the United States, gender differentiation begins in the hospital nursery with the color coding of blue for boys and pink for girls. In parts of the Middle East, public dress is black for women and white for men.

The furisode kimono is distinguished by its fine silk material, long sleeves, and elaborate colors and designs. A girl's twentieth birthday gift is typically a furisode, marking her transition to young adulthood. Only unmarried women wear the furisode, so it is a statement of marital availability. Fluttering the long, wide sleeves at a man is a way to express love for him.

▌ *What meanings do the styles and lengths of sleeves convey in your cultural world?*

Covering or not covering various parts of the body with clothing is another culturally coded matter. Consider the different meanings of women's head or face covering in Egypt and Kuwait (MacLeod 1992). Kuwaiti women's head covering distinguishes them as relatively wealthy, leisured, and honorable, as opposed to the immigrant women workers from Asia, who do not cover their heads. In contrast, head covering in Egypt is done mainly by women from the lower and middle economic levels. For them, it is a way to accommodate conservative Islamic values while preserving their right to work outside the home. In Egypt, the head covering says, "I am a good Muslim and a good wife or daughter," while in Kuwait, the headscarf says, "I am a wealthy Kuwaiti citizen." In many conservative Muslim contexts, it is important for a woman in public to cover more than her head by wearing a full-length loose garment. These rules, along with other patriarchal values, make it difficult for women in some Muslim contexts to participate in sports while in school and in public sporting events such as the international Olympics.

In Japan, the kimono provides an elaborate coding system signaling gender and life-cycle stage (Dalby 2001). The higher one's status, the shorter is the sleeve of one's kimono, but there are gender differences: Men's kimono sleeves come in only one length: short. An unmarried woman's kimono sleeves reach almost to the ground, and a married woman's sleeves are nearly as short as that of a man's.

Communicating with Media and Information Technology

Media anthropology is the cross-cultural study of communication through electronic media such as radio, television, film, recorded music, the Internet, and print media, including newspapers, magazines, and popular literature (Spitulnik 1993). Media anthropology is an important emerging area that links linguistic and cultural anthropology (Allen 1994). Media anthropologists study the media process and media content, the audience response, and the social effects of media presentations. **Critical media anthropology** asks to what degree access to media is liberating or controlling and whose interests the media serve. Critical media anthropologists examine power issues in many areas including journalism, television, movies, advertising, the Internet, social media, and gaming worlds.

A study of Arab media in everyday life reveals major categories of Arab media (Zayani 2011). First, what is Arab media? It is a loose category of public communication using technology that falls under state control. For example, many Arab states have long used radio programs to shape the views of their citizens. Television now dominates public communication in Arab states, though the Internet has increasing importance. Journalism and film are two other major forms of public media. The dynamism and options for social change and empowerment have only begun to be assessed by cultural anthropologists doing research in the Arab world. The Arab spring movement of 2010 would not have been as successful without cell phone communication and other forms of social media.

ADVERTISING FOR LATINOS IN THE UNITED STATES Within the U.S. advertising market, one of the most sought-after segments is the Latino population, also called "the Hispanic market" in the advertising industry (Dávila 2002). Interviews with staff of 16 Latino advertising agencies and content analysis of their advertisements

---

critical media anthropology an approach within the crosscultural study of media that examines how power interests shape people's access to media and influence the contents of its messages.

reveal their approach of treating Latinos as a unified, culturally specific market. The dominant theme, or trope, is that of "the family" as being the most important feature of Latino culture, in contrast to the stereotype of the Anglo population as more individualistic. Recent milk-promotion advertisements for the Anglo population show a celebrity with a milk moustache. The Latino version shows a grandmother cooking a traditional milk-based dessert, and the caption reads, "Have you given your loved ones enough milk today?" (2002:270). In Spanish-language television and radio networks, a kind of "standard" Spanish is used, a generic form with no hint of regionalism or accent.

Latinos are, however, a highly heterogeneous population. By promoting a monolithic image of Latino culture, media messages may be contributing to identity change toward a more monolithic pattern. At the same time, they are certainly missing opportunities to tap into more specialized markets within the Latino population.

A McDonald's billboard targets an immigrant, Spanish-speaking population in South Los Angeles, California, one of the poorest areas of the city. South L.A. has the highest concentration of fast-food restaurants in the city and only a few grocery stores. Health problems associated with a fast-food diet, such as obesity and diabetes, affect many of the half-million people living there.

Cultural and linguistic anthropologists study social media to learn about how it can add to human agency as well as how it connects with the global political economy. (TOP) In Cairo, a woman previews a Facebook Web page showing the picture of an alleged Egyptian victim of torture who was reportedly brutally tortured to death by the police in the city of Alexandria. (BOTTOM) In China, a woman works online in her cubicle at an office in Beijing. China's media sites like Weibo are booming in the world's largest Internet market.

Language, Diversity, and Inequality

9.2   Discuss how communication relates to cultural diversity and social inequality.

This section presents material about language, microcultures, and social inequality. It begins by presenting two models of the relationship between language and culture. Examples follow about class, gender and sexuality, "race" and ethnicity, and age.

Language and Culture: Two Theories

During the twentieth century, two theoretical perspectives were influential in the study of the relationship between language and culture. They are presented here as two distinct models, even though they actually overlap in real life and anthropologists tend to draw on both of them (Hill and Mannheim 1992).

The first was formulated by two early founding figures in linguistic anthropology, Edward Sapir and Benjamin Whorf. In the mid-twentieth century, they formulated an influential model called the **Sapir–Whorf hypothesis**, a perspective that says that people's language affects how they think. If a language has many words for variations of the English word snow, for example, then someone who speaks that language can "think" about snow in more ways than someone can whose language has fewer "snow"

Sapir–Whorf hypothesis a perspective in linguistic anthropology saying that language determines thought.

terms. Among the Saami, whose traditional occupation was reindeer herding (see Culturama, page 188), a rich set of terms exists for snow (review Figure 9.2, page 175). If a language has no word for snow, then someone who speaks that language cannot think of snow. Thus, a language constitutes a thought world, and people who speak different languages inhabit different thought worlds. This catchy phrase became the basis for linguistic determinism, a theory stating that language determines consciousness of the world and behavior. Extreme linguistic determinism implies that the frames and definitions of a person's primary language are so strong that it is impossible to learn another language fully or, therefore, to understand another culture fully. Most anthropologists see value in the Sapir–Whorf hypothesis, but not in its extreme form.

A second approach to understanding the relationship between language and culture comes from scholars working in the area of **sociolinguistics**, a perspective that emphasizes how people's cultural and social context shapes their language and its meanings. Sociolinguists are, therefore, cultural constructionists.

Most anthropologists see some value in both perspectives because language, culture, context, and meaning are highly interactive: Language shapes culture and cultural context shapes language.

Critical Discourse Analysis: Gender and "Race"

Discourse refers to culturally patterned verbal language use including varieties of speech, participation, and meaning. **Critical discourse analysis** is an approach within linguistic anthropology that examines how power and social inequality are reflected in and reproduced through verbal language (Blommaert and Bulcaen 2000). Critical discourse analysis reveals links between language and social inequality, power, and stigma. It also provides insights into agency and resistance through language. The material that follows presents examples of power relations as expressed through language.

GENDER IN EURO-AMERICAN CONVERSATIONS Most languages contain gender differences in word choice, grammar, intonation, content, and style. Early studies of language and gender among white Euro-Americans revealed three general characteristics of female speech (Lakoff 1973):

- Politeness
- Rising intonation at the end of sentences
- Frequent use of **tag questions** (questions seeking affirmation and placed at the end of sentences, such as, "It's a nice day, isn't it?")

In English, male speech, in general, is less polite, maintains a flat and assertive tone in a sentence, and does not use tag questions. Related to politeness is the fact that, during cross-gender conversations, men tend to interrupt women more than women interrupt men.

Deborah Tannen's popular book *You Just Don't Understand* (1990) shows how differences in conversational styles between white Euro-American men and women lead to miscommunication. She says that "women speak and hear a language of connection and intimacy, whereas men speak and hear a language of status and independence" (1990:42). Although both men and women use indirect response (not really answering the question), their different motivations create different meanings embedded in their speech:

> **Michele:** What time is the concert?
> **Gary:** We have to be ready by seven-thirty. (1990:289)

Gary sees his role as one of protector in using an indirect response to Michele's question. He feels that he is simply "watching out for her" by getting to the real point of her question. Michele feels that Gary is withholding information by not answering her directly and is maintaining a power position. By contrast, a wife's indirect response to a question from her husband is prompted by her goal of being helpful in anticipating her husband's underlying interest:

> **Ned:** Are you just about finished?
> **Valerie:** Do you want to have supper now? (1990:289)

Cross-culturally, women's speech is not universally accommodating, subservient, and polite. In cultural contexts in which women's roles are prominent and valued, their language reflects and reinforces their position.

GENDER AND POLITENESS IN JAPANESE, AND THOSE NAUGHTY TEENAGE GIRLS Gender registers in spoken Japanese reflect gender differences (Shibamoto 1987). Certain words and sentence structures convey femininity, humbleness, and politeness. One important contrast between male and female speech is the attachment, by female speakers, of the honorific prefix "o-" to nouns; for example, a woman refers to chopsticks as *ohasi*, while a man calls them *hasi* (Figure 9.4). This addition gives women's speech a more refined and polite tone.

---

sociolinguistics a perspective in linguistic anthropology, which says that culture, society, and a person's social position determine language.

discourse culturally patterned verbal language including varieties of speech, participation, and meaning.

critical discourse analysis an approach within linguistic anthropology that examines how power and social inequality are reflected and reproduced in communication.

tag question a question placed at the end of a sentence seeking affirmation.

	Male	Female
Box lunch	bentoo	obentoo
Money	kane	okane
Chopsticks	hasi	ohasi
Book	hon	ohon

Source: *Language, Gender, and Sex in Comparative Perspective*, by Susan U. Philips, Susan Steele, Chrisitne Tanz. Copyright © Cambridge University Press 1987. Reprinted with permission of Cambridge University Press.

Figure 9.4 Male-Unmarked and Female-Marked Nouns in Japanese

A contrasting pattern of gendered language comes from the *kogals*, young Japanese women between 14 and 22 years of age known for their female-centered coolness (Miller 2004). The kogals have distinctive language, clothing, hairstyles, makeup, attitude, and activities, all of which challenge prescriptive norms for young women. Their overall style is flashy and exuberant, combining global and local elements. Heavy users of cell phones, kogals use a complex and ever-changing set of emoticons,

Over a decade ago, in 2004, a kogal in Tokyo's trendy Shibuyu district displays her cell phone that is covered with stickers. Kogal makeup and dress styles, like kogal language, keep changing.

or "face characters" including icons for "wow," "ouch," "applause," and "I can't hear you." They have also invented a unique text message code for their cell phones that uses mixed scripts such as mathematical symbols and Cyrillic (Russian) letters.

The spoken language of the kogals is a rich and quickly changing mixture of slang, some classic but much newly created. They create new words through compounds and by adding the Japanese suffix "-ru," which turns a noun into a verb, such as *maku-ru* ("go to McDonald's"). They intentionally use strongly masculine language forms, openly talk about sex, and rework taboo sexual terms into new meanings. Reactions from mainstream society to kogals are mixed, ranging from horror to fascination. No matter what, they have cultural influence and are shaking up the gender order and language.

GAY LANGUAGE AND BELONGING IN INDONESIA The national language of Indonesia is referred to as bahasa Indonesia. Many homosexual men in Indonesia speak bahasa gay, or "gay language" (Boellstorff 2004). Indonesia is the world's fourth-largest country in terms of population, with nearly 250 million citizens living on over 6,000 islands and speaking nearly 700 local languages. In spite of this cultural and linguistic diversity, bahasa gay is highly standardized.

Bahasa gay has a distinct vocabulary that plays humorously on mainstream language and provides a political commentary on mainstream life. Some of the vocabulary changes involve sound-alikes; others add a suffix to a standard word. In terms of the state's strongly heterosexual image, Indonesian gays would seem to be a clearly excluded group. Nonetheless, bahasa gay is moving into mainstream linguistic culture, where it conveys agency and freedom from official control.

AFRICAN AMERICAN ENGLISH: PREJUDICE AND PRIDE The topic of African American English (AAE), or African American Vernacular English (AAVE), is complicated by racism of the past and present (Jacobs-Huey 2006). Scholars debate whether AAE/AAVE is a language in its own right or a dialect (nonstandard version) of English. "Linguistic conservatives," who champion Standard American English (SAE), view AAE as an ungrammatical form of English that needs to be "corrected." In the current linguistic hierarchy in the United States, with SAE at the top, speakers of AAE may be both proud of their language and feel stigmatized by those who judge AAE negatively and treat its speakers unfairly (Lanehart 1999).

AAE is a relatively new language, emerging out of slavery to develop a degree of standardization across the United States, along with many local variants. Some of its characteristic grammar results from its African roots. One of the most prominent is the use, or nonuse, of forms of the English verb "to be" (Lanehart 1999:217). In AAE, one says, "She married," which means "She is married" in SAE. Viewed incorrectly by outsiders as "bad" English, "She married" follows a grammatical rule in AAE. That AAE has its own grammar and usage rules is evident in the fact that when non-AAE speakers attempt to speak it or imitate it, they often make mistakes (Jacobs-Huey 1997).

Ethnographic research on African American school-age children in a working-class neighborhood of southwest Philadelphia examined within-gender and cross-gender conversations, including directives (getting someone to do something), argument, he-said-she-said accusations, and storytelling (Goodwin 1990). All these speech activities involve complex verbal strategies that are culturally embedded. In arguments, the children may bring in imaginary events as a "put-on," preceded by the cue term "psych," or use words of a song to create and maintain playfulness within an argument. Much of their arguments involve highly ritualized insults that work quickly to return an insult to the original giver. When a group of girls was practicing some dance steps and singing, a boy said, "You sound terrible." A girl responded, "We sound just like you look" (1990:183). The study revealed the importance of verbal play and art among the children. It also showed that girls often excel at verbal competitions in mixed gender settings.

Children who grow up speaking a version of AAE at home and with peer groups face a challenge in schools, where they are expected to perform in SAE. Just like native Spanish speakers or any non–English-speaking new immigrants, African American children are implicitly expected to become bilingual in AAE and SAE. More than vocabulary and grammar are involved. Teachers should understand that African American children may have culturally distinct styles of expression that should be recognized and valued. For example, in narrative style, African American children tend to use a spiral pattern, skipping around to different topics before addressing the theme, instead of adopting a linear style. Rather than being considered a deficiency, having AAE speakers in a classroom adds cultural diversity to those whose linguistic worlds are limited to SAE.

Inspired by such findings, the Oakland School Board in California approved a resolution in 1996 to recognize Ebonics, or AAE, as the primary language, or vernacular, of African American students. The school developed a special teaching program, called the Bridge Program, in which AAE speakers were encouraged to learn Standard American English through a process of translation between AAE and SAE (Rickford 1997). After several months, students in the Bridge Program had progressed in their SAE reading ability much faster than African American students who were not in the program. Nevertheless, the program received so much negative publicity and raised such sensitive questions about the best way to enhance minority student learning that it was cancelled within the year.

The underlying issues of the so-called Ebonics controversy are still unresolved. One of the thorniest questions debated is whether AAE/AAVE/Ebonics is sufficiently distinct (either as a language separate from SAE or as a dialect) that U.S. schools should address it in their curriculum with special programs.

Language and Communication Change

9.3 **List examples of language change.**

Languages, like the cultures of which they are a part, experience both continuity and change, and for similar reasons. Human creativity and contact lead to linguistic innovation and linguistic borrowing. War, imperialism, genocide, and other forces may destroy languages. This section looks first at what is known about the origins of human language and provides a brief history of writing. Later parts discuss the influence of European colonialism on languages, nationalism and language, world languages, and contemporary language loss and revitalization.

The Origins and History of Language

No one knows how verbal language began. Current evidence of other aspects of human cultural evolution suggests that verbal language began to develop between 100,000 and 50,000 years ago when early modern humans achieved both the physical and mental capacity for symbolic thinking and verbal communication. Facial expressions, gestures, and body postures were likely important features of early human communication, as they are among many nonhuman primate species today.

Early scholars of language were often misled by ethnocentric assumptions that the structure of European languages was normative and that languages with different structures were less developed and deficient. For example, they considered the Chinese language primitive because it lacks the kinds of verbs that European languages have. As discussed at the beginning of this chapter, the Pirahã language appears simpler in many ways compared with English, as does the Pirahã culture, but both Pirahã and English have to be examined within their cultural contexts. Pirahã is a language that works for a rainforest foraging population. English works for a globalizing, technology-driven, consumerist culture. Languages of foraging cultures today can, with caution, provide insights about what foragers' language may have been like thousands of years ago. But they are not "frozen in time" examples of "Stone Age" language.

(LEFT) An African bonobo male waves branches in a display of aggression. (RIGHT) In the United States, women lacrosse players use sticks in a competitive sport invented by American Indians.

Threat is clearly conveyed by the bonobo's behavior. In lacrosse, sticks are used to pass the ball and score points. Is there also a threat aspect to the use of lacrosse sticks during a game?

Historical Linguistics

Historical linguistics is the study of language change through history. It relies on many specialized methods that compare shifts over time and across space in aspects of language such as phonetics, syntax, and meaning. It originated in the eighteenth century with a discovery made by Sir William Jones, a British colonial administrator working in India. During his spare time, he studied Sanskrit, a classical language of India. He noticed marked similarities among Sanskrit, Greek, and Latin in vocabulary and syntax. For example, the Sanskrit word for the English word father is *pitr*; in Greek it is *patéras*, and in Latin it is *pater*. This was an astounding discovery for the time, given the prevailing European mentality that placed its cultural heritage firmly in the classical Graeco–Roman world and depicted the "Orient" as completely separate from "Europe" (Bernal 1987).

Following Jones's discovery, other scholars began comparing lists of words and grammatical forms in different languages: for example, the French *père*, the German *Vater*, the Italian *padre*, the Old English *faeder*, the Old Norse *fadhir*, and the Swedish *far*. These lists allowed scholars to determine degrees of closeness and distance in the relationships among those languages. Later scholars contributed the concept of a **language family**, or groups of languages descended from a parent language (Figure 9.5). Individual languages descended from the same language, such as French and Spanish (both descended from Latin), are referred to as sister languages.

Using comparative evidence from historical and contemporary Eurasian languages, historical linguists developed a hypothetical model of the original parent language, or proto-language, of most Eurasian languages. It is called Proto-Indo-European (PIE). Linguistic evidence suggests that PIE was located in Eurasia, either north or south of the Black Sea (Map 9.4). From its area of origin, between 6,000 and 8,000 years ago, PIE spread into Europe, then into Central, South, and East Asia, where local versions developed over the centuries.

Similar linguistic methods reveal the existence of the original parent form of the Bantu language family, Proto-Bantu, in Africa (Afolayan 2000). Scholars can trace the Bantu expansion starting around 5,000 years ago (Map 9.5). Today, some form of Bantu language is spoken by over 100 million people in Africa, not to mention the number of people in the African diaspora worldwide. Over 600 African languages are derived from Proto-Bantu. According to linguistic analysis, the homeland of Proto-Bantu is the present-day countries of Cameroon and Nigeria, West Africa. It is likely that Proto-Bantu spread through

---

historical linguistics the study of language change using formal methods that compare shifts over time and across space in aspects of language, such as phonetics, syntax, and semantics.

language family a group of languages descended from a parent language.

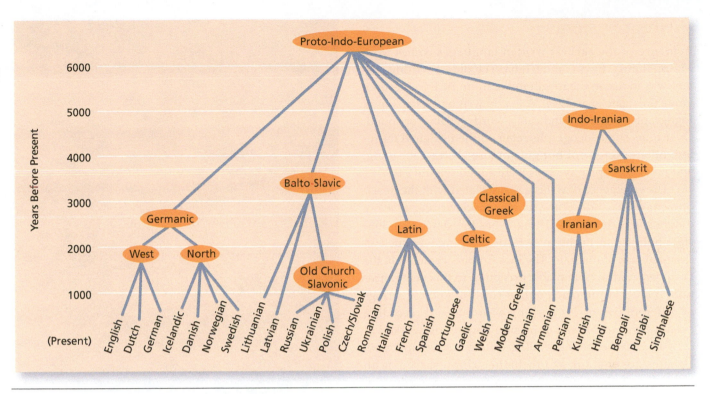

Figure 9.5 **The Indo-European Language Family**

population migration as the farming population expanded and moved, over hundreds of years, into areas occupied by indigenous foragers. Bantu cultural imperialism may have wiped out some local languages, although it is impossible to document any such extinctions. Substantial linguistic evidence, however, suggests some interactions between the farmers and the foragers through which standard Bantu absorbed elements from local languages.

Map 9.4   Two Sites of Proto-Indo-European Origins

Two major theories about the location of PIE exist, with the site south of the Black Sea considered to be earlier.

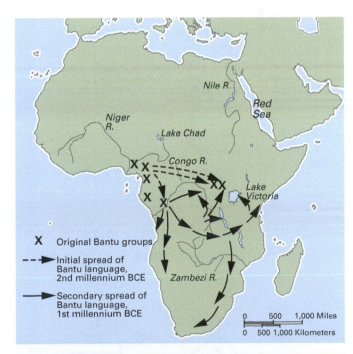

Map 9.5   The Bantu Migrations in Africa

Linguistic evidence for the migrations of Bantu-speaking people relies on similarities between languages in parts of eastern, central, and southern Africa and languages of the original Bantu homeland in West Africa. Over 600 African languages are derived from Proto-Bantu.

Writing Systems

Evidence of the earliest written languages comes from Mesopotamia, Egypt, and China. The oldest writing system was in use in the fourth millennium BCE in Mesopotamia (Postgate et al. 1995). All early writing systems used **logographs**, signs that indicate a word, syllable, or sound. Over time, some logographs retained their original meaning; others were kept but given more abstract meaning, and nonlogographic symbols were added (Figure 9.6).

The emergence of writing is associated with the development of the state. Some scholars take writing as a key diagnostic feature that distinguishes the state from non-state political forms because recordkeeping was such an essential task of the state. The Inca Empire, centered in the Peruvian Andes, is a notable exception to this generalization. It used **khipu** (kee-poo), or cords of knotted strings of different colors, for keeping accounts and recording events. Scholars are not quite sure how khipu worked in the past because the Inca coding system is so complicated. Debates are ongoing as to whether khipu served as an actual language or more simply as an accounting system. Whatever is the answer, the world's largest empire in the fourteenth century relied on khipu.

Two interpretations of the function of early writing systems exist. The first says that early writing was mainly for ceremonial purposes. Evidence for this position

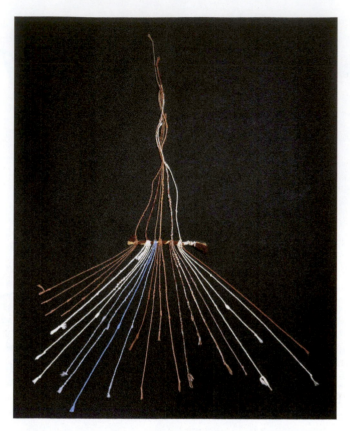

Khipu, or knotted strings, were the basis of state-level accounting in the Incan empire. The knots conveyed substantial information to those who could interpret their meaning.

consists of the prevalence of early writing on tombs, bone inscriptions, and temple carvings. The second says that early writing was mainly for secular use in government recordkeeping and trade. The archaeological record is biased toward durable substances, such as stone. Because ceremonial writing was intended to last, it was more likely to be inscribed on stone. Utilitarian writing, in contrast, was more likely to have been done on perishable materials because people would be less concerned with permanence. (Consider the way you treat shopping lists.) It is likely, however, that more utilitarian writing, as well as other forms of nonceremonial writing, also existed.

Colonialism, Nationalism, and Globalization

European colonialism was a major force of language change. Not only did colonial powers declare their own language as the language of government, business, and education, but they often took direct steps to suppress indigenous languages and literatures. Widespread

---

logograph a symbol that conveys meaning through a picture resembling that to which it refers.

khipu cords of knotted strings used during the Inca empire for keeping accounts and recording events.

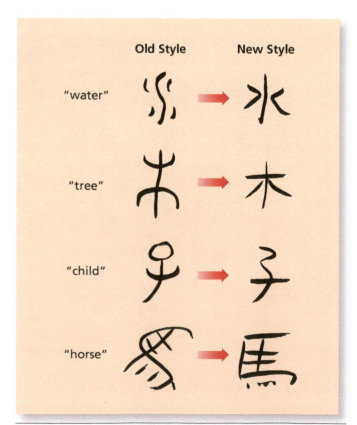

	Old Style	New Style
"water"		
"tree"		
"child"		
"horse"		

Figure 9.6 Logographic and Current Writing Styles in China

bilingualism, or competence in a language other than one's birth language, is one prominent effect of colonialism. Also, globalization is having substantial and complex effects on language.

EUROPEAN COLONIALISM AND CONTACT LANGUAGES Beginning in the fifteenth century, European colonialism had dramatic effects on the people with whom it came into contact, as discussed elsewhere in this book. Language change is an important part of the story of colonialism and indigenous cultures. Depending on the type and duration of contact, it resulted in the development of new languages, the decline of others, and the extinction of many, along with the people who spoke them (Silverstein 1997). Two forms of new languages prompted by European colonialism are pidgins and creoles.

A **pidgin** is a language that blends elements of at least two parent languages and that emerges when two different cultures with different languages come in contact and must communicate (Baptista 2005). All speakers of pidgin have their own native language(s) but learn to speak pidgin as a second, rudimentary language. Pidgins are typically limited to specific functional domains, such as trade and basic social interactions. Many pidgins of the Western Hemisphere were the result of the Atlantic slave trade and plantation slavery. Owners needed to communicate with their slaves, and slaves from various parts of Africa needed to communicate with each other. Pidgins are common throughout the South Pacific.

A pidgin often evolves into a creole, which is a language descended from a pidgin and that subsequently has its own native speakers, a richer vocabulary than a pidgin has, and a more developed grammar. Throughout the

French colonialism added another cultural layer to Arabic influences in Morocco, resulting in many bilingual and trilingual shop signs.

▌ *Where have you seen multilingualism in public use? What languages were used and why?*

Western Hemisphere, many localized creoles have developed in areas such as Louisiana, the Caribbean, Ecuador, and Suriname. Though a living reminder of the heritage of slavery, creole languages and associated literature and music are also evidence of resilience and creativity in the African diaspora.

Tok Pisin (the indigenous pronunciation of "talk pidgin"), originally a pidgin language of Papua New Guinea consisting of a mixture of English, Samoan, Chinese, and Malaysian, is now a creole and is recognized as one of the official languages of Papua New Guinea. Two other creoles are also nationally recognized: Seselwa, a blend including French spoken in the Seychelle Islands in the Indian Ocean and Papiamentu, a blend including Dutch spoken in Curaçao (coo-ruh-sao), the Netherland Antilles, in the Caribbean.

NATIONALISM AND LINGUISTIC ASSIMILATION Nationalist policies of cultural assimilation of minorities have led to the suppression and loss of local dialects and the extinction of many indigenous and minority languages throughout the world. Direct policies of linguistic assimilation include the declaration of a standard language and rules about the language of instruction in public schools. Often, Christian missionaries worked to suppress indigenous languages as part of their attempts to "civilize" "pagan" peoples (see Culturama) on the following page. Indirect mechanisms include discrimination in hiring on the basis of language and social stigma.

GLOBAL LANGUAGES Ninety-six percent of the world's population speaks 4 percent of the world's languages (Crystal 2000). The eight most-spoken languages are Mandarin, Spanish, English, Bengali, Hindi, Portuguese, Russian, and Japanese, in that order. Languages that are gaining widespread currency are called **global languages**, or world languages. Global languages are spoken worldwide in diverse cultural contexts. As they spread to areas and cultures beyond their home area and culture, they take on new, localized identities. At the same time, the "mother language" picks up words and phrases from local languages (Figure 9.7). Global languages may act as both a form of linguistic and economic opportunity and a form of cultural imperialism.

English is the most globalized language in history (Bhatt 2001; Crystal 2003). British English was first transplanted through colonial expansion to the present-day

---

pidgin a contact language that blends elements of at least two languages and that emerges when people with different languages need to communicate.

creole a language directly descended from a pidgin but possessing its own native speakers and involving linguistic expansion and elaboration.

global language a language spoken widely throughout the world and in diverse cultural contexts, often replacing indigenous languages.

Culturama

The Saami of Sápmi, or Lapland

The Saami (SAH-mee) are indigenous people who live in the northernmost parts of Norway, Sweden, Finland, and western Russia (Gaski 1993). The area is called Sápmi, the land of the Saami, or Lapland. The total Saami population is around 100,000 people, with the majority in Norway (Magga and Skutnabb-Kangas 2001).

At the time of the earliest written records of 1,000 years ago, all Saami hunted wild reindeer, among other land and sea species, and may have kept some tamed reindeer for transport (Paine 2004). Over time, herding domesticated reindeer developed and became the economic mainstay.

In the past few hundred years, though, reindeer pastoralism has declined and is now a specialization of about 10 percent of the population. Settled Saami are farmers or work in trade, small-scale industry, handicrafts, services, and the professions.

Traditional Saami reindeer herding has been a family-based system. Men and women cared for the herd, and sons and daughters inherited the rights to the herd equally (Paine 2004). The value of social equality was strong, entailing both rights and privileges.

In their relationships with the modern state, the Saami have experienced discrimination, exclusion, loss of territorial rights, and cultural and linguistic repression. Environmental risks to Saami cultural survival include having been downwind of the prevailing winds after the 1986 Chernobyl disaster, having been near the earlier Soviet atomic testing grounds in Siberia, having had their ancestral territory and sacred spaces lost or damaged by hydroelectric dam construction, and having had grazing lands taken over for use as military training grounds (Anderson 2004).

State policies of cultural assimilation and forced Christianization in the twentieth century marginalized the Saami language and led to language loss (Magga and Skutnabb-Kangas 2001). Several Saami languages and dialects still exist, however, and spatially distant versions are mutually unintelligible (Gaski 1993:116).

Language is of central cultural value to the Saami, and efforts to maintain it have been under way since the 1960s. Besides the Saami language, a traditional song form, the yoik, is of particular importance (Anderson 2005). Yoik lyrics allow a subtle system of double meanings that can camouflage political content (Gaski 1997).

Thanks to Myrdene Anderson, Purdue University, for reviewing this material.

(LEFT) The well-known Saami singer–songwriter Marie Boine performs at the Easter Festival in Kautokeino, Sápmi, northern Norway.

(CENTER) A Saami wedding in Norway with the bride and groom wearing traditional Saami dress. Weddings are held in the spring before the big reindeer migration.

Map 9.6 The Saami of Sápmi, or Lapland

Sápmi extends across Norway, Sweden, Finland, and Russia's Kola Peninsula.

Alcohol	Arabic, Middle East
Avocado	Nahuatl, Mexico/Central America
Banana	Mandingo, West Africa
Bogus	Hausa, West Africa
Candy	Arabic, Middle East
Caucus	Algonquin, Virginia/Delaware, North America
Chimpanzee	Bantu, West and Central Africa
Chocolate	Aztec Nahuatl, Mexico/Central America
Gong	Malaysia, Southeast Asia
Hammock	Arawakan, South America
Hip/hep	Wolof, West Africa
Hurricane	Taino, Caribbean
Lime	Inca Quechua, South America
Moose	Algonquin, Virginia/Delaware, North America
Panda	Nepali, South Asia
Savannah	Taino, Caribbean
Shampoo	Hindi, North India, South Asia
Sugar	Sanskrit, South Asia
Tepee	Sioux, Dakotas, North America
Thug	Hindi, North India, South Asia
Tobacco	Arawak, South America
Tomato	Nahuatl, Mexico/Central America
Tundra	Saami, Lapland, Northern Europe
Typhoon	Mandarin Chinese, East Asia
Zombie	Congo and Angola, Central and West Africa

Figure 9.7 Loan Words in North American English

United States, Canada, Australia, New Zealand, South Asia, Africa, Hong Kong, and the Caribbean. English was the dominant language in the colonies, used in government and commerce and taught in schools. Over time, regional and subregional varieties of English developed, often leading to a "New English" that a native speaker from England cannot understand at all. So many varieties of English now exist that scholars are beginning to talk of the English language family, which includes American English, "Spanglish," "Japlish," and "Tex-Mex."

Textese is a new and emerging variant of English and other languages associated with cell phone communications and involving abbreviations and slang. The limited number of characters allowed, so far, in a cell phone text message has prompted widespread creativity in shortening words and sentences. In English Textese, vowels are often deleted, numbers may stand in for part of a word or an entire word, and a single letter may convey a word. Many stock phrases exist as acronyms, such as lol, that are widely recognized by users.

Endangered Languages and Language Revitalization

The emergence of linguistic anthropology, as mentioned in Chapter 1, was prompted by the need to document disappearing indigenous languages in the United States. Today,

anthropologists and other scholars, as well as descendant language communities themselves, are still concerned about the rapid loss of languages (Fishman 1991; Maffi 2005). The task of documenting declining languages is urgent. It is often accompanied by applied work aimed at preserving and reviving endangered and dying languages (see Think Like an Anthropologist).

Scholars have proposed four phases or degrees of language decline and loss (Walsh 2005):

- Language shift, or language decay, is a category of language decline when speakers have a limited vocabulary in their native language and more often use a new language in which they may be semifluent or fluent (Hill 2001).

- Language endangerment exists when a language has fewer than 10,000 speakers.

- Near-extinction is a situation in which only a few elderly speakers are still living.

- Language extinction occurs when the language has no competent speakers.

Keeping track of endangered and dying languages is difficult because no one is sure how many languages have existed in the recent past or even how many exist now (Crystal 2000). Estimates of the number of living languages today range between 5,000 and 7,000. Part of the

Indigenous language dictionaries and usage guides are increasingly available on the Web and help indigenous peoples, such as these Australian boys, preserve their cultures.

■ *Check out The Internet Guide to Australian Languages.*

Textese an emerging variant of written English and other languages associated with cell phone communication and involving abbreviations and creative slang.

Think Like an Anthropologist
Should Dying Languages Be Revived?

The Western media often carry articles about endangered biological species, such as certain frogs or birds, and the need to protect them from extinction. The reasons for concern about the loss of biological species are many. One major factor is simply that biological diversity is a good thing to have on the earth. Opponents of taking special measures to protect endangered species find support for their position in a Darwinian view that progress involves competition and the survival of those species that can make it. Economic progress might mean building a new shopping center or airport with a massive parking lot. If that means the extinction of a particular species of nonhuman primate, bird, flower, or worm, so be it, in the name of "progress."

Some parallels exist between the survival of endangered languages and that of endangered biological species (Maffi 2005). Supporters of language preservation and revitalization can point to the sheer fact of diversity on earth as a good thing, a sign of a culturally healthy planet with room for everyone's language. They will argue that a people's language is an intrinsic part of their culture. Without language, the culture, too, will die.

Others take the Darwinian view that languages, like species, live in a world of competition. Language survival means that the strong and fit carry on while the weak and unfit die out. They may point out that preserving linguistic heritage is useless because dying languages are part of a past that no longer exists. They resist spending public funds on language preservation and regard revitalization programs as wasteful.

Critical Thinking Questions

- Have you read or heard of an endangered biological species in the media recently? What was the species?
- Have you read or heard of an endangered language in the media lately? What was the language?
- Where do you stand on biological species preservation and on language preservation, and why?

explanation for the fuzzy numbers is the problem in separating languages from dialects. The largest number of languages of any world region is found on the island of New Guinea, which comprises the country of Papua New Guinea and the Indonesian territory of West Papua, and several neighboring small islands (Foley 2000). Over 1,000 languages exist in this area, many from completely separate language families.

Language extinction is especially acute in the Australia–Pacific region, where 99.5 percent of the indigenous languages have fewer than 100,000 speakers (Nettle and Romaine 2000:40). The situation of indigenous languages in the Americas, Siberia, Africa, and South and Southeast Asia is becoming increasingly serious. Over half of the world's languages have fewer than 10,000 speakers, and one-fourth have fewer than 1,000 speakers.

Efforts to revive or maintain local languages face many challenges (Fishman 2001). Political opposition may come from governments that fear local identity movements. Governments are often averse to devoting financial resources to supporting minority language programs. Deciding which version of an endangered language to preserve may have political consequences at the local level (Nevins 2004). Notable achievements have been made, however, with perhaps one of the most robust examples of language maintenance occurring in French-speaking Québec.

Approaches to language maintenance and revitalization must respond to local circumstances and to factors such as how serious the degree of loss is, how many living speakers there are, what version of the language should be maintained or revived, and what resources for maintenance and revitalization programs are available. Major strategies include the following (Walsh 2005):

- Formal classroom instruction
- A master–apprentice system in which an elder teaches a nonspeaker in a one-on-one situation
- Web-based tools and services to support language learning

Each method has both promise and pitfalls. One thing is key: It takes living communities to activate and keep alive the knowledge of a language (Maffi 2003).

9 | Learning Objectives Revisited

9.1 Summarize the ways that humans communicate.

Human communication is the sending of meaningful messages through language. Language is a systematic set of symbols and signs with learned and shared meanings. It may be spoken, hand-signed, written, or conveyed through body movements, marking, or accessories.

Human language has two characteristics that distinguish it from communication systems of other living beings: productivity, or the ability to create an infinite number of novel and understandable messages; and displacement, the ability to communicate about the past, the future, and imaginary things.

Language consists of basic sounds, vocabulary, and syntax. Cross-culturally, languages vary substantially in the details of all three features.

Humans use many forms of nonverbal language to communicate with each other. Sign language is a form of communication that uses mainly hand movements to communicate. Silence is a form of nonverbal communication with its own cultural values and meaning. Body language includes body movements and body placement in relation to other people, body modifications such as tattoos and piercing, dress, and hairstyles.

Media anthropology sheds light on how culture shapes media messages and on the social dynamics that play out in media institutions. Critical media anthropology examines the power relations involved in the media.

9.2 Discuss how communication relates to cultural diversity and social inequality.

The Sapir–Whorf hypothesis emphasizes how language shapes culture. A competing model, called sociolinguistics, emphasizes how one's culture and one's position in it shape language. Each position has merit, and many anthropologists draw on both models.

Critical discourse analysis studies how communication through language can serve the interests of the powerful, maintaining or even increasing social inequality. Although language can reinforce and expand social exclusion, it can also empower oppressed people,

depending on the context. Euro-American women's speech is generally more polite and accommodating than that of men. In Japan, gender codes emphasize politeness in women's speech, but some young Japanese women, the kogals, are creating a new linguistic style of resistance. Gay language in Indonesia is entering the mainstream as an expression of freedom from official control. African American English (AAE), in the view of many experts, has evolved into a standard language with local variants.

9.3 List examples of language change.

The exact origins of human verbal language are not known. Historical linguistics and its discovery of language families provide insights into early human history and settlement patterns. The emergence of writing can be traced to around 6,000 years ago, with the emergence of the state in Mesopotamia. Scripts have spread widely throughout the world, with the Aramaic system the basis of scripts in South and Southeast Asia. The functions of writing vary from context to context. In some situations official recordkeeping predominates, whereas in others writing is important for courtship.

The recent history of language change has been influenced by the colonialism of past centuries and by Western globalization in the current era. Nationalist policies of cultural integration often involve the repression of minority languages and the promotion of a standard language. Colonial contact created the context for the emergence of pidgin languages, many of which evolved into creoles. Western globalization supports the spread of English and the development of localized variants.

In the past 500 years, colonialism and globalization have resulted in the extinction of many indigenous and minority languages. Many others are in danger of dying. Applied linguistic anthropologists seek to preserve the world's linguistic diversity. They document languages and participate in designing programs for teaching dead and dying languages. A key element in language revitalization and survival is having communities use the language.

Key Concepts

big data, p. 174

call system, p. 174

communication, p. 173

creole, p. 187

critical discourse analysis, p. 181

critical media anthropology, p. 179

discourse, p. 181

displacement, p. 174

ethnosemantics, p. 175

global language, p. 187

historical linguistics, p. 184

khipu, p. 186

language, p. 173

language family, p. 184

logograph, p. 186

phoneme, p. 175

pidgin, p. 187

productivity, p. 174

Sapir–Whorf hypothesis, p. 180

sign language, p. 177

sociolinguistics, p. 181

tag question, p. 181

Textese, p. 189

Thinking Outside the Box

1. Try to compose an English sentence with its main verb at the end.
2. Think of occasions when you use silence and see if they involve ambiguity in social relationships or some other factor.
3. Should AAE be suppressed in U.S. public schools in favor of promoting SAE? What are the pros and cons of a mono-language approach in education?

Chapter 10
Religion

Learning Objectives

10.1 Describe how anthropologists define religion and its key features.

10.2 Recognize how globalization has affected world religions.

10.3 Identify examples of religious change in contemporary times.

Anthro Connections

This scene was recorded for the film *Yolngu Boy* that follows three Yolngu (pronounced yo-nen-gu) teenagers as they make the transition from childhood to adulthood. The Yolngu people recently recognized one of their premier artists, Gulumbu Yulpingu, at her death in 2012. She was surrounded by her family and serenaded by sacred songs of the whale. Up to 100 people kept a vigil outside her hospital room. She had always been the first to assist those in need; now her community was with her. She painted the universe, taking traditional Yolngu stories about the Milky Way and extending them to stars beyond: "I have this knowledge my father told me." Her father was a clan leader and artist. He told her stories about the seasons and the stars and how the stars keep people safe.

Source: Eccles 2012

While studying the religious life of people of rural Greece, anthropologist Loring Danforth observed rituals in which participants walk across several yards of burning coals (1989). They do not get burned, they say, because their faith in a saint protects them. Back in the United States, Danforth met an American who regularly walks on fire as part of his New Age faith and who organizes training workshops for people who want to learn how to do it. Danforth himself walked on fire in a ceremony in rural Maine.

Not all anthropologists who study religion undertake such challenges, but they all share an interest in questions about humanity's understanding of the supernatural realm and relationships with it: Why do some religions have many gods and others just one? Why do some religions practice sacrifice? Why do some religions have more participation by women? How do religions respond to changing conditions in the political economy?

Religion has been a cornerstone topic in cultural anthropology since the beginnings of the discipline. The early focus, in the nineteenth century, was on religions of indigenous peoples living in places far from Europe. Now anthropologists also study the religions of state-level societies and the effects of globalization on religious change.

Religion in Comparative Perspective

10.1 Describe how anthropologists define religion and its key features.

This section discusses basic questions in the anthropology of religion, including how to define religion, theories about the origin of religion, and types of religious beliefs, rituals, and religious specialists.

What Is Religion?

Since the earliest days of anthropology, scholars have proposed various definitions of religion. In the late 1800s, British anthropologist Sir Edward Tylor defined religion

Christian firewalkers in northern Greece walking on hot coals. They reaffirm God's protection by not getting burned.

▎*If you have a religious faith, are pain or other physical discomforts involved in any of the rituals?*

A Lao Buddhist temple in Virginia. Religion provides an important source of social cohesion and psychological support for many immigrant groups.

as the belief in spirits. A more comprehensive, current definition says that **religion** consists of beliefs and behavior related to supernatural beings and forces. This definition specifically avoids linking religion with belief in a supreme deity, because some religions have no concept of a supreme deity, whereas others have multiple deities.

Religion is related to, but not the same as, a people's worldview, or way of understanding how the world came to be, its design, and their place in it. Worldview is a broader concept and does not include the criterion of concern with a supernatural realm. An atheist has a worldview, but does not have a religion.

MAGIC VERSUS RELIGION Sir Edward Tylor wrote that magic, religion, and science are alike in that they are different ways in which people have tried to explain the physical world and events in it (1871). He considered science to be the superior, most rational of the three. Sir James Frazer, writing not long after Tylor, defined **magic** as people's attempt to compel supernatural forces and beings to act in certain ways (1978 [1890]). He contrasted magic with religion, which he said is the attempt to please

---

supernatural forces or beings. Frazer differentiated two general principles of magic:

- The law of similarity, the basis of imitative magic, is founded on the assumption that if person or item X is like person or item Y, then actions done to person or item X will affect person or item Y. A familiar example is a voodoo doll. If someone sticks pins into a doll X that represents person Y, then person Y will experience pain or suffering.

- The law of contagion, the basis of contagious magic, says that persons or things once in contact with a person can still have an effect on that person. Common items for working contagious magic include a person's hair trimmings, nail clippings, teeth, saliva, blood, and fecal matter, as well as the placenta of a baby. In cultures where contagious magic is practiced, people are careful about disposing of their personal wastes so that no one else can get hold of them.

Tylor, Frazer, and other early anthropologists supported an evolutionary model (review Chapter 1), with magic preceding religion. They evaluated magic as being less spiritual and ethical than religion and therefore more "primitive." They assumed that, in time, magic would be completely replaced by the "higher" system of religion, which would eventually be replaced by science as the most rational way of thinking. They would be surprised to see the widespread presence of magical religions in the modern world, such as the so-called Wicca, or Neo-Pagan, religion that centers on respect for Earth, nature, and the seasonal cycle. The pentacle is an important Wiccan symbol (Figure 10.1). As of 2007, the U.S. Department of Veterans Affairs added the pentacle to its list of approved

Figure 10.1 A Pentacle.

Sometimes called a pentagram, it is a five-pointed star surrounded by a circle. An important symbol in Neo-Pagan and Wiccan religions, the pentacle is also a magical tool used for summoning energies and commanding spirits.

---

religion beliefs and behavior related to supernatural beings and forces.

magic the attempt to compel supernatural beings and forces to act in certain ways.

religious symbols that can be placed on the headstones of the graves of deceased veterans and their family members.

Many people turn to magical behavior in situations of uncertainty. Magic, for example, is prominent in sports (Gmelch 1997 [1971]). Some baseball players in the United States repeat actions or use charms, including a special shirt or hat, to help them win. This practice is based on the assumption that if it worked before, it may work again. In baseball, pitching and hitting involve more uncertainty than fielding, and pitchers and hitters are more likely to use magic. Magical practices are also common in farming, fishing, the military, and love.

Varieties of Religious Beliefs

Religions comprise beliefs and behavior. Scholars of religion generally address belief systems first because they appear to inform patterns of religious behavior. Religious beliefs are shared by a group, sometimes by millions of people, and are passed on through the generations. Elders teach children through songs and narratives, artists paint the stories on rocks and walls, and sculptors create images in wood and stone that depict aspects of religious belief.

HOW BELIEFS ARE EXPRESSED Beliefs are expressed and transferred over the generations in two main forms:

- **Myth**, stories about supernatural forces or beings
- **Doctrine**, direct statements about religious beliefs

A myth is a narrative that has a plot with a beginning, middle, and end. The plot may involve recurrent motifs, the smallest units of narrative. Myths convey messages about supernatural forces or beings (or, simply, supernaturals) indirectly, through the story itself, rather than by using logic or formal argument. Greek and Roman myths, such as the stories of Zeus, Athena, Orpheus, and Persephone, are world famous. Some people would say that the Bible is a collection of myths; others would object to that categorization as suggesting that the stories are not "real" or "sacred." Myths have long been part of people's oral tradition, and many are still unwritten.

Anthropologists ask why myths exist. Bronislaw Malinowski said that a myth is a charter for society in that it expresses core beliefs and teaches morality (1948). The French anthropologist Claude Lévi-Strauss, arguably the most famous mythologist, saw myths as functional in a philosophical and psychological way (1967). In his view, myths help people deal with the deep conceptual contradictions between, for example, life and death or good and evil, by providing stories in which these dualities find a solution

in a mediating third factor. These mythological solutions are buried within a variety of surface details in the myth. For example, many myths of the Pueblo Indians of the U.S. Southwest juxtapose grass-eating animals (vegetarians) with predators (carnivores). The mediating third character is the raven, which is a carnivore but unlike other meat eaters does not have to kill to eat meat because it is a scavenger.

A cultural materialist perspective, also functionalist, says that myths store and transmit information related to making a living and managing economic crises (Sobel and Bettles 2000). Analysis of 28 myths of the Klamath and Modoc Indians (Map 10.1) reveals that a consistent theme is uncertainty about the availability of food. Other prominent themes are how to cope with hunger, food storage, resource diversification, resource conservation, spatial mobility, reciprocity, and supernatural forces. Thus, myths are repositories of knowledge related to economic survival and environmental conservation.

Doctrine, the other major form in which beliefs are expressed, explicitly defines the supernaturals, the world and how it came to be, and people's roles in relation to the supernaturals and to other humans. Doctrine is written and formal. It is close to law because it links incorrect beliefs and behaviors with punishments. Doctrine is associated with institutionalized, large-scale religions rather than small-scale "folk" religions.

Doctrine, however, can and does change (Bowen 1998). Over the centuries, various popes have pronounced new doctrine for the Catholic Church. A papal declaration of 1854, made with the intent of reinvigorating European Catholicism, bestowed authenticity on the concept of the

Map 10.1 Klamath and Modoc Region in Oregon and California

---

myth a narrative with a plot that involves the supernaturals.

doctrine direct and formalized statements about religious beliefs.

Immaculate Conception, an idea with substantial popular support.

Muslim doctrine is expressed in the Qur'an, the basic holy text of the Islamic faith, which consists of revelations made to the prophet Muhammad in the seventh century and of collections of Muhammad's statements and deeds. In Kuala Lumpur, Malaysia (see Map 6.3, page 117), a small group of highly educated women called the Sisters in Islam regularly debate with members of the local *ulama*, religious authorities who are responsible for interpreting Islamic doctrine, especially concerning families, education, and commercial affairs (Ong 1995). Debates concern such issues as polygamy, divorce, women's work roles, and women's clothing.

BELIEFS ABOUT SUPERNATURAL FORCES AND BEINGS Supernaturals range from impersonal forces to those who look just like humans. Supernaturals can be supreme and all-powerful creators or smaller-scale, annoying spirits that take up residence in people through possession.

The term **animatism** refers to a belief system in which the supernatural is conceived of as an impersonal power. An important example is *mana*, a concept widespread throughout the South Pacific region, including Melanesia, Polynesia, and Micronesia. Mana is a force outside nature that works automatically; it is neither spirit nor deity. It manifests itself in objects and people and is associated with personal status and power, because some people accumulate more of it than others.

Some supernaturals are zoomorphic, deities in the shape, or partial shape, of animals. No satisfactory theory has appeared to explain why some religions develop zoomorphic deities and for what purposes, and why others do not. Religions of classical Greece and Rome and ancient and contemporary Hinduism are especially rich in zoomorphic supernaturals. Anthropomorphic supernaturals, deities in the form of humans, are common but not universal. The human tendency to perceive of supernaturals in their own form was noted 2,500 years ago by the Greek philosopher Xenophanes (zen-AHF-uh-neez), who lived sometime between 570 and 470 BCE. He said,

> But if horses or oxen, or lions had hands and could draw with their hands and accomplish such works as men, horses would draw the figures of their gods as similar to horses and the oxen as similar to oxen, and they would make the bodies of the sort which each of them had. (Lesher 2001:25)

The question of why some religions have anthropomorphic deities and others do not remains unanswered.

Anthropomorphic supernaturals, like humans, can be moved by praise, flattery, and gifts. They have emotions.

They get annoyed if neglected. They can be loving and caring, or they can be distant and nonresponsive. Most anthropomorphic supernaturals are adults, though some are children. Supernaturals tend to have marital and sexual relationships similar to those of the humans who worship them do. Divine marriages are heterosexual, and in some societies male gods have multiple wives. Although many supernaturals have children, grandchildren are not prominent. In pantheons (collectivities of deities), a division of labor reflects specializations in human society. There may be deities of forests, rivers, the sky, wind and rain, agriculture, childbirth, disease, warfare, and marital happiness. The supernaturals have political roles and hierarchies. High gods, such as Jupiter and Juno of classical Roman religion, are all-powerful, with a range of less powerful deities and spirits below them.

In some cultures, deceased ancestors can be supernaturals. Many African, Asian, and American Indian religions have a cult of the ancestors in which the living must do certain things to please the dead ancestors and may also ask for their help in time of need (see Eye on the Environment). In contemporary Japan, ancestor worship is the principal religious activity of many families. Three national holidays recognize the importance of ancestors: the annual summer visit of the dead to their homes and the visits by the living to graves during the two equinoxes.

BELIEFS ABOUT SACRED SPACE Beliefs about sacred space probably exist in all religions, but such beliefs are more prominent in some religions than others. Sacred spaces, such as rock formations or rapids in a river, may or may not be permanently marked (Bradley 2000). Among the Saami (see Culturama in Chapter 9, page 188), traditional religious beliefs were closely tied to sacred natural sites (Mulk 1994). The sites, often unmarked, included rock formations resembling humans, animals, or birds. The Saami sacrificed fish and other animals at these sites until strong pressures from Christian missionaries forced them to repress their practices and beliefs. Many Saami today know where the sacred sites are, but they will not reveal them to outsiders.

Another important form of sacred space that has no permanent mark occurs in a domestic ritual conducted by Muslim women throughout the world. The ritual is called the *khatam quran* (khuh-tum kuh-RAHN), the "sealing" or reading of the holy book of the Qur'an (Werbner 1988). Among Pakistani migrants living in the city of Manchester, northern England (Map 10.3), this ritual involves a gathering of women who read the Qur'an and then share a ritual meal. The reason for gathering is to give thanks or seek divine blessing. During the ritual, the otherwise nonsacred space of the house becomes sacred. A "portable" ritual such as this one is especially helpful in the

---

animatism a belief system in which the supernatural is conceived of as an impersonal power.

Eye on the Environment

Eagle Protection, National Parks, and the Preservation of Hopi Culture

For many generations, young men of the Hopi tribe have searched each spring for golden eaglets in the cliffs of Arizona's Wupatki National Park and other parts of northeastern Arizona (Fenstemeker 2007). They bring the young eagles to the reservation and care for them until the summer, when, as mature birds, they are smothered in a ceremony that the Hopi believe frees the spirits of the birds, which convey messages to their ancestors who reside in the spiritual world. This ceremony is the most important Hopi ritual, but the tribe uses golden eagle feathers in all its rituals. For the Hopi, golden eagles are their link to the spiritual world.

In 1783, the U.S. Continental Congress adopted the bald eagle as the national symbol of the newly independent country. By 1940, numbers of bald eagles had dropped so low that the U.S. Congress passed the Bald Eagle Protection Act to preserve the species that had become established as the symbol of American ideals of freedom. In 1962, Congress amended the act to include golden eagles, because the young of the two species are nearly indistinguishable.

In 1994, President Clinton promoted official accommodation to Hopi beliefs. His administration established a repository for golden eagle feathers and other remains in Colorado. The demand is, however, greater than the supply.

The Hopi have a permit for an annual take of 40 golden eagles in northeastern Arizona, but they are excluded from Wupatki because of its status as a national park. The U.S. policy toward national parks follows the Yellowstone model, which aims to preserve the physical environment and species but excludes indigenous peoples and their cultures. This model has been applied throughout the world to the detriment of peoples who have long successfully lived in regions that are now off limits to them for hunting, fishing, and gathering. Many of these lands are sacred to them, but they are prevented from using them in traditional ways for the sake of "conservation."

Anthropologists and others support environmental and species preservation but not to the exclusion of heritage populations and cultures. They suggest that a case-by-case approach should be followed in considering exemptions to national laws. With regard to the golden eagles of Arizona, they point out that golden eagles are abundant and the Hopi requests for the spring take present no threat to the survival of the species.

Environmentalists are concerned, however, that granting exemptions will establish dangerous precedents that will, over time, destroy pristine environments and precious species. Other environmentalists counter that more eagles are killed every year by airplanes or contact with electrical wires, or they die from eating prey that contains lead bullets.

In contrast to the Yellowstone model, anthropologists advocate for a parks and people approach, which builds on community-based conservation that does not exclude heritage populations from continuing to enjoy the economic and religious benefits of their territory.

Food for Thought

Consider how you would feel if you were told that you could no longer practice the most important annual ritual in your religion but that other people could have a touristic experience at the place where you would normally practice the ritual. For secular students, consider a secular ritual, for example, watching the Super Bowl.

A Kachina doll. Among the Hopi, the word Kachina (kuh-CHEE-nuh) refers to a spirit or "life-bringer." Uncles carve Kachina dolls for their nieces to help them learn about the many spirits that exist in the Hopi religion. Kachina dolls, especially older ones, are highly sought after by non-Indians who collect Indian artifacts.

Map 10.2   Hopi Reservation in Arizona

The Hopi and Navajo tribes once shared the area known as Big Mountain. U.S. Acts of Congress in 1974 and 1996 divided the area into two reservations, leaving the Hopi completely surrounded by the much larger Navajo Nation. About 7,000 people live on the Hopi Reservation.

Map 10.3 England

England is the largest in area and the most populous of the constituent countries of the United Kingdom. Its population of 53 million accounts for 84 percent of the total. DNA analysis reveals that a majority of the English are of Germanic descent, as is their language. The terrain is mainly rolling hills, with some mountains in the north and east. London is by far the largest city, with Manchester and Birmingham competing for second place. English is the dominant language with its diverse regional accents. Many other languages brought into the country by immigrant communities are spoken as first languages, including several South Asian languages, Polish, Greek, and Cantonese. An estimated 250,000 people speak British Sign Language. Although the Church of England is the state religion, everyone in England has the right to religious freedom.

adaptation of migrants to their new contexts, because it can be conducted without a formally consecrated ritual space. All that is required is a place, a supportive group of kin and friends, and the Qur'an.

Religions of the Aboriginal people of Australia are closely tied to sacred space. During a mythological past called the Dreamtime, the ancestors walked the earth and marked out the territory belonging to a particular group. People's knowledge of where the ancestors roamed is secret. In several cases that have recently been brought to the courts, Aboriginal peoples have claimed title to land that is being sought by commercial developers. Some anthropologists provide expert testimony in court, based on their knowledge of a particular culture, to document the validity of the Aboriginal claims (see Anthropology Works on page 200). In one such case, secret Aboriginal knowledge about a sacred place and its associated beliefs was gender specific: It belonged to women and could not be told to men. The anthropologist who was hired to support the women's claims was a woman, so the women could tell her about the sacred places, but she could not convey that knowledge in court to the male judge, a situation that demanded considerable ingenuity on the part of the anthropological consultant.

Ritual Practices

A **ritual** is patterned, repetitive behavior focused on the supernatural realm. Such sacred rituals are the enactment of beliefs expressed in myth and doctrine, for example, the Christian ritual of communion. Sacred rituals are distinct from secular rituals, such as sorority or fraternity initiations, that have no connection to the supernatural realm. Some ritual events combine sacred and secular elements. The U.S. holiday of Thanksgiving originated as a Christian sacred meal with the primary purpose of giving thanks to God for the survival of the Pilgrims (Siskind 1992). Its original Christian meaning is not maintained by everyone who celebrates the holiday today. Secular features of the holiday, such as watching football, may be of greater importance than the ritual aspect of thanking God for plentiful food.

Anthropologists categorize sacred rituals in many ways. One division is based on their timing. Regularly performed rituals are called periodic rituals. Many periodic rituals are performed annually to mark a seasonal milestone such as planting or harvesting or to commemorate an important event. For example, Buddha's Day, an important periodic ritual in Buddhism, commemorates the birth, enlightenment, and death of the Buddha (all on one day). On this day, Buddhists gather at monasteries, hear sermons about the Buddha, and perform rituals such as pouring water over images of the Buddha. Calendrical events, such as the shortest day of the year, the longest day, the new moon, and the full moon, often shape ritual cycles. Nonperiodic rituals, in contrast, occur irregularly, at unpredictable times, in response to unscheduled events, such as a drought or flood, or to mark events in a person's life, such as illness, infertility, birth, marriage, or death. The following material presents highlights of various types of ritual.

LIFE-CYCLE RITUALS A **life-cycle ritual**, or rite of passage, marks a change in status from one life stage to another of an individual or group. Victor Turner's (1969) fieldwork among the Ndembu (en-DEM-boo), horticulturalists of northwestern Zambia, provides insights into the phases of life-cycle rituals. Turner found that, among the

---

ritual patterned behavior that has to do with the supernatural realm.

life-cycle ritual a ritual that marks a change in status from one life stage to another.

Anthropology Works

Aboriginal Women's Culture and Sacred Site Protection

A group of Ngarrindjeri (prounounced NAR-en-jeery) women and their lawyer hired cultural anthropologist Diane Bell to serve as a consultant to them in supporting their claims to a sacred site in southern Australia (Bell 2015). The area on Hindmarsh Island was threatened by the proposed construction of a bridge that would cross sacred waters between Goolwa and the island. The women claimed protection for the area and sought prevention of the bridge building on the basis of their secret knowledge of its sacredness, knowledge passed down in trust from mother to daughter over generations. The High Commission formed by the government to investigate their claim considered it to be a hoax perpetrated to block a project important to the country.

Helping the women prove their case to a White, male-dominated court system was a challenging task for Diane Bell, a White Australian with extensive fieldwork experience among Aboriginal women. Bell conducted research over many months to marshal evidence for the validity of the women's claims. She examined newspaper archives, early recordings of ritual songs, and oral histories of Ngarrindjeri women. She prepared reports for the courtroom about women's sacred knowledge that were general enough to avoid violating the rule of secret, women-only knowledge but detailed enough to convince the High Court judge that the women's knowledge was authentic. In the end, the judge was convinced, and the bridge project was canceled in 1999.

Land developers, however, did not give up, and in 2001, the Federal Court dismissed claims of "secret women's business" as fabricated.

The case is one of the most bitter court conflicts related to "race" in Australia's history—not to mention gender. The senior women who fought for the protection of their sacred place have passed on. Many Ngarrindjeri and those who stood with them during the struggle to stop the construction, will not use the bridge.

In the latest development, in July 2010, high-level officials apologized to the Ngarrindjeri women, acknowledging that their claims were genuine when they objected to the construction of the bridge. Following this public apology, some Ngarrindjeri women, in a peace-making move, walked the bridge for the first time. Others say they will never do so.

Food for Thought

On the Internet, learn more about this case and other disputes in Australia about sacred sites.

The pedestrian bridge from Hindmarsh Island to South Australia.

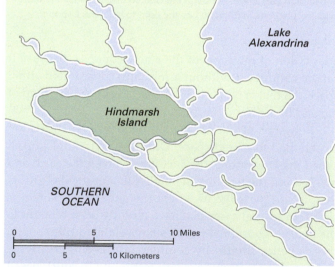

Map 10.4 Hindmarsh Island in Southeast Australia

The Ngarrindjeri name for Hindmarsh Island is Kumarangk.

Ndembu and cross-culturally, life-cycle rituals have three phases: separation, transition, and reintegration.

- In the first phase, the initiate (the person undergoing the ritual) is separated physically, socially, or symbolically from normal life. Special dress may mark the separation. In many cultures of the Amazon and in East and West Africa, adolescents are secluded for several years in separate huts or areas away from the village.

- The transition, or liminal, phase is when the person is no longer in the previous status but is not yet a member of the next stage. Liminality often involves the learning of specialized skills that will equip the person for the new status.

- Reintegration, the last stage, occurs when the initiate emerges and is welcomed by the community as an individual occupying the new status.

Differences in the cross-cultural distribution of puberty rituals for boys and girls reflect the economic value and status of males and females (review Chapter 4). Most societies have some form of puberty ceremony for boys, but puberty ceremonies for girls are less common. In societies where female labor is important and valued, girls have elaborate, and sometimes painful, puberty rites (Brown 1978). Where their labor is not important, menarche is unmarked and there is no puberty ceremony. Puberty rites function to socialize future members of the labor force, among other things. For example, among the Bemba of northern Zambia, during her initiation a girl learns to distinguish 40 kinds of mushrooms and to know which are edible and which are poisonous.

PILGRIMAGE Pilgrimage is round-trip travel to a sacred place or places for purposes of religious devotion or ritual. Prominent pilgrimage places are Varanasi (var-uh-nuh-see) in India (formerly called Banaras or Benares) for Hindus; Mecca in Saudi Arabia for Muslims; Bodh Gaya in India for Buddhists; Jerusalem in Israel for Jews, Christians, and Muslims; and Lourdes in France for Christians. Pilgrimage often involves hardship, with the implication that the more suffering that is involved, the more merit the pilgrim accumulates. Compared with a weekly trip to church or synagogue, pilgrimage removes a person further from everyday life, is more demanding, and therefore is potentially more transformative.

Victor Turner applied the three sequences of life-cycle rituals to pilgrimage: The pilgrim first separates from everyday life, then enters the liminal stage during the actual pilgrimage, and finally returns to be reintegrated into society in a transformed state (1969). A person who has gone on a pilgrimage often gains enhanced public status as well as spiritual benefits.

RITUALS OF INVERSION In a **ritual of inversion**, normal social roles and relations are temporarily inverted. A functionalist perspective says that these rituals allow for social

An Apache girl's puberty ceremony. Cross-cultural research indicates that the celebration of girls' puberty is more likely to occur in cultures in which adult women have valued productive and reproductive roles.

pressure to be released. They also provide a reminder about the propriety of normal, everyday roles and practices to which people must return once the ritual is over.

Carnival (or *carnaval* in Portuguese) is a ritual of inversion with roots in the northern Mediterranean region. It is celebrated widely throughout southern Europe and the Western Hemisphere. Carnival is a period of riotous celebration before the Christian fast of Lent. It begins at different times in different places, but always ends on Mardi Gras (or Shrove Tuesday), the day before the fasting period of Lent begins. The word carnival, from Latin, means "flesh farewell," referring to the fact that believers give up eating meat during Lent.

In Bosa, a town in Sardegna (Sardinia), Italy, carnival involves social-role reversal and the relaxing of usual social norms. Discotheques extend their hours, mothers allow their daughters to stay out late, and men and women flirt with each other in public in ways that are forbidden during the rest of the year (Counihan 1985). Carnival in Bosa has three major phases. The first is impromptu street theater and masquerades that take place over several weeks, usually on Sundays. The skits are social critiques of current events and local happenings. In the masquerades, men dress up as exaggerated women:

> Young boys thrust their padded breasts forward with their hands while brassily hiking up their skirts to reveal their thighs. . . . A youth stuffs his shirt front with melons and holds them proudly out. . . . The high school gym teacher dresses as a nun and lifts up his habit to reveal suggestive red underwear. Two men wearing nothing but bikinis, wigs, and high heels feign a stripper's dance on a table top (1985:15).

---

pilgrimage round-trip travel to a sacred place or places for purposes of religious devotion or ritual.

ritual of inversion a ritual in which normal social roles and order are temporarily reversed.

The second phase occurs on the morning of Mardi Gras, when hundreds of Bosans, mostly men, dress in black, like widows, and flood the streets. They accost passersby, shaking in their faces dolls and other objects that are maimed in some way or bloodied. They shriek at the top of their lungs as if mourning, and they say, "Give us milk, milk for our babies. . . . They are dying, they are neglected, their mothers have been gallivanting since St. Anthony's Day and have abandoned their poor children" (1985:16).

The third phase, called Giolzi, takes place during the evening. Men and women dress in white, wearing sheets for cloaks and pillowcases for hoods. They blacken their faces. Rushing into the street, they hold hands and chant the word Giolzi. They storm at people, pretending to search their bodies for Giolzi and then say, "Got it!" It is not clear what Giolzi is, but whatever it is, it represents something that makes everyone happy.

How does a cultural anthropologist interpret these events? Carnival allows people for a short time to act out roles that are normally denied them. It is also a time when everyone has fun. In this way, rituals of inversion may function as a mechanism for maintaining social order. After a few days of revelry, everyone returns to his or her original place for another year.

SACRIFICE Many rituals involve **sacrifice**, or the offering of something for transfer to the supernaturals. Sacrifice has a long history throughout the world and is probably one of the oldest forms of ritual. It may involve killing and offering animals; making human offerings (of whole people, parts of a person's body, or bloodletting); or offering vegetables, fruits, grains, flowers, or other products. One interpretation of flowers as sacrificial offerings is that they, like vegetables and fruits, are symbolic replacements for former animal sacrifices (Goody 1993).

Spanish documents from the sixteenth century describe the Aztec practice of public sacrifice of humans and other animals to please the gods. The details are gory and involve marching thousands of human victims up to the top of a temple and then cutting out their hearts so that the blood spurts forth. Debate exists among anthropologists as to how many victims were actually sacrificed and why. Cultural materialist Marvin Harris has argued that the numbers were large, up to 100,000 at particular sites, and that the remains of the victims were butchered and eaten by commoners (1977). He maintains that the Aztec state, through such rituals, demonstrated its power and also provided protein to the masses. In opposition to Harris, symbolic anthropologist Peggy Sanday takes an emic perspective and says that the sacrifices were necessary to please the gods and had nothing to do with maintaining the worldly power of leaders (1986).

sacrifice a ritual in which something is offered to the supernaturals.

Religious Specialists

Not all rituals require the presence of a religious specialist, or someone with extensive, formal training, but all require some level of knowledge on the part of the performer(s) about how to do them correctly. Even the daily, household veneration of an ancestor requires some knowledge gained through informal learning. At the other extreme, many rituals cannot be done without a highly trained specialist.

SHAMANS AND PRIESTS General features of the categories of shaman and priest illustrate key differences between these two types of specialists. (Many other specialists fit somewhere in between.) A shaman or shamanka (defined in Chapter 5) is a religious specialist who has a direct relationship with the supernaturals, often by being "called." A potential shaman may be recognized by special signs, such as the ability to go into a trance. Anyone who demonstrates shamanic abilities can become a shaman; in other words, this is an openly available role. Shamans are more often associated with nonstate societies,

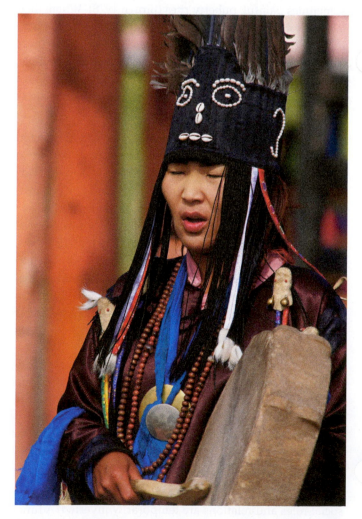

A Mongolian shamanka.

yet faith healers and evangelists of the United States could fit into this category. (Review the discussion in Chapter 5 of shamanic specialists as healers.)

In states, the more complex occupational specialization in religion means that there is a wider variety of types of specialists, especially what anthropologists refer to as priests (not the same as the specific modern role of the Catholic priest), and promotes the development of religious hierarchies and power structures. The terms **priest** and **priestess** refer to a category of full-time religious specialists whose position is based mainly on abilities gained through formal training. A priest may receive a divine call, but more often the role is hereditary, passed on through priestly lineages. In terms of ritual performance, shamans are more involved with nonperiodic rituals. Priests perform a wider range of rituals, including periodic state rituals. In contrast to shamans, who rarely have secular power, priests and priestly lineages often do.

OTHER SPECIALISTS Many other specialized religious roles exist cross-culturally. Diviners are specialists who are able to discover the will and wishes of the supernaturals through techniques such as reading animal entrails. Palm readers and tarot card readers fit into the category of diviners.

Prophets are specialists who convey divine revelations usually gained through visions or dreams. They often possess charisma, an especially attractive and powerful personality, and may be able to perform miracles. Prophets have founded new religions, some long-lasting and others short-lived.

Witches use psychic powers and affect people through emotion and thought. Mainstream society often condemns witchcraft as negative. Some scholars of ancient and contemporary witchcraft differentiate between positive forms that involve healing and negative forms that seek to harm people.

World Religions and Local Variations

10.2 Recognize how globalization has affected world religions.

The term **world religion** was coined in the nineteenth century to refer to religions that were based on written sources, with many followers that crossed country borders and that had a concern with salvation (the belief that human beings require deliverance from an imperfect world). At that time, the term referred only to Christianity, Islam, and Buddhism. It was later expanded to include Judaism,

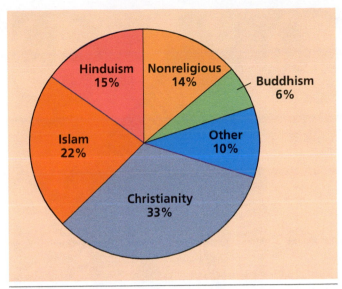

Figure 10.2 Population Distribution of Major World Religions.
Judaism, due to its relatively small numbers, is classified in "Other."

Hinduism, Confucianism, Taoism, and Shintoism. Because of the global importance of the African diaspora that began with the European colonial slave trade, a sixth category of world religions is included here that describes key elements shared among the diversity of traditional African belief systems even though they are oral, not text-based, traditions.

For many centuries, the world religions have traveled outside their original borders through intentional attempts to expand and gain converts or through the migration of believers to new locales. European colonialism was a major force that led to the expansion of Christianity through the missionary work of Protestant sects. The increased rate of population migration since the twentieth century (Chapter 12) and the expansion of television and the Internet give even greater impetus to religious movement and change. Each world religion comprises many local variants, raising a predicament for centrally organized religions in terms of how to maintain a balance between standardization based on core beliefs and the local differences (Hefner 1998).

The material that follows first discusses five long-standing world religions in terms of their history, distribution, and basic teachings (Figure 10.2). (Note: Population statistics for the world religions are rough averages derived from several Internet sources.) They are presented in order by historical age, based on the dates of written texts. For each religion, an example of a local variation is presented. When a world religion moves into a new cultural region, it encounters local religious traditions. In many cases, the incoming religion and local religions

---

priest or **priestess** a male or female full-time religious specialist whose position is based mainly on abilities gained through formal training.

world religion a term coined in the nineteenth century to refer to a religion that is based on written sources, has many followers, is regionally widespread, and is concerned with salvation.

A nineteenth-century painting of the Virgin of Guadalupe by Isidro Escamilla, a Mexican artist. The Virgin of Guadalupe, or Our Lady of Guadalupe, is Mexico's most popular image. Her depiction involves syncretism with the indigenous Aztec goddess Tonantzin, part of a conscious strategy of Christian clergy to convert the Indians. Today, the Virgin of Guadalupe conveys messages of sacrifice and nurturance as well as strength and hope. She appeals to Mexican mothers, nationalists, and feminists alike.

coexist as separate traditions, either as complements or competitors, in what is called **religious pluralism**. In **religious syncretism**, elements of two or more religions blend together. Religious syncretism is most likely to occur when aspects of two religions form a close match with each other. For example, if a local myth involves a hero who has something to do with snakes, there may be a syncretistic link with the Catholic belief in St. Patrick, who is believed to have driven snakes out of Ireland. Many situations of nonfit also exist. For example, Christian missionaries have had difficulty translating the Bible into some indigenous languages because of a lack of matching words or concepts and because of differing kinship and social structures. Some Amazonian groups, such as the Pirahã (review Chapter 9), have no word that corresponds to the Christian

concept of "heaven" (Everett 1995, personal communication). In other cases, matrilineal peoples have found it difficult to understand the significance of the Christian construct of "god the father."

The two world religions that emphasize proselytizing, or seeking converts, are Christianity and Islam. Their encounters with local religions have sometimes been violent, involving the physical destruction of sacred places and objects (Corbey 2003). Common methods include burning, overturning, dismantling, or cutting up sacred objects, dumping them into rivers, and hiding them in caves. European Christian missionaries in the 1800s often confiscated sacred goods and shipped them to Europe for sale to private owners or museums. Both Christian and Islamic conversion efforts frequently involved the construction of their own places of worship on top of the original sacred site. Conflict between these two religions is, unfortunately, not a matter of the past only.

Hinduism

Over 900 million people, or about 15 percent of the world's population, are Hindus. About 97 percent of all Hindus live in India, where Hinduism accounts for 80 percent of the population. The rest live throughout the world in countries such as Bangladesh, Myanmar, Pakistan, Sri Lanka, the United States, Canada, the United Kingdom, Malaysia, Fiji, Trinidad, Guyana, and Hong Kong.

A Hindu is born a Hindu, and Hinduism does not actively seek converts. The core texts of Hinduism are the four Vedas, which were composed in Sanskrit in northern India between 1200 and 900 BCE. Many other scholarly texts, epics and stories, and oral traditions enrich the Hindu tradition. The two most widely known stories are the *Mahabharata* (muh-huh-BHAR-uh-tuh), the story of a war between two patrilineages in which Krishna plays an important role, and the *Ramayana* (ruh-my-uh-nuh), the story of King Rama and his devoted wife, Sita. Throughout India, many local stories also exist, some containing elements from pre-Vedic times.

Hinduism offers a rich polytheism and, at the same time, a philosophical tradition that reduces the multiplicity of deities into oneness. Deities range from a simple stone placed at the foot of a tree to elegantly carved and painted icons of gods such as Shiva and Vishnu and the goddesses Durga and Saraswati. Everyday worship of a deity involves lighting a lamp in front of the god, chanting hymns and mantras (sacred phrases), and taking

---

religious pluralism the condition in which two or more religions coexist either as complementary to each other or as competing systems.

religious syncretism the blending of features of two or more religions.

darshan (dar-shun), which means the act of seeing the deity, usually in the form of an icon (Eck 1985). These acts bring blessings to the worshipper. Local variations of worship often involve deities and rituals unknown elsewhere. For example, fire walking is an important part of goddess worship in southern and eastern India (Freeman 1981) and among some Hindu groups living outside India, notably in Fiji (Brown 1984).

Caste differences in beliefs and practices are also marked, even within the same village. Lower-caste deities prefer offerings of meat sacrifices and alcohol, whereas upper-caste deities prefer flowers, rice, and fruit.

A NAYAR FERTILITY RITUAL The matrilineal Nayars (nie-urs) of Kerala, South India (see Map 13.2, page 265), perform a nonperiodic ritual as a remedy for the curse of the serpent deities who cause infertility in women (Neff 1994). This ritual illustrates the unity of Hinduism in several ritual elements: the use of a camphor flame and incense, the importance of serpent deities, and the offering of flowers to the deity. Locally specific elements are related to the matrilineal cultural context of Kerala.

The all-night ritual includes, first, women painting a sacred design of intertwined serpents on the floor. Several hours of worshipping the deity follow, with the camphor flame, incense, and flowers. Music comes from drumming, playing the cymbals, and singing. The presence of the deity is fully achieved when one of the women goes into a trance. Through her, matrilineal family members may speak to the deity and be blessed.

Among the Nayars, a woman's mother, mother's brothers, and brothers are responsible for ensuring that her desires for motherhood are fulfilled. They share her interest in continuing the matrilineage. What the women say during the trance is important. They typically draw attention to family disharmonies or neglect of the deities. This message diverts blame from the infertile woman for whom the ritual is being held. It reminds family and lineage members of their responsibilities to each other.

HINDU WOMEN AND KARMA IN NORTHERN ENGLAND One of Hinduism's basic concepts is karma, translated as destiny or fate. A person's karma is determined at birth on the basis of his or her previous life and how it was conducted. The karma concept has prompted many outsiders to judge Hindus as fatalistic, lacking a sense of agency. But anthropological research on how people actually think about karma in their everyday lives reveals much individual variation, from fatalism to a strong sense of being in charge of one's destiny. One study looked at women's perceptions of karma among Hindus living in the city of Leeds, northern England (Knott 1996) (see Map 10.3, page 199). Some of the women are fatalistic in their attitudes and behavior. One woman who had a strongly fatalistic view of karma said,

The celebration of Holi, a spring festival popular among Hindus worldwide. Shown here in India, people spray each other with colored powder and water as part of the joyous event. The deeper meaning of Holi is tied to a myth about a demon.

■ *Is the arrival of spring ritually marked in your culture?*

When a baby's born . . . we have a ritual on the sixth day. That's when you name the baby, you know. And on that day, we believe the goddess comes and writes your future . . . we leave a blank white paper and a pen and we just leave it [overnight] . . . So I believe that my future—whatever happens—is what she has written for me. That tells me [that] I have to do what I can do, and if I have a mishap in between I have to accept that. (1996:24)

Another woman said that her sufferings were caused by the irresponsibility of her father and the "bad husband" to whom she had been married. She challenged her karma and left her husband: "I could not accept the karma of being with Nirmal [her husband]. If I had done so, what would have become of my children?" (1996:25). Hindu women's karma dictates that they must be married and have children, so leaving one's husband is a major act of resistance.

Women who seek support when questioning their karmic-defined roles can be religious, such as praying more and fasting, or secular, such as seeking the advice of a psychological counselor or social worker. Some Hindu women in England have themselves become counselors, working in support of other women's independence and self-confidence. They illustrate how human agency can work against traditional religious rules (Map 10.3).

Buddhism

Buddhism originated in a founding figure, Siddhartha Gautama (ca. 566–486 BCE), revered as the Buddha, or Awakened One (Eckel 1995:135). It began in northern India, where the Buddha was born and grew up. From there, it spread throughout the subcontinent, into inner Asia and China, to Sri Lanka, and on to Southeast Asia. Buddhism's popularity declined in India, and Buddhists now constitute less than one percent of India's population. Over the past 200 years, Buddhism has spread to Europe and North America.

Buddhism has a great diversity of doctrine and practice, to the extent that it is difficult to point to a single essential feature other than the importance of Gautama Buddha. No one text is accepted as authoritative for all forms of Buddhism. Many Buddhists worship the Buddha as a deity, but others do not. Instead, they honor his teachings and follow the pathway he suggested for reaching nirvana (nur-VAH-nuh), or release from worldly life. The total number of Buddhists worldwide is around 400 million, or about six percent of the global population.

Buddhism arose as a protest against Hinduism, especially caste inequality, but it retained and revised several Hindu concepts, such as karma. In Buddhism, everyone has the potential through good deeds to achieve a better rebirth with each incarnation, until finally, release from samsara (the cycle of birth, reincarnation, death, rebirth, and so on) is achieved. Compassion toward others, including animals, is a key virtue. Branches of Buddhism have different texts that they consider their canon. Buddhism is associated with a strong tradition of monasticism through which monks and nuns renounce the everyday world and spend their lives meditating and doing good works. Buddhists have many annual festivals and rituals. Some events bring pilgrims from around the world to northern India to visit Sarnath, where the Buddha gave his first teaching, and Gaya, where he gained enlightenment.

LOCAL SPIRITS AND BUDDHISM IN SOUTHEAST ASIA Wherever Buddhism exists outside India, it is never the exclusive religion of the devotees, because it arrived to find established local religions already in place (Spiro 1967). In Myanmar (formerly Burma) (Map 10.5), Buddhism and indigenous traditions coexist without one being dominant. Indigenous beliefs remain strong because they offer a way of dealing with everyday problems. Buddhist beliefs about karma in Myanmar are similar to those in Hinduism: A person's karma is the result of previous births and determines his or her present condition. If something bad happens, the person can do little but suffer through it.

In contrast, indigenous supernaturalism says that the bad things happen because of the actions of capricious spirits called *nats*. Ritual actions, however, can combat the influence of nats. Thus, people can deal with nats but not with karma. The continuity of belief in nats is an example of human agency and creativity. Burmese people kept what was important to them from their traditional beliefs and adopted aspects of the new religion.

Buddhism became an important cultural force and the basis for social integration in Myanmar. A typical village may have one or more Buddhist monasteries and several resident monks. All boys are ordained as temporary members of the monastic order. Almost every villager observes Buddhist holy days. Nonetheless, although Buddhism is held to be the supreme truth, the spirits retain control when it comes to dealing with everyday problems such as a toothache or a monetary loss. In Myanmar, the two traditions exist in a pluralistic situation as two separate options.

Buddhism gained an established footing in Japan in the eighth century. The city of Nara was an important early center of Buddhism. An emperor sponsored the casting of this huge bronze statue of the Buddha.

Is there a Buddhist temple where you live? If so, have you visited it? If not, find out where the nearest one is and visit it if possible.

Map 10.5 Mainland Southeast Asia

Mainland Southeast Asia comprises Myanmar (Burma), Thailand, Laos, Vietnam, Cambodia, and Malaysia. Although each country has a distinct history, the region shares a tropical monsoon climate, emphasis on wet-rice agriculture, and ethnic contrasts between highlanders and lowlanders. Many national and ethnic languages exist. Languages in the Mon-Khmer language family have the most speakers. Theravada Buddhism, Islam, and Christianity are the major religions. Growth in industry and the digital economy have created an economic upsurge in many parts of the region.

Judaism

The first Judaic religious system was defined around 500 BCE, following the destruction of the Temple in Jerusalem by the Babylonians in 586 BCE (Neusner 1995). The early writings, called the Pentateuch (pen-tuh-took), established the theme of exile and return as a paradigm for Judaism that endures today. The Pentateuch is also called the Five Books of Moses, or the Torah. Followers of Judaism share in the belief in the Torah as the revelation of God's truth through Israel, a term for the "holy people." The Torah explains the relationship between the supernatural and human realms and guides people in how to carry out the worldview through appropriate actions. A key feature of all forms of Judaism is the identification of what is wrong with the present and how to escape, overcome, or survive that situation. Jewish life is symbolically interpreted as a tension between exile and return, given its foundational myth in the exile of the Jews from Israel and their period of slavery in Egypt.

Judaism is monotheistic, teaching that God is one, unique, and all powerful. Humans have a moral duty to follow Jewish law, to protect and preserve life and health, and to follow certain duties, such as observing the Sabbath. The high regard for human life is reflected in the general opposition to abortion within Jewish law and in opposition to the death penalty. Words, both spoken and written, are important in Judaism. There is an emphasis on truth telling in life and on the use of established literary formulas at precise times during worship. These formulas are encoded in a *sidur* (sih-door), or prayer book. Dietary patterns distinguish Judaism from other religions; for example, rules of kosher eating forbid the mixing of milk or milk products with meat.

Contemporary varieties of Judaism range from conservative Hasidism to Reform Judaism, which emerged in the early 1800s. One difference between these two perspectives concerns the question of who is Jewish. Jewish law traditionally defined a Jewish person as someone born of a Jewish mother. In contrast, reform Judaism recognizes as Jewish the offspring of a Jewish father and a non-Jewish mother. Currently, the Jewish population numbers about 15 million worldwide, with about half living in North America, a quarter in Israel, and 20 percent in Europe and Russia. Smaller populations are scattered across the globe.

WHO'S WHO AT THE KOTEL The most sacred place to all Jews is the Kotel (ko-TELL), or Western Wall in Jerusalem (Map 10.6, page 208). Since the 1967 war, which brought Jerusalem under Israeli rule, the Kotel has been the most important religious shrine and pilgrimage site of Israel. The Kotel is located at one edge of the Temple Mount (also called Haram Sharif), an area sacred to Jews, Muslims, and Christians. According to Jewish scriptures, God asked Abraham to sacrifice his son Isaac on this hill. Later, King Solomon built the First Temple here in the middle of the tenth century BCE. It was destroyed by Nebuchadnezzsar (neh-boo-kud-NEZZ-er) in 587 BCE, when the Jews were led into captivity in Babylon. Around 500 BCE, the Second Temple was built on the same site. The Kotel is a remnant of the Second Temple. Jews of all varieties, as well as non-Jews, come to the Kotel in vast numbers from around the world. The Kotel plaza is open to everyone, pilgrims and tourists alike. The wall is made of massive rectangular stones weighing between two and eight tons each. At its base is a synagogue area partitioned into men's and women's sections.

This single site brings together a variety of Jewish worshippers and secular visitors. The great diversity among the visitors is evident in the various styles of dress. An orthodox Hasid wearing a fur shtreimel on his head in

The Kotel, or Western Wall, in Jerusalem is a sacred place of pilgrimage, especially for Jews. Men pray in a section marked off on the left, women in the area on the right. Both men and women should cover their heads, and when leaving the wall area, women should take care to keep their faces toward it and avoid turning their backs to it.

▌*Think of some behavioral rules at another sacred place you have visited.*

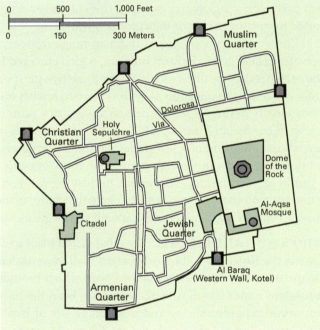

Map 10.6 **Sacred Sites in the Old City of Jerusalem, Israel**

Jerusalem is the holiest city of Judaism, the third holiest city of Islam, and holy to Christians. The section called the Old City is surrounded by walls that have been built, razed, relocated, and rebuilt over several hundred years. The Old City contains four quarters—Armenian, Christian, Jewish, and Muslim—and many sacred sites, such as the Kotel and the Via Dolorosa.

the synagogue area stands next to a man from the United States in shorts, wearing a cardboard skullcap that is available for "secular" visitors. Women from Yemen, wearing traditionally embroidered clothing pray at the Wall alongside women wearing modern Western dress (Storper-Perez and Goldberg 1994:321).

In spite of plaques that state the prohibition against begging, beggars offer to "sell a blessing" to visitors. They may remind visitors that it was the poor who built the wall in the first place. Another category of people is

young Jewish men who, in search of prospective "born again" Jews, "hang around" looking for a "hit" (in their words). Most of the hits are young Americans, who are urged to take their Jewishness more seriously and, if male, to be sure to marry a Jewish woman. Other regulars are Hebrew-speaking men who are available to organize a prayer service. One of the most frequent forms of religious expression at the Kotel is the insertion of written prayers into the crevices of the wall.

The social heterogeneity of the Jewish people is thus transcended in a single space, creating some sense of what Victor Turner (1969) called communitas, a sense of collective unity that bridges individual differences.

PASSOVER IN KERALA The Jews of the Kochi (ko-chee) area of Kerala, South India, have lived there for about 1,000 years (Katz and Goldberg 1989) (see Map 13.2, page 265). The Maharaja of Kochi had respect for the Jewish people, who were mainly merchants. He relied on them for external trade and contacts. In recognition of this relationship, he allowed a synagogue, which is still standing, to be built next to his palace. Syncretism is apparent in Kochi Jewish lifestyle, social structure, and rituals. Basic aspects of Judaism are retained, along with many aspects of Hindu practices.

Three aspects of syncretism with Hinduism are apparent in Passover, one of the most important annual rituals of the Jewish faith. First, the Western/European Passover celebration is typically joyous and a time of feasting. In contrast, the Kochi version has adopted a tone of austerity and is called "the fasting feast." Second, Kochi Passover allows no role for children, whereas, at a traditional Western/European ritual meal, or seder (say-der), children usually ask four questions as a starting point of the narrative. The adult Kochi Jews chant the questions in unison. (In Hinduism, children do not have solo roles in rituals.) Third, a Kochi seder stresses purity even more than standard Jewish requirements do. Standard rules about maintaining the purity of kosher wine usually mean that no gentile (non-Jew) should touch it. But Kochi Jews expand the rule to say that if the shelf or table on which the wine sits is touched by a gentile, the wine is impure. This extra level of "contagion" is influenced by Hindu concepts of pollution.

Christianity

Christianity has many ties with Judaism, from which it sprang. One of the strongest ties is the biblical teaching of a coming savior, or messiah (anointed one). Christianity began in the eastern Mediterranean in the second quarter of the first century (Cunningham 1995). Most of the early believers were Jews who took up the belief in Jesus Christ as the messiah who came to earth in fulfillment of prophesies contained in the Hebrew scriptures.

Today, Christianity is the largest of the world religions, with about two billion adherents, roughly one-third of the world's population. It is the majority religion of Australia, New Zealand, the Philippines, Papua New Guinea, most countries of Europe and of North and South America, and about a dozen southern African countries. Christianity is a minority religion throughout Asia, but Asian Christians constitute 16 percent of the world's Christians and are thus a significant population.

Christians accept the Bible (Old and New Testaments) as containing the basic teachings of their faith, believe that a supreme God sent His son to earth as a sacrifice for the welfare of humanity, and look to Jesus as the model to follow for moral guidance. The three largest branches of Christianity are Roman Catholic, Protestant, and Eastern Orthodox. Within each of these branches, various denominations exist. The greatest growth in Christianity is occurring in sub-Saharan Africa, India, Indonesia, and Eastern Europe.

PROTESTANTISM AMONG WHITE APPALACHIANS Studies of Protestantism in Appalachia describe local traditions that outsiders who are accustomed to standard, urban versions may view as "deviant." For example, some churches in rural West Virginia and North Carolina, called Old Regulars, practice three obligatory rituals: footwashing, communion (a ritual commemorating the Last Supper that Jesus had with his disciples), and baptism (Dorgan 1989). The footwashing ceremony occurs once a year in conjunction with communion, usually as an extension of the Sunday service. An elder is called to the front of the church, and he preaches for 10 to 20 minutes. A round of handshaking and embracing follows. Two deaconesses then come forward to "prepare the table" by uncovering the sacramental elements placed there earlier under a white tablecloth. The elements are unleavened bread, serving plates for the bread, cups for the wine, and a decanter or quart jar or two of wine. The deacons break the bread into pieces and the moderator pours the wine into the cups. Men and women form separate groups as the deacons serve the bread and wine. The deacons serve each other, and then it is time for the footwashing.

The moderator begins by quoting from the New Testament (John 13:4): "He riseth from supper, and laid aside his garments; and he took a towel and girded himself." The moderator takes a towel and basin from the communion table, puts water in it, and selects a senior elder and removes his shoes and socks. The moderator washes his feet slowly and attentively. Other members

(LEFT) Vatican City and St. Peter's Basilica, in Rome, attract more pilgrims/visitors each year than any religious site in the world.
(RIGHT) In the nearby neighborhood, shops cater to pilgrims and tourists by offering a variety of religious and secular goods.

come forward and take towels and basins and take turns washing others' feet and having their feet washed. Soon "the church is filled with crying, shouting, and praising as these highly poignant exchanges unleash a flood of emotions" (Dorgan 1989:106). A functional interpretation of the ritual of footwashing is that it helps maintain social cohesion.

Another feature of worship in some small Protestant churches in Appalachia, especially remote areas of rural West Virginia, involves the handling of poisonous snakes. This practice finds legitimation in the New Testament (Daugherty 1997 [1976]). According to a passage in Mark (16:15–18), "In my name shall they cast out devils; they shall speak with new tongues; they shall take up serpents; and if they drink any deadly thing, it shall not hurt them; they shall lay hands on the sick, and they shall recover." Members of "Holiness-type" churches believe that the handling of poisonous snakes is the supreme act of devotion to God. Biblical literalists, these people choose serpent handling as their way of celebrating life, death, and resurrection and of proving that only Jesus has the power to deliver them from death. Most serpent handlers have been bitten many times, but few have died.

One interpretation says that the risks of handling poisonous snakes mirror the risks of the environment. In Appalachia, unemployment rates are high and many people are economically poor. The structurist view (review Chapter 1) points to the fact that serpent handling increased when local people lost their land rights to big mining and forestry companies (Tidball and Toumey 2003:4). As their lives became more economically insecure, they turned to a way of increasing their sense of stability through a dramatic religious ritual. Outsiders might ask whether such dangerous ritual practices indicate that the people are disturbed. In fact, psychological tests indicate that members of Holiness churches are more emotionally healthy, on average, than members of mainline Protestant churches.

THE LAST SUPPER IN FIJI Among Christians in Fiji (see Map 5.6, page 106), the image of the Last Supper is a dominant motif (Toren 1988). This scene, depicted on tapestry hangings, adorns most churches and many houses. People say, "Christ is the head of this household, he eats with us and overhears us" (1988:697). The image's popularity is the result of its fit with Fijian notions of communal eating and kava drinking. Seating rules at such events place the people of highest status, such as the chief and others close to him, at the "above" side of the room, away from the entrance. Others sit at the "lower" end, facing the highly ranked people. Intermediate positions are located on either side of the person of honor, in ranked order.

Leonardo Da Vinci's fifteenth-century painting of the Last Supper places Jesus Christ in the position of a Fijian chief, with the disciples in an ordered arrangement around him. The disciples and the viewers "face" the chief and eat and drink together, as is appropriate in Fijian society. The positioning parallels the orderly placement of Fijian people around the kava as encountered "virtually every day in the village" (1988:706). This kind of cultural fit is a clear example of religious syncretism.

Islam

Islam is based on the teachings of the prophet Muhammad (570–632 CE) and is thus the youngest of the world religions (Martin 1995:498–513). The Arabic word Islam means "submission" to the will of the one god, Allah, through which peace will be achieved. Followers of Islam, known as Muslims, believe that Muhammad was God's final prophet. Islam has several denominations with essentially similar beliefs but also distinct theological and legal approaches. The two major schools of thought are Sunni

The Hassan II Mosque was built for the sixtieth birthday of Morocco's previous king, Hassan II. It is the second-largest religious monument in the world, after Mecca, with space for 25,000 worshippers inside and another 80,000 outside. The minaret, 210 meters in height, is the tallest in the world.

and Shi'a. About 85 percent of the total Muslim population worldwide is Sunni, and about 15 percent is Shi'a. Sufism is a more mystical variant of Islam, with much smaller numbers of adherents. Many other subgroups exist. The Five Pillars of Islam are profession of faith in Allah, daily prayer, fasting, contributing alms for the poor, and the Hajj (pilgrimage to Mecca). The five pillars are central to Sunni Islam but less so to other branches of Islam, such as the Shi'as and the Sufis.

The total number of Muslims worldwide is about 1.4 billion, making it the second-largest religion with 22 percent of the world's population. Muslim-majority nations are located in northern Africa; the Middle East, Afghanistan, Pakistan, and Bangladesh in South Asia; and several nations in Central Asia and Southeast Asia. Most of the world's Muslims (60 percent) live in South Asia or Southeast Asia. Muslims are minorities in many other countries, including China, where they seek to maintain their religious practices (see Culturama). Although Islam originally flourished among pastoralists, only two percent of its adherents are now in that category.

A common and inaccurate stereotype of Islam prevalent among many non-Muslims is that it is the same no matter where it exists. This erroneously monolithic model tends to be based on an image of conservative Wahhabist Islam as practiced in Saudi Arabia. But Wahhabist Islam is only one of many varieties of Islam.

A comparison of Islam in highland Sumatra (part of Indonesia in Southeast Asia) and Morocco (in North Africa) reveals differences that are the result of local cultural adaptations (Bowen 1992). Eid-ul-Adha (eed-ull-ah-dah), or the Feast of Sacrifice, is celebrated annually by Muslims around the world. It commemorates Ibrahim's willingness to sacrifice his son Ishmael (Isaac in the Christian tradition, Yitzhak in the Jewish) to Allah. It occurs on the tenth of the last month of the year, called Pilgrimage Month, and marks the end of the Hajj. The ritual reminds Muslims of their global unity within the Islamic faith.

An important aspect of this ritual in Morocco (see Map 4.2, page 73) involves the king publicly plunging a dagger into a ram's throat, a reenactment of Muhammad's performance of the sacrifice on the same day in the seventh century. Each male head of household follows the pattern and sacrifices a ram. The size and virility of the ram are a measure of the man's power and virility. Other men of the household stand to witness the sacrifice, while women and children are absent or in the background. After the ram is killed, the men come forward and dab its blood on their faces. In some villages, women play a more prominent role before the sacrifice by daubing the ram with henna (red dye), thus sanctifying it, and using its blood afterward in rituals to protect the household. These state and household rituals are symbolic of male power in the public and private domains—the power of the monarchy and the power of patriarchy.

In Isak (ee-suk), Sumatra (see Map 6.3, page 117), the cultural context is less patriarchal and the political structure does not emphasize monarchy. Isak is a traditionalist Muslim village where people have been Muslims since the seventeenth century. They sacrifice many kinds of animals: chickens, ducks, sheep, goats, and water buffalo. The people believe that so long as the animal's throat is cut and the meat is eaten, the sacrifice satisfies God. Most sacrifices are family affairs and receive little public notice. They are done in the back of the house. Both women and men of the household refer to it as "their" sacrifice, and there are no signs of male dominance. Women may sponsor a sacrifice, as did one wealthy woman trader who sacrificed a buffalo. (The cutting was done by a man.)

The Moroccan ritual emphasizes fathers and sons, whereas the Isak ritual includes attention to a wider range of kin on both the husband's and wife's side, daughters as well as sons, and even dead relatives. In Isak, the ritual carries no centralized political meanings. The differences are not due to the fact that Moroccans know the scriptures better than Sumatrans do. The Isak area has many Islamic scholars who are familiar with the scriptures and regularly discuss them with each other. Rather, the two cultural contexts, including kinship and politics, shape the ritual to local realities.

African Religions

Many African religions are now global. In earlier centuries, they spread outside Africa through the coerced movement of people as slaves. African diaspora religions are especially prominent in the United States, the Caribbean region, and Central and South America. This section summarizes some key features of African religions and then offers two examples of African religions in the Western Hemisphere.

FEATURES OF AFRICAN RELIGIONS With its diverse geography, cultural variation, and long history, Africa encompasses a wide range of religious affiliations, including many Muslims, Christians, Jews, Hindus, practitioners of indigenous religions, and people who follow some combination of these.

Indigenous African religions are difficult to typify, but some of their shared features are as follows:

- Myths about a rupture that once occurred between the creator deity and humans

- A pantheon that includes a high god and many secondary supernaturals ranging from powerful gods to lesser spirits

- Elaborate initiation rituals

Culturama

Hui Muslims of Xi'an, China

The Hui (hway), one of China's largest designated minorities, number around 10 million people. Most live in the northwestern part of the country. The state classifies the Hui as "backward" and "feudal" in comparison to China's majority Han population. Hui residents of Xi'an (shee-ahn), however, reject the official characterization of them as less civilized and less modern than the Han majority (Gillette 2000).

About 60,000 Hui live in Xi'an, mainly in the so-called Old Muslim Quarter, which is dominated by small shops, restaurants, and mosques. The quality of housing and public services is inferior to that found elsewhere in the city. Parents worry that their children are not getting the best education and feel that the state is not providing adequate schooling in their neighborhood. Many Hui have taken steps to improve their houses themselves and to send their children to schools outside the district.

The Hui of Xi'an construct what they consider to be a modern and civilized lifestyle by choosing aspects of Muslim culture and Western culture. Their form of "progress" is visible in many aspects of their daily life, such as eating habits, dress styles, housing, religious practices, education, and family organization.

Being Muslim in China poses several challenges in relation to the dominant Han culture. Diet is one prominent example. The Qur'an forbids four types of food to Muslims: animals that have not been consecrated to God and properly slaughtered, blood, pork, and alcohol (Gillette 2000:116). Three of the four rules apply to meat, and meat is the central part of a proper meal for Muslims. The Hui say that pork is especially impure. This belief differentiates the Hui clearly from other Chinese people, for whom pork is a major food item. Given the Hui belief that the kinds of food one eats affect a person's essence and behavior, they view pork eaters with disdain.

Hui residents consider alcohol even more impure than pork (Gillette 2000:167). Hui of Xi'an do not drink alcohol. They avoid using utensils that have touched alcohol and people who are drinking it. Many Hui of Xi'an, however, make a living in the restaurant business, which caters to Chinese Han and foreign tourists. Although selling alcohol boosts business, many Hui object to it. Some community members say that restricting alcohol has improved the quality of life by making the neighborhood more peaceful and orderly.

In 2003, an urban development project in the Old Muslim Quarter was launched with financial support from the Norwegian government (*People's Daily* 2003). The project will widen the main street, replace "shabby" housing and infrastructure, and restore crumbling buildings of historic interest. A commercial area will be dedicated to restaurants serving Hui food in recognition of the touristic appeal of traditional Hui specialties such as baked beef and mutton, buns with beef, mutton pancake, and mutton soup. It is unclear where alcohol consumption will fit into this plan.

Thanks to Maris Boyd Gillette, Haverford College, for reviewing this material.

(LEFT) At a street stand in Xi'an, Hui men prepare a noodle dish. Like Muslim men in many parts of the world, they wear a white cap.

(CENTER) Hui women in Xi'an participate in a ritual that commemorates Hui people who died in a conflict that spread across northwestern China from 1862 to 1874.

Map 10.7 The City of Xi'an in China

Xi'an, the capital of Shaanxi province, is one of the most economically developed cities in the northwestern part of China.

In Evanston, Illinois, two adopted Haitian-born siblings (left and right) light altar candles. The candles bear the images of Vodou spirits such as the spirit mother, who is the protector and defender of children. The children's adoptive family are Christians who have decided to incorporate some Haitian Vodou practices into their everyday routine.

- Rituals involving animal sacrifices and other offerings, meals, and dances
- Altars within shrines as focal places where humans and deities meet
- Close links with healing

Although these features are fairly constant, African religions are rethought and reshaped locally and over time, with complex and variable results (Gable 1995). In their home locations, they have been influenced by foreign religions, notably Islam and various types of Christianity. The outmigration of African peoples has brought African religions to new locations, where they have been localized and revitalized in their new contexts (Clarke 2004).

Religious syncretisms in North and South America often combine aspects of Christianity with African traditions and elements of indigenous Indian beliefs and practices. Widely popular in Brazil are blended religions such as umbanda, santerí, and condomblé that appeal to people of all social classes, urban and rural, especially for providing social support and alleviation of stress (Burdick 2004).

RAS TAFARI   Also called Rastafarianism, Ras Tafari is an Afro-Caribbean religion with its original roots in Jamaica. It is not known how many Rastafarians there are, because they refuse to be counted (Smith 1995:23). Ras Tafari is a protest religion that shares only a few of the features of the African religions just mentioned. It traces its history to several preachers of the early twentieth century who taught that Ras ("Prince") Tafari, then the Ethiopian emperor Haile Selassie, was the "Lion of Judah" who would lead Blacks to the African promised land.

Rastafarianism does not have an organized set of doctrines or written texts. Shared beliefs of the many diffuse groups in the Caribbean, the United States, and Europe include the belief that Ethiopia is heaven on earth, that Haile Selassie is a living god, and that all Blacks will be able to return to the homeland through his help. Since the death of Haile Selassie in 1975, more emphasis has been placed on pan-African unity and Black power, and less on Ethiopia.

Rastafarianism is particularly strong in Jamaica, where it is associated with reggae music, dreadlocks, and ganja (marijuana) smoking. Variations within the Rastafarian movement in Jamaica range from the belief that one must fight oppression to the position that living a peaceful life brings victory against evil.

Bob Marley, legendary reggae artist and Rastafarian, performing at the Roxy Theater in Hollywood, California, in 1979. Marley died in 1981 at the age of 36, but he is still the most revered reggae musician. He launched the global spread of Jamaican music. Reggae is a genre of Jamaican music associated with Rastafarianism. Its songs address poverty, social injustice, love, and sexuality.

Directions of Religious Change

10.3 **Identify examples of religious change in contemporary times.**

All religions have mythologies and doctrines that provide for continuity in their beliefs and practices. Yet no religion is frozen and unchanging. Cultural anthropologists have traced the resurgence of religions that seemed to be headed toward extinction through colonial forces, and they have documented the emergence of new religions. Likewise, they are observing the contemporary struggle of once-suppressed religions in socialist states to find a new position in the postsocialist world. Religious icons (images, pictures, or other forms of representation), once a prominent feature in Russian Orthodox churches, had been removed and placed in museums. The churches want them back.

Indigenous people's beliefs about the sacredness of their land are an important part of their attempts to protect their territory from encroachment and development by outside commercial interests. The world of religious change offers these examples, and far more, as windows into wider cultural change.

Revitalization Movements

Revitalization movements are social responses to outside forces that seek to reestablish threatened aspects of a religion or adopt new practices and beliefs. These movements arise in the context of rapid cultural change and appear to represent a way for people to try to make sense of their changing world and their place in it. One such movement that emerged as a response of Native Americans to the invasion of their land by Europeans and Euro-Americans was the Ghost Dance movement (Kehoe 1989). In the early 1870s, a shaman named Wodziwob of the Paiute (pie-yoot) tribe in California declared that the world would soon be destroyed and then renewed: Native Americans, plants, and animals would come back to life. He instructed people to perform a circle dance, known as the Ghost Dance, at night.

The movement spread to other tribes in California, Oregon, and Idaho but ended when the prophet died and his prophecy was unfulfilled. A similar movement emerged in 1890, led by another Paiute prophet, Wovoka, who had a vision during a total eclipse. His message was

John Frum Movement supporters stand guard around one of the cult's flagpoles at Sulphur Bay village, on Tanna Island, Vanuatu, in the region of Melanesia. The movement is an example of a cargo cult.

■ *Do Internet research on John Frum.*

the same: destruction, renewal, and the need to perform circle dances in anticipation of the impending event. The dance spread widely and had various effects. Among the Pawnee, it provided the basis for a cultural revival of old ceremonies that had fallen into disuse. The Sioux altered Wovoka's message and adopted a more overtly hostile stance toward the government and White people. Newspapers began to carry stories about the "messiah craze," referring to Wovoka. Ultimately, the government took action against the Sioux, killing Chief Sitting Bull and Chief Big Foot and about 300 Sioux at Wounded Knee. In the 1970s, the Ghost Dance was revived again by the American Indian Movement, an activist organization that seeks to advance Native American rights.

Cargo cults are a type of revitalization movement that emerged throughout Melanesia in response to Western influences. Most prominent in the first half of the nineteenth century, cargo cult behavior emphasized the acquisition of Western trade goods, or cargo in local terms. Typically, a prophetic leader emerged with a vision of how the cargo will arrive. In one instance, the leader predicted that a ship would come, bringing not only cargo but also the people's dead ancestors. Followers set up tables for the expected guests, complete with flower arrangements.

Later, after World War II and the islanders' experiences of aircraft arrivals bringing cargo, the mode of anticipated arrival changed to planes. Once again, people would wait expectantly for the arrival of the plane. Cargo cults emerged as a response to the disruptive effects of new goods being suddenly introduced into indigenous settings. The outsiders imposed a new form of exchange system that emphasized the importance of Western goods and suppressed the importance of indigenous valuables such as shells and pigs. This transformation undermined traditional patterns of gaining status through the exchange of

---

revitalization movement a socioreligious movement, usually organized by a prophetic leader, that seeks to construct a more satisfying situation by reviving all or parts of a religion that has been threatened by outside forces or by adopting new practices and beliefs.

cargo cult a form of revitalization movement that emerged in Melanesia in response to Western and Japanese influences.

indigenous goods. Cargo cult leaders sought help, in the only way they knew, in obtaining Western goods so that they could acquire social status in the new system.

Contested Sacred Sites

Religious conflict is often focused on sacred sites. One place of recurrent conflict is Jerusalem, where many religions and sects within religions compete for control of sacred terrain. Three major religions claim that they have primary rights: Islam, Judaism, and Christianity. Among the Christians, several different sects vie for control of the Church of the Holy Sepulchre (see Map 10.6 on page 208). In India, frequent conflicts over sacred sites occur between Hindus and Muslims. Hindus claim that Muslim mosques have been built on sites sacred to Hindus. On some occasions, the Hindus have destroyed the mosques. Many conflicts that involve secular issues surrounding sacred sites also exist worldwide. In the United States, White racists have burned African American churches. In Israel, some Jewish leaders object to archaeological research because they believe that the ancient Jewish burial places should remain undisturbed.

A similar situation exists among indigenous populations in the Western Hemisphere. Their sacred sites and burial grounds have often been destroyed for the sake of urban growth, petroleum and mineral extraction, and recreational sports. Resistance to such destruction is growing, with indigenous people finding creative ways to protect, restore, and manage their heritage.

Religious Freedom as a Human Right

According to a United Nations Declaration, freedom from religious persecution is a universal human right. Yet violations of this right by countries and by competing religions are common. Sometimes people who are persecuted on religious grounds can seek and obtain sanctuary in other places or nations. Thousands of Tibetan Buddhist refugees, including their leader, the Dalai Lama, fled Tibet after it was taken over by the Chinese. Many Tibetan communities have been established in exile in India, the United States, and Canada, where the Tibetan people attempt to keep their religion, language, and heritage alive.

Religions may be a focal point of conflict and dissension as well as a source of conflict resolution and social resilience in the face of disaster and despair. As an integral part of the heritage of humanity, religions are best understood within a cross-cultural and contextualized perspective. Such an understanding is essential for building a more peaceful future.

---

10 Learning Objectives Revisited

10.1 Describe how anthropologists define religion and its key features.

Early cultural anthropologists defined religion in contrast to magic and suggested that religion was a more evolved form of thinking about the supernatural realm. They collected information on religions of non-Western cultures and constructed theories about the origin and functions of religion. Since then, ethnographers have described many religious systems and documented a rich variety of beliefs, forms of ritual behavior, and types of religious specialists. Beliefs are expressed in either myth or doctrine and often are concerned with defining the roles and characteristics of supernatural beings and how humans should relate to them.

Religious beliefs are enacted in rituals that are periodic or nonperiodic. Some common rituals worldwide are life-cycle rites, pilgrimage, rituals of inversion, and sacrifice. Rituals are transformative for the participants.

Many rituals require the involvement of a trained religious specialist, such as a shaman/shamanka or priest/priestess. Compared with the situation in states, religious specialist roles in nonstate contexts are fewer, less than full time, and less formalized, and they carry less secular power. In states, religious specialists are often organized into hierarchies, and many specialists gain substantial secular power.

10.2 Recognize how globalization has affected world religions.

The so-called world religions are based on texts and generally agreed-on teachings and beliefs shared by many people around the world. In order of historic age, the five long-standing world religions are Hinduism, Buddhism, Judaism, Christianity, and Islam. Christianity has the largest number of adherents, with Islam second and Hinduism third. Because of accelerated global population migration in the past few centuries, many formerly local religions now have a worldwide membership. Because of Western colonialism and slavery, African religions are prominent in the Western Hemisphere, with a variety of syncretistic religions attracting many adherents.

As members of the world religions have moved around the globe, religious beliefs and practices have become contextualized into localized variants. When a new religion moves into a culture, it may be blended with local systems (syncretism), may coexist with indigenous religions in a pluralistic fashion, or may take over and obliterate the original beliefs.

10.3 **Identify examples of religious change in contemporary times.**

Religious movements of the past two centuries have often been prompted by colonialism and other forms of social contact. In some instances, indigenous religious leaders and cults have arisen in an attempt to resist unwanted outside forces of change. In other cases, they evolve as ways of incorporating selected outside elements. Revitalization movements, such as the Ghost Dance movement in the U.S. Plains region, look to the past and attempt to recover lost and suppressed religious beliefs and practices.

Issues of contemporary importance include the increasing amount of conflict surrounding sacred sites, hostilities related to the effects of secular power interests on religious institutions and spaces, and religious freedom as a human right.

Key Concepts

animatism, p. 197
cargo cult, p. 214
doctrine, p. 196
life-cycle ritual, p. 199
magic, p. 195
myth, p. 196

pilgrimage, p. 201
priest or priestess, p. 203
religion, p. 195
religious pluralism, p. 204
religious syncretism, p. 204
revitalization movement, p. 214

ritual, p. 199
ritual of inversion, p. 201
sacrifice, p. 202
world religion, p. 203

Thinking Outside the Box

1. Take careful note of your daily activities and events for a week and assess them in terms of how magic, religion, or science is involved. What did you find?
2. Learn about Oyotunji Village from the Internet. What goes on there? Do people live there? If you went to visit, where would you stay, what would you eat, and what would you do?

3. Think of examples of how particular religious beliefs and practices contribute to human well-being and how, in some circumstances, they do not. How might a cross-cultural perspective provide more insight into the relationship between religion and well-being?

Chapter 11
Expressive Culture

Learning Objectives

11.1 Summarize how culture is expressed through art.

11.2 Illustrate what play and leisure reveal about culture.

11.3 Explain how cultural heritage is a contested resource in contemporary times.

Anthro Connections

A Miao (mee-ow) girl of southwestern China helps her younger sister get ready for the annual Spring Flower Festival. Her headgear is woven from the hair of several generations of women in her family and weighs from four to nearly nine pounds. The Miaos are one of China's 55 officially recognized ethnic minorities. In 2012, (then)

President Hu Jintao attended the fourth Minorities Art Festival of China. President Hu urged the artists to continue to perform for the mainstream theme of ethnic unity and progress and make more contributions toward the prosperity and development of minority art. More than 6,700 ethnic performers participated in the festival.

This chapter considers a vast area of human behavior and thought called **expressive culture**, or behavior and beliefs related to art, leisure, and play. (Definitions of these terms are provided later.) It begins with a discussion of theoretical perspectives on what is art cross-culturally and how anthropologists study art and expressive culture. The second section considers the topics of play and leisure cross-culturally. The last section provides examples of how expressive culture, especially as defined as cultural heritage, is a contested resource, both materially and in terms of individual, local, national, and global identities.

taken, the approach of cultural anthropologists is rather different. Their findings, here as in other cultural domains, stretch and subvert Western concepts and categories and prompt us to look at art within its context. Thus, anthropologists consider many kinds of products, practices, and processes to be art. They also study the artist and the artist's place in society. In addition, they ask questions about how art, and expressive culture more generally, is related to microcultural variation, inequality, and power.

What Is Art?

Are ancient rock carvings art? Is subway graffiti art? An embroidered robe? A painting of a can of Campbell's

Art and Culture

11.1 Summarize how culture is expressed through art.

Compared with the definition of art and how to study the subject as presented in art history classes you may have

expressive culture behaviors and beliefs related to art, leisure, and play.

Painting walls has a long heritage, going back at least to prehistoric cave paintings discovered in Europe and Australia. (LEFT) Graffiti in New York City in the 1980s. (CENTER) A mural in west Belfast, Northern Ireland, where the Irish Republican Army and its opponents expressed their views in murals. These murals are now a tourist attraction. (RIGHT) Albetina Mahalangu paints a wall with Ndebele (en-deb-elly) designs in South Africa. This art is also a tourist attraction.

Think Like an Anthropologist
Probing the Categories of Art

Probably every reader of this book, at one time or another, has looked at an object in an art museum or in an art book or magazine and exclaimed, "But that's not art!"

As a critical thinking research project on "What is art?" visit two museums, either in person or on the Internet. One of these should be a museum of either fine art or modern art. The other should be a museum of natural history.

In the former, examine at least five items on display. In the latter, examine several items on display that have to do with human cultures (that is, skip the bugs and rocks).

Take notes on all the items that you are examining. Then answer the following questions.

Critical Thinking Questions

- What is the object?
- What contextual explanation does the museum provide about the object?
- Was the object intended as a work of art or as something else?
- In your opinion, is it art or not, and why or why not?
- Compare your notes on the objects in the two types of museums. What do your notes tell you about categories of art?

---

soup? Philosophers, art critics, anthropologists, and art lovers have all struggled with the question "What is art?" The issue of how to define art involves more than mere word games. The way art is defined affects the manner in which a person values and treats artistic creations and those who create art (see Think Like an Anthropologist).

Anthropologists propose broad definitions of art to take into account emic definitions cross-culturally. One definition says that **art is the application of imagination, skill, and style to matter, movement, and sound that goes beyond the purely practical** (Nanda 1994:383). Such imagination, skill, and style can be applied to many substances and activities, and the product can be considered art—for example, a beautifully presented meal, a well-told story, or a perfectly formed basket. In this sense, art is a human universal, and no culture can be said to lack artistic activity completely. The Pirahã of the Brazilian Amazon, however, appear to have very little visual art, but they do have verbal art (review Chapter 9).

In addition to studying the art product itself, anthropologists pay attention to the process of making art, the variations in art and its preferred forms cross-culturally, and the way culture constructs and changes artistic traditions. They also consider various categories of art. Within the general category of art, subcategories exist, sometimes denoting eras, such as Paleolithic or modern art. Other subcategories are based on the medium of expression, such as graphic or plastic arts (painting, drawing, sculpture, weaving, basketry, and architecture); decorative arts (interior design, landscaping, gardens, costume design,

and body adornment such as hairstyles, tattooing, and painting); performance arts (music, dance, and theater); and verbal arts (poetry, writing, rhetoric, and telling stories and jokes).

A long-standing distinction in the Western view exists between fine art and folk art. This distinction is based on a Western-centric judgment that defines fine art as rare, expensive art produced by artists usually trained in the Western classical tradition. This is the kind of art that is included in college courses called "Fine Arts." The implication is that all other art is less than fine and is more appropriately called folk art, ethnic art, primitive art, or crafts. Characteristics of Western fine art are as follows: The product is created by a formally schooled artist; it is made for sale on the market; it is clearly associated with a particular artist; its uniqueness is valued; and it is not primarily utilitarian but is rather "art for art's sake." In contrast, all the rest of the world's art that is non-Western and nonclassical is supposedly characterized by the opposite features:

- It is created by an artist who has not received formal training.
- It is not produced for sale.
- The artist is anonymous and does not sign or individually claim the product.
- It is made primarily for everyday use, such as food procurement, processing, or storage; in ritual; or in war.

A closer examination of these two categories is in order. All cultures have art, and all cultures have a sense of what makes something art versus non-art. The term esthetics refers to socially accepted notions of quality (Thompson 1971). Before anthropologists proved otherwise, Western art experts believed that esthetics either did

---

art the application of imagination, skill, and style to matter, movement, and sound that goes beyond what is purely practical.

Yorúbà wood carving follows esthetic principles that require clarity of line and form, a polished surface that creates a play of light and shadows, symmetry, and the depiction of human figures that are neither completely abstract nor completely realistic.

Have you seen African sculptures that follow these principles? Visit an African art museum on the Internet for further exploration.

not exist or was poorly developed in non-Western cultures. We now know that esthetic principles, or established criteria for artistic quality, exist everywhere, whether or not they are written down and formalized. **Ethno-esthetics** refers to culturally specific definitions of what art is. The standards for wood carving in West Africa illustrate the importance of considering cross-cultural variation in the criteria for art (Thompson 1971). Among the Yorúbà (YOR-uh-buh) of Nigeria, esthetic guidelines for wood carving include these:

- Figures should be depicted midway between complete abstraction and complete realism so that they resemble "somebody," but no one in particular. Portraiture in the Western sense is considered dangerous.

- Humans should be depicted at their optimal physical peak, not in infancy or old age.

- Line and form should have clarity.

- The sculpture should have the quality of luminosity achieved through a polished surface and the play of incisions and shadows.

- The piece should exhibit symmetry.

---

ethno-esthetics culturally specific definitions of what art is.

Studying Art in Society

The anthropological study of art seeks to understand not only the products of art but also who makes it and why, the role of art in society, and its wider social meanings. Franz Boas was the first anthropologist to emphasize the importance of studying the artist in society. Functionalism (review Chapter 1) was the most important theory informing anthropological research on art in the first half of the twentieth century. Anthropologists wrote about how paintings, dance, theater, and songs serve to socialize children into the culture, provide a sense of social identity and group boundaries, and promote healing. Art may legitimize political leaders and enhance efforts in war through body painting, adornment, and magical decorations on shields and weapons. Art may also serve as a form of social control, as in African masks worn by dancers who represent deities visiting humans to remind them of the moral order. Art, like language, can be a catalyst for political resistance or a rallying point for ethnic solidarity in the face of oppression.

The anthropology of art relies on a range of methods in data gathering and analysis. The basic method is participant observation, supplemented by collecting and analyzing oral or written material including video and audio recordings. Thus, strong ties often exist between cultural and linguistic anthropologists in the study of art.

Many anthropologists have become apprentices in an artistic tradition. For John Chernoff, learning to play African drums was an important part of building rapport during his fieldwork in Ghana and an essential aspect of his ability to gain an understanding of the importance of music in Ghanaian society (1979). His book, *African Rhythm and African Sensibility*, takes into account the position and role of the ethnographer and how it shapes what the ethnographer learns. Reading the book's introduction will convince you that fieldwork in cultural anthropology is far more than simply gathering the data you think you need for the project you have in mind, especially if your project concerns processes of creativity and expression.

Chernoff argues that only by relinquishing a scientific approach can a researcher learn about creativity and how it is related to society. As one of his drumming teachers said, "The heart sees before the eyes." Chernoff had to do more than practice participant observation. His heart had to participate, too. During his early months in the field, Chernoff often found himself wondering why he was there. To write a book? To tell people back in the United States about Ghana? No doubt, many of the Ghanaians he met wondered the same thing, especially given that his early efforts at drumming were pretty bad, although he did not realize it because he always drank copious amounts of gin before playing. Eventually, he became the student of a master drummer

Expressive culture in Sumba, Indonesia. (TOP) A woman weaves ikat (ih-kut) cloth on a bamboo loom. Ikat is a style of weaving that uses a tie-dye process on either the warp or weft before the threads are woven. The process will create a design in the final product. Double ikat is when both warp and weft threads are tie-dyed before weaving. The motif on this piece of ikat is the Tree of Life flanked by roosters. (BOTTOM) Linguistic anthropologist Joel Kuipers interviews a ritual speaker who is adept at verbal arts performance.

■ *What is a form of verbal art in your culture?*

and went through a formal initiation ceremony. For the ceremony, he had to kill two chickens himself and eat parts of them in a form that most North Americans will never see in a grocery store. Still he was not playing well enough. He went through another ritual to make his wrist "smart" so that it would turn faster, like a cat chasing a mouse. For that ritual, he had to go into the bush, 10 miles outside town, and collect ingredients. The ritual worked. Having a cat's hand was a good thing, but anthropologically it was more important to Chernoff that he had begun to gain an understanding of drumming in its social and ritual contexts.

Chernoff learned about Ghanaian family life and how it is connected to individual performers and to rituals that have to do with music. He also grew to see where his performance fell short and what he needed to do to improve. He gained great respect for the artists who taught him and admiration for their striving for respect. Chernoff's personality was an important ingredient of the learning process. He comments, "I assumed that I did not know what to do in most situations. I accepted what people told me about myself and what I should be doing. . . . I waited to see what people would make of me. . . . By staying cool I learned the meaning of character" (1979:170).

FOCUS ON THE ARTIST In the early twentieth century, Franz Boas urged his students to go beyond the study of the products of art and study the artists. One goal of the anthropologist, he said, is to study art from the artist's perspective. Ruth Bunzel's (1972 [1929]) research with Native American potters in the U.S. Southwest is a classic example of this focus. While undergoing training as an apprentice potter, she asked individual potters about their choices for pot designs. One Zuni (zoo-nee) potter commented, "I always know the whole design before I start to paint" (1972:49). A Laguna potter said, "I learned this design from my mother. I learned most of my designs from my mother" (1972:52). Bunzel discovered the importance of both individual agency and following tradition.

The social status of artists is another aspect of the focus on the artist. Artists may be revered and wealthy as individuals or as a group, or they may be stigmatized and economically marginal. In ancient Mexico, goldworkers were highly respected. In American Indian groups of the Pacific Northwest coast, male carvers and painters had to be initiated into a secret society, and they had higher status than other men. Often a gender division exists. Among the Navajo of Arizona, women weave and men do silversmithing. In the Caribbean, women of African descent are noted for their carvings of calabashes (large gourds). In the contemporary United States, most famous and successful graphic artists are men, although the profession includes many women. Depending on the genre, "race"/ethnicity/indigeneity is another factor shaping success as an artist.

As with other occupations, the performing arts are more specialized in state-level societies. Generally, among free-ranging foragers, little specialization exists. Artistic activity is open to all, and artistic products are shared equally by all. Some people may be especially appreciated as singers, storytellers, or carvers. With increasing social complexity and a market for art, specialized training is required to produce certain kinds of art, and the products are sought after by those who can afford them. Class differences in artistic styles and preferences emerge along with the increasingly complex division of labor.

MICROCULTURES, ART, AND POWER Art forms and styles, like language, are often associated with microcultural groups' identity and sense of pride. For example, the Berbers of highland Morocco are associated with woolen carpets, Maya Indians with woven and embroidered blouses, and the Inuit of Alaska with stone carvings of figurines. Cultural anthropologists provide many examples of linkages between various microcultural dimensions and power issues. In some instances, more powerful groups appropriate the art forms of less powerful groups. In others, forms of art are said to be expressive of resistance.

One study reveals how nationalist interests in Israel result in co-opting Arab art and handicrafts by focusing on souvenirs. Tourists who buy arts and crafts souvenirs rarely learn much about the people who actually made the items. Yet they probably have some mental image of, for example, a village potter sitting at the wheel or a silversmith hammering at a piece of metal in a quaint workshop. Souvenir shops come in different varieties, from street stalls that sell a few items such as embroidered clothing or "ethnic" jewelry to national emporiums that offer a wide range of arts and crafts. An upscale store of the latter category in Israel, called Maskit, caters mainly to tourists (Shenhav-Keller 1993).

Ethnographic study shows how the sellers "put Israeli society on display via its souvenirs." It also reveals how certain artists and craftspeople are selectively rendered invisible. The tourist artifact, or souvenir, can be analyzed like a "text" that contains social messages. In the Maskit stores, three central themes in Israeli society are expressed in the choice and presentation of souvenirs: Israel's attitudes toward its ancient and recent past, its view of its religion and culture, and its approach to Arab Israelis and Palestinians.

Shelly Shenhav-Keller conducted participant observation in the original Maskit store in Tel Aviv and interviewed Jewish Israeli, Arab Israeli, and Palestinian artists and artisans whose products were sold there (1993). Maskit was founded by Ruth Dayan (then the wife of Moshe Dayan) as a Ministry of Labor project in 1954. Its purpose was "to encourage artisans to continue their native crafts in the new surrounding . . . to retain and safeguard the ancient crafts" (Shenhav-Keller 1993:183). Maskit was a success, and a chain of shops was eventually opened. As its status increased, Maskit came to be perceived as an "ambassador of Israel." Dignitaries who traveled from Israel abroad were loaded with gifts from the shop. Official visitors to Israel were given Maskit gifts.

The shop had two floors. The top floor, where the entrance was located, had five sections: fashion (women's clothing, wedding gowns, and dresses with three different styles of Arab embroidery); jewelry; ritual articles (candlesticks, goblets, incense burners); decorative items; and books. The larger lower floor had five thematic sections: the Bar-Mitzvah Corner with prayer books and other ritual items; the children's corner (clothing, games, toys, and T-shirts); the embroidery section (tablecloths, linens, pillow covers, wallets, eyeglass cases); the carpet section; and a large area for ceramics, glassware, and copperware.

Over the years, changes have occurred in who produces the art sold in Maskit. The amount of Jewish ethnic art has declined as older artists have aged and their children have not taken up the craft. Many of the original Jewish Israeli artists gained eminence and opened their own shops. Those who continue to supply Maskit specialize in ceramics, jewelry, carpet design, and ritual articles. These pieces are considered to have the status of art and may be displayed as an "individual collection" within the store. To make up for the decline in objects made by Jewish Israelis, Maskit has turned to Arab artists and craftsmakers.

After the 1967 Six-Day War, Arab Israeli and Palestinian craftsmanship became increasingly available with the incorporation of new areas within Israel, including the Occupied Territories. Most of the Arabs absorbed into the souvenir industry became hired laborers in factories and workshops owned by Maskit or by Israeli artisans who sold their works to Maskit as "Israeli." Maskit provides no information about the artistic role of Israeli Arabs or Palestinians in creating its products. The carpets, for example, are presented simply as handwoven "Israeli" carpets, even though Arab Israelis wove them.

Embroidered Palestinian dresses.

An example of how gender relations play out in expressive culture comes from a study of male strip dancing in Florida (Margolis and Arnold 1993). Advertisements in the media tell women that seeing a male strip dancer is "their chance," "their night out." Going to a male strip show is marketed as a time of reversal of traditional gender roles in which men are dominant and women submissive. Are gender roles actually reversed in a male stripper bar? The short answer is no. Women customers are treated like juveniles. As they stand in line waiting for the show to open, the manager instructs them on how to tip. They are symbolically dominated by the dancers, who take on various roles such as lion tamers. The dive-bomb is further evidence of women's subordinate position. The dive-bomb is a form of tipping the dancer in which the woman customer gets on her hands and knees and tucks a bill held between her teeth into the dancer's g-string. The interpretation of all this behavior is that, rather than reversing the gender hierarchy, it reinforces it.

Not all forms of popular art and performance are mechanisms of social control and maintenance of hierarchies. In the United States, for example, hip-hop and urban Black youths' verbal arts and rap music can be seen as a form of protest through performance (Smitherman 1997). Their lyrics report on their experience of economic oppression, the danger of drugs, and men's disrespect for women. There are many other examples, in addition to the global spread of hip-hop and related music, of marginalized people's music providing an avenue of social mobility.

Performance Arts

The performance arts include music, dance, theater, rhetoric (speechmaking), and narrative (storytelling). One important area has developed its own name: **ethnomusicology**, the cross-cultural study of music. Ethnomusicologists study a range of topics, including the form of the music itself, the social position of musicians, how music interacts with other domains of culture such as religion or healing, and change in musical traditions. This section provides examples about music and gender in Malaysia, music and globalization in Brazil, and theater and society in India.

MUSIC AND GENDER AMONG THE TEMIAR OF MALAYSIA An important topic for ethnomusicologists is gender differences in access to performance roles in music. (For ideas about research on this topic, see Figure 11.1) A cultural materialist perspective would predict that in cultures where gender roles are quite egalitarian, access to and meanings in music will also be egalitarian for males

ethnomusicology the cross-cultural study of music.

If you were doing an ethnographic study of gender roles in musical performance, the following questions would be useful in starting the inquiry. But they would not exhaust the topic. Can you think of questions that should be added to the list?

1. Are men and women equally encouraged to use certain instruments and repertoires?
2. Is musical training available to all?
3. Do male and female repertoires overlap? If so, how, when, and for what reasons?
4. Are the performances of men and women public, private, or both? Are women and men allowed to perform together? In what circumstances?
5. Do members of the culture give equal value to the performances of men and women? On what criteria are these evaluations based, and are they the same for men and women performers?

Source: From "Power and Gender in the Musical Experiences of Women" by Carol E. Robertson, pp. 224–225 in *Women and Music in Cross-Cultural Perspective*, ed. by Ellen Koskoff. Copyright © 1987. Reprinted by permission of the Greenwood Publishing Group, Inc. Westport, CT.

Figure 11.1 Five Ethnographic Questions about Gender and Music

and females. This is the case among the Temiar (tem-ee-yar), foragers of the highlands of peninsular Malaysia (see Map 6.3, page 117). Their musical traditions emphasize balance and complementarity between males and females (Roseman 1987).

Among the Temiar, kinship and marriage rules are flexible and open. Marriages are based on the mutual desires of the partners. Descent is bilineal (review Chapter 6), and marital residence follows no particular rule after a period of bride service. Marriages often end in separation, and serial monogamy is common. Men, however, do have a slight edge over women in political and ritual spheres. They are typically the village leaders, and they are the spirit mediums who sing the songs that energize the spirits.

Although the spirits enter the community through male singers, the male spirit-medium role is not of greater importance or status than a woman's performance role in singing choruses. The singing of the male spirit medium and the female chorus is blurred through overlap between phrases and repetition. The performance is one of general community participation, with integrated male and female roles, as in Temiar society in general.

COUNTRY MUSIC AND GLOBALIZATION IN BRAZIL Linguistic anthropologist Alexander Dent studies the growing popularity of música sertaneja (MOO-see-kah ser-tah-NAY-shah), Brazilian country music (2005). Música sertaneja draws heavily on U.S. country music, but it is significantly localized within Brazilian contexts. Brazilian performers creatively use North American country music songs, such as "Achy Breaky Heart," to convey messages about gender relationships, intimacy, the family, the past, and the importance of the countryside that make sense in the Brazilian context. In their performances and recordings, they use an American genre to critique American-driven processes such as extreme capitalism and globalization and to critique the Brazilian adoption of such Western ways.

A prominent feature of Brazilian country music is performance by a dupla (doo-plah), or two "brothers," who may or may not be biological brothers. They emphasize their similarity by cutting their hair the same way and wearing similar clothes. Musically, they blend their voices, with neither voice dominating the other. When performing, they sing part of a song with their arms over each other's shoulders and gaze at each other affectionately. The dupla and their music emphasize kinship and caring as important aspects of Brazilian tradition that should be preserved.

THEATER AND MYTH IN SOUTH INDIA Theater is a type of enactment that seeks to entertain through movement and through words related to dance, music, parades, competitive games and sports, and verbal art (Beeman 1993). Cross-culturally, strong connections exist among myth, ritual, and performance.

One theatrical tradition that offers a blend of mythology, acting, and music is Kathakali (kuh-tuh-KAH-lee) ritual dance-drama of southern India (Zarrilli 1990). Stylized hand gestures, elaborate makeup, and costumes contribute to the attraction of these performances, which dramatize India's great Hindu epics, especially the *Mahabharata* (review Chapter 10) and the *Ramayana*. Costumes and makeup transform the actor into one of several well-known characters from Indian mythology. The audience easily recognizes the basic character types at their first entrance by the performers' costumes and makeup. Six types of makeup exist to depict characters ranging from the most refined to the most vulgar. Kings and heroes have green facial makeup, reflecting their refinement and moral

---

theater a form of enactment, related to other forms such as dance, music, parades, competitive games and sports, and verbal art, that seeks to entertain through acting, movement, and sound.

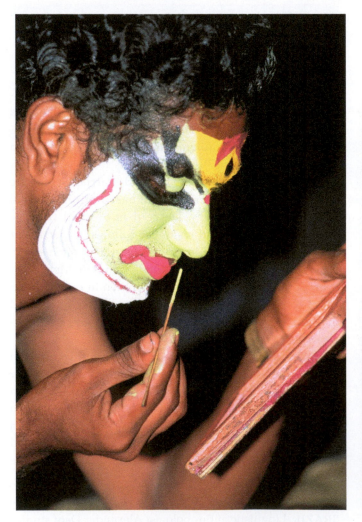

Many forms of theater combine the use of facial makeup, masks, and costumes to transform an actor into someone (or something) else. (LEFT) This Kathakali dancer is applying makeup before a performance in Kerala, South India. (RIGHT) A new use for classical dance-drama in India is for raising social awareness about problems such as excessive dowries and female infanticide. Street theater groups go into neighborhoods and act out skits, drawing members of the audience into dialogue with them.

uprightness. Vulgar characters are associated with black facial makeup and occasionally black beards. With their black faces dotted with red and white, they are the most frightening of the Kathakali characters.

Architecture and Decorative Arts

Like all art forms, architecture is interwoven with other aspects of culture. Architecture may reflect and protect social rank and class differences, as well as gender, age, and ethnic differences (Guidoni 1987). Decorative arts—including interior decoration of homes and buildings, and external design features such as gardens—likewise reflect people's social position and "taste." Local cultures have long defined preferred standards in these areas of expression, but global influences from the West and elsewhere, such as Japan and other non-Western cultures, have been adopted and adapted by other traditions.

ARCHITECTURE AND INTERIOR DESIGN Foragers, being highly mobile, build dwellings as needed and then abandon them. (Refer to photo of Ju/wasi shelter on page 46.) Having few personal possessions and no surplus goods, they need no permanent storage structures. The construction of dwellings does not require the efforts of groups larger than the family unit. Foragers' dwellings are an image of the family and not of the wider society. The dwellings' positioning in relation to each other reflects the relations among families.

More elaborate shelters and greater social cohesiveness in planning occur as foraging is combined with horticulture, as in the semipermanent settlements of the Amazon rainforest. People live in the settlement part of the year but break into smaller groups that spread out into a larger area for foraging. Important decisions concern how the site will fare with respect to the weather, the availability of drinking water, and defensibility. The central plaza

In the politics of architecture, size often matters. (LEFT) The Duomo in Florence, Italy. The Duomo, or Cathedral of Santa Maria del Fiore, was begun in 1296. Its massive dome, designed by architect and sculptor Filippo Brunelleschi, was not completed until 1436. The goal was to surpass all other edifices in height and beauty. The Duomo still physically dominates the city of Florence and also attracts many tourists from around the world. (RIGHT) Burj Dubai, or Dubai Tower, in Dubai, United Arab Emirates, is currently the tallest building in the world. Its immense height signals the importance of Dubai in the modern world and, more generally, the success and prosperity of the Middle East.

must be elevated for drainage and drainage channels dug around the hearths. The overall plan is circular. In some groups, separate shelters are built for extended family groups; in others, they are joined into a continuous circle with connected roofs. In some cases, the headman has a separate and larger shelter.

Pastoralists have designed ingenious portable structures, such as the North American teepee and the Mongolian ger, or yert. The teepee is a conical tent made with a framework of four wooden poles tied at the top with thongs, to which are joined other poles to complete the cone. This frame is then covered with buffalo hide. A ger is also a circular, portable dwelling, but its roof is flatter. The covering is made of cloth. This lightweight structure is easy to set up, take down, and transport, and it is adaptable to all weather conditions. Encampments are often arranged around the teepees or gers in several concentric circles. Social status was the structuring principle, and the council of chiefs and the head chief were located in the center.

With the development of the state, urban areas grew and showed the effects of centralized planning and power, for example, in grid-style planning of streets rather than haphazard placement. The symbolic demonstration of the power, grandeur, and identity of states was and is expressed architecturally through the construction of impressive urban monuments: temples, administrative buildings, memorials, and museums.

Interior decoration of domestic dwellings also became more elaborate. In settled agricultural communities and urban centers, where permanent housing is the norm, decoration is more likely to be found in homes. Wall paintings, sculptures, and other features distinguish the homes of wealthier individuals. Research on interior decoration in contemporary Japan involved studying the contents of home-decorating magazines and doing participant observation within homes (Rosenberger 1992). Findings reveal how people incorporate and localize selected aspects of Western decorating styles.

Home-decorating magazines target middle- and upper-class Japanese housewives who seek to express their status through new consumption styles. A trend is the abandonment of three features of traditional Japanese design: tatami, shoji, and fusuma. Tatami are 2-inch-thick mats that are about 3 feet wide and 6 feet long. A room's size is measured in terms of the number of tatami it holds. Shoji are the sliding screen doors of tatami rooms; one door is covered with glass and the other with translucent rice paper often printed with a design of leaves or waves. Fusuma are sliding wall panels made of thick paper; they are removable so that rooms can be enlarged for gatherings. The tatami room usually contains a low table in the center, with pillows for seating on the floor. A special alcove may contain a flower arrangement,

ancestors' pictures, and a Buddhist altar. Futons are stored in closets around the edges and brought out at night for sleeping.

In distancing themselves from the old style, "modern" Japanese housewives make several changes. The kitchen has a central rather than marginal location and is merged with a space called the DK (dining-kitchen) or LDK (living-dining-kitchen), with wood, tile, or carpeting on the floor. Western products such as carpeting and curtains (instead of the fusuma, the tatami, and shoji) are used to cover surfaces and to separate rooms. The LDK has a couch, a dining set, a television, a stereo, and an array of small items on display, such as Western-style teapots, cuckoo clocks, and knickknacks.

These design choices accompany deeper social changes that involve new aspirations about marriage and family relationships. Home-decorating magazines promote the idea that the modern style brings with it happier children who earn better grades and closer husband–wife ties. Tensions exist, however, between these ideals and the realities of middle- and upper-class life in Japan. Women feel compelled to work either part time or full time to be able to contribute income for satisfying their new consumer needs in spite of societal pressure against careers and for devoting more time to domestic pursuits. Children are in the conflicting position of being indulged as new consumer targets even as the traditional value of self-discipline still holds. Husbands are in the conflicting position of needing to be more attentive to wife and home, whereas the corporate world calls them for a "7–11" working day. Last, the Western image of the happy nuclear family contains no plan for the aged. Only the wealthiest Japanese families manage to satisfy both individualistic desires and filial duties because they can afford a large house in which they dedicate a separate floor for the husband's parents, complete with tatami mats. Less wealthy people have a more difficult time caring for their aged parents.

GARDENS AND FLOWERS Gardens for use, especially for food production, are differentiated from gardens for decorative purposes. The concept of the decorative garden is not a cultural universal. Circumpolar peoples cannot construct gardens in the snow, and highly mobile pastoralists have no gardens because they are on the move. The decorative garden is a product of state-level societies, especially in the Middle East, Europe, and Asia (Goody 1993). Within these contexts, variation exists in what are considered to be the appropriate contents and designs for gardens. A Japanese garden may contain no blooming flowers, focusing instead on the shape and placement of trees, shrubs, stones, and bodies of water.

Elite Muslim culture, with its core in the Middle East, has long been associated with formal decorative gardens.

Flowers appear in many different forms in Islamic art, ranging from single motifs to extended patterns, from more realistic to highly stylized depictions. Flowers appear in architecture, as in this modern mosque in Abu Dhabi (LEFT) as well as on body art, such as women's henna designs (RIGHT).

The Islamic garden pattern involves a square design with a symmetrical layout, fountains, waterways, and straight pathways, all enclosed within walls. A garden, enclosed with four walls, is symbolically equivalent to the concept of paradise. Islamic gardens often surround the tombs of prominent people. India's Taj Mahal, built by a Muslim emperor, follows this pattern, with one modification: The tomb is placed at one edge of the garden rather than in the center. The result is a dramatic stretch of fountains and flowers leading from the main gate to the monument.

The contents of a personal garden, like a dinner menu with all its special ingredients or a collection of souvenirs from around the world with all their memories and meanings, make a statement about its owner's identity and status. For example, in Europe during the height of colonialism, imperial gardens contained specimens from remote corners of the globe, collected through scientific expeditions. Such gardens were created through the collection and placement of plants from many parts of the world and are thus examples of what the French cultural theorist Michel Foucault refers to as a **heterotopia**,

or something formed from elements drawn from multiple and diverse contexts (1970). Heterotopias can be constructed in architecture, cuisine, dress, and more. In the case of the colonial European gardens, the heterotopic message conveyed the owner's worldliness and intellectual status.

Cut flowers are now important economic products. They provide income for gardeners throughout the world, and they are also exchange items. In France, women receive flowers from men more than any other kind of gift (Goody 1993:316). In much of the world, special occasions require gifts of flowers: In the West, as well as in East Asia, funerals are times for displays of flowers. Ritual offerings to the deities in Hinduism are often flowers such as marigolds woven into a chain or necklace.

Flowers are prominent motifs in Western and Asian secular and sacred art, but less so in African art (Goody 1993). Some possible reasons for this variation include

---

heterotopia something formed from elements drawn from multiple and diverse contexts.

ecological and economic factors. Eurasia's more temperate environment possesses a greater variety of blooming plants than Africa's does. Also, sheer economic necessity in low-income countries of Africa limits the amount of space that can be used for decorative purposes. Among wealthy African people, prominent luxury goods include fabrics, gold ornaments, and wooden carvings rather than flowers. This pattern of production is changing with globalization, and many African countries now grow flowers for export to the world market.

Play, Leisure, and Culture

11.2 Illustrate what play and leisure reveal about culture.

This section turns to the area of expressive culture related to what people do for "fun." It is impossible to draw a clear line between the concepts of play or leisure and art or performance, however, because they often overlap. For example, a person could paint watercolors in her leisure time, yet simultaneously be creating a work of art. In most cases, though, play and leisure can be distinguished from other activities (Huizinga, as summarized in Hutter 1996). In the case of play:

- It serves no direct utilitarian purpose for the participants.
- It is limited in terms of time.
- It has rules.
- It may contain chance and tension.

Leisure activities often overlap with play, but many leisure activities, such as reading or lying on a beach, would not be considered play because they lack rules, chance, and tension. Within the broad category of play and leisure activities, several subcategories exist, including varieties of games, hobbies, and recreational travel. Although play and leisure, as well as their subcategories, may be pursued from a nonutilitarian perspective, they are often situated in a wider context of commercial and political interests. Major international competitions are examples of such complexities. South Africa's hosting of the 2010 World Cup soccer games was an opportunity for it to demonstrate its position as a world leader. At the same time, the major advertising sponsors for the events were big-name American companies such as McDonald's, Coca-Cola, and Budweiser.

Cultural anthropologists study play and leisure within their cultural contexts as part of social systems. They ask, for example, why some leisure activities involve teams rather than individuals; what the social roles and statuses of people involved in particular activities are; what the goals of the games are and how those goals are achieved;

how much danger or violence is involved; how certain activities are related to group identity; and how such activities link or separate different groups within or between societies or countries.

Games and Sports as a Cultural Microcosm

Games and sports, like religious rituals and festivals, can be interpreted as reflections of social relationships and cultural ideals. In Clifford Geertz's terms, they are both models of a culture, depicting basic ideals, and models for a culture, socializing people into certain values and ideals (1966). American football can be seen as a model for corporate culture in its clear hierarchy with leadership vested in one person (the quarterback) and its goal of territorial expansion by taking over areas from the competition.

A comparison of baseball as played in the United States and in Japan reveals core values about social relationships in each country (Whiting 1979). The differences emerge clearly when U.S. players are hired by Japanese teams. The U.S. players bring with them an intense sense of individualism, which promotes the value of "doing your own thing." This pattern conflicts with a primary value that influences the playing style in Japan: **wa**, meaning discipline and self-sacrifice for the good of the group. In Japanese baseball, players must seek to achieve and maintain team harmony. Japanese baseball players have a negative view of extremely individualistic, egotistical plays and strategies.

SPORTS AND SPIRITUALITY: MALE WRESTLING IN INDIA In many contexts, sports are closely tied to religion and spirituality. Asian martial arts, for example, require forms of concentration much like meditation, leading to spiritual self-control. Male wrestling in India, a popular form of entertainment at rural fairs and other public events, involves a strong link with spiritual development and asceticism (Alter 1992).

In some ways, these wrestlers are just like other members of Indian society. They go to work, and they marry and have families, but their dedication to wrestling involves important differences. A wrestler's daily routine is one of self-discipline. Every act—defecation, bathing, comportment, devotion—is integrated into a daily regimen of discipline. Wrestlers come to the *akhara* (AKH-uh-ruh), equivalent to a gymnasium, early in the morning for practice under the supervision of a guru or other senior akhara member. They practice moves with different partners for two to three hours. In the early evening, they

---

wa a Japanese word meaning discipline and self-sacrifice for the good of the group.

Wrestlers in a village in northern India. They follow a rigorous regimen of dietary restrictions and exercise to keep their bodies and minds under control.

return for more exercise. In all, a strong young wrestler will do around 2,000 push-ups and 1,000 deep-knee bends a day in sets of 50 to 100.

The wrestler's diet is strictly defined. Most wrestlers are mainly vegetarian. Although they avoid alcohol and tobacco, they do consume bhang, a beverage made of blended milk, spices, almonds, and concentrated marijuana. In addition to regular meals, wrestlers consume large quantities of milk, ghee (clarified butter), and almonds. These substances are sources of strength because, according to traditional dietary principles, they help to build up the body's semen.

Several aspects of the wrestler's life are similar to those of a Hindu sannyasi (sun-YAH-see) or holy man, who renounces life in the normal world. The aspiring sannyasi studies under a guru and learns to follow a strict routine of discipline and meditation called yoga, and he adheres to a restricted diet to achieve control of the body and its life force. Both wrestler and sannyasi roles focus on discipline to achieve a controlled self. Therefore, in India, wrestling does not involve the "dumb jock" stereotype that it sometimes does in North America. Rather, wrestlers have respect because their sport requires perfected physical, spiritual, and moral health.

PLAY, PLEASURE, AND PAIN Many leisure activities combine pleasure and pain. Serious injuries can result from mountain climbing, horseback riding, or playing touch football in the backyard. A more intentionally dangerous category of sports is **blood sports**, competitions that explicitly seek to bring about a flow of blood or even

blood sport a competition that explicitly seeks to bring about a flow of blood from, or even the death of, human–human contestants, human–animal contestants, or animal–animal contestants.

death. Blood sports may involve human contestants, humans contesting against animal competitors, or animals or birds fighting other animals or birds (Donlon 1990). In the United States and Europe, professional boxing is an example of a popular blood sport that few, if any, anthropologists have studied so far. Cultural anthropologists have looked at the use of animals in blood sports such as cockfights and bullfights. These sports are variously interpreted as providing sadistic pleasure, as offering vicarious self-validation (usually of males) through the triumph of their representative pit bulls or fighting cocks, and as the triumph of culture over nature in the symbolism of bullfighting.

Even the seemingly pleasurable leisure experience of a Turkish bath can involve discomfort and pain. One phase involves scrubbing the skin vigorously several times with a rough natural sponge, a pumice stone, or a piece of cork wood wrapped in cloth (Staats 1994). The scrubbing

(TOP) Laotians attend a cockfight on the outskirts of Vientiane, capital of the Lao People's Democratic Republic. Officials of the World Health Organization are concerned that this sport may be one cause of the spread of avian or bird flu in Southeast Asia. (BOTTOM) Jeff Gordon, driver of the No. 24 DuPont Chevrolet, makes a pit stop during a NASCAR Sprint Cup Series race at Phoenix International Raceway in Arizona.

removes layers of dead skin and opens the pores so that the skin will be beautiful. In Turkey, an option for men is a massage that can be quite violent, involving deep probes of leg muscles, cracking of the back, and being walked on by the often weighty masseur. In Ukraine, being struck repeatedly on one's bare skin with birch branches is the final stage of the bath. Violent scrubbing, scraping, and beating of the skin, along with radical temperature changes in the water, are combined with valued social interaction at the bathhouse.

Leisure Travel

Anthropologists who study leisure travel, or tourism, often comment that their research is dismissed as trivial and based on "hanging out" at beautiful beaches or at five-star hotels. Research on tourism, however, is just as challenging as the anthropological study of any other topic.

Tourism is one of the major economic forces in the world, and it has dramatic effects on people and places in tourist destination areas. A large percentage of worldwide tourism involves individuals from Europe, North America, and Japan traveling to less industrialized countries. Ethnic tourism, cultural tourism, and ecotourism are attracting increasing numbers of travelers. They are often marketed as providing a view of "authentic" cultures. Images of indigenous people figure prominently in travel brochures and advertisements (Bruner 2005).

Tourist promotional literature often presents a "myth" of other peoples and places and offers travel as a form of escape to a mythical land of wonder. Research on Western travel literature shows that, from the time of the earliest explorers to the present, it has been full of primitivist images about indigenous peoples who are portrayed as having static or "stone age" traditions, largely unchanged by the forces of Western colonialism, nationalism, economic development, and even tourism. Tourists often seek to find the culture that the tourist industry defines rather than gaining a genuine, more complicated, and perhaps less photogenic view of it. For the tourist, obtaining these desired cultural images through mass tourism involves packaging the "primitive" with the "modern" because most tourists want comfort and convenience along with their "authentic" experience. Thus, advertisements minimize the foreignness of the host country, noting, for example, that English is spoken and that the destination is remote, yet accessible, while simultaneously promoting primitivist and racist imagery.

The tensions involved in accurately presenting a cultural experience, sensationalism, and social stigma emerge clearly in research on tourism in the coal-mining region of Appalachia in Virginia (LaLone 2003). Mary LaLone pinpoints some of the challenges that arise in representing Appalachian culture with accuracy and dignity while

Many international tourists seek "cultural tourism" so that they can participate in what is presented to them as "traditional." Safari tour groups in Africa, as in this visit to Maasailand, combine sightings of exotic wildlife and contact with Maasai people.

Go to the Web to learn about cultural tourism opportunities among the Maasai.

at the same time responding to marketing demands of tourists. For example, in portraying people's everyday lives, accuracy says that it is right to show people wearing shoes and using indoor plumbing, whereas tourists may expect and want to see displays of "hillbilly life" that emphasize poverty, shoelessness, outhouses, feuding, and "moonshining" (producing and consuming illicit alcohol). LaLone suggests that cultural anthropologists can help find a way toward the interpretation and presentation of a region's heritage that provides a more complex view so that hosts retain their dignity, accuracy is maintained, and tourists learn more than they expected.

The anthropology of tourism has focused on the impact of global and local tourism on indigenous peoples and places. Such studies are important in exposing the degree to which tourism helps or harms local people and local ecosystems. For example, the formation of Amboseli National Park in Kenya prevented Maasai herders from accessing traditional water resources (Drake 1991). The project staff promised benefits (such as shares of the revenues from the park) to the Maasai if they stayed off the reserve, but most of the benefits never materialized. In contrast, in Costa Rica, local people were included in the early planning stages of the Guanacaste National Park (Map 11.1), and now they play a greater role in the park management system and share in some of the benefits.

Local people with long-standing rights to land, water, and other resources often attempt to exercise agency and take an active role in transforming the effects of tourism to their advantage, designing and managing tourist projects (Miller 2009; Natcher, Davis, and Hickey 2005). The Gullah people of South Carolina are one such example (see Culturama). The last section of this chapter provides others.

Map 11.1 Costa Rica

The Republic of Costa Rica was the first country in the world to constitutionally abolish its army, and it has largely escaped the violence that its neighbors have endured. Agriculture is the basis of the economy, with tourism—especially ecotourism—playing an increasing role. Most of the 4.6 million inhabitants of Costa Rica are descended from Spanish colonialists. Less than three percent are Afro-Costa Ricans, and less than two percent, or around 50,000, are indigenous people. Seventy-five percent of the people are Roman Catholic and 14 percent Protestant. The official language is Spanish.

High-end tourism in Costa Rica.

Change in Expressive Culture

11.3 Explain how cultural heritage is a contested resource in contemporary times.

Forms and patterns of expressive culture are constantly in motion. Much change is influenced by Western culture through globalization, but influence does not occur in only one direction. African musical styles have transformed the U.S. musical scene since the days of slavery. Japan has exerted a strong influence on upper-class garden styles in the United States. Cultures in which tradition and conformity have been valued in pottery making, dress, or theater find themselves having to make choices about whether to innovate and, if so, how. Many contemporary artists (including musicians and playwrights) from Latin America to China are fusing ancient and "traditional" motifs and styles with more contemporary themes and messages.

Changes occur through the use of new materials and technology and through the incorporation of new ideas, tastes, and meanings. These changes often accompany other aspects of social change, such as colonialism and global tourism.

Colonialism and Syncretism

Western colonialism had dramatic effects on the expressive culture of indigenous peoples. In some instances, colonial disapproval of particular art forms and activities resulted in their extinction. For example, when colonialists banned head-hunting in various cultures, the change also meant that body decoration, weapon decoration, and other related expressive activities were abandoned. This section provides an example of how colonial repression of indigenous forms succeeded, but only temporarily.

In the Trobriand Islands of Papua New Guinea (see Culturama, Chapter 2, page 28), British administrators and missionaries sought to eradicate the frequent tribal warfare as part of a pacification process. One strategy was to replace it with intertribal competitive sports (Leach 1975). In 1903, a British missionary introduced the British game of cricket in the Trobriands as a way of promoting a new morality, separate from the warring traditions. As played in England, cricket involves particular rules of play and a proper look of pure white uniforms. In the early stages of the adoption of cricket in the Trobriands, the game followed the British pattern closely. As time passed and the game spread into more parts of the islands, it developed localized and syncretized versions.

Throughout the Trobriands, the islanders merged cricket into indigenous political competition between big-men (Foster 2006). Big-men leaders urged their followers to increase production in anticipation of a cricket match because matches were followed by a redistributive feast. (Review the discussion of moka in Chapter 8.) The British missionaries discouraged traditional magic in favor of Christian beliefs, but the Trobriand Islanders brought war-related magic into cricket. For example, they used spells against opposing teams, and they decorated bats like war weapons. Weather magic was important, too.

Culturama

The Gullah of South Carolina

Gullah (goo-luh) culture in South Carolina stretches along the coast, going inland about 30 miles (National Park Service 2005). The Gullah are descended from African slaves originating in West and Central Africa. In the early eighteenth century, Charleston, South Carolina, was the location of the largest slave market in British North America.

The enslaved people brought with them many forms of knowledge and practice. Rice was a central part of their African heritage and identity. They knew how to plant it in swamps, harvest it, and prepare it. Gullah ancestors in colonial South Carolina were influential in developing tidal irrigation methods of rice growing, using irrigation and management of the tides to increase yields compared with yields from rainfall-dependent plantings.

Experts at net fishing, the Gullah made handwoven nets that are masterpieces of folk art. Their textile arts include a form of quilting, or sewing strips of cloth together into a larger piece. Gullah women combined their African quilting styles with those of Europeans to form new styles and patterns. Many quilts tell a story in their several panels.

Gullah cuisine combines African elements such as rice, yams, peas, okra, hot peppers, peanuts, watermelon, and sesame seeds with European ingredients and with American Indian foods such as corn, squash, tomatoes, and berries (National Park Service 2005). Popular dishes are stews of seafood and vegetables served over rice.

Rice is the cornerstone of the meal, and the family rice pot is a treasured possession passed down over the generations.

Gullah culture in South Carolina has become a major tourist attraction, including music, crafts, and cuisine. If there is a single item that tourists identify with the Gullah, it is sweetgrass baskets. Basketmaking, once common among all Gullah people in South Carolina, is now a specialized activity. In South Carolina, it is thriving in the Charleston area largely through a combination of tourist demand and the creativity of local artists. Both men and women "sew" the baskets. They sell them in shops in Charleston's historic center and along Highway 17.

As the success of the basketmakers has grown and the popularity of the baskets increased, so, too, has the need for sweetgrass. Sweetgrass baskets thus are a focal point of conflict between Gullah cultural producers and local economic developers who are destroying the land on which the sweetgrass grows. Because tourism in low-country South Carolina is increasingly dependent on cultural tourism, some planners are trying to find ways to devote land to growing sweetgrass.

The story of the Gullah of South Carolina begins with their rich African cultural heritage, through their suffering as slaves, to racism and social exclusion, and to their current situation in which their expressive culture is a key factor in the state economy.

(LEFT) Barbara Manigault, a Gullah artist, with her sweetgrass baskets in Mt. Pleasant, South Carolina.

(CENTER) Drummers at the Gullah Festival in Beaufort (byew-fert). The festival celebrates the culture and accomplishments of the Gullah people.

Map 11.2 The Gullah Region of South Carolina

The heartland of Gullah culture is in the low-country areas of South Carolina, Georgia, and Florida, and on the Sea Islands.

In the Trobriand Islands, British missionaries tried in the late nineteenth century to substitute their game of cricket for intertribal rivalries and warfare. It did not take long, however, for the Trobriand people to transform British rules and style to Trobriand ways.

▌*If you wanted to watch a cricket match, what would be the closest place for you to go?*

If things were not going well, a ritual specialist might use a spell to bring rain and force cancellation of the game.

Over time, the Trobrianders stopped wearing the crisp white uniforms and instead painted their bodies and adorned themselves with feathers and shells. The teams announced their entry into the host village with songs and dances, praising their team in contrast to the opposition. Syncretism is notable in team songs and dances, which draw on Western elements. An example is the famous entry song of the "P-K" team. (P-K is the name of a Western chewing gum.) The P-K team chose its name because the stickiness of gum is like the ability of their bat to hit the ball. Other teams incorporated sounds and motions of airplanes, objects that they first saw during World War II. The songs and dances were explicitly sexual and enjoyed by all, in spite of Christian missionary attempts to suppress the "immoral" aspects of Trobriand culture, which included sexual metaphors in songs about large yams and thrusting hip movements of the dancers among other things.

The Trobrianders also changed some of the rules of play. The home team should always win, but not by too many runs. In this way, guests show respect to the hosts. Winning is not the major goal. The feast after the match is the climax, in which hosts demonstrate their generosity to their guests, establishing the requirement for the next match and feast.

Tourism's Complex Effects

Global tourism has had varied effects on indigenous arts. Often, tourist demand for ethnic arts and souvenirs has led to the mass production of sculpture, woven goods, or jewelry of a lesser quality than was created before the demand. Tourists' interest in seeing an abbreviated form of traditionally long dance or theater performances has led to

the presentation of "cuts" rather than an entire piece. As a result, some scholars say that tourism leads to the decline in quality and authenticity of indigenous arts.

Tourist support for indigenous arts, however, is often the sole force maintaining them because local people in a particular culture may themselves be more interested in foreign music, art, or sports. Vietnamese water puppetry is an ancient performance mode, dating back at least to the Ly Dynasty of 1121 (Contreras 1995). Traditionally, water puppet shows took place in the spring during a lull in the farm work, or at special festival times. The stage for this performance art is either a small natural pond or an artificial water tank with a backdrop that hides the puppeteers from the audience. The puppeteers operate carved and painted wooden figures with bamboo poles, wires, and strings, making them appear to glide over the water on their own. Since the 1980s, water puppetry has grown in popularity among Vietnamese people and international tourists (Foley 2001). It has spread from its core area in the Red River Delta in the northern part of the country to being nationwide and from being a seasonal performance to being year-round.

An even more complicated situation exists in the growth of belly dancing as an essential touristic performance in Istanbul, Turkey (Potuoğlu-Cook 2006). International and Turkish tourists associate belly dancing with the Ottoman past, and it is increasingly available in various venues, including classical concerts, restaurants, and nightclubs in Istanbul and other major cities (see Map 11.3). In spite of Muslim values about female modesty, commercial interests are promoting this performance mode. Even middle-class housewives are taking belly-dancing lessons, a sign that a formerly stigmatized and lower-class activity is gentrifying. The rising popularity of belly dancing is evidence of Turkey's growing cosmopolitanism.

One positive result of global tourism is the growing international and local support for the preservation of **material cultural heritage**, which includes sites, monuments and buildings, and movable objects considered of outstanding world value in terms of history, art, and science (Cernea 2001). UNESCO proposed the basic definition of material cultural heritage in 1972. Since then, several hundred locations worldwide have been placed on its World Heritage List and receive some financial support for preservation. Many other invaluable sites are lost, and will be lost in the future, through destructive engineering projects, urbanization, war, looting, private collecting, and climate change.

Applied anthropologists are involved in promoting improved stewardship of material cultural heritage. Some are motivated by a desire to preserve the record of humanity for future generations or for science. Some know that studying how people interact with

material cultural heritage the sites, monuments, buildings, and movable objects considered to have outstanding value to humanity..

Map 11.3 Turkey

Turkey straddles two continents, with most of its territory being in Asia. Its largest city, Istanbul, is located in the European part. The capital city, Ankara, is located in the Asian part, called Anatolia. Turkey's culture is a blend between East and West. Its population is over 80 million. Under the leadership of Mustafa Kamal Atatürk, a constitutional, representative political system was established in 1923, following the breakup of the Ottoman Empire after World War I. Turkish is the only official language of the country. It is also widely spoken in countries that were once part of the Ottoman Empire, including Albania, Bosnia-Herzegovina, the Republic of Macedonia, Greece, Romania, and Serbia. Over two million Turkish-speaking immigrants live in Germany. Islam is the overwhelmingly predominant religion of Turkey, with 99 percent of the people Muslim. Of these, 75 percent are Sunni, 20 percent Shia, and 5 percent Sufi. According to the constitution, Turkey is a secular state, so there is no official state religion. The most popular sport is football (soccer). The most serious internal security issue is the Kurdish quest for greater cultural autonomy and rights.

A belly dancer performing in Istanbul, Turkey. Belly dancing may have originated in Egypt. In Turkey, it is influenced by Egyptian styles and also by Roma traditions, because many prominent contemporary Turkish belly dancers are Roma. Turkish belly dancing is distinguished by its highly energetic and athletic style and the adept use of *zils*, or finger cymbals.

and perceive the value of a particular site reveals much about culture, identity, and belonging. For example, an ethnographic study of local Korean tourists who visit Changdoek Palace, a World Heritage Site in Seoul, South Korea, offers insights into its role in reinforcing Korean nationalism (Park 2010). Many tourists mention how visiting the site reinforced their sense of being Korean through bringing forth sentiments and feelings about their heritage, even among visitors who said they are not very nationalistic: "It makes my stomach churn to feel that I am naturally connected with this place. I am part of it and it is part of me" (2010:126). Cultural heritage, both material sites and so-called intangible culture are also sources of local economic development, if managed correctly (see Anthropology Works).

In 2003, UNESCO ratified a new policy aimed at protecting **intangible cultural heritage**, or living heritage, manifested in oral traditions, languages, performing arts, rituals and festive events, knowledge and practices about nature and the universe, and craftmaking. Support for this policy is based on the understanding that intangible culture provides people with a sense of identity and continuity, promotes respect for cultural diversity and human creativity, is compatible with the promotion of human rights, and supports sustainable development. Through this initiative, member countries of the United Nations are asked to make lists of valuable forms of intangible culture and take steps to preserve them. This policy has stimulated discussion and debate among cultural anthropologists, who see culture as more than a list of traits—highly contextualized, always changing, and not amenable to being managed or preserved through policy mandates (Handler 2003).

Cultural Heritage as a Contested Resource

Cultural heritage, or claims to a particular cultural identity, set of practices, or location(s), increasingly calls into these issues:

- Who defines cultural heritage in terms of what is authentic or inauthentic
- How to design and carry out cultural heritage preservation in terms of addressing both insider and outsider roles and interests

---

intangible cultural heritage UNESCO's view of culture as manifested in oral traditions, languages, performing arts, rituals and festive events, knowledge and practices about nature and the universe, and craftmaking.

Anthropology Works

A Strategy on Cultural Heritage for the World Bank

With headquarters in Washington, DC, and offices throughout the world, the World Bank is an international organization funded by member nations that works to promote and finance economic development in poor countries. Even though most of its permanent professional staff members are economists, the Bank has begun to pay more attention to noneconomic factors that affect development projects.

A major move in that direction occurred in 1972 when the Bank hired its first anthropologist, Michael Cernea (CHAIR-nyuh). For three decades, Cernea has drawn attention to the cultural dimensions of development, especially in terms of the importance of local participation in development projects and people-centered approaches to resettlement (when, for example, large dams are being planned). He has worked to convince top officials at the World Bank that the Bank should become involved in supporting cultural heritage projects as potential pathways to development.

The World Bank already has in place a "do no harm" rule when it approves projects such as roads, dams, and mines. Cernea agrees that a "do no harm" rule is basic to preventing the outright destruction of cultural heritage, but he points out that it is a passive rule and does nothing to provide resources to preserve sites. Cernea wants the Bank to move beyond its "do no harm" rule. He has written a strategy that is active, not passive. It has two objectives:

- The World Bank should support cultural heritage projects that help to reduce local poverty by creating employment and generating capital from tourism.

- Projects should emphasize the educational value of preserving cultural heritage to local people and international

The UNESCO world Heritage Site of Carthage in Tunisia. Carthage was once the heart of a powerful Phoenician empire that extended throughout the Mediterranean region. The Romans destroyed it in 146 BCE. It later revived to become an important early Christian center until Islamic invaders sacked it in the seventh century.

visitors on the grounds that cultural understanding promotes goodwill and good relations at all levels—local, state, and international.

Cernea offers two suggestions for better management of cultural heritage projects: selectivity in site selection on the basis of the impact of the project on reducing poverty; and building partnerships for project planning and implementation among local, national, and international institutions.

Food for Thought

On the Internet, find the UNESCO World Heritage Site that is nearest to where you live. What does the site contain, and what can you learn about its potential role in generating income for the local people?

- The grim reality of how power, either local or global, can overwhelm local efforts to define and manage cultural heritage for the benefit of local people, especially the poor

Cultural anthropologists point to the fact that the preservation of expressive culture often occurs as a form of local identity claims that may be based on reclamation of the past, and resistance to outside modernizing forces that often erase local heritage or manipulate it for their purposes. One example of insider-driven cultural heritage re-claiming and

redefinition is the resurgence of the hula, a traditional dance form of Hawai'i and other parts of the south Pacific region (Stillman 1996). Beginning in the 1970s, the Hawai'ian Renaissance grew out of political protest, mainly against American colonialism. Hawai'ian youth began speaking out against encroaching development that was displacing indigenous people from their land and destroying their natural resources. They launched a concerted effort to revive the Hawai'ian language, the hula, and canoe paddling, among other things. Since then, hula schools have proliferated, and hula competitions among the islands are widely attended by local people and international tourists.

The 1990s saw the inauguration of the International Hula Festival in Honolulu, which attracts competitors from around the world. Although the hula competitions have helped ensure the survival of this ancient art form, some Hawai'ians voice concerns. First, they feel that allowing non-Hawai'ians to compete is compromising the quality of the dancing. Second, the format of the competition violates traditional rules of style and presentation, which require more time than is allowed, so important dances have to be cut. Third, for Hawai'ians, hula has close ties to religious beliefs and stories about the deities (Silva 2004). Performing hula in a mainly secular format is offensive to the gods and violates the true Hawai'ian way.

Turning to the question of how to preserve cultural heritage, cultural anthropologists tend to support "people-first" cultural heritage projects as opposed to "top-down" projects (Miller 2009). Such grassroots projects are designed by the people whose culture is to be preserved—designed for their benefit and managed by them. A growing number of examples worldwide demonstrate the value of people-first cultural heritage preservation as having strong positive, measurable effects.

An example of people-first heritage preservation with implications for territorial entitlements and cultural survival is the Waanyi Women's History Project in Northern Queensland, Australia (Smith et al. 2003). This is a case of a community-driven project devoted to archiving cultural heritage and to establishing local community management. The "community" is a group of Waanyi (waan-yee) women who value their family history as heritage. The traditional way of maintaining this heritage has been to pass it on verbally from mother to daughter. The women wanted to have a written record of their history and documentation of sites and places of significance to them. They hired an anthropologist consultant to collect and record their narratives. An interesting feature of the case, which contrasts with traditional academic research, is that the knowledge generated cannot be published. The role of the researcher is limited to supporting the aspirations of the Waanyi women.

The project generated new sources of cash income for some Waanyi women through their employment in the National Park as "cultural rangers" responsible for the conservation of women's sites. It thus helped reduce material deprivation and entitlement insecurity and offers a clear case of a locally initiated and locally controlled heritage project with financial benefits going to local people and not to outsiders.

A less hopeful case is that of Hampi, a World Heritage Site in south India (see Map 13.2, page 265), where a strict definition of architectural heritage preservation has brought about the harsh displacement of hundreds of local people. The site includes several medieval temples that are still living temples, that is, they are places of worship as well as heritage buildings (LeDuc 2012). The site also includes the remains of an ancient bazaar (marketplace). Until 2011, the ancient bazaar structure was also part of a living bazaar, nearly a mile long, where many local people lived and maintained shops for tourists as well as providing everyday services for local people such as restaurants and a barbershop for men. In 2011, the state government decreed that local people could no longer live and work in the bazaar area, and their homes and shops were bulldozed. The claim was that their presence is causing damage to the historic heritage site. The contrasting view of the local residents is that their occupancy of the site is rooted in their heritage and the history of the site as a place of living people who worship, shop, eat, and get their hair cut, just as they did hundreds of years ago. But now, to create an "authentic heritage site," those who populated the bazaar as a living site today have been displaced.

Art for Good

Art does more than express people's feelings and experiences of the world. It can also change individuals' feelings and experiences as well as prompt social change more widely.

(LEFT) A small section of the vast Hampi bazaar in which residents resided, shops sold various kinds of goods, and men could get their hair cut in medieval times and until 2011. (RIGHT) Bulldozers removing the modern structures.

Many cultural anthropologists use their deep, local learning to contribute to social awareness through art. For example, while doing doctoral research in a ninth-grade music classroom in Hamburg, Germany, set Emily Joy Rothchild on a path to work with students on a recently released CD and music video that addresses terrorism, Islamophobia, and hate. Rothchild, a singer and pianist, earned her Ph.D. in the anthropology of music from the University of Pennsylvania this spring after conducting research in Hamburg, Germany, for three years. Her dissertation examines a government-funded school in Hamburg that was established to integrate the children and grandchildren of migrants into German society. Students are taught German norms of discipline, punctuality, and professionalism. They also take classes in rap, dance,

"beat-box," and graffiti art. Top students are selected to become part of an elite group of Hip Hop Academy students who travel to other countries as cultural diplomats. Most of the students are Muslims of Turkish, West African, or Middle Eastern descent. Let Me Speak, an album against ISIS, sprang from the students' commitment to stand up to terrorism, ISIS, and daily discrimination based on religion or ethnicity.

Other anthropologists are involved in programs that use art as therapy for post-conflict healing and reconciliation in places that have suffered terrible violence. In Rwanda, for example, art helps survivors of the many years of civil war remember, through art, what they went through and move on to reconciliation.

11 Learning Objectives Revisited

11.1 Summarize how culture is expressed through art.

Cultural anthropologists choose a broad definition of art that takes into account cross-cultural variations. From the anthropological perspective, all cultures have some form of art and a concept of what is good art.

Ethnographers document the ways in which art is related to many aspects of culture: economics, politics, human development and psychology, healing, social control, and entertainment. Art may serve to reinforce social patterns, and it may also be a vehicle of protest and resistance.

Anthropologists who study art examine it within its cultural context. To do this, anthropologists often become apprentices, learning how to make pots or play drums and, in that way, gaining both artistic skills and valuable insights into the culture of art, artists, the meanings of art, the role of the artist in society, and how art changes. A current trend is to examine how art and other forms of expressive culture are related to power issues and social inequality.

Various categories of art exist cross-culturally, and different cultures emphasize different forms. These categories include performance arts, architecture and decorative arts, graphic arts, and more.

11.2 Illustrate what play and leisure reveal about culture.

Anthropological studies of play and leisure examine these activities within their cultural contexts. Cultural anthropologists view games as cultural microcosms, both reflecting and reinforcing dominant social values. Sports and leisure activities, although engaged in for nonutilitarian purposes, are often tied to economic and political

interests. In some contexts, sports are related to religion and spirituality.

Tourism is a rapidly growing part of the world economy with vast implications for culture. Anthropologists who study tourism examine both its impact on local cultures and questions of authenticity in the touristic experience. Tourism companies often market "other" cultures to appeal to consumers, a phenomenon that perpetuates stereotypes and denigrates the "host" culture. Some cultural anthropologists work with the tourism industry and local people to find better ways of representing culture that are more accurate, less stigmatizing to the host culture, and more informative for tourists. Local groups are actively seeking ways to share in the benefits of large-scale tourism and conservation projects and to contribute to cultural and environmental sustainability.

11.3 Explain how cultural heritage is a contested resource in contemporary times.

Major forces of change in expressive culture include Western colonialism, contemporary tourism, and globalization in general. As with other kinds of cultural change through contact, expressive culture may reject, adopt, or adapt new elements. Cultural resistance and syncretism are increasingly frequent, as exemplified in the Trobriand Islanders' co-optation and re-creation of cricket.

In some cases, outside forces have led to the extinction of local forms of expressive culture. In others, outside forces have promoted continuity or the recovery of practices that had been lost. The rising popularity of belly dancing among the middle and upper classes of Istanbul is partly inspired by the demand for its performance by international tourists. Resistance to colonialism and neocolonialism has often inspired cultural revitalization, as in the Hawai'ian Renaissance and community-designed projects in Australia.

UNESCO's policies about the preservation of material cultural heritage and intangible cultural heritage are increasing worldwide attention to, and protection of, many sites and cultural practices. At the same time, tourism may have detrimental effects on the sustainability of a site and the vitality of a cultural practice. In contrast to international policies, many local indigenous groups are taking cultural rights into their own hands and trying to preserve and protect their heritage for themselves and their descendants, rather than for tourists.

Some anthropologists work with local groups to create art that has a social change message, through music for example. Other anthropologists work with public health programs to incorporate art into therapeutic programs for people who have experienced war.

Key Concepts

art, p. 219
blood sport, p. 229
ethno-esthetics, p. 220
ethnomusicology, p. 223

expressive culture, p. 218
heterotopia, p. 227
intangible cultural heritage, p. 234
material cultural heritage, p. 233

theater, p. 224
wa, p. 228

Thinking Outside the Box

1. Think of some occasions in your cultural world in which cut flowers are important. What role do they play?
2. In your cultural world, what are some examples of leisure activities that combine pleasure and pain?
3. Learn which designated cultural heritage sites are in danger from environmental, political, or other factors and consider options for protecting them from harm in each case.

Chapter 12
People on the Move

Learning Objectives

12.1 Describe the major categories of migration.

12.2 Discuss examples of the new immigrants to the United States and Canada.

12.3 Recognize how cultural anthropologists contribute to migration policies and programs.

Anthro Connections

The Marsh Arab people of southern Iraq for long lived in the delta area of the Tigris-Euphrates River, near the Persian Gulf. The Marsh Arabs, who are Shi'ites, suffered under the rule of Saddam Hussein from political repression and his program that drained the marshes. Draining the marshes removed the Marsh Arabs' livelihood by ending their ability to gain food from the rivers, reeds for building houses, and clean water for drinking, cooking, and bathing. It also deprived them of their means of transportation by boat and therefore their ability to maintain social networks. Many Marsh Arabs had to relocate elsewhere in Iraq or in other countries as refugees. Some policy and legal experts claim that Saddam Hussein committed an environmental crime by draining the marshes (Smith 2011). Currently, however, international criminal law does not attach criminal liability to environmental damage. Nor does it attach criminal liability to the effects of large-scale population displacement related to environmental crimes, which could be called crimes against humanity. Some of the marshes have been restored, and many Marsh Arabs have returned to their homeland.

The current generation of North American youth will move more times during their lives than previous generations did. College graduates are likely to change jobs an average of eight times during their careers, and these changes are likely to require relocation.

Environmental, economic, familial, and political factors are causing population movements worldwide at seemingly all-time high levels. Research in anthropology shows, however, that frequent moves during a person's life and mass movements have occurred throughout human evolution. Foragers, horticulturalists, and pastoralists relocate frequently as a normal part of their lives.

Migration is the movement of a person or people from one place to another. Its causes are linked to basic aspects of life, such as providing for one's food or for marriage. It often has profound effects on a person's economic and social status, for better or worse, as well as on health, language, religious identity, and education.

Thus, migration is of great interest to many academics and many professions. Historians, economists, political scientists, sociologists, and scholars of religion, literature, art, and music have studied migration. The professions of law, medicine, education, business, architecture, urban planning, public administration, and social work have specialties that focus on the process of migration and the period of adaptation following a move. Experts working in these areas share with anthropologists an interest in such issues as the kinds of people who migrate, causes of migration, processes of migration, health and psychosocial adaptation to new locations, and implications for planning and policy.

Cultural anthropologists do research on many issues related to migration. They study how migration is related to economic and reproductive systems, health and human development over the life cycle, marriage and household formation, politics and social order, and religion and expressive culture. Because migration affects all areas of human life, it pulls together the material in preceding chapters of this book.

Three tendencies characterize research on migration in cultural anthropology:

- Fieldwork experience in more than one location to understand the places of origin and destination.

- The combination of macro- and microperspectives. Studying migration challenges the traditional fieldwork focus on one village or neighborhood, creating the need to take into account national and global economic, political, and social forces.

- Involvement in applied work. Many opportunities exist for anthropologists to contribute their knowledge to address the situation of people forced to move by war, environmental destruction, and development projects such as dams.

This chapter first presents information on th most important categories of migrants and the opportunities and challenges they face. The second section

---

migration movement from one place to another.

Two scenes of the Chinese diaspora. (LEFT) The Chinatown Cultural Plaza in Honolulu, Hawai'i. Ninety-five percent of Chinese Americans in Hawai'i live in Honolulu. (RIGHT) Chinese Canadians also live mainly in urban areas such as Vancouver and Toronto. In Vancouver, they constitute about 16 percent of the population. Vancouver's Chinatown is a vibrant tourist site and a place where Chinese Canadians reaffirm their cultural heritage, as in the celebration, shown here, of Chinese New Year.

■ *When does Chinese New Year take place, and how is the date determined?*

provides descriptions of several examples of immigrants to the United States and Canada. The last section considers urgent issues related to migration, such as human rights and risk prevention programs.

Categories of Migration

12.1 **Describe the major categories of migration.**

Migration and its effects on people come in many forms. Both vary in terms of the distance involved, the purpose of the move, whether the move was forced or a matter of choice, and the migrant's status in the new destination. Microcultures play an important role in migration and its consequences for the migrant, as the rest of this chapter will document.

Categories Based on Spatial Boundaries

This section reviews the basic features of three categories of population movement defined in terms of the spatial boundaries crossed:

- **Internal migration**, movement within country boundaries
- **International migration**, movement across country boundaries

- **Transnational migration**, movement in which a person regularly moves back and forth between two or more countries and forms a new cultural identity transcending a single geopolitical unit

INTERNAL MIGRATION Rural-to-urban migration was the dominant form of internal population movements in most countries during the twentieth century. A major reason that people migrate to urban areas is the availability of work. According to the **push–pull theory** of labor migration, rural areas are unable to support population growth and rising expectations about the quality of life (the push factor). Cities (the pull factor), in contrast, attract people, especially youths, for employment and lifestyle reasons. According to this theory, rural people weigh the costs and benefits of rural versus urban life and then decide to go or stay. The theory is related to the approach in anthropology that emphasizes human agency, or choice (review

---

internal migration movement within country boundaries.

international migration movement across country boundaries.

transnational migration regular movement of a person between two or more countries, resulting in a new cultural identity.

push–pull theory an explanation for rural-to-urban migration that emphasizes people's incentives to move because of a lack of opportunity in rural areas (the "push") compared with urban areas (the "pull").

An Iraqi girl carries her sister at a camp for internally displaced persons (IDPs) near Falluja in 2004 when Iraq had the most IDPs of any country. Now Syria holds that distinction.

Chapter 1). Many instances of urban migration, however, are shaped by structural forces that are beyond the control of the individual, such as war or poverty.

INTERNATIONAL MIGRATION International migration has grown in volume and significance since 1945 and especially since the mid-1980s. Around 100 million people, or nearly two percent of the world's population, including legal and undocumented immigrants, live outside their home countries. Migrants who move for work-related reasons constitute most of the people in this category. The driving forces behind the trend are economic and political changes that affect labor demands and human welfare (see Think Like an Anthropologist).

The major destination countries of early international immigration were the United States, Canada, Australia, New Zealand, and Argentina. The immigration policies that these countries applied in the early twentieth century are labeled "White immigration" because they explicitly limited non-White immigration (Ongley 1995). In the 1960s, Canada made its immigration policies less racially discriminatory and more focused on skills and experience. The "White Australia" policy formally ended in 1973. In both the Canadian and Australian cases, a combination of changing labor needs and interest in improving those countries' international image prompted the reforms.

During the 1980s and 1990s, the United States, Canada, and Australia experienced large-scale immigration from new sources, especially from Asia, and—to the

United States—from Latin America and the Caribbean. These trends continue in the twenty-first century.

The earlier classic areas of outmigration—northern, western, and southern Europe—are now, instead, receiving many immigrants, including refugees from Africa and the Middle East. International migration flows in the Middle East are complex, with some countries, such as Turkey, experiencing substantial movements both in and out. Millions of Turkish people immigrated to Germany in the later decades of the twentieth century. Turkey, in turn, has received many Iraqi and Iranian Kurdish refugees (review Culturama, Chapter 8, page 169). Over two million Palestinian refugees and their descendants live in Jordan and Lebanon. Israel has attracted Jewish immigrants from Europe, northern Africa, the United States, and Russia.

TRANSNATIONAL MIGRATION Transnational migration is increasing along with other aspects of globalization. It is important to recall, however, that rising rates of transnational migration are related to the creation of state boundaries in recent centuries. Pastoralists with extensive seasonal herding routes were "transnational" migrants long before state boundaries cut across their pathways.

Much contemporary transnational migration is motivated by economic factors. The spread of the global corporate economy is the basis for the growth of one category of transnational migrants nicknamed "astronauts": businesspeople (mainly men) who spend most of their time flying among different cities as investment bankers or corporate executives. At the lower end of the income scale are transnational migrant laborers, who spend substantial amounts of time working in different places and whose movements depend on the demand for their labor.

An important feature of transnational migration is how it affects a migrant's identity, sense of citizenship, and entitlements. Constant movement weakens the sense of having one home and promotes instead a sense of belonging to a community of similar transnational migrants whose lives "in between" take on a new cultural reality.

As a response to the increased rate of transnational migration and the growth of overseas diaspora populations (review the definition in Chapter 7), many "sending" countries (countries that are the source of emigrants, or people who leave) are redefining themselves as transnational countries. A transnational country is a country with a substantial proportion of its population living outside the country's boundaries (Glick et al. 1999). Examples are Haiti, Colombia, Mexico, Brazil, the Dominican Republic, Portugal, Greece, and Philippines. These countries grant continuing citizenship to emigrants and their descendants to foster a sense of belonging and willingness to continue to send **remittances**,

---

remittance the transfer of money or goods by a migrant to his or her family in the country of origin.

Think Like an Anthropologist

Haitian Cane Cutters in the Dominican Republic: Structure or Agency?

The circulation of male labor from villages in Haiti (see Map 13.3, page 269) to work on sugar estates in the neighboring Dominican Republic is the oldest and perhaps largest continuing population movement within the Caribbean region (Martínez 1996). Beginning in the early twentieth century, Dominican sugarcane growers began to recruit Haitian workers, called **braceros** (bruh-SARE-ohs) in Spanish—agricultural laborers permitted entry to a country to work for a limited time. Between 1852 and 1986, an agreement between the two countries' governments regulated and organized the labor recruitment. Since then, recruitment has become a private matter, with men crossing the border on their own or with recruiters working in Haiti without official approval.

Many studies and reports have addressed this system of labor migration. Two competing perspectives exist:

- View 1, the structurist position: The bracero system is neo-slavery and a clear violation of human rights.

- View 2, the human agency position: Braceros are not slaves because they migrate voluntarily.

View 1

Supporters of this position point to interviews with Haitian braceros in the Dominican Republic that indicate, they say, a consistent pattern of labor rights abuses. Haitian recruiters approach poor men, and boys as young as seven years old, and promise them easy, well-paid employment in the Dominican Republic. Those who agree to go are taken to the frontier on foot and then either transported directly to a sugar estate in the Dominican Republic or turned over to Dominican soldiers for a fee for each recruit and then passed on to the sugar estate. Once there, the workers are given only one option for survival: cutting sugarcane, for which even the most experienced workers can earn only a few U.S. dollars a day. Working and living conditions on the estates are bad. The cane cutters are coerced into working even if they are ill, and working hours start before dawn and extend into the night. Many estate owners prevent Haitian laborers from leaving by having armed guards patrol the estate grounds at night. Many of the workers say that they cannot save enough from their meager wages to return home.

View 2

According to this view, reports of coercion are greatly exaggerated and miss the point that most Haitian labor migrants cross the border of their own volition. On the basis of his fieldwork in Haiti, cultural anthropologist Samuel Martínez comments that "Recruitment by force in Haiti seems virtually unheard of. On the contrary, if this is a system of slavery, it may be the first in history to turn away potential recruits" (1996:20). Some recruits have even paid bribes to recruiters to be hired. Most people, even young people, are aware of the terrible working conditions in the Dominican Republic, so they are making an informed choice when they decide to migrate. Repeat migration is common and is further evidence of free choice. The major means of maintaining labor discipline and productivity on the sugar estates is not force but wage incentives, especially piecework. The life histories of braceros show that many of them move from one estate to another, thus discrediting the view that the estates are "concentration camps."

Martínez does, however, raise the issue of how free the "choice" to migrate to the Dominican Republic really is, given the extreme poverty in which many Haitians live. In Haiti, few work opportunities exist, and the prevailing wage for rural workers is very low. Thus, the poor are not truly free to choose to work in their home country: Labor migration to the Dominican Republic becomes a necessity.

In this view, what looks like a free choice to participate in the bracero system is actually a structured choice. It is based on the unavailability of the option to work for a decent wage in Haiti.

Critical Thinking Questions

- What are the comparative strengths of View 1 and View 2?
- What does each perspective support in terms of policy recommendations?
- How does the concept of structured choice change these policy recommendations?

A Haitian migrant laborer. It is a matter of debate how much choice such a laborer has regarding whether he will migrate to the neighboring Dominican Republic for short-term work cutting cane, given the fact that he cannot find paid work in Haiti.

---

bracero an agricultural laborer in Latin America and the Caribbean who is permitted entry to a country to work for a limited time.

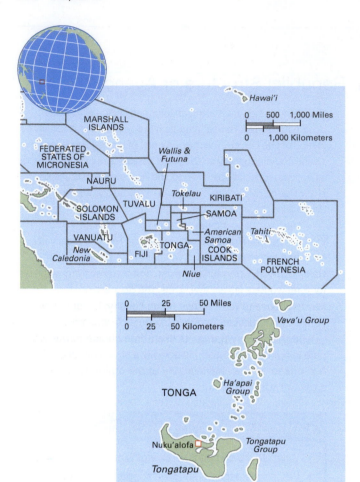

Map 12.1 Tonga

The Kingdom of Tonga is an archipelago of 169 islands, nicknamed by Captain Cook as the Friendly Islands on the basis of his reception there. Tonga is a monarchy, and the current king is Tupou VI who assumed the throne in 2012. Before him, Queen Salote Tupou II reigned from 1918 to 1965. The population is around 106,000, with two-thirds living on the main island, Tongatapu. Rural Tongans are small-scale farmers. Most Tongans are ethnically Polynesian, and Christianity is by far the dominant religion. Languages are Tongan and English. Many Tongans have emigrated, and remittances are a major part of the economy.

or transfers of money or goods from a migrant to his or her family back home. Remittances are an increasingly large, though difficult to quantify, proportion of the global economy and often a large part of a country's economy. For example, at least 60 percent of the gross domestic product of the small Pacific island country of Tonga comes from remittances from members of the Tongan diaspora (Lee 2003:32) (see Map 12.1). India is the country that receives the largest total amount of money through remittances.

Categories Based on Reason for Moving

Migrants are also categorized on the basis of their reason for relocating. The spatial categories just discussed overlap with the categories based on reason. An international migrant, for example, may also be a person who moved for employment

reasons. Migrants experience different kinds of spatial change and, at the same time, have various reasons for moving.

LABOR MIGRANTS Many thousands of people migrate each year to work for a specific length of time. They do not intend to establish permanent residence and are often explicitly barred from doing so. This form of migration, when legally contracted, is called wage labor migration. The period of work may be brief, or it may last several years.

Asian women and girls are the fastest-growing category among the world's more than 214, and they constitute more than half of the 214 million migrant workers (Deen 2015). Most work are in domestic service jobs, and some work as nurses and teachers. Major sending countries are Indonesia, the Philippines, Sri Lanka, and Thailand. Main receiving countries are Saudi Arabia and Kuwait, and, to a lesser degree, Hong Kong, Japan, Taiwan, Singapore, Malaysia, and Brunei. These migrants are usually alone and typically are not allowed to marry or have children in the countries where they are temporary workers. They are sometimes illegally recruited and have no legal protection against unjust working conditions.

Circular migration is a regular pattern of population movement between two or more places. It may occur within or between countries. Internal circular migrants include, for example, female domestic workers throughout Latin America and the Caribbean. These women have their permanent residences in rural areas, but they work for long periods for better-off people in the cities. They may leave their children in the care of grandparents in the country, sending remittances for the children's support.

DISPLACED PERSONS Displaced persons are people who are evicted from their homes, communities, or countries and forced to move elsewhere (Guggenheim and Cernea 1993). Colonialism, slavery, war, persecution, natural disasters, and large-scale mining and dam building are major causes of population displacement. A recent report stated that nearly 44 million people worldwide were displaced from their homes due to conflict or persecution (UNHCR 2011).

Refugees are internationally displaced persons. Many refugees are forced to relocate because they are victims or potential victims of persecution on the basis of their race, religion, nationality, ethnicity, gender, or political views (Camino and Krulfeld 1994). Refugees are a large and growing category of displaced persons. An accurate count of all refugees globally is unavailable, but it is about 16 million people, meaning that about 1 of every 500 people

---

circular migration repeated movement between two or more places, either within or between countries.

displaced person someone who is forced to leave his or her home, community, or country.

refugee someone who is forced to leave his or her home, community, or country.

is a refugee. Eighty percent of the world's refugees are sheltered in poor countries: Pakistan, Iran, and Syria house three million refugees (UNHCR 2011). Around one-fourth of the world's refugees are Palestinians.

Women and children, who form the bulk of refugees, are vulnerable to abuse in refugee camps, including rape and trading sex for food (Martin 2005). Some case studies, however, shed a more positive light on the refugee experience. Many refugee women from El Salvador, for example, learned to read and write in the camps and found positive role models in the humanitarian aid workers and their vision of social equality (Burton 2004).

Internally displaced persons (IDPs) are people who are forced to leave their homes and communities but who remain within their country. They are the fastest-growing category of displaced people, with an estimated number of total IDPs worldwide of 38 million people (Internal Displacement Monitoring Centre 2015), or about one of every 250 people displaced worldwide. Africa is the continent with the most IDPs. Within Africa, Sudan (see Map 13.6, page 275) has the highest number, estimated at 2.7 million people. The conflict in Syria has brought about massive internal population displacement, making Syria the country with the highest number of IDPs, at over seven million.

Following the devastating earthquake in January 2010, somewhere between 1.5 and 2 million Haitians were internally displaced. Out of a total population of around 10 million, therefore, between 15 and 20 percent of its population was displaced. Most of the IDPs went to live with relatives in rural areas; many thousands were housed in tent settlements with inadequate sanitation facilities, food and water, electricity, schools, and security. Many people have left the tent camps, and others have been forcibly removed by the closure of the camps (Ferris and Ferro-Ribeiro 2012). It is still unclear as to the amount of adequate new housing for the displaced people.

Many IDPs, like refugees, live for extended periods in makeshift housing or refugee camps with limited access to basic amenities such as latrines, health care, and schools. Because IDPs do not cross country boundaries, they are not under the purview of the United Nations or other international bodies, which have no authority over problems within countries. Several social activists have taken up the cause of IDPs and worked to raise international awareness of the immensity of the problem including the formal definition of IDPs.

Political violence and conflicts over access to critical resources are major causes of people becoming IDPs. But other factors come into play as well, including natural disasters and large-scale development projects (discussed in Chapter 13). Dam construction, mining, and other projects have displaced millions in the past several decades. Dam construction alone is estimated to have displaced around 80 million people since 1950 (Worldwatch Institute 2003). Forced migration due to development projects is called **development-induced displacement**. Depending on a country's policy, people displaced by development may or may not be compensated financially for the loss of their homes and homeland. Even with monetary compensation, it is rarely possible to replace the life one had and the local knowledge that made life livable.

Mega-dam projects, or dam construction projects that involve costs in the billions of dollars and affect massive areas of land and huge numbers of people, are now attracting the attention of concerned people worldwide who support local resistance to massive population displacement. One of the most notorious cases is India's construction of a series of high dams in its Narmada River Valley, which cuts across the middle of the country from the west coast. This project involves relocating hundreds of thousands of people. The relocation is against the residents' wishes, and government compensation for the loss of their homes, land, and livelihood is inadequate. Thousands of people in the Narmada Valley have organized protests over the many years of construction, and international environmental organizations have lent support. Celebrated Indian novelist Arundhati Roy joined the cause by learning everything she could about the 20 years of government planning for the Narmada dam projects, interviewing people who have been relocated, and writing a passionate statement called *The Cost of Living* (1999) in opposition to the project. In her book, a man who was displaced and living in a barren resettlement area tells how he used to pick 48 kinds of fruit in the forest. In the resettlement area, he and his family have to purchase all their food, and they cannot afford to eat any fruit at all (1999:54–55).

Governments promote mega-dam projects as important to the general welfare of the country. The uncalculated costs, however, are high for the local people who are displaced. In fact, the benefits are skewed toward corporate profits, energy for industrial plants, and energy and water for urban consumers who can pay. In China, the Three Gorges Dam project (Map 12.2), which was completed in 2006, displaced around 1.3 million people. While the government offered financial and other forms of compensation, its efforts have not been sufficient to prevent widespread dissatisfaction and depression (Xi and Hwang 2011).

The manner in which displaced persons are relocated affects how well they will adjust to their new life. Displaced persons in general have little choice about when and where they move, and refugees typically have the least choice of all. The Maya people of Guatemala suffered horribly during years of state violence and genocide. Many became refugees, relocating to Mexico and the United States. Others fit into the category of internally displaced persons (see Culturama, page 247).

---

internally displaced person (IDP) someone who is forced to leave his or her home or community but who remains in the same country.

development-induced displacement the forced migration of a population due to development.

Map 12.2 Site of Three Gorges Dam in China

The Three Gorges Dam, the world's biggest dam, is one of several projects that are transforming China's environment. The dam has created a vast reservoir upstream to Chongqing. Engineers believe that the dam will solve the problem of annual flooding of the Yangtze River, the world's third-largest river, and generate immense amounts of power. Environmentalists point to the downsides, which include the decline of many important fish species, destabilizing slopes, and eroding islands in the Yangtze River delta. Cultural anthropologists are concerned about the forced migration of over one million people from 13 major cities and 140 villages, and the loss of rural farming livelihoods as land is flooded. Archaeologists decry the loss of unknown numbers of prehistoric and historic sites now buried under water. Others mourn the loss of one of the most beautiful places in the world, with its "gumdrop" mountains and breathtaking vistas that have inspired artists for centuries.

Scenes of the Three Gorges dam area in southern China. (TOP) A farmer carries her produce along a trail offering stunning vistas before the dam was built. (BOTTOM) After the Three Gorges dam was opened in 2003, rising water levels upstream from the dam caused unexpected damage to housing that was supposedly safe. This man is carrying his belongings to a higher level, and his house was demolished.

> *Do research so that you can present a five-minute briefing on the social and environmental implications of the Three Gorges Dam to the people in the so-called affected areas.*

Cultural anthropologists have done substantial research on refugee populations, especially those affected by war and other forms of violence and terror (Camino and Krulfeld 1994; Hirschon 1989; Manz 2004). They have discovered some key factors that ease or increase relocation stresses. One critical factor is the extent to which the new location resembles or differs from the home place in features such as climate, language, and food (Muecke 1987). Generally, the more different the places of origin and destination are, the greater are the adaptation demands and stress. Other key factors are the refugee's ability to get a job commensurate with his or her training and experience, the presence of family members, and whether people in the new location are welcoming or hostile to the refugees. Anthropologists' findings about adjustment of refugees displaced by political violence can also be applied to situations in which people are suddenly and forcibly displaced by disasters such as earthquakes, tsunamis, and floods (de Sherbinin et al. 2011). Relocation plans, for example, must be attentive to key social dimensions of the affected population, such as gender roles, age, language,

Culturama

The Maya of Guatemala

The term Maya refers to a diverse range of indigenous people who share elements of a common culture and speak varieties of the Mayan language. (Note: The adjective includes a final *n* only when referring to the language.) Most Maya people live in Mexico and Guatemala, with smaller populations in Belize and the western parts of Honduras and El Salvador. Their total population in Mexico and Central America is about six million.

In Guatemala, the Maya live mainly in the western highlands. The Spanish treated the Maya as subservient, exploited their labor, and took their land. Descendants of a formerly rich and powerful civilization, most Maya now live in poverty and lack basic human rights.

The Maya in Guatemala suffered years of genocide during the country's 36-year civil war, when about 200,000 Maya "disappeared" and were brutally murdered by government military forces (Manz 2004). Many more were forcibly displaced from their homeland, and today around 250,000 Maya live as IDPs (Fitigu 2005). Thousands left the country as refugees, fleeing to Mexico and the United States.

Beatriz Manz tells a chilling story of one group of K'iche' Maya and their struggle to survive during the war (2004). Manz began her fieldwork in 1973 among the Maya living in the rural areas near the highland town of Santa Cruz del Quiché in the province of El Quiché. The Maya farmed small plots, growing maize and other food items, but found it increasingly difficult to grow enough food for their families. An American Catholic priest came to them with an idea for a new settlement, over the mountains to the east, in Santa María Tzeá.

Several Maya from the highlands decided to establish a new village. They divided land into equal-size plots so that everyone had enough to support their families. Over time, more settlers came from the highland village. They cleared land for houses, farms, workshops, and a school.

In the late 1970s, their lives were increasingly under surveillance by the Guatemalan military, who suspected the village of harboring insurgents. In the early 1980s, the military began taking village men away. These men were never seen alive again.

In 1982, a brutal attack left the village in flames and survivors fleeing into the jungle. Some went to Mexico, where they lived in exile for years, and others migrated as refugees to the United States. The peace accords of 1996 officially ended the bloodshed. Many of the villagers returned and began to rebuild.

Thanks to Beatriz Manz, University of California at Berkeley, for reviewing this material.

(LEFT) Maya women pray in a church 55 miles southeast of Guatemala City in 2003. The coffins contain the remains of the victims of a 1982 massacre inside the church.

(CENTER) Maya women are active in market trade.

Map 12.3 Guatemala

Within the Republic of Guatemala, the Maya constitute about 40 percent of the country's population of 14 million.

Militaries often have complex roles including waging war, peacekeeping, and postdisaster assistance. (LEFT) A U.S. platoon being briefed on arrival at an outpost in Afghanistan. (RIGHT) United Nations peacekeepers of China attend a farewell ceremony in Xi'an, capital of northwest China's Shaanxi Province. They are heading for a peacekeeping mission in the Democratic Republic of Congo.

The role of women in the armed forces and in UN peacekeeping operations is an ongoing question. Where do you stand on the issue of including more women in the military, and on what do you base your opinion.

religion, as well as physical factors such as hearing and sight disabilities.

The term "social dimensions" can refer to both key vulnerabilities and strengths that particular people may play in the resettlement and recovery phase. A recent interest of policy makers is in the concept of **resilience**, or the ability of a population to "bounce back" from a traumatic situation. Some cultures appear to have more resilience than others, but the causes of the differences are still being researched.

INSTITUTIONAL MIGRANTS **Institutional migrants** are people who move into a social institution, either voluntarily or involuntarily. They include monks and nuns, the elderly, prisoners, boarding school or college students, and people serving in the military. The following material is about military migrants.

Anthropologists have published little about the effects of migration on people in the military. One matter is clear, however: Military people on assignment need more in-depth training about how to communicate with local people and about the importance of respecting local cultures. A pocket-size handbook on Iraqi etiquette used by some U.S. troops in Iraq provides limited guidelines (Lorch 2003). It says, for example, that one should avoid arguments and should not take more than three cups of coffee or tea if one is a guest. Also, one should not use the "thumbs up" gesture because its meaning is obscene, and one should not sit with one's feet on a desk because that is rude. Such basics are helpful, but they do little to provide more in-depth cultural awareness that can make all the difference in conflict and post-conflict situations.

During wartime, soldiers are trained primarily to seek out and destroy the enemy, not to engage in cross-cultural communication. As mentioned in Chapter 8, winning a war in contemporary times often hinges on what the conquerors do after the outright conflict is over, and that often means keeping troops stationed on foreign soil for a long time. Such

extended assignments take a heavy toll on military personnel's mental health and appear to be linked to high rates of suicide, interpersonal violence, stress-based acts of violence against people in the occupied country, and readjustment problems after returning home. Journalist Sebastian Junger, who has a B.A. in cultural anthropology, spent extended time with an American platoon at a remote and dangerous outpost in the mountains of Afghanistan between 2007 and 2008. His book, *War* (2010) and the documentary film he co-directed, *Restrepo* (2010), are anthropologically informed documentaries of everyday life in a war zone. More than that, Junger's work documents the difficulty for combat soldiers in returning home to their wives and families and the high likelihood that they will opt to return to combat and recreate the strong male bonding of the platoon. Many combat soldiers become circular migrants, moving in and out of combat, never completely comfortable in one place or the other.

The New Immigrants to the United States and Canada

12.2 Discuss examples of the new immigrants to the United States and Canada.

The term **new immigrant** refers to a person who moved internationally since the 1960s. The category of new immigrants worldwide continues to include a large proportion

---

resilience ability of a population to "bounce back" from conflict, a disaster, or other traumatic situation.

institutional migrant someone who moves into a social institution either voluntarily or involuntarily.

new immigrant an international migrant who has moved since the 1960s.

of refugees, most of whom are destitute and desperate for asylum, as well as people seeking improved economic opportunities for themselves and their children in the destination country. Three trends characterize the new international migration in the twenty-first century:

- Globalization: More countries are involved in international migration, leading to increased cultural diversity in both sending and receiving countries.

- Acceleration: Growth in numbers of migrants has occurred worldwide.

- Feminization: Women are a growing percentage of international migrants to and from all regions and in all types of migration; some types exhibit a majority of women.

In the United States, the category of new immigrants refers to people who arrived after the 1965 amendments to the Immigration and Naturalization Act. This change made it possible for far more people from developing countries to enter, especially if they were professionals or trained in some desired skill. Later, the family reunification provision allowed permanent residents and naturalized citizens to bring in close family members. Most of the new immigrants in the United States are from Latin America and the Caribbean and Asia, although increasing numbers are from Eastern Europe, especially Russia (see Figure 12.1).

The United States offers two kinds of visas for foreigners: immigrant visas (also called residence visas) and nonimmigrant visas for tourists and students (Pessar 1995:6). An immigration visa is usually valid indefinitely and allows its holder to be employed and to apply for citizenship. A nonimmigrant visa is issued for a limited period and usually bars its holder from paid employment. Some immigrants are granted visas because of their special skills in relation to labor market needs, but most are admitted under the family unification provision.

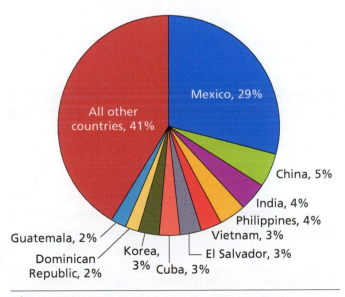

Figure 12.1 Immigrants to the United States as a Percentage of the Total, by National Origin, 2010.

The New Immigrants from Latin America and the Caribbean

Since the 1960s, substantial movements of the Latino or Hispano population (people who share roots in former Spanish colonies in the Western Hemisphere) have occurred, mainly to the United States. Latinos are about 10 percent of the U.S. population, excluding the population of Puerto Rico.

In the United States as a whole, and in some cities, such as Los Angeles, Miami, San Antonio, and New York, Latinos are the largest minority group. Within Latino new immigrants, the three largest subgroups are Mexicans, Puerto Ricans, and Cubans. Large numbers also come from the Dominican Republic, Colombia, Ecuador, El Salvador, Nicaragua, and Peru.

MEXICAN IMMIGRANTS: NEITHER HERE NOR THERE Mexico is by far the major source country of foreign-born immigrants to the United States, constituting 29 percent of all United States immigrants, also referred to as foreign-born people (http://www.migrationinformation.org). Over 12 million foreign-born Mexicans live in the United States. Most live in the traditional destination states of California, Texas, and Illinois, but since the 1990s, more are settling in states such as Georgia, Arkansas, North Carolina, South Carolina, Nebraska, and Ohio. Mexico is also the major source of unauthorized immigration into the United States. Many rural areas in Mexico have been left with mainly elderly people and their grandchildren until the Christmas holidays, when migrant workers return to join their families for a week or two.

Due to the 2008 economic recession in the United States, starting in 2008, two changes in Mexican–U.S. migration occurred (Passel et al. 2012). First is a major reduction in the number of Mexicans migrating to the United States. Second, large numbers of Mexican immigrants to the United States returned to Mexico, taking their children with them who are U.S. citizens and accustomed to life in the United States. As of 2012, the net immigration flow (the number of immigrants compared to the number of out-migrants or emigrants) between Mexico and the United States is less than that of Asian migrants to and from the United States (see Figure 12.2).

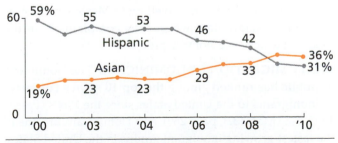

Figure 12.2 Change in Percentage of Hispanic and Asian Immigrants to the United States from 2000 to 2010, as a Percentage of Immigrants to the United States.

New immigrant scenes in the United States. (LEFT) Latino immigrants studying English in a program in Virginia. (RIGHT) A Dominican Day parade in New York City.

Learn about an ethnic festival or event that is being held in the near future. Attend it and observe what signs and symbols of ethnicity are displayed, who attends, and what messages about identity are conveyed.

In spite of these recent shifts, the Mexican immigrant population in the United States is still large and important. While it is impossible to generalize about the vast numbers of migrants to the United States from Mexico, a theme of "neither here nor there" applies to many adult immigrants (Striffler 2007). Through the 1980s, many Mexican men were seasonal labor migrants to the traditional destination areas, working in the United States for several months of the year but always returning home for at least a few months. Due to changing legal and economic conditions in the United States starting in the late 1980s, job opportunities declined in the traditional areas of migration, especially California, and opened up in "heartland" states. A study of poultry processing workers in Arkansas reveals how Mexican immigrants shifted from seasonal work in California to year-around work in a Tyson Foods processing plant (Striffler 2007). This shift made it possible for the men to bring their wives and children to live with them, and the women also started working at the plant.

As seasonal migrants, the men considered "home" to be in Mexico. In Arkansas, as families have been able to reunite, "home" for adults is both here and there, or neither here nor there. For their children, however, the United States is home. For them, travelling to Mexico is a "vacation" to a foreign place where they complain about the food and experience stomach problems.

CHAIN MIGRATION OF DOMINICANS The Dominican Republic has ranked among the top 10 source countries of immigrants to the United States since the 1960s (Pessar 1995) (see Map 13.3, page 269), and Dominicans are one of the fastest-growing immigrant groups in the United States. They live in clusters in a few states, with their highest concentration in New York State.

For Dominican immigrants, as for many other immigrant groups, the *cadena*, or chain, links one immigrant to another (Pessar 1995). **Chain migration** is a form of population movement in which a first wave of migrants comes and then attracts relatives and friends to join them in the destination place. Most Dominicans who are legal immigrants have sponsored other family members. Thus, many Dominicans have entered the United States through the family unification provision. The policy, however, defines a family as a nuclear unit (review Chapter 6) and excludes important members of Dominican extended families, such as cousins and ritual kin (*compadres*). To overcome this barrier, some Dominicans use a technique called the business marriage. In a business marriage, an individual seeking to migrate pays a legal immigrant or citizen a fee, perhaps $2,000, to contract a "marriage" with that person. The migrant then acquires a visa through the family unification provision. A business marriage does not involve cohabitation or sexual relations; it is meant to be broken.

In New York City, most Dominicans work in manufacturing industries, including the garment industry. They are more concentrated in these industries than is any other ethnic group. Recent declines in manufacturing jobs in New York City, and the redefining of better positions into less desirable ones, have therefore disproportionately affected Dominicans. Many Dominicans have established their own retail business, or *bodegas* (bo-DAY-guh). Bodegas are often located in unsafe areas, and some owners have been assaulted or killed. Economic challenges are aggravated by the arrival of even newer immigrants,

---

chain migration a form of population movement in which a first wave of migrants comes and then attracts relatives and friends to join them in the destination.

especially from Mexico and Central America, who are willing to accept lower wages than Dominicans do and worse working conditions.

Although many middle- and upper-class Dominican migrants secured fairly solid employment in the United States on their arrival, they have generally not prospered since then. Dominicans have the highest poverty rate in New York City. Wages are higher for men than women. Poverty is concentrated among women-headed households with young children, and women are more likely than men to be on public assistance.

Still, Dominican women in the United States are more often regularly employed than they would be in the Dominican Republic. This pattern upsets a patriarchal norm in which the nuclear household depends on male earnings and female domestic responsibilities. A woman's earning power means that husband–wife decision making is more egalitarian. A working Dominican woman is likely to obtain more assistance from the man in doing household chores. All of these changes help explain why more Dominican men are eager to return to the Dominican Republic than women are. As one man said, "Your country is a country for women; mine is for men" (Pessar 1995:81). Although most Dominicans left their homeland in search of a better life, many hope to return to the Dominican Republic. A common saying is that in the United States, "there is work but there is no life."

SALVADORANS: ESCAPING WAR TO STRUGGLE WITH POVERTY
Salvadorans make up the fourth-largest Latino population in the United States, numbering around 1,200,000 (http://www.migrationinformation.org). The civil war in El Salvador, which began in 1979 and continued for over a decade, was the major stimulus for Salvadoran emigration (Mahler 1995) (Map 12.4). Most of the refugees came to the United States. About half of all Salvadorans in the United States live in California, especially Los Angeles (Baker-Christales 2004), with another large cluster in the Washington, DC, area. Many also settled around New York City, including many who moved to suburban areas of Long Island.

Middle- and upper-class Salvadorans obtained tourist or even immigration visas relatively easily. The poor, however, were less successful, and many entered the United States illegally as a *mojado* (mo-HAH-do), derogatory slang meaning a "wetback." Like Mexican illegal immigrants, Salvadorans use the term mojado to describe their journey. The Salvadorans, though, had to cross three rivers instead of one. These three crossings are a prominent theme of their escape stories, which are full of physical and psychological hardships, including hunger, arrests, and women being beaten and raped along the way. Once they arrived, things were still not easy, especially in the search for work and housing. Lack of education and marketable skills limit

Map 12.4 El Salvador

In recent times, the Republic of El Salvador has tended to emphasize one or two major export crops, with coffee being dominant. Coffee growing requires high-altitude land, and therefore coffee production has displaced many indigenous people. The country's total population is nearly six million. About 90 percent are mestizo, nine percent of European descent (mostly Spanish), and one percent indigenous. The dominant language is Spanish, although some indigenous people speak Nahuat. Eighty-three percent of the people are Roman Catholic, and Protestants are 15 percent and growing in number.

the job search. For undocumented immigrants, getting a decent job is even harder. These factors make it more likely that Salvadorans work in the informal sector, doing non-salaried work that is not officially registered, where they are easy targets for economic exploitation.

Salvadorans living on Long Island receive low wages and labor in poor conditions. Their jobs involve providing services to better-off households. Men do outside work, such as gardening, landscaping, construction, and pool cleaning. Women work as nannies, live-in maids, house-cleaners, restaurant workers, and caregivers for the elderly. The Salvadorans often hold down more than one job—for example, working at a McDonald's in the morning and cleaning houses in the afternoon. Men's pride prevents them from taking lowly ("women's") jobs such as washing dishes. Women are more flexible and hence are more likely than men to find work. For the poorest Salvadoran refugees, even exploitative jobs may be an economic improvement compared with conditions back home, where they could not support their families at all.

The Salvadorans were attracted to Long Island by its thriving informal economy, a sector where checking for visas was less likely to occur. Unfortunately, the cost of living on Long Island is higher than in many other places. The combination of low wages and high cost of living has kept most Salvadorans in the category of the working poor, with few prospects for improvement. They attempt to cope with high housing costs by crowding many people into units meant for small families. Compared with El Salvador, where most people, except for the urban poor, owned their own homes, only a few Salvadorans on Long Island own homes. Residential space and expenses are shared among extended kin and nonkin who pay rent. This situation causes tension and stress among household members.

The New Immigrants from Asia

The new immigrants from Asia are a highly varied category, ranging from upper-income immigrants from East and South Asia (the Republic of Korea, Japan, China, and India), as well as refugees from war-torn countries (Vietnam, Cambodia, and Nepal). Research on how international migrants from Asia change their behavior in the new destination has therefore addressed a wide variety of topics, including whether different consumption patterns emerge and, if so, how, why, and what effects such changes have on other aspects of their culture, changing youth culture, and religious practices as a social and psychological support.

CHANGING PATTERNS OF CONSUMPTION AMONG HONG KONG CHINESE A Canadian study examined consumption patterns among four groups: Anglo-Canadians, Hong Kong immigrants who had arrived within the previous seven years, long-time Hong Kong immigrants, and Hong Kong residents (Lee and Tse 1994). Since 1987, Hong Kong has been the single largest source of migrants to Canada. The new immigrant settlement pattern in Canada is one of urban clustering. The Hong Kong Chinese have developed their own shopping centers, television and radio stations, newspapers, and country clubs. Because of generally high incomes, Hong Kong immigrants have greatly boosted Canadian buying power.

For most of the poor Hong Kong migrants, however, the move brought a lowered economic situation, reflected in consumption patterns. New immigrants may have to reduce spending on entertainment and expensive items. Primary needs of the new immigrants included items that only about half of all households owned: TVs, a car,

a house, a VCR, carpets, and a microwave oven. Items in the second-needs category were a dining room set, a barbecue, a deep freezer, and a dehumidifier. Long-time immigrants owned more secondary products.

At the same time, businesses in Canada have responded to Hong Kong immigrant tastes by providing Hong Kong–style restaurants, Chinese branch banks, and China-oriented travel agencies. Supermarkets offer specialized Asian sections. Thus, traditional patterns and ties are maintained to some extent. Two characteristics of Hong Kong immigrants distinguish them from other groups discussed in this section: their relatively secure economic status and their high level of education. Still, in Canada, they often have a difficult time finding suitable employment. Some have named Canada "Kan Lan Tai," meaning a difficult place to prosper, a fact that leads many to become "astronauts," or transnational migrants

THREE PATTERNS OF ADAPTATION AMONG VIETNAMESE AMERICANS More than 125 million refugees left Vietnam during and after the wartime 1970s. Most relocated to the United States, but many others went to Canada, Australia, France, Germany, and Britain (Gold 1992). Vietnamese immigrants in the United States constitute the nation's fourth-largest Asian American minority group. Three distinct subgroups are the 1975-era elite, the "boat people," and the ethnic Chinese. Although they interact frequently, they have retained distinct patterns of adaptation.

The first group, the 1975-era elite, avoided many of the traumatic elements of flight. They were U.S. employees and members of the South Vietnamese government and military. They left before having to live under the communists, and they spent little time in refugee camps. Most came with intact families and received generous financial assistance from the United States. Using their education and English language skills, most found good jobs quickly and adjusted rapidly.

The boat people began to enter the United States after the outbreak of the Vietnam–China conflict of 1978. Mainly of rural origin, they had lived for three years or more under communism. Their exit, either by overcrowded and leaky boats or on foot through Cambodia, was dangerous and difficult. More than 50 percent died on the way. Those who survived faced many months in refugee camps in Thailand, Malaysia, the Philippines, or Hong Kong before being admitted to the United States. Because many more men than women escaped as boat people, these refugees are less likely to have arrived with intact families. They were less well educated than the earlier wave, with half lacking competence in English. They faced the depressed U.S. economy of the 1980s. By the time of their arrival, the U.S. government had severely reduced refugee cash assistance and had canceled other benefits. These refugees had a much more difficult time adjusting to life in the United States than the 1975-era elite did.

Vietnamese immigrants in the United States comprise the fourth-largest Asian American group. Many Vietnamese American youth are attaining economic and social success, while others are less fortunate and join urban gangs. (TOP) Vietnamese American college students have fun in a Hollywood nightclub. (BOTTOM) Vietnamese American actress Maggie Q.

The ethnic Chinese, a distinct and socially marginalized class of entrepreneurs in Vietnam, arrived in the United States mainly as boat people. Following the 1987 outbreak of hostilities between Vietnam and China, the ethnic Chinese were allowed to leave Vietnam. Some, using contacts in the overseas Chinese community, were able to reestablish

their roles as entrepreneurs. Most have had a difficult time in the United States because they lacked a Western-style education. They were also sometimes subject to discrimination from other Vietnamese in the United States.

The general picture of first-generation Vietnamese adjustment in the United States shows high rates of unemployment, welfare dependency, and poverty. Interviews with Vietnamese refugees in southern California reveal generational change and fading traditions among youths. Vietnamese teenagers in southern California, for example, have adopted the lifestyle of low-income U.S. teenagers. Their Euro-American friends are more important to them than their Vietnamese heritage is. Given social variations and regional differences in adaptation throughout the United States, however, generalizations about Vietnamese-Americans must be made with extreme caution.

HINDUS OF NEW YORK CITY MAINTAIN THEIR CULTURE With the 1965 change in legislation in the United States, a first wave of South Asian immigrants dominated by male professionals from India arrived (Bhardwaj and Rao 1990). Members of this first wave settled primarily in eastern and western cities. Subsequent immigrants from India, who were less well educated and less wealthy, tend to be concentrated in New York and New Jersey. New York City has the largest population of South Asian Indians in the United States, with about one-eighth of the total number (Mogelonsky 1995).

Members of the highly educated first wave are concentrated in professional fields such as medicine, engineering, and management (Helweg and Helweg 1990). One of the major immigrant groups in Silicon Valley, California, is South Asian Indians. Members of the less educated, later wave find work in family-run businesses or service industries. Indians dominate some trades, such as convenience stores. They have penetrated the ownership of budget hotels and motels and operate nearly half of the total number of establishments in this niche. More than 40 percent of New York City's licensed cab drivers are Indians, Pakistanis, or Bangladeshis (Mogelonsky 1995).

The South Asian Indian population in the United States is one of the better-off immigrant groups and is considered an immigrant success story. South Asian Indians place high value on their children's education and urge them to pursue higher education in fields such as medicine and engineering. They tend to have few children and invest heavily in their schooling and social advancement.

A continuing concern of many members of the first wave is the maintenance of Hindu cultural values in the face of patterns prevalent in mainstream U.S. culture, such as dating, premarital sex, drinking, and drugs (Lessinger 1995). The Hindu population supports the construction of Hindu temples that offer Sunday school classes for young people and cultural events as a way of passing on the

In Flushing, New York, a major Hindu temple holds a ceremony with a priest from India (wearing orange) offering prayers.

Hindu heritage to the next generation. South Asian Hindus attempt to appeal to their youths by accommodating to their lifestyles and preferences in terms of things such as the kind of food served after rituals. Vegetarian pizza is now a common temple menu item for the young people.

Another challenge for Hinduism in the United States and Canada is to establish temples that offer ritual diversity that speaks to Hindus of many varieties. In New York City, the growth of one temple shows how its ritual flexibility helped it to expand. The Ganesha (guh-NAY-shuh) Temple was founded in 1997 under leadership of Hindus from southern India. Temple rituals at first were the same as those conducted in southern Indian temples. Over the years, though, to widen its reach, the temple expanded its

rituals to include those that would appeal to Hindus from other regions of India. The congregation has grown, and the physical structure has expanded to provide for this growth. The daily and yearly cycle has become more elaborate and more varied than what one would find at a typical Hindu temple in southern India.

Migration Policies and Programs in a Globalizing World

12.3 **Recognize how cultural anthropologists contribute to migration policies and programs.**

The major questions related to migration policies and programs concern state and international policies of inclusion and exclusion of particular categories of people. The human rights of various categories of migrants vary dramatically. Migrants of all sorts, including long-standing migratory groups such as pastoralists and horticulturalists, seek ways of protecting their lifestyles, maintaining their health, and creating security for the future.

Protecting Migrants' Health

Health risks to migrants are many and varied, depending on the wide variety of migrant types and destinations. One group of migrants of special concern consists of those whose livelihoods depend on long-standing economic systems requiring spatial mobility, such as foragers, horticulturalists, and pastoralists. The frequency of drought and food shortages in the Sahel region of Africa (Map 12.5) in

Map 12.5 **Sahel Region**

The word sahel comes from the Arabic for "shore" or "border," referring in this case to the area between the Sahara desert and the more fertile regions to the south. Primarily savanna, the region has been the home to many rich kingdoms that controlled Saharan trade routes. Most people make their living from pastoralism and semisedentary cattle raising. The region has recently experienced several major droughts, leading to the widespread death of herd animals, widespread human starvation and malnutrition, and forced population displacement. (Note: Since the time of this map, Sudan has split into two separate countries. See Map 13.6, page 275.)

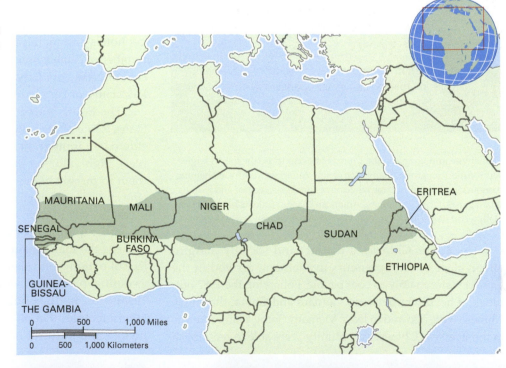

recent decades is prompting research by cultural anthropologists to learn how to prevent such situations through better monitoring and enhanced service provision (see Anthropology Works).

Inclusion and Exclusion

National policies that set quotas on the quantity and types of immigrants who are welcome and that determine how they are treated are dictated largely by political and economic interests. Even in cases of seemingly humanitarian quotas, governments undertake a cost–benefit analysis of how much will be gained and how much will be lost. Governments show their political support or disapproval of other governments through their immigration policies. One of the most obvious economic factors affecting policy is labor flow. Cheap, including illegal, immigrant

---

Anthropology Works

Mapping African Pastoralists' Movements for Risk Assessment and Service Delivery

Pastoralists are often vulnerable to malnutrition as a consequence of climate changes, fluctuations in food supply, war, and political upheaval. Because of their spatial mobility, they are difficult to reach with relief aid during a crisis.

Cultural anthropologists are devising ways to gather and manage basic information about pastoralists' movements in the Sahel region to prevent crises and improve basic service delivery (Watkins and Fleisher 2002). The data required for such proactive planning include the following:

A Tuareg herdsman fights his way through a sandstorm in Mali.

- Information about the number of migrants and the size of their herds in a particular location at a particular time. Such data can inform planners about the level of services required for public health programs, educational programs, and veterinary services. This information can be used to assess the demand on particular grazing areas and water sources and is therefore important in predicting possible future crises.

- Information about patterns of migratory movements. This information can enable planners to move services to where the people are, rather than expecting people to move to the services. Some nongovernmental organizations, for example, are providing mobile banking services and mobile veterinary services. Information about pastoralist movements can be used as an early warning to prevent social conflicts that might result if several groups arrived in the same place at the same time.

Data collection involves interviews with pastoralists, often with one or two key participants, whom the anthropologists select for their specialized knowledge. Interviews cover topics such as the migratory paths followed (both typical and atypical), population levels, the size of herds, and the nutritional and water requirements of people and animals. Given the complex social systems of pastoralists, the data gathering must also include information on group leadership, decision-making practices, and concepts about land and water rights.

The anthropologists organize this information into a computerized database, linking the ethnographic data with other data collected and managed through what is called a geographic information system (GIS). It includes data on the environment and climate information from satellites. The anthropologists then construct various scenarios and assess the relative risks to the people's health. Impending crises can be foreseen, and warnings can be issued to governments and international aid agencies.

Food for Thought

The tracking system described here remains outside the control of the pastoralists themselves. How might it be managed so that they can participate more meaningfully and gain greater autonomy?

In September 2015, residents of Malta, an island country in the Mediterranean, joined other groups around the world in holding a candlelight vigil to show solidarity with refugees and migrants from Africa.

▌*The World Trade Organization supports the free trade of goods between countries. Where does it stand, if at all, on the free movement of*
▌*labor between countries?*

labor is used around the world to maintain profits for businesses and services for the better off. Flows of such labor undermine labor unions and the status of established workers.

State immigration policies are played out in local communities. In some instances, local resentments are associated with a so-called **lifeboat mentality**, a view that seeks to limit enlarging a particular group because of perceived constraints on resources. This perspective may be part of the explanation for many recent outbreaks of hostility throughout the world in which host populations, instead of being gracious and sharing what they have, seek to drive out the immigrants to protect their own entitlements.

Migration and Human Rights

Recent politically conservative trends in many countries around the world have succeeded in reversing earlier, more progressive immigration policies. **Right of return**, or a refugee's entitlement to return to and live in his or her homeland, has been considered a basic human right in the West since the time of the signing of the Magna Carta. It is included in United Nations General Assembly Resolution 194, passed in 1948, and was elevated by the United Nations to an "inalienable right" in 1974.

The right of return is a pressing issue for the hundreds of thousands of Palestinians who fled or were driven from their homes during the 1948 war. They went mainly to Jordan, the West Bank/East Jerusalem, Gaza, Lebanon, Syria, and other Arab states. Jordan and Syria have granted Palestinian refugees rights equal to those of their citizens. In Lebanon, where estimates of the number of Palestinian refugees range between 200,000 and 600,000, the government refuses them such rights (Salam 1994). Israel favors the lower number because it makes the problem seem less

lifeboat mentality a view that seeks to limit growth of a particular group because of perceived resource constraints.

right of return the United Nations' guaranteed right of a refugee to return to his or her home country to live.

severe. The Palestinians favor the higher number to highlight the seriousness of their plight. The Lebanese government also favors the higher number to emphasize its burden in hosting so many refugees. Palestinians know that they are not welcome in Lebanon, but they cannot return to Israel because Israel denies them the right of return. Israel responds to the Palestinians' claims by saying that its acceptance of Jewish immigrants from Arab countries constitutes an equal exchange.

The right of return can be considered, just as validly, within states, even though most have no policy close to that of the United Nations. A stark instance of internal displacement and loss of rights to return home comes from the 2005 hurricanes in New Orleans and the coastal counties of Mississippi and Louisiana. The "racial" lines of displacement are nowhere clearer than in the statistics for the city of New Orleans (Lyman 2006). Before Hurricane Katrina, the population of New Orleans was 54 percent White, 36 percent Black, and six percent Latino. In 2006, the population was 68 percent White and 21 percent Black, with no change in the Latino percentage. The causes of the differential displacement of the Black population are one problem. The fact that many Black Americans, all these many years later, have little chance of returning to their homes, a phenomenon that can be termed differential resettlement, is another.

12 Learning Objectives Revisited

12.1 Describe the major categories of migration.

Migrants are classified as internal, international, or transnational. Another category is based on the migrants' reason for moving. On this dimension, migrants are classified as labor migrants, institutional migrants, or displaced persons. People's adjustment to their new situation depends on the degree of voluntarism involved in the move, the degree of cultural and environmental difference between the place of origin and the destination, and how well expectations about the new location are met, especially in terms of making a living and establishing social ties.

Displaced persons are one of the fastest-growing categories of migrants. Refugees fleeing from political persecution or warfare face serious adjustment challenges because they often leave their home countries with few material resources and frequently have experienced much psychological suffering. The number of internally displaced persons is growing even faster than the number of refugees. Mega-dams and other large-scale development projects result in thousands of people becoming IDPs, and these individuals do not fall under the purview of international organizations such as the United Nations.

12.2 Discuss examples of the new immigrants to the United States and Canada.

Worldwide, the "new immigrants" are contributing to growing transnational connections and to the formation of increasingly multicultural populations within countries. In the United States, the new immigrants from Latin America, especially Mexico, are the largest and fastest-growing category, but their proportion is now declining while that of Asian immigrants is rising.

In the United States, members of most refugee immigrant groups tend to have jobs at the lower end of the economic scale. Jewish refugees from the Soviet Union experience a major gap in what their employment was like in Russia versus their limited options in the United States. Immigrants from East and South Asia, who are more likely than others to have immigrated to the United States voluntarily, have achieved greater levels of economic success than most other new immigrant groups.

Immigrant groups throughout the world often face discrimination in their new destinations. The degree to which discrimination occurs varies with the level of perceived competition for resources. Gender affects immigrant experiences.

12.3 Recognize how cultural anthropologists contribute to migration policies and programs.

Anthropologists have studied national and international migration policies and programs in terms of social inclusion and exclusion. Fieldwork in particular contexts reveals a range of patterns between local residents and immigrants. Working-class resentment among local people against immigrants is not universal and varies with the overall amount and type of employment available.

Anthropologists examine possible infringements of the human rights of migrants, especially as regards the degree of voluntarism in their move and the conditions they face in the destination area. Another human rights issue related to migration is the right of return. The United Nations proclaimed the right of return for internationally displaced populations. Most countries, however, have no such policy. Internally displaced persons, including the evacuees from the 2005 hurricanes in the Gulf region of the United States, have no guarantee that they can return to their home area.

Cultural anthropologists find many roles in applied work related to migration. Gathering data on migratory movements of traditionally mobile people, such as pastoralists, can help make humanitarian aid programs more timely and effective.

Key Concepts

bracero, p. 243
chain migration, p. 250
circular migration, p. 244
development-induced displacement,
    p. 245
displaced person, p. 244
institutional migrant, p. 248

internal migration, p. 241
internally displaced person (IDP),
    p. 245
international migration, p. 241
lifeboat mentality, p. 256
migration, p. 240
new immigrant, p. 248

push–pull theory, p. 241
refugee, p. 244
remittance, p. 242
resilience, p. 248
right of return, p. 256
transnational migration, p. 241

Thinking Outside the Box

1. Find a detailed map that shows the geography of the United States, Mexico, and Central America, including El Salvador. Trace a possible overland migration route from El Salvador to the United States, and find the three rivers that Salvadoran refugees had to cross.
2. Think of a recent experience you had with moving from one location to another. Was your move purely voluntary or not? If not, what were some of the factors influencing your move? How did you deal with your adjustment to the new location?
3. Where do you stand on immigration policy in your home country? Are immigrants good for your country overall or not? If you were in charge of immigration policy, what would be your position and why?

Chapter 13
People Defining Development

Learning Objectives

13.1 Identify what is development and approaches to it.

13.2 Summarize how indigenous peoples and women are redefining development.

13.3 Identify urgent issues in development.

Anthro Connections

A Kayapo Brazilian Indian holds the Holy Fire during the Kari-Oca opening ceremony in 2012 of the Rio + 20 Environmental Summit in Brazil. The Kayapo are a tribe of over 3,000 people and one of the several tribes opposing the construction of a large dam on the Xingu (shin-goo) River in northern Brazil that would destroy thousands of acres of their land. The Rio + 20 Summit brought together representatives from countries around the world that stated commitments to environmental protection. Brazil has experienced remarkable rates of economic growth while at the same time destroying the rainforests and lifeways of its indigenous peoples. For the Kayapo and other Indians, the Brazilian national agenda means possible opportunities for them to enter the global economy, but at what cost to them? Discovery of gold and other valuable resources in Kayapo lands continues to provide economic opportunities to the Kayapo as well as challenges to their integrity as a culture (Darlington 2015).

We have had many visitors to Walpole Island since the French "discovered us" in the seventeenth century in our territory, Bkejwanong. In many cases, these visitors failed to recognize who we were and to appreciate our traditions. They tried to place us in their European framework of knowledge, denying that we possessed our indigenous knowledge. They attempted to steal our lands, water, and knowledge. We resisted. They left and never came back. We continued to share our knowledge with the next visitors to our place. . . . It was a long-term strategy that has lasted more than three hundred years. (Dr. Dean Jacobs, Executive Director of Walpole Island First Nation, from his foreword in VanWynsberghe 2002:ix)

These are the words of a leader of the Walpole Island First Nation, located in southern Ontario, Canada (Map 13.1). They, along with many other indigenous groups worldwide, have taken strong action in recent decades to protect their culture and natural environment. The Walpole Island First Nation organized itself and successfully fought to control industrial waste that was polluting its water and land. In the process, the people have regained their pride and cultural integrity.

The subfield of development anthropology looks at how culture and "development" interact to improve people's lives and reduce poverty. Thus, it has a strong applied component, as well as a critical component that asks hard questions about the causes of poverty. This chapter's first section considers concepts related to change and development and various approaches to development. The second section focuses on development in relation to indigenous peoples and women. The third section looks at urgent issues in development and what cultural anthropology can contribute to them.

Defining Development and Approaches to It

13.1 Identify what is development and approaches to it.

This chapter focuses on the topic of contemporary cultural change as shaped by **development**, or directed change aimed at improving human welfare. A major focus of development efforts is preventing or reducing poverty. As discussed in Chapter 1, poverty is extremely difficult to define, but one workable definition for poverty is lack of access to tangible or intangible resources that contribute to life and the well-being of a person, group, country, or region. Some approaches to eradicating poverty focus on ensuring people's access to basic needs such as adequate food, clean water, housing, and clothing, factors without which a person may die or certainly fail to thrive. More expanded definitions include access to education and personal security (freedom from fear).

Development experts in Paris, Rome, and Washington, DC, who have never lived in poverty or perhaps never even seen it at closer hand than from a taxi from the airport to their

---

development change directed toward improving human welfare.

Canadian Prime Minister Stephen Harper, center (standing), officially apologized for more than a century of abuse and culture loss related to Indian boarding schools at a ceremony in the House of Commons on Parliament Hill in Ottawa, Canada, in 2008. From the nineteenth century to the 1970s, more than 150,000 aboriginal children were required to attend state-funded Christian schools as part of a program to assimilate them into the Canadian state.

Map 13.1 **Walpole Island Reservation in Southern Ontario, Canada**

five-star hotel, spend much time discussing varieties of poverty. They consider how to measure poverty, how to assess whether poverty is increasing or decreasing and why, and what kinds of policies and programs will reduce poverty. They have devised categories such as extreme poverty, defined as serious lack of access to life-supporting resources, and chronic poverty, defined as lack of access to life-supporting resources that endures over a lifetime or over generations.

The causes of poverty deserve an entire book to themselves. For our purposes, we can divide causes into underlying causes or proximate causes. Underlying causes include factors such as climate change; global trade inequalities that place higher-income countries at an advantage compared to

lower-income countries; inequalities within countries that place certain regions or ethnic groups at a disadvantage, as discussed in this chapter's Eye on the Environment box; and gender inequality, which persistently means that women and girls have less of a chance of survival, health, and well-being than men and boys. Proximate causes are those related to short-term factors such as a major natural disaster such as a flood or an earthquake that quickly destroys people's ability to provide for their daily needs, their housing, and their everyday security; or a family member's major health problem that requires large financial expenditures. Underlying causes tend to keep people in poverty and make it difficult for them to escape from poverty. Proximate causes of poverty may mean that people move into poverty and may or may not be able to escape, depending on the resources they have and the context in which they live. Combined, underlying causes and proximate causes prove to be disastrous and lead to extreme and chronic poverty.

Locally, beyond the statistics and policies generated in world capitals, real people in real places experience poverty, in its various manifestations, and attempt to escape from it or deal with it. Analysis of 293 life histories (review Chapter 2 on methods) collected in Bangladesh provides unique insight into how some people manage to exit from poverty and to stay out of poverty over the long term (Davis 2011). Of the entire group, 18 percent had used **micro-credit loans** (small loans made to low-income people to support an income-generating activity). So, even in one of the poorest countries of the world, interventions such as a lending program for the poor can in fact help people escape from poverty over the long term.

micro-credit loan a small cash loan made to low-income people to support an income-generating activity.

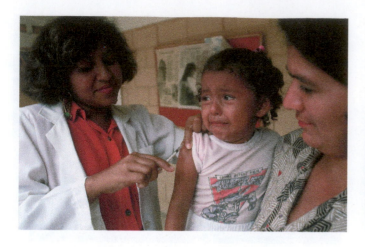
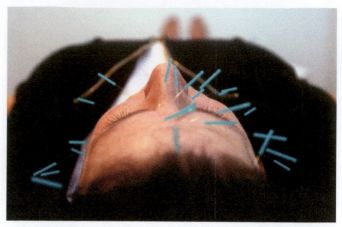

(LEFT) A doctor administering polio vaccine in Ecuador. In 1985, the Pan American Health Organization (PAHO) established a plan for eradicating the polio virus from the Americas by 1990. (RIGHT) A patient rests with acupuncture needles on her face during a "face lift" treatment (to remove wrinkles and make the individual look younger) in New York City. This acupuncture procedure, based in traditional Chinese medicine, follows the theory that the face is where the essence of yin and the energy of yang meet. The procedure seeks to adjust imbalances in yin and yang through the insertion of needles at particular places.

Do research to find out whether traditional Chinese acupuncture had a specialization in "face lifting." If not, can you learn when and where this specialization emerged?

Some readers of this book may have first-hand experiences living in or near poverty. They likely have much to add to the discussion in the following sections of the chapter about poverty around the world and attempts to escape from it, alleviate it, or end it. This section first looks at how culture changes in general. It then turns to the concept of development as a process that seeks to address poverty using both broad processes of change.

Two Processes of Social Change

Two processes underlie all social change. The first is **invention**, the discovery of something new. The second is **diffusion**, the spread of culture through social contact.

INVENTION Most inventions evolve gradually through experimentation and the accumulation of knowledge, but some appear suddenly. Examples of technological inventions that have created cultural change include the printing press, gunpowder, polio vaccine, and satellite communication. Conceptual innovations, such as Jeffersonian democracy, are also inventions.

Many inventions bring about positive cultural change, but not all inventions have positive social outcomes. Inventions inspired by a socially positive goal may have mixed or unintended negative consequences. If you think of some of the major inventions of the past 100 years, such as the automobile, refrigeration/air conditioning, televisions, and cell phones, you can quickly come up with strong pros and cons, with cons including massive environmental costs as well as the growing social divide between people who can afford new commodities and practices versus those who cannot.

DIFFUSION Diffusion is logically related to invention because new discoveries are likely to spread. Diffusion

can occur in several ways. First, in mutual borrowing, two societies that are roughly equal in power exchange aspects of their culture. Second, diffusion sometimes involves a transfer from a dominant culture to a less powerful culture. This process may occur through force or, more subtly, through education or marketing processes that promote the adoption of new practices and beliefs. Third, a more powerful culture may appropriate aspects of a less powerful culture, through cultural imperialism. Lastly, a less powerful and even oppressed cultural group often provides sources of cultural change in a dominant culture.

Changes in a minority culture that make it more like the dominant culture are referred to as **acculturation**. In extreme cases, a culture becomes so thoroughly acculturated that it has experienced **assimilation**, or deculturation—that is, it is no longer distinguishable as having a separate identity. In the most extreme cases, the impact on the minority culture is that it becomes extinct. These processes parallel degrees of language change resulting from contact with dominating cultures and languages. Such changes have occurred among many indigenous people as the result of globalization and the introduction of new technology (see Anthropology Works). Other responses to acculturative influences include the partial acceptance of something new

---

invention the discovery of something new.

diffusion the spread of culture through contact.

acculturation a form of cultural change in which a minority culture becomes more like the dominant culture.

assimilation a form of cultural change in which a culture is thoroughly acculturated, or decultured, and is no longer distinguishable as having a separate identity.

Anthropology Works

The Saami, Snowmobiles, and Social Impact Analysis

How might the adoption of a new belief or practice benefit or harm a particular culture and its various members? Although often difficult to answer, this question must always be asked. A classic study of the snowmobile disaster among a Saami group in Finland offers a careful response to the question in a context of rapid technological diffusion (Pelto 1973).

In the 1950s, the Saami (review Culturama, Chapter 9, page 000) had an economy based on reindeer herding, which provided most of their diet. Besides supplying meat, reindeer had other important economic and social functions. They were used as draft animals, especially for hauling wood for fuel. Their hides were made into clothing and their sinews used for sewing. Reindeer were key items of exchange in both external trade and internal gift-giving. Parents gave a child a reindeer to mark the appearance of the child's first tooth. When a couple became engaged, they exchanged a reindeer with each other to mark the commitment.

By the 1960s, all this had changed because of the introduction of the snowmobile. Previously, people herded the reindeer herds on skis. The use of snowmobiles for herd management had several unintended and interrelated consequences, all of which were detrimental to the herding way of life.

First, the herds were no longer kept domesticated for part of the year, a practice during which they became tame. Instead, they were allowed to roam freely all year and thus became wilder. Second, snowmobiles allowed herders to cover larger amounts of territory at roundup time and to do more than one roundup. As the number of snowmobiles increased, herd sizes declined dramatically. The reasons for the decline included the stress inflicted on the reindeer by the extra distance traveled during roundups, the multiple roundups instead of a single one, and the fear aroused by the noisy snowmobiles. Furthermore, roundups were held at a time when the females were near the end of their pregnancies, a factor that induced reproductive stress.

Negative economic changes occurred, including a new dependence on the outside through the cash economy. Cash is needed to purchase a snowmobile, buy gasoline, and pay for parts and repairs. This delocalization of the economy created social inequality, which had not existed before. Other economic and related repercussions ensued as well:

- The cash cost of effective participation in herding exceeded the resources of some families, which then had to drop out of participation in herding.

- The snowmobile pushed many Saami into debt.

A Saami herder riding a skidoo in northern Norway leads his herd.

- Dependence on cash and indebtedness forced many Saami to migrate to cities for work.

Snowmobiles also changed Saami gender relations by increasing the prominence of young men in herding (Larsson 2005). Before the snowmobiles, reindeer herding was a family operation. Although men did more of the long-distance herding, women also worked closely with the herd. After snowmobiles were adopted, parents began steering their sons toward herding and their daughters toward education and professional careers. Two rationales for such gender tracking are that driving a snowmobile is difficult because the vehicle is heavy and that the driver may get stuck somewhere. The use of snowmobiles also changed the age pattern of reindeer herding in favor of youth over age; thus, older herders were squeezed out.

Pertti Pelto, the anthropologist who first documented this case among the Saami of Finland, calls these transformations a disaster for Saami culture (1973). He offers a recommendation for the future: Communities confronting the adoption of new technology should have a chance to weigh evidence on the pros and cons and make an informed judgment. Pelto's work is one of the early warnings from anthropology about the need for a **social impact assessment**—a study that attempts to predict the potential social costs and benefits of particular innovations before change is undertaken.

---

social impact assessment a study conducted to predict the potential social costs and benefits of particular innovations before change is undertaken.

Food for Thought

If you were a Saami herder, what would you have done if you had been able to consider a social impact assessment of the effects of snowmobiles?

with localization and syncretism, as in the case of the game of cricket in the Trobriand Islands (Chapter 11), or rejection and resistance.

Theories and Models of Development

This subsection reviews theories and models of development and the various kinds of institutions involved in development. It then examines development projects and how anthropologists work with, or sometimes against, those projects.

No single view of development or how to achieve it exists. Debates about these issues are heated and involve experts from many disciplines and governments and local people worldwide. Five theories or models of development are presented here. They differ in terms of the following characteristics:

- The definition of development
- The goal of development
- Measures of development
- Attention to environmental and financial sustainability

MODERNIZATION Modernization is a form of change marked by economic growth through industrialization and market expansion, political consolidation through the state, technological innovation, literacy, and options for social mobility. It originated in Western Europe in the beginning of the seventeenth century with the emerging emphasis on secular rationality and scientific thinking as the pathways to progress (Norgaard 1994). Given the insights of rationality and science, modernization is thought to spread inevitably throughout the world and lead to improvement in people's lives everywhere. The major goals of modernization are material progress and individual betterment.

Supporters and critics of modernization are found in both high-income and low-income countries. Supporters claim that the benefits of modernization (improved transportation, electricity, biomedical health care, and telecommunications) are worth the costs to the environment and society.

Others take a critical view and regard modernization as problematic because of its focus on ever-increasing consumption levels and heavy use of nonrenewable resources. Many cultural anthropologists are critical of Westernization and modernization because their research shows how modernization often brings environmental ruin, increases social inequality, destroys indigenous cultures, and reduces global cultural and biological diversity. In spite of strong cautionary

critiques from anthropologists, environmentalists, and others about the detrimental effects of modernization, most countries worldwide have not slowed their attempts to achieve it. Some governments and citizen groups, however, are promoting lifestyles that rely less on nonrenewable resources and include a concern for protecting the environment.

GROWTH-ORIENTED DEVELOPMENT Development as "induced" change, brought about through applying modernization theory in so-called developing countries, emerged after World War II. At that time, the United States began to expand its role as a world leader, and aid for development was part of its international policy agenda. International development, as defined by major Western development institutions, is similar to modernization in terms of its goals. The process emphasizes economic growth as the most crucial element. According to the growth-oriented development theory, investments in economic growth will lead to improved human welfare through the trickle-down effect: the gradual increase in wealth among the less well-off as it filters down from the more well-off.

Promoting economic growth in developing countries includes two strategies:

- Increasing economic productivity and trade through modernized agriculture and manufacturing and through participation in world markets.

Schoolgirls in Bhutan. The government of Bhutan rejects the Western concept of gross domestic product (GDP) as the best measure of a country's success and instead uses a measurement called gross domestic happiness (GDH).

---

modernization a model of change based on belief in the inevitable advance of science and Western secularism and processes, including industrial growth, consolidation of the state, bureaucratization, a market economy, technological innovation, literacy, and options for social mobility.

Scenes of Kerala. (LEFT) Children attending school via boat in the interior of the state. (RIGHT) Fishing nets on the coast.

■ *Learn more about Kerala and prepare a briefing memo on it for the class with attention to how Kerala differs socially from northern India.*

- Reducing government expenditures on public services such as schools and health to reduce debt and reallocate resources to increase productivity. This strategy, called structural adjustment, has been promoted by the World Bank since the 1980s.

One measure for assessing the achievement of development through this model is the rate of growth of the economy, especially the gross domestic product or GDP.

DISTRIBUTIONAL DEVELOPMENT Distributional development contrasts with growth-oriented development in its emphasis on social equity in benefits, especially in terms of increased income, literacy, and health. It rejects the trickle-down process as ineffective in reaching poor people. Its position is based on evidence that growth-oriented strategies, applied without concern for distribution, actually increase social inequality. In this view, the growth model ensures that "the rich get richer and the poor get poorer."

The distributional approach opposes structural adjustment policies because they further undermine the welfare of the poor by removing the few entitlements they had in the form of services. Advocates of the distributional model see the need for benevolent governments to ensure equitable access to crucial resources to enhance the ability of the poor to provide for their own needs (Gardner and Lewis 1996).

Although conservative, neoliberal economists argue that redistribution is neither realistic nor feasible, supporters of the distributive approach point to cases that have worked. As an example, anthropological research in a village in central Kerala (CARE-uh-luh), a state in southern India (Map 13.2), assessed whether redistribution was an effective development strategy (Franke 1993). The findings showed the answer to be affirmative. Even though Kerala's per capita income is the lowest of any state in India, it has the highest social indicators in the country in health and literacy.

Government attention to distribution in Kerala came about through democratic channels, including demonstrations and pressure on the government by popular

Map 13.2 Kerala, South India

With a population of 344 million, Kerala has living standards, literacy rates, and health indicators that are high compared with the rest of India. Kerala comprises 14 districts and three historical regions: Travancore in the south, Kochi in the central part, and Malabar in the north. Long a socialist democracy, Kerala now allows the free market and foreign direct investment to play larger roles. A major tourist destination because of its tropical ecology and cultural features such as dramatic martial arts and theater, Kerala also hosts a growing Ayurvedic health tourism industry along its coast.

movements and labor unions. These groups forced the state to reallocate land ownership, thereby alleviating social inequality somewhat. In other instances, people pressured government leaders to improve village conditions by providing school lunches for low-income children, increasing school attendance by dalit children (review Chapter 7), and investing in school facilities. Through public action, Nadur village became a better place to live for many people.

HUMAN DEVELOPMENT Another alternative to the growth-first model is called human development, the strategy that emphasizes investing in human welfare. The United Nations adopted the phrase "human development" to emphasize the need for improvements in human welfare in terms of health, education, and personal security and safety. In this model, investments in improving human welfare will lead to economic development. The reverse is not invariably true: The level of economic growth of a country (or region within a country) is not necessarily correlated with its level of human development, as is clear from the case of Kerala. Thus, in this view, economic growth is neither an end in itself nor even a necessary component of development as measured by human welfare. Economic resources, combined with distributive policies, are a strong basis for attaining high levels of human development.

SUSTAINABLE DEVELOPMENT Sustainable development refers to forms of improvement that do not destroy nonrenewable resources and are financially supportable over time. Advocates of sustainable development argue that the economic growth of wealthy countries has been, and still is, costly in terms of the natural environment and people whose lives depend on fragile ecosystems. They say that such growth cannot be sustained at even its present level, not to mention projected demands as more countries become industrialized.

Institutional Approaches to Development

Cultural anthropologists are increasingly aware of the importance of examining the institutions, organizations, and specialists involved in development policy making, programs, and projects. With this knowledge, cultural anthropologists have a better chance of shaping development policies and programs. Institutional research includes studying the management systems of both large-scale institutions such as the World Bank and small-scale organizations in diverse settings. Topics include behavior within the institutions, social interactions with the "client population," and institutional discourse. This

section describes first some large development institutions and then some smaller organizations.

LARGE-SCALE DEVELOPMENT INSTITUTIONS Two major types of large-scale development institutions exist. First are the multilateral institutions—those that include several countries as "donor" members. Second are the bilateral institutions—those that involve only two countries: a "donor" and a "recipient."

The largest multilaterals are the United Nations and the World Bank. Each is a vast and complex social system. The United Nations, established in 1945, includes more than 160 member states. Each country contributes money according to its ability, and each has one vote in the General Assembly. Several United Nations agencies exist, fulfilling a range of functions, such as the United Nations Development Programme (UNDP), the Food and Agriculture Organization (FAO), the World Health Organization (WHO), the United Nations Children's Fund (UNICEF), the United Nations Educational, Scientific, and Cultural Organization (UNESCO), and the United Nations High Commissioner for Refugees (UNHCR).

The World Bank is supported by contributions from over 150 member countries. Founded in 1944, the World Bank is dedicated to promoting the concept of economic growth worldwide. Its main strategy is to promote international investment through loans. The World Bank is guided by a board of governors made up of the finance ministers of member countries. The World Bank system assigns each country a number of votes based on the size of its financial commitment. The economic superpowers, therefore, dominate.

The World Bank group includes the International Bank for Reconstruction and Development (IBRD) and the International Development Association (IDA). Both are administered at the World Bank headquarters in Washington, DC. They lend for similar types of projects and often in the same country, but their loan conditions differ. The IBRD provides loans, with interest, to governments in middle- and low-income countries that are called "credit worthy," that is, they are fairly good investment risks. The IDA, on the other hand, provides interest-free loans and grants to governments of the world's lowest-income countries.

The World Bank group overall promotes change through capitalist-style economic growth models that involve investing in large infrastructure projects versus social projects such as health and schools in terms of overall loans amounts. The 50-year history of the World Bank group has been one of distancing itself from overtly "political" issues, including human rights. A recent ethnographic study conducted inside the World Bank reveals

World Bank headquarters in Washington, DC. The World Bank employs more than 10,000 people from over 160 countries. Two-thirds of its employees are based in Washington.

the internal culture of denying "political" roles while foregrounding supposedly "neutral" practices (Sarfaty 2012). Within the World Bank, a small group of human rights lawyers take a critical position to World Bank lending that, in fact, is in violation of human rights in client countries. The basic message is that there is no such thing as politically neutral lending by the World Bank.

Compared to the World Bank group, the other major development multilateral organizations are those of the United Nations (UN), a sprawling system that includes many units relevant to development, social protection including women and refugees, and cultural heritage. Within the UN group, the Scandinavian countries appear to play a larger role than in the World Bank group. These countries have, for example, promoted for more attention to gender equality through propositions such as the Convention on the Elimination of All Forms of Discrimination against Women (CEDAW), a landmark international agreement that affirms principles of fundamental human rights and equality for women around the world. So far, only a handful of the nearly 200 countries of the world have not ratified CEDAW, and one of them is the United States. Countries that ratify the CEDAW treaty commit to take action to end discrimination against women and girls and affirm principles of fundamental human rights and equality for women and girls. By not ratifying CEDAW, the United States stands with Afghanistan, Somalia, Iran, and a few other countries that are not willing to commit to gender equality.

Prominent bilateral institutions include the Japan International Cooperation Agency (JICA), the United States Agency for International Development (USAID), the Canadian International Development Agency (CIDA), Britain's Department for International Development (DFID), the Swedish Agency for International Development (SIDA), and the Danish Organization for International Development (DANIDA). These agencies vary in terms of the total size of their aid programs, the types of programs they support, and the proportion of aid disbursed as loans that have to be repaid with interest as opposed to aid disbursed as grants that do not require repayment. Compared to other bilaterals, USAID tends to give more loans (which must be repaid, with interest) than grants (which are more like gifts).

Loans and grants also differ in terms of whether they are tied or untied. Tied loans and grants require that a certain percentage of project expenditures go for goods, expertise, and services originating in the donor country. For example, a tied loan to a certain country for road construction would require allocating a designated percentage of the funds to donor country construction companies, to airfare for donor country road experts, and to in-country expenses, such as hotels, food, and local transportation, for donor country experts. When loans or grants are untied, the recipient country may decide freely how to use the funds. USAID offers more tied than untied aid, whereas countries such as Sweden, the Netherlands, and Norway tend to give untied aid.

Another difference among the bilaterals is the proportion of their total aid that goes to the lowest-income countries. The United Kingdom's DFID sends more than 80 percent of its aid to the poorest countries, whereas most of U.S. foreign aid dollars go to Egypt and Israel. Emphasis on certain types of aid also varies from one bilateral institution to another. Cuba has long played a unique role in bilateral aid, concentrating on aid for training health-care providers and for promoting preventive health care (Feinsilver 1993). Its development assistance goes to like-minded socialist countries, including many in Africa and in Latin America. Within Latin America, Brazil and Venezuela are taking on a visible role in development aid to neighboring countries, and they were among the earliest responders to the Haiti earthquake of January 2010.

GRASSROOTS APPROACHES Many countries have experimented with grassroots approaches to development, or locally initiated small-scale projects. This alternative to the top-down development pursued by the large-scale agencies described in the previous section is more likely to be culturally appropriate, supported through local participation, and successful.

The term **social capital** refers to the intangible resources that exist through social ties, trust, and cooperation. Many local grassroots organizations around the world use social capital to provide basic social needs, and they are successful even in the lowest-income countries (see Culturama).

Religious organizations sponsor a wide variety of grassroots development projects. In the Philippines, the Basic Ecclesiastical Community (BEC) movement is based on Christian teachings and follows the model of Jesus as a supporter of the poor and oppressed (Nadeau 2002) (see Map 5.1, page 92). BECs seek to follow the general principles of liberation theology, which blends Christian principles of compassion and social justice, political consciousness raising among the oppressed, and communal activism. In the rural areas, several BECs have successfully built trust among group members and leaders and developed people's awareness of the excesses of global capitalism and the dangers of private greed and accumulation. Part of their success is due to the fact that members were able to pursue new economic strategies outside the constraints of capitalism and that require little capital input, such as organic farming.

A BEC in Cebu City, on the Island of Cebu (suh-BOO), the Philippines, however, was unsuccessful. It faced the challenge of organizing people who make a living scavenging in a nearby city dump. Both adults and children scavenge for materials that are then sorted and sold for recycling, such as plastic. They work for 14 hours a day, seven days a week. It is an organized operation,

Scavenging for a livelihood in an urban dump in the Philippines.
■ *What kind of an entitlement is this?*

with district officials monitoring the dump. Customary arrangements among the scavengers regulate their work areas. Scavenging requires no formal education and few tools—just a basket and a steel hook, and a kerosene lantern for nighttime work. Scavengers earn more than other nonskilled laborers in the city. In the BEC meetings, the scavengers found little on which to build solidarity. Instead, they bickered with each other and complained about each other to the leaders. The sheer poverty of the people was so great that communal values could not compete against their daily economic struggle. In cases of extreme poverty with limited or no options for alternative forms of income generation, government programs may be required to complement faith-based, grassroots initiatives.

The Development Project

Development institutions, whether they are large multilaterals or local nongovernmental organizations (NGOs),

---

social capital the intangible resources existing in social ties, trust, and cooperation.

Culturama

Peyizan Yo of Haiti

Haiti and the Dominican Republic share the island of Hispaniola. Following the island's discovery by Columbus in 1492, Spanish colonialists exterminated the island's indigenous Arawak Indians. In 1697, the French took control of what is now Haiti and instituted an exceptionally cruel system of African plantation slavery. In the late 1700s, the half million slaves revolted. In what is the only successful slave revolution in history, they ousted the French and established the first Black republic in the Western Hemisphere.

Haiti's population of around 10 million people occupies a territory somewhat smaller than the state of Maryland in the United States. The land is rugged, hilly, or mountainous. More than 90 percent of the forests have been cleared.

In economic terms, Haiti is the lowest-income country in the Western Hemisphere. Extreme income inequality exists between the urban elite, who work and live in and near the capital city of Port-au-Prince, and everyone else. The people in the countryside are called *peyizan yo* (the plural form of

peyizan), a Creole term for small farmers who produce for their own use and for the market (Smith 2001). Many also participate in small-scale marketing. Most peyizan yo in Haiti own their land. They grow vegetables, fruits (especially mangoes), sugarcane, rice, and corn.

Haiti has the highest prevalence of HIV/AIDS of any country in the Caribbean region. Medical anthropologist Paul Farmer emphasizes the role of colonialism in the past and global structural inequalities now in causing these high rates (1992). In the nineteenth century, colonial plantation owners grew fabulously rich from this island. Haiti produced more wealth for France than all of France's other colonies combined and more than the 13 colonies in North America produced for Britain.

After the revolution, in 1804, Haiti became the first free country in Latin America and the first in the Western Hemisphere to abolish slavery. Yet, the heritage of colonialism left an imprint of rule by a few and the sheer act of abolishing slavery brought economic and political isolation from slave-holding

countries including the United States, which did not recognize Haiti until after the Civil War. Now, neocolonialism and globalization leave new scars. For decades, the United States has played a major role in supporting conservative political regimes. Powerful drug traffickers use Haiti's coastline as a haven for moving drugs from South America to markets in North America and Europe.

Although the United States and other rich countries pledged billions of dollars to help Haiti "build back better" after the 2010 earthquake, very little of the money pledged has found its way to Haiti, and of that, far less to the people in need.

Yet, the Haitian people—even those still living in camps—find hope and resilience in their families, their faith, and their cultural pride.

Thanks to Jennie Smith-Pariola, Berry College, for reviewing this material.

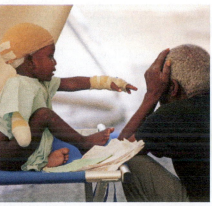

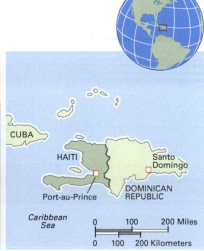

Map 13.3 Haiti

The Republic of Haiti occupies one-third of the Caribbean island of Hispaniola. The population of Haiti is around 10 million.

(LEFT) A woman repays her loan at a small-scale savings and loan business in rural Haiti. Many of the credit union members use their loans to set up small businesses.

(CENTER) A child injured in the January 2010 earthquake sits in a makeshift hospital tent. The 7.0 magnitude earthquake devastated the capital city of Port-au-Prince, killed an estimated 200,000 people, and displaced around 1.5 million people.

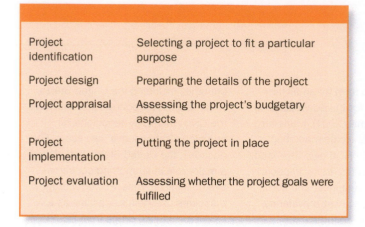

Project identification	Selecting a project to fit a particular purpose
Project design	Preparing the details of the project
Project appraisal	Assessing the project's budgetary aspects
Project implementation	Putting the project in place
Project evaluation	Assessing whether the project goals were fulfilled

Figure 13.1 **The Development Project Cycle**

implement their goals through the **development project**, a set of activities designed to put development policies into action. For example, suppose a government sets a policy of increased agricultural production by a certain percent within a designated period. A development project to achieve the policy goal might be the construction of irrigation canals that would supply water to a targeted number of farmers.

THE DEVELOPMENT PROJECT CYCLE Although details vary among organizations, all development projects have a **project cycle**, or the full process of a project from initial planning to completion (Cernea 1985). The project cycle includes five basic steps from beginning to end (Figure 13.1).

Since the 1970s, applied anthropologists have been involved in development projects. Early on, they were hired primarily to do project evaluations, to determine whether the project had achieved its goals. Their research shows that projects were often dismal failures (Cochrane 1979). Three major reasons for these failures are as follows:

- The project did not fit the cultural and environmental context.

- The project benefits did not reach the target group, such as low-income people in general or women specifically; instead, project benefits went to elites or some other less needy group.

- The intended beneficiaries were worse off after the project than before it.

One factor underlying these three problems is poor project design. The projects were designed by bureaucrats, usually Western economists, who lived in cities far from the project site with no firsthand experience of the lives of the target population. These experts applied a universal formula ("one size fits all") to all situations (Cochrane 2008). The cultural anthropologists who evaluated the projects, in contrast, knew the local people and context and

were therefore shocked by the degree of nonfit between the projects and the people.

Applied anthropologists gained a reputation in development circles as troublemakers—people to be avoided by those who favored a move-ahead approach to getting projects funded and implemented. Applied anthropologists are still considered a nuisance by many development policy makers and planners, but sometimes, at least, a necessary nuisance. On a more positive note, through persistent efforts they have made progress in gaining a role earlier in the project cycle, at the stages of project identification and design.

CULTURAL FIT A review of many development projects over the past few decades reveals the importance of **cultural fit**, or taking the local culture into account in project design (Kottak 1985). A glaring case of nonfit between a project and its target population is a project intended to improve nutrition and health in some South Pacific islands by promoting increased milk consumption (Cochrane 1974). The project involved the transfer of large quantities of powdered milk from the United States to an island community. The local people, however, were lactose intolerant (unable to digest raw milk), and they all soon had diarrhea. They stopped drinking the milk and used the powder to whitewash their houses. Beyond wasting resources, inappropriately designed projects result in the exclusion of the intended beneficiaries. Two examples are when a person's signature is required but the people do not know how to write and when photo identification cards are requested from Muslim women, whose faces may not be shown in public.

Applied anthropologists can provide insights into how to achieve cultural fit to enhance the success of a project. Anthropologist Gerald Murray played a positive role in redesigning a costly and unsuccessful reforestation project supported by USAID in Haiti (1987). Since the colonial era in Haiti (see Map 13.3, page 269), deforestation has been dramatic, with an estimated 50 million trees cut annually. Some of the deforestation is driven by the market demand for wood for construction and for charcoal in the capital city of Port-au-Prince. Another reason is that peyizan yo, or small farmers, need cleared land for growing crops and grazing their goats. The ecological consequences of so much clearing, however, are extensive erosion of the soil and declining fertility of the land.

development project a set of activities designed to put development policies into action.

project cycle the steps of a development project from initial planning to completion: project identification, project design, project appraisal, project implementation, and project evaluation.

cultural fit a characteristic of informed and effective project design in which planners take local culture into account.

In the 1980s, USAID sent millions of tree seedlings to Haiti and the Haitian government urged rural people to plant them. Peyizan yo, however, refused to plant the seedlings on their land and instead fed them to their goats. Murray, who had done his doctoral dissertation on rural Haitian land tenure practices, was called on by USAID to diagnose the problem and suggest an alternative approach. He advised that the kind of seedling promoted be changed from that of fruit trees, in which peyizan yo saw little benefit because they are not to be cut, to that of fast-growing trees, such as eucalyptus, which could be cut as early as four years after planting and sold in Port-au-Prince. Peyizan yo quickly accepted this plan because it would yield profits in the foreseeable future. The cultural nonfit was that USAID wanted trees to stay in place for many years, but peyizan yo viewed trees as things that were meant to be cut in the short term.

THE ANTHROPOLOGICAL CRITIQUE OF DEVELOPMENT PROJECTS The early decades of development anthropology were dominated by what I call **traditional development anthropology**. In traditional development anthropology, the anthropologist takes on a role of helping to make development policies and programs work better. It is the "add an anthropologist and stir" approach to development. Like good applied anthropology in any domain, traditional developmental anthropology does work. For example, an anthropologist familiar with a local culture can provide information about what kinds of consumer goods would be desired by the people or what might persuade people to relocate with less resistance. The anthropologist may act as a cultural broker, someone who uses knowledge of both the donor culture and the recipient culture to devise a workable plan.

Concern exists among many anthropologists about development projects that have negative effects on local people and their environments. For example, a comparison of the welfare of local inhabitants of the middle Senegal River Valley (Map 13.4) before and after the construction of a large dam shows that people's level of food insecurity increased after the dam was built (Horowitz and Salem-Murdock 1993). Before the dam, periodic flooding of the plain provided for a dense population supporting itself with agriculture, fishing, forestry, and herding. After the dam was constructed, water was released less often. The people downstream lacked sufficient water for their crops, and fishing was no longer a dependable source of food. At other times, dam managers released a large flood of water, damaging farmers' crops. Many downstream residents have had to leave the area because of the effects of the dam; they are victims of development-induced displacement (review Chapter 12). Downstream people now have high rates of schistosomiasis, a severely debilitating disease caused by parasites, because the disease spreads quickly in the slow-moving water below the dam.

Map 13.4 Senegal

The Republic of Senegal is mainly rolling sandy plains of the western Sahel. Senegal's economy is mainly agricultural, with peanuts being the main crop. Social inequality is extreme, and urban unemployment is high. The population of Senegal is 13 million, of which 70 percent live in rural areas. Of the many ethnic groups, the Wolof are the largest. Sufi Islam is the major religion, practiced by 94 percent of the population, with Christians making up 4 percent.

Other "dam stories" document the negative effects of dam construction on local people, including the destruction of their economy, social organization, sacred space, sense of home, and environment (Loker 2004). Such mega-projects force thousands, even millions, of people in the affected area to cope with the changes in one way or another. Many leave; others stay and try to replace what they have lost by clearing new land and rebuilding. Most end up in situations far worse than the one in which they lived originally.

The growing awareness of the detrimental effects of many supposedly positive development projects has led to the emergence of what I call **critical development anthropology**. In this approach, the anthropologist takes on a critical-thinking role. The question is not, What can

traditional development anthropology an approach to international development in which the anthropologist accepts the role of helping to make development work better by providing cultural information to planners.

critical development anthropology an approach to international development in which the anthropologist takes a critical-thinking role and asks why and to whose benefit particular development policies and programs are pursued.

I do to make this project successful? Instead, the anthropologist asks, Is this a good project from the perspective of the local people and their environment? If the answer is yes, then an applied anthropologist can take a supportive role. If the answer is no, then the anthropologist can intervene with relevant information, taking on the role of either a whistle-blower to stop the project or an advocate promoting ideas about how to change the project in order to mitigate harm. In the case of the Senegal River dam project, applied anthropologists worked in collaboration with engineers and local people to devise an alternative management plan for the water flow in which regular and controlled amounts of water were released. In many other cases, the process has a less positive outcome, with planners ignoring the anthropologist's advice (Loker 2000).

The baobob tree, also called the tree of life, is in danger throughout southern Africa. Baobabs support natural ecosystems from bugs to small animals. Humans use the bark to make rope, baskets, cloth, musical instrument strings, and waterproof hats. Fresh baobab leaves provide an edible vegetable similar to spinach which is also used medicinally. In Madagascar, for example, the expansion of intensive rice cultivation will bring the death of many baobab trees and threaten the habitats of wild animal species, including lemurs.

Assume that you have just been appointed as Madagascar's minister of people, nature, and development. What do you want your research staff to brief you about during your first month of service?

Development, Indigenous People, and Women

13.2 **Summarize how indigenous peoples and women are redefining development.**

This section considers two categories of people who are increasingly taking an active role in redefining development in their own terms: indigenous people and women. Although the categories overlap, the section presents material about them separately for purposes of illustration.

Indigenous People and Development

Indigenous peoples have been victimized by many aspects of growth-oriented development, as they were by colonialism before it. But now many indigenous groups are redefining development and taking it into their own hands.

As noted in Chapter 1, indigenous people are usually a numerical minority in the states that control their territory. The United Nations distinguishes between indigenous peoples and other minority groups such as African Americans, the Roma, and the Tamils of Sri Lanka. It is more useful to view all "minority" groups as forming a continuum, from purely indigenous groups to minority/ethnic groups that are not geographically original to a place but that share many problems with indigenous peoples as a result of displacement and living within a more powerful majority culture (Maybury-Lewis 1997b).

Indigenous peoples differ from most minorities in that they tend to occupy remote areas and, often, areas rich in natural resources. Remoteness has, to some extent, protected them from outsiders. Now, however, governments, international business, conservationists, and tourists increasingly recognize that the lands of these people contain valuable natural resources, such as gas in the circumpolar region, gold in Papua New Guinea and the Amazon, sapphires in Madagascar, hydroelectric potential in large rivers throughout the world, and cultural attractions.

Accurate statistics on indigenous populations do not exist. Several reasons account for this lack of information (Kennedy and Perz 2000). First, no one agrees about whom to count as indigenous. Second, some governments do not bother to conduct a census of indigenous people, or if they do, they may undercount indigenous people to downplay recognition of their existence. Third, it is often physically difficult, if not impossible, to carry out census operations in indigenous areas. The indigenous people of North Sentinel Island in India's Andaman Islands remain uncounted because Indian officials cannot land on the island without being shot at with arrows (Singh 1994).

The total number of indigenous people worldwide i around 400 million, or about five percent of the world's population (First Peoples Worldwide 2015). The greatest numbers are in Asia, including Central Asia, South Asia, East Asia, and Southeast Asia. Canada's First Nation population is under two million. The American Indian population in the United States numbers around 1 million.

INDIGENOUS PEOPLE AS VICTIMS OF COLONIALISM AND DEVELOPMENT Like colonialism, contemporary global and state political and economic interests often involve the takeover and control of indigenous people's territory. Over the past several hundred years, many indigenous groups and their cultures have been exterminated as a result of contact with outsiders. Death and population decline have resulted from contagious diseases, slavery, warfare, and other forms of violence. With colonialism, indigenous people experienced wholesale attacks as outsiders sought to take their land by force, prevented them from practicing their traditional lifestyles, and integrated them into the colonial state as marginalized subjects. The loss of economic, political, and expressive autonomy has had devastating physical and psychological effects on indigenous peoples. Reduction in the biodiversity of their natural environments is directly linked to impoverishment, despair, and overall cultural decline (Arambiza and Painter 2006; Maffi 2005). These processes are common worldwide, creating unforeseen new risks for indigenous people's welfare.

In Southeast Asia, states use policies of "planned resettlement" that displace indigenous people, or "hill tribes," in the name of progress (Evrard and Goudineau 2004). Development programs for the hill tribes in Thailand, for example, reveal the links among international interests, state goals, and the well-being of the tribes (Kesmanee 1994). The hill tribes include groups such as the Karen, Hmong, Mian, Lahu, Lisu, and Akha. They total about half a million people. International pressures are applied to have the hill tribes replace the cultivation of opium with other cash crops. International aid agencies therefore sponsor alternative agricultural projects and tourism. The Thai government, however, is more concerned with political stability and security in the area, given its strategic location, and therefore promotes development projects such as roads and markets to establish links between the highlands and the lowlands. Either way, the hill tribes are the target of outsiders' interests; thus, they face a challenge to the promotion of their own agendas.

Efforts to find viable substitute crops for opium have been unsuccessful, especially among the Hmong, who are most dependent on opium as a cash crop. Alternative crops require the heavy use of fertilizers and pesticides, which are costly to the farmers and greatly increase environmental pollution; moreover, such crops are less lucrative for the farmers. Logging companies have gained access to the hills and have done far more damage to the forests than the highlanders' horticultural practices have. Increased penetration of the hill areas by lowlanders and international tourists have promoted rising HIV/AIDS rates, illegal trafficking of girls and boys for sex, and opium addiction among the highlanders.

The Thai government, like the government of neighboring Laos, has attempted to relocate highland horticulturalists to the plains through various resettlement schemes. Highlanders who opt for relocation find the lowland plots to be unproductive because of poor soil quality. Relocated highlanders find that their quality of life and economic status decline in the lowlands. Yet another new risk for the resettlers in Thailand and Laos is that they are now heavy consumers of methamphetamines, an addictive, euphoria-inducing compound with serious negative side effects, such as rapid weight loss, tooth decay, diarrhea, nausea, and agitation (Lyttleton 2004). Overall, 50 years of so-called development have been disastrous for Southeast Asia's hill peoples.

INDIGENOUS PEOPLE AND TERRITORIAL ENTITLEMENTS Throughout their history of contact with the outside world, indigenous peoples have actively sought to resist the deleterious effects of "civilization." Since the 1980s, more effective and highly organized forms of protest have become prominent. Indigenous groups now hire lawyers and other experts as consultants to reclaim and defend their territorial rights, gain self-determination, and secure protection from outside risks. Many indigenous people have themselves become trained as lawyers, researchers, and advocates. Conflicts range from lawsuits to attempts at secession (Stidsen 2006).

This section provides an overview on the status of indigenous people's territorial rights claims. Within each large world region, country-by-country variation exists in legal codes and in the adherence to any such codes that may exist.

Latin America Few Latin American countries provide legal protection against encroachment on the land of indigenous groups. Nicaragua, Peru, Colombia, Ecuador, Bolivia, and Brazil have taken the lead in enacting policies that legitimize indigenous rights to land and in demarcating and titling indigenous territories (Stocks 2005). A wide gap often exists, however, between policy and actual protection. Despite these efforts, increasing numbers of Indians throughout the entire region of Latin America have been forced off their land in the past few decades through poverty, violence, and environmental degradation due to encroachment by logging companies, mining operations, ranch developers, and others. In response, many migrate to cities and seek wage labor. Those who remain face extreme poverty, malnutrition, and personal and group insecurities.

A surge of political activism by indigenous people has occurred since the 1990s, sometimes involving physical resistance. Violence continues to erupt between indigenous groups and state-supported power structures, especially in the southern Mexican state of Chiapas

Map 13.5 Nunavut Territory, Canada

Created in 1999, Nunavut is the newest and largest of Canada's territories. It is also the least populated, with 34,000 people. About 85 percent of the people are First Nations peoples, mainly Inuit. Official languages are Inuktitut, Inuinnaqtun, English, and French. The landscape is mainly Arctic tundra. The award-winning movie *Atanarjuat* (*The Fast Runner*) was produced by Inuit filmmakers and filmed in Nunavut.

(see Map 4.3, page 75). In 2005, participants at the First Symposium on Isolated Indigenous Peoples of the Amazon created a group called the International Alliance for the Protection of Isolated Indigenous Peoples. The group seeks to make the relevant state governments aware of the current endangered situation of many indigenous people. These people demand their right to isolation, if that is their choice, and to protection from unwelcome outside contact and encroachment. In 2008, the International Alliance of Forest Peoples formed to push for indigenous people's participation in global climate change talks and to devise a plan whereby wealthy countries would compensate developing countries for conserving tropical forests (Barrionuevo 2008).

Canada In Canada, the law distinguishes between two different types of Native Peoples and their land claims (Plant 1994). Specific claims concern problems arising from previous agreements or treaties, and comprehensive claims are those made by Native Peoples who have not been displaced and have made no treaties or agreements. Most of the former claims have led to monetary compensation. In the latter category, interest in oil and mineral exploration has prompted governments to negotiate with indigenous people in an effort to have the latter's native claims either relinquished or redefined. In some provinces, especially British Columbia, claims affect most of the province. The Nunavut land claim was settled, granting about 25,000 Inuit access to a vast tract of land, including subsurface rights (Jensen 2004) (Map 13.5).

Asia In Asia, most countries have been reluctant to recognize the territorial rights of indigenous people (Plant 1994). In Bangladesh, the Chittagong Hill Tracts area in the southeast is being massively encroached upon by settlers from the crowded plains region (see Map 7.1, page 133). Encroachers from the lowlands now occupy the most fertile land, and the indigenous people and their culture are endangered in many ways, including suffering loss of land and livelihood as well as new health threats. In Thailand, no legal recognition of hill tribes' land rights exists, whereas in Laos and Vietnam, some land has been allocated to indigenous communities (Jensen 2004:5). Indigenous people actively contesting the state's hold over land and resources in the Asia–Pacific region include the Moros of the southern Philippines (see Map 5.1, page 92) and the people of West Papua, the western part of the island of New Guinea controlled by Indonesia (see Map 1.3, page 18). In some cases, indigenous people's fight for secession from the state continues to cost many lives, mainly their own.

Africa   In Africa, political interests of state governments in establishing and enforcing territorial boundaries have created difficulties for indigenous peoples, especially mobile populations such as foragers and pastoralists. Many formerly autonomous pastoralists of the Sahel region (see Map 12.5, page 254) have been transformed into refugees living in terrible conditions. The Tuareg (TWAA-reg), for example, have traditionally lived and herded in a territory that crosses five different countries: Mali, Niger, Algeria, Burkina Faso, and Libya (Childs and Chelala 1994).

Because of political conflict in the region, thousands of Tuareg people live in exile in Mauritania, and their situation is grim. Resistance movements spring up, but states act to suppress them. The people of South Sudan have been living in violence for many years, even now that they have achieved independence from Sudan (Map 13.6). They have been subject to genocide and violent displacement for global and local political and economic reasons, not the least of which involves the rich deposits of oil in areas between Sudan and South Sudan (Warren 2001). As mentioned in the Culturama in Chapter 1 (page 18), South Africa has established more protective legislation for San peoples than have Namibia or Botswana, the other countries with San populations.

Australia and New Zealand   The picture is also mixed in Australia and New Zealand, with more progress in Australia in terms of legal recognition of Aboriginal territorial rights. Urban development, expansion of the non-Aboriginal population, road building, mineral extraction, and international tourism are some of the major threats to both livelihoods and the protection of sacred space. Aboriginal activism has seen some notable successes in achieving what is referred to as native title (Colley 2002). A key turning point in Australia occurred through the efforts of Eddie Koiko Mabo (koy-ko mah-bo), from the Torres Strait Islands. He and his group, the Miriam people, took their claim of

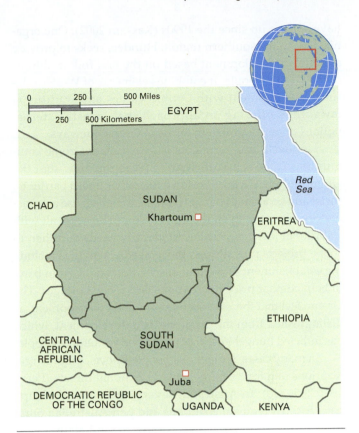

Map 13.6 Sudan and South Sudan

The former Republic of Sudan gained its independence from Britain in 1956. One year before that, a civil war began between the north and the south. In 2003, conflict erupted in the Darfur region. In 2005, a treaty granted southern Sudan the status of an autonomous region for six years, to be followed by a referendum. In 2011, the referendum strongly supported the creation of a separate country of South Sudan with its capital in Juba. Disputes continue between Sudan and South Sudan about the oil revenues, and disputes within South Sudan involve local tribal groups. Other differences relate to religion with Sunni Islam the dominant religion in Sudan while in South Sudan, indigenous religions and Christianity predominate. Arabic is the dominant language of Sudan. In South Sudan where indigenous languages predominate, English is the official language.

rights to their traditional land and water to the High Court, contesting the principle of terra nullius, or "empty land." Colonialists and neocolonialist developers use terra nullius to justify territorial takeovers, claiming that no one lives in a particular place because there is no evidence of property ownership, agriculture, or permanent structures. This claim justified the colonial takeover of large parts of the world occupied by foragers, horticulturalists, and pastoralists. In this landmark case, Mabo convinced the High Court of the legitimacy of the Miriams' claim in 1992 and set a precedent for a series of future land claims by indigenous peoples of Australia.

ORGANIZING FOR CHANGE   Many indigenous peoples have formed organizations for change to promote grassroots development, or development from within. In Ethiopia, for example, several NGOs organized by local people have sprung up since the 1990s (Kassam 2002). One organization in the southern region, Hundee, seeks to provide a model of development based on the oral folk traditions of the Oromo people. It combines elements of Western-defined development with Oromo values and traditional laws, thus offering an approach that recasts external notions of development in terms of Oromo lifeways.

Hundee's long-term goal is to empower Oromo communities to be self-sufficient. It takes the view that the Oromo culture is a positive force for, rather than a barrier to, social and economic change. Hundee members use a participatory approach in all their endeavors. They consult with traditional legal assemblies to identify needs and then to shape projects that address those needs. Activities include the establishment of a credit association and a grain bank to help combat price fluctuations and food shortages. The Oromo feel that these are elements of good development, as distinguished from the outsiders' bad development, which has inflicted hunger and dependency on the Oromo people.

In many cases, indigenous people's development organizations join forces in response to external threats (Perry 1996:245–246). In Australia, several indigenous groups have formed regional coalitions and pan-Australian organizations that have been successful in land claim cases. In Canada, the Grand Council of the Cree collaborates with other northern groups over land issues and opposition to a major hydroelectric dam project (Coon Come 2004; Craik 2004). Indigenous groups worldwide are taking advantage of new technology and media to build and maintain links with each other over large areas.

Although it is tempting to see hope in the newly emerging forms of resistance, self-determination, and organization among indigenous peoples, such hope cannot be generalized to all indigenous groups. While many are making progress in asserting their claims, and their economic status is improving, many others are suffering extreme political and economic repression and possible extinction.

Women and Development

The category of women contrasts with that of indigenous peoples because women, as a group, do not have a recognized territory associated with them. But the effects of colonialism, and now development, on women are similar to their effects on indigenous people: Women have often lost economic entitlements and political power in their communities. Matrilineal kinship, for example, which keeps property in the female line (review Chapter 6), is in decline throughout the world. Westernization and modernization are frequently the cause of this change. Another factor that has had a pervasive negative effect on women's status is the **male bias in development**, or the design and implementation of development projects with men as beneficiaries and without regard to their impact on women's roles and status.

In many countries, a small cookstove is still the main way that families prepare cooked meals. Women are the main users of these cookstoves, and often they are accompanied by small children. Most cookstoves are not fuel-efficient, and they create substantial air pollution. Researchers worldwide are trying to develop improved cookstoves.

THE MALE BIAS IN DEVELOPMENT In the 1970s, researchers began to notice and write about the fact that development projects were male biased (Boserup 1970; Tinker 1976). Many projects completely bypassed women as beneficiaries, targeting men for such initiatives as growing cash crops and learning about new technology. This male bias in development contributed to increased gender inequality by giving men greater access to new sources of income and by depriving women of their traditional economic roles. The development experts' image of a farmer, for example, was male, not female.

Women's projects were typically focused on the domestic domain—for example, infant feeding practices, child care, and family planning. This emphasis led to the domestication of women worldwide, meaning that their lives became more focused on the domestic domain and more removed from the public domain (Rogers 1979). For example, agricultural projects bypassed female horticulturalists, who were taught to spend more time in the house bathing their babies, and political leadership projects focused on men and left women out even in contexts where women traditionally had public political roles.

The male bias in development also contributed to the failure of some projects. In the West African country of Burkina Faso (see Map 12.5, page 254), a reforestation project included men as the sole participants, whose tasks would include planting and caring for the trees. Cultural patterns there, however, dictate that men do not water plants; women do. The men planted the seedlings and left

---

male bias in development the design and implementation of development projects with men as beneficiaries and without regard to the impact of the projects on women's roles and status.

them. Excluding women from the project ensured its failure. The exclusion of women from development continues to be a problem, in spite of many years of attempting to keep women's roles on the development agenda.

The inclusion of women's knowledge, concerns, and voices in research has brought new and important issues to the fore, redefining development to fit women's needs (Figure 13.2). One such issue is gender-based violence. This issue has gained attention even among large multilateral organizations, whose experts now realize that women cannot participate in a credit program, for example, if they fear that their husbands will beat them for leaving the house. The United Nations Commission on the Status of Women drafted a declaration in opposition of violence against women that was adopted by the General Assembly in 1993 (Heise, Pitanguy, and Germain 1994). Article 1 of the declaration states that violence against women includes "any act of gender-based violence that results in, or is likely to result in, physical, sexual or psychological harm or suffering to women, including threats of such acts, coercion or arbitrary deprivations of liberty, whether occurring in public or private life" (Economic and Social Council 1992). This definition cites women as the focus of concern but also includes girls.

WOMEN'S ORGANIZATIONS FOR CHANGE In many countries, women have improved their status and welfare through forming organizations, which are sometimes part of their traditional culture and sometimes a response to outside inspiration. These organizations range from mothers' clubs that help provide for communal child care to credit organizations that give women opportunities to start their own businesses. Some are local and small scale; others are global, such as Women's World Banking, an international organization that started in India and

In the town of San Cristóbal de las Casas, the capital city of Chiapas state in Mexico, a Maya vendor sells her goods. The city is located near the Tzotzil Maya community of Zinacantán.

Bangladesh and grew out of credit programs for low-income working women.

In another case, an informal system of social networks emerged to help support poor Maya women vendors in San Cristóbal, Chiapas, Mexico (Sullivan 1992) (see Map 4.3, page 75). Many of the vendors who work in the city square have fled from the highlands because of long-term political conflict there. They manufacture and sell goods to tourists, earning an important portion of household income. In the city, they find social support in an expanded network that helps compensate for the loss of support from the extensive godparenthood system (review Chapter 6) of the highlands. The vendors' new networks include relatives, neighbors, church members, and other vendors, regardless of their religious, political, economic, or social background.

The networks first developed in response to a series of rapes and robberies that began in 1987. Because the offenders were persons of power and influence, the women did not dare to press charges. Mostly single mothers and widows, they adopted a strategy of self-protection. First, they began to gather during the slow period each afternoon. Second, they always travel in groups. Third, they carry sharpened corset bones and prongs: "If a man insults one of them, the group surrounds him and jabs him in the groin" (Sullivan 1992: 39–40). Fourth, if a woman is robbed, the other women surround her, comfort her, and help contribute something toward compensating her for her loss. The mid-afternoon gatherings developed into support groups that provide financial assistance, child care, medical advice, and training in job skills. The groups have publicly demonstrated against city officials' attempts to prevent them from continuing their vending. Through their collective efforts, they have succeeded in bringing greater security into their lives.

A last example of women's empowerment and personal risk reduction through organized efforts comes from Kazakhstan, Central Asia (see Map 8.2, page 163). In response to the widespread domestic violence of

Prebirth	Sex-selective abortion, battering during pregnancy, coerced pregnancy
Infancy	Infanticide, emotional and physical abuse, deprivation of food and medical care
Girlhood	Child marriage, genital mutilation, sexual abuse by family members and strangers, rape, deprivation of food and medical care, child prostitution
Adolescence	Dating and courtship violence, forced prostitution, rape, sexual abuse in the workplace, sexual harassment
Adulthood	Rape and partner abuse, partner homicide, sexual abuse in the workplace, sexual harassment
Old Age	Abuse and neglect of widows, elder abuse

Source: Adapted from Heise, Pitanguy, and Germain 1994:5.

Figure 13.2 Violence against Girls and Women throughout the Life Cycle

Grameen Bank, a development project launched in Bangladesh, provides small loans to poor people, especially poor women. It has turned out to be, overall, very successful, and the model has spread to other countries around the world. Its founder, Muham-mad Yunus, is a Bangladeshi economist and recipient of the Nobel Peace Prize in 2006.

How does the success of Grameen Bank cause you to question your previous image of Bangladesh?

husbands against wives, an NGO called the Society of Muslim Women (SMW) defines domestic violence as a problem that the Islamic faith should address at the grass-roots level (Snajdr 2005). The organization declines to work with the police and civic activists, who provide secular responses that involve criminalization of the offense, arrest of offenders, and other public procedures. Instead, SMW views domestic violence as a private matter that should be dealt with by using Islamic and Kazakh values. Its three approaches are counseling and shelter for abused women and couples' mediation. SMW's guiding principle is to find a way, if possible, to rebuild the family, something that may sound conservative, and even dangerous, in a situation where wife abuse is reported to occur in four out of five mar-riages. Yet, without funding or professional training, SMW members have provided support for countless women. They help the women overcome isolation by offering shelter, which conforms to the Kazakh custom of hospitality and the Mus-lim virtue of patience. SMW support gives the spouse time to think about their relationship and shifts blame from the vic-tim by invoking Islamic values of familial commitment and gender equality. Nationalist rhetoric shifts blame for men's alcoholism from the individual to the Russian occupation. Thus, SMW works within the bounds of Kazakh culture and uses that culture for positive outcomes within those bounds.

Urgent Issues in Development

13.3 **Identify urgent issues in development.**

This chapter opens with a quotation about the people of Walpole Island Reservation in Canada and their ongoing attempt to recover from the damage that colonialism and

neocolonialism have wreaked on their culture and natu-ral environment. In spite of much progress of local peo-ple and women in redefining development to improve their lives, rather than the lives of external groups such as international businesses and neocolonial states, the bulk of "development" money still goes for mega-projects that do more for people who already have resources than for those with few or no resources.

As discussed earlier in the chapter, development projects are the main mechanism through which development insti-tutions implement their goals. These projects are typically designed by outsiders, often with little local knowledge, and they follow a universal, one-size-fits-all pattern. They range from mega-projects such as massive dams to small projects, with the former being much more damaging to local people than the latter. The so-called beneficiaries or target popu-lation are often not consulted at all about projects that will affect their community. Critics of such externally imposed and often damaging initiatives refer to them as **develop-ment aggression**, the imposition of development projects and policies without the free, prior, and informed consent of the affected people (Tauli-Corpuz 2005). Such development violates the human rights of local people, including their right to pursue a livelihood in their homeland and to pre-vent environmental destruction of their territory. It also con-tributes nothing to prevent or alleviate poverty.

Life Projects and Human Rights

Moving beyond critique, indigenous people, women, and others who are victimized by development aggression are redefining what should be done to improve their lives or

---

development aggression the imposition of development projects and policies without the free, prior, and informed consent of the affected people.

 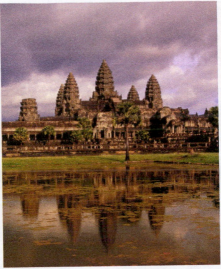 

These World Heritage Sites both benefit and suffer from the designation because of the many tourists drawn to them. (LEFT) Located high in the Peruvian Andes, the fifteenth-century palace complex at Machu Picchu (mah-choo pee-choo) was designated a World Heritage Site in 1983. (CENTER) Angkor Wat, which means "The Temple City," was designated a World Heritage Site in 1983. It was built in the twelfth century as a Hindu temple, but later additions to it were Buddhist. Current tourist numbers are harming the site due to trash, pedestrian traffic, and hotel development. In 1983, fewer than 8,000 tourists visited the site. Projections starting with 2010 are three million and more per year. (RIGHT) Gondolas on the Grand Canal, Venice, Italy. Venice, or Venezia in Italian, is considered to be one of the world's most beautiful cities. It was designated a World Heritage Site in 1987.

Plan a trip to one of these sites and learn whether "green" options exist for accommodations, or if the sites otherwise promote ways to reduce damage from tourists.

protect them from further decline. They propose the concept of the life project rather than the development project. A **life project** is local people's vision of the direction they want to take in life, informed by their knowledge, history, and context, and how to achieve that vision.

Life projects can be considered a human right and thus in accord with the United Nations' Declaration of Human Rights that was ratified in 1948. Development that leads to environmental degradation, including loss of biological diversity, air and water pollution, deforestation, and soil erosion, is a human rights abuse. Many examples exist worldwide of how rich natural resources are improperly exploited to the gain of a few and the detriment of many, turning what could be a blessing into a curse (see Eye on the Environment).

The major extractive industries of mining, oil, and gas are driven by the profit motive to the extent that they are disinclined to take local people's interests and environmental concerns seriously. An **extractive industry** is a business that explores for, removes, processes, and sells minerals, oil, and gas that are found on or beneath the earth's surface and are nonrenewable. The many tragic cases of local violence around the world where local people seek to prevent or remove an extractive industry project from their land, however, have been a wake-up call to some companies. Rio Tinto, one of the largest mining companies in the

world, seeks to use cultural anthropology expertise to find ways to treat "affected peoples" more fairly and to do a better job of ensuring that environmental "mitigation" will occur once a mine is closed (Cochrane 2008).

What drives extractive industries to continue to explore for gold, drill for oil, and cut down trees? What drives countries to build mega-dams and mega-highways? The demand lies with all of us, in our consumerist lifestyle that requires diamonds for engagement rings, gold and platinum for computers and gold and copper for cell phones, electrical power for air conditioning, and fuel to transport us, our food and water, and everything else we buy. Entire mountains in West Virginia are being leveled to provide coal to power the air conditioning used in Washington, DC. Forests in Brazil and New Guinea are taken down so that we can read the newspaper. Corn is being harvested to move vehicles rather than to feed people, and millions of gallons of water are being used to process minerals such as aluminum, rather than being available for human drinking, bathing, and swimming, or for fish and waterfowl. It will take a lot to turn this pattern around from destructive projects to life projects.

Cultural Heritage, Human Rights, and Development: Linking the Past and Present to the Future

Chapter 11 discussed the potential of cultural heritage, both tangible and intangible, in creating employment opportunities for local people through cultural tourism.

life project local people's definition of the direction they want to take in life, informed by their knowledge, history, and context.

extractive industry a business that explores for, removes, processes, and sells minerals, oil, and gas that are found on or beneath the earth's surface and which are nonrenewable.

Eye on the Environment

Oil, Environmental Degradation, and Human Rights in the Niger Delta

During the British colonial era, Nigeria provided wealth for the Crown through the export of palm oil (Osha 2006). In the post-colonial era of globalization, a different kind of oil dominates the country's economy: petroleum. Starting in the 1950s, with the discovery of vast petroleum reserves in Nigeria's Delta region, several European and American companies have explored for, drilled for, and exported crude oil to the extent that Nigeria occupies an important position in the world economy.

(LEFT) A farmer walks through an oil-soaked field. About 500,000 Ogoni people live in Ogoniland, a deltaic region in southern Nigeria. The fertility of the Niger delta has supported farming and fishing populations at high density for many years. Since Shell discovered oil there in 1958, 100 oil wells were constructed in Ogonil and countless oil spills have occurred. (RIGHT) Ogoni author and activist Ken Saro-Wiwa founded the Movement for Survival of Ogoni People (MOSOP) in 1992 to protest Shell's actions in Ogoniland and the Nigerian government's indifference. In 1995, he was arrested, tried for murder under suspicious circumstances, and executed by hanging. Shell has denied any role in his death.

This section goes more deeply into the complicated connections between cultural heritage and improving people's welfare from a life project perspective.

The connection of cultural heritage tourism to development is a double-edged sword, with both benefits and costs (Bauer 2006). Promoting cultural heritage through tourism requires an expansion of supportive infrastructure such as roads and hotels and electricity, the provision of food and other supplies for tourists, and labor to provide services for tourists. Thus, at the same time that it generates revenue, such tourism can preserve and protect cultural heritage, but the presence of the tourism industry and the tourists themselves may damage and even destroy it. Such famous World Heritage Sites as Angkor Wat in Cambodia and Machu Picchu in Peru are physically suffering the strains of huge numbers of tourists. Venice, the world's most touristed city, is also a World Heritage Site. Given its particular attraction as a city of canals, it is at particular risk of overload and environmental degradation from the ever-increasing number of tourist boats in the canals, not to mention the massive amount of solid and liquid trash that tourists leave behind (Davis and

Most local people in the delta, however, have gained few economic benefits from the oil industry and instead have reaped major losses in their agricultural and fishing livelihoods due to environmental pollution. They are poorer now than they were in the 1960s. In addition to economic suffering, they have lost personal security. Many have become victims of the violence that has increased in the region since the 1990s through state and corporate repression of a local resistance movement. Many others have become IDPs (review Chapter 14), leaving the delta region to escape the pervasive violence.

The Ogoni, who live in the southeastern portion of the delta, are one of the most negatively affected groups. Ogoni author Ken Saro-Wiwa founded the Movement for Survival of the Ogoni People (MOSOP) in 1992 to protest Shell's actions in Ogoniland and the Nigerian government's militarized repression in the region. In 1995, he and eight other Ogoni activists were arrested, tried under suspicious circumstances, and executed by hanging.

In a 1992 speech to the United Nations Working Group on Indigenous Populations, Saro-Wiwa eloquently points to the connections among resource extraction, the environment, and Ogoni human rights and social justice:

> Environmental degradation has been a lethal weapon in the war against the indigenous Ogoni people. . . . Oil exploration has turned Ogoni into a wasteland: lands, streams, and creeks are totally and continually polluted; the atmosphere has been poisoned, charged as it is with hydrocarbon vapors, methane, carbon monoxide, carbon dioxide, and soot emitted by gas which has been flared 24 hours a day for 33 years in close proximity to human habitation. . . . All one sees and feels around is death. (quoted in Sachs 1996:13–16)

Many social scientists agree with Saro-Wiwa that such forms of development violate human and cultural rights because they undermine a people's way of life and threaten its continued existence (Johnston 1994).

Food for Thought

Use the Internet to explore the concept of corporate social responsibility, and be prepared to discuss its relationship to the Ogoni situation.

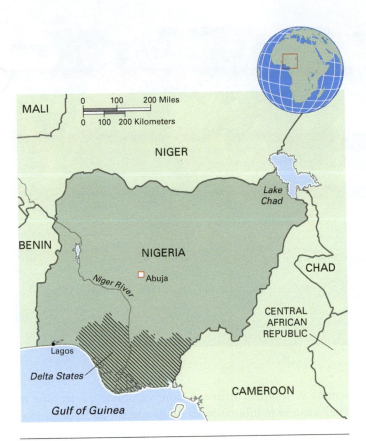

Map 13.7 **Nigeria and the Niger Delta**

Nigeria is the most populous country in Africa, with over 140 million people. It has more than 250 ethnic groups, with the largest being the Fulani, Hausa, Yorùbà, and Igbo. Nigerians speak over 500 languages; English is the official language. Nigeria is Africa's biggest petroleum producer, with an average of two million barrels a day extracted in the Niger Delta. The delta makes up 7.5 percent of Nigeria's landmass, but its population of 31 million accounts for 22 percent of the population. The Niger Delta's petroleum industry supports a high economic growth rate for the country, making it one of the fastest growing economies in the world. Yet little of this wealth filters back to the local people of the delta, who bear the brunt of the environmental and cultural damage caused by the petroleum industry. Oil spills are a frequent problem. One of the world's richest wetlands and richest areas of cultural diversity, with over 40 ethnic groups, is endangered by large-scale petroleum mining that benefits people in the capital city and in other countries.

Marvin 2004). Although promotional literature advertising Venice to tourists shows a romantic scene of a couple in a gondola or sitting alone in the Piazza San Marco, the reality is that the couple would be surrounded by crowds of tourists and heckled by ambitious local entrepreneurs.

A growing area related to cultural heritage preservation is cultural property rights law. Lawyers worldwide are increasingly involved in providing legal definitions and protections of rights to various forms of cultural knowledge and behavior. The legalization of culture is another double-edged sword: On one hand, laws may help

people, such as the San of southern Africa, to gain a share of the profits from the hoodia plant. On the other hand, the legalization of culture can transform much of everyday life into a legal battle requiring expensive legal specialists. For thousands of years, the San had full and unquestioned entitlement to hoodia and its benefits. They did not need to hire international lawyers.

Everything from website addresses that may use tribal names to the designation of what is or is not champagne can now become grounds for litigation. And money, you can be sure, is involved from the start to the finish, as is

Haitian dancers perform on Discover Miami Day at Miami's Little Haiti Caribbean Marketplace. Haitian culture in Miami is an increasingly popular tourist attraction.

the more difficult to quantify sense of identity of people who define themselves in relation to a place, a product, or a taste.

Cultural Anthropology and the Future

Over the next several years, culture will be a major factor in international, regional, and local development and change. Determining how knowledge in cultural anthropology can contribute more effectively to a better future for humanity is a challenge for a field with its intellectual roots in studying what is rather than what might be. You can be part of the future. A timely publication in how to find a career in international development and humanitarian assistance provides step-by-step ideas including taking courses, preparing your cover letter and resume, and doing an internship and volunteering (Gedde 2015).

Just as local people everywhere are redefining development and reclaiming their culture, so are they also helping to redefine the theory, practice, and application of cultural anthropology. Although we live in a time of ongoing war, it is also a time of hope, in which insights and strength often come from those with the least in terms of material wealth but with cultural wealth beyond measure.

13 Learning Objectives Revisited

13.1 Identify what is development and approaches to it.

Several theories or models of development exist, including modernization, growth-oriented development, distributional development, human development, and sustainable development. They differ in terms of how they define development and how to achieve it.

Institutional approaches to development, whether pursued by large-scale or grassroots organizations, tend to rely on the development project as a vehicle of local change. Cultural anthropologists have been hired as consultants on development projects, typically at the end of the project cycle to provide evaluations. Anthropologists have pushed for involvement earlier in the project so that their cultural knowledge can be used in project planning to avoid common errors. A one-size-fits-all project design often results in failed projects.

In traditional development anthropology, anthropological knowledge contributes to a development project by adding insights that will make the project work. In critical development anthropology, anthropological knowledge may suggest that the most socially beneficial path is either to stop the project or to redesign it.

13.2 Summarize how indigenous peoples and women are redefining development.

Indigenous people and women have been affected by international development in various ways, often negatively. They are taking an increasingly active role in redefining development to better suit their vision of the future.

Colonialism, neocolonialism, and globalization have eroded the entitlements of indigenous peoples and women worldwide. Often, such losses are tied to environmental degradation and violence. Indigenous peoples throughout the world suffer because they lack a secure claim to their ancestral territories. They seek social recognition of territorial claims from state governments and protection from encroachment. Some governments are responding to their claims; others are not. Establishing activist organizations has been a major source of strength for promoting indigenous people's rights.

Western development planning and projects have long suffered from a male bias in project design. Excluding women from projects serves to domesticate women and often results in failed projects. Women are stating their needs and visions for the future, thus redefining development in ways that are helpful to them. They have added the issue of violence against women and girls to the policy agendas of development institutions worldwide, including the large multilateral organizations.

13.3 **Identify urgent issues in development.**

Three urgent issues, as informed by cultural anthropology and the views and voices of people themselves, are the redefinition of development projects as life projects, or people-centered projects; the relationship between human rights and development; and the role of cultural heritage in development. Indigenous people, women, and others adversely affected by certain forms of development are promoting these new kinds of development to enhance their prospects for the future.

The concept of the life project is a human right and a right to live in one's cultural world without encroachment, threat, or discrimination. Cultural anthropologists contribute insights from different cultures about perceptions of basic human and cultural rights, and this knowledge, linked to advocacy, may be able to help prevent human/cultural rights abuses in the future.

People's cultural heritage can be a path toward improved welfare, but it is a double-edged sword. Promoting cultural tourism can protect culture but also lead to damage and destruction. An emerging area is the legalization of cultural heritage through intellectual property rights law, another double-edged sword.

Culture is a central issue of our time, and local people are working with cultural anthropologists to address the challenges of an increasingly globalized and insecure, but exciting, world.

Key Concepts

acculturation, p. 262

assimilation, p. 262

critical development anthropology, p. 271

cultural fit, p. 270

development, p. 260

development aggression, p. 278

development project, p. 270

diffusion, p. 262

extractive industry, p. 279

invention, p. 262

life project, p. 279

male bias in development, p. 276

micro-credit loan, p. 261

modernization, p. 264

project cycle, p. 270

social capital, p. 268

social impact assessment, p. 263

traditional development anthropology, p. 271

Thinking Outside the Box

1. Choose two inventions made in your lifetime and assess how they affect your everyday activities, social interactions, and way of thinking.
2. Visit the website of one multilateral development organization and one bilateral organization to learn about their goals, programs, and internship opportunities.

3. What lessons might the Society of Muslim Women (SMW) be able to share with programs that seek to prevent wife abuse in other countries? See page 278 for information about the SMW. (Recall the case of wife abuse in Kentucky presented in Chapter 6, page 125.)

Credits

Text Credits

Chapter 1: **Page 3,** Figure 1.1, Source: © Pearson Education, Inc.; **Page 6,** Source: Spiro, Melford. 1990. On the Strange and the Familiar in Recent Anthropological Thought. In *Cultural Psychology: Essays on Comparative Human Development* (pp. 47–61). James W. Stigler, Richard A. Shweder, and Gilbert Herdt, eds. Chicago: University of Chicago Press.; **Page 6:** Source: Miner, Horace. 1956. Body Ritual among the Nacirema. *American Anthropologist* 58(3):503–507.; **Page 6,** Source: Miner, Horace. 1956. Body Ritual among the Nacirema. *American Anthropologist* 58(3):503–507.; **Page 7,** Figure 1.2, Source: © Pearson Education, Inc.; **Page 10,** Source: Mullings, Leith. 2005. Towards an Anti-Racist Anthropology: Interrogating Racism. *Annual Review of Anthropology* 34:667–693.; **Page 10,** Source: Kroeber, A. L. and Clyde Kluckhohn. 1952. *Culture: A Critical Review of Concepts and Definitions* (p. 81). New York: Vintage Books.; **Page 10,** Source: Harris, Marvin. 1975. *Culture, People, Nature: An Introduction to General Anthropology*, 2nd ed (p. 144). New York: Thomas Y. Crowell.; **Page 11,** Map 1.1, Source: © Pearson Education, Inc.; **Page 14,** Map 1.2, Source: Furst, Peter T. 1989. The Water of Life: Symbolism and Natural History on the Northwest Coast. Dialectical *Anthropology* 14:95–115.; **Page 14,** Map 1.2, Source: © Pearson Education, Inc.; **Page 16,** Figure 1.3, Source: © Pearson Education, Inc.; **Page 16,** Figure 1.4, Source: © Pearson Education, Inc.; **Page 18,** Map 1.3, Source: © Pearson Education, Inc.; **Page 20,** Figure 1.5, Source: Lévi-Strauss, Claude. 1968. *Tristes Tropiques: An Anthropological Study of Primitive Societies in Brazil* (p. 385). New York: Atheneum.; **Page 20,** Figure 1.5, Source: © Pearson Education, Inc.

Chapter 2: **Page 25,** Figure 2.1, Source: © Pearson Education, Inc.; **Page 27,** Source: Weiner, Annette B. 1976. *Women of Value, Men of Renown: New Perspectives in Trobriand Exchange* (p. xvii). Austin: University of Texas Press.; **Page 28,** Source: MacCarthy, Michelle. 2015. 'Like Playing a Game Where You Don't Know the Rules': Investing Meaning in Intercultural Cash Transactions Between Tourists and Trobriand Islanders. *Ethnos: Journal of Anthropology* 80(4):448–471.; **Page 28,** Map 2.1, Source: © Pearson Education, Inc.; **Page 30,** Source: Salamandra, Christa. 2004. *A New Old Damascus: Authenticity and Distinction in Urban Syria* (p. 5). Bloomington: Indiana University Press.; **Page 30,** Source: Hamabata, Matthews Masayuki. 1990. *Crested Kimono: Power and Love in the Japanese Business Family* (pp. 21–22). Ithaca, NY: Cornell University Press.; **Page 30,** Figure 2.2, Source: © Pearson Education, Inc.; **Page 30,** Map 2.2, Source: © Pearson Education, Inc.; **Page 31,** Source: Whitehead, Tony Larry. 1986. Breakdown, Resolution, and Coherence: The Fieldwork Experience of a Big, Brown, Pretty-talking Man in a West Indian Community (pp. 214–215). In *Self, Sex, and Gender in Cross-Cultural Fieldwork* (pp. 213–239). Tony Larry Whitehead and Mary Ellen Conway, eds. Chicago: University of Illinois Press.; **Page 31,** Source: Warren, Carol A. B. 1988. *Gender Issues in Field Research (Qualitative Research Methods)*, Series 9 (p. 18). Newbury Park, CA: Sage Publications.; **Page 32,** Source: Ward, Martha C. 1989. Once Upon a Time (p. 14). In *Nest in the Wind: Adventures in Anthropology on a Tropical Island* (pp. 1–22). Martha C. Ward, ed. Prospect Heights, IL: Waveland Press.; **Page 32,** Source: Beals, Alan R. 1980. *Gopalpur: A South Indian Village. Fieldwork Edition* (p. 119). New York: Holt, Rinehart and Winston.; **Page 32,** Figure 2.3, Source: © Pearson Education, Inc.; **Page 36,** Map 2.3, Source: © Pearson Education, Inc.; **Page 37,** Source: Cátedra, María. 1992. *This World, Other Worlds: Sickness, Suicide, Death, and the Afterlife among the Vaqueiros de Alzada of Spain* (pp. 21–22). Chicago: University of Chicago Press.; **Page 38,** Map 2.4, Source: © Pearson Education, Inc.; **Page 39,** Figure 2.4, Source: From "Social Patterns of Food Expenditure Among Low-Income Jamaicans" by Barbara D. Miller in Papers and Recommendations of the Workshop on Food and Nutrition Security in Jamaica in the 1980s and Beyond, ed. by Kenneth A. Leslie and Lloyd B. Rankine, 1987.

Chapter 3: **Page 44,** Source: Based on http://www.theglobeandmail.com/news/world/two-room-shack-mumbai-slum-asking-price-43000/article2388735/.; **Page 45,** Figure 3.1, Source: © Pearson Education, Inc.; **Page 46,** Figure 3.2, Source: © Pearson Education, Inc.; **Page 47,** Source: Savishinsky, Joel S. 1974. *The Trail of the Hare: Life and Stress in an Arctic Community* (p. xx). New York: Gordon and Breach.; **Page 47,** Source: Savishinsky, Joel S. 1974. *The Trail of the Hare: Life and Stress in an Arctic Community* (p. 169). New York: Gordon and Breach.; **Page 47,** Source: Savishinsky, Joel S. 1974. *The Trail of the Hare: Life and Stress in an Arctic Community* (pp. 169–170). New York: Gordon and Breach.; **Page 47,** Map 3.1, Source: © Pearson Education, Inc.; **Page 48,** Figure 3.3, Source: © Pearson Education, Inc.; **Page 48,** Map 3.2, Source: © Pearson Education, Inc.; **Page 49,** Map 3.3, Source: © Pearson Education, Inc.; **Page 49,** Map 3.4, Source: © Pearson Education, Inc.; **Page 51,** Figure 3.4, Source: © Pearson Education, Inc.; **Page 53,** Figure 3.5, Source: Adapted from "Industrial Agriculture" by Peggy F. Barlett in Economic Anthropology, ed. by Stuart Plattner. Copyright © 1989 by the Board of Trustees of the Leland Stanford Jr. University. All rights reserved. With the permission of Stanford University Press, www.sup.org.; **Page 54,** Figure 3.6, Source: © Pearson Education, Inc.; **Page 55,** Source: Lee, Gary R. and Mindy Kezis. 1979. Family Structure and the Status of the Elderly. *Journal of Comparative Family Studies* 10:429–443.; **Page 55,** Map 3.5, Source: © Pearson Education, Inc.; **Page 56,** Source: Chin, Elizabeth. 2001. *Purchasing Power: Black Kids and American Consumer Culture* (p. 5). Minneapolis: University of Minnesota Press.; **Page 57,** Map 3.6, Source: © Pearson Education, Inc.; **Page 58,** Figure 3.7, Source: © Pearson Education, Inc.; **Page 60,** Source: Bledsoe, Caroline H. 1983. Stealing Food as a Problem in Demography and Nutrition (p. 2). Paper presented at the annual meeting of the American Anthropological Association.; **Page 62,** Map 3.7, Source: © Pearson Education, Inc.; **Page 63,** Map 3.8, Source: © Pearson Education, Inc.; **Page 64,** Source: Milton, Katherine. 1992. Civilization and Its Discontents. *Natural History* 3(92):41. Copyright © 1992 by Natural History Magazine, Inc. Reprinted with permission.

Chapter 4: **Page 69,** Figure 4.1, Source: © Pearson Education, Inc.; **Page 70,** Map 4.1, Source: © Pearson Education, Inc.; **Page 71,** Figure 4.2, Nebel, Bernard J. and Richard T. Wright.

Environmental Science: The Way The World Works, 7th ed. Copyright © 2000. Electronically reproduced by permission of Pearson Education, Inc.; **Page 71**, Figure 4.3, Data from Statistics Bureau, MIC, Ministry of Health, Labor and Welfare.; **Page 73**, Map 4.2, Source: © Pearson Education, Inc.; **Page 74**, Source: Browner, Carole H. 1986. The Politics of Reproduction in a Mexican Village. *Signs: Journal of Women in Culture and Society* 11(4): 714.; **Page 74**, Source: Carstairs, G. Morris. 1967. *The Twice Born* (pp. 83–86). Bloomington: Indiana University Press, quoted in Nag, Moni. 1972. Sex, Culture and Human Fertility: India and the United States. *Current Anthropology* 13:235.; **Page 75**, Map 4.3, Source: © Pearson Education, Inc.; **Page 78**, Source: Frieze, Irene et al. 1978. *Women and Sex Roles: A Social Psychological Perspective* (pp. 73–78). New York: W. W. Norton.; **Page 80**, Source: Mernissi, Fatima. 1987. *Beyond the Veil: Male-Female Dynamics in Modern Muslim Society* (p. xxiv). Revised edition. Bloomington: Indiana University Press.; **Page 80**, Figure 4.4, Source: Based on Whiting, Beatrice B. and John W. M.Whiting. 1975. *Children of Six Cultures: A Psycho-Cultural Analysis*. Cambridge, MA: Harvard University Press.; **Page 81**, Source: Saitoti, Tepilit Ole. 1986. *The Worlds of a Maasai Warrior* (p. 71). New York: Random House.; **Page 81**, Map 4.4, Source: © Pearson Education, Inc.; **Page 82**, Source: Adams, Abigail E. 2002. Dyke to Dyke: Ritual Reproduction at a U.S. Men's Military College. In *The Best of Anthropology Today* (p. 39). Jonathan Benthall, ed. New York: Routledge.; **Page 83**, Source: Ahmadu, Fuambai. 2000. Rites and Wrongs: An Insider/Outside Reflects on Power and Excision. In *Female "Circumcision" in Africa: Culture, Controversy, and Change* (pp. 306, 308). Bettina Shell-Duncan and Ylva Hernlund, eds. London: Lynne Reinner Publishers; **Page 83**, Map 4.5, Source: © Pearson Education, Inc.; **Page 86**, Map 4.6, Source: © Pearson Education, Inc.; **Page 87**, Source: Trelease, Murray L. 1975. Dying among Alaskan Indians: A Matter of Choice. In *Death: The Final Stage of Growth* (p. 35). Elisabeth Kübler-Ross, ed. Englewood Cliffs, NJ: Prentice-Hall.

Chapter 5: Page 90, Source: Rasmussen, Lars Bjørn, Knut Mikkelsen, Margaretha Haugen, Are H. Pripp, Jeremy Z. Fields and Øystein T. Førre. 2012. Treatment of Fibromyalgia at the Maharishi Ayurveda Health Centre in Norway II: A 24-month Follow-up Pilot Study. *Clinical Rheumatology* 31:821–827.; **Page 91**, Source: Thompson, Nile R. and C. Dale Sloat. 2004. The Use of Oral Literature to Provide Community Health Education on the Southern Northwest Coast. *American Indian Culture and Research Journal* 28(3):5.; **Page 91**, Map 5.1, Source: © Pearson Education, Inc.; **Page 92**, Figure 5.1, Adapted from Frake, Charles O. 1961. The Diagnosis of Disease among the Subanun of Mindanao. *American Anthropologist* 63: 118; **Page 93**, Figure 5.2, Source: Based on Chowdhury 1996; Ennis-McMillan, Michael C. 2001. Suffering from Water: Social Origins of Bodily Distress in a Mexican Community. *Medical Anthropology Quarterly* 15(3):368–390; Faiola 2005; Gremillion, Helen. 1992. Psychiatry as Social Ordering: Anorexia Nervosa, a Paradigm. *Social Science and Medicine* 35(1):57–71.; Kawanishi 2004; Rehbun 1994; Rubel, Arthur J., Carl W. O'Nell, and Rolando Collado-Ardon. 1984. *Susto: A Folk Illness*. Berkeley: University of California Press.; **Page 93**, Source: Ngokwey, Ndolamb. 1988. Pluralistic Etiological Systems in Their Social Context: A Brazilian Case Study. *Social Science and Medicine* 26:796.; **Page 93**, Source: Ennis-McMillan, Michael C. 2001. Suffering from Water: Social Origins of Bodily Distress in a Mexican Community. *Medical Anthropology Quarterly* 15(3):368–390.; **Page 94**, Source: Katz, Richard. 1982. *Boiling*

Energy: Community Healing among the Kalahari Kung (p. 34). Cambridge, MA: Harvard University Press.; **Page 95**, Figure 5.3, Source: © Pearson Education, Inc.; **Page 96**, Map 5.2, Source: © Pearson Education, Inc.; **Page 99**, Source: Ashburn 1947:98, quoted in Joralemon, Donald. 1982. New World Depopulation and the Case of Disease. *Journal of Anthropological Research* 38:112.; **Page 99**, Source: Lévi-Strauss, Claude. 1967. *Structural Anthropology*. New York: Anchor Books.; **Page 99**, Map 5.3, Source: © Pearson Education, Inc.; **Page 100**, Map 5.4, Source: © Pearson Education, Inc.; **Page 101**, Source: Dr. Davis-Floyd, Robbie E. 1987. Obstetric Training as a Rite of Passage. *Medical Anthropology Quarterly* 1:292. Reprinted with permission of author.; **Page 102**, Source: Dr. Davis-Floyd, Robbie E. 1987. Obstetric Training as a Rite of Passage. *Medical Anthropology Quarterly* 1:291. Reprinted with permission of author.; **Page 102**, Source: Dr. Davis-Floyd, Robbie E. 1987. Obstetric Training as a Rite of Passage. *Medical Anthropology Quarterly* 1:299. Reprinted with permission of author.; **Page 105**, Map 5.5, Source: © Pearson Education, Inc.; **Page 106**, Map 5.6, Source: © Pearson Education, Inc.

Chapter 6: Page 112, Figure 6.1, Source: © Pearson Education, Inc.; **Page 112**, Map 6.1, Source: © Pearson Education, Inc.; **Page 113**, Figure 6.2, Source: © Pearson Education, Inc.; **Page 113**, Figure 6.3, Source: © Pearson Education, Inc.; **Page 115**, Map 6.2, Source: © Pearson Education, Inc.; **Page 117**, Map 6.3, Source: © Pearson Education, Inc.; **Page 118**, Map 6.4, Source: © Pearson Education, Inc.; **Page 119**, Source: Barnard, Alan and Anthony Good. 1984. *Research Practices in the Study of Kinship* (p. 89). New York: Academic Press.; **Page 120**, Figure 6.4, Source: © Pearson Education, Inc.; **Page 121**, Figure 6.5, Source: © Pearson Education, Inc.; **Page 122**, Figure 6.6, Source: © Pearson Education, Inc.; **Page 124**, Source: Joseph, Suad. 1994. Brother/Sister Relationships: Connectivity, Love, and Power in the Reproduction of Patriarchy in Lebanon. *American Ethnologist* 21:51.; **Page 124**, Source: Joseph, Suad. 1994. Brother/Sister Relationships: Connectivity, Love, and Power in the Reproduction of Patriarchy in Lebanon. *American Ethnologist* 21:52.; **Page 125**, Map 6.5, Source: © Pearson Education, Inc.; **Page 127**, Source: Blackwood, Evelyn. 1995. Senior Women, Model Mothers, and Dutiful Wives. In *Bewitching Women, Pious Men* (pp. 124–158). Ong and Peletz, eds. Berkeley: University of California Press.

Chapter 7: Page 132, Source: Harlan, Tyler and Michael Webber. 2012. New Corporate Uyghur Entrepreneurs in Urumqi, China. *Central Asian* 31:175–191.; **Page 133**, Figure 7.1, Source: © Pearson Education, Inc.; **Page 133**, Map 7.1, Source: © Pearson Education, Inc.; **Page 135**, Source: Stack, Carol. 1974. *All Our Kin: Strategies for Survival in a Black Community* (p. 28). New York: Harper & Row.; **Page 135**, Map 7.2, Source: © Pearson Education, Inc.; **Page 137:** Source: Jourdan, Christine. 1995. Masta Liu (p. 210). In *Youth Cultures: A Cross-Cultural Perspective*. Vered Amit-Talai and Helena Wulff, eds. New York: Routledge.; **Page 137**, Map 7.3, Source: © Pearson Education, Inc.; **Page 139**, Map 7.4, Source: © Pearson Education, Inc.; **Page 141**, Map 7.5, Source: © Pearson Education, Inc.; **Page 143**, Map 7.6, Source: © Pearson Education, Inc.; **Page 144**, Figure 7.2, Source: © Pearson Education, Inc.; **Page 146**, Source: Judd, Ellen. 2002. *The Chinese Women's Movement: Between State and Market* (p. 14). Stanford, CA: Stanford University Press.; **Page 148**, Source: Stephen, Lynn. 1995. Women's Rights Are Human Rights: The Merging of Feminine and Feminist Interests among El Salvador's Mothers of the Disappeared (CO-MADRES). *American Ethnologist* 22(4):814.

Chapter 8: Page 154, Figure 8.1, Source: © Pearson Education, Inc.; **Page 156,** Map 8.1, Source: © Pearson Education, Inc.; **Page 159,** Source: Lacey, Marc. 2002. Where 9/11 News Is Late, But Aid Is Swift. *New York Times* June 3:A1, A7.; **Page 162,** Source: Gale, Faye, Rebecca Bailey-Harris, and Joy Wundersitz. 1990. *Aboriginal Youth and the Criminal Justice System: The Injustice of Justice?* (p. 3). New York: Cambridge University Press.; **Page 163,** Figure 8.2, Aboriginal Youth and the Criminal Justice System: The Injustice of Justice, by Fay Gale, Rebecca Bailey-Harris, Joy Wundersitz, Copyright © Cambridge University Press 1990.; **Page 163,** Map 8.2, Source: © Pearson Education, Inc.; **Page 164,** Source: Clay, Jason W. 1990. What's a Nation: Latest Thinking. *Mother Jones* 15(7):28–30.; **Page 168,** Map 8.4, Source: © Pearson Education, Inc.; **Page 169,** Map 8.3, Source: © Pearson Education, Inc.

Chapter 9: Page 174, Map 9.1, Source: © Pearson Education, Inc.; **Page 175,** Figure 9.1, Source: © Pearson Education, Inc.; **Page 175,** Figure 9.2, Source: "Sami Traditional Terminology" by Nils Jernsletten from SAMI CULTURE IN A NEW ERA: THE NORWEGIAN SAMI EXPERIENCE, edited by Harald Gaski. Published 1997.; **Page 176,** Source: Weine, Stevan M. et al. 1995. Psychiatric Consequences of "Ethnic Cleansing": Clinical Assessments and Trauma Testimonies of Newly Resettled Bosnian Refugees. *American Journal of Psychiatry* 152(4):538.; **Page 176,** Source: Weine, Stevan M. et al. 1995. Psychiatric Consequences of "Ethnic Cleansing": Clinical Assessments and Trauma Testimonies of Newly Resettled Bosnian Refugees. *American Journal of Psychiatry* 152(4):539.; **Page 176,** Source: Weine, Stevan M. et al. 1995. Psychiatric Consequences of "Ethnic Cleansing": Clinical Assessments and Trauma Testimonies of Newly Resettled Bosnian Refugees. *American Journal of Psychiatry* 152(4):541.; **Page 176,** Map 9.2, Source: © Pearson Education, Inc.; **Page 177,** Figure 9.3, Source: Reproduced by permission of the American Anthropological Association from (2004). *The Journal of Linguistic Anthropology* 14(2):186–224. Not for sale or further reproduction.; **Page 178,** Map 9.3, Source: © Pearson Education, Inc.; **Page 180,** Source: Dávila, Arlene. 2002. Culture in the Ad World: Producing the Latin Look. In *Media Worlds: Anthropology on New Terrain* (p. 270). Faye D. Ginsburg, Lila Abu-Lughod, and Brian Larkin, eds. Berkeley: University of California Press.; **Page 181,** Source: Tannen, Deborah. 1990. *You Just Don't Understand: Women and Men in Conversation* (p. 42). New York: Morrow.; **Page 181,** Source: Tannen, Deborah. 1990. *You Just Don't Understand: Women and Men in Conversation* (p. 289). New York: Morrow.; **Page 182,** Source: Boellstorff, Tom. 2004. Gay Language and Indonesia: Registering Belonging. *Journal of Linguistic Anthropology* 14:248–268.; **Page 182,** Figure 9.4, Source: *Language, Gender, and Sex in Comparative Perspective*, by Susan U. Philips, Susan Steele, Chrisitne Tanz. Copyright © Cambridge University Press 1987. Reprinted with permission of Cambridge University Press.; **Page 183,** Source: Goodwin, Marjorie H. 1990. *He-Said-She-Said: Talk as Social Organization among Black Children* (p. 183). Bloomington: Indiana University Press.; **Page 185,** Figure 9.5, Source: © Pearson Education, Inc.; **Page 185,** Map 9.4, Source: © Pearson Education, Inc.; **Page 185,** Map 9.5, Source: © Pearson Education, Inc.; **Page 186,** Figure 9.6, Source: © Pearson Education, Inc.; **Page 188,** Map 9.6, Source: © Pearson Education, Inc.; **Page 189,** Source: Walsh, Michael. 2005. Will Indigenous Languages Survive? *Annual Review of Anthropology* 34:293–315. Copyright © 2005 by Annual Review of Anthropology.

Reprinted with permission.; **Page 189,** Figure 9.7, Source: © Pearson Education, Inc.; **Page 190,** Source: Walsh, Michael. 2005. Will Indigenous Languages Survive? *Annual Review of Anthropology* 34:293–315. Copyright © 2005 by Annual Review of Anthropology. Reprinted with permission.

Chapter 10: Page 194, Source: Based on Eccles, Jeremy. 2012. Artist Saw the Stars Crying: Gulumbu Yunuping, 1945–2012. *Sydney Morning Herald* June 10.; **Page 195,** Source: Frazer, Sir James. 1978[1890]. *The Golden Bough: A Study in Magic and Religion*. New York: Macmillan.; **Page 195,** Figure 10.1, Source: © Pearson Education, Inc.; **Page 196,** Map 10.1, Source: © Pearson Education, Inc.; **Page 197,** Source: Lesher, James H., trans. 2001. *Xenophanes of Colophon: Fragments* (p. 25). Toronto: University of Toronto Press.; **Page 198,** Map 10.2, Source: © Pearson Education, Inc.; **Page 199,** Map 10.3, Source: © Pearson Education, Inc.; **Page 200,** Map 10.4, Source: © Pearson Education, Inc.; **Page 201,** Source: Counihan, Carole M. 1985. Transvestism and Gender in a Sardinian Carnival. *Anthropology* 9(1&2):15.; **Page 202,** Source: Counihan, Carole M. 1985. Transvestism and Gender in a Sardinian Carnival. *Anthropology* 9(1&2):16.; **Page 203,** Figure 10.2, Source: © Pearson Education, Inc.; **Page 205,** Source: Knott, Kim. 1996. Hindu Women, Destiny and Stridharma. *Religion* 26:24. Copyright © 1996 by Taylor and Francis Ltd. Reprinted with permission.; **Page 205,** Source: Knott, Kim. 1996. Hindu Women, Destiny and Stridharma. *Religion* 26:25. Copyright © 1996 by Taylor and Francis Ltd. Reprinted with permission.; **Page 207,** Map 10.5, Source: © Pearson Education, Inc.; **Page 208,** Map 10.6, Source: © Pearson Education, Inc.; **Page 209,** Source: John 13:4. The Holy Bible, Authorized King James Version.; **Page 210,** Source: Dorgan, Howard. 1989. *The Old Regular Baptists of Central Appalachia: Brothers and Sisters in Hope* (p. 106). Knoxville: University of Tennessee Press.; **Page 210,** Source: Mark 16:17–18. The Holy Bible, Authorized King James Version.; **Page 210,** Source: Toren, Christina. 1988. Making the Present, Revealing the Past: The Mutability and Continuity of Tradition as Process. *Man* (n.s.) 23:697.; **Page 210,** Source: Toren, Christina. 1988. Making the Present, Revealing the Past: The Mutability and Continuity of Tradition as Process. *Man* (n.s.) 23:706.; **Page 212,** Map 10.7, Source: © Pearson Education, Inc.

Chapter 11: Page 221, Source: Chernoff, John Miller. 1979. *African Rhythm and African Sensibility: Aesthetics and African Musical Idioms* (p. 170). Chicago: University of Chicago Press.; **Page 221,** Source: Bunzel, Ruth. 1972[1929]. *The Pueblo Potter: A Study of Creative Imagination in Primitive Art* (p. 49). New York: Dover Publications.; **Page 221,** Source: Bunzel, Ruth. 1972[1929]. *The Pueblo Potter: A Study of Creative Imagination in Primitive Art* (p. 52). New York: Dover Publications.; **Page 222,** Source: Shenhav-Keller, Shelly. 1993. The Israeli Souvenir: Its Text and Context. *Annals of Tourism Research* 20:183.; **Page 223,** Figure 11.1, Source: Republished with permission of ABC-CLIO LLC from "Power and Gender in the Musical Experiences of Women" by Carol E. Robertson, pp. 224–225 in Women and Music in Cross-Cultural Perspective, ed. by Ellen Koskoff. Reproduced with permission of GREENWOOD PUBLISHING GROUP, INCORPORATED in the format Republish in a book via Copyright Clearance Center.; **Page 231,** Map 11.1, Source: © Pearson Education, Inc. **232,** Map 11.2, Source: © Pearson Education, Inc.; **Page 234,** Source: Park, Hynug yu. 2010. Heritage Tourism: Emotional Journeys into Nationhood. *Annals of Tourism Research* 37(1):126.; **Page 234,** Map 11.3, Source: © Pearson Education, Inc.

Chapter 12: Page 243, Martínez, Samuel. 1996. Indifference with Indignation: Anthropology, Human Rights, and the Haitian Bracero. *American Anthropologist* 98(1):20.; **Page 244**, Map 12.1, Source: © Pearson Education, Inc.; **Page 246**, Map 12.2, Source: © Pearson Education, Inc.; **Page 247**, Map 12.3, Source: © Pearson Education, Inc.; **Page 249**, Figure 12.1, Source: "Ten Source Countries with the Largest Populations in the United States as Percentages of the Total Foreign-Born Population: 2009," from http://www.migrationinformation.org/datahub/charts/10.2009.shtml. Copyright © 2009 by Migration Policy Institute Data Hub. Reprinted with permission; **Page 249**, Figure 12.2, Source: Figure from Pew Research Center for the People & the Press, 2012. Copyright © 2012 by the Pew Research Center. Reprinted with permission.; **Page 251**, Source: Pessar, Patricia R. 1995. *A Visa for a Dream: Dominicans in the United States* (p. 81). Boston: Allyn and Bacon.; **Page 251**, Map 12.4, Source: © Pearson Education, Inc.; **Page 254**, Map 12.5, Source: © Pearson Education, Inc.

Chapter 13: Page 260, Source: Dr. Dean Jacobs, Executive Director of Walpole Island First Nation, from his foreword in VanWynsberghe, Robert M. 2002. *AlterNatives: Community, Identity, and Environmental Justice on Walpole Island* (p. ix). Boston: Allyn and Bacon.; **Page 261**, Map 13.1, Source: © Pearson Education, Inc.; **Page 265**, Map 13.2, Source: © Pearson Education, Inc.; **Page 269**, Map 13.3, Source: © Pearson Education, Inc.; **Page 270**, Figure 13.1, Source: © Pearson Education, Inc.; **Page 271**, Map 13.4, Source: © Pearson Education, Inc.; **Page 274**, Map 13.5, Source: © Pearson Education, Inc.; **Page 275**, Map 13.6, Source: © Pearson Education, Inc.; **Page 277**, Source: Economic and Social Council. 1992. *Report of the Working Group on Violence against Women.* Vienna: United Nations. E/CN.6/WG.2/1992/L.3.; **Page 277**, Source: Sullivan, Kathleen. 1992. Protagonists of Change: Indigenous Street Vendors in San Cristobal, Mexico, Are Adapting Tradition and Customs to Fit New Life Styles. *Cultural Survival Quarterly* 16:38–40.; **Page 277**, Figure 13.2, Source: Adapted from Heise, Lori L., Jacqueline Pitanguy, and Adrienne Germain. 1994. *Violence against Women: The Hidden Health Burden* (p. 5). World Bank Discussion Papers No. 255. Washington, DC: The World Bank.; **Page 281**, Source: Quoted in Sachs, Aaron. 1996. Dying for Oil. *World Watch Magazine* 9(3):10–21.; **Page 281**, Map 13.7, Source: © Pearson Education, Inc.

Photo Credits

Cover: Travel Pictures/Alamy Stock Photo

Chapter 1: Page 1, Keren Su/Lonely Planet Images/Getty Images; **Page 2**, Silicon Valley Cultures Project; **Page 2**, Lindsay Hebberd/Terra/Corbis; **Page 4**, Scott Sady/AP Images; **Page 4**, Richard A. Gould; **Page 5**, Ramon Espinosa/AP Images; **Page 9**, Alan Tobey/Vetta/Getty Images; **Page 9**, Image Source/Getty Images; **Page 10**, Patricia Tovar; **Page 12**, Kazuyoshi Nomachi/Terra/Corbis; **Page 12**, Dreambigphotos/Fotolia; **Page 13**, Soeren Stache/epa/Corbis; **Page 13**, Pat Roque/AP Images; **Page 14**, Ton Koene/Visuals Unlimited/Encyclopedia/Corbis; **Page 14**, Barbara D. Miller; **Page 16**, Barbara D. Miller; **Page 18**, Washburn/Anthro-Photo File;

Page 18, Louise Gubb/Corbis News/Corbis; **Page 19**, Abbas Dulleh/Associated Press/Corbis

Chapter 2: Page 23, Tronick/Anthro-Photo File; **Page 25**, Cambridge University Press - US - Journals; **Page 25**, Lanita Jacobs; **Page 26**, Pearson Education; **Page 27**, Left Lane Productions/Flirt/Corbis; **Page 28**, Anthro-Photo File; **Page 28**, Albrecht G. Schaefer/Encyclopedia/Corbis; **Page 31**, Liza Dalby; **Page 32**, Courtesy of Isabel Balseiro; **Page 35**, Anthro-Photo File; **Page 35**, Gananath Obeyesekere; **Page 37**, Sue Cunningham/Worldwide Picture Library/Alamy; **Page 37**, Atlantide Phototravel/Latitude/Corbis

Chapter 3: Page 43, Dhiraj Singh/Bloomberg/Getty Images; **Page 46**, Anthro-Photo File; **Page 47**, Dr. Joel Savishinsky; **Page 49**, Ton Koene/ZUMA Press/Corbis; **Page 52**, Jeremy Horner/Documentary Value/Corbis; **Page 52**, Tim Flach/Stone/Getty Images; **Page 55**, Nick Turner/Alamy; **Page 59**, Barbara D. Miller; **Page 59**, Bob Krist/Encyclopedia/Corbis; **Page 61**, Miguel Gandert/Encyclopedia/Corbis; **Page 63**, UBC Museum of Anthropology; **Page 63**, Ubc Museum of Anthropology

Chapter 4: Page 67, Adam eastland/Alamy; **Page 70**, David Turnley/Turnley/Corbis; **Page 70**, Barbara D. Miller; **Page 72**, Diebold George/Superstock/Alamy; **Page 73**, Stephanie Dinkins/Science Source; **Page 75**, Caroline Penn/Alamy; **Page 76**, Bettmann/Corbis; **Page 77**, Scheper-Hughes, Nancy; **Page 79**, Chagnon/Anthro-Photo; **Page 79**, Iryna Tiumentseva/Fotolia; **Page 81**, Adrian Arbib/Encyclopedia/Corbis; **Page 82**, Abigail E. Adams; **Page 84**, Kim Kyung-Hoon/Reuters/Corbis; **Page 85**, Dr. Barry S.Hewlett

Chapter 5: Page 89, Matthew Wakem/Digital Vision/Getty Images; **Page 90**, Andrew Patron/Retna Ltd/Corbis; **Page 94**, Anthro-Photo; **Page 95**, Ricardo Azoury/Corbis; **Page 97**, Ed Kashi/VII/Corbis; **Page 98**, Kcna/Epa/Corbis; **Page 98**, Lynn Johnson/Getty Images; **Page 101**, Bloomberg/Getty Images; **Page 102**, Lara Jo Regan; **Page 103**, Str/Reuters/Corbis; **Page 103**, Barbara D. Miller; **Page 104**, Holly Farrell/Getty Images; **Page 105**, Ed Darack/SuperStock/Corbis; **Page 105**, Pawel Kopczynski/Reuters/Corbis; **Page 107**, Cdc/Phil/Corbis

Chapter 6: Page 110, Jiri PaleniCek/Profimedia International s.r.o./Alamy; **Page 114**, Norbert Schiller/The Image Works; **Page 114**, Christophe Boisvieux/Terra/Corbis; **Page 117**, Robin Laurance/LOOK Die Bildagentur der Fotografen GmbH/Alamy; **Page 117**, Lindsay Hebberd/Terra/Corbis; **Page 119**, Rob Melnychuk/Digital Vision/Getty Images; **Page 122**, Deborah Pellow; **Page 123**, Robert Harding World Imagery; **Page 124**, Image Source/Digital Vision/Getty Images; **Page 126**, Nature Picture Library/Alamy; **Page 126**, Sam Tarling/Corbis; **Page 127**, Kazuhiro Nigo/Afp/Getty Images; **Page 128**, Matthew Amster; **Page 128**, Matthew Amster

Chapter 7: Page 131, Jim Richardson/Terra/Corbis; **Page 134**, David Lees/Documentary Value/Corbis; **Page 135**, Str/Afp/Getty Images; **Page 135**, Ahmad Al Rubaye/Afp/Getty Images; **Page 135**, Streeter Lecka/Getty Images Sport/Getty Images; **Page 136**, Tang Chhin Sothy/Afp/Getty Images; **Page 138**, Charles & Josette Lenars/Corbis; **Page 138**, Skip Nall/Spirit, Corbis; **Page 139**, Donald Nausbaum/Robert Harding Picture Library Ltd/Alamy; **Page 142**, Gideon Mendel/Terra/

Corbis; **Page 143**, David Scheffel; **Page 143**, David Scheffel; **Page 145**, Barbara D. Miller; **Page 145**, Barbara D. Miller; **Page 145**, Raveendran/Afp/Getty Images; **Page 147**, Afp/Getty Images; **Page 148**, Gilles Mingasson/Afp/Getty Images

Chapter 8: Page 151, Christoph Henning/Das Fotoarchiv/ Black Star/Alamy; **Page 153**, Str/Afp/Getty Images; **Page 153**, Jeremy Piper/Bloomberg/Getty Images; **Page 153**, Bertrand Guay/Afp/Getty Images; **Page 155**, Ricardo Azoury/Corbis News/Corbis; **Page 157**, Danny Lehman/Documentary Value/Corbis; **Page 157**, Tobias Bernhard/Flirt/Corbis; **Page 158**, Reuters/Corbis; **Page 158**, Chip Somodevilla/Getty Images News/ Getty Images; **Page 158**, Tim Sloan/Afp/Getty Images; **Page 160**, Philippe Lopez/Afp/Getty Images; **Page 162**, Epa/Corbis; **Page 165**, Antonio Mari; **Page 167**, Stuart Kirsch; **Page 169**, Blickwinkel/Alamy; **Page 169**, Ed Kashi/ VII/Corbis News/Corbis

Chapter 9: Page 172, Charles Cecil/Cecil Images; **Page 173**, Robin Nelson/PhotoEdit; **Page 174**, Daniel Everett; **Page 176**, Fehim Demir/Epa/Corbis; **Page 179**, Around the World in a Viewfinder/Alamy; **Page 180**, Khaled Desouki/Getty Images; **Page 180**, Frederic J. Brown/Staff/Getty Images; **Page 180**, David McNew/Getty Images News/Getty Images; **Page 182**, Eriko Sugita/Reuters/Corbis; **Page 184**, Gallo Images/Terra/Corbis; **Page 184**, Paul A. Souders/Encyclopedia/Corbis; **Page 186**, Sspl/Getty Images; **Page 187**, Barbara D. Miller; **Page 188**, Anders Ryman/Alamy; **Page 188**, Eric CHRETIEN/Contributor/Getty Images; **Page 189**, Robert Essel Nyc/Flirt/Corbis

Chapter 10: Page 193, Penny Tweedie/Alamy; **Page 194**, Loring M. Danforth; **Page 194**, Ruth Krulfeld; **Page 198**, Bob Rowan/Progressive Image/Documentary Value/Corbis; **Page 200**, David Moore/South Australia/Alamy; **Page 201**, Encyclopedia/Corbis; **Page 202**, Tuul and Bruno Morandi/ The Image Bank/Getty Images; **Page 204**, Brooklyn Museum/ Fine Art Museums/Corbis; **Page 205**, Subir Basak/Moment Open/Getty Images; **Page 206**, Jack Heaton; **Page 208**, Barbara D. Miller; **Page 209**, Barbara D. Miller; **Page 210**, Jack Heaton; **Page 212**, Eddie Gerald/Alamy; **Page 212**, Maris Boyd Gillette Professor; **Page 213**, Chicago Tribune/Tribune News Service/ Getty Images; **Page 213**, Michael Ochs/Historical Premium/ Corbis; **Page 215**, Lamont Lindstrom

Chapter 11: Page 217, STR/AFP/Getty Images; **Page 218**, Joseph Sohm/Encyclopedia/Corbis; **Page 218**, Paul Mcerlane/Corbis Wire/Corbis; **Page 218**, Lindsay Hebberd/ Documentary Value/Corbis; **Page 220**, Ibejis, pair of 19th century/Private Collection/Photo © Bonhams, London, UK/

Bridgeman Images; **Page 221**, Lindsay Hebberd/Documentary Value/Corbis; **Page 221**, Joel Kuipers; **Page 222**, Charles Lenars/Documentary Value/Corbis; **Page 224**, Danita Delimont/Pete Oxford/Alamy; **Page 224**, Barbara D. Miller; **Page 225**, Andrew Ward/Life File/Photodisc/Getty Images; **Page 225**, Corbis Wire/Corbis; **Page 227**, Cat/Corbis Flirt/ Alamy; **Page 227**, Robert Harding Picture Library/SuperStock; **Page 229**, Peter Adams/Getty Images; **Page 229**, Vincent Gautier/Corbis Wire/Corbis; **Page 229**, Sam Sharpe/ NewSport/ZUMAPRESS/Alamy; **Page 230**, Gilad Flesch/ PhotoStock-Israel/Alamy; **Page 231**, Jay Dickman/Flirt/Corbis; **Page 232**, Richard Ellis/Alamy; **Page 232**, Bob Krist/Encyclopedia/Corbis; **Page 233**, Courtesy of Michael Schlauch; **Page 234**, David Sutherland/Terra/Corbis; **Page 235**, Felith Belaid/AFP/Getty Images; **Page 236**, Matthew LeDuc; **Page 236**, P.S. Kalidas

Chapter 12: Page 239, Nik Wheeler/Terra/Corbis; **Page 241**, Jon Hicks/Terra/Corbis; **Page 241**, Annie Griffiths Belt/Corbis; **Page 242**, Omar Khodor/Reuters/Corbis; **Page 243**, Edward F. Keller, II; **Page 246**, Keren Su/China Span/Alamy; **Page 246**, China Photos/Reuters; **Page 247**, Mario Linares/ Reuters/Corbis; **Page 247**, Tibor Bognár/Encyclopedia/ Corbis; **Page 248**, Adam Dean/Panos Pictures; **Page 248**, Wu Guoqiang/Xinhua Press/Corbis Wire/Corbis; **Page 250**, Ed Kashi/VII/Corbis News/Corbis; **Page 250**, Ferry, Stephen; **Page 253**, Imaginechina/Corbis Wire/Corbis; **Page 253**, David Butow/Corbis News/Corbis; **Page 254**, Corey Sipkin/ New York Daily News Archive/Getty Images; **Page 255**, Abbie Trayler-Smith/Panos Pictures; **Page 256**, Christian Mangion/Demotix/Corbis

Chapter 13: Page 259, Antonio Scorza/AFP/Getty Images; **Page 261**, Fred Chartrand/The Canadian Press/ Photostream; **Page 262**, Jeremy Horner/Terra/Corbis; **Page 262**, Shannon Stapleton/Reuters/Corbis; **Page 263**, Top-Pics TBK/Alamy; **Page 264**, Rob Howard/Terra/Corbis; **Page 265**, Yogesh More/Ephotocorp/Alamy; **Page 265**, David Sutherland/Encyclopedia/Corbis; **Page 267**, Wim Wiskerke/Alamy; **Page 268**, Jeremy Horner/Alamy; **Page 269**, Gideon Mendel/Encyclopedia/Corbis; **Page 269**, Niko Guido/Corbis News/Corbis; **Page 272**, Attilio Polo's Fieldwork/Moment Open/Getty Images; **Page 276**, Christopher Pillitz/Photonica World/Getty Images; **Page 277**, Gina Martin/National Geographic/Getty Images; **Page 278**, Godong/Alamy Stock Photo; **Page 279**, Getty Images; **Page 279**, Angelo Cavalli/Flirt/Corbis; **Page 279**, Bob Krist/Terra/Corbis; **Page 280**, Reuters/Corbis; **Page 280**, Tim Lamdon/Greenpeace International; **Page 282**, Jeff Greenberg/Alamy

Glossary

acculturation   a form of cultural change in which a minority culture becomes more like the dominant culture.

achieved position   a person's standing in society based on qualities that the person has gained through action.

adolescence   a culturally defined period of maturation from the time of puberty until adulthood that is recognized in some, but not all, cultures.

age set   a group of people close in age who go through certain rituals, such as circumcision, at the same time.

agency   the ability of humans to make choices and exercise free will even within dominating structures.

agriculture   a mode of livelihood that involves growing crops with the use of plowing, irrigation, and fertilizer.

animatism   a belief system in which the supernatural is conceived of as an impersonal power.

anthropology   the study of humanity, including its prehistoric origins and contemporary human diversity.

applied anthropology   the use of anthropological knowledge to prevent or solve problems or to shape and achieve policy goals.

applied medical anthropology   the application of anthropological knowledge to furthering the goals of health-care providers.

archaeology   the study of past human cultures through their material remains.

art   the application of imagination, skill, and style to matter, movement, and sound that goes beyond what is purely practical.

ascribed position   a person's standing in society based on qualities that the person has gained through birth.

asexuality   lack of sexual attraction or interest in sexual activity.

assimilation   a form of cultural change in which a culture is thoroughly acculturated, or decultured, and is no longer distinguishable as having a separate identity.

authority   the ability to take action based on a person's achieved or ascribed status or moral reputation.

balanced exchange   a system of transfers in which the goal is either immediate or eventual equality in value.

band   the form of political organization of foraging groups, with flexible membership and minimal leadership.

big data   sets of information including thousands or even millions of data points that are often generated from Internet and communication sources, such as cell phone use, Facebooking, and Tweeting.

big-man system or **big-woman system**   a form of political organization midway between tribe and chiefdom and involving reliance on the leadership of key individuals who develop a political following through personal ties and redistributive feasts.

bilineal descent   the tracing of descent through both parents.

biological anthropology   the study of humans as biological organisms, including evolution and contemporary variation.

biological determinism   a theory that explains human behavior and ideas as shaped mainly by biological features such as genes and hormones.

blood sport   a competition that explicitly seeks to bring about a flow of blood from, or even the death of, human–human contestants, human–animal contestants, or animal–animal contestants.

bracero   an agricultural laborer in Latin America and the Caribbean who is permitted entry to a country to work for a limited time.

brideprice   the transfer of cash and goods from the groom's family to the bride's family and to the bride.

brideservice   a form of marriage exchange in which the groom works for his father-in-law for a certain length of time before returning home with the bride.

call system   a form of oral communication among nonhuman primates with a set repertoire of meaningful sounds generated in response to environmental factors.

cargo cult   a form of revitalization movement that emerged in Melanesia in response to Western and Japanese influences.

caste system   a form of social stratification linked with Hinduism and based on a person's birth into a particular group.

chain migration   a form of population movement in which a first wave of migrants comes and then attracts relatives and friends to join them in the destination.

chiefdom   a form of political organization in which permanently allied tribes and villages have one recognized leader who holds an "office."

circular migration   repeated movement between two or more places, either within or between countries.

civil society   the collection of interest groups that function outside the government to organize economic and other aspects of life.

collaborative research   an approach to learning about culture that involves anthropologists working with members of the study population as partners and participants rather than as "subjects."

communication   the process of sending and receiving meaningful messages.

community healing   healing that emphasizes the social context as a key component and that is carried out within the public domain.

computational anthropology   a research approach that uses large quantitative datasets available through Google, telephone use, and other computer-based sources to provide large-scale information about human preferences, values, and behavior.

consumerism   a mode of consumption in which people's demands are many and infinite and the means of satisfying them are insufficient and become depleted in the effort to satisfy these demands.

corporate social responsibility (CSR)   business ethics that seek to generate profits for the corporation while avoiding harm to people and the environment.

couvade   customs applying to the behavior of fathers during and shortly after the birth of their children.

creole   a language directly descended from a pidgin but possessing its own native speakers and involving linguistic expansion and elaboration.

critical development anthropology   an approach to international development in which the anthropologist takes a critical-thinking role and asks why and to whose benefit particular development policies and programs are pursued.

critical discourse analysis   an approach within linguistic anthropology that examines how power and social inequality are reflected and reproduced in communication.

critical legal anthropology   an approach within the cross-cultural study of legal systems that examines the role of law and judicial processes in maintaining the dominance of powerful groups through discriminatory practices rather than protecting less powerful people.

critical media anthropology an approach within the crosscultural study of media that examines how power interests shape people's access to media and influence the contents of its messages.

critical medical anthropology an approach within medical anthropology involving the analysis of how economic and political structures shape people's health status, their access to health care, and the prevailing medical systems that exist in relation to them.

cross-cousin offspring of either one's father's sister or one's mother's brother.

cultural anthropology the study of living peoples and their cultures, including variation and change.

cultural broker someone who is familiar with two cultures and can promote communication and understanding across them.

cultural competence among Western-trained health professionals, awareness of and respect for beliefs and practices that differ from those of Western medicine.

cultural constructionism a theory that explains human behavior and ideas as shaped mainly by learning.

cultural fit a characteristic of informed and effective project design in which planners take local culture into account.

cultural materialism an approach to studying culture by emphasizing the material aspects of life, including people's environment, how people make a living, and differences in wealth and power.

cultural relativism the perspective that each culture must be understood in terms of the values and ideas of that culture and not judged by the standards of another culture.

culture people's learned and shared behaviors and beliefs.

culture shock persistent feelings of uneasiness, loneliness, and anxiety that often occur when a person has shifted from one culture to a different one.

culture-specific syndrome a collection of signs and symptoms that is restricted to a particular culture or a limited number of cultures.

dalit the preferred name for the socially defined lowest groups in the Indian caste system; the name means "oppressed" or "ground down."

deductive approach (to research) a research method that involves posing a research question or hypothesis, gathering data related to the question, and then assessing the findings in relation to the original hypothesis.

demographic transition the change from the agricultural pattern of high fertility and high mortality to the industrial pattern of low fertility and low mortality.

descent the tracing of kinship relationships through parentage.

development change directed toward improving human welfare.

development aggression the imposition of development projects and policies without the free, prior, and informed consent of the affected people.

development project a set of activities designed to put development policies into action.

development-induced displacement the forced migration of a population due to development.

diaspora population a dispersed group of people living outside their original homeland.

diffusion the spread of culture through contact.

discourse culturally patterned verbal language including varieties of speech, participation, and meaning.

disease in the disease–illness dichotomy, a biological health problem that is objective and universal.

disease of development a health problem caused or increased by economic development activities that have detrimental effects on the environment and people's relationship with it.

displaced person someone who is forced to leave his or her home, community, or country.

displacement a feature of human language whereby people are able to talk about events in the past and future.

division of labor how a society distributes various tasks depending on factors such as gender, age, and physical ability.

doctrine direct and formalized statements about religious beliefs.

dowry the transfer of cash and goods from the bride's family to the newly married couple.

ecological/epidemiological approach an approach within medical anthropology that considers how aspects of the natural environment and social environment interact to cause illness.

emic insiders' perceptions and categories, and their explanations for why they do what they do.

endogamy marriage within a particular group or locality.

ethnicity a way of categorizing people on the basis of the shared sense of identity based on history, heritage, language, or culture.

ethnocentrism judging another culture by the standards of one's own culture rather than by the standards of that particular culture.

ethno-esthetics culturally specific definitions of what art is.

ethno-etiology a culturally specific causal explanation for health problems and suffering.

ethnography a firsthand, detailed description of a living culture, based on personal observation.

ethnomedicine the study of cross-cultural health systems.

ethnomusicology the cross-cultural study of music.

ethnosemantics the study of the meaning of words, phrases, and sentences in particular cultural contexts.

etic an analytical framework used by outside analysts in studying culture.

exogamy marriage outside a particular group or locality.

expected reciprocity an exchange of approximately equally valued goods or services, usually between people roughly equal in social status.

expressive culture behaviors and beliefs related to art, leisure, and play.

extended household a coresidential group that comprises more than one parent–child unit.

extensive strategy a form of livelihood involving temporary use of large areas of land and a high degree of spatial mobility.

extractive industry a business that explores for, removes, processes, and sells minerals, oil, and gas that are found on or beneath the earth's surface and which are nonrenewable.

family a group of people who consider themselves related through a form of kinship, such as descent, marriage, or sharing.

family farming a form of agriculture in which farmers produce mainly to support themselves but also produce goods for sale in the market system.

female genital cutting (FGC) a range of practices involving partial or total removal of the clitoris and labia.

fertility the rate of births in a population or the rate of population increase in general.

fieldwork research in the field, which is any place where people and culture are found.

foraging obtaining food available in nature through gathering, hunting, or scavenging.

functionalism the theory that a culture is similar to a biological organism, in which parts work to support the operation and maintenance of the whole.

gender a way of categorizing people based on their culturally constructed and learned behaviors and ideas as attributed to males, females, or blended genders.

gender pluralism the existence within a culture of multiple categories of femininity, masculinity, and blurred genders that are tolerated and legitimate.

generalized reciprocity exchange involving the least conscious sense of interest in material gain or thought of what might be received in return.

global language a language spoken widely throughout the world and in diverse cultural contexts, often replacing indigenous languages.

globalization increased and intensified international ties related to the movement of goods, information, and people.

heteronormativity the belief that all people fall into two distinct genders, male and female, with corresponding distinct social roles and adhering to heterosexual relations.

heterotopia something formed from elements drawn from multiple and diverse contexts.

hijra in India, a blurred gender role in which a person, usually biologically male, takes on female dress and behavior.

historical linguistics the study of language change using formal methods that compare shifts over time and across space in aspects of language, such as phonetics, syntax, and semantics.

historical trauma the intergenerational transfer of the detrimental effects of colonialism from parents to children.

horticulture a mode of livelihood based on growing domesticated crops in gardens, using simple hand tools.

household either one person living alone or a group of people who may or may not be related by kinship and who share living space.

humoral healing healing that emphasizes balance among natural elements within the body.

illness in the disease–illness dichotomy, culturally shaped perceptions and experiences of a health problem.

incest taboo a strongly held prohibition against marrying or having sex with particular kin.

indigenous knowledge local understanding of the environment, climate, and other matters related to livelihood and well-being.

indigenous people people who have a long-standing connection with their home territories that predates colonial or outside societies.

inductive approach (to research) a research approach that avoids hypothesis formation in advance of the research and instead takes its lead from the culture being studied.

industrial capital agriculture a form of agriculture that is capital-intensive, substituting machinery and purchased inputs for human and animal labor.

industrialism/digital economy a mode of livelihood in which goods are produced through mass employment in business and commercial operations and through the creation and movement of information through electronic media.

infanticide the killing of an infant or child.

influence the ability to achieve a desired end by exerting social or moral pressure on someone or some group.

informed consent an aspect of fieldwork ethics requiring that the researcher inform the research participants of the intent, scope, and possible effects of the proposed study and seek their consent to be in the study.

institutional migrant someone who moves into a social institution either voluntarily or involuntarily.

intangible cultural heritage UNESCO's view of culture as manifested in oral traditions, languages, performing arts, rituals and festive events, knowledge and practices about nature and the universe, and craftmaking.

intensive strategy a form of livelihood that involves continuous use of the same land and resources.

intercultural health an approach in health that seeks to reduce the gaps between local and Western health systems in promoting more effective prevention and treatment of health problems.

internal migration movement within country boundaries.

internally displaced person (IDP) someone who is forced to leave his or her home or community but who remains in the same country.

international migration movement across country boundaries.

interpretive anthropology or a symbolic approach, seeks to understand culture by studying what people think about, their ideas, and the meanings that are important to them.

interview a research technique that involves gathering verbal data through questions or guided conversation between at least two people.

invention the discovery of something new.

kente cloth a royal and sacred fabric associated with Ghana's Akan people and characterized by geometric shapes, bright colors, and designs associated with proverbs, leaders, events, and plants.

khipu cords of knotted strings used during the Inca empire for keeping accounts and recording events.

kinship system the predominant form of kin relationships in a culture and the kinds of behavior involved.

kula a trading network, linking many of the Trobriand Islands, in which men have long-standing partnerships for the exchange of everyday goods, such as food, as well as highly valued necklaces and armlets.

language a form of communication that is based on a systematic set of learned symbols and signs shared among a group and passed on from generation to generation.

language family a group of languages descended from a parent language.

law a binding rule created through enactment or custom that defines right and reasonable behavior and is enforceable by the threat of punishment.

leveling mechanism an unwritten, culturally embedded rule that prevents an individual from becoming wealthier or more powerful than anyone else.

life project local people's definition of the direction they want to take in life, informed by their knowledge, history, and context.

lifeboat mentality a view that seeks to limit growth of a particular group because of perceived resource constraints.

life-cycle ritual a ritual that marks a change in status from one life stage to another.

linguistic anthropology the study of human communication, including its origins, history, and contemporary variation and change.

localization   the transformation of global culture by local cultures into something new.

logograph   a symbol that conveys meaning through a picture resembling that to which it refers.

magic   the attempt to compel supernatural beings and forces to act in certain ways.

male bias in development   the design and implementation of development projects with men as beneficiaries and without regard to the impact of the projects on women's roles and status.

manioc, or **cassava**   a starchy root crop that grows in the tropics and requires lengthy processing to make it edible, including soaking it in water to remove toxins and then scraping it into a mealy consistency.

market exchange   the buying and selling of commodities under competitive conditions, in which the forces of supply and demand determine value.

marriage   a union, usually between two people who are likely to be, but are not necessarily, coresident, sexually involved with each other, and procreative.

material cultural heritage   the sites, monuments, buildings, and movable objects considered to have outstanding value to humanity.

matriarchy   the dominance of women in economic, political, social, and ideological domains.

matrilineal descent   a descent system that highlights the importance of women by tracing descent through the female line, favoring marital residence with or near the bride's family, and providing for property to be inherited through the female line.

medical pluralism   the existence of more than one health system in a culture; also, a government policy to promote the integration of local healing systems into biomedical practice.

medicalization   the labeling of a particular issue or problem as medical and requiring medical treatment when, in fact, that issue or problem is economic or political.

menarche   the onset of menstruation.

menopause   the cessation of menstruation.

mestizaje   literally, a racial mixture; in Central and South America, indigenous people who are cut off from their Indian roots, or literate and successful indigenous people who retain some traditional cultural practices.

micro-credit loan   a small cash loan made to low-income people to support an income-generating activity.

microculture   a distinct pattern of learned and shared behavior and thinking found within a larger culture.

migration   movement from one place to another.

militarism   the dominance of the armed forces in administration of the state and society.

minimalism   a mode of consumption that emphasizes simplicity, is characterized by few and finite consumer demands, and involves an adequate and sustainable means to achieve them.

mixed methods   data collection and analysis that integrates quantitative and qualitative approaches for a more comprehensive understanding of culture.

mobile money   financial transactions that take place through a cell phone, also called a mobile phone.

mode of consumption   the dominant pattern, in a culture, of using things up or spending resources to satisfy demands.

mode of exchange   the dominant pattern, in a culture, of transferring goods, services, and other items between and among people and groups.

mode of livelihood   the dominant way of making a living in a culture.

mode of reproduction   the predominant pattern, in a culture, of population change through the combined effect of fertility (births) and mortality (deaths).

modernization   a model of change based on belief in the inevitable advance of science and Western secularism and processes, including industrial growth, consolidation of the state, bureaucratization, a market economy, technological innovation, literacy, and options for social mobility.

moka   a strategy for developing political leadership in highland New Guinea that involves exchanging gifts and favors with individuals and sponsoring large feasts where further gift-giving occurs.

monogamy   marriage between two people.

mortality   the rate of deaths in a population.

multisited research   fieldwork conducted in more than one location to understand the culture of dispersed members of the culture or relationships among different levels of culture.

myth   a narrative with a plot that involves the supernaturals.

nation   a group of people who share a language, culture, territorial base, political organization, and history.

new immigrant   an international migrant who has moved since the 1960s.

nuclear household   a domestic unit containing one adult couple (married or partners) with or without children.

parallel cousin   offspring of either one's father's brother or one's mother's sister.

participant observation   basic fieldwork method in cultural anthropology that involves living in a culture for a long time while gathering data.

pastoralism   a mode of livelihood based on keeping domesticated animals and using their products, such as meat and milk, for most of the diet.

patriarchy   the dominance of men in economic, political, social, and ideological domains.

patrilineal descent   a descent system that highlights the importance of men in tracing descent, determining marital residence with or near the groom's family, and providing for inheritance of property through the male line.

personality   an individual's patterned and characteristic way of behaving, thinking, and feeling.

phoneme   a sound that makes a difference for meaning in a spoken language.

phytotherapy   healing through the use of plants.

pidgin   a contact language that blends elements of at least two languages and that emerges when people with different languages need to communicate.

pilgrimage   round-trip travel to a sacred place or places for purposes of religious devotion or ritual.

placebo effect   a positive result from a healing method due to a symbolic or otherwise nonmaterial factor.

policing   the exercise of social control through processes of surveillance and the threat of punishment related to maintaining social order.

political organization   groups within a culture that are responsible for public decision-making and leadership, maintaining social cohesion and order, protecting group rights, and ensuring safety from external threats.

polyandry   marriage of one wife with more than one husband.

polygamy   marriage involving multiple spouses.

polygyny   marriage of one husband with more than one wife.

potlatch   a grand feast in which guests are invited to eat and to receive gifts from the hosts.

poverty   lack of access to tangible or intangible resources that contribute to life and the well-being of a person, group, country, or region.

power   the ability to take action in the face of resistance, through force if necessary.

priest or **priestess**   a male or female full-time religious specialist whose position is based mainly on abilities gained through formal training.

primary group   a social group in which members meet on a face-to-face basis.

productivity   a feature of human language whereby people are able to communicate a potentially infinite number of messages efficiently.

project cycle   the steps of a development project from initial planning to completion: project identification, project design, project appraisal, project implementation, and project evaluation.

pronatalism   an attitude or policy that encourages childbearing.

puberty   a time in the human life cycle that occurs universally and involves a set of biological markers and sexual maturation.

pure gift   something given with no expectation or thought of a return.

push–pull theory   an explanation for rural-to-urban migration that emphasizes people's incentives to move because of a lack of opportunity in rural areas (the "push") compared with urban areas (the "pull").

qualitative data   nonnumeric information.

quantitative data   numeric information.

questionnaire   a formal research instrument containing a preset series of questions that the anthropologist asks in a face-to-face setting, by mail, e-mail, or telephone.

"race"   a way of categorizing people into groups on the basis of supposedly homogeneous and largely superficial biological traits such as skin color or hair characteristics.

rapport   a trusting relationship between the researcher and the study population.

redistribution   a form of exchange that involves one person collecting goods or money from many members of a group, who then, at a later time and at a public event, "returns" the pooled goods to everyone who contributed.

refugee   someone who is forced to leave his or her home, community, or country.

religion   beliefs and behavior related to supernatural beings and forces.

religious pluralism   the condition in which two or more religions coexist either as complementary to each other or as competing systems.

religious syncretism   the blending of features of two or more religions.

remittance   the transfer of money or goods by a migrant to his or her family in the country of origin.

resilience   ability of a population to "bounce back" from conflict, a disaster, or other traumatic situation.

revitalization movement   a socioreligious movement, usually organized by a prophetic leader, that seeks to construct a more satisfying situation by reviving all or parts of a religion that has been threatened by outside forces or by adopting new practices and beliefs.

right of return   the United Nations' guaranteed right of a refugee to return to his or her home country to live.

ritual   patterned behavior that has to do with the supernatural realm.

ritual of inversion   a ritual in which normal social roles and order are temporarily reversed.

sacrifice   a ritual in which something is offered to the supernaturals.

Sapir–Whorf hypothesis   a perspective in linguistic anthropology saying that language determines thought.

secondary group   a group of people who identify with one another on some basis but may never meet with one another personally.

sectarian conflict   conflict based on perceived differences between divisions or sects within a religion.

shaman or **shamanka**   a male and female healer, respectively, whose healing methods rely on communication with the spirit world.

sign language   a form of communication that uses mainly hand movements to convey messages.

social capital   the intangible resources existing in social ties, trust, and cooperation.

social control   processes that, through both informal and formal mechanisms, maintain orderly social life.

social group   a cluster of people beyond the domestic unit who are usually related on grounds other than kinship.

social impact assessment   a study conducted to predict the potential social costs and benefits of particular innovations before change is undertaken.

social justice   a concept of fairness based on social equality that seeks to ensure access to basic human needs and opportunities for disadvantaged members of society.

social norm   a generally agreed-upon standard for how people should behave, usually unwritten and learned unconsciously.

social stratification   a set of hierarchical relationships among different groups as though they were arranged in layers, or "strata."

sociolinguistics   a perspective in linguistic anthropology, which says that culture, society, and a person's social position determine language.

somatization   the process through which the body absorbs social stress and manifests symptoms of suffering.

state   a form of political organization in which a centralized political unit encompasses many communities, a bureaucratic structure, and leaders who possess coercive power.

status   a person's position, or standing, in society.

structural suffering   human health problems caused by such economic and political factors as war, famine, terrorism, forced migration, and poverty.

structurism   a theoretical position concerning human behavior and ideas that says large forces such as the economy, social and political organization, and the media shape what people do and think.

subjective well-being   how people experience the quality of their lives based on their perception of what is a good life.

susto   fright/shock disease, a culture-specific illness found in Spain and Portugal and among Latino people wherever they live; symptoms include back pain, fatigue, weakness, and lack of appetite.

symbol   an object, word, or action with culturally defined meaning that stands for something else; most symbols are arbitrary.

tag question   a question placed at the end of a sentence seeking affirmation.

Textese   an emerging variant of written English and other languages associated with cell phone communication and involving abbreviations and creative slang.

theater   a form of enactment, related to other forms such as dance, music, parades, competitive games and sports, and verbal art, that seeks to entertain through acting, movement, and sound.

trade   the formalized exchange of one thing for another according to set standards of value.

traditional development anthropology   an approach to international development in which the anthropologist accepts the role of helping to make development work better by providing cultural information to planners.

transnational migration   regular movement of a person between two or more countries, resulting in a new cultural identity.

trial by ordeal   a way of determining innocence or guilt in which the accused person is put to a test that may be painful, stressful, or fatal.

tribe   a form of political organization that comprises several bands or lineage groups, each with a similar language and lifestyle and occupying a distinct territory.

unbalanced exchange   a system of transfers in which one party seeks to make a profit.

unilineal descent   the tracing of descent through only one parent.

use rights   a system of property relations in which a person or group has socially recognized priority in access to particular resources such as gathering, hunting, and fishing areas and water holes.

wa   a Japanese word meaning discipline and self-sacrifice for the good of the group.

war   organized and purposeful group action directed against another group and involving lethal force.

Western biomedicine (WBM)   a healing approach based on modern Western science that emphasizes technology for diagnosing and treating health problems related to the human body.

world religion   a term coined in the nineteenth century to refer to a religion that is based on written sources, has many followers, is regionally widespread, and is concerned with salvation.

youth gang   a group of young people, found mainly in urban areas, who are often considered a social problem by adults and law enforcement officials.

References

Abu-Lughod, Lila. 1993. *Writing Women's Worlds: Bedouin Stories*. Berkeley: University of California Press.

Adams, Abigail E. 2002. Dyke to Dyke: Ritual Reproduction at a U.S. Men's Military College. In *The Best of Anthropology Today* (pp. 34–42). Jonathan Benthall, ed. New York: Routledge.

Adams, Vincanne. 1988. Modes of Production and Medicine: An Examination of the Theory in Light of Sherpa Traditional Medicine. *Social Science and Medicine* 27:505–513.

Afolayan, F. 2000. Bantu Expansion and Its Consequences. In *African History before 1885* (pp. 113–136). T. Falola, ed. Durham, NC: Carolina Academic Press.

Ahmadu, Fuambai. 2000. Rites and Wrongs: An Insider/Outside Reflects on Power and Excision. In *Female "Circumcision" in Africa: Culture, Controversy, and Change* (pp. 283–312). Bettina Shell-Duncan and Ylva Hernlund, eds. Boulder, CO: Lynne Reiner Publishers.

Allen, Catherine J. 2002. *The Hold Life Has: Coca and Cultural Identity in an Andean Community*. Washington, DC: Smithsonian Institution Press.

Allen, Susan. 1994. What Is Media Anthropology? A Personal View and a Suggested Structure. In *Media Anthropology: Informing Global Citizens* (pp. 15–32). Susan L. Allen, ed. Westport, CT: Bergin & Garvey.

Alter, Joseph S. 1992. The Sannyasi and the Indian Wrestler: Anatomy of a Relationship. *American Ethnologist* 19(2):317–336.

Amster, Matthew H. 2000. It Takes a Village to Dismantle a Longhouse. *Thresholds* 20:65–71.

Anderson, Benedict. 1991 [1983]. *Imagined Communities: Reflections on the Origin and Spread of Nationalism*. New York: Verso.

Anderson, Myrdene. 2004. Reflections on the Saami at Loose Ends. In *Cultural Shaping of Violence: Victimization, Escalation, Response* (pp. 285–291). Myrdene Anderson, ed. West Lafayette, IN: Purdue University Press.

———. 2005. The Saami Yoik: Translating Hum, Chant and/or Song. In *Song and Significance: Virtues and Vices of Vocal Translation* (pp. 213–233). Dinda Gorlée, ed. Amsterdam: Rodopi.

Applbaum, Kalman D. 1995. Marriage with the Proper Stranger: Arranged Marriage in Metropolitan Japan. *Ethnology* 34(1):37–51.

Arambiza, Evelio and Michael Painter. 2006. Biodiversity Conservation and the Quality of Life of Indigenous People in the Bolivian Chaco. *Human Organization* 65:20–34.

Baker, Colin. 1999. Sign Language and the Deaf Community. In *Handbook of Language and Ethnic Identity* (pp. 122–139). Joshua A. Fishman, ed. New York: Oxford University Press.

Baker-Christales, Beth. 2004. *Salvadoran Migration to Southern California: Redefining El Hermano Lejano*. Gainesville: University of Florida Press.

Baptista, Marlyse. 2005. New Directions in Pidgin and Creole Studies. *Annual Review of Anthropology* 34:34–42.

Barfield, Thomas J. 1994. Prospects for Plural Societies in Central Asia. *Cultural Survival Quarterly* 18(2&3):48–51.

———. 2001. Pastoral Nomads or Nomadic Pastoralists. In *The Dictionary of Anthropology* (pp. 348–350). Thomas Barfield, ed. Malden, MA: Blackwell Publishers.

Barkey, Nanette, Benjamin C. Campbell, and Paul W. Leslie. 2001. A Comparison of Health Complaints of Settled and Nomadic Turkana Men. *Medical Anthropology Quarterly* 15:391–408.

Barlett, Peggy F. 1989. Industrial Agriculture. In *Economic Anthropology* (pp. 253–292). Stuart Plattner, ed. Stanford, CA: Stanford University Press.

Barnard, Alan and Anthony Good. 1984. *Research Practices in the Study of Kinship*. New York: Academic Press.

Barrionuevo, Alexei. 2008. Amazon's "Forest People" Seek a Role in Striking Global Climate Agreements. *New York Times*. April 5:6.

Basso, Keith. H. 1972 [1970]. "To Give Up on Words": Silence in Apache Culture. In *Language and Social Context* (pp. 67–86). Pier Paolo Giglioni, ed. Baltimore: Penguin Books.

Bauer, Alexander A. 2006. Heritage Preservation in Law and Policy: Handling the Double-Edged Sword of Development. Paper presented at the International Conference on Cultural Heritage and Development, Bibliothèca Alexandrina, Alexandria, Egypt, January.

Beals, Alan R. 1980. *Gopalpur: A South Indian Village. Fieldwork Edition*. New York: Holt, Rinehart and Winston.

Beeman, William O. 1993. The Anthropology of Theater and Spectacle. *Annual Review of Anthropology* 22:363–393.

Bernal, Martin. 1987. *Black Athena: The Afroasiatic Roots of Classical Civilization*. New Brunswick, NJ: Rutgers University Press.

Berreman, Gerald D. 1979 [1975]. Race, Caste, and Other Invidious Distinctions in Social Stratification. In *Caste and Other Inequities: Essays on Inequality* (pp. 178–222). Gerald D. Berreman, ed. New Delhi: Manohar.

Bestor, Theodore C. 2004. *Tsukiji: The Fish Market at the Center of the World*. Berkeley: University of California Press.

Beyene, Yewoubdar. 1989. *From Menarche to Menopause: Reproductive Lives of Peasant Women in Two Cultures*. Albany: State University of New York Press.

Bhardwaj, Surinder M. and N. Madhusudana Rao. 1990. Asian Indians in the United States: A Geographic Appraisal. In *South Asians Overseas: Migration and Ethnicity* (pp. 197–218). Colin Clarke, Ceri Peach, and Steven Vertovec, eds. New York: Cambridge University Press.

Bhatt, Rakesh M. 2001. World Englishes. *Annual Review of Anthropology* 30:527–550.

Billig, Michael S. 1992. The Marriage Squeeze and the Rise of Groomprice in India's Kerala State. *Journal of Comparative Family Studies* 23:197–216.

Blackwood, Evelyn. 1995. Senior Women, Model Mothers, and Dutiful Wives: Managing Gender Contradictions in a Minangkabau Village. In *Bewitching Women: Pious Men: Gender and Body Politics in Southeast Asia* (pp. 124–158). Aihwa Ong and Michael Peletz, eds. Berkeley: University of California Press.

Bledsoe, Caroline H. 1983. Stealing Food as a Problem in Demography and Nutrition. Paper presented at the annual meeting of the American Anthropological Association.

Blommaert, Jan and Chris Bulcaen. 2000. Critical Discourse Analysis. *Annual Review of Anthropology* 29:447–466.

Blood, Robert O. 1967. *Love Match and Arranged Marriage*. New York: Free Press.

Bodenhorn, Barbara. 2000. "He Used to Be My Relative." Exploring the Bases of Relatedness among the Inupiat of Northern Alaska. In *Cultures of Relatedness: New Approaches to the Study of Kinship* (pp. 128–148). Janet Carsten, ed. New York: Cambridge University Press.

Boellstorff, Tom. 2004. Gay Language and Indonesia: Registering Belonging. *Journal of Linguistic Anthropology* 14:248–268.

Boserup, Ester. 1970. *Woman's Role in Economic Development*. New York: St. Martin's Press.

Bourgois, Philippe and Jeff Schonberg. 2009. *Righteous Dopefiend*. Berkeley: University of California Press.

Bowen, John R. 1992. On Scriptural Essentialism and Ritual Variation: Muslim Sacrifice in Sumatra. *American Ethnologist* 19(4):656–671.

———. 1998. *Religions in Practice: An Approach to the Anthropology of Religion*. Boston: Allyn and Bacon.

Bradley, Richard. 2000. *An Archaeology of Natural Places*. New York: Routledge.

Brandes, Stanley H. 1985. *Forty: The Age and the Symbol*. Knoxville: University of Tennessee Press.

Brave Heart, Mary Yellow Horse. 2004. The Historical Trauma Response among Natives and Its Relationship to Substance Abuse. In *Healing and Mental Health for Native Americans: Speaking in Red* (pp. 7–18). Ethan Nebelkopf and Mary Phillips, eds. Walnut Creek, CA: AltaMira Press.

Brookes, Heather. 2004. A Repertoire of South African Quotable Gestures. *Journal of Linguistic Anthropology* 14:186–224.

Broude, Gwen J. 1988. Rethinking the Couvade: Cross-Cultural Evidence. *American Anthropologist* 90(4): 902–911.

Brown, Carolyn Henning. 1984. Tourism and Ethnic Competition in a Ritual Form: The Firewalkers of Fiji. *Oceania* 54:223–244.

Brown, Judith K. 1975. Iroquois Women: An Ethnohistoric Note. In *Toward an Anthropology of Women* (pp. 235–251). Rayna R. Reiter, ed. New York: Monthly Review Press.

———. 1978. The Recruitment of a Female Labor Force. *Anthropos* 73(1/2):41–48.

———. 1999. Introduction: Definitions, Assumptions, Themes, and Issues. In *To Have and To Hit: Cultural Perspectives on Wife Beating*, 2nd ed. (pp. 3–26). Dorothy Ayers Counts, Judith K. Brown, and Jacquelyn C. Campbell, eds. Urbana: University of Illinois Press.

Browner, Carole H. 1986. The Politics of Reproduction in a Mexican Village. *Signs: Journal of Women in Culture and Society* 11(4):710–724.

Browner, Carole H. and Nancy Ann Press. 1996. The Production of Authoritative Knowledge in American Prenatal Care. *Medical Anthropology Quarterly* 10(2):141–156.

Bruner, Edward M. 2005. *Culture on Tour: Ethnographies of Travel*. Chicago: University of Chicago Press.

Bunzel, Ruth. 1972 [1929]. *The Pueblo Potter: A Study of Creative Imagination in Primitive Art*. New York: Dover Publications.

Burdick, John. 2004. *Legacies of Liberation: The Progressive Catholic Church in Brazil at the Turn of a New Century*. Burlington, VT: Ashgate Publishers.

Burton, Barbara. 2004. The Transmigration of Rights: Women, Movement and the Grassroots in Latin American and Caribbean Communities. *Development and Change* 35:773–798.

Call, Vaughn, Susan Sprecher, and Pepper Schwartz. 1995. The Incidence and Frequency of Marital Sex in a National Sample. *Journal of Marriage and the Family* 57:639–652.

Camino, Linda A. and Ruth M. Krulfeld, eds. 1994. *Reconstructing Lives, Recapturing Meaning: Refugee Identity, Gender and Culture Change*. Basel: Gordon and Breach Publishers.

Carneiro, Robert L. 1994. War and Peace: Alternating Realities in Human History. In *Studying War: Anthropological Perspectives* (pp. 3–27). S. P. Reyna and R. E. Downs, eds. Langhorne, PA: Gordon and Breach Science Publishers.

Carstairs, G. Morris. 1967. *The Twice Born*. Bloomington: Indiana University Press.

Carsten, Janet. 1995. Children in Between: Fostering and the Process of Kinship on Pulau Langkawi, Malaysia. *Man* (n.s.) 26:425–443.

Cátedra, María. 1992. *This World, Other Worlds: Sickness, Suicide, Death, and the Afterlife among the Vaqueiros de Alzada of Spain*. Chicago: University of Chicago Press.

Cernea, Michael M. 1985. Sociological Knowledge for Development Projects. In *Putting People First: Sociological Variables and Rural Development* (pp. 3–22). Michael M. Cernea, ed. New York: Oxford University Press.

———. 2001. *Cultural Heritage and Development: A Framework for Action in the Middle East and North Africa*. Washington, DC: The World Bank.

Chagnon, Napoleon. 1992. *Yanomamö*, 4th ed. New York: Harcourt Brace Jovanovich.

Chalfin, Brenda. 2004. *Shea Butter Republic: State Power, Global Markets, and the Making of an Indigenous Commodity*. New York: Routledge.

———. 2008. Cars, the Customs Service, and Sumptuary Rule in Neoliberal Ghana. *Comparative Studies in Society and History* 50:424–453.

Chernoff, John Miller. 1979. *African Rhythm and African Sensibility: Aesthetics and African Musical Idioms*. Chicago: University of Chicago Press.

Childs, Larry and Celina Chelala. 1994. Drought, Rebellion and Social Change in Northern Mali: The Challenges Facing Tamacheq Herders. *Cultural Survival Quarterly* 18(4):16–19.

Chin, Elizabeth. 2001. *Purchasing Power: Black Kids and American Consumer Culture*. Minneapolis: University of Minnesota Press.

Chiñas, Beverly Newbold. 1992. *The Isthmus Zapotecs: A Matrifocal Culture of Mexico*. New York: Harcourt Brace Jovanovich.

Clancy, Kathryn B. H, Robin G. Nelson, Julienne N. Rutherford, and Katie Hinde. 2014. Survey of Academic Field Experiences (SAFE): Trainees Report Harassment and Assault. *PLOS ONE* 9(7):e102172.

Clarke, Maxine Kumari. 2004. *Mapping Yorùbá Networks: Power and Agency in the Making of Transnational Communities*. Durham, NC: Duke University Press.

Clay, Jason W. 1990. What's a Nation: Latest Thinking. *Mother Jones* 15(7):28–30.

Cochrane, D. Glynn. 1974. Barbara Miller's class lecture notes in Applied Anthropology, Syracuse University.

———. 1979. *The Cultural Appraisal of Development Projects*. New York: Praeger Publishers.

———. 2008. *Festival Elephants and the Myth of Global Poverty*. Boston: Pearson.

Cohen, Mark Nathan. 1989. *Health and the Rise of Civilization*. New Haven, CT: Yale University Press.

Cole, Douglas. 1991. *Chiefly Feasts: The Enduring Kwakiutl Potlatch*. Aldona Jonaitis, ed. Seattle: University of Washington Press/New York: American Museum of Natural History.

Colley, Sarah. 2002. *Uncovering Australia: Archaeology, Indigenous People and the Public*. Washington, DC: Smithsonian Institution Press.

Comaroff, John L. 1987. Of Totemism and Ethnicity: Consciousness, Practice and Signs of Inequality. *Ethnos* 52(3–4):301–323.

Contreras, Gloria. 1995. Teaching about Vietnamese Culture: Water Puppetry as the Soul of the Rice Fields. *The Social Studies* 86(1):25–28.

Coon Come, Matthew. 2004. Survival in the Context of Mega-Resource Development: Experiences of the James Bay Crees and the First Nations of Canada. In *In the Way of Development: Indigenous Peoples, Life Projects and Globalization* (pp. 153–165). Mario Blaser, Harvey A. Feit, and Glenn McRae, eds. New York: Zed Books in Association with the International Development Research Centre.

Corbey, Raymond. 2003. Destroying the Graven Image: Religious Iconoclasm on the Christian Frontier. *Anthropology Today* 19:10–14.

Counihan, Carole M. 1985. Transvestism and Gender in a Sardinian Carnival. *Anthropology* 9(1&2):11–24.

Craik, Brian. 2004. The Importance of Working Together: Exclusions, Conflicts and Participation in James Bay, Quebec. In *In the Way of Development: Indigenous Peoples, Life Projects and Globalization* (pp. 166–186). Mario Blaser, Harvey A. Feit, and Glenn McRae, eds. Zed Books in Association with the International Development Research Centre.

Crowe, D. 1996. *A History of the Gypsies of Eastern Europe and Russia*. New York: St. Martin's Press.

Crystal, David. 2000. *Language Death*. New York: Cambridge University Press.

———. 2003. *English as a Global Language*, 2nd ed. New York: Cambridge University Press.

Cunningham, Lawrence S. 1995. Christianity. In *The Harper-Collins Dictionary of Religion* (pp. 240–253). Jonathan Z. Smith, ed. New York: HarperCollins.

Dalby, Liza Crihfield. 1998. *Geisha*, 2nd ed. New York: Vintage Books.

———. 2001. *Kimono: Fashioning Culture*. Seattle: University of Washington Press.

Daly, Martin, and Margo Wilson. 1984. A Sociobiological Analysis of Human Infanticide. In *Infanticide: Comparative and Evolutionary Perspectives* (pp. 487–582). Glen Hausfater and Sarah Blaffer Hrdy, eds. New York: Aldine.

Danforth, Loring M. 1989. *Firewalking and Religious Healing: The Anestenaria of Greece and the American Firewalking Movement*. Princeton, NJ: Princeton University Press.

Darlington, Shasta. 2015. Inside Brazil's Battle to Protect the Amazon. CNN October 29. http://www.cnn.com/2015/10/29/world/brazil-logging-climate-change-two-degrees/

Daugherty, Mary Lee. 1997 [1976]. Serpent-Handling as Sacrament. In *Magic, Witchcraft, and Religion* (pp. 347–352). Arthur C. Lehmann and James E. Myers, eds. Mountain View, CA: Mayfield Publishing.

Dávila, Arlene. 2002. Culture in the Ad World: Producing the Latin Look. In *Media Worlds: Anthropology on New Terrain* (pp. 264–280). Faye D. Ginsburg, Lila Abu-Lughod, and Brian Larkin, eds. Berkeley: University of California Press.

Davis, Peter. 2011. Exploring the Long-Term Impact of Development Interventions within Life-History Narratives in Rural Bangladesh. *Journal of Development Effectiveness* 3:263–280.

Davis, Robert C. and Garry R. Marvin. 2004, *Venice, the Tourist Maze: A Cultural Critique of the World's Most Touristed City*. Berkeley: University of California Press.

Davis, Susan Schaefer and Douglas A. Davis. 1987. *Adolescence in a Moroccan Town: Making Social Sense*. New Brunswick: Rutgers University Press.

Davis-Floyd, Robbie E. 1987. Obstetric Training as a Rite of Passage. *Medical Anthropology Quarterly* 1:288–318.

———. 1992. *Birth as an American Rite of Passage*. Berkeley: University of California Press.

de la Cadena, Marisol. 2001. Reconstructing Race: Racism, Culture and Mestizaje in Latin America. *NACLA Report on the Americas* 34:16–23.

de Sherbinin, A., M. Castro, F. Gemenne, M. M. Cernea, S. Adamo, P. M. Fearnside, G. Krieger, S. Lahmani, A. Oliver-Smith, A. Pankhurst, T. Scudder, B. Singer, Y. Tan, G. Wannier, P. Boncour, C. Ehrhart, G. Hugo, B. Pandey, and G. Shi. 2011. Preparing for Resettlement Associated with Climate Change. *Science* 334:456–457.

Deen, Thalif. 2015. Over 100 Million Women Lead Migrant Workers Worldwide. *Inter Press Service*. June 24.

Dent, Alexander Sebastian. 2005. Cross-Culture "Countries": Covers, Conjuncture, and the Whiff of Nashville in *Música Sertaneja* (Brazilian Commercial Country Music). *Popular Music and Society* 28:207–227.

Devereaux, George. 1976. *A Typological Study of Abortion in Primitive Societies: A Typological, Distributional, and Dynamic Analysis of the Prevention of Birth in 400 Preindustrial Societies*. New York: International Universities Press.

digim'Rina, Linus S. 2005. Food Security through Traditions: Replanting Trees and Wise Practices." *People and Culture in Oceania* 20:13–36.

———. 2006. Personal communication.

Dikötter, Frank. 1998. Hairy Barbarians, Furry Primates and Wild Men: Medical Science and Cultural Representations of Hair in China. In *Hair: Its Power and Meaning in Asian Cultures* (pp. 51–74). Alf Hiltebeitel and Barbara D. Miller, eds. Albany: State University of New York Press.

Doi, Yaruko and Masami Minowa. 2003. Gender Differences in Excessive Daytime Sleepiness among Japanese Workers. *Social Science and Medicine* 56:883–894.

Donlon, Jon. 1990. Fighting Cocks, Feathered Warriors, and Little Heroes. *Play & Culture* 3:273–285.

Dorgan, Howard. 1989. *The Old Regular Baptists of Central Appalachia: Brothers and Sisters in Hope*. Knoxville: University of Tennessee Press.

Drake, Susan P. 1991. Local Participation in Ecotourism Projects. In *Nature Tourism: Managing for the Environment* (pp. 132–155). Tensie Whelan, ed. Washington, DC: Island Press.

Duany, Jorge. 2000. Nation on the Move: The Construction of Cultural Identities in Puerto Rico and the Diaspora. *American Ethnologist* 27:5–30.

Duranti, Alessandro. 1997a. *Linguistic Anthropology*. New York: Cambridge University Press.

———. 1997b. Universal and Culture-Specific Properties of Greetings. *Journal of Linguistic Anthropology* 7:63–97.

Durrenberger, E. Paul. 2001. Explorations of Class and Class Consciousness in the U.S. *Journal of Anthropological Research* 57:41–60.

Eccles, Jeremy. 2012. Artist Saw the Stars Crying: Gulumbu Yunuping, 1945–2012. *Sydney Morning Herald* June 10.

Eck, Diana L. 1985. *Darsán: Seeing the Divine Image in India*, 2nd ed. Chambersburg, PA: Anima Books.

Eckel, Malcolm David. 1995. Buddhism. In *The HarperCollins Dictionary of Religion* (pp. 135–150). Jonathan Z. Smith, ed. New York: HarperCollins.

Economic and Social Council. 1992. *Report of the Working Group on Violence against Women*. Vienna: United Nations. E/CN.6/WG.2/1992/L.3.

Englund, Harri. 1998. Death, Trauma and Ritual: Mozambican Refugees in Malawi. *Social Science and Medicine* 46(9):1165–1174.

Ennis-McMillan, Michael C. 2001. Suffering from Water: Social Origins of Bodily Distress in a Mexican Community. *Medical Anthropology Quarterly* 15(3):368–390.

Erickson, Barbra. 2007. Toxin or Medicine? Explanatory Models of Radon in Montana Health Mines. *Medical Anthropology Quarterly* 21:1–21.

Escobar, Arturo. 2002. Gender, Place, and Networks: A Political Ecology of Cyberculture. In *Development: A Cultural Studies Reader* (pp. 239–256). Susan Schech and Jane Haggis, eds. Malden, MA: Blackwell Publishers.

Estrin, Saul. 1996. Co-Operatives. In *The Social Science Encyclopedia* (pp. 138–139). Adam Kuper and Jessica Kuper, eds. New York: Routledge.

Etienne, Mona and Eleanor Leacock, eds. 1980. *Women and Colonization: Anthropological Perspectives*. New York: Praeger.

Evans-Pritchard, E. E. 1951. *Kinship and Marriage among the Nuer*. Oxford: Clarendon.

Everett, Daniel L. 1995. Personal communication.

———. 2008. *Don't Sleep, There Are Snakes: Life and Language in the Amazonian Jungle*. New York: Knopf Publishing Group.

Evrard, Olivier and Yves Goudineau. 2004. Planned Resettlement, Unexpected Migrations and Cultural Trauma in Laos. *Development and Change* 35:937–962.

Fabrega, Horacio, Jr. and Barbara D. Miller. 1995. Adolescent Psychiatry as a Product of Contemporary Anglo-American Society. *Social Science and Medicine* 40(7): 881–894.

Fahey, Dan. 2011. The Trouble with Ituri. *African Security Review* 20:108–113.

Farmer, Paul. 1992. *AIDS and Accusation: Haiti and the Geography of Blame*. Berkeley: University of California Press.

———. 2005. *Pathologies of Power: Health, Human Rights and the New War on the Poor*. Berkeley: University of California Press.

Feinberg, Richard. 2012. Defending "Traditional" Marriage? Whose Definition? What Tradition? *The Huffington Post/American Anthropological Association*. April 30.

Feinsilver, Julie M. 1993. *Healing the Masses: Cuban Health Politics at Home and Abroad*. Berkeley: University of California Press.

Fenstemaker, Sarah. 2007. Conservation Clash and the Case for Exemptions: How Eagle Protection Conflicts with Hopi Cultural Preservation. *International Journal of Cultural Property* 14:315–328.

Ferguson, James. 1994. *The Anti-Politics Machine: "Development," Depoliticization, and Bureaucratic Power in Lesotho*. Minneapolis: University of Minnesota Press.

Ferguson, R. Brian. 1990. Blood of the Leviathan: Western Contact and Amazonian Warfare. *American Ethnologist* 17(1):237–257.

Ferris, Elizabeth and Sara Ferro-Ribeiro. 2012. Protecting People in Cities: The Disturbing Case of Haiti. *Disasters* 36:S43–S63.

First Peoples Worldwide. 2015. http://www.firstpeoples .org/who-are-indigenous-peoples.

Fishman, Joshua A. 1991. *Reversing Language Shift: Theoretical and Empirical Foundations of Assistance to Threatened Languages*. Clevedon, UK: Multilingual Matters Ltd.

———, ed. 2001. *Can Threatened Languages Be Saved? Reversing Language Shift, Revisited: A 21st Century Perspective*. Buffalo, NY: Multilingual Matters Ltd.

Fitigu, Yodit. 2005. Forgotten People: Internally Displaced Persons in Guatemala. www.refugeesinternational.org/ content/article/detail/6344.

Foley, Kathy. 2001. The Metonymy of Art: Vietnamese Water Puppetry as Representation of Modern Vietnam. *The Drama Review* 45(4):129–141.

Foley, William A. 2000. The Languages of New Guinea. *Annual Review of Anthropology* 29:357–404.

Foster, Helen Bradley and Donald Clay Johnson, eds. 2003. *Wedding Dress across Cultures*. New York: Berg.

Foster, Robert J. 2006. From Trobriand Cricket to Rugby Nation: The Mission of Sport in Papua New Guinea. *The International Journal of the History of Sport* 23(5):739–758.

Foucault, Michel. 1970. *The Order of Things: An Archaeology of the Human Sciences*. New York: Random House.

Fox, Robin. 1995 [1978]. *The Tory Islanders: A People of the Celtic Fringe*. Notre Dame: University of Notre Dame Press.

Frake, Charles O. 1961. The Diagnosis of Disease Among the Subanun of Mindanao. *American Anthropologist* 63:113–132.

Franceschet, Susan, Mona Lena Krook, and Jennifer Piscopo. 2012. *The Impact of Gender Quotas*. New York: Oxford University Press.

Franke, Richard W. 1993. *Life is a Little Better: Redistribution as a Development Strategy in Nadur Village, Kerala*. Boulder, CO: Westview Press.

Fratkin, Elliot. 1998. *Ariaal Pastoralists of Kenya: Surviving Drought and Development in Africa's Arid Lands*. Boston: Allyn and Bacon.

Frazer, Sir James. 1978 [1890]. *The Golden Bough: A Study in Magic and Religion*. New York: Macmillan.

Freeman, James A. 1981. A Firewalking Ceremony That Failed. In *Social and Cultural Context of Medicine in India* (pp. 308–336). Giri Raj Gupta, ed. New Delhi: Vikas Publishing.

Frieze, Irene, Jacquelynne E. Parsons, Paula B. Johnson, Diane N. Ruble, and Gail L. Zellman. 1978. *Women and Sex Roles: A Social Psychological Perspective*. New York: W. W. Norton.

Furst, Peter T. 1989. The Water of Life: Symbolism and Natural History on the Northwest Coast. *Dialectical Anthropology* 14:95–115.

Gable, Eric. 1995. The Decolonization of Consciousness: Local Skeptics and the "Will to Be Modern" in a West African Village. *American Ethnologist* 22(2):242–257.

Gale, Faye, Rebecca Bailey-Harris, and Joy Wundersitz. 1990. *Aboriginal Youth and the Criminal Justice System: The Injustice of Justice?* New York: Cambridge University Press.

Gálvez, Alyshia. 2011. *Patient Citizens, Immigrant Mothers: Mexican Women, Public Prenatal Care, and the Birth-Weight Paradox.* New Brunswick, NJ: Rutgers University Press.

Gardner, Katy and David Lewis. 1996. *Anthropology, Development and the Post-Modern Challenge.* Sterling, VA: Pluto Press.

Gaski, Harald. 1993. The Sami People: The "White Indians" of Scandinavia. *American Indian Culture and Research Journal* 17:115–128.

———. 1997. Introduction: Sami Culture in a New Era. In *Sami Culture in a New Era: The Norwegian Sami Experience* (pp. 9–28). Harald Gaski, ed. Seattle: University of Washington Press.

Gedde, Maïa. 2015. *International Development and Humanitarian Assistance: A Career Guide.* New York: Routledge.

Geertz, Clifford. 1966. Religion as a Cultural System. In *Anthropological Approaches to the Study of Religion* (pp. 1–46). Michael Banton, ed. London: Tavistock.

Gillette, Maris Boyd. 2000. *Between Mecca and Beijing: Modernization and Consumption among Urban Chinese Families.* Stanford, CA: Stanford University Press.

Glick Schiller, Nina and Georges E. Fouron. 1999. Terrains of Blood and Nation: Haitian Transnational Social Fields. *Ethnic and Racial Studies* 22:340–365.

Global Times. 2010. China: 24 Million Men to be Mateless by End of Decade. January 11.

Gmelch, George. 1997 [1971]. Baseball Magic. In *Magic, Witchcraft, and Religion* (pp. 276–282). Arthur C. Lehmann and James E. Myers, eds. Mountain View, CA: Mayfield Publishing.

Godelier, Maurice. 2012. *The Metamorphoses of Kinship.* Brooklyn, NY: Verso.

Gold, Stevan J. 1992. *Refugee Communities: A Comparative Field Study.* Newbury Park, CA: Sage Publications.

González, Roberto A. 2009. *American Counterinsurgency: Human Science and the Human Terrain.* Chicago: University of Chicago Press.

Goodwin, Marjorie H. 1990. *He-Said-She-Said: Talk as Social Organization among Black Children.* Bloomington: Indiana University Press.

Goody, Jack. 1993. *The Culture of Flowers.* New York: Cambridge University Press.

Graeber, David. 2011. *Debt: The First 5,000 Years.* Brooklyn, NY: Melville Publishing House.

Greenhalgh, Susan. 2008. *Just One Child: Science and Policy in Deng's China.* Berkeley: University of California Press.

Gregg, Jessica L. 2003. *Virtually Virgins: Sexual Strategies and Cervical Cancer in Recife, Brazil.* Stanford, CA: Stanford University Press.

Gregor, Thomas. 1982. No Girls Allowed. *Science* 82.

Gregory, Chris. 2011. "Skinship:" Touchability as a Virtue in East-Central India. *HAU: Journal of Ethnographic Theory* 1:179–209.

Gremillion, Helen. 1992. Psychiatry as Social Ordering: Anorexia Nervosa, a Paradigm. *Social Science and Medicine* 35(1):57–71.

Grinker, Roy Richard. 1994. *Houses in the Rainforest: Ethnicity and Inequality among Farmers and Foragers in Central Africa.* Berkeley: University of California Press.

Gross, Daniel R. 1984. Time Allocation: A Tool for the Study of Cultural Behavior. *Annual Review of Anthropology* 13:519–558.

Gruenbaum, Ellen. 2001. *The Female Circumcision Controversy: An Anthropological Perspective.* Philadelphia: University of Pennsylvania Press.

Guggenheim, Scott E. and Michael M. Cernea. 1993. Anthropological Approaches to Involuntary Resettlement: Policy, Practice, and Theory. In *Anthropological Approaches to Resettlement: Policy, Practice, and Theory* (pp. 1–12). Michael M. Cernea and Scott E. Guggenheim, eds. Boulder, CO: Westview Press.

Guidoni, Enrico. 1987. *Primitive Architecture.* Trans. Robert Erich Wolf. New York: Rizzoli.

Haddix McCay, Kimber. 2001. Leaving Your Wife and Your Brothers: When Polyandrous Marriages Fall Apart. *Evolution and Human Behavior* 22:47–60.

Hamabata, Matthews Masayuki. 1990. *Crested Kimono: Power and Love in the Japanese Business Family.* Ithaca, NY: Cornell University Press.

Handler, Richard. 2003. Cultural Property and Cultural Theory. *Journal of Social Archaeology* 3:353–365.

Härkönen, Heidi. 2010. Gender, Kinship and Life Rituals in Cuba. *Suomen Antropologi: Journal of the Finnish Anthropological Society* 35:60–73.

Harlan, Tyler and Michael Webber. 2012. New Corporate Uyghur Entrepreneurs in Urumqi, China. *Central Asian* 31:175–191.

Harris, Marvin. 1971. *Culture, Man and Nature.* New York: Thomas Y. Crowell.

———. 1974. *Cows, Pigs, Wars and Witches: The Riddles of Culture.* New York: Random House.

———. 1975. *Culture, People, Nature: An Introduction to General Anthropology,* 2nd ed. New York: Thomas Y. Crowell.

———. 1977. *Cannibals and Kings: The Origins of Culture.* New York: Random House.

———. 1984. Animal Capture and Yanomamo Warfare: Retrospect and New Evidence. *Journal of Anthropological Research* 40(10):183–201.

———. 1993. The Evolution of Human Gender Hierarchies. In *Sex and Gender Hierarchies* (pp. 57–80). Barbara D. Miller, ed. New York: Cambridge University Press.

Hefner, Robert W. 1998. Multiple Modernities: Christianity, Islam, and Hinduism in a Globalizing Age. *Annual Review of Anthropology* 27:83–104.

Heise, Lori L., Jacqueline Pitanguy, and Adrienne Germain. 1994. Violence against Women: The Hidden Health Burden. *World Bank Discussion Papers No. 255.* Washington, DC: The World Bank.

Helweg, Arthur W. and Usha M. Helweg. 1990. *An Immigrant Success Story: East Indians in America.* Philadelphia: University of Pennsylvania Press.

Henshaw, Anne. 2006. Pausing along the Journey: Learning Landscapes, Environmental Change, and Toponymy amongst the Sikusilarmiut. *Arctic Anthropology* 43: 52–66.

Hewlett, Barry S. 1991. *Intimate Fathers: The Nature and Context of Aka Pygmy Paternal Care.* Ann Arbor: University of Michigan Press.

Hill, Jane H. 2001. Dimensions of Attrition in Language Death. In *On Biocultural Diversity: Linking Language, Knowledge, and the Environment* (pp. 175–189). Luisa Maffi, ed. Washington, DC: Smithsonian Institution Press.

Hill, Jane H. and Bruce Mannheim. 1992. Language and World View. *Annual Review of Anthropology* 21:381–406.

Hirschon, Renee. 1989. *Heirs of the Catastrophe: The Social Life of Asia Minor Refugees in Piraeus*. New York: Oxford University Press.

Hoffman, Danny and Stephen Lubkemann. 2005. Warscape Ethnography in West Africa and the Anthropology of "Events." *Anthropological Quarterly* 78:315–327.

Holland, Dorothy C. and Margaret A. Eisenhart. 1990. *Educated in Romance: Women, Achievement, and College Culture*. Chicago: University of Chicago Press.

Hornbein, George and Marie Hornbein. 1992. *Salamanders: A Night at the Phi Delt House*. Video. College Park: Documentary Resource Center.

Horowitz, Irving L. 1967. *The Rise and Fall of Project Camelot: Studies in the Relationship between Social Science and Practical Politics*. Boston: MIT Press.

Horowitz, Michael M. and Muneera Salem-Murdock. 1993. Development-Induced Food Insecurity in the Middle Senegal Valley. *GeoJournal* 30(2):179–184.

Horst, Heather and Daniel Miller. 2005. From Kinship to Link-Up: Cell Phones and Social Networking in Jamaica. *Current Anthropology* 46:755–764, 773–778.

Howell, Nancy. 1979. *Demography of the Dobe !Kung*. New York: Academic Press.

———. 1990. *Surviving Fieldwork: A Report of the Advisory Panel on Health and Safety in Fieldwork*. Washington, DC: American Anthropological Association.

Huang, Shu-Min. 1993. A Cross-Cultural Experience: A Chinese Anthropologist in the United States. In *Distance Mirrors: America as a Foreign Culture* (pp. 39–45). Philip R. DeVita and James D. Armstrong, eds. Belmont, CA: Wadsworth.

Humphrey, Caroline. 1978. Women, Taboo and the Suppression of Attention. In *Defining Females: The Nature of Women in Society* (pp. 89–108). Shirley Ardener, ed. New York: John Wiley and Sons.

Hunte, Pamela A. 1985. Indigenous Methods of Fertility Regulation in Afghanistan. In *Women's Medicine: A Cross-Cultural Study of Indigenous Fertility Regulation* (pp. 44–75). Lucile F. Newman, ed. New Brunswick, NJ: Rutgers University Press.

Hutter, Michael. 1996. The Value of Play. In *The Value of Culture: On the Relationship between Economics and the Arts* (pp. 122–137). Arjo Klamer, ed. Amsterdam: Amsterdam University Press.

Inhorn, Marcia C. 2003. Global Infertility and the Globalization of New Reproductive Technologies: Illustrations from Egypt. *Social Science and Medicine* 56:1837–1851.

———. 2004. Middle Eastern Masculinities in the Age of New Reproductive Technologies: Male Infertility and Stigma in Egypt and Lebanon. *Medical Anthropology Quarterly* 18(2):162–182.

Internal Displacement Monitoring Centre. 2015. http://www.internal-displacement.org/middle-east-and-north-africa/syria/figures-analysis

Jacobs-Huey, Lanita. 1997. Is There an Authentic African American Speech Community: Carla Revisited. *University of Pennsylvania Working Papers in Linguistics* 4(1): 331–370.

———. 2002. The Natives Are Gazing and Talking Back: Reviewing the Problematics of Positionality, Voice, and Accountability among "Native" Anthropologists. *American Anthropologist* 104:791–804.

———. 2006. *From the Kitchen to the Parlor: Language and Becoming in African American Women's Hair Care*. New York: Oxford University Press.

Jankowski, Martín Sánchez. 1991. *Islands in the Street: Gangs and American Urban Society*. Berkeley: University of California Press.

Jenkins, Gwynne. 2003. Burning Bridges: Policy, Practice, and the Destruction of Midwifery in Rural Costa Rica. *Social Science and Medicine* 56:1893–1909.

Jensen, Marianne Wiben, ed. Elaine Bolton, trans. 2004. Land Rights: A Key Issue. *Indigenous Affairs* 4.

Jinadu, L. Adele. 1994. The Dialectics of Theory and Research on Race and Ethnicity in Nigeria. In *"Race," Ethnicity and Nation: International Perspectives on Social Conflict* (pp. 163–178). Peter Ratcliffe, ed. London: University College of London Press.

Johnson, Walter R. 1994. *Dismantling Apartheid: A South African Town in Transition*. Ithaca, NY: Cornell University Press.

Johnston, Barbara Rose. 1994. Environmental Degradation and Human Rights Abuse. In *Who Pays the Price? The Sociocultural Context of Environmental Crisis* (pp. 7–16). Barbara Rose Johnston, ed. Washington, DC: Island Press.

Joralemon, Donald. 1982. New World Depopulation and the Case of Disease. *Journal of Anthropological Research* 38:108–127.

Jordan, Brigitte. 1983. *Birth in Four Cultures*, 3rd ed. Montreal: Eden Press.

Joseph, Suad. 1994. Brother/Sister Relationships: Connectivity, Love, and Power in the Reproduction of Patriarchy in Lebanon. *American Ethnologist* 21:50–73.

Jourdan, Christine. 1995. Masta Liu. In *Youth Cultures: A Cross-Cultural Perspective* (pp. 202–222). Vered Amit-Talai and Helena Wulff, eds. New York: Routledge.

Judah G., P. Donachie, E. Cobb, W. Schmidt, M. Holland, and V. Curtis. 2010. Dirty Hands: Bacteria of Faecal Origin on Commuters' Hands. *Epidemiology and Infections* 138(3):409–414.

Judd, Ellen. 2002. *The Chinese Women's Movement: Between State and Market*. Stanford, CA: Stanford University Press.

Junger, Sebastian. 2010. *Restrepo* (film).

———. 2010. *War*. New York: Twelve.

Kant, Shashi, Ilan Vertinsky, Bin Zheng, and Peggy M. Smith. 2014. Multi-Domain Subjective Wellbeing of Two Canadian First Nations Communities. *World Development* 64:140–157.

Karan, P. P. and Cotton Mather. 1985. Tourism and Environment in the Mount Everest Region. *Geographical Review* 75(1):93–95.

Kassam, Aneesa. 2002. Ethnodevelopment in the Oromia Regional State of Ethiopia. In *Participating in Development: Approaches to Indigenous Knowledge* (pp. 65–81). Paul Sillitoe, Alan Bicker, and Johan Pottier, eds. ASA Monographs No. 39. New York: Routledge.

Kata, Anna. 2010. A Postmodern Pandora's Box: Anti-Vaccination Information on the Internet. *Vaccine* 28: 1709–1716.

Katz, Nathan and Ellen S. Goldberg. 1989. Asceticism and Caste in the Passover Observances of the Cochin Jews. *Journal of the American Academy of Religion* 57(1):53–81.

Katz, Richard. 1982. *Boiling Energy: Community Healing among the Kalahari Kung*. Cambridge, MA: Harvard University Press.

Kaul, Adam. 2004. The Anthropologist as Barman and Tour-Guide: Reflections on Fieldwork in a Touristed Destination. *Durham Anthropology Journal* 12:22–36.

Kehoe, Alice Beck. 1989. *The Ghost Dance: History and Revitalization*. Philadelphia: Holt.

Kendon, A. 1988. Parallels and Divergences between Warlpiri Sign Language and Spoken Warlpiri: Analyses of Spoken and Signed Discourse. *Oceania* 58:239–254.

Kennedy, David P. and Stephen G. Perz. 2000. Who Are Brazil's Indígenas? Contributions of Census Data Analysis to Anthropological Demography of Indigenous Populations. *Human Organization* 59:311–324.

Kerns, Virginia. 1999. Preventing Violence against Women: A Central American Case. In *To Have and To Hit: Cultural Perspectives on Wife Beating*, 2nd ed. (pp. 153–168). Dorothy Ayers Counts, Judith K. Brown, and Jacquelyn C. Campbell, eds. Urbana: University of Illinois Press.

Kesmanee, Chupinit. 1994. Dubious Development Concepts in the Thai Highlands: The Chao Khao in Transition. *Law & Society Review* 28:673–683.

Kim, Hyun-Jun and Karen I. Fredriksen-Goldsen. 2012. Hispanic Lesbians and Bisexual Women at Heightened Risk or Health Disparities. *American Journal of Public Health* 102:e9–e15.

King, Diane E. 2014. *Kurdistan on the Global Stage: Kinship, Land, and Community in Iraq*. New Brunswick, NJ: Rutgers University Press.

Kirksey, Eben. 2012. *Freedom in Entangled Worlds: West Papua and the Architecture of Global Power*. Durham, NC: Duke University Press.

Kirsch, Stuart. 2002. Anthropology and Advocacy: A Case Study of the Campaign against the Ok Tedi Mine. *Critique of Anthropology* 22:175–200.

Knott, Kim. 1996. Hindu Women, Destiny and Stridharma. *Religion* 26:15–35.

Kolenda, Pauline M. 1978. *Caste in Contemporary India: Beyond Organic Solidarity*. Prospect Heights, IL: Waveland Press.

Kondo, Dorinne. 1997. *About Face: Performing "Race" in Fashion and Theater*. New York: Routledge.

Konner, Melvin. 1989. Homosexuality: Who and Why? *New York Times Magazine*. April 2:60–61.

Konvalinka, Nancy. 2013. Caring for Young and Old: The Care-Giving Bind in Late-Forming Families. In *Pathways to Empathy: New Studies on Commodification, Emotional Labor, and Time Binds* (pp. 33–48). Gerttraud Koch and Stefanie Everke Buchanan, eds. New York: Campus Verlag.

Kottak, Conrad Phillip. 1985. When People Don't Come First: Some Sociological Lessons from Completed Projects. In *Putting People First: Sociological Variables and Rural Development* (pp. 325–356). Michael M. Cernea, ed. New York: Oxford University Press.

Kovats-Bernat, J. Christopher. 2002. Negotiating Dangerous Fields: Pragmatic Strategies for Fieldwork Amid Violence and Terror. *American Anthropologist* 104:1–15.

Krantzler, Nora J. 1987. Traditional Medicine as "Medical Neglect": Dilemmas in the Case Management of a Samoan Teenager with Diabetes. In *Child Survival: Cultural Perspectives on the Treatment and Maltreatment of Children* (pp. 325–337). Nancy Scheper-Hughes, ed. Boston: D. Reidel.

Kraybill, Donald B. 2014. *Renegade Amish: Beard Cutting, Hate Crimes, and the Trial of the Bergholz Barbers*. Baltimore, MD: Johns Hopkins University Press.

Kraybill, Donald B. and Steven M. Nolt. 2004. *Amish Enterprise: From Plows to Profits*, 2nd ed. Baltimore, MD: Johns Hopkins University Press.

Kroeber, A. L. and Clyde Kluckhohn. 1952. *Culture: A Critical Review of Concepts and Definitions*. New York: Vintage Books.

Kuipers, Joel C. 1990. *Power in Performance: The Creation of Textual Authority in Weyéwa Ritual Speech*. Philadelphia: University of Pennsylvania Press.

———. 1991. Matters of Taste in Weyéwa. In *The Varieties of Sensory Experience: A Sourcebook in the Anthropology of the Senses* (pp. 111–127). David Howes, ed. Toronto: University of Toronto Press.

Kurin, Richard. 1980. Doctor, Lawyer, Indian Chief. *Natural History* 89(11):6–24.

Kurkiala, Mikael. 2003. Interpreting Honor Killings: The Story of Fadime Sahindal (1975–2002) in the Swedish Press. *Anthropology Today* 19:6–7.

Kuwayama, Takami. 2004. *Native Anthropology: The Japanese Challenge to Western Academic Hegemony*. Melbourne: Trans Pacific Press.

Lacey, Marc. 2002. Where 9/11 News Is Late, But Aid Is Swift. *New York Times* June 3:A1, A7.

Ladányi, János. 1993. Patterns of Residential Segregation and the Gypsy Minority in Budapest. *International Journal of Urban and Regional Research* 17(1):30–41.

Laderman, Carol. 1988. A Welcoming Soil: Islamic Humoralism on the Malay Peninsula. In *Paths to Asian Medical Knowledge* (pp. 272–288). Charles Leslie and Allan Young, eds. Berkeley: University of California Press.

LaFleur, William. 1992. *Liquid Life: Abortion and Buddhism in Japan*. Princeton, NJ: Princeton University Press.

Lakoff, Robin. 1973. Language and Woman's Place. *Language in Society* 2:45–79.

———. 1990. *Talking Power: The Politics of Language in Our Lives*. New York: Basic Books.

LaLone, Mary B. 2003. Walking the Line between Alternative Interpretations in Heritage Education and Tourism: A Demonstration of the Complexities with an Appalachian Coal Mining Example. In *Signifying Serpents and Mardi Gras Runners: Representing Identity in Selected Souths* (pp. 72–92). Southern Anthropological Proceedings, No. 36. Celeste Ray and Luke Eric Lassiter, eds. Athens: University of Georgia Press.

Lanehart, Sonja L. 1999. African American Vernacular English. In *Handbook of Language and Ethnic Identity* (pp. 211–225). Joshua A. Fishman, ed. New York: Oxford University Press.

Larsen, Ulla and Sharon Yan. 2000. Does Female Circumcision Affect Infertility and Fertility? A Study of the Central African Republic, Côte d'Ivoire, and Tanzania. *Demography* 37:313–321.

Larsson, Sara. 2005. Legislating Gender Equality: In Saami Land, Women Are Encouraged to Become Lawyers—But Many Would Rather Be Reindeer Herders. *Cultural Survival Quarterly* 28(4):28–29.

Lassiter, Luke Eric, Hurley Goodall, Elizabeth Campbell, and Michelle Natasya Johnson. 2004. *The Other Side of Middletown: Exploring Muncie's African American Community*. Walnut Creek, CA: AltaMira Press.

Leach, Jerry W. 1975. *Trobriand Cricket: An Ingenious Response to Colonialism*. Video.

LeDuc, Matthew. 2012. Discourses of Heritage and Tourism at a World Heritage Site: The Case of Hampi, India. *Practicing Anthropology* 34:28–32.

Lee, Gary R. and Mindy Kezis. 1979. Family Structure and the Status of the Elderly. *Journal of Comparative Family Studies* 10:429–443.

Lee, Helen Morton. 2003. *Tongans Overseas: Between Two Shores*. Honolulu: University of Hawai'i Press.

Lee, Richard B. 1969. Eating Christmas in the Kalahari. *Natural History*. December 14–22:60–63.

———. 1979. *The !Kung San: Men, Women, and Work in a Foraging Society*. New York: Cambridge University Press.

Lee, Wai-Na and David K. Tse. 1994. Becoming Canadian: Understanding How Hong Kong Immigrants Change Their Consumption. *Pacific Affairs* 67(1):70–95.

Lempert, David. 1996. *Daily Life in a Crumbling Empire*. 2 volumes. New York: Columbia University Press.

Lepani, Katherine. 2012. *Islands of Love, Islands of Risk: Culture and HIV in the Trobriands*. Nashville, TN: Vanderbilt University Press.

Lepowsky, Maria. 1990. Big Men, Big Women, and Cultural Autonomy. *Ethnology* 29(10):35–50.

Lesher, James H., trans. 2001. *Xenophanes of Colophon: Fragments*. Toronto: University of Toronto Press.

Lessinger, Johanna. 1995. *From the Ganges to the Hudson: Indian Immigrants in New York City*. Boston: Allyn and Bacon.

Levin, Dan. 2014. Many in China Can Now Have a Second Child But Say No. *The New York Times*. February 25.

Levine, Robert, Suguru Sato, Tsukasa Hashimoto, and Jyoti Verma. 1995. Love and Marriage in Eleven Cultures. *Journal of Cross-Cultural Psychology* 26:554–571.

Lévi-Strauss, Claude. 1967. *Structural Anthropology*. New York: Anchor Books.

Levy, Jerrold E., Eric B. Henderson, and Tracy J. Andrews. 1989. The Effects of Regional Variation and Temporal Change in Matrilineal Elements of Navajo Social Organization. *Journal of Anthropological Research* 45(4):351–377.

Li, Fabiana. 2009. Documenting Accountability: Environmental Impact Assessment in a Peruvian Mining Project. *Political and Legal Anthropology Review* 32:218–236.

Lin, Xu and Huang Feifei. 2012. China's Old People's Home. *China Daily*. April 12.

Lindenbaum, Shirley. 1979. *Kuru Sorcery: Disease and Danger in the New Guinea Highlands*. Mountain View, CA: Mayfield Publishing.

Lock, Margaret. 1993. *Encounters with Aging: Mythologies of Menopause in Japan and North America*. Berkeley: University of California Press.

Loker, William. 2000. Sowing Discord, Planting Doubts: Rhetoric and Reality in an Environment and Development Project in Honduras. *Human Organization* 59:300–310.

———. 2004. *Changing Places: Environment, Development, and Social Change in Rural Honduras*. Durham, NC: Carolina Academic Press.

Long, Susan Orpett. 2005. *Final Days: Japanese Culture and Choice at the End of Life*. Honolulu: University of Hawai'i Press.

Lorch, Donatella. 2003. Do Read This for War. *Newsweek* 141(11):13.

Lubkemann, Stephen C. 2005. Migratory Coping in Wartime Mozambique: An Anthropology of Violence and Displacement in "Fragmented Wars." *Journal of Peace Research* 42:493–508.

Lutz, Catherine and Anne Lutz Fernandez. 2010. *Carjacked: The Culture of the Automobile and Its Effects on Our Lives*. New York: Palgrave Macmillan.

Lyman, Rick. 2006. Reports Reveal Hurricanes' Impact on Human Landscape. *New York Times*. May 6, p. A16.

Lyttleton, Chris. 2004. Relative Pleasures: Drugs, Development and Modern Dependencies in Asia's Golden Triangle. *Development and Change* 35:909–935.

MacCarthy, Michelle. 2014. Like Playing a Game Where You Don't Know the Rules": Investing Meaning in Intercultural Cash Transactions between Tourists and Trobriand Islanders. *Ethnos* 79(5):1–24.

MacLeod, Arlene Elowe. 1992. Hegemonic Relations and Gender Resistance: The New Veiling as Accommodating Protest in Cairo. *Signs: The Journal of Women in Culture and Society* 17(3):533–557.

Macnair, Peter. 1995. From Kwakiutl to Kwakwaka'wakw. In *Native Peoples: The Canadian Experience*, 2nd ed. (pp. 586–605). R. Bruce Morrison and C. Roderick Wilson, eds. Toronto: McClelland & Stewart.

Maffi, Luisa. 2003. The "Business" of Language Endangerment: Saving Languages or Helping People Keep Them Alive? In *Language in the Twenty-First Century: Selected Papers of the Millennial Conference of the Center for Research and Documentation on World Language Problems* (pp. 67–86). H. Tonkin and T. Reagan, eds. Amsterdam: John Benjamins.

———. 2005. Linguistic, Cultural, and Biological Diversity. *Annual Review of Anthropology* 34:599–617.

Magga, Ole Henrik and Tove Skutnabb-Kangas. 2001. The Saami Languages: The Present and the Future. *Cultural Survival Quarterly* 25(2):26–31.

Mahdavi, Pardis. 2012. Questioning the Global Gays(ze): Constructions of Sexual Identities in Post-Revolution Iran. *Social Identities* 18:223–237.

Mahler, Sarah J. 1995. *Salvadorans in Suburbia: Symbiosis and Conflict*. Boston: Allyn and Bacon.

Major, Marc R. 1996. No Friends but the Mountains: A Simulation on Kurdistan. *Social Education* 60(3):C1–C8.

Malinowski, Bronislaw. 1929. *The Sexual Life of Savages*. New York: Harcourt, Brace & World.

———. 1948. *Magic, Science and Religion, and Other Essays*. Boston: Beacon Press.

———. 1961 [1922]. *Argonauts of the Western Pacific*. New York: E. P. Dutton & Co.

Mamdani, Mahmoud. 1972. *The Myth of Population Control: Family, Caste, and Class in an Indian Village*. New York: Monthly Review Press.

Manz, Beatriz. 2004. *Paradise in Ashes: A Guatemalan Journey of Courage, Terror, and Hope*. Berkeley: University of California Press.

Marcus, George. 1995. Ethnography in/of the World System: The Emergence of Multi-Sited Ethnography. *Annual Review of Anthropology* 24:95–117.

Margolis, Maxine L. and Marigene Arnold. 1993. Turning the Tables? Male Strippers and the Gender Hierarchy in America. In *Sex and Gender Hierarchies* (pp. 334–350). Barbara D. Miller, ed. New York: Cambridge University Press.

Martin, Richard C. 1995. Islam. In *The HarperCollins Dictionary of Religion* (pp. 498–513). Jonathan Z. Smith, ed. New York: HarperCollins.

Martin, Sarah. 2005. *Must Boys Be Boys? Ending Sexual Exploitation and Abuse in UN Peacekeeping Missions.* Washington, DC: Refugees International.

Martínez, Samuel. 1996. Indifference with Indignation: Anthropology, Human Rights, and the Haitian Bracero. *American Anthropologist* 98(1):17–25.

Masquelier, Adeline. 2005. The Scorpion's Sting: Youth, Marriage and the Struggle for Social Maturity in Niger. *Journal of the Royal Anthropological Institute* 11:59–83.

Maybury-Lewis, David. 1997b. *Indigenous Peoples, Ethnic Groups, and the State.* Boston: Allyn and Bacon.

McCallum, Cecilia. 2005. Explaining Caesarean Section in Salvador da Bahia, Brazil. *Sociology of Health and Illness* 27(2):215–242.

McDade, T. W., V. Reyes-Garcia, P. Blackinton, S. Tanner, T. Huanca, and W. R. Leonard. 2007. Ethnobotanical Knowledge is Associated with Indices of Child Health in the Bolivian Amazon. *Proceedings of the National Academy of Sciences* 104:6134–6139.

McElroy, Ann and Patricia K. Townsend. 2008. *Medical Anthropology in Ecological Perspective*, 5th ed. Boulder, CO: Westview Press.

Mead, Margaret. 1928 [1961]. *Coming of Age in Samoa: A Psychological Study of Primitive Youth for Western Civilization.* New York: Dell Publishing.

Meador, Elizabeth. 2005. The Making of Marginality: Schooling for Mexican Immigrants in the Rural Southwest. *Anthropology and Education Quarterly* 36(2): 149–164.

Meigs, Anna S. 1984. *Food, Sex, and Pollution: A New Guinea Religion.* New Brunswick, NJ: Rutgers University Press.

Mencher, Joan P. 1974. The Caste System Upside Down, or The Not-So-Mysterious East. *Current Anthropology* 15(4):469–493.

Mernissi, Fatima. 1987. *Beyond the Veil: Male-Female Dynamics in Modern Muslim Society*, Revised ed. Bloomington: Indiana University Press.

Michaelson, Evelyn Jacobson and Walter Goldschmidt. 1971. Female Roles and Male Dominance among Peasants. *Southwestern Journal of Anthropology* 27:330–352.

Michaud, Catherine M., W. Scott Gordon, and Michael R. Reich. 2005. *The Global Burden of Disease Due to Schistosomiasis.* Cambridge: Harvard School of Public Health, Harvard Center for Population and Development Studies, Schistosomiasis Research Program Working Paper Series. Volume 14, Number 1.

Miller, Barbara D. 1993. Surveying the Anthropology of Sex and Gender Hierarchies. In *Sex and Gender Hierarchies* (pp. 3–31). Barbara D. Miller, ed. New York: Cambridge University Press.

———. 2009. Heritage Management Inside Out and Upside Down: Questioning Top-Down and Outside Approaches. *Heritage Management* 2:5–9.

Miller, Barbara D. and Showkat Hayat Khan. 1986. Incorporating Voluntarism into Rural Development in Bangladesh. *Third World Planning Review* 8(2):139–152.

Miller, Laura. 2004. Those Naughty Teenage Girls: Japanese Kogals, Slang, and Media Assessments. *Journal of Linguistic Anthropology* 14:225–247.

Millward, David. 2012. Arranged Marriages Make a Comeback in Japan. *The Telegraph.* April 16.

Milton, Katherine. 1992. Civilization and Its Discontents. *Natural History* 3(92):37–92.

Miner, Horace. 1965 [1956]. Body Ritual among the Nacirema. In *Reader in Comparative Religion: An Anthropological Approach* (pp. 414–418). William A. Lessa and Evon Z. Vogt, eds. New York: Harper & Row.

Mintz, Sidney. 1985. *Sweetness and Power: The Place of Sugar in Modern History.* New York: Viking.

MIT Technology Review. 2014. The Emerging Science of Computational Anthropology. http://www .technologyreview.com/view/528216/the-emerging-science-of-computational-anthropology/

Miyazawa, Setsuo. 1992. *Policing in Japan: A Study on Making Crime.* Frank G. Bennett, Jr. with John O. Haley, trans. Albany: State University of New York Press.

Modell, Judith S. 1994. *Kinship with Strangers: Adoption and Interpretations of Kinship in American Culture.* Berkeley: University of California Press.

Moerman, Daniel. 2002. *Meaning, Medicine and the "Placebo" Effect.* New York: Cambridge University Press.

Moffat, Tina. 2010. The "Childhood Obesity Epidemic": Health Crisis or Social Construction? *Medical Anthropology Quarterly* 24:1–21.

Mogelonsky, Marcia. 1995. Asian-Indian Americans. *American Demographics* 17(8):32–39.

Moore, Molly. 2008. In France, Prisons Filled with Muslims. *Washington Post* April 29:A1, A4.

Morris, Rosalind. 1994. Three Sexes and Four Sexualities: Redressing the Discourses on Gender and Sexuality in Contemporary Thailand. *Positions* 2:15–43.

Muecke, Marjorie A. 1987. Resettled Refugees: Reconstruction of Identity of Lao in Seattle. *Urban Anthropology* 16(3–4): 273–289.

Mulk, Inga-Maria. 1994. Sacrificial Places and Their Meaning in Saami Society. In *Sacred Sites, Sacred Places* (pp. 121–131). David L. Carmichael, Jane Hubert, Brian Reeves, and Audhild Schanche, eds. New York: Routledge.

Mullings, Leith. 2005. Towards an Anti-Racist Anthropology: Interrogating Racism. *Annual Review of Anthropology* 34: 667–693.

Murdock, George Peter. 1965 [1949]. *Social Structure.* New York: Free Press.

Murray, Gerald F. 1987. The Domestication of Wood in Haiti: A Case Study of Applied Evolution. In *Anthropological Praxis: Translating Knowledge into Action* (pp. 233–240). Robert M. Wulff and Shirley J. Fiske, eds. Boulder, CO: Westview Press.

Myers, James. 1992. Nonmainstream Body Modification: Genital Piercing, Branding, Burning, and Cutting. *Journal of Contemporary Ethnography* 21(3):267–306.

Nadeau, Kathleen M. 2002. *Liberation Theology in the Philippines: Faith in a Revolution.* Westport: Praeger.

Nader, Laura. 1972. Up the Anthropologist—Perspectives Gained from Studying Up. In *Reinventing Anthropology* (pp. 284–311). Dell Hymes, ed. New York: Vintage Books.

Nag, Moni. 1972. Sex, Culture and Human Fertility: India and the United States. *Current Anthropology* 13:231–238.

———. 1983. Modernization Affects Fertility. *Populi* 10:56–77.

Nag, Moni, Benjamin N. F. White, and R. Creighton Peet. 1978. An Anthropological Approach to the Study of the

Economic Value of Children in Java and Nepal. *Current Anthropology* 19(2):293–301.

Nanda, Serena. 1990. *Neither Man nor Woman: The Hijras of India*. Belmont, CA: Wadsworth.

———. 1994. *Cultural Anthropology*. Wadsworth, CA: Wadsworth.

Natcher, David C., Susan Davis, and Clifford G. Hickey. 2005. Co-Management: Managing Relationships, Not Resources. *Human Organization* 64:240–250.

National Park Service. 2005. *Low Country Gullah Culture: Special Resource Study and Final Environmental Impact Statement*. Atlanta: NPS Southeast Regional Office. www .nps.gov.

Neff, Deborah L. 1994. The Social Construction of Infertility: The Case of the Matrilineal Nayars in South India. *Social Science and Medicine* 39(4):475–485.

Nettle, Daniel and Suzanne Romaine. 2000. *Vanishing Voices: The Extinction of the World's Languages*. New York: Oxford University Press.

Neusner, Jacob. 1995. Judaism. In *The HarperCollins Dictionary of Religion* (pp. 598–607). Jonathan Z. Smith, ed. New York: HarperCollins.

Nevins, M. Eleanor. 2004. Learning to Listen: Confronting Two Meanings of Language Loss in the Contemporary White Mountain Apache Speech Community. *Journal of Linguistic Anthropology* 14:269–288.

Newman, Katherine and Ariane De Lannoy. 2014. *After Freedom: The Rise of the Post-Apartheid Generation in Democratic South Africa*. Boston, MA: Beacon Press.

Newman, Lucile. 1972. *Birth Control: An Anthropological View*. Module No. 27. Reading, MA: Addison-Wesley.

———, ed. 1985. *Women's Medicine: A Cross-Cultural Study of Indigenous Fertility Regulation*. New Brunswick, NJ: Rutgers University Pres.

Ngokwey, Ndolamb. 1988. Pluralistic Etiological Systems in Their Social Context: A Brazilian Case Study. *Social Science and Medicine* 26:793–802.

Nichter, Mark. 1996. Vaccinations in the Third World: A Consideration of Community Demand. In *Anthropology and International Health: Asian Case Studies* (pp. 329–365). Mark Nichter and Mimi Nichter, eds. Amsterdam: Gordon and Breach Publishers.

Nolen, Stephanie. 2012. Two-Room Shack, Mumbai Slum. Asking Price: $43,000. *The Globe and Mail*. April 1.

Nordstrom, Carolyn. 1997. *A Different Kind of War Story*. Philadelphia: University of Pennsylvania Press.

Norgaard, Richard B. 1994. *Development Betrayed: The End of Progress and the Coevolutionary Revisioning of the Future*. New York: Routledge.

Obeyesekere, Gananath. 1981. *Medusa's Hair: An Essay on Personal Symbols and Religious Experience*. Chicago: University of Chicago Press.

Ong, Aihwa. 1995. State versus Islam: Malay Families, Women's Bodies, and the Body Politic in Malaysia. In *Bewitching Women, Pious Men: Gender and Body Politics in Southeast Asia* (pp. 159–194). Aihwa Ong and Michael G. Peletz, eds. Berkeley: University of California Press.

Ongley, Patrick. 1995. Post–1945 International Migration: New Zealand, Australia and Canada Compared. *International Migration Review* 29(3):765–793.

Ortner, Sherry. 1999. *Life and Death on Mt. Everest: Sherpas and Himalayan Mountaineering*. Princeton, NJ: Princeton University Press.

Osha, Sanya. 2006. Birth of the Ogoni Protest Movement. *Journal of Asian and African Studies* 41:13–38.

Paine, Robert. 2004. Saami Reindeer Pastoralism: Quo Vadis? *Ethnos* 69:23–42.

Palchykov, Vasyl, Kimmo Kaski, Janos Kertész, Albert-László Barabási, and Robin I. M. Dunbar. 2012. Sex Differences in Intimate Relationships. *Nature* April 19.

Park, Hynug yu. 2010. Heritage Tourism: Emotional Journeys into Nationhood. *Annals of Tourism Research* 37(1):116–135.

Parker, Lyn. 2008. To Cover the Aurat: Veiling, Sexual Morality and Agency among the Muslim Minangkabau, Indonesia. *Intersections: Gender and Sexuality in Asia and the Pacific* 16:1–76.

Parry, Jonathan P. 1996. Caste. In *The Social Science Encyclopedia* (pp. 76–77). Adam Kuper and Jessica Kuper, eds. New York: Routledge.

Pasquino, Gianfranco. 1996. Democratization. In *The Social Science Encyclopedia* (pp. 173–174). Adam Kuper and Jessica Kuper, eds. Routledge: New York.

Passel, Jeffrey, D'Vera Cohn, and Ana Gonzalez-Barrera. 2012. *Net Migration from Mexico Falls to Zero—and Perhaps Less*. Washington, DC: Pew Research Center.

Patterson, Thomas C. 2001. *A Social History of Anthropology in the United States*. New York: Berg.

Peacock, James L. and Dorothy C. Holland. 1993. The Narrated Self: Life Stories in Process. *Ethos* 21(4):367–383.

Peletz, Michael. 2006. Transgenderism and Gender Pluralism in Southeast Asia since Early Modern Times. *Current Anthropology* 47(2):309–325, 333–340.

Pelto, Pertti. 1973. *The Snowmobile Revolution: Technology and Social Change in the Arctic*. Menlo Park, CA: Cummings.

People's Daily. 2003. Xi'an Protects Oldest Residential Area. April 9.

Perry, Richard J. 1996. *From Time Immemorial: Indigenous Peoples and State Systems*. Austin: University of Texas Press.

Pessar, Patricia R. 1995. *A Visa for a Dream: Dominicans in the United States*. Boston: Allyn and Bacon.

Petryna, Adriana, Andrew Lakoff, and Arthur Kleinman, eds. 2007. *Global Pharmaceuticals: Ethics, Markets, Practices*. Durham, NC: Duke University Press.

Pew Research Center. 2010. *The Return of the Multi-Generational Family Household*. Washington, DC: Pew Research Center.

The Pew Charitable Trusts. 2015. Growth in Federal Prison System. *Fact Sheet*. http://www.pewtrusts.org/en/ research-and-analysis/fact-sheets/2015/01/growth-in- federal-prison-system-exceeds-states.

Plant, Roger. 1994. *Land Rights and Minorities*. London: Minority Rights Group.

Plattner, Stuart. 1989. Markets and Marketplaces. In *Economic Anthropology* (pp. 171–208). Stuart Plattner, ed. Stanford, CA: Stanford University Press.

Population Reference Bureau. 2009. *2009 World Population Data Sheet*. Washington, DC: Population Reference Bureau.

Posey, Darrell Addison. 1990. Intellectual Property Rights: What Is the Position of Ethnobiology? *Journal of Ethnobiology* 10:93–98.

Potter, Sulamith Heins. 1977. *Family Life in a Northern Thai Village: A Study in the Structural Significance of Women*. Berkeley: University of California Press.

Potuog˘lu-Cook, Öykü. 2006. Beyond the Glitter: Belly Dance and Neoliberal Gentrification in Istanbul. *Cultural Anthropology* 21:633–660.

Pratt, Jeff. 2007. Food Values: The Local and the Authentic. *Critique of Anthropology* 27:285–300.

Ramesh, A., C. R. Srikumari, and S. Sukumar. 1989. Parallel Cousin Marriages in Madras, Tamil Nadu: New Trends in Dravidian Kinship. *Social Biology* 36(3/4):248–254.

Raphael, Dana. 1975. Matrescence: Becoming a Mother: A "New/Old" *Rite de Passage*. In *Being Female: Reproduction, Power and Change* (pp. 65–72). Dana Raphael, ed. The Hague: Mouton Publishers.

Rasmussen, Lars Bjørn, Knut Mikkelsen, Margaretha Haugen, Are H. Pripp, Jeremy Z. Fields and Øystein T. Førre. 2012. Treatment of Fibromyalgia at the Maharishi Ayurveda Health Centre in Norway II: A 24-month Follow-up Pilot Study. *Clinical Rheumatology* 31:821–827.

Rasmussen, Susan J. 2010. The Slippery Sign: Cultural Constructions of Youth and Youthful Constructions of Culture in Tuareg Men's Face-Veiling. *Journal of Anthropological Research* 66:463–484.

Rathje, William and Cullen Murphy. 1992. *Rubbish! The Archaeology of Garbage*. New York: Harper & Row.

Reiner, R. 1996. Police. In *The Social Science Encyclopedia* (pp. 619–621). Adam Kuper and Jessica Kuper, eds. New York: Routledge.

Reyna, Stephen P. 1994. A Mode of Domination Approach to Organized Violence. In *Studying War: Anthropological Perspectives* (pp. 29–65). S. P. Reyna and R. E. Downs, eds. Langhorne, PA: Gordon and Breach Science Publishers.

Rickford, John. 1997. Unequal Partnership: Sociolinguistics and the African American Speech Community. *Language in Society* 26:161–198.

Roberts, Sean. 2010. Imagining Uyghurstan: Re-evaluating the Birth of the Modern Uyghur Nation. *Central Asian Survey* 28:361–381.

Rogers, Barbara. 1979. *The Domestication of Women: Discrimination in Developing Societies*. New York: St. Martin's Press.

Roseman, Marina. 1987. Inversion and Conjuncture: Male and Female Performance among the Temiar of Peninsular Malaysia. In *Women and Music in Cross-Cultural Perspective* (pp. 131–149). Ellen Koskoff, ed. New York: Greenwood Press.

Rosenberger, Nancy. 1992. Images of the West: Home Style in Japanese Magazines. In *Re-Made in Japan: Everyday Life and Consumer Taste in a Changing Society* (pp. 106–125). James J. Tobin, ed. New Haven, CT: Yale University Press.

Rosenblatt, Paul C., Patricia R. Walsh, and Douglas A. Jackson. 1976. *Grief and Mourning in Cross-Cultural Perspective*. New Haven, CT: HRAF Press.

Ross, Marc Howard. 1993. *The Culture of Conflict: Interpretations and Interests in Comparative Perspective*. New Haven, CT: Yale University Press.

Roy, Arundhati. 1999. *The Cost of Living*. New York: Modern Library.

Rubel, Arthur J., Carl W. O'Nell, and Rolando Collado-Ardon. 1984. *Susto: A Folk Illness*. Berkeley: University of California Press.

Sachs, Aaron. 1996. Dying for Oil. *WorldWatch* June:10–21.

Sahlins, Marshall. 1963. Poor Man, Rich Man, Big Man, Chief. *Comparative Studies in Society and History* 5:285–303.

Saitoti, Tepilit Ole. 1986. *The Worlds of a Maasai Warrior*. New York: Random House.

Salam, Nawaf A. 1994. Between Repatriation and Resettlement: Palestinian Refugees in Lebanon. *Journal of Palestine Studies* 24:18–27.

Salamandra, Christa. 2004. *A New Old Damascus: Authenticity and Distinction in Urban Syria*. Bloomington: Indiana University Press.

Sanday, Peggy Reeves. 1973. Toward a Theory of the Status of Women. *American Anthropologist* 75:1682–1700.

———. 1986. *Divine Hunger: Cannibalism as a Cultural System*. New York: Cambridge University Press.

———. 1990. *Fraternity Gang Rape: Sex, Brotherhood, and Privilege on Campus*. New York: New York University Press.

———. 2002. *Women at the Center: Life in a Modern Matriarchy*. Ithaca, NY: Cornell University Press.

Sanders, Douglas E. 1999. Indigenous Peoples: Issues of Definition. *International Journal of Cultural Property* 8:4–13.

Sanders, William B. 1994. *Gangbangs and Drive-Bys: Grounded Culture and Juvenile Gang Violence*. New York: Aldine de Gruyter.

Sanjek, Roger. 1990. A Vocabulary for Fieldnotes. In *Fieldnotes: The Making of Anthropology* (pp. 92–138). Roger Sanjek, ed. Ithaca, NY: Cornell University Press.

———. 1994. The Enduring Inequalities of Race. In *Race* (pp. 1–17). Steven Gregory and Roger Sanjek, eds. New Brunswick, NJ: Rutgers University Press.

———. 2000. Keeping Ethnography Alive in an Urbanizing World. *Human Organization* 53:280–288.

Sarfaty, Galit. 2012. *Values in Translation: Human Rights and the Culture of the World Bank*. Stanford, CA: Stanford University Press.

Sault, Nicole L. 1985. Baptismal Sponsorship as a Source of Power for Zapotec Women of Oaxaca, Mexico. *Journal of Latin American Lore* 11(2):225–243.

———. 1994. How the Body Shapes Parenthood: "Surrogate" Mothers in the United States and Godmothers in Mexico. In *Many Mirrors: Body Image and Social Relations* (pp. 292–318). Nicole Sault, ed. Brunswick, NJ: Rutgers University Press.

Savishinsky, Joel S. 1974. *The Trail of the Hare: Life and Stress in an Arctic Community*. New York: Gordon and Breach.

———. 1991. *The Ends of Time: Life and Work in a Nursing Home*. New York: Bergin & Garvey.

Schaft, Kai and David L. Brown. 2000. Social Capital and Grassroots Development: The Case of Roma Self-Governance in Hungary. *Social Problems* 47(2):201–219.

Scheffel, David Z. 2004. Slovak Roma on the Threshold of Europe. *Anthropology Today* 20(1):6–12.

Scheper-Hughes, Nancy. 1992. *Death without Weeping: The Violence of Everyday Life in Brazil*. Berkeley: University of California Press.

———. 2012. Mother's Love: Death without Weeping. In *Culture and Conformity*, 14th ed. (pp. 155–164), with new epilogue. James Spradley and David M. McCurdy, eds. Upper Saddle River, NJ: Pearson Education.

Scherrer, Kristin S. 2008. Coming to an Asexual Identity: Negotiating Identity, Negotiating Desire. *Sexualities* 11:621–641.

Schlegel, Alice. 1995. A Cross-Cultural Approach to Adolescence. *Ethos* 23(1):15–32.

Scrimshaw, Susan. 1984. Infanticide in Human Populations: Societal and Individual Concerns. In *Infanticide: Comparative and Evolutionary Perspectives* (pp. 463–486). Glenn Hausfater and Sarah Blaffer Hrdy, eds. New York: Aldine.

Scudder, Thayer. 1973. The Human Ecology of Big Dam Projects: River Basin Development and Resettlement. *Annual Review of Anthropology* 2:45–55.

Semple, Kirk. 2012. With Fanfare, Ashanti People From Ghana Install Their New York Chief. *New York Times*. June 3.

Shachtman, Tom. 2006. *Rumspringa: To Be or Not to Be Amish.* New York: North Point Press.

Shahrani, Nazif M. 2002. War, Factionalism, and the State in Afghanistan. *American Anthropologist* 104:715–722.

Shanklin, Eugenia. 2000. Representations of Race and Racism in American Anthropology. *Current Anthropology* 41(1):99–103.

Shapiro, Danielle. 2011. Islam's Secret Feminists: In an Obscure, Devoutly Muslim Ethnic Group in Indonesia, Women Are Revered—and Own Key Land and Property. *The Huffington Post*. September 4.

Shapiro, Thomas M. 2004. *The Hidden Cost of Being African American.* New York: Oxford University Press.

Shenhav-Keller, Shelly. 1993. The Israeli Souvenir: Its Text and Context. *Annals of Tourism Research* 20:182–196.

Shibamoto, Janet. 1987. The Womanly Woman: Manipulation of Stereotypical and Nonstereotypical Features of Japanese Female Speech. In *Language, Gender, and Sex in Comparative Perspective* (pp. 26–49). Susan U. Philips, Susan Steel, and Christine Tanz, eds. New York: Cambridge University Press.

Shostak, Marjorie. 1981. *Nisa: The Life and Times of a !Kung Woman.* Cambridge, MA: Harvard University Press.

Sidnell, Jack. 2000. *Primus inter pares:* Storytelling and Male Peer Groups in an Indo-Guyanese Rumshop. *American Ethnologist* 27:72–99.

Silva, Noenoe K. 2004. *Aloha Betrayed: Native Hawaiian Resistance to American Colonialism.* Durham, NC: Duke University Press.

Silverstein, Michael. 1997. Encountering Language and Languages of Encounter in North American Ethnohistory. *Journal of Linguistic Anthropology* 6:126–144.

Singh, Holly Donahue. 2014. "The World's Back Womb?": Commercial Surrogacy in India. *American Anthropologist* 116:824–828.

Siskind, Janet. 1992. The Invention of Thanksgiving: A Ritual of American Nationality. *Critique of Anthropology* 12(2):167–191.

Smith, Jennie M. 2001. *When the Hands Are Many: Community Organization and Change in Rural Haiti.* Ithaca, NY: Cornell University Press.

Smith, Jonathan Z., ed. 1995. *The HarperCollins Dictionary of Religion.* New York: HarperCollins.

Smith, Laurajane, Anna Morgan, and Anita van der Meer. 2003. Community-Driven Research in Cultural Heritage Management: The Waanyi Women's History Project. *International Journal of Heritage Studies* 9(1):65–80.

Smith, Tara. 2011. Creating a Framework for the Prosecution of Environmental Crimes in International Criminal Law. In the *Ashgate Research Companion to International Criminal Law: Critical Perspectives* (pp. 45–62). William Schabas, Yvonne McDermott, Niamh Hayes, and Maria Varaki, eds. Burlington, VT: Ashgate Publishing.

Smitherman, Geneva. 1997. "The Chain Remain the Same": Communicative Practices in the Hip Hop Nation. *Black Studies* 28(1):3–25.

Snajdr, Edward. 2005. Gender, Power, and the Performance of Justice: Muslim Women's Responses to Domestic Violence in Kazakhstan. *American Ethnologist* 32: 294–311.

Sobel, Elizabeth and Gordon Bettles. 2000. Winter Hunger, Winter Myths: Subsistence Risk and Mythology among the Klamath and Modoc. *Journal of Anthropological Archaeology* 19:276–316.

Spilde Contreras, Kate. 2006. Indian Gaming in California Brings Jobs and Income to Areas that Need It Most. Indian Gaming. www.indiangaming.com/regulatory/view/?id=35.

Spiro, Melford. 1967. *Burmese Supernaturalism: A Study in the Explanation and Reduction of Suffering.* Englewood Cliffs, NJ: Prentice-Hall.

———. 1990. On the Strange and the Familiar in Recent Anthropological Thought. In *Cultural Psychology: Essays on Comparative Human Development* (pp. 47–61). James W. Stigler, Richard A. Shweder, and Gilbert Herdt, eds. Chicago: University of Chicago Press.

Spitulnik, Deborah. 1993. Anthropology and Mass Media. *Annual Review of Anthropology* 22:293–315.

Springwood, Charles F. 2014. Gun Concealment, Display, and Other Magical Habits of the Body. *Critique of Anthropology* 34:450–471.

Staats, Valerie. 1994. Ritual, Strategy or Convention: Social Meaning in Traditional Women's Baths in Morocco. *Frontiers: A Journal of Women's Studies* 14(3):1–18.

Stack, Carol. 1974. *All Our Kin: Strategies for Survival in a Black Community.* New York: Harper & Row.

Stephen, Lynn. 1995. Women's Rights Are Human Rights: The Merging of Feminine and Feminist Interests among El Salvador's Mothers of the Disappeared (CO-MADRES). *American Ethnologist* 22(4):807–827.

Stidsen, Sille, comp. and ed. Elaine Bolton, trans. 2006. *The Indigenous World 2006.* Rutgers, NJ: Transaction Books.

Stillman, Amy Ku'uleialoha. 1996. Hawaiian Hula Competitions: Event, Repertoire, Performance and Tradition. *Journal of American Folklore* 109(434):357–380.

Stivens, Maila, Cecelia Ng, and Jomo K. S., with Jahara Bee. 1994. *Malay Peasant Women and the Land.* Atlantic Highlands, NJ: Zed Books.

Stocks, Anthony. 2005. Too Much for Too Few: Problems of Indigenous Land Rights in Latin America. *Annual Review of Anthropology* 34:85–104.

Storper-Perez, Danielle and Harvey E. Goldberg. 1994. The Kotel: Toward an Ethnographic Portrait. *Religion* 24:309–332.

Strathern, Andrew. 1971. *The Rope of Moka: Big-Men and Ceremonial Exchange in Mount Hagen, New Guinea.* London: Cambridge University Press.

Striffler, Steve. 2007. Neither Here nor There: Mexican Immigrant Workers and the Search for Home. *American Ethnologist* 34(4):674–688.

Suicide Prevention Resource Center. 2008. *Suicide Risk and Prevention for Lesbian, Gay, Bisexual, and Transgender Youth.* Newton, MA: Education Development Center, Inc.

Sullivan, Kathleen. 1992. Protagonists of Change: Indigenous Street Vendors in San Cristobal, Mexico, Are Adapting Tradition and Customs to Fit New Life Styles. *Cultural Survival Quarterly* 16:38–40.

Sundar Rao, P. S. S. 1983. Religion and Intensity of In-Breeding in Tamil Nadu, South India. *Social Biology* 30(4):413–422.

Suttles, Wayne. 1991. The Traditional Kwakiutl Potlatch. In *Chiefly Feasts: The Enduring Kwakiutl Potlatch* (pp. 71–134). Aldona Jonaitis, ed. Washington, DC: American Museum of Natural History.

Tabac, Lara. 2003. Diary. *Slate*. October 3.

Tannen, Deborah. 1990. *You Just Don't Understand: Women and Men in Conversation.* New York: Morrow.

Tauli-Corpuz, Victoria. 2005. Indigenous Peoples and the Millennium Development Goals. Paper submitted to the Fourth Session of the UN Permanent Forum on Indigenous Issues, New York City, May 16–27. www.tebtebba.org.

Thomas, Frédéric, Francois Renaud, Eric Benefice, Thierry de Meeüs, and Jean-François Guegan. 2001. International Variability of Ages at Menarche and Menopause: Patterns and Main Determinants. *Human Biology* 73(2):271–290.

Thompson, Nile R. and C. Dale Sloat. 2004. The Use of Oral Literature to Provide Community Health Education on the Southern Northwest Coast. *American Indian Culture and Research Journal* 28(3):1–28.

Thompson, Robert Farris. 1971. Aesthetics in Traditional Africa. In *Art and Aesthetics in Primitive Societies* (pp. 374–381). Carol F. Jopling, ed. New York: E. P. Dutton.

Tice, Karin E. 1995. *Kuna Crafts, Gender, and the Global Economy.* Austin: University of Texas Press.

Tidball, Keith G. and Christopher P. Toumey. 2003. Signifying Serpents: Hermeneutic Change in Appalachian Pentecostal Serpent Handling. In *Signifying Serpents and Mardi Gras Runners: Representing Identity in Selected Souths* (pp. 1–18). Southern Anthropological Society Proceedings, No. 36. Celeste Ray and Luke Eric Lassiter, eds. Athens: University of Georgia Press.

Tierney, Patrick. 2000. *Darkness in El Dorado: How Scientists and Journalists Devastated the Amazon.* New York: W. W. Norton.

Tinker, Irene. 1976. The Adverse Impact of Development on Women. In *Women and World Development* (pp. 22–34). Irene Tinker and Michele Bo Bramsen, eds. Washington, DC: Overseas Development Council.

Tooker, Elisabeth. 1992. Lewis H. Morgan and His Contemporaries. *American Anthropologist* 94(2):357–375.

Toren, Christina. 1988. Making the Present, Revealing the Past: The Mutability and Continuity of Tradition as Process. *Man* (n.s.) 23:696–717.

Torri, Maria Costanza. 2012. Intercultural Health Practices: Towards an Equal Recognition Between Indigenous Medicine and Biomedicine? A Case Study from Chile. *Health Care Analysis* 20:31–49.

Trelease, Murray L. 1975. Dying among Alaskan Indians: A Matter of Choice. In *Death: The Final Stage of Growth* (pp. 33–37). Elisabeth Kübler-Ross, ed. Englewood Cliffs, NJ: Prentice-Hall.

Trotter, Robert T. II. 1987. A Case of Lead Poisoning from Folk Remedies in Mexican American Communities. In *Anthropological Praxis: Translating Knowledge into Action* (pp. 146–159). Robert M. Wulff and Shirley J. Fiske, eds. Boulder, CO: Westview Press.

Trouillot, Michel-Rolph. 1994. Culture, Color, and Politics in Haiti. In *Race* (pp. 146–174). Steven Gregory and Roger Sanjek, eds. New Brunswick, NJ: Rutgers University Press.

———. 2001. The Anthropology of the State in the Age of Globalization. *Current Anthropology* 42:125–133, 135–138.

Tucker, Bram, Amber Huff, Tsiazonera, Jaovola Tombo, Patricia Hajasoa, and Charlotte Nagnisaha. 2011. When the Wealthy Are Poor: Poverty Explanations and Local Perspectives in Southwestern Madagascar. *American Anthropologist* 113:291–305.

Turner, Victor W. 1969. *The Ritual Process: Structure and Anti-Structure.* Chicago: Aldine.

Tylor, Edward Burnett. 1871. *Primitive Culture: Researchers into the Development of Mythology, Philosophy, Religion, Art, and Custom.* 2 volumes. London: J. Murray.

Uhl, Sarah. 1991. Forbidden Friends: Cultural Veils of Female Friendship in Andalusia. *American Ethnologist* 18(1): 90–105.

UNHCR. 2011. *Global Trends Report 2020.* New York: United Nations, United Nations High Commissioner for Refugees.

VanWynsberghe, Robert M. 2002. *AlterNatives: Community, Identity, and Environmental Justice on Walpole Island.* Boston: Allyn and Bacon.

Varley, Emma. 2010. Targeted Doctors, Missing Patients: Obstetric Health Services and Sectarian Conflict in Northern Pakistan. *Social Science and Medicine* 70:61–70.

Vellinga, Marcel. 2004. *Constituting Unity and Difference: Vernacular Architecture in a Minangkabau Village.* Leiden: KITLV Press.

Walmsley, Roy. 2010. World Prison Population List. *International Centre for Prison Studies.* http://www.idcr.org.uk/wp-content/uploads/2010/09/WPPL-9-22.pdf.

Walsh, Michael. 2005. Will Indigenous Languages Survive? *Annual Review of Anthropology* 34:293–315.

Ward, Martha C. 1989. Once Upon a Time. In *Nest in the Wind: Adventures in Anthropology on a Tropical Island* (pp. 1–22). Martha C. Ward, ed. Prospect Heights, IL: Waveland Press.

Warren, Carol A. B. 1988. *Gender Issues in Field Research. Qualitative Research Methods, Volume 9.* Newbury Park, CA: Sage Publications.

Warren, D. Michael. 2001. The Role of the Global Network of Indigenous Knowledge Resource Centers in the Conservation of Cultural and Biological Diversity. In *Biocultural Diversity: Linking Language, Knowledge and the Environment* (pp. 446–461). Luisa Maffi, ed. Washington, DC: Smithsonian Institution Press.

Watkins, Ben and Michael L. Fleisher. 2002. Tracking Pastoralist Migration: Lessons from the Ethiopian Somali National Regional State. *Human Organization* 61:328–338.

Watson, James, L., ed. 1997. *Golden Arches East: McDonald's in East Asia.* Stanford, CA: Stanford University Press.

Watson, Rubie S. 1986. The Named and the Nameless: Gender and Person in Chinese Society. *American Ethnologist* 13(4):619–631.

Weatherford, J. 1981. *Tribes on the Hill.* New York: Random House.

Websdale, Neil. 1995. An Ethnographic Assessment of the Policing of Domestic Violence in Rural Eastern Kentucky. *Social Justice* 22(1):102–122.

Webster, Gloria Cranmer. 1991. The Contemporary Potlatch. In *Chiefly Feasts: The Enduring Kwakiutl Potlatch* (pp. 227–250). Aldona Jonaitis, ed. Washington, DC: American Museum of Natural History.

Weine, Stevan M., Daniel F. Becker, Thomas H. McGlashan, Dori Laub, Steven Lazrove, Dolores Vojvoda, and Leslie Hyman. 1995. Psychiatric Consequences of "Ethnic Cleansing": Clinical Assessments and Trauma Testimonies of Newly Resettled Bosnian Refugees. *American Journal of Psychiatry* 152(4):536–542.

Weiner, Annette B. 1976. *Women of Value, Men of Renown: New Perspectives in Trobriand Exchange.* Austin: University of Texas Press.

———. 1988. *The Trobrianders of Papua New Guinea.* New York: Holt, Rinehart and Winston.

Whitehead, Tony Larry. 1986. Breakdown, Resolution, and Coherence: The Fieldwork Experience of a Big, Brown, Pretty-talking Man in a West Indian Community. In *Self, Sex, and Gender in Cross-Cultural Fieldwork* (pp. 213–239). Tony Larry Whitehead and Mary Ellen Conway, eds. Chicago: University of Illinois Press.

Whiting, Beatrice B. and John W. M. Whiting. 1975. *Children of Six Cultures: A Psycho-Cultural Analysis.* Cambridge, MA: Harvard University Press.

Whiting, Robert. 1979. You've Gotta Have "Wa." *Sports Illustrated* September 24:60–71.

Whyte, Martin King. 1993. Wedding Behavior and Family Strategies in Chengdu. In *Chinese Families in the Post-Mao Era* (pp. 189–216). Deborah Davis and Stevan Harrell, eds. Berkeley: University of California Press.

Wikan, Unni. 1977. Man Becomes Woman: Transsexualism in Oman as a Key to Gender Roles. *Man* 12(2):304–319.

Williams, Brett. 1984. Why Migrant Women Feed Their Husbands Tamales: Foodways as a Basis for a Revisionist View of Tejano Family Life. In *Ethnic and Regional Foodways in the United States: The Performance of Group Identity* (pp. 113–126). Linda Keller Brown and Kay Mussell, eds. Knoxville: University of Tennessee Press.

Williams, Walter. 1992. *The Spirit and the Flesh: Sexual Diversity in American Indian Cultures*, 2nd ed. Boston: Beacon Press.

Wolf, Charlotte. 1996. Status. In *The Social Science Encyclopedia* (pp. 842–843). Adam Kuper and Jessica Kuper, eds. New York: Routledge.

World Bank. 2003. *Roma Poverty Remains Key Hurdle to Shared Prosperity in Central and Eastern Europe.* Washington, DC: The World Bank. www.worldbank.org/roma.

Worldwatch Institute. 2003. *Vital Signs 2003: The Trends That Are Shaping Our Future.* Washington, DC: Worldwatch Institute/W. W. Norton.

Wu, David Y. H. 1990. Chinese Minority Policy and the Meaning of Minority Culture: The Example of Bai in Yunnan, China. *Human Organization* 49(1):1–13.

Xi Juan, Sean-Shong Huang, and Patricia Drentea. 2013. Experiencing a Forced Relocation at Different Life Stages: The Effects of China's Three Gorges Project-Induced Relocation on Depression. *Society and Mental Health* 3(1):59–76.

Zaidi, S. Akbar. 1988. Poverty and Disease: Need for Structural Change. *Social Science and Medicine* 27:119–127.

Zarrilli, Phillip B. 1990. Kathakali. In *Indian Theatre: Traditions of Performance* (pp. 315–357). Farley P. Richmond, Darius L. Swann, and Phillip B. Zarrilli, eds. Honolulu: University of Hawaii Press.

Zayani, Mohammed. 2011. Toward a Cultural Anthropology of Arab Media. *History and Anthropology* 22:37–56.

Index

Italicized page numbers indicate photos, figures, or maps.